ZAGAT®

Movie
Guide
2009

EDITOR
Curt Gathje

COORDINATOR
Larry Cohn

Published and distributed by
Zagat Survey, LLC
4 Columbus Circle
New York, NY 10019
T: 212.977.6000
E: movies@zagat.com
www.zagat.com

ACKNOWLEDGMENTS

We thank the Arizona Film Society, DC Independent Film Festival, MSC Film Society, Olympia Film Society, Peachtree Film Society, University Film Society, Yale Film Society, Carol Bialkowski, Jason Briker, Kimberly Butler, Ed Dwyer, Gwen Hyman, Marilyn Laurie, David Margolick, Joshua Mooney, Pia Nordlinger, Maura O'Connell, Bernard Onken, Jane Rosenthal, Arthur Schlesinger Jr. and Bill Wolf, as well as the following members of our staff: Josh Rogers (associate editor), Reni Chin, Jeff Freier, Michelle Golden, Roy Jacob, Natalie Lebert, Mike Liao, Dave Makulec, Andre Pilette, Becky Ruthenburg, Sharon Yates and Kyle Zolner.

© 2008 Zagat Survey, LLC
ISBN-13: 978-1-57006-996-3
ISBN-10: 1-57006-996-4
Printed in the
United States of America

Contents

Ratings & Symbols

Title, Director, Cast, Running Time

Z Tim & Nina Uncut ◑   ▽ 25 | 19 | 25 | 12

2001 | Directed by Quentin Tarantino | With Brad Pitt, Angelina Jolie | 90 minutes | Rated PG

Review, surveyor comments in quotes

Tim and Nina's "courtship in Paris" is the "ooh-la-la" subject of this chop-socky/docudrama hybrid (think *Breathless* meets *Rush Hour*) that "inspires" the insipid but is "boring as heck" for everyone else; all applaud Pitt's "butch but tender" take on Tim as a "young buck", while Jolie is "so adorable" as "Nina in love" that many "want to adopt *her*"; P.S. the interminable cinéma-vérité "dinner scenes in bed" aren't for the squeamish, and Angie is rumored to have gotten pregnant during the mashed-potatoes course.

Ratings   **Overall Quality, Acting, Story** and **Production Values** are rated on the Zagat 0 to 30 scale.

0	-	9	poor to fair
10	-	15	fair to good
16	-	19	good to very good
20	-	25	very good to excellent
26	-	30	extraordinary to perfection
	▽		low response	less reliable

Symbols

Z	Zagat Top Movie (highest ratings, popularity and importance)
✉	Oscar winner for Best Picture, Actor, Actress, Director, Screenplay, Foreign Language Film
◑	filmed in black & white
F	foreign language film
∅	not yet on DVD

About This Survey

 Here are the results of our **2009 Movie Survey,** our seventh edition of the ultimate moviegoer's guide, covering 2,300 outstanding films. We've added 40 films from the last year as well as 310 earlier titles for a total of 350 new entries since our last edition. Like all of our guides, this one is based on the collective opinions of thousands of savvy consumers.

WHO PARTICIPATED: Input from 18,951 avid moviegoers forms the basis for the ratings and reviews in this guide (their comments are shown in quotation marks within the reviews). Viewing an average 2.2 movies per week (or 114 per year), these surveyors collectively see films well over two million times annually and they are quick to give us their opinions on each and every one. We sincerely thank each of these participants – this book is really "theirs."

HELPFUL LISTS: Our top lists and indexes can help you find exactly the right film. See Top New Releases (page 7), Favorite Films of All Time (page 8), Top Ratings (pages 9–31) and Top Foreign Language Films (page 32). We've also provided 67 handy indexes. Though the vast majority of films in this book are currently available on DVD, we have flagged those that are not with the following icon - Ø.

ABOUT ZAGAT: This marks our 29th year reporting on the shared experiences of consumers like you. What started in 1979 as a hobby involving 200 of our friends has come a long way. Today we have over 350,000 surveyors and now cover airlines, bars, clubs, dining, entertaining, golf, hotels, lounges, movies, music, resorts, shopping, spas, theater and tourist attractions worldwide.

VOTE AND COMMENT: We invite you to join any of our upcoming surveys at **ZAGAT.com.** There you can rate and review pretty much any subject year-round. In exchange for participating you will receive a free copy of the resulting guide when published.

AVAILABILITY: Zagat guides are available in all major bookstores as well as on **ZAGAT.com,** the award-winning **ZAGAT.mobi** (for web-enabled mobile phones) and **ZAGAT TO GO** (for smartphones). These products also enable you to reserve at thousands of places with just one click.

FEEDBACK: There is always room for improvement, thus we invite your comments and suggestions about any aspect of our performance. Tell us when we're wrong. Tell us what additional features you would like us to include. Just contact us at **movies@zagat.com.**

New York, NY
September 10, 2008

Nina and Tim

Nina and Tim Zagat

What's New

For this seventh edition of our *Movie Guide*, we've surveyed the new releases of the last 12 months and included our Top 40 list (see opposite page). As always, our surveyors' votes and comments reveal much about the national moviegoing mood.

 PARAMOUNT PICTURES: For the second year running, the top-rated film was a foreign language entry, *The Diving Bell and the Butterfly*. No. 2 was *Iron Man*, part of the ever-popular Action/Adventure/Fantasy genre that also included *The Chronicles of Narnia: Prince Caspian* and *Transformers*. Animation had a middling year with one strong showing (*Ratatouille*, No. 3), one not so strong (*Horton Hears a Who!*, No. 24). Musicals continued to burgeon with *Across the Universe*, *Hairspray*, *Once* and *Sweeney Todd*.

THEMATICS: Trendwise, surveyors liked movies depicting strong women (*Elizabeth: The Golden Age*, *Juno*, *La Vie en Rose*, *A Mighty Heart*, *Sex and the City*) and flawed men (*The Bucket List*, *Before the Devil Knows You're Dead*, *Charlie Wilson's War*, *Lars and the Real Girl*, *Michael Clayton*). Petty thieves got a lift with *The Bank Job*, *Before the Devil Knows You're Dead*, *Eastern Promises* and *In Bruges*, while the fluid of choice this season was blood, and lots of it (*No Country for Old Men*, *Sweeney Todd*, *There Will Be Blood*).

FRANCHISE FRENZY: After a lackluster showing last year, sequels bounced back this time out via *The Bourne Ultimatum*, *The Chronicles of Narnia* and *Harry Potter and the Order of the Phoenix*. In addition, a number of future franchises were hatched: *Hairspray*, *Iron Man* and *Transformers* all have sequels in the works.

THE HOT LIST: Regarding the season's hardest-working actors, three players garnered triple appearances in the Top 40: **Amy Adams** (*Charlie Wilson's War*, *Enchanted*, *Miss Pettigrew Lives for a Day*), **Josh Brolin** (*American Gangster*, *In the Valley of Elah*, *No Country for Old Men*) and **Philip Seymour Hoffman** (*Before the Devil Knows You're Dead*, *Charlie Wilson's War*, *The Savages*). Double-feature runners-up included **Russell Crowe** (*American Gangster*, *3:10 to Yuma*), **Morgan Freeman** (*The Bucket List*, *Gone Baby Gone*), **Tommy Lee Jones** (*In the Valley of Elah*, *No Country for Old Men*), **Shia LaBeouf** (*Indiana Jones and the Kingdom of the Crystal Skull*, *Transformers*) and **Denzel Washington** (*American Gangster*, *The Great Debaters*).

DVD WANT LIST: We annually ask voters to name their favorite films not available on DVD that should be. This year's mentions included perennial contender *The African Queen*, along with *Betrayal*, *The Devils*, *Enchanted April*, *Isadora*, *Let It Be*, *Looking for Mr. Goodbar*, *The Magnificent Ambersons*, *Song of the South*, *That Man from Rio*, *A Thousand Clowns*, *White Mischief* and *Yentl*.

New York, NY
September 10, 2008

Curt Gathje

Top New Releases

Excludes films with low votes, unless indicated by a ∇.

<u>26</u>] Diving Bell & the Butterfly
Iron Man
Ratatouille

<u>25</u>] Juno
Bourne Ultimatum
La Vie en Rose
Great Debaters
Once

<u>24</u>] Harry Potter/Order of Phoenix
Kite Runner
No Country for Old Men
Eastern Promises
Michael Clayton
Gone Baby Gone

<u>23</u>] There Will Be Blood
American Gangster
In Bruges
Into the Wild
Savages, The
Sweeney Todd

Before the Devil Knows . . .
Bank Job
Chronicles of Narnia: Caspian
Horton Hears a Who!
Enchanted
3:10 to Yuma
Sicko

<u>22</u>] In the Valley of Elah
Sex and the City
Charlie Wilson's War
Lars and the Real Girl
Across the Universe
Atonement
Stardust

<u>21</u>] Miss Pettigrew Lives for a Day
Hairspray
Transformers
Elizabeth: The Golden Age
Mighty Heart
Bucket List

Favorite Films of All Time

1. Godfather, The
2. Casablanca
3. Star Wars
4. Gone with the Wind
5. Shawshank Redemption
6. Braveheart
7. Lord of the Rings/Fellowship
8. Citizen Kane
9. Godfather Part II
10. Raiders of the Lost Ark
11. American Beauty
12. When Harry Met Sally...
13. Beautiful Mind
14. It's a Wonderful Life
15. African Queen
16. Schindler's List
17. Matrix, The
18. Princess Bride
19. Wizard of Oz
20. Annie Hall
21. Usual Suspects*
22. Pretty Woman
23. Sound of Music
24. Moulin Rouge!
25. Pulp Fiction
26. 2001: A Space Odyssey
27. Gladiator
28. Affair to Remember
29. Breakfast at Tiffany's
30. Goodfellas*
31. Almost Famous
32. Saving Private Ryan
33. Singin' in the Rain*
34. Apocalypse Now
35. Lawrence of Arabia
36. Bridget Jones's Diary
37. Star Wars V/Empire Strikes*
38. Shrek
39. Silence of the Lambs*
40. Animal House
41. Forrest Gump
42. All About Eve
43. Top Gun
44. Blade Runner
45. Memento*
46. E.T. The Extra-Terrestrial
47. Chocolat
48. Graduate, The
49. Dr. Strangelove
50. To Kill a Mockingbird*
51. Dirty Dancing
52. Airplane!
53. Blazing Saddles*
54. Shakespeare in Love*
55. Die Hard
56. Doctor Zhivago*
57. Harry Potter/Sorcerer's Stone
58. American Pie
59. American President
60. Willy Wonka/Choc. Factory
61. 12 Angry Men
62. As Good As It Gets
63. English Patient*
64. Ferris Bueller's Day Off
65. Rear Window
66. Amadeus
67. Caddyshack
68. Chinatown*
69. Fargo
70. Good Will Hunting*
71. Maltese Falcon
72. Sixth Sense
73. Dead Poets Society
74. Grease*
75. Great Escape

* Indicates a tie with film above

Top Overall Quality Ratings

For Top Foreign Language Films, see page 32.

CLASSIC (PRE-1960)

29 Casablanca

28 Wizard of Oz
Lady Eve
Singin' in the Rain
Rear Window
It Happened One Night
Citizen Kane
All About Eve
African Queen
Third Man
Best Years of Our Lives
Grapes of Wrath
On the Waterfront
Paths of Glory
Fantasia
Bridge on the River Kwai
Some Like It Hot
Sunset Boulevard
All Quiet on Western Front
Gone with the Wind
North by Northwest
High Noon
12 Angry Men
Double Indemnity
Maltese Falcon

27 Sweet Smell of Success
Snow White
Philadelphia Story
Woman of the Year
Treasure of the Sierra Madre
Heiress, The
Notorious
Searchers, The*
Ox-Bow Incident
Brief Encounter
Duck Soup
Holiday
It's a Wonderful Life
Christmas Carol
Great Expectations
Witness for the Prosecution
Big Sleep
Night of the Hunter
Hamlet
Sullivan's Travels
Streetcar Named Desire
Stalag 17
How Green Was My Valley
Quiet Man
Top Hat

MODERN (1960 TO DATE)

29 Godfather, The
Godfather Part II
Schindler's List
Lawrence of Arabia
To Kill a Mockingbird

28 Star Wars
Shawshank Redemption
Pianist, The
Finding Nemo
Dr. Strangelove
Lord of the Rings/Return
Spellbound
Man for All Seasons
Lion in Winter
Hotel Rwanda
Sound of Music
Psycho | 1960
Raiders of the Lost Ark

27 One Flew Over Cuckoo's...
My Fair Lady

I Never Sang for My Father
Usual Suspects
West Side Story
Taxi Driver
Young Frankenstein
Silence of the Lambs
Manchurian Candidate | 1962
Chinatown
Apocalypse Now
Lord of the Rings/Fellowship
Patton
Annie Hall
Sting, The
Chicago
Lord of the Rings/Two Towers
Gandhi
Great Escape
Million Dollar Baby
Advise & Consent
Wild Bunch
Princess Bride

Graduate, The
Spirited Away
Goodfellas
Mad Hot Ballroom*
Toy Story

Days of Wine and Roses
Doctor Zhivago
Breaker Morant
Fitzcarraldo

BY GENRE

ACTION/ADVENTURE

CLASSIC

27	Treasure of the Sierra Madre
25	Adventures of Robin Hood
	Mutiny on the Bounty
	King Kong
	Captains Courageous
24	Rio Bravo
23	Captain Blood
22	Mark of Zorro
	Around the World in 80 Days
21	Tarzan and His Mate

MODERN

29	Lawrence of Arabia
28	Lord of the Rings/Return
	Raiders of the Lost Ark
27	Lord of the Rings/Fellowship
	Lord of the Rings/Two Towers
	Great Escape
26	Papillon
	Magnificent Seven
	Spartacus
25	Man Who Would Be King

AMERICANA

CLASSIC

28	Best Years of Our Lives
	Grapes of Wrath
27	It's a Wonderful Life
26	Shadow of a Doubt
	Meet Me in St. Louis
	Mr. Smith Goes to Washington
25	Yankee Doodle Dandy
	Member of the Wedding
	Mr. Deeds Goes to Town
	All the King's Men

MODERN

29	To Kill a Mockingbird
26	Christmas Story
25	Music Man
	Badlands
	Seabiscuit
24	Stand by Me
	American Graffiti
	Far From Heaven
	Forrest Gump
	Straight Story

ANIMATED

CLASSIC

28	Fantasia
27	Snow White
26	Pinocchio
	Cinderella
	Bambi
	Lady and the Tramp
25	Peter Pan
	Sleeping Beauty
24	Dumbo
	Alice in Wonderland

MODERN

28	Finding Nemo
27	Spirited Away
	Toy Story
26	Shrek
	Beauty/Beast
	Shrek 2
	Incredibles, The
	Monsters, Inc.
	Ratatouille
	Toy Story 2

BIOGRAPHY

CLASSIC

25	Yankee Doodle Dandy
	Sergeant York
24	Scarlet Empress▽
23	Diary of Anne Frank
	Viva Zapata!
	Lust for Life
	Anastasia
22	Song of Bernadette
	Pride of the Yankees

MODERN

29	Lawrence of Arabia
28	Man for All Seasons
27	Patton
	Gandhi
26	Raging Bull
	Amadeus
	Becket
	Ray
	Anne of the Thousand Days
	Last Emperor

CHILDREN/FAMILY

CLASSIC

28	Wizard of Oz
27	It's a Wonderful Life
	Christmas Carol
24	Lili
	Bells of St. Mary's
	National Velvet
	Old Yeller
	Jungle Book
23	Father of the Bride
22	20,000 Leagues Under Sea

MODERN

28	Sound of Music
27	Princess Bride
	Mary Poppins
26	E.T. The Extra-Terrestrial
	Christmas Story
	Sounder
	Willy Wonka
25	Babe
	Whale Rider
24	Harry Potter/Goblet of Fire

COMEDY

CLASSIC

28	Some Like It Hot
27	Woman of the Year
	Mister Roberts
26	Adam's Rib
	Great Dictator
	Man Who Came to Dinner*
	Monkey Business
	Harvey
25	Auntie Mame
	Lavender Hill Mob

MODERN

27	Young Frankenstein
	Annie Hall
	Graduate, The
26	This Is Spinal Tap
	When Harry Met Sally...
	Manhattan
	Local Hero
25	Waiting for Guffman
	Blazing Saddles
	Tootsie

CRIME

CLASSIC

28	Rear Window
	On the Waterfront
26	Arsenic and Old Lace
	Anatomy of a Murder
25	Public Enemy
	Lavender Hill Mob
	High Sierra
	Dial M for Murder
	To Catch a Thief
24	Little Caesar

MODERN

29	Godfather, The
	Godfather Part II
27	Usual Suspects
	Sting, The
	Chicago
	Goodfellas
26	Departed, The
	Pulp Fiction
	Capote
	Mystic River

CULT

CLASSIC

29	Casablanca
28	Wizard of Oz
	All About Eve
	Fantasia
27	It's a Wonderful Life
	Gun Crazy
26	Red Shoes
25	Forbidden Planet
23	Freaks
20	7th Voyage of Sinbad

MODERN

28	Star Wars
	Shawshank Redemption
	Dr. Strangelove
	Sound of Music
27	Manchurian Candidate	1962
	Princess Bride
26	Monty Python/Holy Grail
	Breakfast at Tiffany's
	Blade Runner
	Willy Wonka

DRAMA

CLASSIC

28	Citizen Kane
	Best Years of Our Lives
	Grapes of Wrath
	On the Waterfront
	Paths of Glory
	High Noon
	12 Angry Men
27	Heiress, The
	Ox-Bow Incident
	Great Expectations

MODERN

29	Godfather, The
	Godfather Part II
	Schindler's List
	To Kill a Mockingbird
28	Shawshank Redemption
	Pianist, The
	Lion in Winter
	Hotel Rwanda
27	I Never Sang for My Father
	Taxi Driver

DRAMEDY

CLASSIC

28	All About Eve
	African Queen
27	It's a Wonderful Life
	Sullivan's Travels
	Stalag 17
	Dinner at Eight
26	Women, The
	Mr. Smith Goes to Washington
25	Sabrina
	Lady Vanishes

MODERN

27	One Flew Over Cuckoo's...
	Sting, The
26	Breakfast at Tiffany's
	Crimes and Misdemeanors
	Sense and Sensibility
	Charade
	Bend It Like Beckham
	Cool Hand Luke
25	Apartment, The
	Fargo

EPIC

CLASSIC

28	Bridge on the River Kwai
	Gone with the Wind
26	Ben-Hur
25	Mutiny on the Bounty
	Gunga Din
24	Ten Commandments
	Giant
23	Duel in the Sun
22	Around the World in 80 Days
	Robe, The

MODERN

29	Lawrence of Arabia
27	Gandhi
	Doctor Zhivago
26	Last Emperor
	2001: A Space Odyssey
	Braveheart
	Spartacus
25	Empire of the Sun
	Once Upon a Time/West
	Passage to India

FANTASY

CLASSIC

28	Wizard of Oz
27	Christmas Carol
26	Harvey
25	Miracle on 34th Street
	King Kong
	Lost Horizon
24	Ghost and Mrs. Muir
	Brigadoon
20	Topper
	7th Voyage of Sinbad

MODERN

28	Lord of the Rings/Return
27	Lord of the Rings/Fellowship
	Lord of the Rings/Two Towers
	Princess Bride
	Spirited Away
	Toy Story
	Mary Poppins
26	Willy Wonka
24	Harry Potter/Goblet of Fire
	Harry Potter/Order of Phoenix

FILM NOIR

CLASSIC

28	Third Man
	Sunset Boulevard
	Double Indemnity
	Maltese Falcon
27	Sweet Smell of Success
	Big Sleep
	Night of the Hunter
	Gun Crazy
	Laura
26	Out of the Past

MODERN

27	Chinatown
26	Blade Runner
	L.A. Confidential
	Memento
25	Fargo
	Cape Fear | 1962
24	Body Heat
	Blood Simple
23	Seven
22	Last Seduction

HORROR

CLASSIC

25	Frankenstein
	Bride of Frankenstein
24	Dracula
	Invasion/Body Snatchers
	Mummy, The
23	Freaks
	Cat People
	Thing, The
22	Invisible Man
21	House of Wax

MODERN

25	Exorcist, The
	Shining, The
24	Rosemary's Baby
	Hush... Hush, Sweet Charlotte
23	Army of Darkness
	Thing, The
22	Poltergeist
	Halloween
	Carrie
	Pit and the Pendulum

MUSICAL

CLASSIC

28	Wizard of Oz
	Singin' in the Rain
27	Top Hat
	King and I
26	American in Paris
	Band Wagon
	Meet Me in St. Louis
	Swing Time
25	Yankee Doodle Dandy
	Shall We Dance

MODERN

28	Sound of Music
27	My Fair Lady
	West Side Story
	Chicago
	Mary Poppins
26	Fiddler on the Roof
	Cabaret
	Funny Girl
25	Music Man
	That's Entertainment!

ROMANCE

CLASSIC

29	Casablanca
28	Lady Eve
	It Happened One Night
	African Queen
	Gone with the Wind
27	Philadelphia Story
	Notorious
	Brief Encounter
	Holiday
	How Green Was My Valley

MODERN

27	My Fair Lady
	West Side Story
	Annie Hall
	Graduate, The
	Doctor Zhivago
26	Room with a View
	Charade
	Manhattan
	Romeo and Juliet
25	Harold and Maude

SCI-FI

CLASSIC

26	On the Beach
25	Forbidden Planet
	Day the Earth Stood Still
24	Invasion/Body Snatchers
23	War of the Worlds
	Thing, The
22	20,000 Leagues Under Sea
20	Fly, The
19	Journey to Center of Earth
16	Godzilla

MODERN

28	Star Wars
26	E.T. The Extra-Terrestrial
	Star Wars V/Empire Strikes
	Iron Man
	Blade Runner
	2001: A Space Odyssey
25	Matrix, The
	Alien
24	Star Wars VI/Return of Jedi
	Close Encounters

THRILLER

CLASSIC

28	Rear Window
	Third Man
	North by Northwest
27	Notorious
	Night of the Hunter
	Vertigo
	39 Steps
26	Shadow of a Doubt
	Gaslight
	Strangers on a Train

MODERN

28	Psycho | 1960
27	Taxi Driver
	Silence of the Lambs
	Manchurian Candidate | 1962
26	Jaws
	Pulp Fiction
	Memento
	Seven Days in May
	Sixth Sense
25	Counterfeit Traitor

WAR

CLASSIC

29	Casablanca
28	Best Years of Our Lives
	Paths of Glory
	Bridge on the River Kwai
	All Quiet on Western Front
	Gone with the Wind
27	Stalag 17
	Caine Mutiny
	Mister Roberts
26	To Have and Have Not

MODERN

29	Schindler's List
	Lawrence of Arabia
28	Pianist, The
27	Apocalypse Now
	Patton
	Great Escape
26	MASH
	Saving Private Ryan
	Henry V
	Fog of War

WESTERN

CLASSIC

28	High Noon
27	Searchers, The
	Ox-Bow Incident
	Stagecoach
26	Red River
	Shane
25	My Darling Clementine
	Destry Rides Again
24	Oklahoma!
	She Wore a Yellow Ribbon

MODERN

27	Wild Bunch
26	Butch Cassidy/Sundance Kid
	Hud
	Unforgiven
	Magnificent Seven
25	Outlaw Josey Wales
	Once Upon a Time/West
	Man Who Shot Liberty Valance
24	No Country for Old Men
	Good, the Bad and the Ugly

BY DECADE

1910s/1920s

28	General, The
	Gold Rush
	Napoléon
27	Potemkin
	Metropolis
26	Cabinet of Dr. Caligari
	Nosferatu
25	Birth of a Nation
24	Cocoanuts, The
	Thief of Bagdad

1930s

28	Wizard of Oz
	It Happened One Night
	All Quiet on Western Front
	Gone with the Wind
27	Snow White
	Duck Soup
	Holiday
	Top Hat
	Dinner at Eight
	Wuthering Heights

1940s

29	Casablanca
28	Lady Eve
	Citizen Kane
	Third Man
	Best Years of Our Lives
	Grapes of Wrath
	Fantasia
	Double Indemnity
	Maltese Falcon
27	Philadelphia Story

1950s

28	Singin' in the Rain
	Rear Window
	All About Eve
	African Queen
	On the Waterfront
	Paths of Glory
	Bridge on the River Kwai
	Some Like It Hot
	Sunset Boulevard
	North by Northwest

1960s

29	Lawrence of Arabia
	To Kill a Mockingbird
28	Dr. Strangelove
	Man for All Seasons
	Lion in Winter
	Sound of Music
	Psycho
27	My Fair Lady
	West Side Story
	Manchurian Candidate

1970s

29	Godfather, The
	Godfather Part II
28	Star Wars
27	One Flew Over Cuckoo's...
	I Never Sang for My Father
	Taxi Driver
	Young Frankenstein
	Chinatown
	Apocalypse Now
	Patton

1980s

28	Raiders of the Lost Ark
27	Gandhi
	Princess Bride
	Breaker Morant
	Fitzcarraldo
26	E.T. The Extra-Terrestrial
	Raging Bull

Amadeus
Star Wars V/Empire Strikes
Soldier's Story

1990s

29 Schindler's List
28 Shawshank Redemption
27 Usual Suspects
Silence of the Lambs
Goodfellas
Toy Story
26 Saving Private Ryan
Beauty/Beast
Hoop Dreams
Pulp Fiction

2000s

28 Pianist, The
Finding Nemo

Lord of the Rings/Return
Spellbound
Hotel Rwanda
27 Lord of the Rings/Fellowship
Chicago
Lord of the Rings/Two Towers
Million Dollar Baby
Spirited Away
Mad Hot Ballroom
26 March of the Penguins
Shrek
Shrek 2
Iron Man
Beautiful Mind
Incredibles, The
Crash
Departed, The
Ray

BY DIRECTOR

Robert Aldrich

25 Flight of the Phoenix
24 Kiss Me Deadly
Hush... Hush, Sweet Charlotte

Woody Allen

27 Annie Hall
26 Crimes and Misdemeanors
Manhattan

Pedro Almodóvar

26 Talk to Her
25 All About My Mother
24 Women on the Verge

Robert Altman

26 MASH
25 3 Women
23 McCabe & Mrs. Miller

Paul Thomas Anderson

23 There Will Be Blood
20 Magnolia
19 Boogie Nights

Wes Anderson

23 Rushmore
22 Bottle Rocket
20 Royal Tenenbaums

Michael Apted

24 Amazing Grace
Coal Miner's Daughter
22 Gorky Park

Hal Ashby

26 Being There
25 Harold and Maude
23 Coming Home

Bruce Beresford

27 Breaker Morant
24 Tender Mercies
Driving Miss Daisy

Ingmar Bergman

27 Seventh Seal
Persona
26 Wild Strawberries

Bernardo Bertolucci

26 Conformist, The
Last Emperor
22 1900

Peter Bogdanovich

23 Last Picture Show
22 Paper Moon
21 What's Up, Doc?

Kenneth Branagh

26 Henry V
24 Hamlet
22 Dead Again

James L. Brooks

25 Terms of Endearment
23 Broadcast News
22 As Good As It Gets

Mel Brooks
27 Young Frankenstein
26 Producers, The
25 Blazing Saddles

Richard Brooks
25 Elmer Gantry
   In Cold Blood
   Cat on a Hot Tin Roof

Tim Burton
23 Sweeney Todd
22 Big Fish
21 Edward Scissorhands

James Cameron
24 Terminator, The
23 Aliens
   Terminator 2: Judgment Day

Frank Capra
28 It Happened One Night
27 It's a Wonderful Life
26 Arsenic and Old Lace

John Cassavetes
24 Woman Under the Influence
22 Faces
   Gloria

Charles Chaplin
28 City Lights
   Gold Rush
   Modern Times

Joel Coen
25 Fargo
24 Blood Simple
   No Country for Old Men

Francis Ford Coppola
29 Godfather, The
   Godfather Part II
27 Apocalypse Now

Sofia Coppola
21 Lost in Translation
20 Virgin Suicides
17 Marie Antoinette

David Cronenberg
24 Eastern Promises
22 History of Violence
21 Dead Zone

Cameron Crowe
23 Say Anything
   Almost Famous
21 Jerry Maguire

Alfonso Cuarón
24 Little Princess
   Harry Potter/Prisoner
   Y Tu Mamá También

George Cukor
27 My Fair Lady
   Philadelphia Story
   Holiday

Michael Curtiz
29 Casablanca
26 Mildred Pierce
25 Yankee Doodle Dandy

Jonathan Demme
27 Silence of the Lambs
25 Stop Making Sense
24 Philadelphia

Brian De Palma
22 Carlito's Way
   Scarface
   Carrie

Vittorio De Sica
27 Bicycle Thief
25 Two Women
   Garden of the Finzi-Continis

Stanley Donen
28 Singin' in the Rain
26 Charade
24 Funny Face

Clint Eastwood
27 Letters from Iwo Jima
   Million Dollar Baby
26 Unforgiven

Blake Edwards
27 Days of Wine and Roses
26 Breakfast at Tiffany's
25 Experiment in Terror

Federico Fellini
27 La Strada
   Nights of Cabiria
26 8½

Victor Fleming
28 Wizard of Oz
   Gone with the Wind
25 Captains Courageous

John Ford
28 Grapes of Wrath
27 Searchers, The
   How Green Was My Valley

Milos Forman

27 One Flew Over Cuckoo's...
26 Amadeus
21 Ragtime

Bob Fosse

26 Cabaret
24 Lenny
All That Jazz

John Frankenheimer

27 Manchurian Candidate
26 Seven Days in May
22 Birdman of Alcatraz

Stephen Frears

26 Queen, The
24 Dangerous Liaisons
23 Dirty Pretty Things

Mel Gibson

26 Braveheart
22 Passion of the Christ
19 Apocalypto

Terry Gilliam

26 Monty Python/Holy Grail
24 Brazil
22 Twelve Monkeys

Christopher Guest

25 Waiting for Guffman
24 Best in Show
23 Mighty Wind

Curtis Hanson

26 L.A. Confidential
21 Wonder Boys
19 8 Mile

Howard Hawks

27 Big Sleep
Bringing Up Baby
26 Red River

Werner Herzog

27 Fitzcarraldo
25 Aguirre: The Wrath of God
22 Nosferatu the Vampyre

George Roy Hill

27 Sting, The
26 Butch Cassidy
22 Slaughterhouse-Five

Alfred Hitchcock

28 Rear Window
North by Northwest
Psycho

Ron Howard

26 Beautiful Mind
25 Cinderella Man
24 Apollo 13

John Hughes

23 Ferris Bueller's Day Off
22 Breakfast Club
Sixteen Candles

John Huston

28 African Queen
Maltese Falcon
27 Treasure of the Sierra Madre

Alejandro González-Iñárritu

26 Amores Perros
22 21 Grams
Babel

James Ivory

26 Room with a View
24 Remains of the Day
22 Howards End

Peter Jackson

28 Lord of Rings/Return
27 Lord of Rings/Fellowship
Lord of Rings/Two Towers

Jim Jarmusch

24 Down by Law
18 Coffee and Cigarettes
16 Broken Flowers

Lawrence Kasdan

24 Body Heat
Silverado
23 Big Chill

Philip Kaufman

26 Right Stuff
22 Quills
21 Unbearable Lightness of Being

Elia Kazan

28 On the Waterfront
27 Streetcar Named Desire
26 Gentleman's Agreement

Stanley Kramer

26 Inherit the Wind
On the Beach
Judgment at Nuremberg

Stanley Kubrick

28 Dr. Strangelove
Paths of Glory
26 2001: A Space Odyssey

Akira Kurosawa

29 Seven Samurai
   Rashomon
28 Yojimbo

David Lean

29 Lawrence of Arabia
28 Bridge on the River Kwai
27 Brief Encounter

Ang Lee

26 Sense and Sensibility
25 Eat Drink Man Woman
24 Crouching Tiger

Spike Lee

23 Malcolm X
   Do the Right Thing
   Inside Man

Sergio Leone

25 Once Upon a Time/West
24 Good, the Bad and the Ugly
   Once Upon a Time/America

Richard Lester

24 Hard Day's Night
22 Three Musketeers
   Funny Thing Happened...

Barry Levinson

25 Rain Man
   Diner
24 Avalon

George Lucas

28 Star Wars
24 American Graffiti
23 Star Wars III/Revenge of Sith

Baz Luhrmann

23 Moulin Rouge!
   Strictly Ballroom
19 Romeo + Juliet

Sidney Lumet

28 12 Angry Men
26 Pawnbroker, The
24 Fail-Safe

David Lynch

24 Elephant Man
   Straight Story
22 Blue Velvet

Terrence Malick

25 Badlands
23 Days of Heaven
19 Thin Red Line

Louis Malle

27 Au Revoir Les Enfants
24 Atlantic City
22 Damage

Joseph L. Mankiewicz

28 All About Eve
25 Sleuth
24 Ghost and Mrs. Muir

Michael Mann

25 Insider, The
22 Last of the Mohicans
   Heat

Anthony Minghella

23 Truly Madly Deeply
22 Cold Mountain
   English Patient

Vincente Minnelli

26 American in Paris
   Band Wagon
   Meet Me in St. Louis

Mike Nichols

27 Graduate, The
25 Who's Afraid of V. Woolf?
   Catch-22

Alan J. Pakula

26 Sophie's Choice
25 All the President's Men
24 Parallax View

Alan Parker

24 Commitments, The
   Midnight Express
23 Mississippi Burning

Arthur Penn

25 Miracle Worker
   Bonnie and Clyde
24 Little Big Man

Roman Polanski

28 Pianist, The
27 Chinatown
24 Rosemary's Baby

Sydney Pollack

25 Tootsie
   Out of Africa
24 Way We Were

Otto Preminger

27 Advise & Consent
   Laura
26 Anatomy of a Murder

Robert Redford
- 25 Ordinary People
- 22 River Runs Through It
- 21 Quiz Show

Rob Reiner
- 27 Princess Bride
- 26 This Is Spinal Tap
- When Harry Met Sally...

John Sayles
- 25 Lone Star
- 24 Eight Men Out
- 23 Brother from Another Planet

Franklin J. Schaffner
- 27 Patton
- 26 Papillon
- 24 Boys from Brazil

Martin Scorsese
- 27 Taxi Driver
- Goodfellas
- 26 Raging Bull

Ridley Scott
- 26 Blade Runner
- 25 Alien
- 23 Gladiator

Bryan Singer
- 27 Usual Suspects
- 24 X2: X-Men United
- 19 X-Men

Steven Soderbergh
- 23 Traffic
- 21 Out of Sight
- Erin Brockovich

Steven Spielberg
- 29 Schindler's List
- 28 Raiders of the Lost Ark
- 26 E.T. The Extra Terrestrial

George Stevens
- 27 Woman of the Year
- Place in the Sun
- 26 Shane

Oliver Stone
- 25 Platoon
- 22 Wall Street
- 21 Salvador

John Sturges
- 27 Great Escape
- 26 Magnificent Seven
- 24 Bad Day at Black Rock

Preston Sturges
- 28 Lady Eve
- 27 Sullivan's Travels
- 25 Palm Beach Story

Quentin Tarantino
- 26 Pulp Fiction
- 25 Kill Bill Vol. 2
- 24 Reservoir Dogs

François Truffaut
- 27 400 Blows
- Day for Night
- 25 Shoot the Piano Player

Gus Van Sant
- 24 Good Will Hunting
- 22 Finding Forrester
- 19 My Own Private Idaho

John Waters
- 19 Polyester
- Hairspray
- 18 Pink Flamingos

Peter Weir
- 25 Gallipoli
- 24 Picnic at Hanging Rock
- Year of Living Dangerously

Orson Welles
- 28 Citizen Kane
- 26 Touch of Evil
- 25 Lady from Shanghai

Wim Wenders
- 25 Buena Vista Social Club
- 24 Wings of Desire
- 22 Paris, Texas

Billy Wilder
- 28 Some Like It Hot
- Sunset Boulevard
- Double Indemnity

Robert Wise
- 28 Sound of Music
- 27 West Side Story
- 25 Day the Earth Stood Still

William Wyler
- 28 Best Years of Our Lives
- 27 Heiress, The
- Roman Holiday

Fred Zinnemann
- 28 Man for All Seasons
- High Noon
- 26 From Here to Eternity

Top Acting Ratings

CLASSIC (PRE-1960)

29 All About Eve
Hamlet
On the Waterfront
Brief Encounter
African Queen

28 Casablanca
Streetcar Named Desire
12 Angry Men
Lady Eve
Now, Voyager
Adam's Rib
Philadelphia Story
Sweet Smell of Success
Little Foxes
White Heat
Night of the Hunter
Born Yesterday
Kind Hearts and Coronets
Grapes of Wrath
Heiress, The
Woman of the Year
Caine Mutiny
Sunset Boulevard

Witness for the Prosecution
Bridge on the River Kwai
It Happened One Night
Third Man
Ball of Fire
Snake Pit
His Girl Friday
Bad Day at Black Rock

27 Treasure of the Sierra Madre
Jezebel
Citizen Kane
Some Like It Hot
Rear Window
Double Indemnity
Room at the Top
East of Eden
Bringing Up Baby
Man Who Came to Dinner
Notorious
Paths of Glory
To Have and Have Not
Desk Set
Mister Roberts

MODERN (1960 TO DATE)

29 Godfather Part II
Godfather, The
One Flew Over Cuckoo's...
Monster
Capote
Ray
Lion in Winter
Taxi Driver
Queen, The
Becket
To Kill a Mockingbird
Schindler's List
Away from Her
Last King of Scotland
Pianist, The

28 Hotel Rwanda
Beautiful Mind
Million Dollar Baby
Silence of the Lambs
Days of Wine and Roses
Gandhi
Man for All Seasons
Patton

Shawshank Redemption
Lawrence of Arabia
Raging Bull
Notes on a Scandal
Inherit the Wind
Mystic River
Sophie's Choice
Iris
Prime of Miss Jean Brodie
My Left Foot
Midnight Cowboy
TransAmerica
Chinatown
Vera Drake
Departed, The
Apartment, The
Hud
Walk the Line
Savages, The
Sleuth*
Frances
American History X
Raisin in the Sun

Ben Affleck

25 Good Will Hunting
19 Chasing Amy
Changing Lanes

Woody Allen

26 Annie Hall
Crimes and Misdemeanors
24 Husbands and Wives

Julie Andrews

25 Sound of Music
24 Mary Poppins
Victor/Victoria

Jennifer Aniston

22 Good Girl
21 Office Space
20 Friends with Money

Ann-Margret

26 Carnal Knowledge
24 Grumpy Old Men
18 Bye Bye Birdie

Fred Astaire

26 On the Beach
24 Funny Face
23 Top Hat

Lauren Bacall

27 To Have and Have Not
Big Sleep
26 Key Largo

Anne Bancroft

28 Miracle Worker
27 Graduate, The
Elephant Man

Antonio Banderas

24 Women on the Verge
21 Tie Me Up! Tie Me Down!
19 Interview with the Vampire

Drew Barrymore

23 Confessions/Dangerous Mind
22 E.T. The Extra-Terrestrial
19 Music and Lyrics

Kathy Bates

26 About Schmidt
25 Fried Green Tomatoes
24 Misery

Warren Beatty

25 Bonnie and Clyde
Splendor in the Grass
23 Parallax View

Annette Bening

27 Being Julia
American Beauty
26 Grifters, The

Ingrid Bergman

28 Casablanca
27 Notorious
Gaslight

Gael García Bernal

26 Bad Education
Amores Perros
25 Motorcycle Diaries

Halle Berry

26 Monster's Ball
21 X2: X-Men United
19 X-Men: The Last Stand

Cate Blanchett

28 Notes on a Scandal
27 Elizabeth
25 Veronica Guerin

Humphrey Bogart

29 African Queen
28 Casablanca
Caine Mutiny

Marlon Brando

29 Godfather, The
On the Waterfront
28 Streetcar Named Desire

Matthew Broderick

26 Glory
24 Election
22 Biloxi Blues

Richard Burton

29 Becket
27 Who's Afraid of V. Woolf?
Anne of the Thousand Days

Nicolas Cage

26 Adaptation
25 Moonstruck
24 Leaving Las Vegas

James Cagney

28 White Heat
27 Mister Roberts
25 Public Enemy

Michael Caine
28 Sleuth
26 Man Who Would Be King
Quiet American

Jim Carrey
24 Eternal Sunshine
22 Truman Show
Man on the Moon

Charles Chaplin
28 Gold Rush
City Lights
27 Great Dictator

Don Cheadle
28 Hotel Rwanda
27 Crash
24 Reign Over Me

Cher
26 Silkwood
25 Moonstruck
24 Mask

Julie Christie
29 Away From Her
26 Doctor Zhivago
Billy Liar

Montgomery Clift
27 From Here to Eternity
Place in the Sun
26 Suddenly, Last Summer

George Clooney
27 Good Night, and Good Luck
26 Michael Clayton
24 Syriana

Glenn Close
26 Dangerous Liaisons
24 Big Chill
23 Fatal Attraction

Jennifer Connelly
28 Beautiful Mind
27 House of Sand and Fog
Requiem for a Dream

Sean Connery
26 Man Who Would Be King
25 Wind and the Lion
24 Finding Forrester

Gary Cooper
28 Ball of Fire
26 High Noon
For Whom the Bell Tolls

Kevin Costner
26 Upside of Anger
24 Silverado
23 Open Range

Joan Crawford
26 Grand Hotel
Women, The
25 Mildred Pierce

Russell Crowe
28 Beautiful Mind
Insider, The
27 Cinderella Man

Tom Cruise
27 Rain Man
26 Few Good Men
24 Collateral

Tony Curtis
28 Sweet Smell of Success
27 Some Like It Hot
19 Operation Petticoat

Matt Damon
25 Good Will Hunting
24 Syriana
23 Bourne Ultimatum

Bette Davis
29 All About Eve
28 Now, Voyager
Little Foxes

Daniel Day-Lewis
28 My Left Foot
There Will Be Blood
25 In the Name of the Father

James Dean
27 East of Eden
24 Rebel Without a Cause
23 Giant

Judi Dench
28 Notes on a Scandal
Iris
Mrs. Brown

Catherine Deneuve
25 Last Metro
Belle de Jour
Indochine

Robert De Niro
29 Taxi Driver
28 Raging Bull
Deer Hunter

Johnny Depp

27] Finding Neverland
26] Sweeney Todd
25] Pirates Caribbean/The Curse

Cameron Diaz

24] Being John Malkovich
20] In Her Shoes
Holiday, The

Leonardo DiCaprio

28] Departed, The
26] Blood Diamond
25] What's Eating Gilbert Grape

Kirk Douglas

27] Paths of Glory
26] Out of the Past
25] Lust for Life

Michael Douglas

25] China Syndrome
24] Traffic
Wonder Boys

Robert Downey Jr.

27] Chaplin
26] Iron Man
22] Guide to Recognizing Saints

Richard Dreyfuss

24] Apprenticeship/Duddy Kravitz
23] Goodbye Girl
American Graffiti

Faye Dunaway

28] Chinatown
25] Network
Bonnie and Clyde

Clint Eastwood

28] Million Dollar Baby
26] Unforgiven
23] Outlaw Josey Wales

Dakota Fanning

25] I Am Sam
Man on Fire
22] Charlotte's Web

Colin Farrell

25] In Bruges
22] Home at the End of the World
20] Phone Booth

Mia Farrow

26] Crimes and Misdemeanors
25] Hannah and Her Sisters
Rosemary's Baby

Will Ferrell

23] Stranger Than Fiction
21] Elf
19] Blades of Glory

Sally Field

27] Norma Rae
25] Steel Magnolias
Absence of Malice

Laurence Fishburne

26] Akeelah and the Bee
What's Love Got to Do with It
22] Boyz N the Hood

Henry Fonda

28] 12 Angry Men
Lady Eve
Grapes of Wrath

Jane Fonda

27] Julia
On Golden Pond
26] Coming Home

Harrison Ford

24] Fugitive, The
Raiders of the Lost Ark
Witness

Jodie Foster

28] Silence of the Lambs
Accused, The
26] Alice Doesn't Live Here

Jamie Foxx

29] Ray
24] Dreamgirls
Collateral

Brendan Fraser

27] Gods and Monsters
26] Quiet American
17] Mummy Returns

Morgan Freeman

28] Million Dollar Baby
Shawshank Redemption
27] Driving Miss Daisy

Clark Gable

28] It Happened One Night
27] Gone with the Wind
25] Mutiny on the Bounty

Greta Garbo

27] Ninotchka
26] Camille
Grand Hotel

Ava Gardner
26 Night of the Iguana
On the Beach
25 Killers, The

Judy Garland
26 Wizard of Oz
Star Is Born
24 Meet Me in St. Louis

Richard Gere
26 Chicago
25 Primal Fear
24 Unfaithful

Paul Giamatti
26 Sideways
25 American Splendor
24 Illusionist, The

Mel Gibson
25 Year of Living Dangerously
Gallipoli
24 Braveheart

Whoopi Goldberg
27 Color Purple
21 Ghost
18 Sister Act

Cuba Gooding Jr.
25 Radio
22 Boyz N the Hood
Jerry Maguire

Cary Grant
28 Philadelphia Story
His Girl Friday
27 Bringing Up Baby

Hugh Grant
23 Bridget Jones's Diary
Love Actually
About a Boy

Jake Gyllenhaal
26 Brokeback Mountain
24 Zodiac
23 Donnie Darko

Gene Hackman
26 Conversation, The
Unforgiven
French Connection

Tom Hanks
27 Philadelphia
26 Road to Perdition
Forrest Gump

Ethan Hawke
27 Training Day
Before the Devil Knows . . .
25 Dead Poets Society

Goldie Hawn
23 Butterflies Are Free
22 Cactus Flower
20 Everyone Says I Love You

Audrey Hepburn
27 My Fair Lady
Two for the Road
26 Children's Hour

Katharine Hepburn
29 Lion in Winter
African Queen
28 Adam's Rib

Charlton Heston
24 Touch of Evil
23 Ben-Hur
Agony and the Ecstasy

Dustin Hoffman
28 Midnight Cowboy
27 Graduate, The
Rain Man

Philip Seymour Hoffman
29 Capote
28 Savages, The
27 Before the Devil Knows . . .

William Holden
28 Born Yesterday
Sunset Boulevard
Bridge on the River Kwai

Anthony Hopkins
28 Silence of the Lambs
27 Elephant Man
Remains of the Day

Rock Hudson
23 Giant
22 Magnificent Obsession
20 Pillow Talk

William Hurt
25 Children of a Lesser God
Body Heat
Kiss of the Spider Woman

Anjelica Huston
26 Crimes and Misdemeanors
Grifters, The
24 Prizzi's Honor

Jeremy Irons
27] Being Julia
26] Reversal of Fortune
25] French Lieutenant's Woman

Samuel L. Jackson
26] Pulp Fiction
23] Red Violin
Black Snake Moan

Scarlett Johansson
26] Ghost World
24] Lost in Translation
23] Girl with a Pearl Earring

Angelina Jolie
24] Mighty Heart
23] Good Shepherd, The
Girl, Interrupted

Tommy Lee Jones
27] Coal Miner's Daughter
No Country for Old Men
In the Valley of Elah

Diane Keaton
26] Annie Hall
Something's Gotta Give
25] Crimes of the Heart

Gene Kelly
28] Inherit the Wind
26] Singin' in the Rain
23] American in Paris

Grace Kelly
27] Rear Window
26] High Noon
Country Girl

Nicole Kidman
28] Hours, The
25] Others, The
Dogville

Ben Kingsley
29] Schindler's List
28] Gandhi
27] House of Sand and Fog

Kevin Kline
28] Sophie's Choice
24] Fish Called Wanda
Big Chill

Burt Lancaster
28] Sweet Smell of Success
27] Elmer Gantry
Atlantic City

Jessica Lange
28] Frances
27] Tootsie
25] Crimes of the Heart

Jude Law
26] Road to Perdition
24] Cold Mountain
23] Closer

Heath Ledger
26] Brokeback Mountain
21] Patriot, The
18] Casanova

Vivien Leigh
28] Streetcar Named Desire
27] Gone with the Wind
25] Ship of Fools

Jack Lemmon
28] Days of Wine and Roses
Apartment, The
27] Odd Couple

Laura Linney
28] Savages, The
26] You Can Count on Me
Kinsey

Shirley MacLaine
28] Apartment, The
27] Being There
26] Terms of Endearment

Tobey Maguire
25] Seabiscuit
24] Wonder Boys
Cider House Rules

John Malkovich
26] Dangerous Liaisons
Killing Fields
25] Shadow of the Vampire

Steve Martin
24] Dirty Rotten Scoundrels
23] All of Me
Planes, Trains/Automobiles

Marx Brothers
25] Duck Soup
Night at the Opera
24] Monkey Business

Matthew McConaughey
25] Lone Star
24] Amistad
22] Frailty

Frances McDormand
<u>27</u> Fargo
<u>26</u> North Country
<u>25</u> Man Who Wasn't There

Ewan McGregor
<u>24</u> Big Fish
<u>23</u> Moulin Rouge!
<u>22</u> Trainspotting

Ian McKellen
<u>27</u> Gods and Monsters
<u>26</u> Lord of Rings/Return
<u>25</u> Lord of Rings/Fellowship

Steve McQueen
<u>27</u> Papillon
<u>26</u> Sand Pebbles
Great Escape

Liza Minnelli
<u>25</u> Cabaret
<u>21</u> Arthur
New York, New York

Marilyn Monroe
<u>27</u> Some Like It Hot
<u>24</u> Misfits, The
<u>23</u> Seven Year Itch

Julianne Moore
<u>28</u> Hours, The
<u>27</u> Far From Heaven
<u>24</u> End of the Affair

Eddie Murphy
<u>22</u> Trading Places
<u>19</u> Beverly Hills Cop
<u>18</u> 48 HRS.

Bill Murray
<u>25</u> Rushmore
<u>24</u> Lost in Translation
<u>20</u> Broken Flowers

Liam Neeson
<u>29</u> Schindler's List
<u>26</u> Kinsey
<u>24</u> Mission, The

Paul Newman
<u>28</u> Hud
Sweet Bird of Youth
<u>27</u> Cat on a Hot Tin Roof

Jack Nicholson
<u>29</u> One Flew Over Cuckoo's...
<u>28</u> Chinatown
<u>27</u> Five Easy Pieces

Nick Nolte
<u>25</u> Affliction
<u>24</u> Cape Fear
<u>21</u> Prince of Tides

Edward Norton
<u>28</u> American History X
<u>25</u> Painted Veil
Fight Club

Kim Novak
<u>26</u> Vertigo
<u>24</u> Picnic
<u>22</u> Bell, Book and Candle

Laurence Olivier
<u>29</u> Hamlet
<u>28</u> Sleuth
<u>27</u> Wuthering Heights

Ryan O'Neal
<u>23</u> Paper Moon
<u>20</u> What's Up, Doc?
<u>18</u> Barry Lyndon

Peter O'Toole
<u>29</u> Lion in Winter
Becket
<u>28</u> Lawrence of Arabia

Clive Owen
<u>25</u> Inside Man
<u>24</u> Children of Men
<u>23</u> Closer

Al Pacino
<u>29</u> Godfather Part II
Godfather, The
<u>28</u> Insider, The

Gwyneth Paltrow
<u>25</u> Shakespeare in Love
<u>23</u> Emma
<u>22</u> Proof

Gregory Peck
<u>29</u> To Kill a Mockingbird
<u>27</u> Gentleman's Agreement
<u>26</u> Cape Fear

Sean Penn
<u>28</u> Mystic River
<u>27</u> 21 Grams
<u>26</u> Dead Man Walking

Michelle Pfeiffer
<u>26</u> Dangerous Liaisons
<u>25</u> I Am Sam
<u>24</u> Age of Innocence

Brad Pitt
25 Fight Club
   Babel
23 Seven

Sidney Poitier
28 Raisin in the Sun
27 In the Heat of the Night
   Guess Who's Coming...

Robert Redford
26 Sting, The
   Butch Cassidy
   All the President's Men

Vanessa Redgrave
27 Julia
23 Blowup
21 Camelot

Burt Reynolds
26 Deliverance
21 Boogie Nights
20 Starting Over

Tim Robbins
28 Shawshank Redemption
28 Mystic River
24 Bob Roberts

Julia Roberts
25 Charlie Wilson's War
23 Closer
   Erin Brockovich

Kurt Russell
26 Silkwood
23 Miracle
22 Tombstone

Meg Ryan
25 When Harry Met Sally...
22 Sleepless in Seattle
20 You've Got Mail

Adam Sandler
24 Reign Over Me
20 Punch-Drunk Love
   Spanglish

Susan Sarandon
27 Atlantic City
26 Dead Man Walking
25 Thelma & Louise

Peter Sellers
28 Dr. Strangelove
27 Being There
24 Lolita

Omar Sharif
28 Lawrence of Arabia
26 Doctor Zhivago
25 Funny Girl

Martin Sheen
27 Apocalypse Now
   Badlands
24 Gettysburg

Frank Sinatra
27 From Here to Eternity
26 Manchurian Candidate
   Man with the Golden Arm

Will Smith
25 Pursuit of Happyness
24 Six Degrees of Separation
22 I Am Legend

Sissy Spacek
27 Badlands
27 Coal Miner's Daughter
26 In the Bedroom

Kevin Spacey
28 Usual Suspects
27 L.A. Confidential
   American Beauty

Rod Steiger
29 On the Waterfront
28 Pawnbroker, The
27 In the Heat of the Night

James Stewart
28 Philadelphia Story
27 Rear Window
   Anatomy of a Murder

Ben Stiller
21 Meet the Fockers
   Meet the Parents
19 There's Something/Mary

Meryl Streep
28 Sophie's Choice
   Hours, The
26 Adaptation

Barbra Streisand
25 Funny Girl
   Way We Were
21 On a Clear Day You Can See...

Donald Sutherland
27 Ordinary People
26 Don't Look Now
25 MASH

Hilary Swank
- 28 Million Dollar Baby
- 27 Boys Don't Cry
- 23 Freedom Writers

Elizabeth Taylor
- 27 Who's Afraid of V. Woolf?
- Cat on a Hot Tin Roof
- Place in the Sun

Charlize Theron
- 29 Monster
- 27 In the Valley of Elah
- 26 North Country

Emma Thompson
- 27 Sense and Sensibility
- Remains of the Day
- 26 Howards End

Billy Bob Thornton
- 27 Sling Blade
- 26 Monster's Ball
- 25 Man Who Wasn't There

Uma Thurman
- 26 Pulp Fiction
- 24 Kill Bill Vol. 2
- 22 Kill Bill Vol. 1

Spencer Tracy
- 28 Adam's Rib
- Inherit the Wind
- Woman of the Year

John Travolta
- 26 Pulp Fiction
- 23 Love Song for Bobby Long
- 22 Get Shorty

Kathleen Turner
- 25 Body Heat
- 24 Prizzi's Honor
- Accidental Tourist

Jon Voight
- 28 Midnight Cowboy
- 26 Coming Home
- Deliverance

Mark Wahlberg
- 21 Invincible
- Boogie Nights
- Three Kings

Christopher Walken
- 28 Deer Hunter
- 25 Man on Fire
- 24 Catch Me If You Can

Denzel Washington
- 27 Philadelphia
- Training Day
- 26 American Gangster

John Wayne
- 25 Red River
- Searchers, The
- Quiet Man

Sigourney Weaver
- 25 Year of Living Dangerously
- 23 Holes
- 22 Alien

Orson Welles
- 28 Third Man
- 27 Citizen Kane
- Jane Eyre

Gene Wilder
- 26 Producers, The
- Young Frankenstein
- 22 Blazing Saddles

Robin Williams
- 26 Awakenings
- Dead Poets Society
- 25 Good Will Hunting

Bruce Willis
- 26 Pulp Fiction
- 25 Sixth Sense
- 23 Twelve Monkeys

Kate Winslet
- 27 Finding Neverland
- Sense and Sensibility
- Little Children

Reese Witherspoon
- 28 Walk the Line
- 24 Election
- 23 Importance of Being Earnest

Natalie Wood
- 25 Splendor in the Grass
- 24 West Side Story
- Rebel Without a Cause

Renée Zellweger
- 27 Cinderella Man
- 26 Chicago
- 24 Cold Mountain

Catherine Zeta-Jones
- 26 Chicago
- 24 Traffic
- 22 Terminal, The

Top Story Ratings

CLASSIC (PRE-1960)

28
Hamlet
Casablanca
All Quiet on Western Front
Paths of Glory
Witness for the Prosecution
Grapes of Wrath
Wizard of Oz
Great Expectations
Best Years of Our Lives
Double Indemnity
Rear Window
Christmas Carol

27
All About Eve
Wuthering Heights
On the Beach
Citizen Kane
Heiress, The
12 Angry Men
Bridge on the River Kwai
39 Steps
Place in the Sun
Strangers on a Train
Dial M for Murder

Gone with the Wind
It's a Wonderful Life
Rebecca
Searchers, The
Gun Crazy
Sunset Boulevard
Third Man
Brief Encounter
Maltese Falcon
Anatomy of a Murder
Of Mice and Men
North by Northwest
Stalag 17
Laura
Gentleman's Agreement
Lady Eve
Vertigo

26
Ox-Bow Incident
Sweet Smell of Success
Hunchback/Notre Dame
Some Like It Hot
Diary of Anne Frank
Member of the Wedding

MODERN (1960 TO DATE)

29
Godfather, The
To Kill a Mockingbird

28
Schindler's List
Godfather Part II
Shawshank Redemption
Usual Suspects
Star Wars
Manchurian Candidate | 1962
Hotel Rwanda
Seven Days in May

27
Man for All Seasons
Henry V
Great Escape
Dr. Strangelove
Raiders of the Lost Ark
Breaker Morant
Romeo and Juliet
Lord of the Rings/Return
Psycho | 1960
Christmas Story
Pianist, The
House of Games
Sting, The

One Flew Over Cuckoo's...
Day of the Jackal
Killing Fields
Lord of the Rings/Fellowship
Princess Bride
Lawrence of Arabia
Inherit the Wind
Spellbound*
Sixth Sense
I Never Sang for My Father
Lion in Winter
West Side Story*
Gandhi
My Fair Lady
Memento
Sound of Music
Wait Until Dark
Fiddler on the Roof
Advise & Consent
Silence of the Lambs

26
Doctor Zhivago
Lord of the Rings/Two Towers
Chinatown

Top Production Values Ratings

CLASSIC (PRE-1960)

29 Fantasia
Wizard of Oz
Gone with the Wind

28 Singin' in the Rain
Citizen Kane
Ben-Hur
Bridge on the River Kwai
Third Man

27 North by Northwest
Searchers, The
King and I
American in Paris
Casablanca
Quiet Man
Sunset Boulevard
Snow White
Red River
Ten Commandments
Rear Window

26 Gold Diggers of 1933
Band Wagon
Paths of Glory

Top Hat
Great Expectations
Some Like It Hot
Notorious
Lady from Shanghai
Vertigo
Ziegfeld Follies
African Queen
Heiress, The
Bambi
Night of the Hunter
Touch of Evil
Sweet Smell of Success
Gigi
All About Eve
Moulin Rouge
Red Shoes
Cinderella
Star Is Born
Woman of the Year
Pinocchio
42nd Street
Laura

MODERN (1960 TO DATE)

29 Lord of the Rings/Return
Finding Nemo
Lord of the Rings/Two Towers
Lawrence of Arabia
Lord of the Rings/Fellowship
Godfather, The
Star Wars
Chicago
Godfather Part II
Schindler's List

28 Winged Migration
Star Wars V/Empire Strikes
Matrix, The
Last Emperor
March of the Penguins
Saving Private Ryan
Toy Story
Raiders of the Lost Ark
Pianist, The
Shrek 2
Doctor Zhivago
Spirited Away
Sound of Music

Shrek
Monsters, Inc.
Incredibles, The
Iron Man
Apocalypse Now
Star Wars VI/Return of Jedi
Toy Story 2
Star Wars III/Revenge of Sith
Nightmare Before Christmas

27 Howl's Moving Castle
2001: A Space Odyssey
Beauty/Beast
West Side Story
Jurassic Park
Ratatouille
My Fair Lady
Patton
Braveheart
Brazil
Cars
Gandhi
Last Samurai
Blade Runner

Top Foreign Language Films

CLASSIC (PRE-1960)

29 Seven Samurai | *Japan*
Rashomon | *Japan*

28 Children of Paradise | *France*
Beauty/Beast | *France*
Grand Illusion | *France*
Open City∇ | *Italy*

27 Bicycle Thief | *Italy*
Seventh Seal | *Sweden*
Rules of the Game∇ | *France*
La Strada | *Italy*
Nights of Cabiria | *Italy*
Triumph of the Will* | *Germany*
400 Blows | *France*

Wages of Fear | *France*

26 Wild Strawberries | *Sweden*
Black Orpheus | *France*
Rififi | *France*
Smiles of a Summer Night | *Sweden*
Alexander Nevsky | *Russia*
M | *Germany*
Diabolique | *France*
Mon Oncle | *France*

25 Mr. Hulot's Holiday | *France*
Blue Angel | *Germany*

MODERN (1960 TO DATE)

29 Sorrow and the Pity | *France*

28 Shoah | *France*
Lives of Others | *Germany*
Battle of Algiers | *Italy*
Yojimbo | *Japan*
Das Boot | *Germany*

27 Ran | *Japan*
Life Is Beautiful | *Italy*
Downfall | *Germany*
Persona | *Sweden*
Born into Brothels | *U.S.*
Au Revoir Les Enfants | *France*
Letters from Iwo Jima | *U.S.*
Jean de Florette | *France*
Pan's Labyrinth | *Spain*
Shop on Main Street | *Czech*
Day for Night | *France*

26 Cinema Paradiso | *Italy*
Conformist, The | *Italy*
Diving Bell & the Butterfly | *France*
King of Hearts | *France*
City of God | *Brazil*
Babette's Feast | *Denmark*
Black Book | *Holland*
8½ | *Italy*
Amarcord | *Italy*
Fanny and Alexander | *Sweden*
Z | *France*
Cries and Whispers | *Sweden*
Talk to Her | *Spain*
Delicatessen | *France*
Amélie | *France*

Seven Beauties | *Italy*
Central Station | *Brazil*
Amores Perros | *Mexico*

25 Two Women | *Italy*
Sea Inside | *Spain*
Antonia's Line | *Holland*
Garden of the Finzi-Continis | *Italy*
Leopard, The | *Italy*
Hiroshima, Mon Amour | *France*
Aguirre: The Wrath of God | *Germany*
Maria Full of Grace | *U.S.*
Scenes from a Marriage | *Sweden*
Farewell My Concubine | *China*
La Dolce Vita | *Italy*
Marriage of Maria Braun | *Germany*
All About My Mother | *Spain*
Contempt | *France*
Hero | *China*
My Life As a Dog | *Sweden*
Like Water for Chocolate | *Mexico*
Shoot the Piano Player | *France*
Juliet of the Spirits | *Italy*
Breathless | *France*
Eat Drink Man Woman | *Taiwan*
La Vie en Rose | *France*

24 Jules and Jim | *France*

MOVIE
DIRECTORY

	OVERALL	ACTING	STORY	PROD.

About a Boy
21 | 23 | 22 | 21

2002 | Directed by Chris Weitz, Paul Weitz | With Hugh Grant, Toni Collette, Nicholas Hoult, Rachel Weisz | 101 minutes | Rated PG-13

This "wonderfully funny romantic comedy" features Grant's "best work" as a "rich, self-absorbed" "skirt-chaser pretending to be a single dad" who strikes up a "sweet friendship" with a "lonely young boy" and "redeems himself in the end"; those who "expect the usual superficial" "chick-flick fluff" are "pleasantly surprised" by this "clever" adaptation of the Nick Hornby novel.

About Last Night. . .
17 | 16 | 17 | 16

1986 | Directed by Edward Zwick | With Rob Lowe, Demi Moore, James Belushi, Elizabeth Perkins | 113 minutes | Rated R

"Brat pack" fans still find this "very '80s" romantic comedy "relatable" for its interpretation of "young" lovers as they struggle "to commit or not to commit" (it's based on the David Mamet play *Sexual Perversity in Chicago* with "not much resemblance to the original"); admirers of the "pre-fame" Moore and "at-his-prime" Lowe call it a "true guilty pleasure", even if the "silly", "self-absorbed" milieu is "so 20 years ago."

About Schmidt
21 | 26 | 20 | 21

2002 | Directed by Alexander Payne | With Jack Nicholson, Kathy Bates, Hope Davis, Dermot Mulroney | 125 minutes | Rated R

It's a "change of pace for Nicholson" ("no eyebrow raising"), who plays a "lethargic" "Middle America everyman" trying "to give his life purpose before it's too late" in this "heartbreaking" yet "hilarious" dramedy "guaranteed to scare anyone approaching retirement"; though it "drags at times", the "brilliant acting overcomes any plot shortcomings" – and the "Kathy Bates hot-tub scene" "will leave your head spinning."

Absence of Malice
21 | 25 | 21 | 20

1981 | Directed by Sydney Pollack | With Paul Newman, Sally Field, Bob Balaban | 116 minutes | Rated PG

"Newman and Field ignite the screen" in this "textured" "hard-hitting" courtroom drama demonstrating how "guilt by association" causes a "newspaper to ruin a man's career"; most say that the "irresponsible press" is a topic made for the movies, but some feel this "slight" effort "should have been better" – starting with the "not-believable ending."

Absent-Minded Professor, The ◐
19 | 17 | 19 | 17

1961 | Directed by Robert Stevenson | With Fred MacMurray, Nancy Olson, Keenan Wynn | 97 minutes | Rated PG

Despite its "charming", "classic Disney" formula, this "bouncy tale" involving an invention dubbed "flubber" divides voters: flubbergasted fans claim it "stands up well over time", but deflators find it "kinda corny", adding it "may not appeal" to small fry, since its black-and-white cinematography "looks old"; although popular enough to inspire a couple of remakes, the "original is the best."

Abyss, The
20 | 19 | 19 | 25

1989 | Directed by James Cameron | With Ed Harris, Mary Elizabeth Mastrantonio | 146 minutes | Rated PG-13

"Eye-popping" special effects – notably the "breakout use of morphing" – are the raison d'être of this "underwater opus", a "fun"

subscribe to ZAGAT.com

cocktail comprised of a "little sci-fi, a little action and a little romance"; it's also a little "long" and "sputters" at the finale, so diehards recommend the (even longer) "director's cut", which "fleshes out the far-too-abrupt ending in the original version."

Accidental Tourist, The

1988 | Directed by Lawrence Kasdan | With William Hurt, Kathleen Turner, Geena Davis | 121 minutes | Rated PG

This "zany" romantic drama about love, loss and "alphabetizing the groceries in your cupboard" is "as good as" Anne Tyler's best-seller and might "break and mend your heart in one sitting"; its "perfect cast" includes a "terrific" Hurt and an "offbeat", "pitch-perfect" Davis (who "copped an Oscar"), though some argue the picture is "too quirky" and "inert" for mainstream audiences.

Accused, The ✉

1988 | Directed by Jonathan Kaplan | With Kelly McGillis, Jodie Foster, Bernie Coulson | 108 minutes | Rated R

Not for the "faint of heart", this "white-knuckle" thriller about a gang rape and its courtroom consequences is "based on true events" and dominated by a "phenomenal" Foster, who won a "thoroughly deserved" Oscar for her "captivating performance"; the "excruciating", "very graphic" reenactment of the crime is "definitely for mature audiences" – but far from gratuitous given the picture's "socially responsible" message.

Ace Ventura: Pet Detective

1994 | Directed by Tom Shadyac | With Jim Carrey, Courteney Cox, Sean Young | 86 minutes | Rated PG-13

The "vulgar", "puerile humor" of this "silly, turn-your-brain-off" comedy about a pet detective tracking down a kidnapped dolphin was "Carrey's breakthrough", though some would "rather eat dirt" than sit through it; still, the "rubber-faced" star is so "over the top" that few notice this venture is "inanely short on plot."

Across the Universe

2007 | Directed by Julie Taymor | With Evan Rachel Wood, Jim Sturgess, Joe Anderson, Dana Fuchs | 133 minutes | Rated PG-13

"Psychedelic '60s nostalgia" underlies this "different" musical fantasia via "zeitgeist-tapper" Taymor, a "fun ride" that uses the "amazing Beatles catalog" (re-recorded and sung by the actors) to illuminate that turbulent era; the "clichéd", "cut-and-paste" story and "preachy" undertone are trumped by "sumptuous", "visually stunning" set pieces and "cameos galore" (Bono, Joe Cocker, Eddie Izzard); in the end, "if you love the music, you'll love the film."

⚡ Adam's Rib ◑

1949 | Directed by George Cukor | With Spencer Tracy, Katharine Hepburn, Judy Holliday | 101 minutes | Not Rated

"Chemistry abounds" in this "sparkling" matchup of Tracy and Hepburn, "probably the best pairing" of these "two pros", who are so "delightful" that many "wish they'd made even more movies together"; plotwise, this "battle-of-the-sexes" comedy concerns "married attorneys on opposing sides of a case", but fans say it's worth watching for the "effortless comedic timing" alone.

	OVERALL	ACTING	STORY	PROD.

Adaptation
22 | 26 | 21 | 22

2002 | Directed by Spike Jonze | With Nicolas Cage, Meryl Streep, Chris Cooper | 114 minutes | Rated R

"You'll either love or hate" this "story within a story within a story", a "dark", "twisted" "head trip" about a screenwriter trying to adapt an unadaptable book; some find it "confusing", and even fans feel the "ending seemed to belong to a different film" ("perhaps that's the point"), but still "it's one of the most original movies ever made", bolstered by "superb acting."

Addams Family, The
17 | 19 | 16 | 20

1991 | Directed by Barry Sonnenfeld | With Anjelica Huston, Raul Julia, Christopher Lloyd | 102 minutes | Rated PG-13

That "creepy, kooky" family spawned from the *New Yorker* cartoons" and popularized by the '60s TV series makes its "ookie" screen debut with all its "madcap", ghoulish antics intact; "like MTV's *The Osbournes*", the story revolves around "misunderstood but lovable" types doing "quirky, offbeat" things.

Adventures in Babysitting
19 | 16 | 19 | 17

1987 | Directed by Chris Columbus | With Elisabeth Shue, Keith Coogan, Anthony Rapp, Penelope Ann Miller | 102 minutes | Rated PG-13

A standard on the "slumber-party" circuit, this "classic '80s" teen comedy stars the "adorable" Shue as a "girl next door" type babysitting some "misfit kids" and taking them on a "wild ride" through Chicago; an "enjoyable time-waster", it's worth fast-forwarding to the "scene in the R&B bar" and Vincent D'Onofrio's "great cameo."

Adventures of Priscilla, Queen of the Desert, The
23 | 24 | 22 | 22

1994 | Directed by Stephan Elliott | With Terence Stamp, Guy Pearce, Hugo Weaving | 104 minutes | Rated R

"Outlandish drag queens" and the "Australian outback" collide in this "razor-sharp" road comedy, a "flaming romp" about "boas, false eyelashes" and a bus "ride through the desert"; highlights include Stamp's "campy" performance as a "post-op transsexual looking for love" and a "fabulous" soundtrack that will thrill "ABBA fans"; P.S. yup, "that's really Guy Pearce!"

Adventures of Robin Hood, The
25 | 22 | 24 | 24

1938 | Directed by Michael Curtiz, William Keighley | With Errol Flynn, Olivia de Havilland | 102 minutes | Not Rated

This "swashbuckliest swashbuckler of them all" is the "definitive telling" of the tale, filmed in "gorgeous Technicolor" and "acted with verve" by a "charismatic" Flynn and a "perfect" de Havilland; ok, it might be "a bit dated", but its "lightning-quick dialogue", "exciting" swordplay and those famous "green tights" are "still engaging" enough to inspire a "whole genre of films" – plus a "whole lot of parodies."

☑ Advise & Consent ◑
27 | 27 | 27 | 24

1962 | Directed by Otto Preminger | With Henry Fonda, Charles Laughton, Walter Pidgeon, Don Murray | 139 minutes | Not Rated

A "grown-up study of Washington" (which should be "required viewing for all of Congress"), this "interesting", "behind-the-scenes" drama stars Fonda as a Cabinet candidate whose confirmation hearings inaugurate a "gutsy" exposé of hardball politics; voters consent it's a "talky chestnut", but it's still a front-runner for "one of Preminger's best."

⚡ Affair to Remember, An   26 | 25 | 25 | 23

1957 | Directed by Leo McCarey | With Cary Grant, Deborah Kerr, Richard Denning | 119 minutes | Not Rated

The "ultimate chick flick", this "three-hanky tearjerker" begins with a "glamorous" "shipboard romance" that turns "tragic" after an "unexpected twist" at the "Empire State Building"; though the "inspiration for many other weepies" (notably *Sleepless in Seattle*), this one's the "standard", thanks to the "captivating banter", ultra-"suave Grant" and some "classic NY" scenery; just don't bother to see it with your boyfriend – men "don't get it."

Affliction   20 | 25 | 19 | 19

1998 | Directed by Paul Schrader | With Nick Nolte, Sissy Spacek, James Coburn | 113 minutes | Rated R

Granted, it's "grim, grim, grim", but this "disquieting" adaptation of Russell Banks' novel of "family dysfunction" in New Hampshire is still "eminently watchable" due to its "strong performances": Nolte's "wrenching" work and Coburn's "scary", Oscar-winning turn in particular; though admittedly a "great exposé on abuse", some of the afflicted find it so "mind-numbingly downbeat" that they want to "slash their wrists" afterward.

⚡ African Queen, The ✉∅   28 | 29 | 26 | 26

1951 | Directed by John Huston | With Humphrey Bogart, Katharine Hepburn, Robert Morley | 105 minutes | Not Rated

"Curmudgeonly riverboat captain" Bogie and "feisty missionary" Hepburn "sizzle" as they take a "trip up a hellish river" and "discover love, courage" and the "best use of leeches since the Middle Ages" in this "beautifully crafted" drama; its "legendary reputation" owes a lot to Huston's "no-nonsense direction", James Agee's "witty" screenplay, the fine "location shots" of "deepest Africa" and, of course, that "undeniable chemistry" between the two shining stars; in sum, "they don't make 'em like this anymore."

After Hours   21 | 20 | 22 | 19

1985 | Directed by Martin Scorsese | With Griffin Dunne, Rosanna Arquette, Teri Garr | 96 minutes | Rated R

From the ever-"creative" Scorsese comes this "offbeat" cult curio, a "pitch-black comedy" set in '80s SoHo recounting the after-hours adventures of a "straight-laced guy" out on the town and out of cash in a "pre-ATM" world; the "numerous subplots" (involving an "ice cream truck", a "headbanger nightclub" and a potty-mouthed sculptress) strike the straightlaced as "confusing" verging on "weird", but most tout its "razor-sharp performances" and "deft" wit.

After the Sunset   17 | 18 | 17 | 19

2004 | Directed by Brett Ratner | With Pierce Brosnan, Salma Hayek, Woody Harrelson | 97 minutes | Rated PG-13

The "non-Bond" Brosnan is "still cool" in this romance about a jewel thief on a "Caribbean jaunt" enticed into "one last heist" with the "spicy" Hayek (with a "quirky" FBI guy in hot pursuit); the "banter", "lush scenery" and "gratuitous bikini" shots make for some good "eye candy", but even with a last-reel "twist", it's a "no-brainer caper" and non-takers "yawn good night."

Against All Odds | 18 | 19 | 18 | 18 |
1984 | Directed by Taylor Hackford | With Rachel Ward, Jeff Bridges, James Woods, Jane Greer | 128 minutes | Rated R

A "decent remake" of *Out of the Past,* this "twisted", "oversexed" romance finds a "hot, hot, hot" Bridges as a "washed-up quarterback" (with "remarkable abs") entwined in a "tense love triangle" with a "knockout" Ward and the "sinister" Woods; "steamy" love scenes and a "cool" car chase make for a "good rainy-day flick", but what really stays with viewers is that prime example of "'80s cheese", "Phil Collins' theme song."

Age of Innocence, The | 22 | 24 | 22 | 26 |
1993 | Directed by Martin Scorsese | With Daniel Day-Lewis, Michelle Pfeiffer, Winona Ryder | 139 minutes | Rated PG

"Scorsese does Edith Wharton justice" in this "exquisite period drama" concerning "forbidden love" among "upper-class NYers" in the "opulent" "Gilded Age"; Day-Lewis gives a "subtle, understated" performance as the "tortured" lover, while the "gorgeous production" supplies a "sumptuous feast for the eyes" that "captures the smallest details in a languorous way" – maybe that's why the pace is a little on the "slow" side.

Agnes of God | 21 | 25 | 22 | 19 |
1985 | Directed by Norman Jewison | With Jane Fonda, Anne Bancroft, Meg Tilly | 98 minutes | Rated PG-13

Make sure to "be in a serious mood" for this "disturbing" yet "powerful" drama about a "hysterical nun who may or may not be pregnant"; while there's some mighty "serious acting by some great women", voters split on the story ("compelling" vs. "convoluted") and the overall quality ("thought-provoking" vs. "underbaked"); either way, it's "worth sitting through just for the ending."

Agony and the Ecstasy, The | 23 | 23 | 22 | 24 |
1965 | Directed by Carol Reed | With Charlton Heston, Rex Harrison, Diane Cilento | 138 minutes | Not Rated

"All who love art" can get a "romanticized history lesson" via this "well-made epic" featuring Heston as Renaissance man Michelangelo, commissioned to limn the ceiling of the Sistine Chapel while "sparring" with "foil" Pope Julius (the "excellent" Harrison); "good storytelling" makes for an "unparalleled study of the artistic process", even if a few philistines agonize "could this movie be any longer?"

Aguirre: The Wrath of God | 25 | 25 | 23 | 25 |
1977 | Directed by Werner Herzog | With Klaus Kinski, Helena Rojo | 100 minutes | Not Rated

"Shot on a small budget under unbelievable conditions", this "staggering" saga of 16th-century Spaniards seeking El Dorado by crossing the Andes and then descending the Amazon stars Kinski as a "hopelessly mad" "megalomaniac conquistador" opposite "more monkeys than you can shake a stick at"; the film's "hauntingly beautiful" but "static" pacewise, and it's "hard to tell who's more obsessed – the characters in the movie or the director and actors who made it."

A.I.: Artificial Intelligence | 16 | 20 | 15 | 23 |

2001 | Directed by Steven Spielberg | With Haley Joel Osment, Jude Law, Frances O'Connor | 146 minutes | Rated PG-13

"*Pinocchio*" meets "*Blade Runner*" in this "mesmerizing" tale of a "robot boy who wants to be loved" in a devastated, tech-sprawled future; while the "brilliant" Osment brings real life to this artificial world, the scenario is a "strange mélange", one part Stanley Kubrick's "brooding" vision (he first optioned the story), one part Spielberg's "sugar"-coated "sentimentalism"; biggest "downer": that "Amazingly Inept ending."

Air Force One | 18 | 19 | 18 | 21 |

1997 | Directed by Wolfgang Petersen | With Harrison Ford, Gary Oldman, Glenn Close | 124 minutes | Rated R

The "furrowed-browed" Ford plays a "butt-kicking" American president whose plane is hijacked by a "Russian madman" in this "escapist" thriller, a gripping mix of "edge-of-your-recliner suspense" and multi-"million-dollar stunts"; granted, cynics nix its "far-fetched", "action-by-the-numbers" plot but admit that this piece of "harmless, jingoistic fun" "works best with a big bowl of popcorn" nearby.

Airplane! | 24 | 19 | 20 | 19 |

1980 | Directed by Jim Abrahams, David Zucker, Jerry Zucker | With Robert Hays, Julie Hagerty, Lloyd Bridges, Leslie Nielsen, Peter Graves, Robert Stack | 88 minutes | Rated PG

"Funny as heck", this "laugh-a-second spoof" mocks "'70s-era disaster films" with a "scatter-gag" barrage of "relentless slapstick", "constant plays on words" and the "best appearance by Ethel Merman in decades"; granted, it's "infantile" and some of the humor might be perceived as "politically incorrect" today, but there are so many "one-liners you'll remember years later" – 'don't call me Shirley!' – that it's no surprise this flick "launched a thousand imitators."

Airport | 17 | 15 | 18 | 18 |

1970 | Directed by George Seaton | With Burt Lancaster, Helen Hayes, Dean Martin, George Kennedy | 137 minutes | Rated G

The "first" and arguably the "best" of the "disaster flick" genre, this "gripping", "old-fashioned" drama unfolds on one particular night when nothing's going right at a major airport; given the "big, lumbering production" with a bevy of nearly "out-of-work actors" spouting "soap opera–city" dialogue, it's become a "guilty pleasure", though in its heyday it inspired "myriad sequels and spoofs."

ℤ Akeelah and the Bee | 26 | 26 | 25 | 24 |

2006 | Directed by Doug Atchison | With Laurence Fishburne, Angela Bassett, Keke Palmer | 112 minutes | Rated PG

"All ages" are "pleasantly surprised" by this "entirely uplifting" drama featuring Palmer's "phenomenal debut" as a single-parent schoolgirl vying for a national spelling-bee title; she "holds her own" in a "feel-good" tale that "makes you want to break out the dictionary", and even if it "pulls your heartstrings blatantly" right up to the "triumphant ending", it's still "compelling" viewing – like *Rocky* for intelligent people."

Akira

23 | – | 21 | 26

1990 | Directed by Katsuhiro Otomo | Animated | 124 minutes | Rated R
"Defining the anime genre", this "groundbreaking" "classic" "based on the Japanese comic book" is "blazingly kinetic", though "more violent than it needs to be" and thus "not for younger viewers"; the "confusing" sci-fi plot (something to do with "how power corrupts") might "make you wonder if something was lost in translation", but it's so "visually stunning" you won't care.

Aladdin

24 | – | 22 | 25

1992 | Directed by Ron Clements, John Musker | Animated | 90 minutes | Rated G
Disney's "fast-moving" animated version of the Aladdin story is "stolen" by Robin Williams' "infectiously manic", "whirlwind" vocal performance as a "genius" genie; overall, its "likable characters" and "humorous storyline" appeal to both "adults and kids alike", while the "enchanting" Oscar-winning soundtrack will leave you "singing for days."

Alamo, The

18 | 18 | 20 | 21

1960 | Directed by John Wayne | With John Wayne, Richard Widmark, Laurence Harvey | 167 minutes | Not Rated
A "big-as-Texas" slice of "Americana", this "entertaining" rendition of the Battle of the Alamo still "appeals as a period film", although it strikes some as "overblown", "hokum history" with a "surprisingly boring" Wayne as Davy Crockett; even so, that "slam-bang, operatic finale" "mostly justifies" the "dreary opening hour."

☑ Alexander Nevsky ❶🅵

26 | 22 | 25 | 26

1939 | Directed by Sergei Eisenstein | With Nikolai Cherkassov | 107 minutes | Not Rated
"Propaganda" was never better than this "exceptional" war epic, made to rally Soviet support for Stalin; shot in "haunting" black-and-white and set to a "superb Prokofiev score", it recounts the trials and tribulations of a 13th-century Russian prince, and even if the "clanky" script "ultimately collapses under the weight of all the ideological baggage", it's still a "triumph of expressionism" from "genius" director Eisenstein.

Alfie

22 | 26 | 22 | 20

1966 | Directed by Lewis Gilbert | With Michael Caine, Shelley Winters, Vivien Merchant, Jane Asher | 114 minutes | Not Rated
This "little charmer" of a drama stars the "phenomenal" Caine in the career-making role of a "philandering playboy who gets his comeuppance" after dalliances with a flock of '60s birds; although it seems "a bit dated" and might be "politically incorrect" today, its "brutally honest" script still "asks the important questions" – and there's an "excellent" Sonny Rollins score as a bonus.

Alfie

12 | 17 | 13 | 15

2004 | Directed by Charles Shyer | With Jude Law, Susan Sarandon, Sienna Miller, Marisa Tomei, Nia Long | 103 minutes | Rated R
A "cocky", "commitment-phobic womanizer" is the subject of this "lighter", "slicker" remake of the British dramedy, transposing the action to modern-day NYC but retaining the "talking-to-the-camera bit" and "bittersweet ending" of its predecessor; no kidding, Law's "scrumptious", but most agree "Caine was a better cad."

	OVERALL	ACTING	STORY	PROD.

Alice
20 | 23 | 21 | 21

1990 | Directed by Woody Allen | With Mia Farrow, William Hurt, Judy Davis, Joe Mantegna | 102 minutes | Rated PG-13

As usual, the "Manhattan locations play a starring role" in Woody Allen's "modern-day New York version of *Alice in Wonderland*", wherein an uptight Upper East Side matron undergoes a spiritual (and sexual) awakening after ingesting herbal potions; it's among the "least stereotypical" of the director's films, both "funny and touching", if rather "underappreciated."

Alice Doesn't Live Here Anymore ✉
24 | 26 | 23 | 21

1974 | Directed by Martin Scorsese | With Ellen Burstyn, Kris Kristofferson, Jodie Foster | 112 minutes | Rated PG

In this "early Scorsese" drama, Burstyn won an Oscar for her role as a "blue-collar" gal "trying to find herself" after a marriage breakup, and the "poignant", very "real" outcome marked a "watershed" for "feminists" in a "time when men and women were changing their roles."

Alice in Wonderland
24 | - | 25 | 25

1951 | Directed by Clyde Geronimi, Wilfred Jackson, Hamilton Luske | Animated | 75 minutes | Rated G

Disney's wonderfully "wacky" animation transforms Lewis Carroll's children's book into an "intelligent cartoon" rife with "hidden messages" and a slightly "schizophrenic" edge to boot; indeed, "family entertainment" mavens say this "imaginative" production is such a "terrific adaptation" that it "almost makes you forget the classic Tenniel illustrations."

⌷ Alien
25 | 22 | 25 | 26

1979 | Directed by Ridley Scott | With Sigourney Weaver, Tom Skerritt, Veronica Cartwright | 117 minutes | Rated R

"Often imitated but never equaled", this "fierce" sci-fi "horror classic" could pass as a "Hitchcock-in-space" thriller thanks to its "jaw-dropping visuals" and "heart-pounding" plot about an outer space "survey team" that inadvertently brings a "new guest" home to dinner; "Weaver rocks" in "macho-man" mode and is only upstaged by the "slimy", "really gross" title character, the "best movie monster this side of Frankenstein."

Aliens
23 | 21 | 22 | 26

1986 | Directed by James Cameron | With Sigourney Weaver, Michael Biehn, Bill Paxton | 137 minutes | Rated R

This "second installment" in the *Alien* franchise is just as "scream-out-loud scary" as its predecessor, with a "*Rambo*-esque" emphasis; expect the "same high-quality production values" and "edge-of-your-seat tension", and if there's debate as to whether it "trumps" or "just lives up to" the original, one thing's certain: Weaver is still one "bad-ass" chick.

⌷ All About Eve ✉◗
28 | 29 | 27 | 26

1950 | Directed by Joseph L. Mankiewicz | With Bette Davis, Anne Baxter, Gary Merrill, George Sanders, Celeste Holm | 138 minutes | Not Rated

"Fasten your seatbelts" – the "ladies lunch on each other" in this "scalding", "wickedly funny" look at the "vicious world of showbiz"; a "boffo" Davis is "electrifying" as the "fading star" (opposite a "strong" Baxter as the rising one), but both are indebted to Mankiewicz's "perfect script", a "catty" catalog of "sharp-tongued dialogue" that "puts today's scenarios to shame"; in sum, this is one of the "best backstage bitchfests of all time."

All About My Mother ✉🅕   25 | 26 | 25 | 23
1999 | Directed by Pedro Almodóvar | With Cecilia Roth, Penélope Cruz, Marisa Paredes | 101 minutes | Rated R

Though "all the major characters are women", this "captivating story" via Spanish director Almodóvar is definitely "not a chick flick": rather, this "unusual", Oscar-winning drama about a mother searching for her dead son's transsexual dad provides a very "modern definition of what makes a family"; fans single out Roth's "stunning" work and Cruz's "breakout performance" – that is, when they're not "crying their hearts out" or "laughing their heads off."

All Dogs Go to Heaven   17 | - | 17 | 18
1989 | Directed by Don Bluth, Gary Goldman, Dan Kuenster | Animated | 89 minutes | Rated G

"Great for toddlers and young children", this "cute" animated flick about a "ghostly canine" sent from heaven to do good on earth might be a "non-Disney film" but still boasts "Disney quality"; surveyors split on the end result: a "listless, uninspired cartoon" vs. a "wonderfully sweet tearjerker."

All of Me   21 | 23 | 20 | 20
1984 | Directed by Carl Reiner | With Steve Martin, Lily Tomlin, Victoria Tennant, Richard Libertini | 93 minutes | Rated PG

Steve and Lily supply "some of the funniest physical humor ever put on film" in this "zany" Carl Reiner comedy about an "unhappy lawyer" and a dying heiress who undergo a "mind-body switcheroo" via a "swami guy" (the "hilarious" Libertini); granted, it may be a little "dated", but it's still remembered for the immortal line "put Edwina back in bowl."

🅩 All Quiet on the Western Front ✉◗   28 | 26 | 28 | 25
1930 | Directed by Lewis Milestone | With Lew Ayres, Louis Wolheim, Raymond Griffith | 131 minutes | Not Rated

"One of the first anti-war films" (and the "last word" on the subject for many), this "devastating" WWI saga is a "harrowing" glimpse at the "unglorious nature" of battle; over 75 years later, it "still packs a wallop", and though a bit "slow" by modern standards, this "faithful adaptation of the novel" will "stay with you."

All That Jazz   24 | 23 | 22 | 26
1979 | Directed by Bob Fosse | With Roy Scheider, Jessica Lange, Ann Reinking, John Lithgow | 123 minutes | Rated R

A "brilliantly original" "autobiopic" from Bob Fosse about Bob Fosse, this "prescient" drama might be "self-indulgent" and plainly "inspired by 8½", but it's also a "warts-and-all" "character sketch" with, no surprise, "imaginative choreography"; look for a "great star turn" by Scheider and lots of "sardonic" dialogue.

🅩 All the King's Men ✉◗   25 | 26 | 25 | 22
1949 | Directed by Robert Rossen | With Broderick Crawford, John Ireland, Mercedes McCambridge | 109 minutes | Not Rated

The "American dream goes sour" in this "classic political drama" adapted from the Pulitzer Prize–winning novel about the rise and fall of a Huey Long–esque Louisiana politician "corrupted by power"; this Best Picture winner is memorable for its "strong story" – and "even stronger acting by Crawford" (who also won a statuette).

All the King's Men | 15 | 19 | 18 | 17 |

2006 | Directed by Steven Zaillian | With Sean Penn, Jude Law, Anthony Hopkins, Kate Winslet | 128 minutes | Rated PG-13

Despite the casting of some of the "best actors alive", this "disappointing" reexamination of Robert Penn Warren's novel about a "Louisiana political legend" is "nowhere near as good" as the source material – or the "superior 1949 film version"; a minority says it's "better than the critics give it credit for", but neigh-sayers snort it's "hooey" – "all the king's horses couldn't help this one."

All the President's Men | 25 | 26 | 26 | 23 |

1976 | Directed by Alan J. Pakula | With Robert Redford, Dustin Hoffman, Jason Robards | 138 minutes | Rated PG

"History comes alive" in this "truth-is-stranger-than-fiction" account of the "Watergate" scandal, a "riveting", torn-"from-the-headlines thriller" that "captures you every time" "even though you know the outcome"; as reporters Woodward and Bernstein, Redford and Hoffman are truly "memorable" (ditto those "ties and sideburns"), and in the end this "gripping" effort brings "clarity to the events of that confusing time."

All the Right Moves | 16 | 15 | 16 | 15 |

1983 | Directed by Michael Chapman | With Tom Cruise, Craig T. Nelson, Lea Thompson | 91 minutes | Rated R

"Rookie" Cruise shows his youthful "promise" tackling this "teen drama" about a "rebel football hero" who's determined to escape "small-town life", facing off with "unlikable coach" Nelson and love interest Thompson as he "learns to play by his own rules"; the "predictable formula" leaves many unmoved, but as a flashback to the star's "pre-couch hopping days", it's "ok escapist fare."

Almost Famous ⊠ | 23 | 24 | 24 | 22 |

2000 | Directed by Cameron Crowe | With Billy Crudup, Frances McDormand, Kate Hudson | 122 minutes | Rated R

"Almost perfect" filmmaking, director Crowe's "feel-good" "semi-autobiographical story" about his work as a "teenage *Rolling Stone* reporter" who's "on the road with a rock band" is half "coming-of-age" romance, half unadulterated "love song" to the 1970s; while Crudup's "underrated" portrayal of a rocker and McDormand's "outstanding" mother earn kudos, "Hudson steals the show" as the quintessential "vulnerable groupie."

Along Came a Spider | 16 | 20 | 18 | 18 |

2001 | Directed by Lee Tamahori | With Morgan Freeman, Monica Potter, Michael Wincott | 104 minutes | Rated R

Playing a forensic psychologist trying to rescue a senator's daughter from a psychopathic kidnapper, "Freeman carries" this "better-than-average" thriller adapted from the James Patterson book; but even though this "prequel of sorts to *Kiss the Girls*" is "competent" enough, foes fret it's "pretty predictable" and "close to thrill-free", except for that "nice twist at the end."

| | OVERALL | ACTING | STORY | PROD. |

Along Came Polly
15 | 17 | 14 | 16

2004 | Directed by John Hamburg | With Ben Stiller, Jennifer Aniston, Philip Seymour Hoffman, Debra Messing | 90 minutes | Rated PG-13

"Opposites" attract in this "silly", "by-the-numbers" romantic comedy pairing a "neurotic nebbish" with a "free spirit"; Ben and Jen are "pretty funny" (albeit "more pretty than funny") and "Hank Azaria looks good in a thong", but most viewers say the picture's just a "warmed-over" retread of "*There's Something About Mary*."

Alpha Dog
19 | 21 | 21 | 19

2007 | Directed by Nick Cassavetes | With Ben Foster, Shawn Hatosy, Emile Hirsch, Sharon Stone, Justin Timberlake, Bruce Willis | 122 minutes | Rated R

"Unexpectedly deep" insights underlie this "powerful" drama based on a true story about a pack of "gangsta-wannabe" SoCal teens who "kidnap an innocent boy to get back at his brother"; even though "Timberlake's surprisingly good" and the goings-on reasonably "compelling", that "what-a-downer" ending is a total bummer.

Altered States
19 | 20 | 20 | 20

1980 | Directed by Ken Russell | With William Hurt, Blair Brown, Bob Balaban | 102 minutes | Rated R

"Sometimes you don't know which end is up" in this "mind-bending" sci-fi "journey" starring Hurt as a scientist experimenting with sensory deprivation via an isolation chamber and select hallucinogens; although the "trippy" visuals and "convoluted" plot were considered "shocking" at the time, it may now look "like a relic from another era."

ℤ Amadeus ✉
26 | 27 | 25 | 27

1984 | Directed by Milos Forman | With F. Murray Abraham, Tom Hulce, Elizabeth Berridge | 158 minutes | Rated PG

"Genius thwarted by mediocrity" is the theme of this "lively" Mozart biopic that's admittedly "not historically accurate", given its depiction of the "tortured" composer as something of a cross between a "twerp" and a "rock god"; awash in "lush period details", "timeless music" and "surprisingly nuanced performances" by Abraham and Hulce, it even manages to "make classical music seem racy" – and was quite the Oscar magnet, taking home eight of them.

ℤ Amarcord ✉ 🄵
26 | 25 | 25 | 26

1975 | Directed by Federico Fellini | With Magali Noël, Bruno Zanin, Pupella Maggio | 127 minutes | Rated R

"Fellini's warmhearted look back to his childhood", this Foreign Language Oscar winner is a "wonderful depiction" of "small-town life" in 1930s "fascist Italy", an "evocative" film that's simultaneously "lyric, tragic, vulgar and comic"; fans say this "beautiful reminiscence" reveals the famed director "at his most accessible" – and most "surreal."

Amazing Grace
24 | 25 | 24 | 24

2007 | Directed by Michael Apted | With Ioan Gruffudd, Romola Garai, Albert Finney | 111 minutes | Rated PG

Appropriately "amazing", this account of an 18th-century British abolitionist's "noble fight" to "end the slave trade in England" highlights an "important" piece of human-rights history "largely unknown in the

U.S."; Welsh star Gruffudd is a "charming presence", ditto the "excellent" Finney, whose supporting turn lends the "sumptuous" period production some extra "shine."

⊠ Amélie 🅵   26 | 26 | 24 | 25

2001 | Directed by Jean-Pierre Jeunet | With Audrey Tautou, Mathieu Kassovitz | 122 minutes | Rated R

"Sweet as *sucre*", this "candy-coated" "picture postcard" of a romance concerns a "modern-day Pollyanna from Montmartre" "who wants to fix everyone's life" to make up for "what's missing in hers"; in the title role, a "new star has arrived" in "gamine" Tautou, a "21st-century Audrey Hepburn" whose "doe-eyed", "cute-as-a-button" looks alone will "put a huge grin on your face"; indeed, this "brimming-with-goodwill" picture is so "magical", you'll "hardly notice the subtitles."

⊠ American Beauty ⊠   24 | 27 | 23 | 24

1999 | Directed by Sam Mendes | With Kevin Spacey, Annette Bening, Wes Bentley, Thora Birch | 121 minutes | Rated R

The "desperation of modern suburban life" is the theme of this "engrossing" Best Picture winner that polarizes viewers: fans hail this tale of a man's "midlife awakening" and "resurrection" as a "truthful commentary on American society", but thornier types fuss it's a "pretentious", "angry" tract "disguised as existentialist philosophy"; nonetheless, there are plenty of bouquets for Spacey's "dead-on" performance and Alan Ball's "seriously meaty", "rapierlike screenplay."

American Gangster   23 | 26 | 23 | 24

2007 | Directed by Ridley Scott | With Denzel Washington, Russell Crowe, Ruby Dee | 157 minutes | Rated R

Denzel is one "amazing bad guy" in this "powerful" crime epic that traces (and maybe "glamorizes") the rise and fall of a real-life "Harlem drug kingpin" who amassed riches selling heroin in the '70s; on the law-and-order side, Crowe is equally "outstanding" as an "honest cop" pitted against a "worthy opponent" in this "deliciously violent", if somewhat "overlong", picture.

American Gigolo   19 | 19 | 18 | 19

1980 | Directed by Paul Schrader | With Richard Gere, Lauren Hutton, Nina Van Pallandt, Hector Elizondo | 117 minutes | Rated R

The "eye candy can't be beat" in this "stylish" (albeit "so '80s") drama about a "cool-drink-of-water" callboy – the "first true metrosexual" – who's suspected of murder; it was "Gere's breakout part", though some say he's upstaged by his "Giorgio Armani" duds and that "cool" Giorgio Moroder soundtrack.

American Graffiti   24 | 23 | 23 | 23

1973 | Directed by George Lucas | With Richard Dreyfuss, Ron Howard, Cindy Williams | 110 minutes | Rated PG

"Spot future stars" (including an early Harrison Ford) in this "end-of-an-era" dramedy that "launched a dozen careers" and proves that "Lucas once directed actors, not just pixels"; "covering one night" in 1962 – "but what a night" – it "captures a time and place" in teenage, West Coast America by mixing "cool cars", "period jukebox hits" and "Wolfman Jack" into a "classic growing-up story" that really "makes nostalgia compelling."

American History X

25 | 28 | 24 | 23

1998 | Directed by Tony Kaye | With Edward Norton, Edward Furlong, Beverly D'Angelo | 119 minutes | Rated R

"Neo-Nazi violence" and "racism" lie at the heart of this "scalding" drama about "white supremacists" that's "like a punch in the gut" thanks to the "gifted" Norton's "all-too-convincing" portrait of a "scary" "skinhead"; though surely "horrifying", this "powerful" film will also "make you think."

⊠ American in Paris, An ⊠

26 | 23 | 22 | 27

1951 | Directed by Vincente Minnelli | With Gene Kelly, Leslie Caron, Oscar Levant, Nina Foch | 113 minutes | Not Rated

A "debonair" Kelly and "beautiful Caron" "dance up a storm" in this "unforgettable" Gershwin musical that might tempt you to "visit Paris"; sure, the "silly story" is a bit "hackneyed", but "who cares?" when the production's so "visually compelling" (especially that climactic ballet "integrating Impressionist art" in its settings); no surprise, it took home six Oscars, including Best Picture.

Americanization of Emily, The ◑

24 | 24 | 22 | 21

1964 | Directed by Arthur Hiller | With James Garner, Julie Andrews, James Coburn, Melvyn Douglas | 115 minutes | Not Rated

"Considered controversial in its day", this "powerful anti-war" film tells the story of a "cynical" American naval officer scheming to avoid duty in the D-day invasion while romancing a priggish English lass; Andrews is "quite good" in her "first role to depart from her sweet image", though Paddy Chayefsky's screenplay gets mixed notices: "literate" vs. "preachy."

American Pie

19 | 16 | 18 | 18

1999 | Directed by Paul Weitz | With Jason Biggs, Shannon Elizabeth, Tara Reid | 95 minutes | Rated R

"You'll never look at an apple pie the same way" after a gander at this "drop-dead funny" slice of "raunch" about some teenage dudes, "hormones a-raging", who "vow to lose their virginity on prom night"; while bluenoses berate its "toilet humor" as "moronic", "baked-goods" buyers say its "laugh-a-minute" plot is an "intelligent grossout", the "Gen-X" version of *Porky's*."

American President, The

21 | 22 | 21 | 21

1995 | Directed by Rob Reiner | With Michael Douglas, Annette Bening, Martin Sheen | 114 minutes | Rated PG-13

"Only in Hollywood" could the "President openly date a lobbyist", but no one "believes it for a second – or cares" – since this "feel-good" romance is so darned "entertaining"; voters like Douglas' "humanized" Chief Exec and Bening's "luminous" gal pal but reject the "rose-colored" script and its "telegraphed happy ending", sighing "pass the popcorn."

American Psycho

19 | 22 | 18 | 19

2000 | Directed by Mary Harron | With Christian Bale, Chloë Sevigny, Willem Dafoe, Reese Witherspoon | 101 minutes | Rated R

Dark comedies don't get much more "pitch black" than this stylishly "freaky" look at a "yuppie psychopath" whose "decadent '80s lifestyle", "status worship" and "serial killing" is alternately "sick, disturbing and hilarious"; Bale is "to die for", the soundtrack's "killer" and the "witty" script still manages to conjure up the "heebie-jeebies" – even if the violence is "rather bland compared to the book."

American Splendor
`23` `25` `22` `22`

2003 | Directed by Shari Springer Berman, Robert Pulcini | With Paul Giamatti, Hope Davis, Harvey Pekar | 101 minutes | Rated R

An "average slob" gets the big-screen treatment in this "subversive" biopic of underground comics scribe Harvey Pekar, a "schlubby" "anti-hero" complete with a "file-clerk" day job; deftly employing "three parallel realities" – "actors, cartoons" and Harvey himself – to tell its story, this "offbeat" picture is really "original", though some feel it "falls short of its potential" and wonder "what does it amount to in the end?"

American Tail, An
`21` `-` `21` `22`

1986 | Directed by Don Bluth | Animated | 77 minutes | Rated G

"One of the first good non-Disney" pieces of animation, this "wonderful" "story of the immigrant experience" follows the adventures of a Russian mouse separated from his kin after arriving in America; a "real family favorite", its "clever" concept with a "touch of pathos" makes many "hearts melt."

American Werewolf in London, An
`20` `17` `21` `21`

1981 | Directed by John Landis | With David Naughton, Jenny Agutter, Griffin Dunne | 97 minutes | Rated R

"Filmed with style and wit", this "tragicomic gorefest" "shows some bite" as it follows the misadventures of two American "zombies" abroad; best remembered for its "transformation scene" combining "superior makeup" and "amazing special effects" – and second-best known for Agutter's "hot shower scene" – this one's so "suspenseful and creepy" that it "helped revitalize the horror genre" in the early '80s.

Amistad
`21` `24` `22` `24`

1997 | Directed by Steven Spielberg | With Morgan Freeman, Djimon Hounsou, Matthew McConaughey | 152 minutes | Rated R

Examining the "dark underside of American history", this "little-known" true story of 19th-century "Africans forced into slavery" "starts on a slave ship and culminates in court"; while some say this "gripping", "difficult" story is an "underappreciated" Spielberg opus, others find it so "heavy-handed" and "manipulative" that they're left "out to sea."

Amityville Horror, The
`18` `15` `19` `18`

1979 | Directed by Stuart Rosenberg | With James Brolin, Margot Kidder, Rod Steiger | 117 minutes | Rated R

"Do your research" could be the motto of this "frightening look into home ownership", a horror "classic" about a couple who move into one of the creepiest houses in filmdom; despite "less-than-believable" emoting, it "kept a lot of people awake in the '80s", though by "today's standards" it's kind of "cheesy" and "not that scary."

☒ Amores Perros ☒
`26` `26` `25` `23`

2001 | Directed by Alejandro González Iñárritu | With Gael García Bernal, Emilio Echevarría, Álvaro Guerrero | 154 minutes | Rated R

"One tough flick", this "powerful (and difficult)" drama relates three "skillfully interwoven tales" linked together by a horrific car crash in Mexico City; it's "not for everyone" – particularly the "queasy dog-fighting scenes" – and can be "a bit hard to follow", but the result is something "you won't find in Hollywood movies", enhanced by a "riveting" performance by Bernal that "shot him to stardom."

Analyze That
14 | 17 | 12 | 15

2002 | Directed by Harold Ramis | With Robert De Niro, Billy Crystal, Lisa Kudrow, Joe Viterelli, Cathy Moriarty | 96 minutes | Rated R

That the "novelty" of mobsters in therapy is "worn out beyond belief" doesn't stop Billy and Bobby from reuniting for this "lame" sequel to *Analyze This*, a "profanity"-fest with "few laughs" fashioned from a "one-joke concept"; in the final analysis, most shrink from recommending this "disappointment", saying they'd rather "sleep with the fishes."

Analyze This
18 | 21 | 18 | 18

1999 | Directed by Harold Ramis | With Robert De Niro, Billy Crystal, Lisa Kudrow, Chazz Palminteri | 103 minutes | Rated R

"*Sopranos*" nuts see some familiar plot threads in this "funny Mafia movie" featuring the "hilarious pairing" of "De Niro as a mobster with anxiety attacks" and Crystal as his reluctant shrink; though some analysts shrug it off as a "flat" "trifle", supporters call it an "amusing send-up" that may be "ridiculous, but it works."

Anastasia ⊠
23 | 27 | 24 | 23

1956 | Directed by Anatole Litvak | With Ingrid Bergman, Yul Brynner, Helen Hayes | 105 minutes | Not Rated

The Oscar-winning, ever "appealing" Bergman and a "great" Brynner make quite a "combo" in this dramatic biography of Anastasia, the legendary daughter of the last Russian czar and pretender to the throne – or is she?; told with "sympathy and empathy", it's a "cuddle-up-with-your-honey" picture with acting "so good you find yourself rooting for those inept royals"; "is it true?" – c'mon, "does it matter?"

Anastasia
20 | - | 19 | 22

1997 | Directed by Don Bluth, Gary Goldman | Animated | 94 minutes | Rated G

"Disney isn't the only one" making "amazing animation" these days: this cartoon version of a lost (and found) Russian princess is an "astonishingly good feature", although it "doesn't seem to be kid material"; still, it's a "visually appealing" extravaganza oozing "style", even if the "bat steals the show."

☒ Anatomy of a Murder ◑
26 | 27 | 27 | 24

1959 | Directed by Otto Preminger | With James Stewart, Lee Remick, Ben Gazzara, Arthur O'Connell | 160 minutes | Not Rated

Stewart "pulls out all the stops" as a "down-to-earth" lawyer in this courtroom drama that's a "spellbinding" look at a "sensational" "backwoods" revenge killing; "considered risqué" in the '50s given Remick's "sultry" turn and its use of the then-verboten word "'panties'", it remains as "riveting" as ever.

Anchorman: The Legend of Ron Burgundy
14 | 16 | 12 | 15

2004 | Directed by Adam McKay | With Will Ferrell, Christina Applegate, Steve Carell | 94 minutes | Rated PG-13

"Sideburns", "leisure suits" and shameless "male chauvinism" set the "'70s flashback" mood of this "dimwitted" comedy about a "fatuous" TV news anchor pitted against a woman trying to break into the "old boys' club of the newsroom"; while the "sophomoric" proceedings recall a *Saturday Night Live* sketch that goes on too long", it's worth watching for that "hilarious", "cameo"-laden "rumble scene."

And Justice for All   23 | 26 | 22 | 22

1979 | Directed by Norman Jewison | With Al Pacino, Jack Warden, Christine Lahti | 119 minutes | Rated R

The "innocent get tossed by the wayside" in this "compelling" courtroom drama about an "honest young lawyer" defending a "risk-taking" judge accused of rape; Pacino is in "vintage" form, delivering an "incandescent" performance highlighted by an "explosive rant": "you're out of order, the whole trial is out of order!"

Andromeda Strain, The   20 | 18 | 25 | 20

1971 | Directed by Robert Wise | With Arthur Hill, David Wayne, James Olson, Kate Reid | 131 minutes | Rated G

"Science provides the thrills" in this piece of "thinking man's sci-fi" based on the early "Michael Crichton thriller" concerning a "dangerous" virus from outer space; though it may be "low-tech" (with "out-of-date special effects" and "sprayed-on perspiration"), it supplies enough "palpable tension" to keep things "interesting."

Angela's Ashes   22 | 24 | 25 | 22

1999 | Directed by Alan Parker | With Emily Watson, Robert Carlyle | 145 minutes | Rated R

The "poverty, disease and damp" of early 20th century Ireland are "vividly portrayed" in this "bleak but uplifting" family drama adapted from Frank McCourt's memoir; thanks to a "brilliant" cast, "breathtaking" cinematography and a knack for "finding humor amid harsh reality", it's an "inspirational celebration" of "mankind's indomitable spirit."

Angel Heart   18 | 18 | 18 | 18

1987 | Directed by Alan Parker | With Mickey Rourke, Robert De Niro, Lisa Bonet, Charlotte Rampling | 113 minutes | Rated R

A 1950s gumshoe fends off noirish "seediness" and supernatural "creepiness" in this "atmospheric" thriller charting the search for a "missing big-band crooner" in locales ranging from the Big Apple to the Big Easy; though Rourke's in full "freaky-deaky" mode and De Niro flaunts "nice fingernails", the picture is renowned for Bonet's super-"steamy", "voodoo"-charged sex scene.

Angels with Dirty Faces ◐   24 | 24 | 22 | 20

1938 | Directed by Michael Curtiz | With James Cagney, Pat O'Brien, Humphrey Bogart | 97 minutes | Not Rated

Two toughs from the slums take different career paths – one becoming a "lowlife", the other a priest – in this "cautionary melodrama" from the days when "good was good and bad was bad"; "cliché-ridden" though it may be, it was designed to "scare the bejesus out of would-be delinquents" – or at least have them "doing Cagney impersonations for weeks" afterward.

Anger Management   13 | 18 | 13 | 16

2003 | Directed by Peter Segal | With Adam Sandler, Jack Nicholson, Marisa Tomei | 106 minutes | Rated PG-13

The "unlikely" pairing of "silly" Sandler with "versatile" Nicholson as patient and therapist is a "cute idea gone awry" in this "disappointing" comedy flush with "juvenile bathroom humor"; when cooler heads prevail, primary blame goes to the "ridiculous premise", an "incoherent" affair which neither "great cameos" (Heather Graham, Woody Harrelson) nor a "surprise ending" can temper.

☒ Animal Crackers ◑

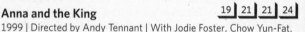

26 | 24 | 18 | 20

1930 | Directed by Victor Heerman | With the Marx Brothers, Lillian Roth, Margaret Dumont | 97 minutes | Rated G

"Hooray for Captain Spaulding!"; this "timeless" Marx Brothers "romp" is best remembered for Groucho's "priceless entrance" and "fabulously stupid" quips ("I shot an elephant in my pajamas, but how he got in my pajamas, I'll never know"); needless to say, the "storyline isn't the point" here, but the "zany" pace doesn't leave time for logic anyway.

☒ Animal House

24 | 20 | 21 | 20

1978 | Directed by John Landis | With John Belushi, Tim Matheson, Tom Hulce, John Vernon | 109 minutes | Rated R

"Raunchy and vulgar", this much-admired "granddaddy of the frat boy gross-out comedies" features the much-"missed" Belushi "at his side-splitting best" as Bluto Blutarsky, a "seven-year college" vet; "no, it ain't Shakespeare", but rather a "textbook" study of "toga parties", "road trips", "food fights" and "anarchic libidos on parade" that's so much of a "guy's movie" that some fellas say they "thought it was a documentary."

Anna and the King

19 | 21 | 21 | 24

1999 | Directed by Andy Tennant | With Jodie Foster, Chow Yun-Fat, Tom Felton | 148 minutes | Rated PG-13

Take a "trip to Thailand" via this "touching" romance that's a "nonmusical rendition" of *The King and I*, based on the true story of Brit school teacher Anna Leonowens; though "slow" pacing and the "absence of chemistry" between Foster and Yun-Fat leave things "rather flat", at least this "lush" production ("magnificent scenery", "elaborate costumes") is "gorgeous to look at."

Anna Christie ◑

▽ 26 | 27 | 24 | 23

1930 | Directed by Clarence Brown | With Greta Garbo, Charles Bickford, Marie Dressler | 89 minutes | Not Rated

The "amazing Garbo" is in "fabulous voice" for her talking pictures "breakout", this adaptation of Eugene O'Neill's "deep" drama about a hard-luck Swedish lass whose connections to her father and sweetheart are haunted by her "waterfront hooker" past; it's "definitely a classic" that "leaves an impact", and just beholding Greta at her "peak" is "reason enough to watch."

☒ Anna Karenina ◑

26 | 26 | 26 | 25

1935 | Directed by Clarence Brown | With Greta Garbo, Fredric March, Freddie Bartholomew | 95 minutes | Not Rated

"Let's hear it for Tolstoy", whose "huge novel" gets a "brilliant" celluloid spin in this romance of "choices and consequences", starring "Garbo at her best" as the restless Russian who trades mundane wedlock with husband Rathbone for notoriety with the "marvelous" March; classicists insist it's a "moving" ride "from the second it starts" to the climactic encounter between Anna and "the train."

	OVERALL	ACTING	STORY	PROD.

⚡ Anne of the Thousand Days — 26 | 27 | 26 | 26

1969 | Directed by Charles Jarrott | With Richard Burton, Geneviève Bujold, Irene Papas | 145 minutes | Rated PG-13

"History buffs" and "Anglophiles" like this "top-notch" period drama, a "powerful" recounting of "Henry VIII's inability to commit", featuring "brilliant" work by Burton as the "boorish" king and Bujold as the "sensuous Anne Boleyn"; the "beautiful production" is alternately "transporting" and "heart-wrenching", while the Oscar-winning "costumes alone are worth the watch."

Annie — 19 | 19 | 20 | 20

1982 | Directed by John Huston | With Albert Finney, Carol Burnett, Aileen Quinn, Tim Curry | 126 minutes | Rated PG

Little Orphan Annie's "rags-to-riches" saga morphs into a "colorful" "children's musical" with a "splendid cast" in this "stylized" "adaptation of the comic strip" that first bowed on Broadway; parents say it's "perfect for kids", and even those who find it "bloated" and "boring" find themselves leaving the theater humming 'Tomorrow.'

⚡ Annie Hall ✉ — 27 | 26 | 25 | 24

1977 | Directed by Woody Allen | With Woody Allen, Diane Keaton, Tony Roberts | 93 minutes | Rated PG

"Every neurotic's favorite comedy", this Oscar-winning Allen film about an "insecure" "Jewish nebbish" smitten with a nutty, "la-di-da"-spouting "shiksa" is "among his deftest creations"; its "pitch-perfect NY" setting, "pure-genius script" and "very funny" set pieces (the "lobster-cooking episode", the "split-screen family dinner scene") make for "essential Woody."

Anniversary Party, The — 18 | 23 | 17 | 17

2001 | Directed by Alan Cumming, Jennifer Jason Leigh | With Alan Cumming, Jennifer Jason Leigh, Phoebe Cates, Kevin Kline, Jennifer Beals, Gwyneth Paltrow | 115 minutes | Rated R

"Hollywood shallowness" gets the "cinema verité" treatment in this "dark", "low-budget" tale of a "dysfunctional" writer and actress celebrating their wedding anniversary with various friends and hangers-on; party-poopers don't dig the "unsympathetic" characters and all that "talk, talk, talk", but others relish the "smart" skewering of "Southern California culture" by the "engrossing" ensemble cast.

Ant Bully, The — 18 | - | 18 | 21

2006 | Directed by John A. Davis | Animated | 88 minutes | Rated PG

"Cute" ant-ics ensue after a boy "shrinks down to the size of an insect" in this "appealing" animated adventure; "wonderful" visuals and a "good environmental message" make it a natural for "family" viewing, even if some swat its "resemblance to *Antz* and *A Bug's Life.*"

Antonia's Line ✉⏹ — 25 | 26 | 25 | 24

1996 | Directed by Marleen Gorris | With Willeke van Ammelrooy, Els Dottermans | 102 minutes | Rated R

"About women and for women", this "liberating" Dutch drama recounts 50 years in one lady's life, told in "flashback" from her "death bed"; "shockingly feminist" to chauvinists, its "charming performances" and "empowering message" are so "unforgettable" that it more than "deserves the Best Foreign Film Oscar" it received.

Antwone Fisher

23 | 26 | 24 | 22

2002 | Directed by Denzel Washington | With Derek Luke, Denzel Washington, Joy Bryant | 120 minutes | Rated PG-13

"Buy a box of tissues before you rent" this "inspiring true-life story about a boy from the 'hood who makes something of himself despite many obstacles"; this "emotional roller coaster" is "wonderfully acted" and represents a "terrific directorial debut by Denzel", who "manages to bring realism to what could have been a manipulative storyline."

Antz

20 | - | 19 | 23

1998 | Directed by Eric Darnell, Tim Johnson | Animated | 87 minutes | Rated PG

Opinion splitz on this fully computer-animated feature about an insect's "rebellion" against conformity; fans buzz that this "highly creative" film "for all ages" tells a "well-executed" story, yet drones swat it for "ugly animation" and a "subversive socialist subtext" that's "not recommended" for "younger children"; P.S. Woody Allen's voice-over as a "neurotic ant is a must-hear."

Any Given Sunday

17 | 20 | 17 | 20

1999 | Directed by Oliver Stone | With Al Pacino, Cameron Diaz, Dennis Quaid, James Woods, Jamie Foxx | 150 minutes | Rated R

A football coach "in the twilight of his career", an upstart QB and a "tough heiress" collide in this look at the "competitive challenges" as well as the "business side" of pro ball; "realistic", "brilliantly choreographed" gridiron action delivers "all the punch and crunch of front-row seats", though Stone's typically "over-the-top" direction "misses greatness by a few yards."

Apartment, The

25 | 28 | 25 | 23

1960 | Directed by Billy Wilder | With Jack Lemmon, Shirley MacLaine, Fred MacMurray | 125 minutes | Not Rated

"Sex in the big, bad city" has never been as "realistic" or "touching" as in this "sad-edged romance", recounting the exploits of a "hapless" "junior exec in love with his boss' mistress"; it pits a "baby-faced" Lemmon opposite a "tender" MacLaine and "understated" MacMurray, and besides being "very amusing", it's also a "powerful social comment masquerading as comedy."

☒ Apocalypse Now

27 | 27 | 25 | 28

1979 | Directed by Francis Ford Coppola | With Martin Sheen, Marlon Brando, Robert Duvall | 153 minutes | Rated R

The "Vietnam nightmare" meets Joseph "Conrad's *Heart of Darkness*" in this "landmark" Coppola opus that's one part "gut churner", one part "acid trip" as it examines the "insanity of war"; true, it's "long", the "last half hour is disappointing" and many wonder "what the heck Brando's saying", but ultimately this "sprawling" "meditation on the human mind" just plain "grabs you"; P.S. the expanded version (*Apocalypse Now Redux*) divides voters.

Apocalypto ☐

19 | 20 | 18 | 23

2006 | Directed by Mel Gibson | With Rudy Youngblood, Dalia Hernández, Raoul Trujillo | 139 minutes | Rated R

"Love him or hate him", polarizing director Gibson shows he can pull off "visually spectacular", "action-packed" entertainment with this "fascinating tale of survival" set during the "fall of ancient Mayan civilization"; be prepared for a cast of "unknowns" speaking in (subtitled) "native dialects", along with Mel's trademark use of "extreme blood and gore."

Apollo 13 | 24 | 24 | 25 | 26 |

1995 | Directed by Ron Howard | With Tom Hanks, Bill Paxton, Kevin Bacon, Gary Sinise | 140 minutes | Rated PG

"Even though you [presumably] know the outcome", this "space race" drama based on the "remarkable true story" of the "perilous voyage of Apollo 13" stays "suspenseful"; with a roster of "big-name actors" exuding the "right stuff", it delivers "get-up-and-cheer escapism" that might be "a tad corny" but will "make you proud to be an American" – "isn't history wonderful?"

Apprenticeship of Duddy Kravitz, The | 22 | 24 | 24 | 20 |

1974 | Directed by Ted Kotcheff | With Richard Dreyfuss, Micheline Lanctôt, Jack Warden | 120 minutes | Rated PG

A "nice Jewish boy in Montreal comes of age" and tries to ascend the "slippery slope of success" in this "little-known comic gem" "tinged with sadness"; a "moving" adaptation of Mordecai Richler's novel, it's a "genius" "showcase for Dreyfuss" as the titular "hustling" "mensch."

Apt Pupil | 18 | 23 | 20 | 18 |

1998 | Directed by Bryan Singer | With Ian McKellen, Brad Renfro, Bruce Davison, David Schwimmer | 111 minutes | Rated R

A "teen identifies his neighbor as a former Nazi" leading to "mind games" and "blackmail" in this "creepy" adaptation of the Stephen King novella; the pairing of "rebel" Renfro with the "always amazing" McKellen compensates for the "slightly unbelievable" plot twists and "so-so" production values.

Armageddon | 15 | 14 | 14 | 21 |

1998 | Directed by Michael Bay | With Bruce Willis, Billy Bob Thornton, Ben Affleck, Liv Tyler | 144 minutes | Rated PG-13

An "asteroid hurtles toward the earth" in this "high testosterone" "explosionfest" with a "far-fetched" "patriotic story" involving a *Dirty Dozen*–style space mission" and "tongue-in-cheek heroics"; foes say this "blockbuster" is "all budget and no brain" with "state-of-the-art special effects as the real star of the film."

Army of Darkness | 23 | 17 | 20 | 19 |

1993 | Directed by Sam Raimi | With Bruce Campbell, Embeth Davidtz | 81 minutes | Rated R

"Leading with his chin", "B-movie god" Campbell plays a "chainsaw"-wielding, "time-traveling" slacker pitted against Dark Ages hordes in this "witty" horror comedy (known in geekdom as the "third episode of the *Evil Dead* series"); "deliberately cheesy" production values and an "abundance of quotable lines" – i.e. "gimme some sugar, baby" – have earned it "cult-classic" status.

Around the World in 80 Days | 22 | 20 | 22 | 25 |

1956 | Directed by Michael Anderson | With David Niven, Cantinflas, Shirley MacLaine | 175 minutes | Rated G

"It's the scenery, stupid" that makes this globe-trotting "epic" "travelogue" based on "Jules Verne's classic book" "worth watching", though lots of "stars popping up in cameo roles" add to the "visual cornucopia"; however, some find it a "boring", "three-hour ride" and "can't believe" it snagged a Best Picture Oscar.

⚡ Arsenic and Old Lace ◑ | 26 | 26 | 25 | 22 |

1944 | Directed by Frank Capra | With Cary Grant, Priscilla Lane, Raymond Massey | 118 minutes | Not Rated

"Elderberry wine" makes for "murderous fun" in this "macabre" black comedy about two "vengeful old ladies" killing off bachelors while "chewing the scenery"; as their nephew, a "frantic" Grant "hams it up unashamedly" and delivers the "world's best double takes" in this "funny" adaptation of the Broadway hit.

Arthur | 20 | 21 | 19 | 19 |

1981 | Directed by Steve Gordon | With Dudley Moore, Liza Minnelli, John Gielgud | 117 minutes | Rated PG

There's "not a dull moment" in this "silly" yet "tender" romantic comedy about a "falling-down-drunk" millionaire looking for love; although top billing goes to "sexy short guy" Dudley Moore opposite "Liza Minnelli as Liza Minnelli", this "priceless" picture arguably belongs to Gielgud, who delivers its most "classic line" – "I'll alert the media" – "as if he were playing Hamlet."

As Good As It Gets ✉ | 22 | 25 | 21 | 21 |

1997 | Directed by James L. Brooks | With Jack Nicholson, Helen Hunt, Greg Kinnear | 139 minutes | Rated PG-13

Fans feel the "title says it all": this "smart comedy" about the "unlikely pairing" of a "cantankerous" "obsessive-compulsive jerk" and a "kooky" "single-mom waitress" crackles with "sharp", "NY neurotic" dialogue; but even though both Hunt and Nicholson grabbed Oscars for their "tour-de-force" turns, some shrug they "play themselves" in this "overhyped" and "overrated" flick.

Asphalt Jungle, The ◑ | 24 | 24 | 24 | 23 |

1950 | Directed by John Huston | With Sterling Hayden, Louis Calhern, Sam Jaffe | 112 minutes | Not Rated

Sure, this "prime example of juicy film noir" is one of the "original caper" pictures, about a "carefully planned" "jewel heist gone terribly wrong", but it's also appealing for an "early" turn by Marilyn Monroe in a "blow-you-away" bit part; otherwise, this "dark tale" of "greed" and "emotion" supplies enough "twists and compelling characters" to make it "one of Huston's most underrated films."

Assassination of Richard Nixon, The | 18 | 25 | 18 | 18 |

2004 | Directed by Niels Mueller | With Sean Penn, Naomi Watts, Don Cheadle | 95 minutes | Rated R

Based on a "real-life incident" that "will send you Googling to learn more", this "fascinating character study" of a "downtrodden", mentally imbalanced man reminds many of "De Niro in *Taxi Driver*"; but even though Penn delivers his usual "amazing" work, this "vision of the flip-side of the American dream" may be "too nihilistic" for some.

Assault on Precinct 13 | 16 | 16 | 16 | 17 |

2005 | Directed by Jean-François Richet | With Ethan Hawke, Laurence Fishburne, John Leguizamo, Maria Bello | 109 minutes | Rated R

There's "lots of testosterone" on display in this "bloodier-than-a-slaughterhouse" "B-movie", a reworking of John Carpenter's "schlocky" 1976 thriller about a "siege on a Detroit police precinct"; despite "credible" casting and "reasonably good action", critics contend this "unnecessary remake" is too "contrived."

Atlantic City

| | 24 | 27 | 22 | 22 |

1980 | Directed by Louis Malle | With Burt Lancaster, Susan Sarandon, Kate Reid | 104 minutes | Rated R

This "valentine to a lost city" pairs a "stunning" Lancaster and Sarandon as unlikely lovers "trying to redeem their lives" in the "bleak atmosphere" of a "dying" town; "sad, bittersweet" and "overlooked", it boasts a "superb" John Guare script full of "characters worth caring about" but is most remembered for the scene of "our heroine bathing herself with sliced lemons."

Atlantis: The Lost Empire

| | 16 | - | 14 | 21 |

2001 | Directed by Gary Trousdale, Kirk Wise | Animated | 95 minutes | Rated PG

Centering on the search for the "legendary" sunken civilization, this "sophisticated action" flick is a Disney production featuring elements of "Jules Verne" and "Japanese anime" but no "song-and-dance numbers" or cute talking animals; though its blend of traditional and CGI animation is "visually stunning", some say the story's "subpar" and a bit "too violent for minors."

Atonement

| | 22 | 24 | 22 | 25 |

2007 | Directed by Joe Wright | With James McAvoy, Keira Knightley, Saoirse Ronan | 130 minutes | Rated R

"Remarkable performances" by Knightley and McAvoy and "gorgeous" camerawork illuminate this "haunting", "Merchant-Ivory"-esque romance about two lovers in pre-World War II England whose lives are "irreparably changed" by a child's "misunderstanding"; whether the finale is a "shocker" or a "disappointment" is debatable, but either way most say its arrival takes "too long"; best moment: the "spectacular five-minute tracking shot of soldiers on the beach at Dunkirk."

Auntie Mame

| | 25 | 25 | 24 | 25 |

1958 | Directed by Morton DaCosta | With Rosalind Russell, Forrest Tucker, Coral Browne | 143 minutes | Not Rated

"Defining diva-dom for generations", this hilariously "stylish" comedy about a wide-eyed kid's "wacky rich" auntie stars a "larger-than-life Rosalind Russell" as a "great old broad"-cum-"force of nature"; it might be "overlong and underplotted", but "great one-liners" barbed with "sharp wit" ("life is a banquet and most poor suckers are starving to death") assure its reputation as the "campiest of camp classics."

ⓩ Au Revoir Les Enfants 🄵

| | 27 | 26 | 27 | 24 |

1987 | Directed by Louis Malle | With Gaspard Manesse, Francine Racette | 104 minutes | Rated PG

"Powerful and haunting", this "must-see" drama explores "anti-Semitism" in WWII "occupied France" via its depiction of a "Jewish boy hidden" in a French school; though there's certainly "no happy ending" here, it "brings the events of the Holocaust to a personal level" so devastatingly that you'll "never forget" it.

Austin Powers: International Man of Mystery

19 18 17 19

1997 | Directed by Jay Roach | With Mike Myers, Elizabeth Hurley, Michael York | 90 minutes | Rated PG-13

"No-brainer" alert: this "shagadelic" "spoof of James Bond movies" delivers "tons of laughs" with "dumb" jokes and overall "retro '60s silliness" – "oh, behave!" – courtesy of "comic genius" Myers in a dual role as a spy with "mossy teeth" and a villain with a pet pussycat; there's debate over its "crude" "toilet humor" but wide agreement that you needn't "bother with the sequels."

Austin Powers: The Spy Who Shagged Me

19 18 16 19

1999 | Directed by Jay Roach | With Mike Myers, Heather Graham, Michael York, Verne Troyer | 95 minutes | Rated PG-13

The second installment of Myers' James Bond parody, this "totally sophomoric" satire is as "politically incorrect" as the original, though some groan it "hasn't aged well", citing the "same old jokes" and Graham's "wooden" turn; still, it did "introduce Mini-Me and Fat Bastard into popular culture" and that "Jerry Springer footage" is "gloriously silly."

Austin Powers in Goldmember

16 16 12 19

2002 | Directed by Jay Roach | With Mike Myers, Beyoncé Knowles, Seth Green, Michael York, Michael Caine | 94 minutes | Rated PG-13

After a "funny, star-studded opening sequence", it's "all downhill" in this "inane" third episode of the 007-lampooning franchise; diehards are "totally randy" over the "cheesy insanity" and Beyoncé's "hot" turn as "Foxxy Cleopatra", but most groan this "played-out" series should be "put to bed."

Auto Focus

16 22 17 18

2002 | Directed by Paul Schrader | With Greg Kinnear, Willem Dafoe, Rita Wilson, Maria Bello | 105 minutes | Rated R

The "rise and fall" of "sick puppy" sitcom star Bob Crane is charted in this "raw" look at a "mid-level actor turned sex addict" and his enabler buddy; even though Kinnear and Dafoe are "suitably creepy" as "partners in grime", straitlaced surveyors find it "hard to empathize with the characters and their obsessions" and feel the film is "devoid of any uplifting moments" – it's "like watching a train wreck."

Avalon

24 25 24 23

1990 | Directed by Barry Levinson | With Aidan Quinn, Elizabeth Perkins, Armin Mueller-Stahl | 126 minutes | Rated PG

"Touching" and "oh-so-true", this third installment of director Levinson's "semi-autobiographical" "homage to the immigrant experience" (and "growing up in Baltimore") follows a "bravura cast" across several generations; the "wistful humor" and "nostalgic" sense of time and place make for a "rare" dose of "heartfelt" entertainment, best summed up by its most renowned line: "why did you cut the turkey?"

Aviator, The

23 25 22 27

2004 | Directed by Martin Scorsese | With Leonardo DiCaprio, Cate Blanchett, Kate Beckinsale, John C. Reilly | 170 minutes | Rated PG-13

Martin Scorsese takes off with a "bottomless budget" in this "sweeping" biopic of "eccentric" gazillionaire Howard Hughes, where the lift-off is supplied by "sumptuous" production design (including one of the "most realistic plane crashes" ever filmed) and Cate Blanchett's "dead-on", Oscar-grabbing take on Kate Hepburn; more debatable is Leo's title turn ("formidable" or "hollow"), though most agree on the "too-long" running time and "soulless", "conventional" windup.

Awakenings
22 26 23 20
1990 | Directed by Penny Marshall | With Robert De Niro, Robin Williams, John Heard | 121 minutes | Rated PG-13

A true story about the search for a "cure for comatose patients" gets "thought-provoking" treatment in this "touching" drama, featuring Williams "playing it straight" for a change opposite a "memorable" De Niro; while some berate its "sentimental", "hanky-wringing" edge, most find it both "amusing and moving", despite the "potentially mawkish" subject matter.

☒ Away From Her
26 29 25 25
2007 | Directed by Sarah Polley | With Julie Christie, Gordon Pinsent, Olympia Dukakis, Michael Murphy | 110 minutes | Rated PG-13

Depicting the "emotional impact" of Alzheimer's disease on "patient and family", this "beautiful yet heartbreaking" love story may be "hard to take" but is nonetheless a "must-see" for Christie's "brilliant" portrayal of a housewife "lost in her own world"; a "triumphant" directorial debut from the "poised" Polley, it's "riveting" filmmaking "with hardly a false move, word or gesture."

Awful Truth, The ✉◑
25 26 24 23
1937 | Directed by Leo McCarey | With Irene Dunne, Cary Grant, Ralph Bellamy, Alexander D'Arcy | 91 minutes | Not Rated

"Two spoiled rich people" on the verge of divorce try to "win each other back" in this "laugh-out-loud" romantic comedy top-billing the "classic combo" of Grant and Dunne; it's "one of the better screwball" pictures "from the golden age of Hollywood" with enough "crackling dialogue" and sheer "fun" to leave nostalgics wishing "Hollywood would make more films like this."

Babe
25 22 25 26
1995 | Directed by Chris Noonan | With James Cromwell, Magda Szubanski, Danny Mann | 89 minutes | Rated G

"Believe the hype": fans are in "hog heaven" over this "porcine" comedy about a "talking pig" who "wants to be a sheepherder so he won't get eaten"; "cute without being cutesy", it features Oscar-winning "computer effects" that allow "animals to interact" with humans so realistically that it may "turn you into a vegetarian."

Babel ▣
22 25 21 24
2006 | Directed by Alejandro González Iñárritu | With Brad Pitt, Cate Blanchett, Adriana Barraza, Rinko Kikuchi | 143 minutes | Rated R

Sort of an "international version of *Crash*", this "tapestry" of "cleverly intertwined" tales makes you "ponder life" as it leaps across continents to prove "we're connected to people we don't know" and to lament the "barriers between cultures"; Pitt and crew are "uniformly excellent", but some find it too "confusing" and "not as good as critics want you to think."

	OVERALL	ACTING	STORY	PROD.

☒ Babette's Feast ✉🅵
26 | 26 | 26 | 25

1988 | Directed by Gabriel Axel | With Stéphane Audran, Bibi Andersson, Jarl Kulle | 102 minutes | Rated G

"Sumptuous enough to make vegetarians drool" (though "slow as molasses"), this "classic foodie" dramedy is an "unusual" tale based on the Isak Dinesen story about the "power of redemption" cooked up in one "magnificent meal"; "still mouthwatering after all these years", this "intriguing" Danish treat is so "delectable" and "savory" that it could be the "Zagat signature movie."

Baby Boom
19 | 20 | 20 | 18

1987 | Directed by Charles Shyer | With Diane Keaton, Sam Shepard, Harold Ramis | 103 minutes | Rated PG

"Career vs. home and family" is the theme of this "very '80s" "light comedy" starring a "sharp, understated" Keaton as a "woman who wants it all" – and gets it when she inherits a baby and hooks up with Shepard; though tough guys dismiss it as a "feel-good chick flick", "warm-and-fuzzy" folk find it a "likable" tale of "triumphant romance."

Baby Doll ◐
20 | 23 | 19 | 20

1956 | Directed by Elia Kazan | With Carroll Baker, Karl Malden, Eli Wallach, Mildred Dunnock | 114 minutes | Not Rated

"One of the steamier movies of the '50s" (and "still racy" today), this "darkly amusing" "cult classic" via Tennessee Williams revolves around the misfortunes of a frustrated Southerner whose "19-year-old bride won't let him touch her until she turns 20"; Baker's "Lolita"-esque title turn "riled the Legion of Decency" at the time, particularly that scene of her "curled up in a crib, sucking her thumb."

Backdraft
18 | 18 | 18 | 23

1991 | Directed by Ron Howard | With Kurt Russell, William Baldwin, Scott Glenn, Robert De Niro | 132 minutes | Rated R

"Big fires and cute firemen" sum up the appeal of this disaster thriller aflame with a "stellar cast" and some mighty "eye-opening", "amazingly realistic" special effects; ok, the "melodramatic storyline's a bit soft" and the actors struggle with the "moronic dialogue", but the action sequences will "keep you hanging on until the end."

Back to the Future
23 | 20 | 25 | 24

1985 | Directed by Robert Zemeckis | With Michael J. Fox, Christopher Lloyd, Lea Thompson | 111 minutes | Rated PG

A "time-traveling DeLorean" propels the "delectably dimpled Fox" into a "fun ride to the past" (and an opportunity to observe his parents as "goofy teenagers") in this "perfect blend of sci-fi, fantasy and pop culture"; "irrepressibly entertaining" and very popular, it spawned an "incredible ride" at the Universal theme park as well as two "terrible sequels."

Bad and the Beautiful, The ✉◐
24 | 25 | 24 | 24

1952 | Directed by Vincente Minnelli | With Lana Turner, Kirk Douglas, Walter Pidgeon, Dick Powell | 118 minutes | Not Rated

Douglas is at his "jaw-clenching best" playing a "manipulative producer" in this knowing, "behind-the-scenes" look at Tinseltown that could be "Hollywood's best movie about itself"; told in a series of flashbacks by a director, an actress and a screenwriter, it's "lush,

| | OVERALL | ACTING | STORY | PROD. |

hammy" stuff that's "over the top in just the right way"; P.S. "never loan Lana Turner your car."

Bad Day at Black Rock
24 | 28 | 24 | 22

1955 | Directed by John Sturges | With Spencer Tracy, Robert Ryan, Anne Francis | 81 minutes | Not Rated

This "taut little thriller" is "mean, lean" moviemaking about "bigotry and intolerance" in a "small town with a secret", starring an "excellent" Tracy in "one of his more unusual roles"; although somewhat "forgotten" today, it's "just as relevant as it was in the post-McCarthy '50s", "giving you plenty to think about" as it "profiles American prejudices."

Bad Education 🇫
23 | 26 | 23 | 24

2004 | Directed by Pedro Almodóvar | With Gael García Bernal, Fele Martínez, Daniel Giménez Cacho | 106 minutes | Rated R

"Bad boy" director Almodóvar proves he's at the "head of the class" with this "visually hypnotic", "gender-bending" mystery that pays homage to both "film noir" and "Hitchcock"; boasting a "bravura" performance by rising star Bernal (who's just as "sexy in drag"), this "out-there" flick is rife with "racy", "taboo"-smashing material (e.g. "drugs", "transvestites", "priest abuse") and "not for the easily offended."

🅉 Badlands
25 | 27 | 24 | 24

1973 | Directed by Terrence Malick | With Martin Sheen, Sissy Spacek, Warren Oates | 95 minutes | Rated PG

The "banality of evil" is dissected in this "dark, disturbing" depiction of a true-life teen crime spree; playing "shallow", "disaffected" lovers on the run, a "very young" Spacek and Sheen are "first rate", while Malick's "trademark sweeping cinematography" acts as "visually stunning" counterpoint to the "bitingly tragic" story; in short, it's "gutsy", "twisted" and "not nearly as well known as it should be."

Bad News Bears, The
18 | 16 | 19 | 15

1976 | Directed by Michael Ritchie | With Walter Matthau, Tatum O'Neal, Vic Morrow | 102 minutes | Rated PG

A "must-see for any Little Leaguer", this "cute" sports comedy pitches a story about a curmudgeonly drunk roped into coaching a "truly awful" kids' baseball team; though perhaps "better then than now" (with "foul but funny language" that might raise parental eyebrows), its sequels are definitely "bad news for moviegoers."

Bad Santa
18 | 20 | 17 | 17

2003 | Directed by Terry Zwigoff | With Billy Bob Thornton, Tony Cox, John Ritter, Bernie Mac | 91 minutes | Rated R

"Rude, crude and awfully funny", this "fearless" black comedy toplines Thornton as a "burnt-out", "mean-spirited" Santa who robs department stores with his partner, a "potty-mouthed" elf; no question, it's "sick, sick, sick" and "definitely not for kids" ("it ain't rated R for nothing"), but "twisted" types label it the "perfect antidote to phony Christmas cheer."

Bad Seed, The 🅞
22 | 23 | 25 | 20

1956 | Directed by Mervyn LeRoy | With Nancy Kelly, Patty McCormack, Eileen Heckart | 129 minutes | Not Rated

"Not for the faint of heart", this "very creepy" thriller is the story of a "perky little deranged girl" who's the "world's most evil child" (think

"Ted Bundy in a pinafore"); "unsettling and unforgettable" in its time, it's still "way, way over the top", and even if the Broadway play "had a better ending", this one will positively "send chills down your spine."

Ⓩ Ball of Fire ◑

| 26 | 28 | 24 | 23 |

1941 | Directed by Howard Hawks | With Gary Cooper, Barbara Stanwyck, Oskar Homolka, Dana Andrews | 111 minutes | Not Rated

Fired-up admirers praise the "classic" hilarity in this "delightful" screwball comedy, wherein "sassy" burlesque queen Stanwyck holes up with "eight straight-laced" linguists to school them in "early '40s slang"; add Cooper in a "droll", "deadpan" turn as a "timid bookworm", and sparks fly as the "splendid cast" lets fly with the "witty" repartee.

Ⓩ Bambi

| 26 | – | 25 | 26 |

1942 | Directed by David Hand | Animated | 70 minutes | Rated G

"Don't forget those tissues" before settling into this dear coming-of-age story that's best remembered for the "absolutely heart-wrenching" "death of Bambi's mother", a "cruel lesson in life" that will "make you think twice about showing it" to young children; otherwise, it's arguably the "most beautiful" example of vintage Disney animation, "warm and fuzzy" but "not mawkish."

Bananas

| 23 | 20 | 22 | 19 |

1971 | Directed by Woody Allen | With Woody Allen, Louise Lasser, Carlos Montalban | 82 minutes | Rated PG-13

"For Allen purists mostly", this "early" comic romance "relies heavily on sight gags and slapstick humor" in its "anarchic" story of a nebbish turned "Latin American dictator" that's a "zany" satire to some, but "intermittently funny shtick" to others; P.S. hang on for a "young" Sylvester Stallone's cameo as a "thug on the subway."

Ⓩ Band Wagon, The

| 26 | 21 | 20 | 26 |

1953 | Directed by Vincente Minnelli | With Fred Astaire, Cyd Charisse, Nanette Fabray, Oscar Levant | 111 minutes | Not Rated

A "worthy companion to *Singin' in the Rain*", this "solid musical" comedy boasts the "most romantic moment in movie history" – the "hauntingly lovely 'Dancing in the Dark' number in Central Park" – performed by Astaire and Charisse; thanks to its "fantastic music" and "delightful cast", nostalgists regret that Hollywood got off this bandwagon.

Bang the Drum Slowly

| 23 | 25 | 24 | 18 |

1973 | Directed by John Hancock | With Michael Moriarty, Robert De Niro, Vincent Gardenia | 96 minutes | Rated PG

Moriarty and De Niro deliver "two moving performances" in this memorably "sad" drama about a hayseed baseball catcher with a terminal illness and the star pitcher who befriends him; both a "real tearjerker" and a "powerful story of friendship", it's a "well done", "humbling" experience that still has "staying power."

Bank Job, The

| 23 | 22 | 24 | 23 |

2008 | Directed by Roger Donaldson | With Jason Statham, Saffron Burrows, David Suchet | 111 minutes | Rated R

A "good, old-fashioned bank heist" is the foundation of this solid, "highly entertaining" picture, supposedly based on a "real-life" caper with a "royal plotline" (i.e. the theft of some racy photographs of

Princess Margaret); despite a "fine" Statham, "fast-paced" action and an out-of-nowhere "twist ending", it remains something of a "sleeper."

Barbarella
13 | 9 | 11 | 15

1968 | Directed by Roger Vadim | With Jane Fonda, John Phillip Law, Anita Pallenberg, Milo O'Shea | 98 minutes | Rated PG

Über-"babe" Fonda "pushes the boundaries of sexuality" (at least the 1968 boundaries) with her "zero-g striptease" and other "amusing" outfit-free antics in this "campy" sci-fi "cult classic"; if you can just "forget the story" and the "terrible", "bad-high-school-play" production values, you'll have "great fun" with all that young Jane "eye candy."

Barbarian Invasions, The ✉🅵
24 | 25 | 23 | 23

2003 | Directed by Denys Arcand | With Rémy Girard, Stéphane Rousseau | 99 minutes | Rated R

"Skillfully written" and "palpably human", this "moving" Canadian drama mines the "ambiguities of life" in its story of a terminally ill left-wing professor tended to by his estranged, capitalistic son; doling out alternately "acerbic" and "emotional" observations about "modern" times and "human relationships", it took home the Best Foreign Film Oscar for its efforts.

Barbershop
20 | 20 | 20 | 18

2002 | Directed by Tim Story | With Ice Cube, Cedric the Entertainer, Eve | 102 minutes | Rated PG-13

An "old-time barbershop where everyone hangs out" is the centerpiece of this "enjoyable, day-in-the-life" comedy that may be "set in a black neighborhood" but will "appeal to all hair colors"; Cedric the Entertainer's "timing steals the show", and even if the "Rosa Parks" and "Jesse Jackson" gibes seem "politically incorrect", the picture ultimately offers a "solid message about community."

Barefoot Contessa, The
24 | 25 | 23 | 23

1954 | Directed by Joseph L. Mankiewicz | With Humphrey Bogart, Ava Gardner, Edmond O'Brien | 128 minutes | Not Rated

"Romantic to the nth degree", this "enjoyable" drama centers on a "ravishing" performance by the "amazing Ava" as a "gorgeous" ingenue who rises to "old Hollywood" stardom and ultimately marries into minor royalty; if some say the "thin plot" reveals feet of clay, it's still loaded with "elegance" and "real quality" – "those were movies!"

Barefoot in the Park
23 | 24 | 22 | 21

1967 | Directed by Gene Saks | With Robert Redford, Jane Fonda, Charles Boyer, Mildred Natwick | 106 minutes | Rated G

Channeling "how delightful the first rush of true love is", this "light" romantic comedy pairs "ingénue" Fonda with "heartthrob" Redford in a "cute tale" of newlyweds who "try on marriage in a small NY flat"; there's "great chemistry" between the "beautiful" leads and Neil Simon's script is "witty", even if some say its "strong period quality" makes the film feel "a bit dated" today.

Barfly
18 | 21 | 17 | 16

1987 | Directed by Barbet Schroeder | With Mickey Rourke, Faye Dunaway, Frank Stallone | 100 minutes | Rated R

"Down and out" in LA the Charles Bukowski way, this "painful look" at "burnt-out alcoholics" stars Rourke and Dunaway as "rummies on the skids" uttering "heavy dialogue" over "tacky/cool" background music; some swat it for being "relentlessly depressing", but for most it's a "gritty, poignant look at the fringes of society" with some mighty "great acting" as a bonus.

Barry Lyndon

20 | 18 | 21 | 27

1975 | Directed by Stanley Kubrick | With Ryan O'Neal, Marisa Berenson, Leon Vitali | 184 minutes | Rated PG

"Kubrick's classic adaptation" of the Thackeray novel depicts the "rise and fall of an Irish lad whose luck finally runs dry" with "amazing period detail" and "gorgeous photography"; but although this "thing of beauty" is a "feast for the eyes", the "acting's from hunger" and the "dull, plodding" pace leaves some sighing "what you see isn't what you get."

Barton Fink

20 | 24 | 19 | 22

1991 | Directed by Joel Coen | With John Turturro, John Goodman, Judy Davis, Michael Lerner | 116 minutes | Rated R

"Delightfully weird", this Coen brothers drama about a gone-Hollywood playwright with a colossal case of writer's block "alternates between fascinating and frustrating" given a "surreal", "terribly odd" storyline that's "brain candy" for intellectuals; despite "fantastic acting" from an "exceptional" Turturro and "absolutely sinister" Goodman, this "out-there" picture is "not for everyone."

Basic Instinct

19 | 19 | 20 | 19

1992 | Directed by Paul Verhoeven | With Michael Douglas, Sharon Stone, Jeanne Tripplehorn | 123 minutes | Rated R

Aside from Sharon Stone's notorious "uncrossed legs" "money shot", this "leering erotic thriller" offers enough "noir-esque dialogue" and "gratuitous sex" to make for one "highly provocative" "hormone movie"; though detractors deem it "unintentionally funny trash", "mired in leftover '80s hedonism", fans find it "surprisingly entertaining" – just "don't make the mistake of watching it with your parents."

Basketball Diaries, The

22 | 24 | 21 | 19

1995 | Directed by Scott Kalvert | With Leonardo DiCaprio, Lorraine Bracco, Mark Wahlberg | 102 minutes | Rated R

Jim Carroll's "tell-all" memoir about his youthful rebound from "drug abuse" to "redemption" in "gritty NYC" shoots to the silver screen via this "well-done" adaptation, featuring a slam-dunk performance from "then-rising star" DiCaprio; though the cast of "dysfunctional" teens is "not always pleasant to watch", it's an undeniably "gripping" look at the "nasty side of the street."

Basquiat

17 | 20 | 19 | 17

1996 | Directed by Julian Schnabel | With Jeffrey Wright, Benicio Del Toro, David Bowie | 108 minutes | Rated R

It "feels as though you've lived, not just watched", this "insightful biopic" about the rise and fall of a "promising prodigy imploding" in the NY art scene; directed by fellow artist Schnabel, "excellently scored" by ex-Velvet Undergrounder John Cale and featuring a "beautifully cast" Bowie as pop conduit Andy Warhol, it's a "dark", tragic ride that "ends abruptly – like Basquiat's life did."

	OVERALL	ACTING	STORY	PROD.

Batman
20 | 19 | 19 | 24

1989 | Directed by Tim Burton | With Michael Keaton, Jack Nicholson, Kim Basinger | 126 minutes | Rated PG-13

The "first and best of the bat franchise", this "brilliantly shot" fantasy-adventure flick reflects the "dark side of the comic book" thanks to the "dynamic duo" of "visionary" director Burton and "top-notch" "caped crusader" Keaton; Nicholson's an "awesome" Joker and the *Blade Runner*–esque Gotham City is "realized to stunning effect", so even if the "sequels stink", this one "rocks."

Batman Begins
23 | 21 | 23 | 26

2005 | Directed by Christopher Nolan | With Christian Bale, Michael Caine, Katie Holmes | 141 minutes | Rated PG-13

After a "worrisome decline" into "cartoonish goofery", the Batman franchise is "back on track" with this "quality" revival, a "rollicking ride" that revels in the "dark" tone of the "original comic book" as it recounts the Caped Crusader's "early years"; as for acting, the "brooding" Bale "soars" in the lead role, shedding "insight" into his character's "inner turmoil", though romantic interest Holmes is deemed the "weak link."

Batman Returns
16 | 17 | 15 | 21

1992 | Directed by Tim Burton | With Michael Keaton, Danny DeVito, Michelle Pfeiffer | 126 minutes | Rated PG-13

The "last of the dark deco Batman" pictures, this "freak show of a sequel" is "another atmospheric Burton production" that keeps Keaton as the caped crusader and is "spiced up" by a "sizzling" Pfeiffer playing an "S&M version of Catwoman"; spoilsports say "they should've stopped" after the original, bemoaning what happens when "marketing takes over a movie."

Batteries Not Included
19 | 20 | 20 | 20

1987 | Directed by Matthew Robbins | With Hume Cronyn, Jessica Tandy, Elizabeth Peña, Frank McRae | 106 minutes | Rated PG

"Cute little alien robots" descend from above to "save the elderly tenants of an apartment building" from eviction in this "sweet" family flick via executive producer Steven Spielberg; the "always-worth-watching" Cronyn-Tandy tandem provide some "funny" geriatric shtick, abetted by "clever" FX "for their time."

Z Battle of Algiers, The ⓞⒻ
28 | 24 | 27 | 26

1967 | Directed by Gillo Pontecorvo | With Jean Martin, Yacef Saadi | 117 minutes | Not Rated

"Terrorism and military response" are the up-to-the-minute subjects of this "decades-ahead-of-its-time" feature delineating the Algerian struggle for independence from French rule; the "riveting" footage is "so lifelike" that it "looks like a documentary", but even as a "docudrama" it remains "timely, essential" viewing.

Beaches
22 | 23 | 22 | 21

1988 | Directed by Garry Marshall | With Bette Midler, Barbara Hershey, John Heard | 123 minutes | Rated PG-13

Alternately "heartwarming and heartbreaking", this "major chick flick" (a "10-hanky" special) captures the "intensity of friendship" as it recounts the "lifelong" alliance of "two opposites": the "always passionate" Midler and the more "detached" Hershey; hard-hearted sorts yawn it's a "sappy soap opera", but others say when you need a "good cathartic cry", this "guilty pleasure" is the "one to watch."

ⓩ Beau Geste ◑   25 | 23 | 25 | 22

1939 | Directed by William A. Wellman | With Gary Cooper, Ray Milland, Robert Preston | 120 minutes | Not Rated

"Heroic heroes and villainous villains" populate this "ultimate" war picture about "friendship and honor" that's "perhaps the best Foreign Legion movie" ever made; ok, there are "no special effects" and it might seem "corny" today, but it still supplies plenty of "first-class adventure" right up to that "majestic ending."

ⓩ Beautiful Mind, A ✉   26 | 28 | 25 | 25

2001 | Directed by Ron Howard | With Russell Crowe, Ed Harris, Jennifer Connelly | 134 minutes | Rated PG-13

"What *Rain Man* did for autism", this "absorbing" Oscar winner about a "brilliant mathematician's" battle with mental illness "does for schizophrenia", revealing the "thin line between genius and insanity"; "phenomenally acted" by Crowe and Connelly, it "celebrates the triumph of the human spirit" – though foes say its "Hollywoodized" script "strays too far from historical accuracy."

ⓩ Beauty and the Beast ◑🄵   28 | 25 | 27 | 28

1947 | Directed by Jean Cocteau | With Jean Marais, Josette Day, Marcel André | 93 minutes | Not Rated

Enter a "highly stylized universe" in this "hallucinatory" take on the classic "fairy tale" that's both "dreamlike" and "complex" owing to "Cocteau's wit and imagination"; "still unsurpassed by more lavish productions", this "amazing visual feast" demonstrates the artistry possible with "ancient technology" – and enough "sexuality beneath the surface" to keep things throbbing.

Beauty and the Beast   26 | - | 25 | 27

1991 | Directed by Gary Trousdale, Kirk Wise | Animated | 84 minutes | Rated G

A "sensational score" complements the cast of "lovable characters" in this "magical milepost" that "set the bar for a new wave of animated classics"; told with a "fresh approach", it has an "intelligent" "heroine with chutzpah" trilling "catchy", "singable songs"; in short, this "modern masterpiece" – the first animated film ever nominated for Best Picture – is nothing less than "Disney at its high-flying best."

Because of Winn-Dixie   19 | 20 | 20 | 19

2005 | Directed by Wayne Wang | With AnnaSophia Robb, Jeff Daniels, Cicely Tyson, Dave Matthews | 106 minutes | Rated PG

The reliable pairing of "cute" youngster with "loveable" canine infuses this "heartwarming" family picture, a doggedly "sweet" production presented in an "old-fashioned" way that "doesn't depend on noise and fast editing" to hold your attention; rocker Dave Matthews supplies some "nice" supporting relief from all the "saccharine" goings-on.

ⓩ Becket ✉   26 | 29 | 26 | 26

1964 | Directed by Peter Glenville | With Richard Burton, Peter O'Toole, John Gielgud | 148 minutes | Not Rated

"Big drama writ large", this biopic about England's King Henry II and his "deep bond with Thomas Becket" features the "brilliant teaming" of "two high-powered actors" – the "winning" O'Toole and "wonderful" Burton – in "histrionic, bellowing performances"; sure, it's "a bit talky", but otherwise this "beautifully filmed period piece" is living proof of the way "history should be experienced."

Bedazzled
20 | 19 | 21 | 16

1967 | Directed by Stanley Donen | With Dudley Moore, Peter Cook, Raquel Welch | 104 minutes | Not Rated

This "immensely clever" "takeoff on the Faust legend" relocated to "swinging '60s London" is a "wickedly funny" comedy full of "vintage Brit humor" and "witty" "double entendres" in its story of "poor dweeb Moore selling his soul" to the devil in exchange for "true love"; ok, it may be "slow in spots", but it's still "far superior to the 2000 remake."

Bee Movie
19 | – | 18 | 22

2007 | Directed by Steve Hickner, Simon J. Smith | Animated | 90 minutes | Rated PG

Lending his voice to a scrappy bumblebee rebelling against hive life by exploring the frontiers of "insect/human romance", Jerry Seinfeld plays to "kids and adults alike" in this "mildly entertaining" cartoon with an "eco-conscious" message; however, despite "well-done animation" and "clever" zingers, some drone the "trite" concept "doesn't fly."

Beethoven
16 | 14 | 16 | 16

1992 | Directed by Brian Levant | With Charles Grodin, Dean Jones, Bonnie Hunt, Stanley Tucci | 87 minutes | Rated PG

"Dog lovers" dig this "cute" exercise in "good, clean family fun" about a "slobbery", "scene-stealing" St. Bernard who wreaks havoc in the house while deftly avoiding the clutches of an evil vet; though grumps growl about the "average acting", "predictable storyline" and "laboratory villains", "kids love it" – enough said.

Beetlejuice
20 | 19 | 21 | 22

1988 | Directed by Tim Burton | With Michael Keaton, Geena Davis, Alec Baldwin, Winona Ryder | 92 minutes | Rated PG

"Netherworld antics" animate this "demented haunted-house comedy", a "bizarre" yet "enchanting" flick from "twisted" director Burton that's "endlessly inventive and endearingly funny"; built around a "genius" performance by Keaton as the "wonderfully disgusting" title character, it's also notable for a "macabre" turn from Ryder as an "unusual teenager."

Before Night Falls
22 | 26 | 22 | 20

2000 | Directed by Julian Schnabel | With Javier Bardem, Johnny Depp, Olivier Martinez | 133 minutes | Rated R

Based on the true life story of "gay Cuban poet" Reinaldo Arenas, this "historically significant" biodrama is a "serious" reminder not to "take freedom for granted" as it details the hero's struggles against an "oppressive regime" bent on "silencing" him; look for an "excellent" Bardem in a "beautiful", "fully realized" performance.

Before Sunrise
23 | 23 | 22 | 21

1995 | Directed by Richard Linklater | With Ethan Hawke, Julie Delpy | 105 minutes | Rated R

A "thinking person's" romance, this "bittersweet gem" examines a "passionate meeting of the minds" between Hawke and the "enchanting" Delpy as "star-crossed" Euroailing students who hook up for a single night; the duo's "winning chemistry" is framed by "beautiful" Viennese backdrops, and "what might have been" will dawn on those who catch the "10-years-later follow-up", *Before Sunset*.

Before Sunset
21 | 23 | 20 | 21

2004 | Directed by Richard Linklater | With Ethan Hawke, Julie Delpy | 80 minutes | Rated R

After their "magical" one-night "chance encounter" in *Before Sunrise*, Hawke and Delpy – now "older and somewhat wiser" – meet again in "atmospheric" Paris for a one-day "second chance" in this "intelligent romance"; while their "nonstop" conversation seems to "drag" for some, it's a "fairy tale" for those mesmerized by the stars' "amazing chemistry."

Before the Devil Knows You're Dead
23 | 27 | 23 | 22

2007 | Directed by Sidney Lumet | With Philip Seymour Hoffman, Ethan Hawke, Albert Finney, Marisa Tomei | 117 minutes | Rated R

"Crime doesn't pay" in this "dark" "American tragedy" about two brothers' botched robbery of a mom-and-pop store owned by their own mom and pop; Hoffman and Hawke are "killer" as the "morally bankrupt" siblings, and their "downward spiral" is rife with "unpredictable plot twists," although you might want to avert your eyes from "Phil's nude scene."

Being John Malkovich
22 | 24 | 24 | 22

1999 | Directed by Spike Jonze | With John Cusack, Cameron Diaz, John Malkovich, Catherine Keener | 112 minutes | Rated R

"'Original' does not even begin to describe" this "surreal romp" that mixes "dark fantasy" with "smart comedy" in its "off-the-wall" story of a regular guy who finds a portal that takes him "inside the head" of actor John Malkovich; though it "rewards rather than insults the audience's intelligence", it's definitely "not for everybody", being either "engrossing", "audacious fun" or "confusing as hell."

Being Julia
23 | 27 | 21 | 24

2004 | Directed by István Szabó | With Annette Bening, Jeremy Irons | 104 minutes | Rated R

Bening "steals the show" with her "luminous" portrayal of a "fading English actress undertaking one last fling" with a young Yank in this "enjoyable" Brit "comedy of manners" based on the Somerset Maugham novella; overall, it's a "fluffy period piece" perhaps best suited for devotees of the "theatuh", but it's still "worth watching" all the way through for that "deliciously wicked climax."

☑ Being There
26 | 27 | 25 | 23

1979 | Directed by Hal Ashby | With Peter Sellers, Shirley MacLaine, Melvyn Douglas | 130 minutes | Rated PG

"Politics and hypocrisy" get a skewering in this "classic allegory" about a "slow-thinking" gardener who proves that "80 percent of life is just showing up"; "Sellers glows" in this "faithful" adaptation of Jerzy Kosinski's story, which "requires patience with its slow pace" but does "allow you to form your own conclusions."

Bell, Book and Candle
22 | 22 | 22 | 21

1958 | Directed by Richard Quine | With Kim Novak, James Stewart, Jack Lemmon | 106 minutes | Not Rated

Stewart and Novak "have fun with witchcraft" in this romantic comedy based on the Broadway hit about a "man falling for a woman who's a witch"; fans claim that this "old chestnut" was responsible for many cats being "named Pyewacket" and note that the "enchanting" title refers to the Roman Catholic rite of exorcism.

☑ Belle de Jour 🇫 | 24 | 25 | 23 | 23 |

1968 | Directed by Luis Buñuel | With Catherine Deneuve, Jean Sorel | 101 minutes | Rated R

Deneuve was "never sexier" than in this "marvelously perverse" French drama, a peek at the "dark side" of a "chichi housewife" pent up in "bourgeois" wedlock whose "S&M fantasies" compel her to take a "side job" at the local bordello; more "Dali painting" than *Playboy* centerfold, it's a "stylish", "complex" window into director Buñuel's "surreal world", and the leading lady's "intense", "alluring" performance spices up the "slow" spots.

Bells Are Ringing | 24 | 24 | 22 | 22 |

1960 | Directed by Vincente Minnelli | With Judy Holliday, Dean Martin, Fred Clark | 127 minutes | Not Rated

A "funny" Broadway musical becomes a "fine vehicle" for the "wonderful" Holliday in this story of a singing switchboard girl hung up on a playwright (the slightly "out-of-his-league" Martin); yet despite a "classic" score and a "famous song" ('The Party's Over'), some say this "stage-bound" production's "outdated."

Bells of St. Mary's, The ◑ | 24 | 25 | 23 | 23 |

1945 | Directed by Leo McCarey | With Bing Crosby, Ingrid Bergman | 126 minutes | Not Rated

Bergman and "ring-a-ding Bing" take turns "tugging your heart" in this "*Going My Way* sequel", a "heartwarming" drama (and "Christmas fave") about a crooning clergyman sent to a parochial school's rescue with a message of "selfless giving"; the "old-fashioned sweetness" strikes a "treacly" note for cynics, but "sentimental" sorts still delight in its "touching", "keep-a-hanky-handy" style of filmmaking that's "now extinct."

Bend It Like Beckham | 26 | 24 | 25 | 23 |

2003 | Directed by Gurinder Chadha | With Parminder K. Nagra, Keira Knightley, Jonathan Rhys Meyers | 112 minutes | Rated PG-13

"Bend it like anything you want" – this "thoroughly entertaining", "cross-cultural feel-good movie" about an "Indian girl in England who wants to play soccer" scores with its "empowering" storyline and "fantastic ensemble acting"; a "true delight" "for young and old alike", it's the "best ethnic-themed movie since *My Big Fat Greek Wedding*" – "but no TV series, please."

☑ Ben-Hur ✉ | 26 | 23 | 25 | 28 |

1959 | Directed by William Wyler | With Charlton Heston, Jack Hawkins, Stephen Boyd | 212 minutes | Rated G

Unleashed four decades "before *Gladiator*", this "bigger than big" sword-and-sandals "masterpiece" features Heston exuding "hammy", bare-chested "bravura" as a Judean prince betrayed into Roman slavery only to seek payback via "breathtaking" bouts of action (including that "stunner" of a "chariot race"); a colossal hit and major Oscar magnet, it epitomizes the "grand Hollywood historical epic", built on "biblical" bedrock.

Benji

19	16	18	17

1974 | Directed by Joe Camp | With Patsy Garrett, Peter Breck | 86 minutes | Rated G

The "must-see" flick for the "mid-'70s" single-digit demo, this fetching "doggy adventure" features a star turn from a "cute", shaggy-browed mutt who trots to the rescue after his young owners are kidnapped; nostalgists recall a "sappy" but "wonderful" "childhood favorite", albeit with "low-rent" production values.

Benny & Joon

21	24	21	19

1993 | Directed by Jeremiah Chechik | With Johnny Depp, Mary Stuart Masterson, Aidan Quinn | 98 minutes | Rated PG

"Misfits find true love" in this ultra-"quirky" romance featuring the early "Depp in his element", exuding "priceless subtlety" as he "channels Buster Keaton" and Charlie Chaplin routines to win over his "kooky", "special-needs" housemate Masterson; ok, it's "more than a little strange"(even for an "underground hit"), but when "different" is this "engaging", "who needs normal?"

Best in Show

24	25	23	22

2000 | Directed by Christopher Guest | With Christopher Guest, Eugene Levy, Catherine O'Hara | 90 minutes | Rated PG-13

"Three woofs" and "four paws up" for this "quirky riot" of a mockumentary about a "gaggle of fanatical dog show participants" and their "pedigreed pooches"; the wacky repartee makes for a "beautifully inappropriate", "laugh-a-minute satire" that "can be viewed 100 times without becoming dog-eared."

Best Little Whorehouse in Texas, The

14	13	15	17

1982 | Directed by Colin Higgins | With Burt Reynolds, Dolly Parton, Dom DeLuise, Charles Durning | 114 minutes | Rated R

"Harmless" enough "escapism", this "fair" rendering of the hit Broadway musical portrays the "daily grind" of "Texas hookers" whose titular establishment is threatened to close; most find Burt and Dolly too "hokey", though the picture's best little scene is that "song and dance" routine by "what-a-scream" Durning.

Z Best Years of Our Lives, The ✉◐

28	27	28	25

1946 | Directed by William Wyler | With Myrna Loy, Fredric March, Dana Andrews, Teresa Wright | 172 minutes | Not Rated

"Have the Kleenex handy" – there's no denying the "pure heart" of this "compelling" drama exploring the "uneasy readjustment" of WWII "vets coming home" to Main Street USA; its all-around "riveting" acting and "no-miss script" perfectly capture the "next-door" post-war mood, taking Best Picture (plus six more Oscars) and resonating as a "quintessentially American period piece."

Beverly Hills Cop

20	19	19	19

1984 | Directed by Martin Brest | With Eddie Murphy, Judge Reinhold, John Ashton | 105 minutes | Rated R

This action/comedy "breakthrough" is a "star vehicle" for Murphy, cast as an "inner-city" flatfoot with a "trademark laugh" who upstages his "goofy" El Lay counterparts in pursuit of a friend's killer; though the typically "'80s" foolery and "cheesy storyline" have cooled over time, this "hoot" still works as "feel-good" fare to fill a "Saturday afternoon."

| | OVERALL | ACTING | STORY | PROD. |

Beyond the Sea
19 | 22 | 19 | 20

2004 | Directed by Kevin Spacey | With Kevin Spacey, Kate Bosworth, John Goodman | 118 minutes | Rated PG-13

A bona fide "labor of love", this "enjoyable" bio of '50s bopper Bobby Darin was directed, co-written and enacted by the "many hat"-wearing Spacey, who's his "usual riveting self" – and even does his own "first-rate singing"; still, sinkers say Kevin's "too old for the part" and compare this "self-indulgent" "vanity project" to "singing into a hairbrush in front of a mirror."

☑ Bicycle Thief, The ✉◑ᕒ
27 | 26 | 27 | 24

1949 | Directed by Vittorio De Sica | With Lamberto Maggiorani, Enzo Staiola | 93 minutes | Not Rated

"Poetry put on film", this early slice of "Italian neorealism" is "so sad" but so "beautifully executed" that it's ultimately "not a downer"; using "nonprofessional actors" in a drama of a father and son searching impoverished post-war Rome for the stolen bike that's key to their livelihood, De Sica tugs hearts with a "timeless pathos" that's most "affecting" for its "charm and simplicity."

Big
23 | 24 | 24 | 22

1988 | Directed by Penny Marshall | With Tom Hanks, Elizabeth Perkins, Robert Loggia | 104 minutes | Rated PG

Getting literal with its "inner child", this "cute" "kid-in-a-man's-body" comedy stars a "winning", "never-so-lovable" Hanks, who "makes the movie" (and moves into the big time) as a 13-year-old who "becomes an adult overnight" and gains entrée to NYC's corporate playground; though some of the "fantasy" is "on the sappy side", a large contingent calls it "most rewatchable."

Big Business
19 | 20 | 18 | 18

1988 | Directed by Jim Abrahams | With Bette Midler, Lily Tomlin, Fred Ward | 97 minutes | Rated PG

Playing "two sets of twins" separated at birth, "Midler and Tomlin and Midler and Tomlin" star in this "hilariously cheesy" mistaken identity comedy set in NY's Plaza Hotel; a "guilty pleasure" for fans of '80s "polyester clothes and big hair", it "doesn't really hold up" for others who sniff it's "silly" and suggest that "Bette should stick to music."

Big Chill, The
23 | 24 | 22 | 21

1983 | Directed by Lawrence Kasdan | With Glenn Close, William Hurt, Kevin Kline, Jeff Goldblum, Mary Kay Place, JoBeth Williams, Tom Berenger | 105 minutes | Rated R

Trace the tracks of their tears as this '60s-era "nostalgia" trip tries to "define a generation" via a "superb ensemble", an "iconic soundtrack" and the "soul-searching" premise of "boomers regathering" at a friend's funeral (fun fact: Kevin Costner "plays the stiff"); anyone bummed by the "contrived" setup and "smug" "yuppie angst" can still groove to the "perfect" tune selection.

Big Clock, The ◑
25 | 25 | 25 | 23

1948 | Directed by John Farrow | With Ray Milland, Charles Laughton, Maureen O'Sullivan, Elsa Lanchester | 95 minutes | Not Rated

"Nice and twisty", this "classic noir" stars Ray Milland as a crime magazine editor in a "real predicament" after witnessing "his publisher killing his lover"; the "suspenseful" story was filmed again in 1987 as *No Way Out,* but pundits say the original "dances rings around" the remake.

Big Daddy
17 | 16 | 17 | 17

1999 | Directed by Dennis Dugan | With Adam Sandler, Joey Lauren Adams, Jon Stewart | 93 minutes | Rated PG-13

Big on "typical" Sandler "guy" appeal, this "untraditional comedy" about a "man-boy trying to be a father" has enough "cute child interaction" to make it one of the star's "most accessible" vehicles (it "mercifully lacks the crude humor" of his usual work); true believers find it "hard not to laugh", though some pan it as a "nonsensical" outing that "gives stupid a bad name."

Big Easy, The
22 | 22 | 22 | 20

1987 | Directed by Jim McBride | With Dennis Quaid, Ellen Barkin, Ned Beatty, John Goodman | 108 minutes | Rated R

Emitting the "same sweaty humidity as its New Orleans locale", this "steamy", "sultry" drama is the story of a "less than perfect cop" and an "easy-on-the-eyes" assistant D.A. who meet during a "police corruption investigation"; Quaid's at his "bad-boy best", Barkin's "sizzlin'" and their "explosive chemistry" comes to a boil in "one of the best love scenes" ever filmed.

Big Fish
22 | 24 | 23 | 25

2003 | Directed by Tim Burton | With Ewan McGregor, Albert Finney, Billy Crudup, Jessica Lange | 125 minutes | Rated PG-13

The "guy equivalent of a chick flick", this "bittersweet" story of a "complicated father-and-son relationship" reels in sentimentalists with equal parts of "whimsy and schmaltz"; "less twisted" than director Burton's usual fare, it still has its "oddball" moments via a "patchwork", *Forrest Gump*-like script, and if cynics yawn it's "sappy" and "slow", many more laud its "vivid imagery and good message" – plus, it's a relief to "see McGregor without a light saber" for a change.

⚡ Big Heat, The ◑
25 | 25 | 24 | 22

1953 | Directed by Fritz Lang | With Glenn Ford, Gloria Grahame, Lee Marvin, Carolyn Jones | 90 minutes | Not Rated

"Considered daring in its time", this "ultimate noir picture" features a rogues' gallery of hard-boiled "tough guys" and gals in a story about an honest cop "obsessed with getting revenge" following his wife's murder; though tepid types say the heat's "cooled off over the years", there's "one horrifying scene" involving a pot of "scalding hot coffee" that's still quite a "shocker."

Big Lebowski, The
20 | 22 | 19 | 20

1998 | Directed by Joel Coen | With Jeff Bridges, John Goodman, Julianne Moore, Steve Buscemi | 117 minutes | Rated R

The brothers Coen "strike again" with this "shaggy-dog" comedy, an "homage to slobs" that gets rolling when Bridges' "aging" "slacker/ stoner character" and his "bizarre bowling buddies" become embroiled in a surreal kidnapping; though an "acquired taste" and certainly "strange for its own sake" ("dude, where's my plot?"), it has "cult" followers citing "quotable" lines and swearing "you'll laugh" your head off.

Big Night

	OVERALL	ACTING	STORY	PROD.
	24	26	23	23

1996 | Directed by Campbell Scott, Stanley Tucci | With Stanley Tucci, Tony Shalhoub, Minnie Driver | 107 minutes | Rated R

"Yum": this "quirky", "thoroughly enjoyable" dramatic "feast" tracks two "Italian immigrant brothers" in their "endearing" effort to keep their restaurant and culinary "vision" alive on the '50s-era Jersey coast; hailed as an "overlooked gem", its slow-simmering pace allows admirers to "savor" "brilliant performances" that are rivaled only by "stunning food shots" – "don't catch it on an empty stomach."

☑ Big Sleep, The ◑

	27	27	24	24

1946 | Directed by Howard Hawks | With Humphrey Bogart, Lauren Bacall, Martha Vickers | 114 minutes | Not Rated

"Whodunit? who cares?" as long as the legendary Bogie and Bacall keep up the "snappy" patter and "heavy-lidded" "chemistry" in this "dizzying" film noir "classic" featuring Bogart as "fast-talking" gumshoe Philip Marlowe prowling Raymond Chandler territory (1940s Los Angeles at its most "atmospheric"); if the notoriously "incomprehensible plot" is seriously in need of a clue, at least the "crackling" pace and "salty" repartee always "entertain and enthrall."

Big Trouble in Little China

	19	16	18	18

1986 | Directed by John Carpenter | With Kurt Russell, Kim Cattrall, Dennis Dun | 99 minutes | Rated PG-13

"Chopsocky" meets "schlock" in this "absurd but entertaining" martial-arts action picture about a "truck driver who gets in over his head with a Chinese gang"; there are "cheesy effects" and "crazy" dialogue galore, but it's attained "cult status" solely because of the "bad-ass" Russell, who tears it up opposite a "young", "unknown" Cattrall.

Bill & Ted's Excellent Adventure

	15	10	15	13

1989 | Directed by Stephen Herek | With Keanu Reeves, Alex Winter, George Carlin | 90 minutes | Rated PG

"Two goof-offs" about to flunk out of high school time-travel to the past in a desperate attempt to graduate in this "totally tubular" slacker comedy, a budding "cult classic" that just may be "better than you remember it"; sure, this "sophomoric", "truly mindless" flick could have "typecast Keanu" forever, and even if it's "not very good, it's still lots of fun, dude."

Billy Elliot

	25	26	25	23

2000 | Directed by Stephen Daldry | With Julie Walters, Jamie Bell | 110 minutes | Rated PG-13

It takes *Swan Lake* to break the "working-class shackles" of a Northern England mining town in this "coming-of-age" drama about a "boy who loves ballet" and his hardscrabble dad; behind the "thick British accents", fans discover a "captivating" if "unlikely tale" propelled by "talent, desire" and lots of "fancy footwork", with an "uplifting" finale that's apt to inspire "a good cry."

Billy Liar ◑

	22	26	23	20

1963 | Directed by John Schlesinger | With Tom Courtenay, Julie Christie, Wilfred Pickles | 98 minutes | Not Rated

A prime example of British "kitchen-sink realism", this "poignant comic gem" relates the story of a daydreamer–cum–pathological liar itching to escape his humdrum, blue-collar existence; in the "challenging" title role, Courtenay's a "charmer", but the picture is stolen by the "scrumptious young" Christie in her first major film role.

Biloxi Blues
21 | 22 | 22 | 20

1988 | Directed by Mike Nichols | With Matthew Broderick, Christopher Walken, Penelope Ann Miller | 106 minutes | Rated PG-13

WWII-era "basic training" gets the Neil Simon treatment in this "fair adaptation" of his "semi-autobiographical" stage comedy about a raw recruit confronted with a "crazed drill sergeant" in the "sweltering" South; a "sweet" "sequel of sorts to *Brighton Beach Memoirs*", it's "not momentous" but does manage to muster some "spirit of the times."

Birdcage, The
22 | 25 | 22 | 22

1996 | Directed by Mike Nichols | With Robin Williams, Nathan Lane, Gene Hackman, Dianne Wiest | 117 minutes | Rated R

Reset in South Beach, director Nichols' "slick" take on the "classic" French farce *La Cage aux Folles* soars "over the top" on the wings of the "perfect comedic combination" of Williams and Lane, cast as a pair of "flamboyant" gay cabaret owners obliged to "play it straight" for their son's "uptight" in-laws-to-be; busy with burlesque and "insight", it's widely welcomed as a "laugh-out-loud" "blast", though holdouts chirp "stick with the original."

Birdman of Alcatraz ◐
22 | 25 | 22 | 20

1962 | Directed by John Frankenheimer | With Burt Lancaster, Karl Malden, Thelma Ritter | 147 minutes | Not Rated

Lancaster is "at the top of his game" in this saga of "a man, a prison and some birds", the "fascinating" bio of Rock lifer Robert Stroud who struggles under the screws' authority but "finds love and friendship" when he becomes a famed ornithologist; it's generally judged a "keeper" as a "gritty" but "entertaining" penal drama that's also a "touching" "examination of survival."

Birds, The
24 | 20 | 24 | 25

1963 | Directed by Alfred Hitchcock | With Tippi Hedren, Rod Taylor, Jessica Tandy, Suzanne Pleshette | 119 minutes | Rated PG-13

"Nature strikes back, Hitchcock style", in this "improbably terrifying" "nail-biter" about "birds gone mad" that "still packs enough of a punch" to leave the timid "traumatized"; though critics aren't chirping about the "hokey", "no-rhyme-or-reason" plot that takes "too long to get going", ultimately you'll "never think of pigeons in the same way" after a gander at this one.

Birdy
23 | 25 | 22 | 21

1984 | Directed by Alan Parker | With Matthew Modine, Nicolas Cage | 120 minutes | Rated R

Much "emotional" flutter marks this "haunting" drama that "gets into the psyches" of a "pair of outcasts": Modine as a "traumatized" Vietnam-era vet with a "disturbing" fixation on "birdlike" behavior and a "brilliant" Cage as the childhood friend out to revive him; thanks to the leads' "breadth and heart", it's a "neglected minor classic" nested within a "surreal" story – "this film can fly."

⚡ Birth of a Nation, The ◑

25 | 20 | 19 | 27

1915 | Directed by D.W. Griffith | With Lillian Gish, Mae Marsh, Henry B. Walthall | 190 minutes | Not Rated

A "masterful" technical feat that could be the "most influential movie ever made", Griffith's "landmark" silent epic "wrote the book" on "camera movement" and "cinema as storytelling" while offering a "morally irresponsible" version of Reconstruction replete with "blatantly racist" "stereotyping" and the "Ku Klux Klan presented as heroes"; so even though this work marks the "birth of the feature" film, be prepared for a storyline that's a "mess" – "even by 1915" standards.

Bishop's Wife, The ◑

24 | 24 | 24 | 23

1947 | Directed by Henry Koster | With Cary Grant, Loretta Young, David Niven | 105 minutes | Not Rated

Although "less well known" than some of its "holiday movie" peers, this "Christmasy" romance stars Grant as a "guardian angel" blessed with "elegance and style" ("duh!") who's sent to "restore faith" to a clergyman and his spouse but "falls in love" along the way; overall, it's an "amusing, touching" display of "old-fashioned" "star power" that sentimental souls will "never forget."

Blackboard Jungle ◑

23 | 24 | 22 | 19

1955 | Directed by Richard Brooks | With Glenn Ford, Anne Francis, Vic Morrow, Sidney Poitier | 101 minutes | Not Rated

See "the '50s in a new way" via this "gritty" drama, a standout of the "juvenile delinquent genre" set in an "inner-city school" where "danger is only a heartbeat away" as idealistic teacher Ford is forced to "tame" a horde of punks; notable for Hollywood's "first use of a rock 'n' roll" soundtrack, it may "feel a bit dated", though cynics shrug "schools haven't changed" that much.

⚡ Black Book 🄵

26 | 27 | 26 | 27

2007 | Directed by Paul Verhoeven | With Carice van Houten, Sebastian Koch, Thom Hoffman, Derek de Lint | 145 minutes | Rated R

Set in Nazi-occupied Holland, this WWII Dutch resistance drama "balances a taut thriller with an intimate character study" in its story of a Jewish Mata Hari who "infiltrates the Gestapo" by "sleeping with the enemy"; there's "moral ambiguity" aplenty – "what would you do to survive?" – not to mention "bone-chilling" violence, "explicit nudity" and "breathtaking" acting from the "sexy" van Houten and "dishy" Koch.

Black Cauldron, The

19 | - | 19 | 20

1985 | Directed by Richard Rich, Ted Berman | Animated | 80 minutes | Rated PG

Adapted from Lloyd Alexander's "classic" fantasy book series, this "enjoyable" swords 'n' sorcery cartoon adventure merges the search for a magic cauldron with a "coming-of-age story"; it's "a little darker" than Disney's typical output, with some "unusually sinister" scenes that may be "too scary" for small tots.

Black Hawk Down

23 | 21 | 23 | 26

2001 | Directed by Ridley Scott | With Josh Hartnett, Ewan McGregor, Tom Sizemore | 144 minutes | Rated R

It's "hard to watch, but it's even harder to turn away" from this "astoundingly gripping" (and "surprisingly accurate") account of a 1993

Mogadishu "military misadventure", which pitted a handful of U.S. Army Rangers against a huge enemy force; "Scott puts you on the ground with the soldiers", "brilliantly showing the total chaos of the Somalian battle" in all its "gory", "graphic" and "grueling" detail; indeed, even peaceniks agree this "salute to our servicemen" "doesn't simplify or sensationalize" combat.

☑ Black Orpheus ✉🖪

| | 26 | 23 | 25 | 25 |

1959 | Directed by Marcel Camus | With Marpessa Dawn, Breno Mello | 100 minutes | Rated PG

"Brazilian backdrops" and "bossa nova" rhythms cast their "spell" over Greek legend in this "enchanting", "lyrical" foreign flick, an "exotic retelling" of the Orpheus and Eurydice myth transposed to "modern-day Rio" during Carnival; "sexy", "lush" and full of "beautiful shots" of "cinema verité" revelry, it takes its Dionysian devotees to Hades and back in "unmatched" style – and oh, that "moving-in-your-seat" soundtrack!

Black Snake Moan

| | 20 | 23 | 19 | 19 |

2007 | Directed by Craig Brewer | With Samuel L. Jackson, Christina Ricci, Justin Timberlake | 116 minutes | Rated R

"Tennessee Williams" meets "exploitation cinema" in this "raunchy" "story of redemption" about a "sex-obsessed country girl" who's "chained to a radiator" by a do-gooder "determined to save her"; the "over-the-top" approach means it "ain't for all tastes", but compensations include a "fantastic" blues soundtrack and a "great" supporting turn by Timberlake – "who knew?"

Black Stallion, The

| | 24 | 20 | 23 | 25 |

1979 | Directed by Carroll Ballard | With Mickey Rooney, Kelly Reno, Teri Garr | 118 minutes | Rated G

Equestrians of "all ages" ponder the "bond between boy and horse" in this "captivating" family film about an Arabian steed who's shipwrecked with a youngster on a desert island only to be entered in a turf race after they're rescued and resettled to a Western ranch; though saddled with a "somber" side, it "wins the roses" with a "skillful blend" of "breathtaking" scenery and "luminous cinematography."

Black Sunday

| | 19 | 19 | 21 | 20 |

1977 | Directed by John Frankenheimer | With Robert Shaw, Bruce Dern, Marthe Keller | 143 minutes | Rated R

Terrorists "try to blow up the Super Bowl" in this "paranoia" thriller that's "hard to forget whenever you walk into a packed stadium"; both "exciting" and "ahead of its time", the picture is stolen by a downright "eerie" Dern playing a seemingly "clean-cut" pilot hiding some explosive "mental baggage."

Blade

| | 18 | 15 | 19 | 21 |

1998 | Directed by Stephen Norrington | With Wesley Snipes, Stephen Dorff, Kris Kristofferson | 120 minutes | Rated R

A "moody" plotline whetted with "extreme action" makes for a "bloody good time" in this "style-laden" comic-book redo, with Snipes showing some "edge" as a "half-human, half-vampire" superhero who uses his "ninja" skills to "fight the underworld"; though the spectacle is so "slick" that it "created a franchise", those after something sharper may be "disappointed."

	OVERALL	ACTING	STORY	PROD.

⚡ Blade Runner
26 | 22 | 25 | 27

1982 | Directed by Ridley Scott | With Harrison Ford, Rutger Hauer, Sean Young, Daryl Hannah | 117 minutes | Rated R

This "awesome" "blueprint" for "modern sci-fi" is a "visually stunning" picture best watched with "your brain switched on"; an ultra-"stylish" "noir take" on LA as a 21st-century "dystopia" where "commercialism and biotech run amok", it's also a "hard-boiled morality play" with one of "Ford's best acting jobs" as a PI "hunting cyborg replicants while falling in love with one"; connoisseurs run right for the "superior director's cut."

Blades of Glory
19 | 19 | 17 | 19

2007 | Directed by Josh Gordon, Will Speck | With Will Ferrell, Jon Heder, Will Arnett, Amy Poehler | 93 minutes | Rated PG-13

Ferrell and Heder "kick ice" in this "funny figure-skating spoof", a "dorky adolescent" comedy that "boldly goes where no straight man has gone before"; keep moving "if you're expecting Shakespeare", but otherwise brace yourself for lots of "stupid", "belly laugh"–inducing stunts performed in skin-tight "unitards."

Blair Witch Project, The
10 | 10 | 13 | 10

1999 | Directed by Daniel Myrick, Eduardo Sánchez | With Heather Donahue, Joshua Leonard, Michael Williams | 86 minutes | Rated R

This "shoestring"-budgeted, faux-documentary horror flick about the search for a legendary witch was a big box-office hit when released thanks to an "excellent marketing" campaign; but nowadays most feel the project "got drowned in its own hype" and find fault with the "endlessly whining" cast and "jiggly", "Dramamine"-worthy camerawork.

⚡ Blazing Saddles
25 | 22 | 23 | 23

1974 | Directed by Mel Brooks | With Cleavon Little, Gene Wilder, Harvey Korman, Madeline Kahn | 93 minutes | Rated R

"You'll never look at a horse the same way" after a peek at this "decidedly un-PC" comedy via Mel Brooks, an "off-the-wall" Wild West "spoof" that "insults everyone" with a mix of "slapstick", "eminently quotable one-liners" and infamously "tasteless" routines (like the sound effects–ridden "campfire scene"); most call it "enjoyable" if "overdone."

Blood Diamond
25 | 26 | 25 | 26

2006 | Directed by Edward Zwick | With Leonardo DiCaprio, Djimon Hounsou, Jennifer Connelly | 143 minutes | Rated R

"You'll rethink your jewelry purchases" after a look at this "engaging" production mining the "horror of the African diamond trade" for "socially relevant" drama and featuring an "intense" DiCaprio as an "unlikable" smuggler whose "hint of a golden heart" helps a father – the "spectacular" Hounsou – find his kidnapped son; "violent" action scenes drive home the "savagery" of the conflict while indicting the "wealth-obsessed" culture that nurtures it.

Blood Simple
24 | 25 | 25 | 22

1985 | Directed by Joel Coen | With Frances McDormand, John Getz, Dan Hedaya | 97 minutes | Rated R

"Complex" is more like it as the Coen brothers' first feature "pumps new blood" into the "low-budget crime thriller" in this "brilliant" "film noir homage" filled with "wicked" "thrills delivered with a drawl"; it's a "twisty", "nerve-jangling" tale of betrayal and revenge in a dusty Texas town, told with a "quirky" slant that "foreshadows" the filmmakers' "masterpiece, *Fargo.*"

Blood Work
17 | 18 | 17 | 18

2002 | Directed by Clint Eastwood | With Clint Eastwood, Jeff Daniels, Anjelica Huston, Wanda De Jesus | 110 minutes | Rated R

A retired FBI profiler with a heart transplant is drawn into "pursuing the killer of his donor" in this generally "solid genre piece" laced with "lots of twists and turns"; while die-hard Clint fans applaud a "veteran at work", contras contend he's "too long in the tooth" to play a romantic lead.

Blow
22 | 24 | 22 | 22

2001 | Directed by Ted Demme | With Johnny Depp, Penélope Cruz, Ray Liotta | 124 minutes | Rated R

Both the "glamour and the consequences of drug trafficking" are depicted in this "gritty" true story charting the "rise and fall" of George Jung, the "premier coke dealer" of the '70s; as usual, Johnny's the "definition of cool", Penélope not as much ("lacks Deppth"), while the picture's "glorification of hedonism" leaves some "disappointed" by its "glossy Hollywood undertone."

Blow Out
19 | 19 | 21 | 20

1981 | Directed by Brian De Palma | With John Travolta, Nancy Allen, John Lithgow, Dennis Franz | 108 minutes | Rated R

De Palma's "ode to *Blowup*", this "smart thriller" features a "particularly good" Travolta as a movie soundman who stumbles upon evidence of a "politically motivated murder" with a "Chappaquiddick" ring to it; Allen's "innocent prostitute" and Lithgow's "creepy murderer" ratchet up the "gripping" mood, though voters split on the windup: "suspenseful" vs. "contrived."

◪ Blowup
26 | 23 | 25 | 25

1966 | Directed by Michelangelo Antonioni | With David Hemmings, Vanessa Redgrave, Sarah Miles | 111 minutes | Not Rated

"Forget *Austin Powers*", baby, "this is the *real* Swinging London": a "riveting existential thriller" that tracks a happening fashion photographer obsessed with both Redgrave and a "mysterious death in a park"; hipsters hail it as an "enigmatic" (or "infuriating") milestone of the "alienation genre" possessed by the "spirit of the '60s" – and that tasty "period flavor" is still "too cool for words."

◪ Blue Angel, The ❶🅕
25 | 27 | 24 | 22

1931 | Directed by Josef von Sternberg | With Marlene Dietrich, Emil Jannings | 99 minutes | Not Rated

Behold the "magnificent Dietrich" "at her best" in this "Weimar-era" German drama, the story of "naughty Lola", a garter-flashing chanteuse who "seduces an old fool" of a schoolmaster and expedites his "descent into the gutter"; though it's a "dated" dose of "ennui and moral rot" in a "world now lost", fräulein Marlene's "tour-de-force", career-launching turn is "music to the eyes."

Blues Brothers, The
22 | 19 | 19 | 21

1980 | Directed by John Landis | With John Belushi, Dan Aykroyd, John Candy | 133 minutes | Rated R

"Ignore the plot" and "get out the popcorn" for this "good-time" comedy, powered by Belushi and Aykroyd on a "full tank of gas" as sibs

Jake and Elwood, who accept a "mission from God" to provoke "hilarity" and find out "how many cars they can wreck"; if it's (ahem) "not a critics' choice", those with a hankering for "hot" "soul 'n' blues" numbers liberally chased with "dumb fun" insist "you gotta love it."

Blue Velvet
22 | 23 | 20 | 23

1986 | Directed by David Lynch | With Kyle MacLachlan, Isabella Rossellini, Dennis Hopper | 120 minutes | Rated R
"One sick puppy of a movie", this pretty "kinky" yet totally "enthralling" look at the "seedy underbelly" "beneath the surface of suburbia" is "love-it-or-hate-it" filmmaking from the "warped" mind of "surrealist auteur Lynch"; despite applause for Hopper's "creepy" portrayal of the "gas-inhaling pervert" ("worth seeing for the Pabst Blue Ribbon scene alone"), sensitive souls find the flick "ugly, pointless" and "not as good as its reputation."

Bob and Carol and Ted and Alice
17 | 19 | 17 | 17

1969 | Directed by Paul Mazursky | With Natalie Wood, Robert Culp, Elliott Gould, Dyan Cannon | 104 minutes | Rated R
"Remember the '60s?" – this "social satire" of wannabe swingers experimenting with free love "captures the era to a T", though what was once "hip 'n' happening" seems more "quaint" today; still, many find themselves "laughing at the outfits, the decor", the "dated" dialogue and that "priceless" ending.

Bobby
20 | 22 | 21 | 22

2006 | Directed by Emilio Estevez | With Laurence Fishburne, Heather Graham, Anthony Hopkins, Helen Hunt, Lindsay Lohan, William H. Macy, Demi Moore, Sharon Stone | 120 minutes | Rated R
An "everybody-who's-anybody" ensemble cast populates this "moving", "Altman"-esque patchwork of "vignettes" set in LA's Ambassador Hotel on "the day that Bobby Kennedy was assassinated"; director Estevez makes "great use of newsreel footage" to capture the "turbulent '60s" – an era when "people running for office actually stood for something" – even if a minority sees "too many stars" and "too little point."

Bob Roberts
22 | 24 | 22 | 20

1992 | Directed by Tim Robbins | With Tim Robbins, Alan Rickman, Gore Vidal | 102 minutes | Rated R
The satire "cuts like a chainsaw" in this "left"-leaning political satire, a "timeless" "mockumentary" following the Senate campaign of a "folk-singing Republican" whose "rebel" image masks a "mean-spirited ideologist"; overall, it's "more cynical than funny", but voters say writer/director/composer/star Robbins shines brightest in the "fun soundtrack."

Bodyguard, The
14 | 13 | 15 | 16

1992 | Directed by Mick Jackson | With Kevin Costner, Whitney Houston | 130 minutes | Rated R
This "melodramatic" romance finds Whitney testing her "star potential" as a "diva" pop singer ("what range!") who falls for Costner's "hot hunk" of a bodyguard; some endorse it as "watchable fluff", but just as many seek protection from a "witless yawner" whose "only redeeming quality" is its "hit songs."

	OVERALL	ACTING	STORY	PROD.

Body Heat
24 | 25 | 25 | 23

1981 | Directed by Lawrence Kasdan | With William Hurt, Kathleen Turner, Richard Crenna, Mickey Rourke | 113 minutes | Rated R

"Whew!" this "palpably steamy" "noir thriller" stars "what-a-babe" Turner as a trophy wife who "burns up the screen" as she seduces "small-town lawyer" Hurt into a "spiraling" web of "deceit" that "keeps you guessing" to the last frame; in short, it's a sexed-up "version of the old help-me-kill-my-husband story", a kind of "*Double Indemnity* for a new generation."

Boiler Room
18 | 19 | 20 | 18

2000 | Directed by Ben Younger | With Giovanni Ribisi, Vin Diesel, Nicky Katt, Nia Long | 118 minutes | Rated R

"Gordon Gekko" would appreciate this "homage to *Wall Street* and *Glengarry Glen Ross*" offering an "insider look" at a "sleazy stock firm" commandeered by soulless brokers out for "easy money"; though few are bullish about the "superfluous" romantic subplot, the good news is "Diesel can actually act if given decent material."

Z Bonnie and Clyde
25 | 25 | 24 | 25

1967 | Directed by Arthur Penn | With Warren Beatty, Faye Dunaway, Gene Hackman, Estelle Parsons | 111 minutes | Rated R

More a piece of "film history than real history", this "stunning" 1930s "crime-spree" biopic "broke a lot of old rules" in its "revisionist" take on the title characters, real-life "losers" reconceived by Beatty and Dunaway as the "screen's best-ever antiheroes"; the "letter-perfect" cast, "impeccable" direction and "gorgeously gory" photography all add up to way-"ahead-of-its-time" moviemaking, even if the "indelible images" of the "bloody ballet at the end" unsettle the squeamish.

Boogie Nights
19 | 21 | 19 | 19

1997 | Directed by Paul Thomas Anderson | With Mark Wahlberg, Burt Reynolds, Julianne Moore, John C. Reilly | 152 minutes | Rated R

Set in the '70s "disco era", this "dead-on look" at the "ins and outs (so to speak) of the porn industry" features "inspired performances" – "Burt returns!", "Marky Mark grows up!" – even if the "XXX film stars" portrayed "don't have much going on upstairs"; though the "sex-drugs-and-roller-skates" plot is "shamelessly entertaining" for the "first 2/3" of the picture, the "violent", "depressing" final act can be "emotionally draining."

Boondock Saints, The
23 | 23 | 24 | 21

2000 | Directed by Troy Duffy | With Willem Dafoe, Sean Patrick Flanery, Norman Reedus | 110 minutes | Rated R

A pair of "bad-ass Irish brothers" dole out "vigilante justice" with an "iron fist" in this "fast-paced" pulp fictioner set in Boston's tough "Southie" neighborhood; "classic lines", "relentless violence" and an "over-the-top" turn by Dafoe as a gay FBI agent are all prime suspects for the flick's "cult following."

Borat
18 | 19 | 16 | 16

2006 | Directed by Larry Charles | With Sacha Baron Cohen, Ken Davitian, Pamela Anderson | 84 minutes | Rated R

"Nothing's sacred" in this "squirmingly funny", "marvelously offensive" mockumentary about a "Kazakhstani reporter documenting the

American way of life" while wreaking "equal opportunity bigotry" on everything in his path ("it makes *Jackass* look like *My Fair Lady*"); the "easily offended" blast the "low-budget" look, "mean-spirited" script and overall "sophomoric antics", but admit it does "push the envelope" – even if "you'll need a shower afterwards"; P.S. "watch the wrestling scene at your own peril."

Born Free
24 | 19 | 24 | 23

1966 | Directed by James Hill | With Virginia McKenna, Bill Travers, Geoffrey Keen | 95 minutes | Rated PG

The "theme song alone" is enough to set off "shameless weeping" as this "well-told" family flick unfolds, focusing on a husband and wife in "wild Africa" and their effort to "protect the lioness Elsa"; a "major tearjerker" in its day, it remains "vivid" for boomers who tell of "loving it as a child" even though it's "so sad."

☑ Born into Brothels ☒
27 | - | 27 | 24

2004 | Directed by Zana Briski, Ross Kauffman | Documentary | 85 minutes | Rated R

An "emotionally devastating" glimpse of the "poverty and suffering" endured by the "children of Calcutta's red-light district", this "remarkable", Academy Award–winning documentary takes a "humanistic" approach to its "tough subject", adding a dash of hope for a "brighter future"; indeed, supporters say the "brave filmmakers" "deserve a Nobel Prize more than an Oscar."

Born on the Fourth of July ✉
20 | 21 | 20 | 20

1989 | Directed by Oliver Stone | With Tom Cruise, Kyra Sedgwick, Willem Dafoe | 145 minutes | Rated R

"Cruise excels" in one of Stone's "most accomplished works", a "potent", "well-done" bio of Vietnam vet Ron Kovic that's an "intense", "heart-wrenching" study of "flag-waving patriotism"; though it draws fire for being "contrived" and "overwrought", it does offer convincing "proof that Tom can act."

☑ Born Yesterday ✉◑
26 | 28 | 25 | 23

1950 | Directed by George Cukor | With Judy Holliday, Broderick Crawford, William Holden | 103 minutes | Not Rated

"Still magical today", this "zany" screwball comedy has to do with a "not-so-dumb blonde" in Washington, DC who undergoes a *My Fair Lady*-like transformation and "breaks out of her bimbo chains"; thanks to a unique voice and "great timing", the "perfectly cast" Holliday took home an Best Actress Academy Award for her "pure gold" performance, a "pièce de résistance" that the 1993 remake just "can't match."

Bottle Rocket
22 | 20 | 21 | 17

1996 | Directed by Wes Anderson | With Owen Wilson, Luke Wilson, James Caan | 92 minutes | Rated R

Anderson's "offbeat" directorial debut, this "charmer" of a comedy sends off "quirky" fireworks, letting the "Wilson boys" rock as "would-be gangsters" on the run whose "hijinks-laden" exploits can be "surprisingly funny"; the "obviously low-budget" production "doesn't always gel", but it remains an "overlooked precursor" of "what was to come."

	OVERALL	ACTING	STORY	PROD.

Bourne Identity, The
20 | 19 | 20 | 21

2002 | Directed by Doug Liman | With Matt Damon, Franka Potente, Chris Cooper | 119 minutes | Rated PG-13

An "amnesiac" CIA assassin struggles to recover his identity in this "adrenaline-rush" thriller based on the Robert Ludlum best-seller that features "riveting action" scenes (including "one of the better car chases in recent memory"), but only "decent chemistry" between the leads; though Matt's performance provokes debate – "cool and capable" versus "lightweight" – in the end the scenic European "locations redeem the picture."

Bourne Supremacy, The
21 | 21 | 21 | 23

2004 | Directed by Paul Greengrass | With Matt Damon, Joan Allen, Julia Stiles | 108 minutes | Rated PG-13

Damon is "re-Bourne" as a "secret agent turned wanted man" out for "payback" in this "sharp-shooting sequel", a "spy caper with a brain" that's "as good as the original", packing fresh "cat-and-mouse action", "high-tech twists" and "gorgeous" Euro backdrops; its "herky-jerky" camera coverage can be "dizzying", though, so "take Dramamine" during those "fantastic" car chases that are one "wicked ride."

☒ Bourne Ultimatum, The
25 | 23 | 23 | 26

2007 | Directed by Paul Greengrass | With Matt Damon, Julia Stiles, David Strathairn | 115 minutes | Rated PG-13

"From the opening scene" through the "amazing" windup, the "action doesn't stop" in this "outstanding" Bourne threequel, an "adrenaline"-soaked "cherry on top of the franchise" packed with "cloak-and-dagger intrigue", "dizzying" car chases and "exotic international locales"; reprising his role as the titular amnesiac spy, Damon proves again he was "born to play the part", and fans hope the "door's open for more" installments.

Bowling for Columbine
22 | - | 21 | 19

2002 | Directed by Michael Moore | Documentary | 120 minutes | Rated R

Moore's "provocative" yet "surprisingly funny" docudrama is a "punch in the jaw to anyone who is completely pro-gun"; "even if the events were staged, the message massaged and the view decidedly one-sided", it's still an "important movie" that "everyone should see", so "watch it before passing judgment" – "you'll have something to talk about for hours."

Boys Don't Cry ✉
23 | 27 | 23 | 21

1999 | Directed by Kimberly Peirce | With Hilary Swank, Chloë Sevigny, Peter Sarsgaard | 118 minutes | Rated R

Turning a "dark situation" into a "tough" study of "intolerance", this "disturbing" drama is a "faithful telling of the story of Teena Brandon", a small-town girl who "dresses and acts the part" of a boy, leading to "powerful" complications; though the Oscar-winning Swank is "beyond convincing", the "brutal" ending is "not easy to watch", but "will stay with you" – "unfortunately, it's true."

Boys from Brazil, The
24 | 26 | 25 | 22

1978 | Directed by Franklin J. Schaffner | With Gregory Peck, Laurence Olivier, Steve Guttenberg, James Mason | 123 minutes | Rated R

"Old Nazis" plan new terror via a brood of "Hitler clones" in this "taut thriller" starring the "powerful" Olivier as a war-criminal tracker who goes "mano a mano" with Peck's "evil Dr. Mengele"; it's a trove of "delightfully creepy" scenes, and the "over-the-top" scenario still holds up given that a "genetic-engineering nightmare" is "even scarier now."

Boys on the Side
15 | 18 | 15 | 16

1995 | Directed by Herbert Ross | With Whoopi Goldberg, Mary-Louise Parker, Drew Barrymore | 117 minutes | Rated R

"Girl power" is alive and well in this "epitome of a chick flick" charting the offbeat adventures of three gals headed cross country; the "touching" story, one part road movie and one part feminist tract, proves that "friendship is a great thing", while also demonstrating that "Drew can act if she picks the right material."

Boyz N the Hood
23 | 22 | 24 | 21

1991 | Directed by John Singleton | With Ice Cube, Cuba Gooding Jr., Laurence Fishburne | 107 minutes | Rated R

The "gangsta flick" that "sets the bar" for the competition "keeps it real" as it takes a "hard-core" look at ghetto "gang wars in South Central" LA; an "important" breakthrough with some "surprising acting turns", it's a "fantastic first film" from Singleton, whose later work doesn't "get anywhere near this one."

☒ Braveheart ✉
26 | 24 | 25 | 27

1995 | Directed by Mel Gibson | With Mel Gibson, Sophie Marceau, Catherine McCormack | 177 minutes | Rated R

"It's got everything" say fans of this "awe-inspiring" medieval "history lesson" about an "underdog" Scottish hero ("Mel in a kilt") "knocking heads" in an anti-Brit rebellion; the "gory", "hackin'-and-hewin'" battles, "heartfelt" acting and "huge scope" help justify Gibson's Best Director win, even if some warn of three "long", "melodramatic" hours.

Brazil
24 | 23 | 23 | 27

1985 | Directed by Terry Gilliam | With Jonathan Pryce, Robert De Niro, Bob Hoskins | 131 minutes | Rated R

Even as "fantasy", Monty Python alum Gilliam's "twisted", "utterly original" vision of a "part-Orwell, part-Python" future is "a little out there"; it demands "perseverance" – what with its "baffling" "whirlwind" of "bizarre" effects and chin-scratching "black comedy" plot about one man's struggle with a "Kafka-esque" "bureaucracy" – but rewards those who hang in there with a "totally crazy ride."

Breach
23 | 26 | 24 | 23

2007 | Directed by Billy Ray | With Chris Cooper, Ryan Phillippe, Laura Linney | 110 minutes | Rated PG-13

Based on the "actual events" surrounding the case of Robert Hanssen, the notorious FBI agent caught "spilling the beans to the Soviets", this "taut" espionage thriller pits the "brilliant" Cooper against an "amazing" Phillippe in a "chess game of the minds" that has you "engaged from the get-go"; don't expect any "over-the-top pyrotechnics" or "easy answers" here, just good old "edge-of-your-seat tension" that doesn't quit "even if you know the ending."

☒ Breaker Morant
27 | 27 | 27 | 24

1980 | Directed by Bruce Beresford | With Jack Thompson, Edward Woodward, Bryan Brown | 107 minutes | Rated PG

"Guy's-flick" fans salute this "solid Aussie" drama of "kangaroo" justice, a "small masterpiece" in its "gripping" depiction of "betrayal" at a military trial during the Boer War; told with "moving realism", it tackles the "question of morals in warfare" using a "top-notch" cast to "demonstrate bravery" and "bravura", turning the fate of "appointed scapegoats" into an "inspiration."

⏣ Breakfast at Tiffany's

	OVERALL	ACTING	STORY	PROD.
	26	26	24	24

1961 | Directed by Blake Edwards | With Audrey Hepburn, George Peppard, Patricia Neal | 115 minutes | Rated PG
In the "role she was born to play", a "mesmerizing" Hepburn brings Truman Capote's "messed-up" "free spirit" Holly Golightly to life in "peerless style"; devotees find everything about it "irresistible" – "Henry Mancini's divine score", Audrey's "timeless clothes", the "love-letter-to-New-York" cinematography – and call this "dream-making, heartbreaking" tribute to the "power of romance" their "all-time favorite."

Breakfast Club, The

	22	21	22	19

1985 | Directed by John Hughes | With Emilio Estevez, Anthony Michael Hall, Judd Nelson, Molly Ringwald | 92 minutes | Rated R
Any card-carrying "child of the '80s" is apt to "know all the lines" of this "engaging" high school yukfest, a "Gen-X" "time capsule" about a group of "Brat Pack all-stars" "stuck in detention" and left to compare and contrast "confused personalities"; a "hoot" with a "sensitive" side, it's rerun "ad infinitum", since it "speaks to teenagers in a way that *American Pie* will never be able to."

Breakfast on Pluto

	19	24	18	20

2005 | Directed by Neil Jordan | With Cillian Murphy, Liam Neeson, Stephen Rea | 135 minutes | Rated R
Thanks to Murphy's "beyond amazing" performance as a "hapless" Irish transvestite seeking "self-actualization" in 1970s Great Britian, this "edgy" drama whips IRA "turmoil", "tongue-in-cheek" repartee, "T-Rex" and a "totally bitchin' wardrobe" into one "fabulous" eye-opener; but while its story of a "tragicomic innocent" is "compelling", a few feel the "odd flights of fancy" lie somewhere "between involving and cloying."

Breaking Away ✉

	24	21	24	20

1979 | Directed by Peter Yates | With Dennis Christopher, Dennis Quaid, Daniel Stern | 100 minutes | Rated PG
A "rousing ride", this *Rocky*-esque "Hoosier tale" is a "coming-of-age" drama on two wheels, with Christopher leading a cast of "cutie-pie" "underdogs" as a cyclist who pedals straight into a "town-and-gown" "class conflict"; it's cheered on as a "big-hearted" "buddy film" that delivers a "socko" bike race finale.

Breaking the Waves

	23	27	20	20

1996 | Directed by Lars von Trier | With Emily Watson, Stellan Skarsgård | 153 minutes | Rated R
"Be prepared" for "emotionally devastating" doings in this "raw" drama of "delusion" and "doomed romance" about a "dimwitted girl" who "sacrifices everything for her paralyzed husband"; most pronounce it "strange" yet "so well done it's painful" (the "musical interludes give one time to weep"), though foes call it a "silly" parable that's a most "depressing" picture of "female martyrdom."

| | OVERALL | ACTING | STORY | PROD. |

Break-Up, The ▣▣

15 | 17 | 14 | 16

2006 | Directed by Peyton Reed | With Vince Vaughn, Jennifer Aniston | 105 minutes | Rated PG-13

"Misleadingly marketed as a romantic comedy", there's "not a lot of love or laughs" in this "surprisingly serious" Aniston-Vaughn dramedy mapping the trajectory of a "relationship gone awry"; "downright ugly" fight scenes and a "depressing ending" "hit too close to home" for most – a "real break-up is less painful."

Breathless ❶▣

25 | 24 | 21 | 23

1961 | Directed by Jean-Luc Godard | With Jean-Paul Belmondo, Jean Seberg | 87 minutes | Not Rated

"So hip" and as "refreshing" now as at its debut, this French "New Wave masterpiece" breathes "pure pleasure" into a "silly gangster story" with "luscious" leads Belmondo and Seberg as lovers on the lam (even the late-'50s Paris setting is a "terrific character"); while scholars speak of genre-"defining" technical feats – the "jump cut is born!" – most simply find it "charming" and way "ahead of its time."

Bride & Prejudice

20 | 18 | 19 | 23

2005 | Directed by Gurinder Chadha | With Aishwarya Rai, Martin Henderson, Daniel Gillies | 111 minutes | Rated PG-13

Equal parts "Bollywood, Jane Austin and Merchant-Ivory", this "silly" yet "delightful" musical transposes *Pride and Prejudice* to "present-day India" with "lush" scenery, "gorgeous clothes" and "showstopping numbers"; viewers "new to the genre" should "keep their minds open" – and their eyes too, given an "attractive" cast led by Aishwarya Rai, said to be the "most beautiful woman in the world."

Bride of Frankenstein, The ❶

25 | 21 | 23 | 23

1935 | Directed by James Whale | With Boris Karloff, Colin Clive, Elsa Lanchester | 75 minutes | Not Rated

Bolt-necked Frankie gets "his one shot at love" in this "excellent sequel" to the hoary "'30s horror classic", wherein Karloff reprises his signature role with "panache" and Lanchester's shocked fiancée simply has "great hair"; fright fiends cherish the "creepy" results as "campy", "funny" and not a little "whacked."

Bride Wore Black, The ▣

▽ 25 | 26 | 25 | 22

1968 | Directed by François Truffaut | With Jeanne Moreau, Michel Bouquet, Jean-Claude Brialy | 107 minutes | Not Rated

The "original *Kill Bill*", this psychological thriller based on the Cornell Woolrich novel stars a "sterling" Moreau as a widow hell bent on avenging her husband's murder; it's an out-and-out "homage to Hitchcock" and plain that director Truffaut "knows the territory well", even engaging Hitch favorite Bernard Herrmann as its composer.

▣ Bridge on the River Kwai, The ✉

28 | 28 | 27 | 28

1957 | Directed by David Lean | With William Holden, Alec Guinness, Jack Hawkins, Sessue Hayakawa | 161 minutes | Rated PG

Those "stiff upper lips" do some "memorable" whistling in director Lean's "grand", "engrossing" Japanese POW camp epic, an "old-fashioned" yarn about the "timeless themes" of "honor", "conviction" and the "madness" of war; a lock for the top Oscars of 1957, it "succeeds" mightily with "great performances" – led "heart and soul" by a "hubris"-afflicted Guinness – enhanced by "splashy" scenery and an "explosive ending."

Bridges of Madison County, The | 19 | 23 | 20 | 20 |

1995 | Directed by Clint Eastwood | With Clint Eastwood, Meryl Streep, Annie Corley | 135 minutes | Rated PG-13

Director/leading man Eastwood unveils his "gentle side" in this "bittersweet" romance recounting the "middle-aged" passion between a "roving" photographer and a "lonely housewife"; some cite the "banal", "snail's-pace" plot as a big "yawn", but to fans it's "lovably sappy" – and "way better" than the "treacly" book.

Bridget Jones's Diary | 21 | 23 | 22 | 21 |

2001 | Directed by Sharon Maguire | With Renée Zellweger, Hugh Grant, Colin Firth | 97 minutes | Rated R

This "everygirl" "chick flick" is a "charming" romance that logs the progress of the "fab" Zellweger, doing a "knockout job" in the title role as a "twentysomething singleton" "desperately seeking a spouse" but beleaguered by "faux pas", "weight gain" and a "perfect cad" of a boss; followers find it "hilarious yet so true" but won't commit as to whether it "nails the book" or not.

Bridget Jones: The Edge of Reason | 14 | 18 | 13 | 16 |

2004 | Directed by Beeban Kidron | With Renée Zellweger, Hugh Grant, Colin Firth | 108 minutes | Rated R

A "disappointing" sequel to *Bridget Jones's Diary*, this "vapid" chick flick picks up where the original left off, following a "pudgy" British "klutz" who's "seesawing between two beaux" – but "without the cleverness" this time; although "it never hurts to watch Grant and Firth" in action, otherwise there's "no edge" and "no reason" to see it.

Bridge to Terabithia | 22 | 22 | 22 | 24 |

2007 | Directed by Gabor Csupo | With Josh Hutcherson, Anna Sophia Robb, Zooey Deschanel | 95 minutes | Rated PG

Roping together "imaginative" fantasy and "touching" drama, this "well-done" coming-of-ager about a pair of pre-teen "outsiders" who "find each other" in a "make-believe" world hews "very close to the book" it's based on and boasts "delightful" work by leads Hutcherson and Robb; still, parents caution the "shocking climax" may take a toll on tots.

⊠ Brief Encounter ◑ | 27 | 29 | 27 | 25 |

1946 | Directed by David Lean | With Celia Johnson, Trevor Howard, Stanley Holloway | 86 minutes | Not Rated

For a "truly romantic" fix, this "quiet" "masterpiece of yearning" from David Lean (via Noël Coward) is "right up there" in the running as the "definitive tearjerker"; the "never better" Johnson and Howard play "ordinary people" whose meeting on a commuter line develops into a "short but intense" "connection", with swells of Rachmaninoff to seal the deal; in brief, an "unforgettable" trip.

Brigadoon | 24 | 21 | 22 | 24 |

1954 | Directed by Vincente Minnelli | With Gene Kelly, Van Johnson, Cyd Charisse | 108 minutes | Not Rated

A Lerner and Loewe "stage show turned into a movie", this "lesser-known" MGM musical is set in a mythical Scottish town that can be visited by outsiders only once every 100 years; though some criticize the "corny" concept, "phony accents" and "cardboard back-lot" sets, most "suspend disbelief" once the music starts and the "magical" Kelly and Charisse begin "dancing in the heather."

Bright Lights, Big City | 15 | 16 | 15 | 16 |

1988 | Directed by James Bridges | With Michael J. Fox, Kiefer Sutherland, Phoebe Cates, Dianne Wiest | 107 minutes | Rated R

Fox abandons *Family Ties* for cocaine highs in this "depressing", "not so bright" portrait of a struggling writer's "downward spiral" into drugs and debauchery in '80s NYC; big pity this "snorefest" is such a "tame" treatment of Jay McInerney's zeitgeist-catching novel – many say "they shouldn't have even tried to adapt it."

Brighton Beach Memoirs | 22 | 23 | 23 | 20 |

1986 | Directed by Gene Saks | With Jonathan Silverman, Blythe Danner, Judith Ivey | 108 minutes | Rated PG-13

Pre-war Brooklyn "lives on in folklore" via this "nostalgic" coming-of-age drama that kicks off author Neil Simon's "autobiographical" trilogy with "bittersweet" reminisces of '30s "Jewish culture"; the "period-piece" POV can be "schmaltzy", but the "three-dimensional portrayals" from a "talented cast" leave "little to kvetch about."

Bringing Down the House | 19 | 21 | 17 | 19 |

2003 | Directed by Adam Shankman | With Steve Martin, Queen Latifah, Eugene Levy, Joan Plowright | 105 minutes | Rated PG-13

Steve and Queenie are a "modern day George and Gracie" in this "laugh-out-loud" comedy about a "staid" lawyer and an "outrageous" bank robber who meet in an online chat room; the script may be "vulgar" with too many "outdated racial stereotypes", but at least it's "equal opportunity offensive" – and it's always "nice to see plus-size girls get their props."

☒ Bringing Up Baby ◑ | 27 | 27 | 24 | 24 |

1938 | Directed by Howard Hawks | With Katharine Hepburn, Cary Grant | 102 minutes | Not Rated

"One continuous roar", director Hawks' "screwiest of screwball comedies" is propelled at a "frenetic pace" by the Hepburn-Grant "chemistry" and a "tons-of-fun" scenario touching on "dinosaur bones, crazy rich folk" and a lost leopard; it's an old-school "madcap" "champ", and fans of "farce" still bring it up as the "funniest movie ever."

Bring It On | 17 | 15 | 16 | 16 |

2000 | Directed by Peyton Reed | With Kirsten Dunst, Eliza Dushku, Gabrielle Union | 98 minutes | Rated PG-13

"One for the tweens", this "frothy" high-school comedy about "rival cheerleading squads" brings on "bouncy" pom-pommer Dunst, depending on "team spirit" as she copes with "cliques" and "cattiness" on the way to a "competitive" showdown; for sure, the plot's strictly "cookie-cutter", but "turn your brain off" and you just may feel like "15 again."

Broadcast News | 23 | 25 | 22 | 20 |

1987 | Directed by James L. Brooks | With William Hurt, Albert Brooks, Holly Hunter | 127 minutes | Rated R

"Appearance over substance" is the subject of this "smart" "send-up of the media" about a "love triangle" in a "career-driven", *Network*-esque TV newsroom that hums with "behind-the-scenes" one-upmanship; nominated for a slew of Oscars (but winner of none), this "ahead-of-its-time" comedy remains "totally engaging", due to the efforts of its "sharp-as-a-tack" cast.

Broadway Danny Rose ◑

22	22	22	20

1984 | Directed by Woody Allen | With Woody Allen, Mia Farrow, Nick Apollo Forte | 84 minutes | Rated PG

Woody and Mia (in rosier days) light up this comedy about a "Mafia tootsie who melts" for the "ultimate mensch", a small-time talent agent clinging to the "underbelly" of "borscht-belt" showbiz; although infused with a "NY sensibility", some say the "shaggy-dog" plot "doesn't quite deliver."

Brokeback Mountain ✉

24	26	23	26

2005 | Directed by Ang Lee | With Heath Ledger, Jake Gyllenhaal, Michelle Williams, Anne Hathaway | 134 minutes | Rated R

Widely pegged as the "gay cowboy movie", this "star-crossed" "Romeo-and-Romeo" romance is as "controversial" as they come, yet its "gimmick-free" rendition of "forbidden love" "avoids sensationalism" thanks to an "understated" performance by Ledger (and an "underrated" one by Gyllenhaal), backed up by "stunning scenery", a "ravishing score" and "Angst" Lee's "heartfelt", Oscar-winning direction; ultimately, this "timeless" film has had a "real cultural influence", even if it's best remembered for the "most spoofed line of the year": "I wish I knew how to quit you."

Broken Flowers

16	20	15	17

2005 | Directed by Jim Jarmusch | With Bill Murray, Julie Delpy, Sharon Stone | 106 minutes | Rated R

Murray's "dry delivery" and director Jarmusch's "minimalism" are the "thin" soil for this "oddball", "low-key" indie drama about a "middle-aged Everyman" who "hits the road" to "revisit the women in his life" in order to find the "son he never knew"; "subtle" smarts aside, many say "enough already" of a "slow trip" made even more "infuriating" by an "arty ending."

Brother Bear

21	-	21	23

2003 | Directed by Aaron Blaise, Bob Walker | Animated | 85 minutes | Rated G

"Sweet" yet "not overly sentimental", this "politically correct" Disney feature tells the tale of a boy turned into a bear, learning to "respect all living things" along the way; despite "old-fashioned" animation and a "slow-moving" pace, it redeems itself with a "message of love"; P.S. a pair of moose voiced by SCTV's McKenzie brothers provide a breath of "over-the-top" relief for grown-ups.

Brother from Another Planet, The

23	22	23	19

1984 | Directed by John Sayles | With Joe Morton, Steve James, Bill Cobbs | 108 minutes | Rated R

"Truly original for its time", this "low-budget" "cult favorite" via John Sayles examines "race relations and urban life" in its "offbeat" story of a black extraterrestrial who lands in Harlem; despite the sci-fi underpinnings, it's more of a "funny social commentary" about "what it means to be human", with a mute title character (the very "likable" Morton) and one of the "greatest on-screen card tricks ever."

| | OVERALL | ACTING | STORY | PROD. |

Brotherhood of the Wolf 🇫

18 17 17 21

2002 | Directed by Christophe Gans | With Samuel Le Bihan, Vincent Cassel, Monica Bellucci, Mark Dacascos | 142 minutes | Rated R

"Historical epic" meets "Hong Kong action film" in this "bizarre" Gallic production about a werewolf on the loose in 18th-century France that tosses equal parts of "horror", "martial arts", "costume drama" and "Harlequin romance" into the "genre blender"; sure, it "wins points for originality", but it's best enjoyed if you "leave logic at the door."

Brothers McMullen, The

19 19 19 16

1995 | Directed by Edward Burns | With Edward Burns, Mike McGlone, Jack Mulcahy | 98 minutes | Rated R

"Indie darling" Burns' "low-budget" first flick is an "engaging" drama that serves up a "slice of Irish-American life", tracking a trio of "working-class" brothers through their amorous ups and downs; though some find this tale of "loyalty and commitment on Long Island" a tad "amateurish", this "little gem" generated "big buzz" – so "what happened to this guy?"

Bruce Almighty

18 20 18 19

2003 | Directed by Tom Shadyac | With Jim Carrey, Jennifer Aniston, Morgan Freeman | 101 minutes | Rated PG-13

"Heaven help us": Carrey of the renowned "rubber face" portrays an "ordinary man" turned Supreme Being and actually "delivers laughs" plus a "positive message" in this "enjoyable", "lighthearted" chuckler co-starring the "lovable" Aniston and "elegant" Freeman; a warning to those who pray for "something edgy": this one might feel like "religion class."

Bucket List, The

21 24 20 21

2007 | Directed by Rob Reiner | With Jack Nicholson, Morgan Freeman | 97 minutes | Rated PG-13

"Old pros" Nicholson and Freeman prove they're "not past their prime" in this "super-sentimental", "Hallmark-quality" buddy flick about two cancer patients with "only months to live", who "fulfill their dying wishes" with a "last romp around the world"; a lot "funnier than its subject material might suggest", it allows the actors plenty of "scenery-chewing" opportunities en route to its "predictable" denouement.

Buck Privates ◑

22 19 16 18

1941 | Directed by Arthur Lubin | With Abbott & Costello, the Andrews Sisters | 84 minutes | Not Rated

A coupla clowns go to boot camp and "frivolity" ensues in this "classic Abbott and Costello" comedy, which "evokes an era" thanks to the "duo's rapid-fire patter" and USO-worthy tunes by the "Andrews Sisters at their peak"; despite "patchwork" plotting, it "ranks up there" in Bud and Lou's oeuvre and works as a swell "Sunday morning" indulgence.

Buddy Holly Story, The

21 23 21 20

1978 | Directed by Steve Rash | With Gary Busey, Don Stroud, Charles Martin Smith | 113 minutes | Rated PG

Busey hits the "top of the charts" with his "flawless" singing impersonation of "pioneering rocker" Buddy Holly in this "convincing" biopic that charts the star's "rise to greatness" on the strength of seminal songs and "iconic glasses" that "invented geek chic"; indeed, the '50s "maverick spirit" is so "bravura", you wish they could "rewrite history" for a "happier ending."

| | OVERALL | ACTING | STORY | PROD. |

Buena Vista Social Club
25 | - | 24 | 24

1999 | Directed by Wim Wenders | Documentary | 101 minutes | Rated G

"Revelatory – and danceable" – this documentary is a "love letter to a vanishing breed" of musicians, "aging" vets of the "Afro-Cuban jazz" scene who volunteer "personal histories" of "trials and tribulations" in the "shadow of Castro", interspersed with "irresistible" live jams; it "builds slowly" in a haze of "washed-out tropical colors" to a narrative of "great charm" and "insight", backed by a soundtrack that's as "captivating" as they come.

Bug's Life, A
24 | - | 22 | 26

1998 | Directed by John Lasseter, Andrew Stanton | Animated | 96 minutes | Rated G

"Even parents" bug out on the "mind-blowing creativity" of the Disney/Pixar team's "step-ahead animation" in this "cute" parable of "insect politics" rendered in "sharp, colorful" computer graphics that "look incredible", even if the "social satire" is "geared for kids"; most maintain it's "superior to *Antz*" and advise sticking around for the fake outtakes as the credits roll (the "best part").

Bugsy
18 | 19 | 18 | 19

1991 | Directed by Barry Levinson | With Warren Beatty, Annette Bening, Harvey Keitel, Ben Kingsley | 135 minutes | Rated R

"Long but fascinating", this bio of mobster Bugsy Siegel (the "gangster who created Las Vegas out of desert dust") is a "graphic" film about high-rolling "lowlifes"; though a few yawn it's a "Beatty vanity project", at least the "bewitching cinematography" makes the already "beautiful cast even more ravishing"; fave line: "why don't you run outside and jerk yourself a soda?"

Bull Durham
22 | 22 | 22 | 20

1988 | Directed by Ron Shelton | With Kevin Costner, Susan Sarandon, Tim Robbins | 108 minutes | Rated R

"Life and love in minor-league baseball" equal "diverting" comedy in this "funny and realistic" sports pic, juiced by "sexy", "laid-back acting" from Sarandon and Costner, a "great pair" out to take the "American spirit" into extra innings; fans cheer it on as a "smart home run" that's "one of the best" of the hardball yarns.

Bullets Over Broadway
21 | 23 | 21 | 21

1994 | Directed by Woody Allen | With John Cusack, Dianne Wiest, Jennifer Tilly, Chazz Palminteri | 98 minutes | Rated R

A "quirky, colorful" shot of "period" atmosphere, this "backstage comedy" concerns a Jazz Age dramatist and a "gangster who rewrites his Broadway play"; it's "likable" enough for its "witty dialogue" and "over-the-top" cast, though as usual for a "post-*Hannah*" Allen opus, some wish it were "just a little funnier."

Bullitt
22 | 20 | 20 | 24

1968 | Directed by Peter Yates | With Steve McQueen, Robert Vaughn, Jacqueline Bisset | 113 minutes | Rated PG

Arguably "the mother of all cop films", this "solid" action thriller stars an "icy-cool" McQueen, "acting by not acting" as a no-bull SFPD detective who takes on a corrupt system; set in Frisco "before too many high-rises" arrived, it's famed for a "definitive car chase" ("wheee!")

that's "still the best" after "countless" knockoffs, though some find the ride "pretty straightforward" plotwise.

Bus Stop
21 | 21 | 20 | 20

1956 | Directed by Joshua Logan | With Marilyn Monroe, Don Murray, Eileen Heckart | 96 minutes | Not Rated

Proving herself "at home on the range", Monroe brings "depth" to romantic comedy as a "vulnerable" "Western chantoosie" with "impossible dreams" adrift in an otherwise "slightly sappy" tale of a cowpoke's "crazy love"; though Marilyn proves she's more than "just a pretty face", skeptics of her "serious actress" mode say they "want to get off."

Z Butch Cassidy & the Sundance Kid ✉
26 | 26 | 25 | 25

1969 | Directed by George Roy Hill | With Paul Newman, Robert Redford, Katharine Ross | 110 minutes | Rated PG

"Compulsive charmers" Newman and Redford play a pair of wise-cracking, "magnetic" "antiheroes" trying to stay ahead of the law in this "outstanding" Western "buddy movie", loaded with "adventure and humor"; it fuses a "snappy" script, Burt Bacharach soundtrack and "too many classic scenes to count" into a "sentimental favorite" that's "never boring" from start to "unforgettable" finish.

Butterfield 8 ✉
23 | 26 | 24 | 23

1960 | Directed by Daniel Mann | With Elizabeth Taylor, Laurence Harvey, Eddie Fisher, Dina Merrill | 109 minutes | Not Rated

A "bombshell" call girl with a "taste for the good life" and "fabulous furs" falls for a "rich, married heartbreaker" in this "expertly done" drama that landed Taylor her first Oscar; no question, Liz "sizzles", but some say this "dated", sanitized version of the 1935 John O'Hara novel is "hardly one for the ages."

Butterflies Are Free
21 | 23 | 21 | 20

1972 | Directed by Milton Katselas | With Goldie Hawn, Edward Albert, Eileen Heckart | 109 minutes | Rated PG

"Great casting" floats this "charming comedy" from Broadway to the big screen, with a "young Goldie" playing a "goofy free spirit" out to "befriend/seduce" a blind attorney who's in thrall to an "overprotective mother"; while the "realities of disability" are "touching", it's the "priceless chemistry" that has most aflutter.

Butterfly Effect, The
17 | 18 | 22 | 18

2004 | Directed by Eric Bress, J. Mackye Gruber | With Ashton Kutcher, Amy Smart, Melora Walters | 113 minutes | Rated R

Get some "mental exercise" courtesy of this "original" if "confusing" psychological thriller about a traumatized fellow who travels back in time to exorcise his demons; just be aware that the "everything-is-connected-to-everything" storyline is pretty "dark" (with "child abuse" and "animal torture" subplots) and thus too "disturbing" for impressionable types.

Bye Bye Birdie
19 | 18 | 18 | 20

1963 | Directed by George Sidney | With Janet Leigh, Dick Van Dyke, Ann-Margret | 112 minutes | Rated G

The high "fun quotient" bolsters this "upbeat" musical from the "long-ago world" of 1963, a look at the hoopla surrounding an Elvis-like singer's farewell gig before he goes off to the army; though Ann-

Margret is "one heck of a talented sex kitten" doing some athletic song-and-dance numbers that – whew! – "stay with you", detractors wave it off as "cheesy" fare that's "woefully dated now."

☒ Cabaret ✉
26 | 25 | 25 | 27
1972 | Directed by Bob Fosse | With Liza Minnelli, Michael York, Joel Grey | 124 minutes | Rated PG
Comprised of equal parts "love, angst", "singing, dancing and Nazis", this "seminal modern musical" set in pre-WWII Berlin is a "touchstone" of the genre that "hasn't lost its luster"; old chums cheer Fosse's "superb direction" and the "starmaking performances" from Minnelli and Grey (who all took home Oscars), and even though the mood of the piece can career from "dark" to "raunchy", it's always "fun to watch."

☒ Cabinet of Dr. Caligari, The ◑
26 | 21 | 24 | 26
1921 | Directed by Robert Wiene | With Conrad Veidt, Werner Kraus | 67 minutes | Not Rated
"They don't get any freakier" than this "fascinating antique", a "menacingly atmospheric" silent horror flick that uses "German expressionism" and "twisted sets" to kindle a "nightmare" tale of murder told by a "tortured mind"; "stark, powerful" and "spooky" right down to the pioneering "surprise ending", it's "still being imitated" and still makes many modern chillers "look lame."

Cabin in the Sky ◑
24 | 23 | 23 | 22
1943 | Directed by Vincente Minnelli | With Ethel Waters, Eddie "Rochester" Anderson, Lena Horne | 98 minutes | Not Rated
A "rare major studio release with an all African-American cast", this "classic musical" is worth seeing since nearly "every black actor or singer of the era was in it"; the rather "dated" plot – something to do with a husband's temptation and its consequences – pales in comparison to the "wonderful music", including "gems" like 'Taking a Chance on Love' and 'Happiness is a Thing Called Joe.'

Cable Guy, The
11 | 14 | 11 | 13
1996 | Directed by Ben Stiller | With Jim Carrey, Matthew Broderick, Leslie Mann, Jack Black | 96 minutes | Rated PG-13
Carrey "shows the cruel side of his humor" in this "blackest of comedies" about a "flat-out weird" cable technician who becomes the "psycho stalker" of a customer ("uncomfortable straight man" Broderick); though fans insist it's "misunderstood", more shrug "not funny."

Cactus Flower
21 | 22 | 20 | 20
1969 | Directed by Gene Saks | With Walter Matthau, Ingrid Bergman, Goldie Hawn | 103 minutes | Rated PG
This "cute" if "dated" comedy about the affairs of a philandering dentist might be "romantic fluff", but it's redeemed by a "strong cast", particularly the "radiant" Bergman and the "delightful", Oscar-winning Hawn "in her screen debut"; sticklers say "even Matthau can't save" the "weak story", though "he does try."

Caddyshack
24 | 20 | 19 | 19
1980 | Directed by Harold Ramis | With Chevy Chase, Rodney Dangerfield, Bill Murray | 99 minutes | Rated R
"Dumb as it is", this "goofy" comedy of "golfers gone amok" is a "classic" of "un-ironic" (some say "sophomoric") humor featuring a "price-

less" ensemble cast and a fake gopher; "ok, it's a guy thing", but it "stands the test of time" as "oft-quoted" "mindless fun."

◪ Caine Mutiny, The

OVERALL	ACTING	STORY	PROD.
27	28	26	23

1954 | Directed by Edward Dmytryk | With Humphrey Bogart, Jose Ferrer, Van Johnson | 124 minutes | Not Rated

This "briny" blend of "powerful wartime story" and "engrossing" courtroom drama gets its ballast from Bogart's "brilliant", "pull-out-all-the-stops" turn as Queeg, the "demented sea captain" compulsively "click, click, clicking" a set of "steel balls"; the "classic script" follows a "totally believable" high-seas rebellion to a court-martial and is "must-see" material for maritime mavens.

Calendar Girls
23	25	23	22

2003 | Directed by Nigel Cole | With Helen Mirren, Julie Walters, John Alderton | 108 minutes | Rated PG-13

"Older can be beautiful" is the "serious message behind the tea and scones" of this comic tale of "plucky", middle-aged English gals who pose for a nude calendar to raise funds for a cancer center; the "talent-laden cast" does a "charming" job with this "female version of *The Full Monty*", and let's face it, "who doesn't love Helen Mirren naked?"; wags note certain parts "sag" a bit.

Caligula
12	14	12	16

1980 | Directed by Tinto Brass | With Malcolm McDowell, Helen Mirren, John Gielgud, Peter O'Toole | 156 minutes | Rated NC-17

"Pagan Rome" gets the "adults-only" treatment in this "sick" mix of "big stars", "excessive mayhem" and "hard-core porn" depicting the life and times of an "out-of-control" Roman emperor with an "overactive libido"; a prime contender for the "worst film ever made", it's "campy", "laughable" stuff that's "much ado about pretty much nothing."

Camelot
21	21	23	23

1967 | Directed by Joshua Logan | With Richard Harris, Vanessa Redgrave, Franco Nero | 179 minutes | Rated G

Lerner and Loewe's Broadway musical of the "well-worn" King Arthur legend receives "faithful" treatment in this tale of pomp and "passion in medieval England"; admirers of the "gorgeous" sets and "beautiful music" sing its praises as a "magical" "diversion", though folks take a tilt at the "ponderous excess" and note "no one in the cast can carry a tune."

◪ Camille ◑
26	26	25	26

1937 | Directed by George Cukor | With Greta Garbo, Robert Taylor, Lionel Barrymore | 109 minutes | Not Rated

The "epitome of classic romance", this ultra-"tragic love story" stars "Garbo at her peak" playing a 19th-century Parisian courtesan with a cough who falls for a rather naïve young man; although Taylor is "marginal in an admittedly thankless role", his leading lady's "charm" and "breathtaking beauty" is "fascinating" enough to keep admirers enthralled; P.S. "have plenty of Kleenex on hand."

Candidate, The ✉

20	22	22	20

1972 | Directed by Michael Ritchie | With Robert Redford, Peter Boyle, Melvyn Douglas | 109 minutes | Rated PG

A "prescient" civics lesson, this political drama tracks a "social activist seduced into selling his soul" when he runs for the Senate; a "most convincing" Redford leads the pack of "top-notch performances" as the novice campaigner who's "in far over his head", presenting a "cynical view" of the process that registers as "timely" over 30 years later.

Cannonball Run, The

| | 17 | 14 | 15 | 16 |

1981 | Directed by Hal Needham | With Burt Reynolds, Roger Moore, Farrah Fawcett, Dom DeLuise | 95 minutes | Rated PG

"Zany, not brainy", this "sophomoric" comedy sends a "mugging" Reynolds and "half of 1981 Hollywood" on a "race across America" with "fast cars, hot women" and miles of "mindless fun" in lieu of an "actual plot"; though "incredibly cheesy" and "showing its age", it's still loaded with "good laughs", especially if you "don't want to think too hard."

Ⓩ Cape Fear ◐

| | 25 | 26 | 26 | 23 |

1962 | Directed by J. Lee Thompson | With Gregory Peck, Robert Mitchum, Polly Bergen | 105 minutes | Not Rated

It's high tide for "rage and revenge" in this "doozy" of a noir thriller, a real "nail-biter" starring Peck as an upright dad who "gets down in the gutter" to protect his family from a "deeply frightening" ex-con at large in the marsh and "as evil as they come"; most rate it "scarier than the remake", "without the histrionics."

Cape Fear

| | 20 | 24 | 21 | 20 |

1991 | Directed by Martin Scorsese | With Robert De Niro, Nick Nolte, Jessica Lange, Juliette Lewis | 128 minutes | Rated R

Count on "fear for sure" as Scorsese's "well-done" redo of the killer '62 thriller heads for "over-the-top territory", working up "sustained suspense" as a "terrifying" De Niro "has a ball" portraying a vengeance-bent "wacko"; it's an "edge-of-your-seat" ride, with the "cameos" from the "previous cast" that are a "nice touch."

Ⓩ Capote ✉

| | 26 | 29 | 24 | 25 |

2005 | Directed by Bennett Miller | With Philip Seymour Hoffman, Catherine Keener, Chris Cooper | 114 minutes | Rated R

Not content to do a mere "uncanny impression", "genius" Hoffman delves "inside the mind" of "flamboyant" writer Truman Capote to render the "iconoclast" "in all his complexity" – while nabbing a "well-deserved" Oscar along the way – in this "fascinating" biopic, a behind the scenes look at the writing of Tru's "watershed" book *In Cold Blood*; abetted by Keener's "sturdy" supporting turn, this "world-class study" also works well as a "meditation on journalistic ethics."

Captain Blood ◐

| | 23 | 21 | 20 | 21 |

1935 | Directed by Michael Curtiz | With Errol Flynn, Olivia de Havilland, Basil Rathbone | 119 minutes | Not Rated

Avast, there's "salty" "popcorn fun" aplenty in this "smashing" swashbuckler, featuring "Flynn's first starring role" as an enslaved wretch who becomes a "devil-may-care" pirate of the Caribbean; armchair buccaneers jump on board for the "roguish" baddies, "high-seas action" and "men in tights", not minding that the old vessel is "on the creaky side."

Ⓩ Captains Courageous ✉◐

| | 25 | 26 | 24 | 21 |

1937 | Directed by Victor Fleming | With Spencer Tracy, Freddie Bartholomew, Lionel Barrymore | 115 minutes | Not Rated

Fashioned from a Kipling tale that's "every boy's dream of excitement", this "tearjerker" adventure story stars Bartholomew as a bratty rich kid who's rescued at sea and matures under the helm of a salty sailor, the Oscar-winning Tracy; the lad's "highly touching" transformation is conveyed through "phenomenal" acting that's "too often forgotten."

Carlito's Way
22 | 25 | 22 | 22

1993 | Directed by Brian De Palma | With Al Pacino, Sean Penn, Penelope Ann Miller | 145 minutes | Rated R

Scarface cohorts De Palma and Pacino go "gangster" again in this "tight, tense" crime thriller about a Latino drug lord just out of prison who's "trying to go straight but not getting there"; with the principals "in peak form" (Penn "steals the show" as a "slimy, coke-addicted" lawyer), it's a "cool", if "underrated" look at the underworld with a "subtle" slant.

Carmen Jones
23 | 23 | 23 | 23

1954 | Directed by Otto Preminger | With Dorothy Dandridge, Harry Belafonte, Pearl Bailey | 105 minutes | Not Rated

A "modern", "Americanized" version of Bizet's "classic" *Carmen*, this "beautiful reimagining" was a "breakthrough for its time" given its all-black cast, led by the "sassy" Dorothy and "hot" Harry; while the concept's "superb" and the music "beautiful", it's docked a few points since the stars' songs were dubbed by "real opera singers."

Carnal Knowledge
22 | 26 | 21 | 21

1971 | Directed by Mike Nichols | With Jack Nicholson, Candice Bergen, Art Garfunkel, Ann-Margret | 98 minutes | Rated R

"Literate people talk dirty" in this "bitter but engrossing" look at "two self-absorbed buddies who measure life in terms of their sexual conquests", and though these "pretty sad characters" can be "hard to watch", the "perfect cast" expertly evokes its theme of "innocence lost"; still, the jaded jeer what was "bold for its time" is now rather "tame."

Carousel
24 | 22 | 22 | 25

1956 | Directed by Henry King | With Gordon MacRae, Shirley Jones, Cameron Mitchell | 128 minutes | Not Rated

"Girl meets wrong boy" at the traveling show in this silver screen go-round of Rodgers and Hammerstein's "sentimental" musical, which draws on a "lovely" score and "fine cast" of "first-rate" singers to spin a tale that's "romantic, sad" and "not always pretty"; while it's regarded as a "neglected great" to devotees, it's also seen as a squandering of "talent" on a "corny", "tarnished-with-age" storyline.

Carrie
22 | 22 | 23 | 21

1976 | Directed by Brian De Palma | With Sissy Spacek, Piper Laurie, Amy Irving, John Travolta | 98 minutes | Rated R

"Stephen King done right", this "bloody good" horror pic headlines Spacek as a "bug-eyed" "telekinetic outcast" (with a "nut bar" of a mom) who repays the "casual cruelty of high-schoolers" with a prom-night "flip-out" that's gorier than a bucket of "pig's blood"; with "character-oriented" carnage that's a cut above "shock schlock", it's "white knuckles all the way" to that "grabber" of an ending.

Cars
24 | - | 23 | 27

2006 | Directed by John Lasseter, Joe Ranft | Animated | 116 minutes | Rated G

Disney/Pixar's "well-oiled" animation outfit rigs a "familiar fish-out-of-water story" ("*Doc Hollywood*", anyone?) to "talking cars" and rolls out this "delightful" joyride featuring "exceptional" renderings and "adorable" vocal characterizations by Owen Wilson, Paul Newman and comic Larry The Cable Guy; parents appreciate the "great" soundtrack and "offbeat" cultural references – real lifesavers when the young 'uns "watch it for the 30th time."

Car Wash
17 | 16 | 15 | 16

1976 | Directed by Michael Schultz | With Richard Pryor, George Carlin, The Pointer Sisters | 97 minutes | Rated PG

It's "'70s flashback" time via this "light comedy" depicting a "day in the life" of an LA service station where a "silly" crew hoses down autos and cracks wise to a disco beat; Pryor drums up "big laughs" in a "small role", but ultimately it's "a bit dated" now – you probably "remember the soundtrack more than the movie."

☑ Casablanca ✉◑
29 | 28 | 28 | 27

1942 | Directed by Michael Curtiz | With Humphrey Bogart, Ingrid Bergman, Paul Henreid, Claude Rains | 102 minutes | Rated PG

We'll always have the "magic" of this "most compelling" of romances, a showcase for "legendary" turns from an "enigmatic" Bogart, "radiant" Bergman and "top-shelf" supporting cast set against the "unforgettable" backdrop of WWII occupied North Africa; the "fast-paced" plot of passion and "intrigue" is an "unsurpassed" model of good, "old-fashioned storytelling" and a bona fide "runner-up to Shakespeare" for "classic lines" – there's no choice but to "play it again and again."

Casanova
16 | 18 | 16 | 20

2005 | Directed by Lasse Hallström | With Heath Ledger, Sienna Miller, Jeremy Irons, Oliver Platt, Lena Olin | 108 minutes | Rated R

"Eighteenth-century Venice" sparkles in this "light", *Tom Jones*"-ish bio of the "legendary lothario", nicely played by the "easy-on-the-eyes" Ledger; on the other hand, critics call it a "narrow depiction of a complex man", noting that there's "more bodice heaving than ripping" going on in this relatively sex-free exercise.

Casino
21 | 24 | 21 | 22

1995 | Directed by Martin Scorsese | With Robert De Niro, Sharon Stone, Joe Pesci, James Woods | 178 minutes | Rated R

A crash course in "pre-corporate casino management", this "flashy" crime saga of "mob life" in "seedy Vegas" relates a "dark" tale that deals out "violence, drugs and self-loathing" in spades; proponents lay their money down for De Niro as a dapper hood, Pesci's "insane mob guy" bit and a "sizzling" Stone proving she "can actually act"; still, those who yawn it's "way too long" say bets are off, since they could be "watching *Goodfellas* instead."

Casino Royale
23 | 22 | 21 | 26

2006 | Directed by Martin Campbell | With Daniel Craig, Eva Green, Mads Mikkelsen, Judi Dench | 144 minutes | Rated PG-13

A "strong reboot for the franchise", this "excellent prequel" based on Ian Fleming's first 007 novel goes "back to basics" with "fewer gadgets" and "more brains" to give the long-running series a "needed jolt"; "blond Bond" Daniel Craig's "blue-collar" take on the character makes him a "worthy successor to Connery, Sean Connery", and though the picture "bogs down in the card scenes", it's worth seeing for that "amazing opening foot chase" alone.

Casper | 15 | 14 | 15 | 19 |
1995 | Directed by Brad Silberling | With Christina Ricci, Bill Pullman, Cathy Moriarty | 100 minutes | Rated PG
The "special effects are worth the ticket price" of this "typical family movie" that's also notable for its "really cute" title character, a ghost who's referred to as 'living impaired'; though some say the "sappy" storyline's "charmless", at least it's "not annoyingly adorable."

Cast Away | 20 | 25 | 18 | 23 |
2000 | Directed by Robert Zemeckis | With Tom Hanks, Helen Hunt | 143 minutes | Rated PG-13
"Hanks does Crusoe" in this "well-made" adventure based on Tom's "almost-one-man-show" as a "pudgy FedEx" pilot marooned after a crash landing and forced to "slim down", don a "loincloth" and start "talking to a volleyball"; though "feeling his loneliness" may be "inspiring", foes say the action's beached by "slow-moving" stretches and a "trite" windup that's too "predictable."

Casualties of War | 20 | 23 | 21 | 21 |
1989 | Directed by Brian De Palma | With Michael J. Fox, Sean Penn, John C. Reilly, John Leguizamo | 113 minutes | Rated R
A portrait of "war stripped of all romantic notions", this "sobering", "thought-provoking" account of a "brutal rape" by American soldiers during the Vietnam conflict is both "haunting" and harrowing; Fox (an "innocent" GI who's the film's moral conscience) and Penn (his "tough" superior) deliver "unforgettable" performances in this "disturbing" metaphor for American imperialism.

Cat Ballou ✉ | 21 | 22 | 19 | 20 |
1965 | Directed by Elliot Silverstein | With Lee Marvin, Jane Fonda, Michael Callan | 97 minutes | Not Rated
"Not your typical Western", this comic oater "with a heart" stars Fonda as a righteous lady outlaw but is stolen by Oscar-winner Marvin, who horses around in two roles, including that of a whiskey-addled gunslinger; a "hoot in its day", it's nearing its ninth life but is still "fun to watch."

Catch Me If You Can | 23 | 24 | 25 | 24 |
2002 | Directed by Steven Spielberg | With Leonardo DiCaprio, Tom Hanks, Christopher Walken | 141 minutes | Rated PG-13
Spielberg's "witty, fast-paced" "cat-and-mouse game" ("based on a true story" about a charming con man) is "mischievous fun from the delightful opening credits until the final frame", with "lots of '60s color" and "awesome acting" by the "engaging DiCaprio" and "rock-solid" Hanks; it's an "exciting, wild ride" that shows us "sometimes crime *does* pay."

⛟ Catch-22 | 25 | 25 | 25 | 23 |
1970 | Directed by Mike Nichols | With Alan Arkin, Jon Voight, Anthony Perkins, Bob Newhart, Art Garfunkel, Orson Welles, Richard Benjamin, Paula Prentiss | 122 minutes | Rated R
A "faithful" adaptation of Joseph Heller's "classic novel", this "wicked black comedy" about the "absurdity of war" skewers the "brutality and bureaucracy" of combat in its "devastating" look at a squadron of

WWII flyboys (played by a "sterling" ensemble cast led by Arkin); simultaneously "hilarious" and "appalling", it's a "cultural artifact" of the "cynical '60s" to some, "never more relevant" to others.

ℤ Cat on a Hot Tin Roof
25 | 27 | 24 | 23

1958 | Directed by Richard Brooks | With Elizabeth Taylor, Paul Newman, Burl Ives | 108 minutes | Not Rated

"Man, these people have problems": "steamy Liz" "in that white slip" and a "dynamite" Newman "couldn't possibly look better" as they "burn up the screen" in this "sex-soaked" Tennessee Williams drama of "love, rejection" and "Southern family politics"; the "towering" Ives presides as the ragin' Big Daddy, adding an "incredibly interesting" *Lear*-like thread to all that "eye candy."

Cat People ◑
23 | 20 | 21 | 22

1942 | Directed by Jacques Tourneur | With Simone Simon, Kent Smith, Tom Conway, Jane Randolph | 73 minutes | Not Rated

"More scary than many modern films", this "wonderfully weird" "low-budget" horror flick tells the story of a "tortured soul" who believes "she's cursed to become a killer panther"; it may be "relatively tame by today's standards" (and "not for *Friday the 13th* fans"), but does achieve an "eerie tension" via its "mysterious characters", "dark sets" and "incredible use of light and shadow."

Cat People
16 | 17 | 18 | 18

1982 | Directed by Paul Schrader | With Nastassja Kinski, Malcolm McDowell, John Heard, Annette O'Toole | 118 minutes | Rated R

"Pretty on the eye if fuzzy on the brain", this "atmospheric" remake of the 1942 "Simone Simon cult classic" is a "stylish but forgettable" fantasy having to do with panthers and "sexual politics"; fans purr about its "creepy", "feline performances" and "nifty special effects", but seen-it-alls say the "David Bowie theme song" is the "best thing about it."

Cat's Meow, The
18 | 20 | 18 | 20

2002 | Directed by Peter Bogdanovich | With Kirsten Dunst, Eddie Izzard, Edward Herrmann, Cary Elwes | 114 minutes | Rated PG-13

The "mysterious" 1924 death of a "Hollywood mogul" aboard William Randolph Hearst's yacht is the "speculative springboard" for this "clever" whodunit; though "a bit slow", it's energized by an "entertaining" cast channeling "rich and famous" Jazz Age types, most notably Izzard's "wonderfully lascivious" spin on Charlie Chaplin.

Cellular
16 | 17 | 17 | 17

2004 | Directed by David R. Ellis | With Kim Basinger, Chris Evans, Jason Statham, William H. Macy | 94 minutes | Rated PG-13

Telecommunications gets a "suspenseful" spin in this "breakneck-paced", "woman-in-distress" thriller about a kidnap victim who phones a complete stranger and manages to enlist his help; some call it a "blatant rip-off of *Phone Booth*", while others are hung up by its "generic Ken doll" hero and "implausible", "coincidence"-laden plot.

Celluloid Closet, The
25 | - | 25 | 24

1995 | Directed by Robert Epstein, Jeff Friedman | Documentary | 102 minutes | Rated R

Learn to "appreciate" certain classics in a "whole new" way via this documentary "revelation" that traces "gay themes and undercurrents" in Hollywood history using film clips and "insightful" interviews; it takes an "unsparing look at prejudice" that's also a "very entertaining" glimpse into a "crowded closet" – even if some wish there were more than "mild surprises behind the door."

☑ Central Station 🄵 26 | 27 | 25 | 22

1998 | Directed by Walter Salles | With Fernanda Montenegro, Marília Pêra, Vinícius de Oliveira | 113 minutes | Rated R

The unexpected bonding between a "world-weary woman" and a "sweet young boy" lies at the heart of this "flawless" Brazilian drama hailed for its "absorbing performances" ("Fernanda Montenegro is a revelation") played out against "stark inner city" and "colorful countryside" locales; a "tug-at-your-heart" "tearjerker" if there ever was one, its "haunting" "story of redemption" makes for one "very special movie."

Changing Lanes 16 | 19 | 17 | 17

2002 | Directed by Roger Michell | With Ben Affleck, Samuel L. Jackson | 99 minutes | Rated R

A freeway fender-bender turns into "road rage" of epic proportions in this "fast-moving" "urban melodrama" pitting an "affluent", "smarmy" lawyer against a "poor, down-and-out" dad, both suffering from "too much testosterone" and bent on one-upmanship; admirers like its "small scope" and Jackson's "fine" performance but not the "just-along-for-the-ride" Affleck or that "wussy", "cop-out" ending.

Chaplin 22 | 27 | 22 | 22

1992 | Directed by Richard Attenborough | With Robert Downey Jr., Moira Kelly, Kevin Kline, Anthony Hopkins | 143 minutes | Rated PG-13

Downey is "simply brilliant" in the title role of this "well-done" biopic, going "beyond impersonation into pure embodiment" of the silent-screen film legend, whose politics and "love of young women" fueled much controversy; "lovely" production design and an "exceptional" supporting cast (including Geraldine Chaplin, "playing her own grandmother") offset the rather "long" running time.

☑ Charade 26 | 25 | 26 | 25

1963 | Directed by Stanley Donen | With Cary Grant, Audrey Hepburn, Walter Matthau | 113 minutes | Not Rated

Expect "plenty of plot twists" in this "quintessential romantic comedy/thriller" (the "best Hitchcock flick that Hitchcock didn't make") about the scramble for a missing fortune; its very "easy-on-the-eyes" stars, "luscious Paris" scenery, magical "Mancini melodies" and "Audrey's fab wardrobe" make for "perfect" moviemaking – "murder was never so much fun."

☑ Chariots of Fire ✉ 26 | 25 | 25 | 25

1981 | Directed by Hugh Hudson | With Ben Cross, Ian Charleson, Ian Holm | 123 minutes | Rated PG

Remembered for "running off with" a Best Picture Oscar, this "inspiring" drama paces itself in "superb" style as it follows the "trials and triumph" of a British track team bound for the 1924 Olympics; thanks to "uplifting" legwork and a very "hummable" soundtrack, it breaks the tape as a "never boring" movie.

Charlie and the Chocolate Factory   18 | 20 | 20 | 24

2005 | Directed by Tim Burton | With Johnny Depp, Freddie Highmore, Helena Bonham Carter | 115 minutes | Rated PG

Burton's "edgy imagination" molds this "ambitious reimagining" of the family classic into an "eye-popping" "morality tale" about a poor kid's visit to a candyland run by the "warped" Depp (who channels his version of Willy Wonka with enough "Michael Jackson" to "give you the willies"); though "truer to Roald Dahl's book" than the original, some say this go-round is "less sweet" – all that "manic dementia" adds up to "empty calories."

Charlie's Angels   13 | 11 | 10 | 17

2000 | Directed by McG | With Cameron Diaz, Drew Barrymore, Lucy Liu, Bill Murray | 98 minutes | Rated PG-13

"Girl power" gets a glam "MTV" makeover replete with "bootylicious" babes and "high-flying action" in this "fluffy", "nonsensical" send-up of the '70s TV series about foxy femme crime-fighters; no doubt, "it doesn't have the best acting ever" ("did Murray lose a bet?") and the "storyline's completely far-fetched", but charitable souls say it's "good when you want something mind-numbing."

Charlie Wilson's War   22 | 25 | 24 | 23

2007 | Directed by Mike Nichols | With Tom Hanks, Julia Roberts, Philip Seymour Hoffman, Amy Adams | 102 minutes | Rated R

Have a "good laugh over a crazy war" (and "learn a lot" about "current political predicaments") via this "clever" satire recounting the "real-life" exploits of a "corrupt" congressman whose cause célèbre – "defeating the Soviets in Afghanistan" – may have "altered the course of world history"; as for the "high-caliber" talent, Hanks "shines" and Hoffman "steals the show" as a "renegade CIA operative."

Charlotte's Web   23 | 22 | 25 | 24

2006 | Directed by Gary Winick | With Dakota Fanning | 97 minutes | Rated G

There are "no surprises" in this "delightful rendering" of E. B. White's "classic" farm fable, just "sweet" storytelling made "magical" by the "amazing" Fanning and a barnyard bunch brought to life by "believable" effects and "wonderful" celeb voice work ("Julia Roberts is fabulous as Charlotte"); though an itsy-bitsy minority maintains the 1973 animated version "can't be beat", most exalt this "much-needed break" from today's family-unfriendly fare.

Charly ✉   21 | 25 | 22 | 17

1968 | Directed by Ralph Nelson | With Cliff Robertson, Claire Bloom, Leon Janney | 103 minutes | Rated PG

A bright idea grafting drama onto a "believable" sci-fi scenario, this "original" flick gives Best Actor honoree Robertson a chance to "shine" as a "man who goes from retardation to genius and back again" after a round of brain surgery; tutor Bloom adds romantic interest to make the doings "supremely touching" – "if a bit sappy" for cynics.

Chasing Amy   20 | 19 | 20 | 17

1997 | Directed by Kevin Smith | With Ben Affleck, Joey Lauren Adams, Jason Lee | 111 minutes | Rated R

Director Smith's trademarks – "Jersey-speak", "coarse humor", "semi-realistic situations" – are all apparent in this "offbeat" romantic comedy, featuring Affleck in the role of a comic-book scribe bewitched by a lesbian with a "nails-on-chalkboard" voice; it "rocks" fans with an "entertainingly different" mix of "smart" talk and "slacker cool", but foes claim it's a "sentimental" ode to "geek life" that's "not really funny."

Cheaper By the Dozen

22 | 22 | 23 | 19

1950 | Directed by Walter Lang | With Clifton Webb, Jeanne Crain, Myrna Loy | 85 minutes | Not Rated

Set at the turn of the last century, this "warm family comedy" relates the "wonderful", fact-based story of a pair of efficiency experts bringing up 12 "cute" children, with a "droll" Webb stealing the show as the "pompous" head of the brood; sure, it strays into "precious" territory but oldsters attest it "wears well over time."

Cheaper By the Dozen

17 | 18 | 16 | 18

2003 | Directed by Shawn Levy | With Steve Martin, Bonnie Hunt, Piper Perabo, Hilary Duff | 98 minutes | Rated PG

For a "good, old-fashioned movie experience", try this "wholesome" comedy about a "big crazy family" uprooted by dad and mom's new jobs; granted, it's "very different" from the original 1950 flick and "not really a remake except for the number of children", but the "kids are cute" and there are "some funny moments"; best scene: that "breakfast disaster of epic proportions."

⚡ Chicago ✉

27 | 26 | 25 | 29

2002 | Directed by Rob Marshall | With Renée Zellweger, Catherine Zeta-Jones, Richard Gere, Queen Latifah | 113 minutes | Rated PG-13

"Bob Fosse would have been proud" of this "absolutely brilliant" adaptation of his boffo Broadway "tale of murder, greed and corruption" in 1920s Chicago; "astounded" surveyors swear this "razzle-dazzle" "visual masterpiece" "deserved every Oscar it won" thanks to its "phenomenal acting", "sexy cinematography", "spine-tingling music" ("who knew the big three could sing?") and "major dance moves that'll leave you gasping for air"; even critics who complain of "miscasting" and "MTV camerawork" hope it sparks a "return to old-fashioned movie musicals."

Chicken Little

19 | - | 17 | 22

2005 | Directed by Mark Dindal | Animated | 81 minutes | Rated G

Disney lays a *War of the Worlds* spin on a "classic" children's fable and hatches some "good clean fun" in this "cute" cartoon featuring "excellent" animation and some "amusing" moments; the scattered nuggets of adult "belly laughs" earn parental praise, though a few critics chirp it "should have spent a little more time in the incubator."

Chicken Run

23 | - | 23 | 27

2000 | Directed by Peter Lord, Nick Park | Animated | 84 minutes | Rated G

Pure "poultry in motion", this "ingenious", "touching" barnyard saga uses "fantastic" claymation to portray a "darn appealing" bunch of British fowl and their "valiant struggle" to get off the farm; "subtle references" make it a "hilarious take" on all the *Stalag 17*-style POW pics, so while kids can enjoy the "innocent" animated escapade, it "doesn't chicken out" on "tongue-in-cheek", grown-up undertones; in an eggshell, a "good run for the money."

Children of a Lesser God

23 | 25 | 22 | 21

1986 | Directed by Randa Haines | With Marlee Matlin, William Hurt, Piper Laurie | 119 minutes | Rated R

This "touching" drama "does justice to the original play" on the strength of "sexy, compelling" turns from Hurt as a speech teacher at a school for the deaf and Best Actress winner Matlin, "signing throughout" as a hearing-impaired woman with a complex past; expect "moving scenes" as their intimacy develops, and though an "enjoyable" intro to the "deaf community", it might be a "little overdramatized."

Children of Men

22 | 24 | 22 | 24

2006 | Directed by Alfonso Cuarón | With Clive Owen, Julianne Moore, Michael Caine | 109 minutes | Rated R

Dubbed "Blade Runner for Generation X", this "dystopian" vision of a "not-too-distant future" in which "women can no longer conceive" revolves around Owen's "outstanding" turn as an "unwilling hero" out to "save the human race"; references to "war", "totalitarianism" and "immigration" sharpen the "contemporary bite", leaving it to Caine's "unconventional" cameo as a "hippie pothead" to provide some "levity."

☒ Children of Paradise ◑ ⓕ

28 | 27 | 27 | 26

1946 | Directed by Marcel Carné | With Arletty, Jean-Louis Barrault, Pierre Renoir | 190 minutes | Not Rated

Filmed in France "under the noses of the Nazis", this "legendary" romance "lovingly re-creates 1840s Paris" in a "multilayered" story of a "lovesick" mime's passion for a vampish stage siren; built on "profound" themes and "stylized" performances (that come off as "melodramatic" but are rich with "beauty and feeling"), it "continues to fascinate" as a "masterpiece of world cinema" and the big screen's "greatest tribute to live theater."

Children's Hour, The ◑

24 | 26 | 24 | 22

1961 | Directed by William Wyler | With Audrey Hepburn, Shirley MacLaine, James Garner, Miriam Hopkins | 107 minutes | Not Rated

"Way ahead of its time", this "groundbreaking" adaptation of the Lillian Hellman play examines "scandal and reputation", specifically what happens after a "malicious child" fingers two schoolteachers as lesbians; despite a "predictable" ending and subject matter that's "tragic" verging on "depressing", the "performances still pack a wallop."

China Syndrome, The

22 | 25 | 24 | 20

1979 | Directed by James Bridges | With Jack Lemmon, Jane Fonda, Michael Douglas | 122 minutes | Rated PG

The going gets "scary" as a nuclear power facility heads for meltdown in this "intelligent thriller" starring a "terrific" Lemmon as the plant supervisor and "Fonda at her peak" as a frustrated TV reporter; the "couldhappen" story is "well-crafted", but conservatives contend that the "melodramatic" matchup of "bad-guy corporate players" against "good-guy idealists" makes it into the "definitive liberal" "message film."

☒ Chinatown ☒

27 | 28 | 26 | 26

1974 | Directed by Roman Polanski | With Jack Nicholson, Faye Dunaway, John Huston | 131 minutes | Rated R

This "taut drama" about "stolen water" and "bottled-up emotion" in 1930s Los Angeles is a "nearly perfect" exercise in "Technicolor film noir" that's simultaneously "funny, bleak and knowing"; credit the "dynamite" cast, "ravishingly beautiful" cinematography and "superb script" by Robert Towne (that concludes with a "shocking", "untypical-Hollywood ending") for its success; most memorable scene: Dunaway's "slap"-happy "she's-my-sister-she's-my-daughter" tour de force.

Chocolat 22 | 24 | 22 | 23

2000 | Directed by Lasse Hallström | With Juliette Binoche, Alfred Molina, Johnny Depp | 121 minutes | Rated PG-13

A "yummy escape" "bordering on a fairy tale", this "funny" romance finds "lovely" "rebel spirit" Binoche pitted against "petty-minded villagers" when she opens a chocolate shop in a French hamlet and takes up with Depp; the blend of a "beautiful setting" mixed with some "uplifting whimsy" makes for one "tasty bonbon."

Chorus Line, A 19 | 19 | 21 | 21

1985 | Directed by Richard Attenborough | With Michael Douglas, Alyson Reed, Michelle Johnston | 113 minutes | Rated PG-13

"Dance lovers never tire" of the "stay-in-your-head" songs and snappy "kick-line" choreography of this "delightful" musical about "Broadway hopefuls" auditioning for chorus jobs; still, voters split on the end result – a "singular sensation" vs. "doesn't hold a candle to the stage production" – though all are pleased that it was at least "recorded for posterity."

Christine 17 | 16 | 20 | 19

1983 | Directed by John Carpenter | With Keith Gordon, John Stockwell, Alexandra Paul | 110 minutes | Rated R

"Boy meets car, boy falls for car" in this adaptation of Stephen King's fantasy/horror tale about an "evil" 1958 Plymouth Fury with a mind of its own, featuring enough "freaky" touches and flying "shards of glass" to make "public transportation" more palatable; many say the titular auto drives away with "best acting" honors.

Christmas Carol, A ◑ 27 | 26 | 28 | 23

1951 | Directed by Brian Desmond Hurst | With Alastair Sim, Kathleen Harrison, Mervyn Johns | 86 minutes | Not Rated

"Sim is the best Scrooge ever" in this Dickens of a "holiday delight", a "magical adaptation" of the "timeless" fable concerning a rich old paragon of "grouchiness" transformed by a Yuletide visit from a posse of ghosts; cherished as "superb" family fare that "inspires" without drowning in the "happily-ever-after tone" of other versions, it has fans replaying it "religiously" because there's "no way" to do "Christmas without it."

☑ Christmas Story, A 26 | 23 | 27 | 22

1983 | Directed by Bob Clark | With Peter Billingsley, Melinda Dillon, Darren McGavin | 94 minutes | Rated PG

A "sweet but not sugary" look at the "debacle that's Christmas in America", this "irresistible" family fave takes a "fond glimpse back" with a "funny-till-it-hurts" "exposition of a '40s childhood" centered on a kid bent on a "BB gun" under the tree; "most rewatchable" and "quotable" thanks to its "excellent cast and script", it's "good clean fun" for all ages and now widely deemed a seasonal "must."

| | OVERALL | ACTING | STORY | PROD. |

Chronicles of Narnia: Prince Caspian   23 | 21 | 22 | 27

2008 | Directed by Andrew Adamson | With Ben Barnes, Georgie Henley, Skandar Keynes, William Moseley | 144 minutes | Rated PG

The Pevensie children return to the magical realm of Narnia to find it threatened by an "evil king" in this "darker" but "fun" follow-up, a "sweeping" saga that's "as grand as the first" and equally "respectful" of novelist C.S. Lewis' "timeless" vision; the young cast "continues to delight", the production's "breathtaking" and the big battle scenes are both "exhilarating" and "goreless", for the ultimate in "kid enjoyment."

Chronicles of Narnia: 23 | 21 | 24 | 26
The Lion, the Witch & the Wardrobe

2005 | Directed by Andrew Adamson | With Georgie Henley, Skandar Keynes, Tilda Swinton | 140 minutes | Rated PG

C.S. Lewis' "classic" children's fantasy is "faithfully" rendered on celluloid via this "masterful production", a veritable "feast for the eyes" whose mane highlights include "lovely" performances, "beautiful" costumes and "spectacular" effects ("you can almost touch Aslan"); its "religious overtones" court controversy, however, with defenders declaring the "Christian themes are dealt with appropriately" and skeptics suggesting "it feels like a sermon."

Chronicles of Riddick, The   14 | 12 | 14 | 19

2004 | Directed by David Twohy | With Vin Diesel, Colm Feore, Thandie Newton, Judi Dench | 119 minutes | Rated PG-13

"Spectacular pyrotechnics" and "Vin's sculpted bod" provide distraction from the "cardboard characters" in this "Riddick-ulous" sci-fi sequel to cult fave *Pitch Black*; playing an outer-space fugitive pursued by bounty hunters, Diesel shows his "campy" side trading "cheesy lines" with Dame Judi Dench, but otherwise it's pretty "bloated", "bombastic" stuff.

Cider House Rules, The ✉   22 | 24 | 23 | 22

1999 | Directed by Lasse Hallström | With Tobey Maguire, Charlize Theron, Michael Caine | 126 minutes | Rated PG-13

Presenting "life choices" in a '30s-era Maine orphanage, this "thought-provoking tearjerker" is a story of "compassion" with some "tough subject matter sneaked in" that gives Maguire his "breakout role" and proves "Caine really can act"; despite a few objections to the "cloying" tone and "watered-down" treatment of John Irving's novel, "satisfied" customers rule it an "absorbing" "feel-good" flick that "doesn't pander to the Hallmark crowd."

Cincinnati Kid, The   24 | 25 | 22 | 22

1965 | Directed by Norman Jewison | With Steve McQueen, Edward G. Robinson, Ann-Margret, Karl Malden | 102 minutes | Rated PG

This "gritty" drama that "predates today's poker craze" still "antes up" some "real entertainment" thanks to a "royal flush of a cast" led by the "never-cooler" McQueen, whose portrayal of a "professional card sharp" pays off in a "riveting, big-game sequence"; though basically "*The Hustler* with cards", bettors wager it's one of the all-time "best gambling flicks."

Z Cinderella 26 | - | 25 | 26

1950 | Directed by Clyde Geronimi, Wilfred Jackson, Hamilton Luske | Animated | 74 minutes | Rated G

"You know the drill": "breathtaking" animation from "Disney's golden age" merges with the stuff "girlish dreams" are made of in this "beautiful fantasy" about an "overworked orphan" who bags her Prince Charming with a little help from her fairy godmother and some finely feathered friends; if "short on characterization", it remains an "old-fashioned favorite" that's a shoe-in to be a "classic for generations to come."

Cinderella Liberty 19 | 23 | 20 | 17

1973 | Directed by Mark Rydell | With James Caan, Marsha Mason, Kirk Calloway | 117 minutes | Rated R

"Great chemistry" between the leads buoys this "honest" but "often-overlooked" romance about a lonesome shore-patrol swabbie who falls for a "tender-hearted prostitute" and becomes a real father figure to her "mixed-race son"; an "excellent" Caan plays well against Mason's "sympathetic" portrayal of the "hooker who doesn't know any other way to live"; all in all, a shipshape effort.

Cinderella Man 25 | 27 | 25 | 25

2005 | Directed by Ron Howard | With Russell Crowe, Renée Zellweger, Paul Giamatti | 144 minutes | Rated PG-13

The "dreary" "look of the Great Depression" permeates this "superbly crafted" sports biopic 'bout James Braddock, the "down-on-his-luck pug" who "battled back" from poverty and injury for a "shot at the heavyweight title"; given its "superb" combo of the "incredibly believable" Crowe and "wonderful" Giamatti, fans feel this "worthy" contender "should have been a bigger hit."

Z Cinema Paradiso ⊠⦿ 26 | 26 | 26 | 25

1990 | Directed by Giuseppe Tornatore | With Philippe Noiret, Jacques Perrin | 123 minutes | Rated R

This Italian "heart-warmer" is an "endearing" look at "love and loss" and a "nostalgic valentine" to the "magic of cinema"; based on the "utterly charming" story of a "projectionist in the local movie house" who "mentors a fatherless child", it rolls a "colorful" cast, *bellissimo* camerawork and a "lovely" score into an "engrossing", frankly "sentimental" film.

Z Citizen Kane ⊠◑ 28 | 27 | 27 | 28

1941 | Directed by Orson Welles | With Orson Welles, Joseph Cotten, Agnes Moorehead, Everett Sloane | 119 minutes | Rated PG

"Loosely based on the life of William Randolph Hearst", this "magnum opus" about a "ruthless megalomaniac" who "mourns the loss of his innocent childhood" is an "undisputed masterpiece" that's "often imitated, never duplicated" and "as fresh as ever"; starring and directed by wunderkind Welles, it "revolutionized the cinema" and forever changed the meaning of the word "rosebud" – "by comparison, all other films are home movies."

City Hall 18 | 22 | 18 | 18

1996 | Directed by Harold Becker | With Al Pacino, John Cusack, Bridget Fonda, Danny Aiello | 111 minutes | Rated R

Hopefully not "what real politics is like", this crime thriller lets "Pacino and Cusack excel" as a populist "New York City mayor" and his deputy doing damage control after a police shooting unravels "big-city corruption" between officialdom and the mob; supporters say "don't fight it", but even the "can't-go-wrong" cast flounders with the "disappointing" storyline.

Z City Lights ◐

28 | 28 | 26 | 25

1931 | Directed by Charles Chaplin | With Charles Chaplin, Virginia Cherrill | 87 minutes | Not Rated

"Humor, pathos and poignancy" make this silent "Chaplin masterpiece" glow with "old-fashioned sentimentality" as the Little Tramp's "devotion for a blind flower girl" leads to a series of "classic" sequences; from famed bits like the "balletic boxing match" to the "heartbreaking" closing, this early flicker is a testament to a master "on top of his game."

Z City of God F

26 | 25 | 26 | 25

2003 | Directed by Kátia Lund, Fernando Meirelles | With Matheus Nachtergaele, Seu Jorge | 130 minutes | Rated R

"Even those who are allergic to subtitles" will be more than "captivated" by this "shattering portrait" of "street kids in Brazil" who "grow up to become a gang of murderous drug dealers"; it's a "harrowing, gut-wrenching" "tour de force" that's "dynamically acted" by "nonactors" and made "edgy and fresh" by "hypnotic visuals"; the "extreme violence and brutality" may "leave you feeling ill", but "you can't look away."

City Slickers

20 | 20 | 20 | 19

1991 | Directed by Ron Underwood | With Billy Crystal, Daniel Stern, Jack Palance | 112 minutes | Rated PG-13

"Yee-haw!"; a "super" Crystal rides high in this "tons-of-fun" "buddy comedy" about three NYers who go west for a dude-ranch vacation and wind up having a "midlife crisis during a cattle drive"; the "right-on" cast (particularly the "just-too-funny Palance") has a way with "wisdom and great one-liners", rounding up applause for "good fun" that doesn't shy from its "moving" side.

Civil Action, A

20 | 21 | 23 | 19

1998 | Directed by Steven Zaillian | With John Travolta, Robert Duvall, Kathleen Quinlan, William H. Macy | 115 minutes | Rated PG-13

Filed in the same docket as "*Erin Brockovich*", this "compelling" David-vs.-Goliath courtroom drama recounts the "true story" of a suit filed against two "multibillion-dollar corporations" for "poisoning a Massachusetts town's drinking water"; it's a "gripping" portrayal of "corruption and greed way before Enron", and Travolta's "excellent" as a showboating, "clay-footed" attorney.

Claire's Knee F

23 | 24 | 22 | 23

1971 | Directed by Eric Rohmer | With Jean-Claude Brialy, Aurora Cornu, Laurence de Monaghan | 105 minutes | Rated PG

The "antithesis of an action movie", this "insightful" look at "erotic desire done without conventional sex scenes" tells the story of a "midlife crisis"–bound Frenchman "obsessed with, well, the title says it all"; knockers rap all the "cerebral ooh-la-la" as too "talky", though admirers insist this "sweet paean to romantic longing" is "probably the high point of Rohmer's career."

Clash of the Titans   18 | 14 | 20 | 17

1981 | Directed by Desmond Davis | With Harry Hamlin, Judi Bowker, Laurence Olivier, Maggie Smith | 118 minutes | Rated PG

"Hamlin looks great in next to nothing" as he battles everyone from Medusa to a two-headed dog in this "campy" "sandal saga" based on classical Greek mythology; despite plenty of "star power", cynics nix the Olympian "bad acting" ("was Olivier just feeding his ego as Zeus?"), and the "dated" special effects split voters: modernists yawn "cheesy", but nostalgic types salute FX legend Ray Harryhausen, whose "claymation monsters" and "stop-motion animation" are "always entertaining."

Clear and Present Danger   20 | 21 | 22 | 20

1994 | Directed by Phillip Noyce | With Harrison Ford, Willem Dafoe, Anne Archer | 141 minutes | Rated PG-13

Clearly "great popcorn fodder", this "provocative action" flick is "one of the better Clancy adaptations", with Ford in "fine form" reprising his role as "what-a-man" CIA agent Jack Ryan pitted against a Colombian dope cartel; though some call it "escapist stuff", it's so "exciting" and "patriotic", you can't help but root for this "smart movie hero."

Clearing, The   16 | 22 | 16 | 17

2004 | Directed by Pieter Jan Brugge | With Robert Redford, Helen Mirren, Willem Dafoe | 95 minutes | Rated R

A "grudge-holding" ex-employee kidnaps a businessman and inadvertently sets the exec's marriage unraveling in this somewhat "intriguing", distinctly "low-key" psychological thriller; still, what's "polished" to some is "lackluster" to others, save for the "superb cast" struggling to overcome the relentlessly "slow pace" and "unfulfilling ending."

Cleopatra   19 | 18 | 19 | 25

1963 | Directed by Joseph L. Mankiewicz | With Elizabeth Taylor, Richard Burton, Rex Harrison | 192 minutes | Not Rated

"Grand, gaudy and tons of fun", this epic bio of the queen of the Nile (renowned for "breaking all production-cost records") is either a "guilty pleasure" or an "incredible waste of time"; devotees dig its "huge scale", over-the-top "entertainment" value and Liz's "exquisite" beauty, but cynics nix the flick's "bloated" look and "draggy" pace, advising that you "hit the clicker" immediately after Cleo's "showstopping entrance into Rome."

Clerks ◑   23 | 17 | 22 | 16

1994 | Directed by Kevin Smith | With Brian O'Halloran, Jeff Anderson, Marilyn Ghiglimi | 92 minutes | Rated R

"Crude" acting and "bottom-of-the-barrel production" values are redeemed by "wicked black humor" and "inspired", "raunchy" dialogue in this "microbudget indie" effort, a "fast-paced" comedy that pumps life into the "dead-end job" scene with a "realistic" look at "minimart" wage slavery; the "first foray" in Smith's "New Jersey series", it's a "slacker" "cult classic" that's "painfully funny" but unsafe for the "squeamish."

Clerks II   18 | 17 | 17 | 18

2006 | Directed by Kevin Smith | With Brian O'Halloran, Jeff Anderson, Rosario Dawson, Trevor Fehrman | 97 minutes | Rated R

The "first slackers of moviedom" are back in this "funny" sequel, now working behind the register of a fast-food joint but just as "crude" and "lewd" as ever; maybe "not as groundbreaking as the original", it's a mix of "the witty, the witless" and the "overly sentimental", peppered with the usual "gross-out" moments (i.e. that "over-the-edge donkey scene").

Click
16 | 17 | 17 | 18

2006 | Directed by Frank Coraci | With Adam Sandler, Kate Beckinsale, Christopher Walken, David Hasselhoff | 107 minutes | Rated PG-13

"Channel surfers" can relate to this "harmless" Sandler vehicle about a "whiney wimp" with a "magic remote control" that allows him to fast-forward or freeze-frame his own life; while the "cool story" has some "hilarious" moments, it gets "too preachy" in the final act when it descends into "careful-what-you-wish-for" territory.

Client, The
17 | 19 | 19 | 18

1994 | Directed by Joel Schumacher | With Susan Sarandon, Tommy Lee Jones, Brad Renfro | 120 minutes | Rated PG-13

Ok, it's "not great literature or art", but this adaptation of the John Grisham best-seller makes for a "good evening of entertainment" with its "linear story" of a youngster fleeing mobsters *and* the FBI; though too "predictable" for some, the "enjoyable Sarandon" and "impressive Renfro" keep things "interesting" enough.

Cliffhanger
15 | 12 | 15 | 19

1993 | Directed by Renny Harlin | With Sylvester Stallone, John Lithgow, Janine Turner | 113 minutes | Rated R

"*Rocky* on the rocks" sums up this "usual Stallone" action vehicle, with Sly heading a mountain rescue team beset by "nasty guys" crash-landed in the mountains; its "panoramic" backdrops and "nail-biter" sequences definitely "keep guys on the couch", but the "wooden performances" and a "quick freefall" into "implausibility" lead some to dub it a "dud" – "too bad there wasn't an avalanche."

ℤ Clockwork Orange, A
25 | 24 | 24 | 25

1971 | Directed by Stanley Kubrick | With Malcolm McDowell, Patrick Magee | 137 minutes | Rated R

"Not for the weak of heart", this "ingenious Kubrick" cult parable is a "bold", "nightmarish" "mix of sex, ultraviolence" and "mind control" set in a "freaky", "futuristic" Britain; following the travails of "unhinged" "bad boy" McDowell (the "sinister yet strangely likable" head of a "vicious gang of droogies") through his "chilling" crimes to his "brainwashing" rehab, it threads "brilliant visuals" and "twisted" "social satire" into "riveting", "artful stuff" – helped by a bit of the old "Ludwig van."

ℤ Close Encounters of the Third Kind
24 | 22 | 25 | 27

1977 | Directed by Steven Spielberg | With Richard Dreyfuss, François Truffaut, Teri Garr | 135 minutes | Rated PG

"It's ok to believe in UFOs" thanks to this "landmark" sci-fi "spectacle", a "mesmerizing", "believable contact film" wherein Spielberg's "sense of wonder" first embraces the "aliens-come-to-earth" formula; the "hopeful" plotline involves a race to "figure it all out" when strange signals arrive from the sky, and the result is a "mind-blowing" "visual treat" with plenty of "heart" (and "mountains of mashed potatoes") that delivers a "jaw-dropping" climax with a "sentimental streak" a light-year wide.

Closer

	OVERALL	ACTING	STORY	PROD.
	19	23	18	19

2004 | Directed by Mike Nichols | With Jude Law, Julia Roberts, Natalie Portman, Clive Owen | 104 minutes | Rated R

"Possibly the worst first-date movie ever", this "chilly", "caustic" look at four "seriously flawed" folks involved in a "love trapezoid" is a "feel-bad flick" alright, even if defenders "love that Clive" as well as the "intelligent direction" and "brutally honest" script; but many find the "dirty talk", "unlikable characters" and "joyless" mood too "uncomfortable to watch."

Clueless

21	19	20	20

1995 | Directed by Amy Heckerling | With Alicia Silverstone, Paul Rudd, Brittany Murphy | 97 minutes | Rated PG-13

Totally "sneaky-smart", this "lively" "update of *Emma*" with a "*90210*" twist is a "winning" comedy about LA's "spoiled rich" kids and stars a "delightful", "not-quite-acting" Silverstone, who juggles romantic uncertainty, a variety of "Valley catch phrases" and a "'90s" wardrobe "to die for"; despite a few hints of "fluff" – "whatever" – it offers "pure enjoyment" as a "pivotal teen movie" and some of the "sharpest" "bubblegum" out there.

Coach Carter

21	22	21	20

2005 | Directed by Thomas Carter | With Samuel L. Jackson | 136 minutes | Rated PG-13

"Reliably cool" Jackson hits nothin' but net with this "inspiring" tale ("based on a true story") of a "get-tough" high school hoops coach who leads his "underdog" squad to the Big Game; sure, the "feel-good" outcome may be "a bit predictable", but at the final buzzer fans cheer the "valuable" stay-in-school message, not to mention those "slam 'n' jam" B-ball scenes.

Coal Miner's Daughter ⊠

24	27	23	22

1980 | Directed by Michael Apted | With Sissy Spacek, Tommy Lee Jones, Levon Helm | 125 minutes | Rated PG

Kentucky moonshine and "bravura performances" brighten this "charming biopic" of country crooner Loretta Lynn, led by the Oscar-winning Spacek as the daughter of Appalachia who "makes it huge" in Nashville; a down-home, "down-to-earth fairy tale", its "realistic portrayal" of a star's "rise to fame" and bout with burnout plays like an "interesting" C&W take on *Behind the Music.*

Cocktail

16	15	14	16

1988 | Directed by Roger Donaldson | With Tom Cruise, Bryan Brown, Elisabeth Shue, Kelly Lynch | 104 minutes | Rated R

As "easily forgotten" as a "booze-soaked vacation", this "lightweight" romantic concoction stars a "likable" (if "mugging") Cruise as a "hot" NYC "flair bartender" who "bottle-twirls" his way to love with "rich chick" Shue; nevertheless, teetotalers groan this "watered-down highball" is nothing more than "*Top Gun* behind a bar."

Cocoanuts, The ◐

24	22	19	19

1929 | Directed by Robert Florey, Joseph Santley | With the Marx Brothers, Kay Francis | 96 minutes | Not Rated

Never mind the "technical primitiveness", this first Marx Brothers comedy is as "zany" as their later work; though this "crude" rendering of the sibs' Broadway show is burdened with "trite musical numbers" and a "weak" story involving Florida real estate, die-hard Marxists say ya "gotta love" it as an "intriguing mess" that's at worst a guarantee of "better things to come."

Cocoon

20 | 21 | 21 | 20

1985 | Directed by Ron Howard | With Don Ameche, Wilford Brimley, Hume Cronyn | 117 minutes | Rated PG-13

"Old duffers" meet "pod people" in this "warm" sci-fi tale, which spins a "clever story" of an intergalactic meet-up between extraterrestrials and Florida rest-home residents, whose backyard pool becomes a fountain of youth; the "delightful" setup and "complete characters" give some of Hollywood's elder statesmen room to "romp", while director Howard makes it all "credible" – if a bit too "warm and cuddly" for some.

Coffee and Cigarettes ◑

18 | 20 | 16 | 19

2003 | Directed by Jim Jarmusch | With Roberto Benigni, Cate Blanchett, Iggy Pop, Tom Waits, Bill Murray | 95 minutes | Rated R

Filmed episodically over 17 years, this collection of 11 black-and-white vignettes depicting conversations over caffeine and ciggies is a "hit-or-miss" proposition: sometimes "brilliant", sometimes "monotonous"; fans single out Blanchett's "amazing" double role and that "hoot" of a scene pairing Bill Murray with Wu-Tang Clan, but ultimately this one's "more for Jarmusch fans than for the general public."

Cold Mountain

22 | 24 | 22 | 26

2003 | Directed by Anthony Minghella | With Jude Law, Nicole Kidman, Renée Zellweger | 152 minutes | Rated R

The "cinematic equivalent of a coffee table book", this "beautifully shot" Civil War saga of separated lovers "adapted from Homer's *Odyssey*" stars a "smokin'" Law opposite a "too-beautiful" Kidman, ever the "fashion plate" when she's "supposed to be starving"; never mind the too-"long" running time, "watching-the-grass-grow" pacing and controversy over Renée's Oscar win ("much deserved" vs. "Granny Clampett"), at the very least, this one is "worth falling asleep on the sofa for."

Collateral

21 | 24 | 21 | 22

2004 | Directed by Michael Mann | With Tom Cruise, Jamie Foxx, Jada Pinkett Smith | 120 minutes | Rated R

Cruise sports a silver hairdo and plays "against type" as a "psychopathic" contract killer pitted against Foxx's "unassuming everyman" for one "nightmare evening" in this "taut", "edge-of-your-seat" thriller from "master-of-moods" auteur Mann; devotees say the "incongruous plot", "tacked-on romance" and "generic conclusion" are "forgivable" due to the "morally challenging" situations – and "LA never looked so beautiful and dangerous."

Collector, The

23 | 26 | 25 | 22

1965 | Directed by William Wyler | With Terence Stamp, Samantha Eggar | 119 minutes | Not Rated

A "deeply disturbed recluse" kidnaps a "lovely young woman" in this "chilling story of obsession" adapted from John Fowles' "devastating" first novel; "terrific acting by Stamp and Eggar" keeps folks "fascinated", and if this "creepy stalker film" can be "hard to watch" at times, it's still "wonderfully done."

	OVERALL	ACTING	STORY	PROD.

Color of Money, The ✉ | 16 | 21 | 16 | 17 |

1986 | Directed by Martin Scorsese | With Paul Newman, Tom Cruise, Mary Elizabeth Mastrantonio | 119 minutes | Rated R

Something different from Martin Scorsese, this "generation-later" "follow-up to *The Hustler*" details how a washed-up billiards baron molds an up-and-comer into his protégé; though somewhat "predictable", "excellent acting" from the "powerhouse Cruise" and the "finely tuned", Oscar-winning Newman "saves it."

⚡ Color Purple, The | 26 | 27 | 26 | 25 |

1985 | Directed by Steven Spielberg | With Whoopi Goldberg, Danny Glover, Oprah Winfrey | 154 minutes | Rated PG-13

A "heartfelt" reading of Alice Walker's "breakthrough" best-seller, this "moving" drama of "empowerment" "really hits home" with its depiction of a "post-slavery black family" in the Deep South and a wronged woman's "redemption and liberation"; the "breathtaking" lenswork, "Goldberg's best-ever showing" and a "brilliant" supporting cast ("Oprah can act!") make for a "teary" "triumph" that some cite as "Oscar's biggest snub."

Colors | 20 | 22 | 20 | 19 |

1988 | Directed by Dennis Hopper | With Sean Penn, Robert Duvall, Maria Conchita Alonso | 120 minutes | Rated R

"One of the first" looks at the LA gang scene, this "intense" crime flicker takes on the Crips-vs.-Bloods face-off "from the perspective of the police", i.e. Duvall and the colorful "young" Penn as, respectively, a "senior officer and a rookie"; though "worth seeing" for its "superb cast" alone, the "run-of-the-mill cop" plot "doesn't fulfill its lofty social-commentary" promise.

Coma | 19 | 19 | 22 | 18 |

1978 | Directed by Michael Crichton | With Geneviève Bujold, Michael Douglas, Richard Widmark, Rip Torn | 113 minutes | Rated PG

"Hospitals are scary" places in this "taut" conspiracy thriller based on Robin Cook's best-seller whose "clever premise" involves deliberate medical malpractice; maybe it's "lost its punch over the years" ("we've become used to the fact that hospitals screw up all the time"), yet defenders argue this "forgotten classic" is "still relevant."

Coming Home ✉ | 23 | 26 | 23 | 21 |

1978 | Directed by Hal Ashby | With Jane Fonda, Jon Voight, Bruce Dern, Penelope Milford | 126 minutes | Rated R

"Jon and Jane are magic together" in this "ultimate anti-war message" drama–cum–love triangle involving a paraplegic Vietnam vet, an "inconveniently married" hospital volunteer and a gung-ho marine; expect "moving performances" (Voight and Fonda took home Oscars) and "loads of emotion" that manage to convey a "coming of age for both the characters – and the times."

Coming to America | 18 | 18 | 17 | 17 |

1988 | Directed by John Landis | With Eddie Murphy, Arsenio Hall, James Earl Jones | 116 minutes | Rated R

"Sidesplitting", "multiple-character tour de force" showcasing the talents of "total riot" Murphy and "hilarious" Hall in a "goofy", "fish-out-of-water" comedy about an African prince who logically "heads to

Queens" to find a royal mate; hard-core groupies who can "repeat the whole movie by heart" reveal their favorite scene: "pre-*ER* Eriq Le Salle's Soul Glow" routine.

Commitments, The
24 | 23 | 23 | 21

1991 | Directed by Alan Parker | With Robert Arkins, Andrew Strong, Colm Meaney | 118 minutes | Rated R

Roddy Doyle's "classic" tale of "lower-class" Dublin youths trying to bring soul music to Ireland is a "poignant", "feel-good" take on the "passions and perils of putting your dreams into flight"; but it's the "infectious", "toe-tapping" soundtrack that really "steals the show", making this "charming" film "eminently watchable" – and "rewatchable."

Company, The
19 | 18 | 15 | 22

2003 | Directed by Robert Altman | With Neve Campbell, Malcolm McDowell, James Franco | 112 minutes | Rated PG-13

Going "behind the curtain of a dance company", this "fly-on-the-wall" look at Chicago's Joffrey Ballet is primarily a "beautiful choreography showcase" peppered with some "backstage" backbiting between numbers to tie it all together; "not one of Altman's best", it's "interesting but far from electrifying" since there's "no discernable plot."

Con Air
14 | 15 | 14 | 18

1997 | Directed by Simon West | With Nicolas Cage, John Cusack, John Malkovich, Steve Buscemi | 115 minutes | Rated R

"Hardened criminals" en route to a "high-security prison" skyjack their plane in this "popcorn action flick" that's a "no-brainer" if you're ready for an "enjoyably obnoxious" experience; foes protest this "testosteronefest" has "little plot" and "just-collecting-a-paycheck" acting, but worst of all is Cage's "horrific mullet."

Conan the Barbarian
16 | 9 | 15 | 18

1982 | Directed by John Milius | With Arnold Schwarzenegger, James Earl Jones | 129 minutes | Rated R

The flick that "brought Arnold to everyone's attention", this "archetypal sword-and-sorcery fantasy" about a "barbarian butt-kicker" is "all a teenage boy could want" in a movie, conjuring up a pulpy, "no-holds-barred world of lust and vengeance"; even though Schwarzenegger's "acting isn't that great" – it was "before he learned to talk" – his "muscles are expressive" enough.

Confessions of a Dangerous Mind
19 | 23 | 19 | 20

2003 | Directed by George Clooney | With Sam Rockwell, Drew Barrymore, George Clooney | 113 minutes | Rated R

"Odd but oddly compelling", this bio of "game show guru" Chuck Barris is a "real eyebrow-raiser", intercutting his antics as host of *The Gong Show* with his "secret life" as a "CIA hit man"; while the dual careers are too "preposterous" and "bizarro" for many to swallow ("puhleeze"), some confess the picture "grows on you the more you watch it" – what it lacks in logic, "it makes up for in nerve."

Confidence
18 | 21 | 19 | 19

2003 | Directed by James Foley | With Edward Burns, Rachel Weisz, Andy Garcia, Dustin Hoffman | 97 minutes | Rated R

"First-rate" casting and a "twist-and-turn"-till-you-drop heist plot provide the uplift in this "solid" caper that also earns kudos for

Hoffman's turn as a "delightfully sleazy" crime boss; comparisons to *The Sting* abound, with converts cheering this one's "just as good", while contras shrug it's "nothing you haven't seen before."

☑ Conformist, The ⬛   26 | 26 | 27 | 26

1971 | Directed by Bernardo Bertolucci | With Jean-Louis Trintignant, Stefania Sandrelli, Dominique Sanda | 115 minutes | Rated R
Director "Bertolucci is at his absolute best" in this "supercool, super-stylized" Italian psychological drama set in the '30s about an "emotionally troubled civil servant" turned "fascist agent"; nonconformists warn "beware the dubbed version" but concur that Vittorio Storaro's "haunting" cinematography transcends dialogue; hottest moment: that "erotic tango" between Sanda and Sandrelli.

Constant Gardener, The   23 | 26 | 23 | 24

2005 | Directed by Fernando Meirelles | With Ralph Fiennes, Rachel Weisz | 129 minutes | Rated R
The "politically pertinent" topic of pharmaceutical companies' alleged "exploitation of third-world citizens" forms the "fascinating" backdrop of this "tautly woven" thriller–cum–"haunting" love story featuring the "ever dependable" Fiennes as an "uptight English diplomat" who unravels a "mystery" involving his activist wife (the "fabulous" Weisz); based on John Le Carré's "complex" novel, it's undoubtedly "more exciting than its title might suggest", and provides plenty of "food for thought."

Constantine   16 | 15 | 18 | 21

2005 | Directed by Francis Lawrence | With Keanu Reeves, Rachel Weisz, Shia LaBeouf | 121 minutes | Rated R
"Stylish" is the word for this supernatural thriller adapted from the *Hellblazer* comic books revolving around a world-weary exorcist enacted by a "wooden" Reeves (replete with a man-in-black wardrobe "right out of *The Matrix*"); critics wish the "dialogue was as refined as the special effects", but admit its "ridiculousness factor" can be mesmerizing.

Contact   20 | 21 | 20 | 22

1997 | Directed by Robert Zemeckis | With Jodie Foster, Matthew McConaughey, Tom Skerritt | 153 minutes | Rated PG
This "thinking person's" sci-fi flick asks the "Big Question" – "are we alone" in the universe?; true believers cite the "excellent special effects", "fascinating" story and a fine Foster "near the top of her form", but the alienated dismiss it as "long-winded" and "preachy", opting to "read Carl Sagan's excellent book" instead.

Contempt ⬛   25 | 24 | 22 | 24

1964 | Directed by Jean-Luc Godard | With Brigitte Bardot, Michel Piccoli, Jack Palance, Fritz Lang | 104 minutes | Not Rated
The "struggle between commerce and artistic integrity" gets the Godard treatment in this "scathing" "movie about movies" that details a screenwriter's struggle to adapt James Joyce's *Ulysses* and simultaneously keep his marriage from unraveling; with a "coquettish" Bardot and a "full-throttle" Palance on board, "stunning" Mediterranean vistas in CinemaScope and a "cameo from director Fritz Lang", it's a fine example of "classic French New Wave" that's "showy, smart" and "enjoyably pretentious."

Contender, The

2000 | Directed by Rod Lurie | With Joan Allen, Gary Oldman, Jeff Bridges, Christian Slater | 126 minutes | Rated R

In this Clinton White House–ish "Washington soap opera" (that will keep you "guessing till the end"), a "scrappy" female pol "stays true to her principles" at great cost to her reputation and career; though Allen is "superb" and Bridges would make a "fine" real-life prez, some pundits protest the drama's "tackling of big issues" as "overblown melodrama."

Conversation, The

1974 | Directed by Francis Ford Coppola | With Gene Hackman, John Cazale, Frederic Forrest | 113 minutes | Rated PG

A "brilliant" thriller about a "paranoid" surveillance specialist who comes undone, this "little-known" Coppola feature features a "virtuoso performance by Hackman", whose gradual "deterioration is amazing" (there's also an appearance by a very young Harrison Ford); though a bit "slow-moving", the script is so "superbly constructed" that "if this flick doesn't put you on edge, nothing will."

Cook, the Thief, His Wife & Her Lover, The

1990 | Directed by Peter Greenaway | With Michael Gambon, Helen Mirren, Richard Bohringer, Alan Howard | 124 minutes | Rated NC-17

Definitely "not for the timid", this "disturbingly dark" "art-house" comedy takes gastronomic and sexual "debauchery" to the furthest extremes (think cannibalism) in its depiction of adultery and "revenge" in a French restaurant; "gorgeous production design", a "superb" cast and an "intellectual", "unorthodox" plot make it "worth suffering through the icky bits."

Cooler, The

2003 | Directed by Wayne Kramer | With William H. Macy, Maria Bello, Alec Baldwin | 101 minutes | Rated R

"Losing is winning" for the perpetually "unlucky" title character in this "quirky" dramedy about a Vegas shill hired by a casino to "jinx high-rollers' winning streaks"; an "unglamorous" spin on the usual gambling yarn, it boasts "riveting acting" and a "believable love story", though some say the "gratuitous violence" and Macy's "racy" nude scenes are more of a "crapshoot."

∃ Cool Hand Luke

1967 | Directed by Stuart Rosenberg | With Paul Newman, George Kennedy, Strother Martin | 126 minutes | Not Rated

"One of the best movie lines ever" ('what we have here is a failure to communicate') and that "famous hard-boiled egg scene" make this "damn great" Deep South prison drama memorable – not to mention the efforts of "consummate pro" Newman playing one cool con on a "chain gang", abetted by a "strong" Kennedy, who grabbed an Oscar for his supporting work.

Cool Runnings

1993 | Directed by Jon Turteltaub | With John Candy, Doug E. Doug, Leon, Malik Yoba | 98 minutes | Rated PG

Granted, it might be "silly", but this "cute", "underrated" comedy "based on the true" tale of the '88 Olympics' "Jamaican bobsled team" is "fun for the whole family" (despite "a bit too much profanity");

cheerleaders say its "come-from-behind" story will "touch anyone's heart", particularly those who "miss John Candy."

Cop Land
| 17 | 19 | 18 | 17 |

1997 | Directed by James Mangold | With Sylvester Stallone, Harvey Keitel, Ray Liotta, Robert De Niro | 104 minutes | Rated R

"Crooked NYC cops" face off against a "small-town" NJ sheriff in this "way-before-*The-Sopranos*" crime drama that builds to a "violent", *High Noon*-ish climax; it's a natural "if you like Italian actors", with a "surprisingly solid performance" from Stallone, who packed on enough extra pounds for the role to hold his own against the "heavyweight" cast.

Corpse Bride, The
| 20 | - | 19 | 25 |

2005 | Directed by Tim Burton, Mike Johnson | Animated | 76 minutes | Rated PG

From the "macabre" mind of Tim Burton and in the spirit of "*The Nightmare Before Christmas*" comes this "ghoulishly entertaining" fairy tale pulsing with "eye-popping" stop-motion animation and "raucous" musical numbers; make no bones about it, Johnny Depp's voicing of a "groom who's stolen away to the world of the dead" is an added "pleasure", though some maligners mourn the "trite" story.

Cotton Club, The
| 20 | 20 | 19 | 23 |

1984 | Directed by Francis Ford Coppola | With Richard Gere, Gregory Hines, Diane Lane, Bob Hoskins | 127 minutes | Rated R

Coppola's "ambitious", big-budget "homage to the Jazz Age" pits "heartsick lovers" against murderous "mobsters" in a "period" Harlem nightclub setting; although it's somewhat "uneven" due to a "meandering" plot that "never comes together", compensations include "wonderful" acting, "beautiful set design" and "brilliant musical numbers", especially that "not-to-be-missed" "tap duel" by the Hines brothers.

Counterfeit Traitor, The
| 25 | 25 | 26 | 23 |

1962 | Directed by George Seaton | With William Holden, Lili Palmer, Hugh Griffith | 140 minutes | Not Rated

"Based on a true story", this "classy" (albeit "forgotten") WWII spy thriller revolves around a Swedish "quisling" blacklisted by the Allies after trading with the Nazis; in the title role, the "dashing" Holden is in his "gracefully aging prime", though some say the "deeply moving" Palmer steals the show as his "noble" confederate.

Count of Monte Cristo, The
| 19 | 20 | 22 | 22 |

2002 | Directed by Kevin Reynolds | With James Caviezel, Guy Pearce, Richard Harris | 131 minutes | Rated PG-13

"Revenge is sweet" in this "well-crafted" swashbuckler about a man wrongfully imprisoned plotting epic payback; fans like its "old-fashioned", "golden-age-of-Hollywood" approach ("great swordplay", "excellent production values", "enough romance to keep the girls interested"), but foes yawn that this "500th remake of the Dumas classic" is "nothing new" and "not particularly engaging."

Country Girl, The ✉◑
| 24 | 26 | 23 | 23 |

1954 | Directed by George Seaton | With Bing Crosby, Grace Kelly, William Holden | 104 minutes | Not Rated

Kelly ventures "out of her normal range" into Oscar-winning territory as a "frumpy" gal married to an alcoholic "actor on the skids" in this

| | OVERALL | ACTING | STORY | PROD. |

"top-notch" drama adapted from the Clifford Odets play; Crosby also "plays against type" to "memorable" effect, while the "brilliant" Holden completes the trifecta by supplying the romantic "tension."

Cousin, Cousine 🄵∅

21 20 21 19

1976 | Directed by Jean-Charles Tacchella | With Marie-Christine Barrault, Victor Lanoux | 95 minutes | Rated R

This "sweet but naughty" French farce about romantically involved cousins-by-marriage offers a "refreshing" take on family dynamics; while some say it's "much better than the American" remake (*Cousins*), those suffering from memory lapses "can't recall anything" except – *zut alors!* – Barrault's "naked breasts."

Crash ✉

26 27 26 25

2005 | Directed by Paul Haggis | With Sandra Bullock, Don Cheadle, Matt Dillon, Brendan Fraser, Terrence Howard, Ludacris, Thandie Newton, Ryan Phillippe | 113 minutes | Rated R

"Everyone's a little bit racist" according to this "provocative" treatment of "prejudice in America", a Best Picture Oscar grabber about "intertwined lives" in LA that "break down stereotypes" and "make you rethink your values"; with a "dream-team cast" enlivening the "incredible writing", expect to collide with some "tough", "wonderfully unpredictable" scenes that deliver a "powerful message."

☑ Cries and Whispers 🄵

26 28 24 26

1972 | Directed by Ingmar Bergman | With Harriet Andersson, Liv Ullmann, Ingrid Thulin | 106 minutes | Rated R

"Compelling is an understatement" when it comes to this "tortured masterpiece", a "raw", "close-in study of three sisters and their prickly relationship" that's "quintessential Bergman"; although it's "well acted" and "handsomely mounted", its depiction of "pain" is so "hard to watch" that some ask "are you sure 'angst' isn't a Swedish word?"

Crimes and Misdemeanors

26 26 25 24

1989 | Directed by Woody Allen | With Woody Allen, Mia Farrow, Anjelica Huston, Martin Landau | 107 minutes | Rated PG-13

"Crime does pay" in this "deeply serious" Allen dramedy with dual plotlines, one about a murderous philanderer, the other a "socially inept" filmmaker; "ruthlessly truthful", it manages to be alternately "scathing", "thought-provoking" and "hilarious", with "dead-on casting" and an "expert" scenario to boot.

Crimes of the Heart

21 25 21 21

1986 | Directed by Bruce Beresford | With Diane Keaton, Jessica Lange, Sissy Spacek | 105 minutes | Rated PG-13

"Three big-name movie stars" play three "loopy" Southern sisters in this "touching" drama about a weepy reunion brought about after one of the gals has shot her husband; adapted by Beth Henley from her Pulitzer Prize–winning play, it's a prominent contender in the "chick-flick" pantheon, but be prepared for a "determinedly wacky" point of view.

Crimson Tide

21 24 22 22

1995 | Directed by Tony Scott | With Denzel Washington, Gene Hackman, George Dzundza | 116 minutes | Rated R

"Gripping", "tightly plotted" action flick relating the "macho machinations aboard a submarine" as two officers square off over a nuclear launch that could trigger an "unprovoked war"; given the "smart", "thought-provoking" acting of "big-screen titans" Washington and Hackman, you can expect a "first-rate" ride, even if some shrug it off as a "*Hunt for Red October* wannabe."

Crocodile Dundee
17 | 14 | 17 | 16

1986 | Directed by Peter Faiman | With Paul Hogan, Linda Kozlowski | 98 minutes | Rated PG-13

This "surprise hit from Down Under" is a classic "fish-out-of-water" comedy about a transplanted Aussie "clashing with the ways of the modern world"; though critics split on Hogan's appeal – "charming" vs. "better in Subaru commercials" – overall, it's "lightweight" fun.

Crossing Delancey
23 | 23 | 23 | 21

1988 | Directed by Joan Micklin Silver | With Amy Irving, Peter Riegert, Sylvia Miles | 97 minutes | Rated PG

This "romantic comedy with a Jewish twist" earns "*mazel tovs*" for its "endearing" story of an "intellectual" striver, set up with a "pickle vendor" thanks to "old-school matchmaking" from her "meddling" bubbe; despite crossing into "schmaltzy" territory, it's "well acted" and "relevant for all those single gals" who hope "all's well that ends well."

Crouching Tiger, Hidden Dragon ✉🅕
24 | 23 | 21 | 28

2000 | Directed by Ang Lee | With Chow Yun-Fat, Michelle Yeoh, Zhang Ziyi | 120 minutes | Rated PG-13

Whether it's a "kung fu chick flick", a "thinking person's" martial arts film or "'chop-socky' translated into art", this "surreal" fantasy is full of "eye-popping fight sequences" that are half "ballet", half "Bruce Lee"; most memorable for its "strong female characters" and that "encounter in the bamboo forest", it's nothing less than a "breath of fresh air on the stale movie landscape."

Crow, The
21 | 19 | 21 | 22

1994 | Directed by Alex Proyas | With Brandon Lee, Michael Wincott, Bai Ling | 102 minutes | Not Rated

"Channel your inner Goth" via this "wonderfully dark", blazingly "stylish" comic book adaptation about a corpse brought back to life as an "avenging angel", played out against an "awesome" alt-rock soundtrack; sadly, it's best known for the "tragic death" of its star, Brandon Lee, "accidentally killed when a gun misfired" during production.

Crucible, The
19 | 21 | 23 | 19

1996 | Directed by Nicholas Hytner | With Daniel Day-Lewis, Winona Ryder, Joan Allen, Paul Scofield | 124 minutes | Rated PG-13

Arthur Miller's "classic" play gets a "first-rate" stage-to-screen transfer in this "devastating", "depressing" drama in which the "Salem witch trials" of the 1690s stand in for the Cold War "mass hysteria" of the 1950s; "strong performances" from Day-Lewis and Allen compensate for the "scarcely believable" Ryder.

Cry-Baby
17 | 16 | 15 | 16

1990 | Directed by John Waters | With Johnny Depp, Amy Locane, Susan Tyrrell | 85 minutes | Rated PG-13

"Kinda dumb" in a "classic B-movie" way, this "wacko" John Waters comedy set in 1950s Baltimore tells the story of a "boring square" who decides she's "tired of being good" and falls for a "troublemaking greaser"; given its "similarities to *West Side Story*", some call it the director's "most mainstream" work, but a few babies cry about "caricatures rather than characters" and "emoting rather than emotion."

Crying Game, The ✉   22 | 24 | 24 | 20
1992 | Directed by Neil Jordan | With Stephen Rea, Miranda Richardson, Jaye Davidson | 112 minutes | Rated R
"Violence and pathos" are served in the "right amounts" in this "disturbing" British drama about an "IRA recruit who's not really committed to his cause"; most famed for its whopper of a "surprise twist" (that leaves some "still flabbergasted"), this "intense vision of terrorism" offers enough nuanced "questions about race, sex and country" to justify a Best Screenplay Oscar.

Cujo   17 | 16 | 19 | 18
1983 | Directed by Lewis Teague | With Dee Wallace, Danny Pintauro, Christopher Stone | 91 minutes | Rated R
"Dog lovers beware": this "intense" frightfest following a rabid St. Bernard on a "scary" rampage may put you off "canine companions" forever; yet young pups brought up on "high-tech horror" shrug it "doesn't cut it" – the "tension of Stephen King's novel isn't there" and they even "changed the original ending."

Curious George   19 | - | 19 | 21
2006 | Directed by Matthew O'Callaghan | Animated | 86 minutes | Rated G
"Belly laughs for the diaper set" abound in this "cuddly" animated feature (based on the "beloved storybook") that tells the tale of the "man in the yellow hat" and the "cutest monkey ever" with enough "simple innocence" to be "completely safe" for all ages; some say all that "kid stuff" can be "kinda boring", but "preschoolers" will be "glued to the screen."

Curse of the Golden Flower 𝔽   21 | 21 | 18 | 27
2006 | Directed by Zhang Yimou | With Chow Yun-Fat, Gong Li, Liu Ye | 114 minutes | Rated R
Think "Shakespeare filtered through Confucius" to get the gist of this "eye-popping" production that "re-creates the wonders of ancient China" in its "convoluted" tale of palace intrigue and "family loyalty gone bad"; "lavish sets", "awe-inspiring action" and a "cast of thousands" compensate for a somewhat "depthless" story infused with "too much majesty" and "not enough intimacy."

Damage   22 | 25 | 21 | 21
1992 | Directed by Louis Malle | With Jeremy Irons, Juliette Binoche, Miranda Richardson, Rupert Graves | 111 minutes | Rated R
The "penalties of infidelity" infuse this "mesmerizing tale of sexual obsession", wherein a "middle-aged man" embarks on a "cringe-inducing" affair with his son's fiancée; the acting's "galvanizing" and the "art-house sex" scenes "acrobatic", so whether the end result is "profound" or "pretentious", it's decidedly good "dinner-party"-debate fodder.

Damned, The   23 | 24 | 21 | 23
1969 | Directed by Luchino Visconti | With Dirk Bogarde, Helmut Berger, Ingrid Thulin, Charlotte Rampling | 157 minutes | Rated R
Steel yourself for "decadence on parade" in this "sick, slick" look at a family of "jaded" German industrialists who ally themselves with

the Nazis on the eve of WWII; both "absorbing and repellent in equal measure", it's "kinky" alright, though "outstanding production values" and the "beautiful Rampling" make it slightly more palatable for general audiences.

Damn Yankees
24 | 23 | 23 | 24

1958 | Directed by George Abbott, Stanley Donen | With Gwen Verdon, Tab Hunter, Ray Walston | 111 minutes | Not Rated

This screen adaptation of the Faust-influenced Broadway musical recounts how a "man makes a pact with the devil" to guarantee that the "Washington Senators win the pennant"; reprising their stage roles, Walston is at his "evil best" as Lucifer, while the "too-rarely-seen" Verdon gets what she wants as his sidekick, Lola; it's a "perfect evocation of the national optimism of the '50s" with a "great score" and a bonus: "Bob Fosse's mambo."

Dancer in the Dark
22 | 23 | 20 | 22

2000 | Directed by Lars von Trier | With Björk, Catherine Deneuve, David Morse | 140 minutes | Rated R

A "musical like no other", this "dynamic" if "depressing" film "pushes the genre to the limit" in its account of an immigrant Czech "factory worker going blind who finds redemption only in music"; while foes find it "difficult to watch" – "even painful" – artistes laud its "wondrously strange" feel and praise pop star Björk's "amazing acting chops" and "compelling" vocal work.

Dances with Wolves ✉
23 | 20 | 22 | 25

1990 | Directed by Kevin Costner | With Kevin Costner, Mary McDonnell, Graham Greene | 183 minutes | Rated PG-13

For once, American Indians are portrayed in a "human light" in this "picturesque, sweeping epic" about a Civil War soldier who goes West, joins the Sioux and finds love along the way; although "beautifully shot" and quite the Oscar magnet (seven statuettes, including Best Picture), this "guy flick that women love" has critics citing a "monotonous", way-"too-long" running time.

Dangerous Beauty
21 | 21 | 20 | 24

1998 | Directed by Marshall Herskovitz | With Catherine McCormack, Rufus Sewell, Oliver Platt, Jacqueline Bisset | 111 minutes | Rated R

"Glittery" Renaissance Venice "in all its glory" is no match for an "outstanding" McCormack, playing an "intriguing" courtesan opposite "heartthrob" Sewell in this "pleasing" period love story; "beautiful cinematography" and "marvelous costumes" add to its "chick-flick" appeal, while "clever" commentary on "gender roles" complements the "eye feast."

Dangerous Liaisons ✉
24 | 26 | 24 | 26

1988 | Directed by Stephen Frears | With Glenn Close, John Malkovich, Michelle Pfeiffer | 119 minutes | Rated R

"Malkovich quietly chews up the scenery" opposite "perfectly evil" "ice queen" Close in this "flawless" drama set in "decadent", 17th-century France rife with "treachery, betrayal and sexual games" among the "upper classes" ("no wonder the peasants revolted"); still, its "sumptuous production" and Oscar-winning screenplay make the "manipulating" characters more palatable.

OVERALL | ACTING | STORY | PROD.

Dangerous Lives of Altar Boys, The | 19 | 21 | 19 | 19

2002 | Directed by Peter Care | With Kieran Culkin, Jena Malone, Emile Hirsch, Jodie Foster | 104 minutes | Rated R

"If you're into comic books or went to Catholic school", this "coming-of-age" drama "captures the essence" of "teen angst" among "mischievous" parochial kids and boasts an "inventive" visual style "mixing live action" with "cool" cartoon segments; it showcases Culkin's "great promise", and if skeptics shrug at "discombobulated" plotting, acolytes applaud a "solidly crafted" effort.

Daredevil | 14 | 14 | 14 | 19

2003 | Directed by Mark Steven Johnson | With Ben Affleck, Jennifer Garner, Colin Farrell | 103 minutes | Rated PG-13

"Ben Affleck in tights" may be a "big draw in Greenwich Village", but he's pretty "disappointing" everywhere else as the title character of this action/adventurer based on Marvel Comics' blind superhero, a lawyer by day turned freelance vigilante at night; despite the "delicious" Garner, "over-the-top" Farrell and "high-energy", Hong Kong–style fight sequences, most advise "watch *Spiderman* instead."

Darjeeling Limited, The | 17 | 19 | 16 | 20

2007 | Directed by Wes Anderson | With Owen Wilson, Adrien Brody, Jason Schwartzman | 91 minutes | Rated R

Wes Anderson's latest "quirky" "mystery tour" follows three estranged, "Salinger-esque" brothers who reunite on a subcontinental train ride, making stops for "witty", "existential" and "heartfelt" observations along their "journey to self-awareness"; despite "touching" performances and "breathtaking" shots of the Indian countryside, some say it's too "plodding" – like "going nowhere with heavy suitcases."

Dark Crystal, The | 24 | - | 24 | 26

1982 | Directed by Jim Henson, Frank Oz | With puppet characters | 93 minutes | Rated PG

"Sinister muppets" take the stage in this "classic" "all-puppet feature", a "magical fairy tale" with an "otherworldly good and evil" storyline that represents the "culmination of Jim Henson's imagination"; while the "stunning visuals" please crowds, some warn that the "dark" plot "may be too scary" for smaller fry.

Z Dark Victory ◑ | 25 | 27 | 23 | 23

1939 | Directed by Edmund Goulding | With Bette Davis, George Brent, Humphrey Bogart | 104 minutes | Not Rated

"Sensational" Bette at her "Warner Brothers peak" "turns camp into classic" in this melodramatic "tearjerker" about an heiress who's got everything – including a brain tumor; sob sisters say it's "worth every hanky" for Davis' "valiant" turn (one of the "best performances of 1939") and keep their eye out for a "young Ronald Reagan" in a supporting role.

Darling ✉◑ | 22 | 25 | 20 | 21

1965 | Directed by John Schlesinger | With Julie Christie, Dirk Bogarde, Laurence Harvey | 128 minutes | Not Rated

Get a "glimpse of the Swinging '60s" via this "quintessential" story of a "self-absorbed" "model/party girl" who "makes it to the top" only to find "there's nothing there"; if the film feels "a bit dated", at least it's "cast to perfection" – the "smashing", Oscar-winning Christie is "at the height of her beauty and acting powers" here.

☒ Das Boot 🇫

28 | 26 | 26 | 27

1982 | Directed by Wolfgang Petersen | With Jürgen Prochnow, Herbert Grönemeyer | 149 minutes | Rated R

When it comes to "underwater über alles" action, it's hard to top this "sweaty, claustrophobic" saga of "doomed German sailors" engaged in a "battle of egos" in a U-boat at the "bottom of the ocean"; though it's almost an "anti-recruiting film" given its "harrowing" realism, it exhibits enough "depth" to prove that "fear has no nationality" – you'll almost "root for" the Nazis.

Dave

21 | 22 | 22 | 20

1993 | Directed by Ivan Reitman | With Kevin Kline, Sigourney Weaver, Frank Langella | 110 minutes | Rated PG-13

"Kline's adorable, as usual" in this "funny" political satire about an average "doofus" who looks so much like the President that he's asked to pinch-hit and winds up putting "faith back in government"; a latter-day *Mr. Smith Goes to Washington*", this comedy has a "serious message", though conspiracy theorists say the message is "proof that liberals really do run Hollywood."

☒ David Copperfield ◐

▽ 27 | 26 | 27 | 25

1935 | Directed by George Cukor | With Freddie Bartholomew, W.C. Fields, Lionel Barrymore | 130 minutes | Not Rated

"One of the gems" of the Hollywood versions of "classic novels", this "wonderfully atmospheric", "very Dickensian" production may be a bit "creaky", though ultimately most of its "scenes are truly effective"; credit the "brilliant acting" from the MGM "repertory company", an "inspired" bunch headed up by Fields, whose "agile, hilarious" performance as Mr. Micawber is a "joy to watch."

Da Vinci Code, The

19 | 18 | 21 | 22

2006 | Directed by Ron Howard | With Tom Hanks, Audrey Tautou, Ian McKellen | 149 minutes | Rated PG-13

Despite "all the hype", surveyors split on this "glossy" adaptation of Dan Brown's mega-popular "page-turner" about a "human" Jesus who "married Mary Magdalene": admirers call it a "well-crafted" thriller packed with "fun puzzles", "magnificent" European settings and "intriguing" "intellectual banter", but contras say the "hard-to-follow" story "leaves little room" for the actors to strut ("Hanks is sleepwalking"), feeling that what was "fast-paced" in the novel is "lumberingly slow" here; ultimately, the "book was better" – "aren't they always?"

Dawn of the Dead

19 | 12 | 19 | 17

1978 | Directed by George A. Romero | With David Emge, Ken Foree, Scott Reiniger, Gaylen Ross | 128 minutes | Rated R

"It's not just another day at the mall" as director Romero (*Night of the Living Dead*) brings his zombie franchise "back to life" via this "graphic gorefest" about survivors of an "apocalyptic nightmare" trapped in a shopping center besieged by hordes of the "walking dead"; a "morbidly funny" "critique of consumerism" with plenty of "heart and guts" (not to mention "cheesy" effects and "bad acting"), this is "seminal" horror.

Dawn of the Dead   19 | 16 | 17 | 21

2004 | Directed by Zack Snyder | With Sarah Polley, Ving Rhames, Jake Weber, Mekhi Phifer | 101 minutes | Rated R

The "old horror classic" set in a ghoul-infested shopping mall receives a "fresh update" (i.e. "faster zombies") in this "excellent remake" that "does its predecessor proud"; "scary when it's supposed to be" and similarly "funny" at the right moments, it's an "entertaining" look at a "world gone mad – and then some"; P.S. "stay with the end credits" for some extra "bonus thrills."

Day After Tomorrow, The   16 | 14 | 14 | 24

2004 | Directed by Roland Emmerich | With Dennis Quaid, Jake Gyllenhaal, Emmy Rossum, Ian Holm | 124 minutes | Rated PG-13

"Weather is the enemy" in this "high-gloss" sci-fi "thrill ride" with a "virtuous environmental message" underlying its story of a "killer ice age" ironically brought on by "global warming"; alright, the "impressive special effects" are a "helluva lot of fun" (notably the "destruction of all your favorite landmarks"), but critics "cringe" at the "bad science", "hammy acting" and "check-your-brain-at-the-door" plot; for many, this one's "not a disaster movie", simply a "disaster."

Day at the Races, A ◑   24 | 21 | 20 | 19

1937 | Directed by Sam Wood | With the Marx Brothers, Maureen O'Sullivan, Margaret Dumont | 111 minutes | Not Rated

The "Marx Brothers at their zenith of zaniness" horse around in this "very funny" comedy about a veterinarian turned human doctor; though some say it's a "slightly second-tier" also-ran (only "sporadically funny" and even a tad "racist"), it was nevertheless one of the boys' "biggest box office hits."

☑ Day for Night ✉🅵   27 | 25 | 25 | 25

1973 | Directed by François Truffaut | With Jacqueline Bisset, Valentina Cortese, Jean-Pierre Léaud | 115 minutes | Rated PG

"Truffaut's homage to American filmmaking", this "quintessential movie about making movies" "perfectly captures" all the "behind-the-scenes" "neuroses" and "joy" from an insider's point of view; though it shows the director "at his lightest", the "magical" result was both "charming" and "wacky" enough for it to take home a Best Foreign Language picture Oscar.

☑ Day of the Jackal, The   25 | 24 | 27 | 22

1973 | Directed by Fred Zinnemann | With Edward Fox, Michael Lonsdale, Delphine Seyrig | 145 minutes | Rated PG

"Grip the edge of your seat and hang on" for a "fast-paced" game of "cat and mouse" as this "riveting" thriller follows the race to foil a "legendary" hit man's "plot to assassinate Charles de Gaulle"; a "top-notch cast" and "true-to-the-book intelligence" keep things "tense until the very end", so fans of "crackling suspense" call it the "real deal" – and wonder "why they bothered to remake it."

Day of the Locust, The   20 | 21 | 21 | 21

1975 | Directed by John Schlesinger | With Donald Sutherland, Karen Black, Burgess Meredith, William Atherton | 144 minutes | Rated R

"Hollywood's penchant for crushing dreams" gets the John Schlesinger treatment in this "really dark" adaptation of Nathanael

West's "cautionary satire" about down-and-out types scrambling to make it big in Tinseltown during the Depression; it's "powerful, disturbing" stuff with "fine" work from Sutherland and an ending so "frightening" that many "still can't be in a crowd without thinking about it."

Days of Heaven 23 | 21 | 20 | 25

1978 | Directed by Terrence Malick | With Richard Gere, Brooke Adams, Sam Shepard | 95 minutes | Rated PG

"Underseen but not underappreciated", this "gorgeous" if "bleak" drama detailing a love triangle between two dirt-poor migrant workers and a loaded landowner "broke new ground" in its use of "beautiful cinematography" to take the place of conventional exposition; though it "speaks volumes without much dialogue", low-attention-span types yawn "not terribly compelling."

☑ Days of Wine and Roses ◑ 27 | 28 | 25 | 24

1962 | Directed by Blake Edwards | With Jack Lemmon, Lee Remick, Charles Bickford | 117 minutes | Not Rated

For a "tough look" at a "serious issue", this "harrowing" drama about the "ravages of alcoholism" was a "huge breakthrough in its day" and remains "relevant" thanks to "tear-your-heart-out" performances from Lemmon and Remick as "desperate" young marrieds "lost in the bottom of the bottle"; "Henry Mancini's haunting title song" won the Oscar and "says it all."

Day the Earth Stood Still, The ◑ 25 | 20 | 26 | 21

1951 | Directed by Robert Wise | With Michael Rennie, Patricia Neal, Sam Jaffe | 92 minutes | Rated G

"Fifties-era real-life fears about the fate of humanity" are the backbone of this "Cold War sci-fi" flick about a "benevolent alien" invasion of Washington, DC; sure, the "less-is-more special effects" seem "dated" and "primitive by today's standards", but the "underlying message" – "world peace or else!" – makes this one "very enlightened for its time."

Dazed and Confused 22 | 19 | 20 | 18

1993 | Directed by Richard Linklater | With Jason London, Rory Cochrane, Sasha Jenson | 103 minutes | Rated R

Revolving around the "shameless" antics of a bunch of teenagers "getting loaded, laid and in trouble" on the "last day of school", this "coming-of-age" flick recalls *American Graffiti* transposed to the 1970s and induces "big laughs" from "characters you quickly fall in love with"; throw in a "killer soundtrack", and it's just the ticket for a "brainless afternoon."

Dead Again 22 | 24 | 24 | 22

1991 | Directed by Kenneth Branagh | With Kenneth Branagh, Andy Garcia, Emma Thompson | 107 minutes | Rated R

There are "good twists and mind tricks" aplenty in this "stylish, pseudo-noir thriller" about a detective drawn into a decades-old murder mystery; deadheads dig its "riveting performances", "Dali-esque imagery" and that "wonderful twist at the end", swearing you'll never look at a "pair of scissors" the same way after seeing this "over-the-top" "nail-biter."

Dead Calm 20 | 21 | 21 | 19

1989 | Directed by Phillip Noyce | With Nicole Kidman, Sam Neill, Billy Zane | 96 minutes | Rated R

A "married couple" yachting "on the high seas" are terrorized by an "over-the-top psychopath" in this "creepy open-water thriller" that delivers "nail-biting" chills plus an "early look at La Kidman" enduring "desperation" (and "frightfully mismanaged hair"); it's a dead-on "popcorn flick" that'll "make you jump" – and also "think twice about chartering a boat."

Dead Man Walking ✉ 23 | 26 | 23 | 21

1995 | Directed by Tim Robbins | With Susan Sarandon, Sean Penn, Robert Prosky | 122 minutes | Rated R

"Based on a true story", this "enlightening" study of capital punishment is also a "profound lesson in human compassion" thanks to "poignant" turns from a "riveting" Penn as a "condemned killer" and the Oscar-winning Sarandon as a nun bent on leading him to "redemption"; although "unsettling and disturbing" overall, the picture "provides both sides of the death-penalty argument" in an "objective", "unflinching" manner.

Dead Men Don't Wear Plaid ◑ 20 | 20 | 18 | 22

1982 | Directed by Carl Reiner | With Steve Martin, Rachel Ward | 89 minutes | Rated PG

Martin's "satirical look at noir films" involves the "clever use of old footage" (featuring stars like Humphrey Bogart, Ingrid Bergman and Lana Turner) that's intercut into a "silly" story about a deadbeat, '40s-era detective; fans of splice comedies say this one was way "ahead of its time", long before "mashups and remixes", though a few opine it's only "fun for movie buffs and a curiosity for everyone else."

☒ Dead Poets Society ✉ 24 | 25 | 24 | 23

1989 | Directed by Peter Weir | With Robin Williams, Robert Sean Leonard, Ethan Hawke | 128 minutes | Rated PG

"Living with rules" vs. "living with passion" gets the big-screen treatment in this "uplifting" drama about an "inspirational teacher" who admonishes his students with a ringing "'carpe diem!'"; thanks to the Oscar-winning screenplay and Williams' ultra-"convincing" turn as the "influential mentor", many say this "wake-up call" of a movie should be "mandatory classroom viewing."

Dead Pool, The 19 | 20 | 19 | 19

1988 | Directed by Buddy Van Horn | With Clint Eastwood, Patricia Clarkson, Liam Neeson | 91 minutes | Rated R

Dead serious Dirty Harry "cleans up San Francisco once again" in this "enjoyable" final installment of Clint's "classic" crime series, this time revolving around a murderous celebrity stalker; look for a "unique car chase" (involving a "remote-controlled bomb") and a scenery-chewing bit from a then-unknown Jim Carrey as an "Axl Rose–like rock star."

Dead Ringers 18 | 23 | 19 | 19

1988 | Directed by David Cronenberg | With Jeremy Irons, Geneviève Bujold | 115 minutes | Rated R

Ok, it's "beyond weird", but this "cold, clinical" tale of "twin gynecologists" "descending into madness" strikes followers of things "depraved" as a "deliciously creepy" picture, given its fascination with "prescription drugs", "kinky sex" and some mighty "bizarre" surgical instruments; despite Irons' "astounding dual performance", very vocal opponents call it "really offensive" with "no redeeming value", maybe the "ickiest movie ever"; proceed at your own risk.

Dead Zone, The
OVERALL 21 | ACTING 23 | STORY 24 | PROD. 19

1983 | Directed by David Cronenberg | With Christopher Walken, Brooke Adams, Martin Sheen, Tom Skerritt | 103 minutes | Rated R
"Twilight Zone fans" dig the "spooky" premise of this supernatural thriller, starring an "eerily sympathetic" Walken as an "inadvertent psychic" whose "disturbing" ability to foresee the future sets up a dead reckoning with a presidential contender; the "budget's a little low", but supporters say this is "one of the better Stephen King adaptations."

Death at a Funeral
20 | 22 | 20 | 19

2007 | Directed by Frank Oz | With Matthew Macfadyen, Alan Tudyk, Peter Dinklage, Rupert Graves | 90 minutes | Rated R
A "dead man, his gay dwarf lover", his "dysfunctional family" – oh, and a bottle of "psychedelic drugs" – collide in this "nothing-sacred", "thigh-smacking" British comedy concerning one "wacky funeral"; while the "zany" brand of "pure-bred English humor" is certainly an "acquired taste", most praise the "over-the-top" emoting in this "delightful romp."

Death in Venice
24 | 26 | 24 | 24

1971 | Directed by Luchino Visconti | With Dirk Bogarde, Marisa Berenson, Bjorn Andresen, Silvana Mangano | 130 minutes | Rated PG
"Delicious but depressing", this "exquisitely sad meditation on love and loss" adapted from the Thomas Mann novella stars a "memorable" Bogarde as a man who becomes obsessed by a boy while on holiday in circa-1910 Venice; though the scenery's certainly "beautiful to look at" (and the "take-your-breath-away" Mahler soundtrack equally "haunting"), the film's "slow" pace and long, "languid" shots make some shrug "gorgeous but tedious."

Death on the Nile
19 | 20 | 23 | 21

1978 | Directed by John Guillermin | With Peter Ustinov, Bette Davis, Angela Lansbury | 140 minutes | Rated PG
"Everyone looks properly shifty-eyed and guilty" in this "decent" enough adaptation of the Agatha Christie whodunit that takes place on a cruise down the River Nile; though foes grouse it's a "lightweight" "follow-up to Murder on the Orient Express", cast with "out-of-work actors", fans find it "suspenseful" enough and single out the "outrageous" Lansbury and Oscar-winning costumes for praise.

Deathtrap
22 | 24 | 25 | 20

1982 | Directed by Sidney Lumet | With Michael Caine, Christopher Reeve, Dyan Cannon | 116 minutes | Rated PG
Mystery "mindbenders" don't come more "clever" than this "amusing" take on Ira Levin's Broadway "whodunit" that "keeps you guessing and guessing" ("mostly incorrectly") in its story of a blocked playwright planning murder most foul in order to pilfer a script; "masterful casting" offsets any stagey "static", while all the "twists" are "wickedly absorbing."

Death Wish
16 | 14 | 17 | 15

1974 | Directed by Michael Winner | With Charles Bronson, Hope Lange, Vincent Gardenia | 93 minutes | Rated R

"Brash, politically incorrect and extremely macho", this '70s "revenge fantasy" was quite "scary" (and controversial) in its time, given its story of a "do-gooder" architect turned vicious "vigilante" after the murder of his wife; in the role that made him a star, Bronson is "more bad-ass than Clint Eastwood ever was", although four sequels later some say "he should have stopped after the first one."

Deconstructing Harry
16 | 19 | 17 | 17

1997 | Directed by Woody Allen | With Woody Allen, Richard Benjamin, Kirstie Alley, Judy Davis | 96 minutes | Rated R

"Uncompromising self-examination" is the heart of this "dark" Woody Allen film about a "neurotic" novelist who uses his life as fodder for his writing; though the finicky fuss about his "treatment of women" and "abundance of dirty-mouthed" talk, fans call it his "strongest work in the last decade"; favorite character: Robin Williams' (literally) "unfocused" actor.

Deep, The
17 | 16 | 17 | 19

1977 | Directed by Peter Yates | With Robert Shaw, Jacqueline Bisset, Nick Nolte | 123 minutes | Rated PG

From the "same era" that gave us *Jaws* comes this "underwater" adventure about "dangerous sunken treasure", a damp "guilty pleasure" best remembered for that "infamous" image of "Jackie Bisset in a sopping-wet T-shirt"; though "not a match" for Peter Benchley's best-selling novel, it's still "solid", "cheesy fun."

Deep End of the Ocean
19 | 22 | 20 | 19

1999 | Directed by Ulu Grosbard | With Michelle Pfeiffer, Treat Williams, Whoopi Goldberg, Jonathan Jackson | 106 minutes | Rated PG-13

"Loss and redemption" are the "serious chords" struck by this "moving" tale of a family's discovery of their "kidnapped son", nine years after his disappearance; like the best-seller it was adapted from, the picture's a "downer", but the "reunion scenes" and the cast's uniformly "good" work keep the "depressing" material afloat.

Deep Impact
15 | 14 | 15 | 19

1998 | Directed by Mimi Leder | With Robert Duvall, Téa Leoni, Elijah Wood, Vanessa Redgrave | 120 minutes | Rated PG-13

Impending "mass destruction" (via a comet plummeting toward the earth) is the subject of this "world-coming-to-an-end" "disaster flick", a "strangely moving" endeavor portraying "people preparing for a known death"; though there are comparisons to *Armageddon*'s "similar storyline", "this one has heart, a brain and a bonus – no bad Bruce Willis performance."

⌷ Deer Hunter, The ✉
26 | 28 | 24 | 24

1978 | Directed by Michael Cimino | With Robert De Niro, Christopher Walken, Meryl Streep, John Cazale, John Savage | 183 minutes | Rated R

"Ordinary guys from an ordinary American town" undergo the "ravages" of Vietnam in this "unforgettable war film", a "deeply moving", "epic-in-every-way" work that netted five Oscars (including Best Picture); brace yourself for "tough-as-nails" performances from De Niro and Walken, some "profound" if "heavy-handed symbolism" plotwise and a wrenching "Russian roulette scene" that will "leave you drained"; P.S. it also features "someone new named Streep."

Déjà Vu　　　　　19 | 21 | 19 | 21

2006 | Directed by Tony Scott | With Denzel Washington, Paula Patton, Val Kilmer, Jim Caviezel | 128 minutes | Rated PG-13

A lawman goes the "time-travel", "parallel-universes" route to "prevent a terrorist attack" in this "suspenseful" sci-fi thriller marking "another great collaboration" between director Scott and the "excellent-in-anything" Washington; filmed in a decimated, "post-Katrina" New Orleans, it leans on a Hollywood specialty – "big explosions" – to distract from the "plot holes."

☑ Delicatessen ◨　　26 | 23 | 24 | 26

1992 | Directed by Jean-Pierre Jeunet, Marc Caro | With Dominique Pinon, Jean-Claude Dreyfus | 99 minutes | Rated R

Cannibalism is on the menu of this "wonderfully twisted" black comedy about a *boulangerie* serving cuts of meat fit for "Hannibal Lecter" or Sweeney Todd; definitely "not for everyone", it's certainly "original", with enough "quirky characters" and "macabre" twists to make for an "inventive", if offbeat, "late-night snack."

Deliverance　　　　25 | 26 | 25 | 23

1972 | Directed by John Boorman | With Jon Voight, Burt Reynolds, Ned Beatty, Ronny Cox | 109 minutes | Rated R

This "allegorical nightmare" about four "city slickers" on a "weekend canoe trip" "did for camping in the woods what *Jaws* did for swimming in the ocean", mainly because of that infamous "squeal-like-a-pig" "rape scene" (to the tune of "those damn 'Dueling Banjos'"); more important, it also "proves that thought and testosterone can coexist" and "debunks the long-held myth that Reynolds can't act."

De-Lovely　　　　20 | 22 | 19 | 22

2004 | Directed by Irwin Winkler | With Kevin Kline, Ashley Judd | 125 minutes | Rated PG-13

"You can hum along (if you're old enough)" to the "wonderful score" of this Cole Porter biopic, an "informative" effort that doesn't shy away from the composer's "messy" love life; while some are "desappointed" by the "movie-of-the-week" screenplay and "gimmicky" musical numbers "decimated by modern singers", at least Kline's "usual fine performance" "gets the beguine begun."

☑ Departed, The ✉　　26 | 28 | 25 | 26

2006 | Directed by Martin Scorsese | With Leonardo DiCaprio, Matt Damon, Jack Nicholson, Mark Wahlberg | 151 minutes | Rated R

Scorsese brought home a "well-deserved and long-overdue" Oscar for directing this "dynamite" Boston "crime opera", a "complex" cops 'n' mobsters flick that's "overflowing with superstars" (though "Jack steals the show") but so "violent" that "your ears will ring from the gunshots"; set to an "excellent" soundtrack and featuring a finale that will have you "picking your jaw up off the floor", this "instant classic" simply "delivers on all cylinders."

Derailed
16 | 18 | 18 | 17

2005 | Directed by Mikael Håfström | With Clive Owen, Jennifer Aniston, Vincent Cassel | 107 minutes | Rated R

An "adman's extramarital affair" sinks into a web of "blackmail" in this "serviceable" adultery thriller starring the "easy-on-the-eyes" Owen opposite an "against-type", "femme fatale" Aniston; problem is, the pair "don't exude enough big-screen chemistry" and the "not-so-surprising ending" can be seen coming "a mile away."

Descent, The
18 | 16 | 18 | 20

2006 | Directed by Neil Marshall | With Shauna Macdonald, Natalie Mendoza | 99 minutes | Rated R

"Claustrophobes beware": this "creepy" horror flick about spelunkers fighting off "freaky" monsters in a cave will "play with your fears" and "jangle your nerves"; an "all-female cast" of "tough chicks" supplies the "intensity", even when the script veers off into "far-fetched" territory.

Desk Set
25 | 27 | 23 | 23

1957 | Directed by Walter Lang | With Katharine Hepburn, Spencer Tracy, Gig Young, Joan Blondell | 103 minutes | Not Rated

Set in the "dawn of the computer age", this "brisk" romantic comedy brings the "battle of the sexes into the workplace" by pitting "efficiency expert" Tracy against "research librarian" Hepburn; while the "two pros" display "perfect chemistry" and "flawless timing", a few say it's "not their finest hour" – though "Kate's wardrobe" alone makes it "worth the rental" for fashionistas.

Desperately Seeking Susan
15 | 13 | 14 | 13

1985 | Directed by Susan Seidelman | With Rosanna Arquette, Madonna, Aidan Quinn | 104 minutes | Rated PG-13

This "quintessential '80s" flick set in NYC's SoHo has to do with a case of mistaken identity but is best known as Madonna's "breakout vehicle" (despite Arquette's "underappreciated" starring role); though the verdict on the Material Girl's thespian abilities is lukewarm – she "basically plays herself" – the picture's still "fun."

Destry Rides Again ◐
25 | 25 | 23 | 23

1939 | Directed by George Marshall | With Marlene Dietrich, James Stewart, Mischa Auer | 94 minutes | Not Rated

A "surprisingly modern approach to the code of the Old West", this "funny" oater tells the tale of a "reluctant", "soft-spoken" lawman aiming to tame a corrupt town; there's "strong chemistry" between Stewart's "aw-shucks" deputy and Dietrich's "heart-of-gold" floozy, not to mention a "classic saloon fight" and an "irresistible" song – 'The Boys in the Backroom' – later "parodied in *Blazing Saddles*."

Detective, The
20 | 21 | 19 | 19

1968 | Directed by Gordon Douglas | With Frank Sinatra, Lee Remick, Ralph Meeker, Jack Klugman | 114 minutes | Not Rated

"Anything with Frank in it has to be good", and "one of the best" in his acting oeuvre is this "powerful" crime story about a NYPD vet who re-opens a murder case and uncovers corruption in the seedy side of the city; it's a "winner in the dramatic department", but some detect a "depressing" tone that leaves "a bad feeling" about New York, New York.

Devil in a Blue Dress

19 | 22 | 19 | 20

1995 | Directed by Carl Franklin | With Denzel Washington, Jennifer Beals, Tom Sizemore, Don Cheadle | 102 minutes | Rated R

Playing a punchy sleuth in post-WWII LA, Denzel encounters "noir-style intrigue" in this "solid adaptation" of Walter Mosley's detective novel about the search for a missing woman; the "steamy" production design supplies "nice period" detail, while an "amazing" Cheadle "steals the show" as a baby-faced, gold-toothed killer.

Devil's Advocate, The

19 | 19 | 20 | 20

1997 | Directed by Taylor Hackford | With Keanu Reeves, Al Pacino, Charlize Theron | 144 minutes | Rated R

"Lawyers as the devil's minions" is this thriller's "delightfully sinister" setup, with a "creep-a-delic" Pacino in "hammy overdrive" as a "modern-day Satan" ("be very afraid") who leads "hot-shot" legal eagle Reeves into temptation with a "Faust-like offer he can't refuse"; it's "required viewing for young attorneys", even if a few feel the "over-the-top" storyline is "one hell of a mess."

Devil's Own, The

17 | 18 | 17 | 17

1997 | Directed by Alan J. Pakula | With Harrison Ford, Brad Pitt, Rubén Blades, Treat Williams | 107 minutes | Rated R

An IRA terrorist flees Belfast for Staten Island in this "intriguing" (if "generic") political thriller best remembered for the onscreen pairing of Pitt and Ford; too bad the stars "don't have the chemistry of a great screen team" – the acting seems to be more of the "mutual-admiration-society" school – but hang in there for the "fun action scenes."

Devil Wears Prada, The

22 | 25 | 21 | 23

2006 | Directed by David Frankel | With Meryl Streep, Anne Hathaway, Emily Blunt, Stanley Tucci | 109 minutes | Rated PG-13

Streep's "absolutely delicious" as an "ice queen" "boss from hell" in this "haute couture comedy" delineating the "cutthroat world" of fashion journalism; although the "off-the-rack" storyline strikes some as "more Gap than Prada", the picture is a must-see "if you're into shoes and belts", and "so much better" than the "second-rate book"; best moment: the "coat montage."

∃ Diabolique ⊙F

26 | 25 | 28 | 23

1955 | Directed by Henri-Georges Clouzot | With Simone Signoret, Véra Clouzot | 116 minutes | Not Rated

"Leave it to the French" to serve up this "nasty little thriller" about a murderous love triangle set in a boarding school that "scares the socks" off surveyors; granted, it "looks pretty primitive today", but ultimately "Signoret still smolders", the "clever plot twists" keep coming and "whoa, what an ending!"

∃ Dial M for Murder

25 | 24 | 27 | 24

1954 | Directed by Alfred Hitchcock | With Ray Milland, Grace Kelly, Robert Cummings | 105 minutes | Rated PG

A "jilted husband seeks revenge on his philandering wife" in this "taut" Hitchcock thriller, a "stagey story" transformed into a "suspenseful" movie (fun fact: it was "originally shot in 3-D"); actingwise, "Kelly shines", Milland is "subtly sinister" and Cummings "drags down every scene he appears in."

Diamonds Are Forever

20 | 18 | 18 | 21

1971 | Directed by Guy Hamilton | With Sean Connery, Jill St. John, Charles Gray | 125 minutes | Rated PG

"007 goes Vegas, baby" in this sixth installment of the series, chock-full of the usual "gadgets" and gals, including the "hot", high-"cheekboned" St. John; in his next-to-last appearance as the stirred-but-never-shaken spy, Connery's at his "dashing, womanizing best" while Gray, as a "hilarious Howard Hughes type", makes a "great villain"; still, Fleming fanatics fret it's "one of the sillier" in the canon.

Diary of a Mad Black Woman

19 | 19 | 18 | 18

2005 | Directed by Darren Grant | With Tyler Perry, Kimberly Elise, Steve Harris, Shemar Moore | 116 minutes | Rated PG-13

Meeting the demand for "more films starring black women", this "entertaining" soap opera about a jilted wife's revenge on her spouse will "keep you laughing" as it ladles out a you-go-girl message; sure, it's "a bit corny" and "over the top", but what's "silly" to some is "inspirational" to others.

Diary of a Mad Housewife ∅

20 | 24 | 21 | 19

1970 | Directed by Frank Perry | With Richard Benjamin, Carrie Snodgress, Frank Langella | 104 minutes | Rated R

This "satire about urban living and values" examines the disintegration of a loveless marriage between a "self-absorbed" man and a woman "lacking in self-esteem"; Snodgress is "perfection" in an Oscar-nominated performance, but Benjamin (as the "ultimate nightmare husband") elicits the most heated response: a few want to "punch him" by the end of the movie; best scene: the "opening elevator sequence."

Diary of Anne Frank, The ◑

23 | 23 | 26 | 21

1959 | Directed by George Stevens | With Millie Perkins, Shelley Winters, Richard Beymer | 180 minutes | Not Rated

"Every young person should see" this true story of a Jewish family hiding from the Nazis in an Amsterdam attic that "brings to life a dark time in history"; "man's inhumanity to man" is depicted "from a child's point of view" and "though we know the outcome", the "suspense" is truly "heartbreaking."

Dick Tracy

13 | 13 | 13 | 20

1990 | Directed by Warren Beatty | With Warren Beatty, Madonna, Al Pacino, Glenne Headly | 105 minutes | Rated PG

It's "visually stunning", it's "star-studded", it's got "great Sondheim songs" – but this "classy", "colorful" adaptation of the long-running comic strip is still "nothing special" due to a "vapid" script and an overall sense of "wretched excess"; the good news: this could be "Madonna's best film appearance."

Die Another Day

19 | 17 | 16 | 23

2002 | Directed by Lee Tamahori | With Pierce Brosnan, Halle Berry, Toby Stephens | 133 minutes | Rated PG-13

Equipped with "everything you expect from a James Bond film", this 20th installment sports "cool gadgets", "fast cars", "easy-on-the-eyes" stars and "Schwarzenegger-like one-liners" in a story that has something to do with the "current political crisis with North Korea" despite quibbles about an "absurd plot" and "too many CGI effects" diehards declare there's nothing wrong with the "yummy" Halle and her "homage-to-Ursula-Andress" bikini.

Die Hard
23 | 19 | 22 | 24

1988 | Directed by John McTiernan | With Bruce Willis, Bonnie Bedelia, Alan Rickman | 131 minutes | Rated R

This "flawless" "granddaddy of the '80s action" flick spawned "countless imitations but no equals" thanks to its "thrill-a-minute" mix of suspense, explosions and "comic one-liners"; die-hard diehards tout Willis' "ass-kicking" turn as a "loser whom fate requires to be a hero" as well as "chic bad guy" Rickman, who supplies the "cool quips and fashion tips."

Diner
25 | 25 | 23 | 22

1982 | Directed by Barry Levinson | With Steve Guttenberg, Mickey Rourke, Kevin Bacon, Ellen Barkin | 110 minutes | Rated R

Levinson's first Baltimore drama "centers on the lives of a group of '50s high school grads" "who spent their youth in diners"; a "finely observed" "guy flick" that's both "smart and funny", it features a "wonderful ensemble cast" that delivers the snappy patter so "brilliantly" it served as a "springboard" for the careers of "many future stars."

☒ Dinner at Eight ◑
27 | 27 | 24 | 25

1933 | Directed by George Cukor | With Marie Dressler, John Barrymore, Jean Harlow | 113 minutes | Not Rated

It seems as if "every star at MGM appears" in this frothy dramedy about a social-climbing hostess' "high society" dinner party where nothing goes as planned; look for plenty of "art deco sparkle" productionwise, a "joy" of a script and "suave, understated" performances from Dressler and John Barrymore; biggest surprise: Harlow's "snappy" turn as a gum-popping, gold-digging hussy.

Dinner Rush
▽ 23 | 24 | 23 | 22

2000 | Directed by Bob Giraldi | With Danny Aiello, Edoardo Ballerini, Kirk Acevedo | 99 minutes | Rated R

A "great flick for foodies", this "well-done" indie drama unfolds over one tumultuous night at a trendy Manhattan eatery where the cast of characters includes low-down gangsters, high-strung chefs, put-upon waiters and spoiled food critics; maybe it's "not as endearing as *Big Night*", but fans savor the "excellent" Aiello – and that "nice twist" at the end.

Dinosaur
19 | - | 17 | 24

2000 | Directed by Eric Leighton, Ralph Zondag | Animated | 82 minutes | Rated PG

"Kids interested in dinosaurs" dig this Disney flick for its "extraordinary animation", "wonderful music" and "fabulous" meteor shower scene; but despite some "exciting moments", soreheads lament that it's "lacking in the plot department" and not much more than a "dull remake of *The Land Before Time*."

Dirty Dancing
21 | 17 | 20 | 20

1987 | Directed by Emile Ardolino | With Patrick Swayze, Jennifer Grey, Jerry Orbach | 96 minutes | Rated PG-13

Whether it's a "girls'-night-in" "entertainment" or a "Sunday afternoon vacation", this "cult classic" is the cinematic equivalent of "comfort food" and even works as an "excellent date movie" after all these years; its "heart-melting story" centers on the romance between "hot, sexy teen dream" Swayze and "cute gamine" Grey, who "shake their booties" just "like the Solid Gold dancers" used to do to pop hits in a "'60s Catskills resort."

Dirty Dozen, The

| 21 | 19 | 22 | 20 |

1967 | Directed by Robert Aldrich | With Lee Marvin, Ernest Borgnine, Charles Bronson | 145 minutes | Not Rated
This "delightful" war adventure exudes a "healthy dose of cynicism" in telling the tale of a "merry band of cutthroats" "brought together to do good in WWII"; the "early-in-their-careers" actors are "awesome", "super-macho" types (particularly "ultimate tough guy" Marvin playing as their leader), while the "rough-and-tumble", action-packed plot still seems "fun after all these years."

Dirty Harry

| 21 | 18 | 20 | 19 |

1971 | Directed by Don Siegel | With Clint Eastwood, Harry Guardino, Reni Santoni | 102 minutes | Rated R
Clint's at his "steely-eyed, gravelly voiced best" in this "modern cop" flick that "struck a chord in the '70s" and "created a fast-and-furious" subgenre "solid" enough to "spawn a host of imitators"; throw in some "great views of San Francisco" and a moodily "muted jazz score" and you just might "feel lucky, punk."

Dirty Pretty Things

| 23 | 24 | 24 | 21 |

2003 | Directed by Stephen Frears | With Chiwetel Ejiofor, Audrey Tautou, Sergi López | 97 minutes | Rated R
London's illegal "immigrant underworld" goes under the microscope in this "atmospheric", "suspenseful" crime thriller detailing "shady goings-on" (think prostitution, drug dealing and "macabre" trafficking in human organs) at a "swanky UK hotel"; the "low-budget look" works well with the "gritty performances", "thought-provoking" scenario and "unexpected ending."

Dirty Rotten Scoundrels

| 22 | 24 | 22 | 20 |

1988 | Directed by Frank Oz | With Steve Martin, Michael Caine, Glenne Headly | 110 minutes | Rated PG
Right up there in the "pantheon of silly", this "inspired" farce (remade from 1964's *Bedtime Story*) has the "perfect cast": Martin and Caine as "competing con men" on the French Riviera "trying to outdo each other" in a Lothario's challenge to "grift an heiress"; the "fencing" between the "two pros" yields "high hilarity" and "quotable scenes galore."

Discreet Charm of the Bourgeoisie, The ✉ 🄵

| 24 | 23 | 23 | 22 |

1972 | Directed by Luis Buñuel | With Fernando Rey, Delphine Seyrig, Stéphane Audran | 102 minutes | Rated PG
"Controversial" in its day, this Oscar-winning "satirical portrait of the French bourgeoisie" tells the "elliptical" tale of "six people in search of a hot meal" who are "confounded at every turn" by bizarre goings-on; Buñuel serves up enough "dream-within-a-dream sequences" to turn this dark comedy into a "thoughtful, surreal delight" that further enhances his reputation as the "Dali of cinema."

| | OVERALL | ACTING | STORY | PROD. |

Disturbia
21 22 22 22

2007 | Directed by D.J. Caruso | With Shia LaBeouf, Sarah Roemer, Carrie-Anne Moss, David Morse | 105 minutes | Rated PG-13

"*Rear Window* for a younger generation", this "well-done" thriller about a teen under house arrest who spies on his neighbors is "entertaining" enough, though all agree "no one does it like Hitchcock"; thus, there are "no surprises if you've seen the original", save for the "very likable" LaBeouf (the "kid's going to be a star") and the "resoundingly creepy" Morse.

Diva ▣
24 20 24 24

1982 | Directed by Jean-Jacques Beineix | With Wilhelmenia Fernandez, Frederic Andrei | 123 minutes | Rated R

Perhaps the "greatest opera/action flick ever", this "oh-so-stylish" French thriller creates a "complicated world" about a "scooter-riding kid" obsessed by a "reclusive soprano"; "glorious to look at", with "wonderful images of Paris", it's most memorable for that "fast-paced motorcycle chase" in the Métro.

Divine Secrets of the Ya-Ya Sisterhood
16 20 17 17

2002 | Directed by Callie Khouri | With Sandra Bullock, Ellen Burstyn, James Garner, Ashley Judd | 116 minutes | Rated PG-13

A "disappointing adaptation of an amazing book", this Southern-fried "quintessential chick flick" tells the tale of a complicated "mother-and-daughter relationship" with "not a whit of the sass or charm of the novel"; though many find the performances "terrific" ("older actresses rock"), the "schmaltzy", "*Fried Green Magnolias*" script strikes some sisters as "more yo-yo than ya-ya."

☑ Diving Bell and the Butterfly, The ▣
26 28 26 26

2007 | Directed by Julian Schnabel | With Mathieu Amalric, Emmanuelle Seigner, Marie-Josée Croze, Max von Sydow | 112 minutes | Rated PG-13

Overcoming its "depressing subject" matter with "intelligence, humanity" and even "humor", this "heartfelt" true story of a "playboy incapacitated by a stroke" who can communicate "only by blinking a single eyelid" certainly "puts life in perspective"; though much of the film is "shot through the victim's eye", you "can tell the director is a painter" given the "artistic sensibility" and "remarkable visuals"; indeed, it's "full of feeling", but there's "not a sentimental moment in it."

Divorce Italian Style ✉ ◑ ▣
24 25 23 22

1962 | Directed by Pietro Germi | With Marcello Mastroianni, Daniela Rocca, Stefania Sandrelli | 104 minutes | Not Rated

"Mastroianni's a hoot" playing an "unfortunately married" man "lusting for greener pastures" in this "*molto bene*" comedy set way back when divorce was illegal in Italy; its "silly but sweet" Oscar-winning screenplay is both a "condemnation of the law" as well as a "nice satire", and if it "loses a little in translation", it compensates with black-and-white cinematography that's "lusher than most color films."

D.O.A. ◑
22 22 26 21

1950 | Directed by Rudolph Maté | With Edmond O'Brien, Pamela Britton, Luther Adler | 83 minutes | Not Rated

"One of the best opening lines" – "I want to report a murder . . . mine" – sets in motion the "intriguing plot" of this "elaborate time-runs-backward" drama in which an "innocent man must find his own killer before he dies"; set against a backdrop of "great location shots of LA and San Francisco", it's "gritty, bleak" noir that's "compelling as hell", even if a few deadbeats declare it "promises more than it delivers."

☑ Doctor Zhivago ✉
	OVERALL	ACTING	STORY	PROD.
	27	26	26	28

1965 | Directed by David Lean | With Omar Sharif, Julie Christie, Geraldine Chaplin, Rod Steiger | 197 minutes | Rated PG-13

Lean's "timeless" – others say "long" – Oscar-winning evocation of Boris Pasternak's "sweeping" novel of "love and war" is the "epic to end all epics", merging "brilliant historical storytelling" with "romantic extravaganza"; set during the Russian Revolution, it "humanized the USSR during the Cold War" due to the "tear-jerking" relationship between Christie and Sharif – though its "balalaika"-heavy theme song and the scenes in that "winter wonderland" of an "ice palace" resonate most.

Dodgeball
16 | 16 | 15 | 16

2004 | Directed by Rawson Marshall Thurber | With Vince Vaughn, Ben Stiller, Christine Taylor, Rip Torn | 92 minutes | Rated PG-13

A "sophomoric spoof of the sporting world", this "manic" comedy fields a "Frat Pack" "matchup" of "deadpan" Vaughn vs. "sadistic meathead" Stiller, playing owners of "dueling gyms" who use the "goofball playground game" to settle a score; fans of "crude slapstick" say "don't dodge this one", but other spectators "may want to duck."

Dog Day Afternoon ✉
24 | 27 | 22 | 20

1975 | Directed by Sidney Lumet | With Al Pacino, John Cazale, Chris Sarandon, Charles Durning | 124 minutes | Rated R

This "funny/sad" true tale of a botched "bank heist" committed by "hapless" amateurs is transformed into a "deep, character-driven" example of director Lumet "at his best"; expect "great performances from the entire cast" (from the nervous bank tellers "right down to the pizza delivery guy"), with particular kudos to an "ass-kicking" Pacino and a "brilliant" Sarandon as his gay lover.

Dogville
21 | 25 | 20 | 21

2004 | Directed by Lars von Trier | With Nicole Kidman, Harriet Andersson, Lauren Bacall, Paul Bettany | 178 minutes | Rated R

Decidedly "not for everyone", this avant-garde "morality play" about a woman on the run taken in by a small town is "risky", "controversial" stuff, starting with its "minimalist", stagelike setting and "terribly long" running time; some growl it's too "self-important" (and maybe even "anti-American"), but those willing to "take a deep breath and plunge in" find it "daring" and "thought-provoking" – "art films don't get much artier than this."

Donnie Brasco
20 | 24 | 22 | 20

1997 | Directed by Mike Newell | With Al Pacino, Johnny Depp, Anne Heche | 127 minutes | Rated R

In this true story, an undercover FBI agent "befriends the man he's supposed to entrap" and takes you "inside the inner workings of the mob" to reveal a "more realistic side to the underworld"; a "sympathetic", "nuanced" Pacino does the "gangster-as-loser" thing right, while Depp's titular turn is similarly "excellent"; like the 'family' it portrays, this one "never lets go of you."

Donnie Darko

22 | 23 | 23 | 21

2001 | Directed by Richard Kelly | With Jake Gyllenhaal, Drew Barrymore, Mary McDonnell | 113 minutes | Rated R

"*Harvey*" meets "*Psycho*" in this indie "cult favorite" that combines "trippy sci-fi" FX with "John Hughes high-school angst" in its story of a "delusional" teen who sees visions of "demonic bunny rabbits"; sure, you might "need a few viewings to understand it", but its "huge fan base" goes bonkers over the "original" script, "top-notch soundtrack" and the "solid" Jake, in the breakout role that made him a star.

Don't Look Back ◐

25 | - | 22 | 23

1967 | Directed by D.A. Pennebaker | Documentary | With Bob Dylan, Joan Baez, Donovan | 96 minutes | Not Rated

This "revealing" "slice of musical history" "captures the young Bob Dylan in all his contradictory charm and churlishness" as an "artist in transition" and is an "indelible" "reminder of what all the fuss was about"; perhaps the "most referenced" rockumentary ever, "it's improved with time" and includes one of the "first music videos" ever: the famed cue-cards clip for 'Subterranean Homesick Blues.'

Don't Look Now

24 | 26 | 24 | 24

1973 | Directed by Nicolas Roeg | With Julie Christie, Donald Sutherland | 110 minutes | Rated R

"Venice at its most eerie" is the backdrop for this "disturbing" psychological thriller with an "atmosphere of dread" so pervasive that you'll be "on the edge of your gondola" throughout; based on a Daphne du Maurier story about "grieving parents" mourning the death of their child, it weaves a "blind clairvoyant" and a "murderous dwarf" into its "thoroughly adult" web – and tops things off with "one of the best sex scenes in the history of cinema."

Door in the Floor, The

19 | 23 | 19 | 19

2004 | Directed by Tod Williams | With Jeff Bridges, Kim Basinger, Jon Foster | 111 minutes | Rated R

"Nice looking and well acted", this "textured" adaptation of "the first third of John Irving's novel *A Widow for One Year*" relates the "sad, bleak" tale of a successful, "self-centered author whose marriage has fallen apart"; Bridges is "brilliant", Basinger the "same vulnerable mess, as usual", and although the picture certainly "has its moments", some slam it as "ultimately unengaging."

Doors, The

20 | 22 | 20 | 21

1991 | Directed by Oliver Stone | With Val Kilmer, Kyle MacLachlan, Meg Ryan, Crispin Glover | 140 minutes | Rated R

"Jim Morrison is alive and well and living inside Val Kilmer", who's "spooky good" in this "excellent" glimpse into the "inner workings of one of rock's greatest bands"; the "tragic" trajectory of its "decadent", "visionary" singer is delineated against a backdrop of "trippy" effects, "fun period details" and, needless to say, "great music."

Do the Right Thing

23 | 23 | 22 | 21

1989 | Directed by Spike Lee | With Spike Lee, Danny Aiello, Ossie Davis, Ruby Dee | 120 minutes | Rated R

"Italian-American pizza parlor owners in Brooklyn" and the "African-American community who patronize the shop" clash "on the hottest day of the year" in this "anatomy of a race riot" from Spike Lee, who "deftly balances tragedy with comedy" to telegraph a "message as clear as black and white" that still "resonates years later."

☒ Double Indemnity ◑ | 28 | 27 | 28 | 25 |

1944 | Directed by Billy Wilder | With Fred MacMurray, Barbara Stanwyck, Edward G. Robinson | 107 minutes | Not Rated

"From the chiaroscuro settings to the world-weary voice-over", Wilder's "refreshingly sour" slice of "hard-boiled" noir "sets the standard for the genre"; the story of "another dumb cluck done in by a woman", it features a "fast-talking" MacMurray, a "knockout" Stanwyck ("love the anklet") and a "fantastic" Robinson, with enough plot "twists" and sly "killer banter" to make it the cinematic equivalent of "bonded bourbon"; best scene: shopping at the "supermarket."

Double Jeopardy | 16 | 18 | 19 | 18 |

1999 | Directed by Bruce Beresford | With Tommy Lee Jones, Ashley Judd, Annabeth Gish | 105 minutes | Rated R

"Diverting" enough, this "clever" thriller finds Judd playing a "kick-ass bitch" wrongfully imprisoned for murder and hell-bent on "revenge"; legal eagles rule it's "completely implausible" (even its title "premise is false") and add that "Jones' cop thing is getting old", but it's "enjoyable nonetheless" if you like "a lot of twists."

Down and Out in Beverly Hills | 17 | 19 | 17 | 17 |

1986 | Directed by Paul Mazursky | With Nick Nolte, Richard Dreyfuss, Bette Midler | 103 minutes | Rated R

The "Jean Renoir classic" *Bondu Saved from Drowning* is "given an American spin" in this "spoof of the upper class", Beverly Hills–style, wherein a "bum interacts in the lives of a wealthy family" with "hilarious" results; Bette's "divine" as a "neurotic wife and even if the humor verges on the "crude", it's still "winning" enough.

Down by Law ◑ | 24 | 23 | 23 | 22 |

1986 | Directed by Jim Jarmusch | With Tom Waits, John Lurie, Roberto Benigni | 107 minutes | Rated R

A "trio of unlikely fugitives" – a DJ, a pimp and an Italian tourist – takes it on the lam from a Louisiana slammer in this "odd" comedy that's best remembered for "introducing Benigni" to American audiences; but even though this "original" has attained "compulsory" "cult classic" status over time, a few say its "slow pace is not for everyone."

☒ Downfall 🅕 | 27 | 28 | 26 | 25 |

2005 | Directed by Oliver Hirschbiegel | With Bruno Ganz, Alexandra Maria Lara, Corinna Harfouch | 155 minutes | Rated R

"Unlike any WWII movie you've seen", this "extremely well-done" German production provides an "engrossing look" at the last days inside "Hitler's bunker" during the "fall of Berlin"; true, the film's "a little long" and Ganz's "humanizing" take on the "fallen dictator" may be a "tough pill to swallow", but in the end it's "riveting" and "utterly believable."

Down with Love | 18 | 19 | 17 | 23 |

2003 | Directed by Peyton Reed | With Renée Zellweger, Ewan McGregor, David Hyde Pierce | 101 minutes | Rated PG-13

"Not everyone's cup of tea", this "stylized homage" spoofs "Camelot-era" sex comedies with its "frothy" tale of a "lady-killer" journalist out

| | OVERALL | ACTING | STORY | PROD. |

to seduce a "wily" writer, and fans "dig the clothes" and the wink-wink "double entendres"; but foes fume "fluffy", citing a "thin" plot and "little chemistry" between the leads ("Doris and Rock did it better"), although Pierce "out-Tony Randalls Tony Randall."

Dracula ◑
24 | 21 | 23 | 20

1931 | Directed by Tod Browning | With Bela Lugosi, Helen Chandler, Dwight Frye | 75 minutes | Not Rated

Granted, the "special effects are nonexistent", but this "definitive Dracula" is still "scarier than anything made today", leaving "plenty of room for imagination" thanks to Lugosi's "riveting" take on the "immortal vampire"; though it uses music sparingly to evoke an "eerie atmosphere", a new, souped-up DVD with a "Philip Glass score" is highly touted; best line: "I never drink . . . wine."

Dracula
20 | 19 | 22 | 25

1992 | Directed by Francis Ford Coppola | With Gary Oldman, Winona Ryder, Anthony Hopkins, Keanu Reeves | 130 minutes | Rated R

"You can sink your teeth" into Coppola's "highly underrated" "retelling of Bram Stoker's tale" of a "lovelorn", bloodthirsty Romanian count; "stylish" costumes, Oscar-winning sets, a "stunning" Oldman and the spectacle of "Tom Waits eating bugs" make for "visionary" moviemaking, even if some nix the "laughable miscasting" of Reeves.

Dragonslayer
18 | 14 | 19 | 20

1981 | Directed by Matthew Robbins | With Peter MacNicol, Caitlin Clarke, Ralph Richardson | 109 minutes | Rated PG

Nearly "20 years older than the *Lord of the Rings* films", this swords 'n' sorcery saga about a sorcerer's apprentice bent on slaying a fire-breathing beast still manages to conjure up some "entertaining" hocus-pocus with "great special effects (for their time")"; the story may be a little "hokey", but the "dragon has to be seen to be believed."

Dr. Dolittle
16 | 17 | 17 | 18

1998 | Directed by Betty Thomas | With Eddie Murphy, Ossie Davis, Peter Boyle | 85 minutes | Rated PG-13

Both "kids and kids at heart" "crack up" over this "priceless" Murphy vehicle in which he "shines" playing a doc who can "talk to animals"; based vaguely on Hugh Lofting's "perennially popular" children's stories, this update employs state-of-the-art animatronics and computer graphics to make the animalspeak both realistic and "entertaining."

Dreamer
21 | 22 | 21 | 21

2005 | Directed by John Gatins | With Kurt Russell, Dakota Fanning, Elisabeth Shue | 106 minutes | Rated PG

"Great family entertainment" is trotted out when "girl meets horse" in this "feel-good" flick with an "anything's-possible-if-you-work-hard" message; promoters promise that the "beautiful Kentucky scenery", "cute-as-a-button" Fanning and "old-fashioned" racing thrills will "keep you glued to the screen", despite the "pretty predictable" windup.

Dreamers, The
17 | 19 | 17 | 19

2004 | Directed by Bernardo Bertolucci | With Michael Pitt, Eva Green, Louis Garrel | 115 minutes | Rated NC-17

Themes of "cinematic and political freedom" (not to mention "graphic sex scenes") "keep your interest" in Bertolucci's "adults-only" drama set in the "tumultuous" Paris of 1968 that intercuts "actual footage" from classic films with a story of three "beautiful young idealists" involved in an "explicit" ménage à trois; whether it's a "fearless homage" to the "French New Wave" or a "pretentious" dose of "gratuitous porn" is one of the "challenging" issues raised.

Dreamgirls
23 | 24 | 22 | 26

2006 | Directed by Bill Condon | With Jamie Foxx, Beyoncé Knowles, Eddie Murphy, Jennifer Hudson | 131 minutes | Rated PG-13

This "glitzy" Motown musical chronicles the "roller-coaster" fortunes of a "Supremes"-like trio and marks the "breathtaking" big-screen debut of "*American Idol*" manqué Hudson, who "pours on the pathos" with an "exquisite" Beyoncé and "dy-no-mite" Murphy at her side; busting out "gorgeous" costumes to accompany the "top-notch" tunes, it "feels like being at a Broadway show – minus the ticket prices."

Dressed to Kill
20 | 22 | 19 | 20

1980 | Directed by Brian De Palma | With Michael Caine, Angie Dickinson, Nancy Allen | 105 minutes | Rated R

"Swirling camerawork, split screens, tracking shots that go on for miles" – yup, it's another "stylishly bloody" De Palma thriller, replete with "violent slashings, sensuous showers and sexual confusion" as it tells the adventures of a "happy hooker, an unhappy housewife and a shrink"; though an "inspiring" Angie provides the "sexy" "goose bumps", foes say it's "too derivative of Hitchcock."

Driving Miss Daisy ✉
24 | 27 | 23 | 22

1989 | Directed by Bruce Beresford | With Morgan Freeman, Jessica Tandy, Dan Aykroyd | 99 minutes | Rated PG

"Race relations" in the South and the "loss of dignity" that can come with aging are "wonderfully depicted" in this "heartwarming" story of an "unconventional friendship" between a matriarch and her chauffeur; the "sterling" Tandy and Freeman exhibit "incredible onscreen chemistry" (she drove home with an Oscar) in this "uplifting yet down-to-earth" drama.

Dr. No
23 | 20 | 22 | 23

1963 | Directed by Terence Young | With Sean Connery, Ursula Andress, Jack Lord | 110 minutes | Rated PG

The "first Bond outing" is a "lean and mean" thriller "unhindered by political correctness", with "fewer gadgets" and gals than usual (though the image of Andress in that "white bikini" is "seared forever onto many a man's brain"); while the "dashing" Connery "makes it all look effortless", "purists" note this "unadulterated" "template" is the "closest they ever came to Ian Fleming's vision."

☑ Dr. Strangelove ◐
28 | 28 | 27 | 26

1964 | Directed by Stanley Kubrick | With Peter Sellers, George C. Scott, Sterling Hayden | 93 minutes | Rated PG

"Nuclear annihilation was never funnier" than in Kubrick's "stinging Cold War satire", a "chillingly comic" examination of "distressingly familiar government officials" and their "precious bodily fluids"; as members of "our military at work", Scott is "magnificent" and Sellers "phenomenal" (in "three, count 'em, roles"), while "Slim Pickens riding the bomb" remains one of the cinema's most indelible images; doomsday devotees dub it "apocalypse now and forever."

Drugstore Cowboy
| 19 | 21 | 19 | 18 |

1989 | Directed by Gus Van Sant | With Matt Dillon, Kelly Lynch, James Le Gros | 100 minutes | Rated R

Van Sant's grittily "accurate depiction" of narcotics addicts robbing drugstores for drugs is loaded with "precise, unexpected performances" and a surprise bonus: William Burroughs as a junkie ex-priest; though habit-ues hail it as a "highly original dark comedy", nonsupporters say it "doesn't hold up well."

⊠ Duck Soup ◑
| 27 | 25 | 23 | 22 |

1933 | Directed by Leo McCarey | With the Marx Brothers, Margaret Dumont | 70 minutes | Not Rated

"Hail, hail Freedonia" cry fans of the "anarchic" Marx foursome, whose trademark "lunacy" is at its "peak" in this "political satire" about a "mythical dictatorship"; "absurdly funny" – it includes the "legendary mirror scene with Groucho and Harpo" – it's the brothers' "finest hour" and voted top of the Marxes in this Survey.

Duel in the Sun
| 23 | 22 | 22 | 24 |

1946 | Directed by King Vidor | With Jennifer Jones, Gregory Peck, Joseph Cotten, Lillian Gish | 146 minutes | Not Rated

Producer David O. Selznick "goes for baroque" in this "overripe", "overacted", "overly long" horse opera about a "hot" half-breed and the two brothers who desire her; its "shockingly sexual" undercurrent led to its "nickname, *Lust in the Dust*", though what's "campy" and "over the top" for some is "epic" and "operatic" to others; no question, "they don't make 'em like this anymore."

Dumb and Dumber
| 15 | 16 | 12 | 14 |

1994 | Directed by Peter Farrelly, Bobby Farrelly | With Jim Carrey, Jeff Daniels, Lauren Holly | 106 minutes | Rated PG-13

No duh, the "title says it all" in this maiden effort from the Farrelly brothers, a "gross-out" "guilty pleasure" about a "moronic duo" "traveling cross country" with a briefcase stuffed with cash; fans say the "vulgar" antics (think "potty jokes", "disgusting noises") "grow on you", though foes sneer the "puerile", "not-for-adults" storyline makes for the "ultimate" in "lowbrow humor."

Dumbo
| 24 | - | 23 | 24 |

1941 | Directed by Ben Sharpsteen | Animated | 64 minutes | Rated G

"Elephants fly" in this "short but sweet" animated Disney classic message movie "about the importance of being yourself"; though the politically correct disparage its "racist undertones" and find it "too sad" for smaller fry, fans laud its "fabulous", Oscar-winning score and "unforgettable sequences" – particularly the "tripped-out" "hallucination" of those pink pachyderms on parade.

Dune
| 14 | 13 | 18 | 18 |

1984 | Directed by David Lynch | With Kyle MacLachlan, Francesca Annis, Jürgen Prochnow, Sting | 137 minutes | Rated PG-13

"Beautiful to look at but incoherent" plotwise, this "problematic" adaptation of Frank Herbert's "iconic" sci-fi novel is either a "heroic mess" or an "unjustly maligned" work that "gets better after repeated viewings"; many argue that the "complicated storyline" (something to do with warring factions in the far-off year of 10191) is practically "un-filmable", but whether the end result is worth seeing for director Lynch's trademark "high weirdness" or just a "waste of celluloid" is up to you.

Dying Gaul, The
17 | 23 | 16 | 18

2005 | Directed by Craig Lucas | With Peter Sarsgaard, Campbell Scott, Patricia Clarkson | 101 minutes | Rated R

Art versus commerce is the "interesting premise" of this "edgy" drama wherein a "shattered gay man" sells a vaguely autobiographical screenplay to a Hollywood studio, only to undergo "betrayal heaped on betrayal" as it goes through rewrites; fans like the "never-saw-it-coming" ending and "terrific" cast "flexing their talent", but the blasé yawn the picture is "just not compelling" enough.

Eastern Promises
24 | 27 | 23 | 23

2007 | Directed by David Cronenberg | With Viggo Mortensen, Naomi Watts, Vincent Cassel | 100 minutes | Rated R

Fasten your seatbelts for a "brutal" slice of gangster life depicted in this "stomach-clenching" thriller starring a "stunning" Mortensen as a Russian mobster with "nice tattoos" caught in a vicious "spiral of murder"; the "strong" supporting cast and "killer ending" supply bonus thrills, but the "take-your-breath-away" moment is Viggo's Full Monty "steam room fight scene."

Easter Parade
22 | 21 | 17 | 24

1948 | Directed by Charles Walters | With Judy Garland, Fred Astaire, Ann Miller | 107 minutes | Not Rated

"It isn't really Easter" till you've watched this "grand Irving Berlin musical" boasting 17 songs and "lots of frills upon it" – including Fred and Judy at their "singing and dancing best" in their "only screen appearance together"; the slender story has Astaire trying to make a star out of chorus girl Garland, but this "wonderful" MGM "showcase" transcends its plot with sheer star power.

East of Eden
24 | 27 | 24 | 23

1955 | Directed by Elia Kazan | With James Dean, Julie Harris, Raymond Massey, Jo Van Fleet | 115 minutes | Not Rated

An "unforgettable" Dean eats "every actor on the set for breakfast" in his "searing" big-screen debut as the "proverbial bad seed" in this adaptation of John Steinbeck's tale of "sibling rivalry"; sure, there are also "beautiful" CinemaScope panoramas and an Oscar-winning turn from Van Fleet, but Jimmy makes it "memorable" – "to think he only made three films is amazing."

Easy Rider
23 | 23 | 20 | 20

1969 | Directed by Dennis Hopper | With Peter Fonda, Dennis Hopper, Jack Nicholson | 94 minutes | Rated R

"Sex, drugs and rock 'n' roll" explode on the silver screen in this "seminal" "road movie" that "defined a generation" by capturing the essence of the "tumultuous" '60s; famed for "Nicholson's starmaking performance" and Hopper's "manic", "revolutionary" direction, this "trippy" "time capsule" might have also "invented the music video" thanks to that "amazing soundtrack"; still, Gen-Y types protest it "doesn't hold up" today, unless you "get high" first.

Eat Drink Man Woman 🄵
25 | 24 | 24 | 24 |

1994 | Directed by Ang Lee | With Sihung Lung, Wu Chien-Lien, Yang Kuei-Mei, Wang Yu-Wen | 123 minutes | Not Rated

Gourmands eat up this "tasty" Taiwanese look at a "different culture" that tells the story of a traditional "Asian father who shows his love by cooking for his daughters"; director Lee's "visual feast" contrasts "ticklish relationships" with "stupendous food scenes" so adroitly that many "get hungry just thinking about it."

Eating Raoul
18 | 18 | 21 | 15 |

1982 | Directed by Paul Bartel | With Paul Bartel, Mary Woronov, Robert Beltran | 90 minutes | Rated R

"Not everyone can stomach" this "blacker-than-black" "bizarro" "cult" comedy, but there's agreement that its "absurd" plot (about a Moral Majority–esque couple luring swingers to their deaths) is the "trailer-park" version of *Sweeney Todd*; "kind of sick", this "deadpan" "low-budget" "B movie" is also kind of "fun" – and "probably for grown-ups only."

Educating Rita
18 | 21 | 19 | 18 |

1983 | Directed by Lewis Gilbert | With Michael Caine, Julie Walters | 110 minutes | Rated PG-13

Caine and Walters exhibit "great chemistry" in this "interesting" tale of an "alcoholic professor" who tutors a "working-class" gal; though the "pseudo-*Pygmalion*" plot "isn't quite convincing" for some, others relate perfectly to the "believable" title character, a "woman who won't allow herself to be held back by social class."

Edward Scissorhands
21 | 22 | 22 | 24 |

1990 | Directed by Tim Burton | With Johnny Depp, Winona Ryder, Dianne Wiest | 100 minutes | Rated PG-13

Burton's "oddball" opus spins a "delightfully bent" "love story" around an ultimate "outsider" – a "misfit boy with garden tools for hands" – living in "conformist suburbia"; "Depp shows he has the big-screen stuff" (and "makes a hell of a topiary"), while the "primary-colored" art direction creates an "alternative universe disturbingly close to home"; best line: Wiest's perky "Avon calling!"

Ed Wood ◑
20 | 23 | 19 | 21 |

1994 | Directed by Tim Burton | With Johnny Depp, Martin Landau, Sarah Jessica Parker | 127 minutes | Rated R

"Schlockmeister" director Ed Wood gets the full Tim Burton treatment in this "loving tribute" that's also an "entertaining glimpse into grade Z filmmaking"; look for an "enthusiastic", "totally sympathetic" Depp in the title role opposite an Oscar-winning Landau as a "drugged-out" Bela Lugosi – "never before have the talentless been so brilliantly rendered by the talented."

Eiger Sanction, The
22 | 20 | 23 | 22 |

1975 | Directed by Clint Eastwood | With Clint Eastwood, George Kennedy, Vonetta McGee, Jack Cassidy | 123 minutes | Rated R

Its premise may "sound strange" – "an art professor climbing a Swiss mountain to assassinate a spy" – but this "gritty" Eastwood thriller provides "great escapism" via "fantastic" locales and plenty of "cliff-hanging" action (all the more gripping since Clint "does his own stunts"); keep an eye on the "wonderful" Cassidy, who "acts up a storm" as a "slimy" secret agent.

☑ 8½ ⊠◐▣ | 26 | 26 | 24 | 26

1963 | Directed by Federico Fellini | With Marcello Mastroianni, Claudia Cardinale, Anouk Aimée | 145 minutes | Not Rated

"Navel-gazing has never been more profound" than in this "semi-autobiographical" "Italian masterpiece" from the "extraordinary" Fellini about a blocked "director trying to make a film" by using his "life as material for his work"; told in "stream of consciousness", it also features "luscious" art direction and a "career-defining turn by Mastroianni" – no wonder many call this "heartfelt" flick the "definitive movie about movies."

Eight Below | 22 | 19 | 24 | 24

2006 | Directed by Frank Marshall | With Paul Walker, Bruce Greenwood, Moon Bloodgood | 120 minutes | Rated PG

The "astounding canine cast" does the "best acting" in this live-action Disney adventure, an "uplifting" true story about a sled dog team's "struggle to survive" after the humans evacuate in the wake of a "monster snow storm in Antarctica"; though "weepy for sure", it's a "wholesome family flick" iced with enough "thrills" to ensure that you "won't be bored."

Eight Men Out | 24 | 24 | 25 | 23

1988 | Directed by John Sayles | With John Cusack, David Strathairn, D.B. Sweeney, Charlie Sheen | 119 minutes | Rated PG

A "black eye for baseball" gets a "dark" retelling in Sayles' "insightful" sports story, recounting the "legendary 1919 Black Sox scandal" that left eight players "forever banned" for "throwing the World Series"; with a "superb" ensemble cast (who "actually look like ballplayers") and an "uncanny re-creation" of "post-WWI" times, it's pitched as a "contender" for best diamond drama.

8 Mile | 19 | 18 | 17 | 19

2002 | Directed by Curtis Hanson | With Eminem, Kim Basinger, Brittany Murphy, Mekhi Phifer | 110 minutes | Rated R

Take *Rocky*, add *Purple Rain*, "go to Detroit" and top everything off with some "sweet freestyle scenes", and you've got this "quality" "retread" of the "poor-boy-claws-his-way-out-of-the-neighborhood" story; while Eminem's "semi-autobiographical" performance is ("surprise!") "raw and touching", this "gritty" flick (and its "7 mile"–long string of "F-words") gets truly "compelling" in the last "rap-off."

El Cid | 19 | 16 | 20 | 23

1961 | Directed by Anthony Mann | With Charlton Heston, Sophia Loren, Raf Vallone | 182 minutes | Not Rated

This early '60s epic is a "guy's delight" that finds Heston once again inhabiting the skin of a "larger-than-life" figure, this time the legendary 11th-century Spaniard who defended his country against the Moors; "lots of action" elates thrill-seekers, though foes lambaste it as "bombastic and overblown."

	OVERALL	ACTING	STORY	PROD.

Election `22` `24` `22` `20`

1999 | Directed by Alexander Payne | With Reese Witherspoon, Matthew Broderick | 103 minutes | Rated R

"Student council elections" as an "allegory for real political life" underscore this "whip-smart" "black comedy" about a "goody two-shoes" "high-school overachiever" and a teacher bent on putting a stop to her rise; voters find "no fraud" in this "spot-on" "social satire", adding that "unless you were home-schooled, you'll relate."

Elephant `19` `18` `19` `21`

2003 | Directed by Gus Van Sant | With Alex Frost, Eric Deulen | 81 minutes | Rated R

"Wildly original", this "disturbing" examination of a "Columbine-esque" high-school massacre splits surveyors: fans praise the "dreamlike" plot, "cinema verité"–style photography and "moving" work by a cast of "nonprofessionals", but cynics say it's "insightless" and "boring"; both sides agree it's "tough to watch" and "definitely open to interpretation."

Elephant Man, The ◐ `24` `27` `25` `23`

1980 | Directed by David Lynch | With Anthony Hopkins, John Hurt, Anne Bancroft | 125 minutes | Rated PG

The "dignity in deformity" is defined in this "unflinching" true story about a "Victorian-era" freak who "tests the compassion of a horrified society"; "brilliant acting and makeup" make it a "gloriously Gothic" "voyage into the human heart" – a "perfect match of director and material", it will "touch you deep inside."

Elf `21` `21` `20` `20`

2003 | Directed by Jon Favreau | With Will Ferrell, James Caan, Bob Newhart, Zooey Deschanel | 95 minutes | Rated PG

Imbued with the "real spirit of Christmas", this "surprisingly sweet-natured" holiday comedy stars "funny man Ferrell" as a "human being raised by elves" at the North Pole who travels to NYC to find his birth parents; granted, there's "nothing to tax your mind" in this "old-fashioned romp", but Will's a "hoot", "Deschanel looks gorgeous" and the "deadpan" Newhart is "consistently hilarious."

Elizabeth `24` `27` `23` `26`

1998 | Directed by Shekhar Kapur | With Cate Blanchett, Geoffrey Rush, Joseph Fiennes | 124 minutes | Rated R

"Captivating" Cate displays "unbelievable range" in this bio of England's "Virgin Queen" that follows her progress from "lusty young woman" to "ice-cold, calculating icon"; though it "feels like a fantasy version of Elizabeth I's life" to skeptics, scholars swear it's "historically on the mark", with "beautiful sets", "excellent costume design" and a "gripping" storyline.

Elizabeth: The Golden Age `21` `25` `19` `25`

2007 | Directed by Shekhar Kapur | With Cate Blanchett, Geoffrey Rush, Clive Owen | 114 minutes | Rated PG-13

Cate's "commanding" reprise of Queen Elizabeth I and a "meticulous" re-creation of "glorious Olde England" make for "period piece pleasure" in this "lavish" sequel tracing the events leading up to the Spanish Armada in 1588; still, critics carp it's "historically dubious", a "bit of a soap opera" and "not in the same class as its predecessor."

| | OVERALL | ACTING | STORY | PROD. |

Elizabethtown
14 | 16 | 14 | 15

2005 | Directed by Cameron Crowe | With Orlando Bloom, Kirsten Dunst, Susan Sarandon | 123 minutes | Rated PG-13

"Nothing really clicks" in this "overblown" chick flick, a mix of "*Jerry Maguire*" and "*Garden State*" that tells the story of an ambitious hot-shot who loses both his job and his father in the same week, only to find romance and "healing" when he returns to his hometown; a "mix tape"-worthy soundtrack can't overcome the "rambling" story and "bland" stars with "zero chemistry."

Ella Enchanted
19 | 19 | 19 | 21

2004 | Directed by Tommy O'Haver | With Anne Hathaway, Hugh Dancy, Cary Elwes | 96 minutes | Rated PG

"Tween girls" are the target audience of this "cute" fairy tale, a "fun gloss" on a "Cinderella"-like maiden hexed by a spell that makes her "obey all commands"; underneath it all is a "modern", pop-culture sensibility with a "catchy soundtrack" and a "grrl-power" message, leading some to compare it to a "live action version of *Shrek*" – even if the special effects "look fake."

Elmer Gantry ✉
25 | 27 | 24 | 23

1960 | Directed by Richard Brooks | With Burt Lancaster, Jean Simmons, Shirley Jones | 146 minutes | Not Rated

Disciples of this "rip-roaring" adaptation of the Sinclair Lewis novel testify that Lancaster's Oscar-winning, "fire-and-brimstone" performance as a "street preacher"-cum-"con man" in a "hypocritical" traveling ministry is the "best of his career" (while some "get religion" watching Jones' take on a jilted prostitute); its "excellent script" detailing a "flesh vs. the spirit" conflict also took home a statuette.

Elvira Madigan 🄵
20 | 19 | 20 | 24

1967 | Directed by Bo Widerberg | With Pia Degermark, Thommy Berggren | 91 minutes | Rated PG

Both "visually stunning" and "wonderfully dated", this Swedish sobfest recounts the "heartbreaking" affair between "two AWOL lovers" – a tightrope walker and a married army officer – who are "beautiful" and, of course, "doomed"; although memorable for its "lovely scenery" and the Mozart piano concerto it popularized, it's forgettable to those who see it as "tiresome" "romantic fluff."

Emma
22 | 23 | 23 | 24

1996 | Directed by Douglas McGrath | With Gwyneth Paltrow, Jeremy Northam, Greta Scacchi | 121 minutes | Rated PG

Jane Austen's "charming" story of "matchmaking at its best and worst" gets an "engaging" spin in this "delightful period piece" starring a "perfect" Paltrow opposite a "laconically charming" Northam; its "cheery" tone and dryly "humorous approach" make it a natural to "watch back-to-back with *Clueless*, since they're both based on the same novel."

Emmanuelle 🄵
16 | 14 | 14 | 15

1974 | Directed by Just Jaeckin | With Sylvia Kristel, Alain Cuny, Marika Green | 95 minutes | Rated R

Long before "Cinemax", this "leader" of "soft-core porn" features finds Kristel looking "very feminine" (and "sans silicone") in the part of a naive but libidinous diplomat's spouse out to explore the "erotic" possibilities available within R-rated limits; considered "sexy for its day", it remains "scenic in many ways" but rather "tame for this century."

Emperor's Club, The
19 | 22 | 19 | 19

2002 | Directed by Michael Hoffman | With Kevin Kline, Emile Hirsch, Embeth Davidtz, Paul Dano | 110 minutes | Rated PG-13
Kline adds a "worthy" notch to his acting curriculum vitae in this "sentimental" but "thought-provoking" tale of a "devoted" teacher "reaching out to a troubled student"; cynics say the classroom setting and "inspirational" lessons about "what makes a man" look "familiar" – it's really *Dead Poets Society* with a different name."

Emperor's New Groove, The
20 | - | 18 | 20

2000 | Directed by Mark Dindal | Animated | 78 minutes | Rated G
A "selfish, smart-mouthed emperor becomes a llama" with extremely humbling results in this "quirky", "overlooked cartoon" that effortlessly merges both "standard and CGI animation" with "superb voice acting"; sure, aesthetes complain of a "low-budget", "slapped-together" look, but most find it "highly entertaining" with "lots of great gags" and a script that's "actually funny."

☑ Empire of the Sun
25 | 23 | 24 | 26

1987 | Directed by Steven Spielberg | With Christian Bale, John Malkovich | 154 minutes | Rated PG
Perhaps Spielberg's most "underappreciated" picture, this "touching story of a British child's internment in a World War II Japanese prison camp" is an "ambitious" epic replete with "dazzling" acting, "David Lean-worthy" imagery and an "especially moving John Williams score"; maybe the "storyline drags" a bit midway, but overall its "sheer power" supplies the "magic moments."

Enchanted
23 | 22 | 22 | 25

2007 | Directed by Kevin Lima | With Amy Adams, Patrick Dempsey, James Marsden | 107 minutes | Rated PG
Disney simultaneously "parodies and pays homage" to itself in this "clever" musical fairy tale about a maiden from a generic "cartoon world" (complete with talking "woodland creatures") who's unwittingly transposed to "rough-and-tumble" NYC; look for amusingly "kitschy" song-and-dance routines and "lovely chemistry" between the "exuberant" Adams and "McDreamy" Dempsey.

☑ Enchanted April ∅
24 | 26 | 22 | 25

1992 | Directed by Mike Newell | With Joan Plowright, Miranda Richardson, Josie Lawrence | 95 minutes | Rated PG
For a "wonderfully rich pick-me-up", take a look at this "genteel" "getaway" of a movie about four "risk-taking" women who decide to "leave their dreary English lives behind" and are "transformed" during an April vacation in "lush, sunny" Tuscany; the perfect "antidote to winter", it's "more complex than it first appears", and Plowright's "terrific performance" will brighten any "rainy day."

Endless Summer, The
24 | - | 20 | 23

1966 | Directed by Bruce Brown | Documentary | 95 minutes | Not Rated
"Cowabunga" – this "quintessential" surfing documentary is a bona fide "'60s relic"-cum-"classic travelogue" that puts some in the mood

to "grab a board and move to Hawaii"; ok, there's "not much of a storyline" (two surfers traveling the globe "in search of the perfect wave"), but armchair beachcombers seeking a "great escape" claim it "stands the test of time."

End of the Affair, The

OVERALL	ACTING	STORY	PROD.
20	24	20	22

1999 | Directed by Neil Jordan | With Ralph Fiennes, Julianne Moore, Stephen Rea | 102 minutes | Rated R

"Faith, love and loss" underlie this "terrific" adaptation of Graham Greene's "tragic romance" set in "rainy" WWII London about a "conflicted, adulterous Englishwoman" and her "jealous, angry lover"; this "difficult story" succeeds thanks to a "flashback"-heavy, "multilayered" scenario and "wonderful screen chemistry" between a "powerful" Fiennes and a "smoldering" Moore modeling "glamorous slips and retro suits."

Enemy at the Gates

OVERALL	ACTING	STORY	PROD.
21	22	23	23

2001 | Directed by Jean-Jacques Annaud | With Jude Law, Ed Harris, Rachel Weisz, Joseph Fiennes | 131 minutes | Rated R

"Soviet Communists and Nazis" scrap on the Russian front in this "gripping" war pic, putting WWII's "hellish" siege of Stalingrad "on a very personal level", featuring Harris and Law as "two dueling snipers" with their sights set on "cleverly choreographed standoffs"; the "rousing action" and "engrossing characterizations" are "powerful stuff" that make this "violent", "sprawling" saga "worth the effort."

Enemy of the State

OVERALL	ACTING	STORY	PROD.
19	19	20	21

1998 | Directed by Tony Scott | With Will Smith, Gene Hackman, Jon Voight | 131 minutes | Rated R

"Privacy and civil liberties" issues take center stage in this ultra-"engaging", ultra-"paranoid" thriller about "Big Brother"-ish "government agents" pursuing a DC lawyer who's unwittingly holding an incriminating videotape; so "fast moving" that there's barely time to "catch your breath", it mixes "high-tech" effects with a "low-concept" idea to come up with something that's "very exciting" indeed.

⚡ English Patient, The ✉

OVERALL	ACTING	STORY	PROD.
22	24	21	25

1996 | Directed by Anthony Minghella | With Ralph Fiennes, Juliette Binoche, Kristin Scott Thomas | 160 minutes | Rated R

"Love it or hate it", there's no question that this "lush" WWII romance (winner of nine Oscars) boasts an "old-Hollywood scope", swoonworthy cinematography, "brilliant writing" and "magnetic" performances from Fiennes and Scott Thomas as star-crossed lovers "in the desert sands of North Africa"; but those who "agree with Elaine on *Seinfeld*" claim this patient requires "patience", thanks to a pace so "laborious" that it's "recommended for treating insomnia."

Enigma

OVERALL	ACTING	STORY	PROD.
18	20	20	19

2002 | Directed by Michael Apted | With Dougray Scott, Kate Winslet, Jeremy Northam, Saffron Burrows | 119 minutes | Rated R

"Cryptography and romance" collide in this WWII spy thriller wherein a British "math guy" attempts to "decipher Nazi transmissions" while searching for his missing girlfriend; although it's decidedly "more intellectual than action-oriented", the story's "well told" and the casting "solid", notably a dowdy, "almost unrecognizable" Winslet.

	OVERALL	ACTING	STORY	PROD.

Enron: The Smartest Guys in the Room — 25 | - | 26 | 22

2005 | Directed by Alex Gibney | Documentary | 109 minutes | Not Rated

Learn how "arrogant corruption" and "greed run amok" led to the collapse of energy trader Enron's "house of cards" in this "compelling" documentary that "reveals the downside of American corporate culture"; "full of information", it reduces a "complicated", "numbers-centered" scheme into an "easy-to-follow" account that manages to both "disgust and fascinate", without resorting to "Michael Moore hysteria."

Enter the Dragon — 23 | 16 | 17 | 20

1973 | Directed by Robert Clouse | With Bruce Lee, John Saxon, Jim Kelly | 98 minutes | Rated R

"Martial arts" mavens maintain that this "all-time best kung fu" flicker is "butt-kicker" Lee's "magnum opus", the "standard by which all karate films are judged"; sure, the "production's cheesy" and its "James Bond" "rip-off" plot is "unoriginal", but the "balletic, ballistic" fight scenes are so "spectacular" that this one "spawned many forgettable imitators" – not to mention many "video games."

Eragon — 16 | 15 | 17 | 20

2006 | Directed by Stefen Fangmeier | With Edward Speleers, Jeremy Irons, Sienna Guillory, John Malkovich | 104 minutes | Rated PG

Riding on the tailwind of "*Star Wars* and *The Lord of the Rings*", this "daring-young-man-riding-a-firebreathing-dragon" fantasy is "visually appealing" but otherwise "average" due to "subpar" emoting and a "flimsy", "cliché-ridden" script; devotees still "hope for sequels", though most "pray this was a onetime deal."

Eraser — 14 | 12 | 14 | 17

1996 | Directed by Chuck Russell | With Arnold Schwarzenegger, Vanessa Williams, James Caan | 115 minutes | Rated R

"Not one of Arnie's best", this "middling" action flick about a witness protection program operative helping people jettison their former identities and assume new ones "doesn't live up to the promise" of its pricey production; sure, the effects are "cool", but the "ridiculous" storyline and all that "technical mumbo-jumbo" is ultimately "forgettable."

Eraserhead ◑ — 21 | 17 | 17 | 19

1977 | Directed by David Lynch | With Jack Nance, Charlotte Stewart | 90 minutes | Not Rated

Director Lynch's "trippy", "dread-inducing" debut is an "eerie glimpse of a marriage gone horribly awry" that "replicates the logic of a nightmare" (i.e. "you don't know what's going on half the time"); gird yourself for some "disturbing pictures, disturbing music" and "no discernable plot", but at least this "cult classic" is "willing to take risks."

Erin Brockovich ✉ — 21 | 23 | 23 | 21

2000 | Directed by Steven Soderbergh | With Julia Roberts, Albert Finney, Aaron Eckhart | 130 minutes | Rated R

"Roberts proves her worth" with a "boffo", Oscar-winning turn in this "uplifting", "push-up bra"–laden true story about "standing up to a big corporation and winning"; ok, its "socially conscious", "don't-mess-with-the-little-people" screenplay might owe a lot to "*Norma Rae*", but ultimately this "polished production" works as both a "star vehicle and a compelling story."

| | OVERALL | ACTING | STORY | PROD. |

Escape from Alcatraz
23 22 23 21

1979 | Directed by Don Siegel | With Clint Eastwood, Fred Ward, Patrick McGoohan | 112 minutes | Rated PG

"Actually filmed on The Rock", this "edge-of-your-seat thriller" based on a real-life "amazing escape" from the "infamous" prison stars Eastwood as a "likable bad guy" in one of his "best non-Western performances"; the "good pace" and "solid action" are "thoroughly entertaining", with some "socially conscious" commentary thrown in to boot.

Escape from New York
15 13 17 18

1981 | Directed by John Carpenter | With Kurt Russell, Lee Van Cleef, Ernest Borgnine | 99 minutes | Rated R

A "hoot and a half", this "tongue-in-cheek" action-adventurer is set in "post-apocalyptic" Manhattan that has morphed into a maximum security prison where the President is being held hostage; to the rescue comes Russell as Snake Plissken, a "cartoon character" but still a "very appealing hero", who manages to keep the "novel premise amusing" enough to make for some "silly", "cheesy fun."

Eternal Sunshine of the Spotless Mind
23 24 24 23

2004 | Directed by Michel Gondry | With Jim Carrey, Kate Winslet, Tom Wilkinson, Mark Ruffalo, Kirsten Dunst | 108 minutes | Rated R

A "one-of-a-kind experience", this "quirky romantic" fantasy follows a "balanced" Carrey and "winning" Winslet as broken-up lovers who biologically erase their memories of each other, then struggle to erase the erasure; though "not everyone's cup of tea", the "zany" script is "cerebral", "comical" and "complex" (given a "juggled time sequence" à la "*Memento*"), yet skillfully steered by director Gondry's "deft hand."

⊠ E.T. The Extra-Terrestrial
26 22 26 27

1982 | Directed by Steven Spielberg | With Dee Wallace, Henry Thomas, Drew Barrymore | 115 minutes | Rated PG

Arguably the "*Wizard of Oz* for a brand-new generation", this "irresistible" sci-fi "fairy tale" is the "endearing story of a boy", the "cutest alien of all time" and their attempts to "phone home"; there's agreement that Spielberg's "incredibly imaginative" "genius strikes again", managing to express "every human emotion in less than two hours", so gather the "entire family" along with a "big bowl of Reese's Pieces" and get ready for some "true magic."

Everybody's All-American
19 21 21 18

1988 | Directed by Taylor Hackford | With Jessica Lange, Dennis Quaid, Timothy Hutton, John Goodman | 127 minutes | Rated R

A "sports hero's rise and fall" is the subject of this "memorable" drama about an "LSU football jock", his "smart-cookie girlfriend" and their attempt to "hold on to the past" as they grow older; foes say it veers between "sentimental" and "depressing", but fans find this "reality check behind the end zone" reasonably "compelling."

Everyone Says I Love You
18 20 17 19

1996 | Directed by Woody Allen | With Alan Alda, Goldie Hawn, Woody Allen, Julia Roberts, Edward Norton, Drew Barrymore, Tim Roth | 101 minutes | Rated R

Woody Allen does "musical comedy" in this "high-concept", "refreshingly whimsical" picture with a "powerhouse cast" and "magnificent backdrops" ("Paris never looked so romantic"); brace yourself for some of the "most unfortunate singing this side of the shower curtain", though standout numbers include the "Groucho Marx costume party" and "Goldie's song and dance."

Everything You Always Wanted to Know About Sex

| 21 | 20 | 20 | 19 |

1972 | Directed by Woody Allen | With Woody Allen, Gene Wilder, Lou Jacobi, Louise Lasser, Lynn Redgrave, John Carradine, Burt Reynolds, Tony Randall | 87 minutes | Rated R

"Nothing like the book of the same name", this "early Woody Allen" feature is comprised of seven "kinky" comedy sketches "illustrating questions from a sex manual"; despite the "dated" feel and "inconsistent quality" (some of the vignettes "run far too long"), sex addicts say it "hits more than it misses"; P.S. fast-forward to Gene Wilder's "hilarious" turn as a "therapist in love with a sheep."

Every Which Way But Loose

| 16 | 16 | 15 | 16 |

1978 | Directed by James Fargo | With Clint Eastwood, Sondra Locke, Geoffrey Lewis, Beverly D'Angelo | 110 minutes | Rated PG

"Just plain dopey fun", this "slightly different" Eastwood vehicle tells the story of a barroom-brawling truck driver chasing after a country-music singer with his pet orangutan in tow; though "Clint holds his own", the monkey "steals the show" (and "strikes the funny bone") while "swinging from chandeliers" and "punching people out"; best line: "right turn, Clyde."

Evil Dead, The

| 22 | 14 | 18 | 17 |

1982 | Directed by Sam Raimi | With Bruce Campbell, Ellen Sandweiss, Betsy Baker | 85 minutes | Rated NC-17

"Not for the weak-stomached", this "scary, scary, scary" "gorefest" with "abundant blood" and lots of "energy" is "dumb", "campy horror at its best"; alright, the acting's "questionable", the dialogue "lame", the story "hackneyed" and the effects very "low-budget", but it "blows Hollywood blockbusters away" because it's "so much fun."

Evita

| 19 | 17 | 21 | 24 |

1996 | Directed by Alan Parker | With Madonna, Antonio Banderas, Jonathan Pryce | 134 minutes | Rated PG

"Sleazy politics come alive" in this "visually rich" celluloid version of the Andrew Lloyd Webber stage musical based on the life of Argentina's Eva Peron, an all-singing, dialogue-free production that seems to some like an "extended MTV video"; though surveyors split on Madonna's title turn ("surprisingly good" vs. "doesn't have the chops"), the "smoldering", "powerful" Banderas is a hit and overall this "entertaining" epic is at the very least "watchable."

Excalibur

| 22 | 19 | 22 | 23 |

1981 | Directed by John Boorman | With Nigel Terry, Nicol Williamson, Helen Mirren, Nicholas Clay | 140 minutes | Rated R

The Holy Grail for "King Arthur junkies", this "grown-up version" of the round table legend is a "dark" take on Camelot with "sumptuous" visuals, "racy love scenes" and a "Wagnerian" soundtrack that "set the bar" for "sensual" fantasy; forsooth, it's "long and self-important", but fans exult over a "compelling" telling of a "tale you thought you knew."

| | OVERALL | ACTING | STORY | PROD. |

Exodus
23 23 26 25

1960 | Directed by Otto Preminger | With Paul Newman, Eva Marie Saint, Sal Mineo | 210 minutes | Not Rated

An "all-star cast" drives this story of the "founding of modern Israel", a "stunning", "satisfying" Preminger epic "faithfully" adapted from Leon Uris' best-seller; fans single out the star turn from a "too-gorgeous-for-words" Newman "in his prime", and if the plot has some "bathos" mixed into its "high drama", it's ultimately a "moving" moving picture.

Exorcism of Emily Rose, The
17 19 19 19

2005 | Directed by Scott Derrickson | With Laura Linney, Tom Wilkinson, Campbell Scott, Jennifer Carpenter | 119 minutes | Rated PG-13

Equal parts "courtroom drama" and "psychological horror flick", this "interesting" hybrid "loosely based on a true story" crosscuts the murder trial of an exorcist with flashbacks of a "possessed" young woman's "creepy" demise; the "harrowing yet skeptically distanced" approach works for most, but hard-core horrorites harrumph it's "not really scary – unless you consider lawyers scary."

Exorcist, The ✉
25 24 26 25

1973 | Directed by William Friedkin | With Ellen Burstyn, Max von Sydow, Linda Blair | 122 minutes | Rated R

"Horror and religion" collide in this "head-spinning", "nightmare-inducing" "shocker" about a child possessed by the devil that "grossed out America" with its "revolting" language and that infamous "pea-soup vomit scene"; though some say it's "slid into camp" over the years, most maintain it's still "one of the scariest movies ever" – but stick to the "original" cut that's much more "terrifying" than the recent 'restored' reissue.

Experiment in Terror ◑
25 24 25 23

1962 | Directed by Blake Edwards | With Glenn Ford, Lee Remick, Stefanie Powers, Ross Martin | 123 minutes | Not Rated

A rare thriller from Blake Edwards, this "little-known gem" is "one of the better woman-in-danger pictures" thanks to "chilling" performances by Remick as a "sexy" bank teller and Martin as an "asthmatic" extortionist; a jazzy Henry Mancini soundtrack and "mesmerizing" San Francisco settings (particularly that knockout windup at Candlestick Park) supply the atmosphere.

Eye of the Needle
23 25 26 22

1981 | Directed by Richard Marquand | With Donald Sutherland, Kate Nelligan, Christopher Cazenove | 112 minutes | Rated R

"Overlooked but worthwhile", this "engrossing" WWII thriller about a Nazi spy out to alert Hitler about D-day is suspenseful enough to "keep your heart in your throat" throughout; Sutherland is "fantastic" as the "creepy" lead, somehow "convincing you to cheer for him", especially when conducting a "waves-crashing-against-the-rocks" romance with the "excellent" Nelligan.

Eyes Wide Shut
13 15 12 19

1999 | Directed by Stanley Kubrick | With Tom Cruise, Nicole Kidman, Sydney Pollack | 159 minutes | Rated R

"Stanley Kubrick's final hurrah", this "would-be erotic thriller" about "marital infidelity" disappoints most voters, especially given the big "build-up before its release"; critics condemn Cruise's "cardboard-cutout" acting, the "plodding" plot, the "Chinese water torture" soundtrack and the director's "overall failure of vision" – but not the "polished, sexy" Kidman, who's the "only thing worth watching" in this "maddening" picture.

Eyewitness

23 **24** **23** **21**

1981 | Directed by Peter Yates | With William Hurt, Sigourney Weaver, Christopher Plummer | 103 minutes | Rated R

"Early starring roles" bear witness to the promise of "sexy" Bill and "stunning" Sigourney, who "both do excellent work" in this "absorbing" thriller about a janitor fixated on a TV newswoman, who meet after he discovers a murder victim; it's a "solid enough plot", and the "noir" atmosphere is enhanced by the "lovely" NYC settings.

Fabulous Baker Boys, The

20 **22** **18** **19**

1989 | Directed by Steven Kloves | With Jeff Bridges, Michelle Pfeiffer, Beau Bridges | 114 minutes | Rated R

"Sibling rivalry" gets "compelling" treatment in this "great date movie" about two "journeyman musicians" competing for the attentions of their "slinky, sexy" girl singer; the Bridges brothers exude the "art of cool" and Pfeiffer "slithers around so deliciously" that no one minds that this "slice-of-life" story "doesn't go anywhere", given the "enjoyable" ride; most memorable scene, no question: Michelle "draped over a piano" crooning 'Makin' Whoopee' – "who knew she could sing?"

Face/Off

18 **19** **18** **21**

1997 | Directed by John Woo | With John Travolta, Nicolas Cage, Joan Allen, Gina Gershon | 138 minutes | Rated R

"Hong Kong auteur" John Woo "goes Hollywood" in this "hyperkinetic" action flick that "fires on all pistons", despite an "unashamedly preposterous scenario" in which "over-the-top" archenemies Travolta and Cage "switch places" (and faces); be prepared for "twists and turns galore", "lots of violence" and enough "mindless fun" to put this one at the very top of your "guilty pleasures list."

Faces ◑

22 **27** **18** **19**

1968 | Directed by John Cassavetes | With John Marley, Gena Rowlands, Lynn Carlin, Seymour Cassel | 130 minutes | Rated PG-13

The "beginning of independent filmmaking as we know it", this "ultra-low-budget" drama really "put Cassavetes on the map as a director" with its "revealing" insights on infidelity and the meaninglessness of life; it "remains as avant-garde" as ever thanks to the "fierce performances" alone, and is just the thing "when you want to take a breather from feel-good fare."

Fahrenheit 451

21 **19** **25** **19**

1966 | Directed by François Truffaut | With Oskar Werner, Julie Christie, Cyril Cusack | 110 minutes | Not Rated

"Truffaut's first English-language picture" is an "excellent adaptation" of Ray Bradbury's "Big Brother"-ish sci-fi novel, a "social commentary" about "censorship by book burning" in the not-too-distant future (the title is the temperature at which paper ignites); though zealots praise the "thoughtful" presentation of an "important topic", nonbelievers flame it as "plodding" and suggest you "read the book" instead.

| | OVERALL | ACTING | STORY | PROD. |

Fahrenheit 9/11
21 | - | 22 | 19

2004 | Directed by Michael Moore | Documentary | 122 minutes | Rated R

Conveyed "with all the subtlety of a carpet bombing", Moore's "un-apologetically biased" polemic against George W. Bush's "policies and leadership" elicits passionate praise and bitter condemnation alike, with defenders calling it a "daring exposé" of the "real truth" and foes crying it's a "complete fraud on every level"; though unlikely to "change your opinion", it's still a "must-see for anyone remotely interested in what's going on in the Washington world of today."

Fail-Safe ◑
24 | 25 | 26 | 21

1964 | Directed by Sidney Lumet | With Henry Fonda, Walter Matthau, Larry Hagman | 112 minutes | Not Rated

The "Cold War gets hot" in this "chilling", "hypnotic" nuclear-war melodrama about an American President forced to make some "horrifying choices" as an atom bomb hurtles its way toward Moscow; devotees note that the storyline is strikingly similar to that of *Dr. Strangelove* (though decidedly laugh-free) but insist its "what if?" plot is especially "gripping – and hopefully not prophetic."

Failure to Launch
15 | 17 | 16 | 16

2006 | Directed by Tom Dey | With Matthew McConaughey, Sarah Jessica Parker, Kathy Bates | 97 minutes | Rated PG-13

This "light" comedy lifts off with McConaughey as a "dreamy" slacker "still living with his parents", who hire Parker (in full *Sex and the City* persona) to "coax" him out of the nest; with "few surprises" other than a "TMI" take of "Terry Bradshaw in the buff", it's either a "disposable date movie" or a "cliché-ridden" "dud" that "should have been scrubbed."

Falcon and the Snowman, The
21 | 23 | 21 | 19

1985 | Directed by John Schlesinger | With Timothy Hutton, Sean Penn, Lori Singer | 132 minutes | Rated R

"Compelling" and "thought-provoking", this "fact-based" drama recounts the story of two "suburban dudes" with a "lack of morals" who matter-of-factly "sell state secrets" to the Russians; though a minority says it's "unmemorable", there's agreement that "sensitive" turns by Hutton and Penn supply the "watchability."

Fame
21 | 18 | 21 | 20

1980 | Directed by Alan Parker | With Irene Cara, Lee Curreri, Eddie Barth, Laura Dean | 134 minutes | Rated R

"Little girls who sing in front of the mirror" relate to this "feel-good" musical set in "NY's High School of Performing Arts", where "talented", "leg warmer–wearing teenagers" spend their days "dancing in the streets" and "struggling for fame"; ok, it's a bit "overdone" and "very dated now", but "crank up the volume" and you'll "enjoy the energy" all the same.

Family Man, The
16 | 17 | 18 | 17

2000 | Directed by Brett Ratner | With Nicolas Cage, Téa Leoni, Don Cheadle | 125 minutes | Rated PG-13

A "harried, unmarried exec wakes up with a new life and family" in this "what-if?" picture, an "update of *It's a Wonderful Life*" that may be "a

| | OVERALL | ACTING | STORY | PROD. |

bit far-fetched" but still "questions all the choices we make"; Leoni is "adorable", Cage "more affecting than expected" and despite the "slow" pace, most leave "believing wholeheartedly in true love."

Family Stone, The
16 | 19 | 16 | 18

2005 | Directed by Thomas Bezucha | With Sarah Jessica Parker, Diane Keaton, Rachel McAdams, Dermot Mulroney | Rated PG-13
A "type-A girl" meets her boyfriend's "type-B family" at Christmastime in this "mildly entertaining" dramedy that lies somewhere between "heartwarming", "heart-wrenching" and "girlie" "fluffy fluff"; while most agree on the "first-class talent" (including "national treasure" Keaton and a "fun" Parker playing against type as a "cold bitch"), there are catcalls for the "unlikable characters", "flip-flopping" storyline and that too "tidy ending."

☒ Fanny and Alexander ⊠ 🄵
26 | 25 | 25 | 26

1983 | Directed by Ingmar Bergman | With Pernilla Allwin, Bertil Guve, Gunn Wallgren | 188 minutes | Rated R
"Proof that Bergman wasn't miserable all the time", this "semi-autobiographical look back at his childhood" in Sweden "told from two siblings' point of view" features the "master" "at his most accessible"; sure, the "pacing's slow" and the film "long" (in fact, it's a pared-down version of a six-hour TV miniseries), yet the overall "visual magnificence" makes for something "rich and interesting."

☒ Fantasia
28 | - | - | 29

1940 | Directed by Ben Sharpsteen et al | Animated | 120 minutes | Rated G
Disney's "magnificent merger" of "mind-blowing" animation with a symphonic orchestra conducted by "maestro Leopold Stokowski" is a piece of "unbeatably creative" "eye candy" that's "never been equaled"; though a "flop when it first came out", it was later revived as a "'60s head movie" (thanks to trippy sequences like those "dancing hippos in tutus" and "Mickey Mouse as the sorcerer's apprentice"); modernists maintain this "original music video" remains a "perfect way to introduce a child to classical" sounds.

Fantasia 2000
24 | - | - | 27

1999 | Directed by James Algar et al | Animated | 75 minutes | Rated G
The "perfect companion" to the 1940 "classic", this "worthy" sequel marrying animation to music of great composers is "terrific Disney" that might be "more for adults than kids" for a change; it "keeps the spirit of the original beautifully" (right down to the "cloying celebrity" intros to each vignette), and although the "flamingo-with-the-yo-yo" scene enthralls many, the "best segment" is "'Rhapsody in Blue' via Al Hirschfeld."

Fantastic Four
14 | 13 | 14 | 19

2005 | Directed by Tim Story | With Ioan Gruffudd, Jessica Alba, Chris Evans, Michael Chiklis | 106 minutes | Rated PG-13
The "first family of comics" comes to life in this "CGI"-centric actioner celebrating the "tight-costumed" quartet of "superhuman misfits" as they "fight the evil Dr. Doom"; though "inoffensive" "summer bubblegum" for some, foes fume that the "simplistic story" and

"plastic" acting make for a "fantastic bore" that's "hard to watch" for "anyone over eight."

Fantastic Four: Rise of the Silver Surfer `15` `13` `15` `21`

2007 | Directed by Tim Story | With Ioan Gruffudd, Jessica Alba, Chris Evans, Michael Chiklis | 92 minutes | Rated PG

"Fast-moving" action, "shiny special effects" and Ms. Alba's "form-fitting" costume keep this "lackluster" comic book sequel within the realm of "escapist fun", despite the "cardboard" acting and "weak" storytelling; geeks are galled by supervillain Galactus' on-screen depiction ("a big dark cloud?"), though they award the chrome-domed Silver Surfer "best character" honors "since he doesn't talk much."

Fantastic Voyage `19` `12` `23` `21`

1966 | Directed by Richard Fleischer | With Stephen Boyd, Raquel Welch, Edmond O'Brien | 100 minutes | Rated PG

"Outrageous in its day", this sci-fi fantasy for "thinking" folks "still wows" the wide-eyed with its story about scientists shrunken and then "injected into a human body" to repair a blood clot; despite "wooden acting" and a "dumb ending", the "special effects are impressive for its time" – and Raquel sure looks swell in and out of that skintight diving outfit.

Farewell My Concubine **F** `25` `26` `24` `26`

1993 | Directed by Chen Kaige | With Leslie Cheung, Gong Li, Zhang Feng-Yi | 171 minutes | Rated R

"Worthy of David Lean on every level", this "sumptuous", "epic achievement" traces a complex friendship between two Peking Opera singers over a "fascinating sweep of history" from the '30s to the '70s; "stunning both visually and emotionally", it boasts "superb acting" and "outstanding scenery", but make sure to sit up straight: its "over-long" running time can be "draining."

Far From Heaven `24` `27` `23` `26`

2002 | Directed by Todd Haynes | With Julianne Moore, Dennis Quaid, Dennis Haysbert | 107 minutes | Rated PG-13

Haynes' "gorgeous homage to director Douglas Sirk's '50s melodramas" takes a "grippingly bittersweet" look at the "reality of the suburban picket-fence dream" and "genteel Northern racism"; though the pace is "slow" and the story "a little weak", it remains a "must-see" thanks to "flawless performances" from Moore and Quaid as well as "colorful", "stunning cinematography" that "captures the time period with brilliance" – the "costumes alone are close to heaven."

Z Fargo `25` `27` `25` `25`

1996 | Directed by Joel Coen | With Frances McDormand, William H. Macy, Steve Buscemi | 98 minutes | Rated R

This "comic noir" treatment of "crime in the heartland" shows "how funny Minnesota can be" in the hands of the Coen brothers, who "spin a folksy", violent yarn that makes the "outrageous seem everyday" and the "mundane interesting"; but the pièce de résistance is McDormand's "deadpan", Oscar-winning turn as a "pregnant" "crime-stopper" whose "goofy dialogue" alone is – "you betcha" – worth the price of admission.

	OVERALL	ACTING	STORY	PROD.

Fast Food Nation

18 | 16 | 19 | 16

2006 | Directed by Richard Linklater | With Greg Kinnear, Catalina Sandino Moreno, Ashley Johnson, Ehtan Hawke, Kris Kristofferson | 116 minutes | Rated R

This "fictionalized" rendering of a journalist's "eye-opening" vivisection of the fast-food industry uses "multiple narratives" to expose the "big bad corporations" greasing the American diet; activists say it will "make you a vegan – for a few days, at least" – but analysts sense a "bland" re-hash of "Super Size Me."

Fast Times at Ridgemont High

22 | 19 | 21 | 18

1982 | Directed by Amy Heckerling | With Sean Penn, Judge Reinhold, Jennifer Jason Leigh | 92 minutes | Rated R

One of the "crown jewels of the teen-comedy" genre, this "totally killer" "coming-of-age" "favorite" is an indelible "snapshot of the '80s" that made a star of Penn in the immortal role of "surfer stoner dude" Jeff Spicoli; adapted from Cameron Crowe's book, it showcases a "sprawling cast in interweaving stories" (like a kind of "teenage Nashville") and, among other things, "inspired a generation of in-school pizza orderers"; best "gratuitous scene": "Phoebe Cates on the diving board."

Fatal Attraction

22 | 23 | 23 | 21

1987 | Directed by Adrian Lyne | With Michael Douglas, Glenn Close, Anne Archer | 119 minutes | Rated R

"Anyone contemplating an extramarital affair" should take a hard look at this "genuinely creepy" "cautionary tale", dominated by a "demented" Close as a "licentious hubby's worst nightmare"; though the plot "goes overboard" occasionally and Douglas "plays the same character as in 47 other movies", the picture had tremendous "cultural impact" in its day and is "still hair-raising" – particularly the "yikes"-inducing "boiled-bunny" scene.

Father of the Bride ◑

23 | 25 | 21 | 20

1950 | Directed by Vincente Minnelli | With Spencer Tracy, Joan Bennett, Elizabeth Taylor | 92 minutes | Not Rated

Hollywood legends Tracy (in the "harried" title role) and Taylor (as the bride) walk down the aisle together in this "heartwarming" chestnut about the "havoc surrounding the planning of a wedding"; while most vow it's something that "all fathers and daughters should watch" together, a few pronounce it "dated and slow."

Father of the Bride

20 | 20 | 19 | 20

1991 | Directed by Charles Shyer | With Steve Martin, Diane Keaton, Martin Short | 105 minutes | Rated PG

"Faster-moving than the original", this "engaging" comedy captures the "chaos of wedding planning" thanks to a "hilarious" Martin (as the "clueless dad") and an equally "hysterical" Short; sure, it can be rather "silly", but ultimately goes down "like soothing chocolate pudding", and it "won't inflict pain on guys", even though it's a bona fide "chick flick."

Fear and Loathing in Las Vegas

15 | 20 | 15 | 18

1998 | Directed by Terry Gilliam | With Johnny Depp, Benicio Del Toro, Craig Bierko | 119 minutes | Rated R

"You'll either love or loathe" this "whirlwind cult film", a "faithful adaptation" of Hunter S. Thompson's "unadaptable" book detailing his "psychedelic" escapades in Las Vegas; despite kudos for Depp and Del Toro's "bizarre but authentic" performances, loathers find the film "essentially unpleasant" with "no plot", just a bunch of "idiots doing drugs."

Fearless 🅵 | 20 | 19 | 19 | 21 |

2006 | Directed by Ronny Yu | With Jet Li, Nathan Jones, Shido Nakamura | 103 minutes | Rated PG-13

"Stunningly choreographed" fight scenes are the heart of this "solid" martial-arts epic loosely based on the life of Chinese *wushu* master Huo Yuanjia; even though there's "hardly any storyline at all", no one cares what with "action" galore and Jet Li's "awesome" chopsocky.

🅩 Ferris Bueller's Day Off | 23 | 22 | 23 | 21 |

1986 | Directed by John Hughes | With Matthew Broderick, Alan Ruck, Mia Sara | 98 minutes | Rated PG-13

"Every teen's fantasy" of "ditching high school" for the day is realized in this "brilliant comedy" about a "sly slacker" on the loose in Chicago who "gets away with everything" and "does it with style"; the "smug-mugged" Broderick exudes "bravado" in the role that "launched his career", while "underappreciated" director Hughes offhandedly produces a picture so "influential" that it "belongs in a time capsule of the '80s."

Fever Pitch | 20 | 19 | 21 | 19 |

2005 | Directed by Bobby Farrelly, Peter Farrelly | With Drew Barrymore, Jimmy Fallon | 103 minutes | Rated PG-13

"Sports and love" are the themes of this "surprisingly tame outing" from the Farrelly brothers, a "feel-good" rom-com about an alpha gal who falls for an "obsessed" Red Sox fan; though the "chemistry's believable" between the "watchable" Fallon and the "adorable" Barrymore, the overall call is "harmless" – "not a home run", but maybe a "solid triple."

Few Good Men, A | 23 | 26 | 23 | 22 |

1992 | Directed by Rob Reiner | With Tom Cruise, Jack Nicholson, Demi Moore, Kevin Bacon | 138 minutes | Rated R

"Star-driven", "crackerjack courtroom drama" about a military murder investigation that's both "intelligent and entertaining"; no question, there are more than a few good performances, especially the "adorable-as-ever" Cruise in a "gritty", change-of-pace role playing against Nicholson's "riveting" if "pompous" marine colonel, who delivers the picture's most "infamous line: 'you can't handle the truth.'"

🅩 Fiddler on the Roof | 26 | 25 | 27 | 26 |

1971 | Directed by Norman Jewison | With Topol, Leonard Frey, Norma Crane | 181 minutes | Rated G

One of the "last of the epic musicals", this "uplifting" adaptation of the "Broadway classic" finds "wide-screen resonance" in its "memorable" score and "elaborate production" values; despite the unmusical subject matter (19th-century "Jews fleeing the pogroms"), it's still a "joyous" film that's as "moving as a moving picture can be."

Field of Dreams | 22 | 21 | 23 | 22 |

1989 | Directed by Phil Alden Robinson | With Kevin Costner, Amy Madigan, Ray Liotta, James Earl Jones | 107 minutes | Rated PG

"Even non-sports fans can love" this "feel-good" fantasy/drama about "baseball, ghosts" and "one man's search to find himself" in an Iowa cornfield; its "realistic sporting sequences, great storyline" and "touching" Costner turn ("before he lost it") make for a flick that "gets better every time you see it"; even those who find it too "sentimental" agree it's a "must-see for any father and son."

Fifth Element, The　　19 | 15 | 19 | 23

1997 | Directed by Luc Besson | With Bruce Willis, Gary Oldman, Milla Jovovich | 126 minutes | Rated PG-13

"Hyperkinetic", "loud" and "fast-paced", this "slick" sci-fi "actionfest" is about as substantial as a "big ball of cotton candy, but a hoot nonetheless"; sure, "Willis saves the planet – again" – but in this "loopy" "send-up of the genre", the "tongue-in-cheek" plot plays a distinct second fiddle to the "visually spectacular" effects; still, shirkers shrug it off as a "messy example of why more isn't always better."

50 First Dates　　18 | 18 | 19 | 19

2004 | Directed by Peter Segal | With Adam Sandler, Drew Barrymore, Rob Schneider | 99 minutes | Rated PG-13

"Comedy power couple" Sandler and Barrymore have the "chemistry" down pat in this "surprisingly touching", "well-thought-out" romance about a womanizer enthralled by a woman with short-term memory loss (i.e. she can't remember what she did on her last date); fans sigh it's "sweet" and "light-hearted", foes say "juvenile" and "farfetched", but at least they "didn't cop out with a cheap Hollywood ending."

Fight Club　　23 | 25 | 24 | 24

1999 | Directed by David Fincher | With Brad Pitt, Edward Norton, Helena Bonham Carter | 139 minutes | Rated R

"Love-it-or-hate-it" moviemaking is alive and well in this "testosterone-ridden" "cult classic" that uses "top-notch effects", "twisted humor" and a "killer" soundtrack in its depiction of "ultraviolent, disenfranchised males"; an "amazing Norton" and "underrated Pitt" provide the fireworks in this "gore"-drenched drama, with a "surprise finish" that's either "mind-blowing" or "nonsensical", depending on who's talking.

Fighting Temptations, The　　17 | 17 | 16 | 17

2003 | Directed by Jonathan Lynn | With Cuba Gooding Jr., Beyoncé Knowles | 123 minutes | Rated PG-13

A "great" gospel soundtrack blesses this otherwise "predictable" comedy spinning the tale of a soulless ad exec turned choir leader in order to collect an inheritance; Cuba "overacts" his way through the "trite" script, while Beyoncé should "stick to singing."

Finding Forrester　　22 | 24 | 22 | 20

2000 | Directed by Gus Van Sant | With Sean Connery, Rob Brown | 136 minutes | Rated PG-13

Plenty of "feel-good" "male bonding" turns up in this "inspirational" "cross-race" drama, with Connery as a literary "curmudgeon" playing "unlikely mentor" to an "inner-city kid" studying at a tony prep school; it works thanks to "excellent acting" that elevates the "clichéd" themes, though some find Van Sant's Good Will Hunting "very similar."

❸ Finding Nemo　　28 | - | 25 | 29

2003 | Directed by Andrew Stanton, Lee Unkrich | Animated | 100 minutes | Rated G

"No matter what your age", you'll be "riveted to your seat" by this "Pixar masterpiece" about a "neurotic father fish searching for his son" in a "beautifully rendered undersea world"; voters insist it's "one of the best animated films of all time", blending "superb visual effects" with a "touching" yet "hilarious script" (laced with "adult references that the tots will certainly miss") and "fully developed, brilliantly voiced characters."

Finding Neverland
| 25 | 27 | 24 | 26 |

2004 | Directed by Marc Forster | With Johnny Depp, Kate Winslet, Julie Christie | 106 minutes | Rated PG

"Even if you're a rock-hearted cynic", get out your handkerchiefs for this "pixie dust–coated", "semi-biographical" reflection on *Peter Pan* playwright J.M. Barrie's "fantastic imagination" and the people who inspired it; "do-no-wrong" Depp and Winslet "fly high" with "stellar performances", though most agree it's the "adorable child" actors who "steal the show" demonstrating the "simple power of play."

Finian's Rainbow
| 21 | 21 | 20 | 22 |

1968 | Directed by Francis Ford Coppola | With Fred Astaire, Petula Clark, Tommy Steele, Keenan Wynn | 141 minutes | Rated G

This "last musical" starring the "lighter-than-air Astaire" was "directed by Coppola, of all people", who supplies an "inventive" take on the genre in this story of Irish folks (and a leprechaun) transplanted to a Southern town; although "dated" to a few, it's "underrated" to others.

Firefox
| 17 | 17 | 18 | 18 |

1982 | Directed by Clint Eastwood | With Clint Eastwood, Freddie Jones, Warren Clarke | 136 minutes | Rated PG

A "top-notch American flier" embarks on a mission to "steal a Soviet superjet" equipped with a "thought"-controlled weapons system in this "straightforward" Cold War spy thriller; it's an "easy watch" thanks to the "cool planes" and Eastwood channeling "James Bond", even if the pace is "slow" and the special effects "dated."

Firestarter
| 17 | 18 | 19 | 18 |

1984 | Directed by Mark L. Lester | With Drew Barrymore, Martin Sheen, George C. Scott, David Keith | 114 minutes | Rated R

"Stephen King freaks" light up at the mention of this pyrotechnics-laden rendition of the horrormeister's book about a child with the "supernatural ability" to kindle fires; but wet blankets feel the "novel is way better", bashing the "campy" dialogue and all-too-familiar-"variation-on-*Carrie*" premise.

Firewall
| 15 | 16 | 16 | 17 |

2006 | Directed by Richard Loncraine | With Harrison Ford, Paul Bettany, Virginia Madsen | 105 minutes | Rated PG-13

With Ford putting his "aging bones back into action" as a high-tech security exec out to rescue his kidnapped family, this thriller heats up suspense at a "slow simmer" spiced up with "cyber-twists" for "IT geeks"; still, cynics nix the "ho-hum" momentum and advise the star to shed the "same ol'" roles and "start acting your age."

Firm, The
| 17 | 17 | 20 | 18 |

1993 | Directed by Sydney Pollack | With Tom Cruise, Jeanne Tripplehorn, Gene Hackman | 154 minutes | Rated R

"Nail-biters" say this "slick" adaptation of John Grisham's "solid" best-seller about an "honest lawyer and his evil employers" succeeds mainly because of its "quirky supporting performances"; but foes argue this "not-too-thrilling thriller" "rarely lives up to the book", particularly since they went and "changed the ending."

First Blood: Rambo
18 | 13 | 19 | 18

1982 | Directed by Ted Kotcheff | With Sylvester Stallone, Richard Crenna, Brian Dennehy | 97 minutes | Rated R

A "great kick-butt movie" "bolstered by a muscular score", this "simplistic but satisfying revenge tale" about a Vietnam vet harassed by small-town cops "delivers some punch"; the "studly", "steroidal" Stallone makes a bloody decent "action god", if not a silver-tongued thespian ("he should never talk"), though compadres caution it's his "last good movie before getting lost in sequel land."

First Wives Club, The
17 | 19 | 18 | 17

1996 | Directed by Hugh Wilson | With Bette Midler, Goldie Hawn, Diane Keaton, Maggie Smith | 102 minutes | Rated PG

The "heavyweight talent" of its "all-star cast" made this "lightweight battle-of-the-sexes farce", a revenge comedy pitting "strong women" against "rotten men", into a big hit at the box office; still, foes say it's as "fluffy as Goldie's lips", citing a "ridiculous plot" that's an "embarrassment for all involved"; P.S. it's "not a good date movie" either.

Fish Called Wanda, A
23 | 24 | 22 | 21

1988 | Directed by Charles Crichton | With John Cleese, Jamie Lee Curtis, Kevin Kline | 108 minutes | Rated R

It's easy getting hooked on this "nonstop", "kitchen-sink comedy" about a heist perpetrated by a "bumbling gang" portrayed by a "few chaps of Python fame" as well as the "show-stealing", Oscar-winning Kline; be prepared for "lots of giggles", but "forget political correctness", as "stutterers" and some unfortunate "goldfish" are gleefully abused.

Fisher King, The
21 | 24 | 21 | 21

1991 | Directed by Terry Gilliam | With Jeff Bridges, Robin Williams, Mercedes Ruehl, Amanda Plummer | 137 minutes | Rated R

Grail-seekers gravitate to this "strange" mix of "comedy, fantasy and drama", a "powerful" story of a high-flying radio shock jock who falls to earth only to be rescued by a homeless man; some find the plot "confusing" and "a little too out there", but loyal subjects say the "incredible visual effects in the Grand Central Station" scene alone "make it worth watching."

Fistful of Dollars, A
19 | 17 | 18 | 17

1967 | Directed by Sergio Leone | With Clint Eastwood, Marianne Koch, Mario Brega | 99 minutes | Rated R

The "pasta flows" in this "early spaghetti Western" as Clint "defines coolness" with his "prototypical" "Man With No Name" caught between two rival families; though a "couple notches down from *The Good, the Bad and the Ugly*" ("maybe something was lost in the translation"), this "classic" is "still fun" on a rainy day.

ⓩ Fitzcarraldo
27 | 26 | 26 | 27

1982 | Directed by Werner Herzog | With Klaus Kinski, Claudia Cardinale | 158 minutes | Rated PG

"Absolute perseverance" verging on "outlandish obsession" is the theme of this "very bizarre" story of a "quixotic" fellow determined to "build an opera house in the middle of the South American jungle"; "awe-inspired" types say "you've never seen anything like it", starting with that "scene of a ship being carried over a mountain", done with "no special effects"; P.S. try it as a "double feature with *Burden of Dreams*", the "spectacular making-of documentary."

Five Easy Pieces
24 | 27 | 22 | 21

1970 | Directed by Bob Rafelson | With Jack Nicholson, Karen Black, Lois Smith | 96 minutes | Rated R

"Nicholson's at the height of his powers" in this "deliberately paced character study" about "disaffection", "wasted ambition and dreams" that's a "must-see" for die-hard Jack fans; it "captures the restlessness of its era" with an expert "mix of comedy and serious drama" – and offers explicit instructions on "how not to be a waitress" in that "unforgettable chicken-salad sandwich" scene.

5,000 Fingers of Dr. T., The
20 | 17 | 21 | 24

1953 | Directed by Roy Rowland | With Tommy Rettig, Hans Conried, Peter Lind Hayes | 88 minutes | Not Rated

"Imaginative, absurd, trippy and a million other crazy things", this "ahead-of-its-time" musical "written by Dr. Seuss" depicts a "bizarre world" where a boy battles a piano teacher bent on world domination; though this "quirky little masterpiece" boasts a "growing cult following", it might be a little too "dark" and "frightening" for smaller fry.

Flags of Our Fathers
23 | 23 | 23 | 26

2006 | Directed by Clint Eastwood | With Ryan Phillippe, Jesse Bradford, Adam Beach | 132 minutes | Rated R

As an "elegiac" tribute to "our military heroes", Clint's snapshot of the "real history" behind the "Iwo Jima flag-raisers" – subjects of the "famous photo" that "won WWII" – focuses on the "flipside of heroism" to document the "brutal realities" encountered "both on and off the battlefield"; the ensemble cast is "outstanding", the action scenes "gritty" (if a bit "hard to follow") and the "insights" into "government propaganda" specially resonant "in today's climate."

Flashdance
16 | 14 | 15 | 18

1983 | Directed by Adrian Lyne | With Jennifer Beals, Michael Nouri | 96 minutes | Rated R

"Break dancing, leg warmers and sweatshirts worn off the shoulder" got their start in this "breakthrough" musical about a "Cinderella"-esque steel worker yearning to be a ballerina; granted, the "politically incorrect" story is "somewhat lacking", yet this "guilty pleasure" features a "soundtrack that nails the early '80s" and was "one of the highest grossing films" of its time – "what a feeling", indeed.

Flatliners
18 | 18 | 19 | 18

1990 | Directed by Joel Schumacher | With Kiefer Sutherland, Julia Roberts, Kevin Bacon, Oliver Platt | 115 minutes | Rated R

Med school students conduct "risky" experiments to bring themselves near death, only to wind up "battling their inner demons" in this heart-stopping thriller best remembered as a "starter movie" for a clutch of "up-and-coming actors"; maybe the "intriguing" premise verges on "implausible", but it still manages to "scare the bejesus" out of most, "without any gore."

	OVERALL	ACTING	STORY	PROD.

Fletch
| | 19 | 18 | 18 | 16 |

1985 | Directed by Michael Ritchie | With Chevy Chase, Joe Don Baker, Tim Matheson | 98 minutes | Rated PG

This "goofball" "cult" comedy represents "Chase's peak" in his "ultimate" role as an "undercover reporter who changes his ID more often than his underwear"; fools for "tomfoolery" swear it's "possibly the most quotable movie" ever, thanks to a flurry of "great one-liners" that only get "funnier every time you see it."

Flicka
| | 18 | 19 | 19 | 20 |

2006 | Directed by Michael Mayer | With Tim McGraw, Maria Bello, Alison Lohman | 95 minutes | Rated PG

Girl meets horse in this "wholesome", "mother-and-daughter" entertainment (an update of the old chestnut My Friend Flicka) about a teen who tames a wild mustang; panoramic tableaux of "beautiful Wyoming" and "surprisingly good" acting by country crooner McGraw add some extra giddy-up to its "importance-of-family" theme.

Flight of the Phoenix, The
| | 25 | 26 | 24 | 21 |

1965 | Directed by Robert Aldrich | With James Stewart, Richard Attenborough, Peter Finch | 147 minutes | Not Rated

"Jimmy Stewart can fly anything" and does in this post–Spirit of St. Louis adventure flicker about a desert plane crash that leaves its survivors facing a "seemingly hopeless future"; "realistically shot" and "brilliantly acted", it's a "feel-good", "can-do" kind of picture "without violence" that "really stays with you."

Flightplan
| | 18 | 21 | 17 | 19 |

2005 | Directed by Robert Schwentke | With Jodie Foster, Peter Sarsgaard, Sean Bean | 98 minutes | Rated PG-13

After clearing for a "promising takeoff", this "head-scratcher" thriller finds Foster in "stressed single mom" mode ("à la Panic Room"), "frantic" to convince sky marshal Sarsgaard she's "lost her daughter" aboard a "supersized plane"; those leery of "plot holes" so big that "you could fly a 747 through" should plan on a "bumpy ride", but with a "terrific" Jodie always "keeping you guessing", it's still intermittently "engrossing."

Flushed Away
| | 19 | - | 19 | 23 |

2006 | Directed by Sam Fell, David Bowers | Animated | 85 minutes | Rated PG

"From the brilliant minds that brought you Wallace & Gromit" comes this "enjoyable" animated adventure in which a "spoiled house mouse" is reluctantly subjected to a taste of London's "sewer life"; overflowing with enough "English humour", "potty" gags and "singing slugs" to satisfy all ages, it's "entertaining" if "not up to the classics."

Fly, The
| | 20 | 18 | 22 | 18 |

1958 | Directed by Kurt Neumann | With Vincent Price, David Hedison, Patricia Owens | 94 minutes | Not Rated

The "golden age of B movies" lives on in this wonderfully "camp classic" about a scientist "who pushes the envelope too far and becomes a fly"; fans buzz it remains "truly horrifying", especially that "unforgettable" shot of our hero "stuck in the spider's web" ("help me!") that makes up for any quaintness in the execution.

Fly, The

16 | 17 | 17 | 20

1986 | Directed by David Cronenberg | With Jeff Goldblum, Geena Davis | 96 minutes | Rated R

A "reinterpretation, not a rehash" of the "campy original", this "graphic, gruesome" remake explores Cronenberg's "obsession about the relationship between biology and technology"; sure, "special effects rule the day" here, yet there's also an "effective" love story amid the otherwise "dark" doings.

Fly Away Home

22 | 20 | 24 | 24

1996 | Directed by Carroll Ballard | With Anna Paquin, Jeff Daniels, Dana Delany | 107 minutes | Rated PG

Get out your "biggest bowl of popcorn" for this "deeply felt family film" about a young girl, her estranged dad and the flock of baby geese she takes under her wing; fans "honk" about its "captivating story" and "beautiful" Canadian scenery, saying it's "not just for kids", but rather a "quite uplifting", "lovely movie for all."

Flyboys

18 | 17 | 19 | 22

2006 | Directed by Tony Bill | With James Franco, Jennifer Decker, Jean Reno | 140 minutes | Rated PG-13

"Realistic" renderings of WWI aerial combat propel this "rousing" salute to the "American heroes" who volunteered to fly for France's Lafayette Escadrille despite "small chances of survival"; an "outrageously good-looking" cast provides some uplift to the pretty "predictable" proceedings, though the picture's a natural for anyone who "likes airplanes."

Flying Down to Rio ◑

23 | 19 | 16 | 25

1933 | Directed by Thornton Freeland | With Dolores del Rio, Gene Raymond, Fred Astaire, Ginger Rogers | 89 minutes | Not Rated

It was made as a Dolores del Rio vehicle, but this "often overlooked" musical is best remembered as the "first pairing" of "scene stealers" Fred and Ginger who are "pure heaven" performing the "infectious" 'Carioca'; most choose to "forget the plot" and "fast-forward to the dance routines", particularly the "amazing" "girls-dancing-on-airplane-wings" number.

Fog, The

17 | 15 | 18 | 16

1980 | Directed by John Carpenter | With Adrienne Barbeau, Jamie Lee Curtis, Janet Leigh, Hal Holbrook | 89 minutes | Rated R

Long-"dead pirates" return as "revenge-seeking ghosts" who terrorize a Northern California coastal town in this "creepy" horror flick with "gore" and "violence" aplenty; sure, it's "old-school" and may seem "borderline cheesy" now (even "inadvertently funny" at times), but busty "B-movie" babe Barbeau and Carpenter's moody score "intensify the impact."

Fog of War, The

26 | - | 25 | 23

2003 | Directed by Errol Morris | Documentary | 95 minutes | Rated PG-13

"Controversial" former U.S. Secretary of Defense Robert S. McNamara recounts his involvement in WWII and the Cuban missile crisis, as well as his role as one of the "architects of the Vietnam War", in this "eye-opening", Oscar-winning documentary that's "amazingly relevant" considering the current political climate; director Morris' "fascinat ing yet maddening" work underscores McNamara's "brilliance and fallibility" while "neither condemning nor excusing him entirely."

Footlight Parade ◖

23	21	18	25

1933 | Directed by Lloyd Bacon | With James Cagney, Joan Blondell, Ruby Keeler, Dick Powell | 104 minutes | Not Rated

A "low-budget troupe" of show folk struggles to stay afloat during the Depression in this "zany" musical that's worth seeing for "Busby Berkeley's grand production numbers", as well as the chance to "watch James Cagney" cut a rug; maybe the "dated" story's just "so-so", but the "amazing" dance routines (including 'By a Waterfall', 'Honeymoon Hotel' and 'Shanghai Lil') are nothing short of "electric."

Footloose

17	15	16	17

1984 | Directed by Herbert Ross | With Kevin Bacon, Lori Singer, John Lithgow, Dianne Wiest | 107 minutes | Rated PG

A "town that's banned dancing" is the setting for this "classic '80s rebellion flick", a "guilty pleasure" that "started it all for Kevin Bacon" and is best remembered for its hit-heavy soundtrack and "jumping" theme song; though "silly fluff" to detractors, it's "all-around fun" for "toe-tappers" who "take it for what it is."

For a Few Dollars More

23	21	21	20

1967 | Directed by Sergio Leone | With Clint Eastwood, Lee Van Cleef, Gian Maria Volontè | 130 minutes | Rated R

"No one's tougher than Clint" (who "doesn't smile once" but sure "looks good in a poncho") in this "tasty spaghetti western", the second installment in the Man With No Name trilogy; even though the dialogue's "dubbed", the characters "cardboard" and the bounty-hunter plot "weird", this "guilty pleasure" is still "fun to watch" – and "oh, that music!"

Forbidden Planet

25	18	25	24

1956 | Directed by Fred M. Wilcox | With Walter Pidgeon, Anne Francis, Leslie Nielsen | 98 minutes | Rated G

Its long-before-digital FX "may seem quaint" today, but this "top-notch psychological thriller" represents the "true start of the sci-fi genre" to many; despite a compelling storyline "based on Shakespeare's *Tempest*" and some halfway decent acting from the humans, "Robby the Robot is the real star" here.

Foreign Correspondent ◖

24	22	24	22

1940 | Directed by Alfred Hitchcock | With Joel McCrea, Laraine Day, Herbert Marshall, George Sanders | 120 minutes | Not Rated

One of Hitchcock's "forgotten movies", this "crackling" espionage drama set on the eve of WWII follows a political reporter across Europe, and is worth seeing for its "terrific set pieces" (the "famous windmill scene", those "umbrellas in the rain"); still, a minority finds the "pro-American" sentiment a tad "too preachy", saying the director is "more the master of propaganda than the master of suspense" here.

Forgetting Sarah Marshall

20	20	20	19

2008 | Directed by Nicholas Stoller | With Jason Segel, Kristen Bell, Mila Kunis, Russell Brand | 112 minutes | Rated R

A "dumped boyfriend tries to get over his ex" on a tropical vacation in this "wickedly funny" breakup farce from the "Judd Apatow comedy factory", offering a trademarked blend of "raunch and tenderness" jazzed up with some "great Hawaii scenery"; as a "nerdy guy in love", star/writer Segel "bares more than his soul" with lots of "sex jokes" and "full-frontal nudity."

⚡ Forrest Gump ✉ 24 | 26 | 24 | 25

1994 | Directed by Robert Zemeckis | With Tom Hanks, Robin Wright, Gary Sinise | 142 minutes | Rated PG-13

"Even macho guys" get misty over this "sentimental" story of "hope and perseverance" that explores recent American history through the "unlikely eyes" of a "simple-minded", Zelig-like hero (the "triumphant", Oscar-winning Hanks); though picky viewers find "not much assortment in this box of chocolates", they're overruled by "enchanted" believers who say its "basic good-heartedness" makes it "remarkably touching."

Fort Apache ◑ 23 | 22 | 23 | 22

1948 | Directed by John Ford | With John Wayne, Henry Fonda, Shirley Temple, Ward Bond | 125 minutes | Not Rated

This "great" Golden-Age-of-Hollywood Western is the first of the Ford trilogy that both mythologized and humanized the cavalry; Fonda's effectively "cast against type" as a by-the-numbers commander who takes over a frontier fort and can't connect with his men or the local Indians, while Wayne is "perfect" as the more understanding captain with whom he clashes; tame for the TV generation, its fight scenes are "remarkable for its era."

Fort Apache, The Bronx 21 | 23 | 21 | 20

1981 | Directed by Daniel Petrie | With Paul Newman, Ken Wahl, Rachel Ticotin, Ed Asner | 125 minutes | Rated R

Considered "shocking in its day", this "gritty" snapshot of a "city overtaken by crime" set a "new standard for cop dramas" with its "tell-it-like-it-is" depiction of hookers, junkies and the NYPD; "not-bad-on-the-eyes" Newman is "at his acting best" as the veteran "good guy" on the force, with strong backup from a "wonderful ensemble."

Fortune Cookie, The ◑ 23 | 25 | 22 | 21

1966 | Directed by Billy Wilder | With Walter Matthau, Jack Lemmon | 125 minutes | Not Rated

The first (and many say the "best") pairing of the Lemmon-Matthau combo", this biting black comedy via Billy Wilder takes aim at our litigious society in its story of a sports cameraman faking an injury in exchange for insurance money; a "top-notch script" intertwining "big laughs" and "nonstop snickers" keeps things moving at a fast clip, even if the ending "veers uncomfortably between drama and humor."

48 HRS. 19 | 18 | 18 | 17

1982 | Directed by Walter Hill | With Nick Nolte, Eddie Murphy, Annette O'Toole | 92 minutes | Rated R

The "blueprint" for "buddy action flicks", this "entertaining" crime thriller about a "surly white cop teaming up with a loud-mouthed black convict" features "stroke-of-genius" casting pairing Nolte and Murphy; ok, it's "brainless fun" and a "little too violent", but worth catching for Eddie's "starmaking" screen debut alone – especially his "great rendition of 'Roxanne.'"

	OVERALL	ACTING	STORY	PROD.

42nd Street ◑
24 | 18 | 20 | 26

1933 | Directed by Lloyd Bacon | With Ruby Keeler, Ginger Rogers, Bebe Daniels | 89 minutes | Not Rated

Alright, it's a "bit corny by modern standards", but this "brassy" "mother of all backstage musicals" showcases choreographer "Busby Berkeley at his glossy best" applying his "inventive" genius to all those "dancing feet"; "every actress' dream" come true, it's a real "classic", so just ignore the "hackneyed" plot and Keeler's "clunky" footwork.

40 Year Old Virgin, The
19 | 20 | 19 | 18

2005 | Directed by Judd Apatow | With Steve Carell, Catherine Keener, Paul Rudd | 116 minutes | Rated R

Alright, the title portends a hopeless "one-trick pony", but funnyman Carell actually "pulls it off", delivering "loads of laughs" and even some "surprising charm" as a "sweet", middle-aged "nerd" chasing his first score in this "wickedly funny" sex farce; no surprise, prudes protest the "unapologetically vulgar" content and complain the story takes "too long" to climax; P.S. "body wax", anyone?

For Whom the Bell Tolls
25 | 26 | 26 | 22

1943 | Directed by Sam Wood | With Gary Cooper, Ingrid Bergman, Katina Paxinou | 170 minutes | Not Rated

Fans swear this adaptation of Hemingway's Pulitzer Prize–winner about an American fighting fascism in '30s Spain "gets every single nuance right", starting with its "poignant", "old-fashioned love story" right down to the very convincing battle sequences; though a minority dubs it "schmaltz in macho drag", it strikes a chord as a "true classic by any measure" for most bell-ringers.

For Your Consideration
17 | 22 | 16 | 17

2006 | Directed by Christopher Guest | With Catherine O'Hara, Eugene Levy, Christopher Guest, Jennifer Coolidge, Parker Posey | 86 minutes | Rated PG-13

Christopher Guest and his loyal "stock company" "break their mockumentary mold" to make funny the conventional way in this "satire of the Hollywood awards season" that simultaneously "skewers the Oscars" and the "shallowness of the entertainment industry"; "bright moments" aside, foes fret the story is waif-"thin" and "uninspired", not unlike the "industry insiders" it lampoons.

For Your Eyes Only
18 | 16 | 18 | 21

1981 | Directed by John Glen | With Roger Moore, Carole Bouquet, Topol, Julian Glover | 127 minutes | Rated PG

A "solid" entry in the Bond blitz, this spy flicker focuses less on "super-gadgets" and more on Moore, leading many to label it his "best" outing as the ever-suave 007; the "realistic villains", "exotic locations" and "jaw-dropping" ski chases entice "even die-hard nonfans" – although the "fight scenes are never believable."

Foul Play
21 | 19 | 20 | 19

1978 | Directed by Colin Higgins | With Goldie Hawn, Chevy Chase, Dudley Moore | 116 minutes | Rated PG

Goldie "at her cute, giggly best" and a "terrific" Chevy make a "charming couple" in this "lightweight murder mystery" that's a loose "take-off on Hitchcock's *The Man Who Knew Too Much*"; its "international-

"assassination plot" seesaws between "hilarity and suspense", while Moore deftly walks away with the picture as a lecherous swinger with a memorably equipped bachelor pad.

Fountainhead, The ◑   22 | 22 | 23 | 22

1949 | Directed by King Vidor | With Gary Cooper, Patricia Neal, Raymond Massey | 114 minutes | Not Rated

Ayn Rand's mammoth novel "brought to life", this Hollywood version fortunately "doesn't take six months to watch" as it profiles the life of a "Frank Lloyd Wright"-esque architect intent on being a "genuine individual"; foes find it too talky and "hokey" (except for the "delicious Neal") and advise you "read the book before seeing the movie."

Four Brothers   17 | 18 | 18 | 18

2005 | Directed by John Singleton | With Mark Wahlberg, Tyrese Gibson, André Benjamin, Garrett Hedlund | 109 minutes | Rated R

"Tough guys with hearts" flaunt their "badass style" in this "gritty" action drama about a quartet of "misfit foster brothers" primed for "revenge" and "lots of gunplay" after their "non-biological mother" is murdered; it's near kin to a "typical" "B-level shoot 'em up", but "intense" doses of "realistic inner-city turmoil" ensure "you won't fall asleep."

Four Feathers, The   16 | 17 | 19 | 22

2002 | Directed by Shekhar Kapur | With Heath Ledger, Wes Bentley, Kate Hudson, Djimon Hounsou | 131 minutes | Rated PG-13

Re-creating the "imperial" heyday of Victorian England, this "beautiful" epic follows a British officer who confronts his own "cowardice" during a colonial war in the Sudan; although the stars and settings are equally "photogenic" ("nice sand"), the script "lacks subtlety" and the "miscast" Hudson is "out of her league."

☒ 400 Blows, The ◑🅵   27 | 26 | 25 | 24

1959 | Directed by François Truffaut | With Jean-Pierre Léaud, Robert Beauvais | 94 minutes | Not Rated

"Anyone who survived adolescence" can relate to this French "coming-of-age" film, a "semi-autobiographical" effort that marked Truffaut's directorial debut; as his "great alter ego", Léaud "depicts the pain and joy of growing up" in a winsomely "giddy" turn, though the picture earned its "place in film history" by "breaking a lot of rules" while demonstrating a "true love of movies."

Four Seasons, The   21 | 23 | 21 | 21

1981 | Directed by Alan Alda | With Alan Alda, Carol Burnett, Rita Moreno, Jack Weston, Sandy Dennis | 107 minutes | Rated PG

Director/star Alda's comedy of "real life" is a "well-done character study" about three married couples who compare "quippy" notes on "divorce and middle age" when they meet for quarterly "joint vacations"; it's seasoned with "spectacular locations" and "endearing" moments perfectly synched to a "Vivaldi score", though cynics call it a "sappy" *Big Chill* for 50-year-olds."

Four Weddings and a Funeral   21 | 21 | 21 | 20

1994 | Directed by Mike Newell | With Hugh Grant, Andie MacDowell, Kristin Scott Thomas | 117 minutes | Rated R

This "entertaining" marriage of "sweet and savvy" wrings "unexpected" laughs out of the "ups and downs of modern love" and "every bad wedding" you've ever endured; notable for "putting Hugh Grant on the map", it also boasts a "sparkling script" and a "quirky" ensemble cast, though the less said about the "wooden", "whiny" MacDowell the better.

Fox and the Hound, The
18 | - | 19 | 18

1981 | Directed by Ted Berman, Richard Rich, Art Stevens | Animated | 83 minutes | Rated G

As the title canines become unlikely pals, kids can learn about the "meaning of friendship" from this "cute" Disney film, but it's not all tail-wagging "family" fun: the "bittersweet" tone "tugs at those heartstrings with no mercy", and bashers bark at the "copy-machine" quality of the early '80s animation.

Fracture
22 | 26 | 22 | 22

2007 | Directed by Gregory Hoblit | With Anthony Hopkins, Ryan Gosling, David Strathairn, Rosamund Pike | 112 minutes | Rated R

Up-and-comer Gosling goes "toe to toe" with "scene-stealing" Sir Anthony and "holds his own" in this "smart" "cat-and-mouse" crime thriller deploying a "decent formula" to "Hitchcockian" effect; if the truckload of "twists and turns" don't leave you "wondering how it ends", at least the "witty" repartee between the leads will "hold your attention."

Frailty
20 | 22 | 21 | 19

2002 | Directed by Bill Paxton | With Bill Paxton, Matthew McConaughey, Matt O'Leary | 100 minutes | Rated R

A "small film packing a big wallop", this "spooky" exercise in psychological horror concerns a "religious fanatic" dad with traumatized kids and a homicidal agenda; thankfully, most of the bloodletting is rendered "offscreen", yet this "unsettling" picture still gives many "the willies" and concludes with a "shocker ending" right out of *The Twilight Zone.*

Frances
23 | 28 | 23 | 22

1982 | Directed by Graeme Clifford | With Jessica Lange, Kim Stanley, Sam Shepard | 140 minutes | Rated R

"Disturbing" but still "quite fine", this "harrowing" biography of "Hollywood nonconformist" Frances Farmer pulls no punches in its exploration of the actress' "demons" and "society's response to her mental illness"; in the title role, Lange is "magical" (and "matched by Stanley as her mother"), but this one's "not for the timid" given its ultimately "desperate, depressing" tone.

Frankenstein ❶
25 | 21 | 25 | 23

1931 | Directed by James Whale | With Boris Karloff, Colin Clive, Mae Clarke | 71 minutes | Not Rated

The "granddaddy of all horror films" adds a touch of "pathos" and "camp" to its story of a mad scientist who "goes against nature" and builds a creature "prone to violence"; beyond monster-mashing, it also explores the "theme of loneliness" via Karloff's "heartbreaking" ghoul, and though "a bit overacted", it's still "goose-bumps time when Colin Clive shouts *'it's alive!'*"

Frankie & Johnny
20 | 23 | 20 | 19

1991 | Directed by Garry Marshall | With Al Pacino, Michelle Pfeiffer, Nathan Lane, Kate Nelligan | 118 minutes | Rated R

"Pfeiffer and Pacino show their chops" in this "unconventional" romance that gets "honest" about "real relationship" tangles between a "charming" short-order cook and a "weary waitress"; maybe Michelle's "a little too glamorous for this", but the performances are certainly "convincing enough" to make for a "sweet tale of love and second chances."

Freaks ◐

23 | 18 | 22 | 19

1932 | Directed by Tod Browning | With Wallace Ford, Leila Hyams, Olga Baclanova | 64 minutes | Not Rated

"Dated" perhaps, but "as creepy as ever", this "subversive" look at "circus sideshow" performers still shocks 75 years later since it casts "actual human oddities" – real midgets, pinheads and Siamese twins – in leading roles; "banned for years" after its initial release and "hardly politically correct", it's either "exploitative", "sympathetic" or a "nightmare-inducing" "train wreck" that "you can't take your eyes off of."

Freaky Friday

18 | 17 | 21 | 16

1976 | Directed by Gary Nelson | With Barbara Harris, Jodie Foster, John Astin | 95 minutes | Rated G

A "kooky" idea – a teenage girl and her mom trade bodies for a day – powers this "fun" '70s "family film" that's a step up from the "usual body-swapping" comedies; thanks to a "smart script" and "brilliant" performances from Harris and Foster, some mothers and daughters watch it together for a "great bonding experience."

Freaky Friday

21 | 22 | 20 | 20

2003 | Directed by Mark Waters | With Jamie Lee Curtis, Lindsay Lohan, Mark Harmon | 97 minutes | Rated PG

"Nicely adapted to the 21st century", this "surprisingly entertaining" remake of the '70s comedy about mother-and-daughter body-swapping is "in many ways better than the original" thanks to "smart, funny" performances by the "spirited" Lindsay and "still-a-babe" Jamie Lee; it's just the ticket when "you don't feel like thinking too hard", with plenty of "family appeal" that extends beyond the "Disney Channel crowd."

Freedom Writers

22 | 23 | 23 | 20

2007 | Directed by Richard LaGravenese | With Hilary Swank, Patrick Dempsey, Scott Glenn | 123 minutes | Rated PG-13

Alright, the "fish-out-of-water-teacher-teaching-rough-urban-youths" story is as "clichéd" as they come, but this "inspirational" iteration earns high marks thanks to its "true-life" source material and Swank's "home-run" swing as a "creative" pedagogue who urges her "challenging" students to "pour their hearts out in journals"; extra credit is awarded for the "attempt to show the real side of growing up poor and non-white in America."

Free Willy

17 | 14 | 18 | 18

1993 | Directed by Simon Wincer | With Jason James Richter, Lori Petty | 112 minutes | Rated PG

"Everyone cries at the end" of this "family favorite", the "touching" story of an unhappy street kid who befriends an unhappy "killer" whale" to "inspiring" results; it's "captivating" enough to work as a good "babysitter" for the kiddies, though seen-it-all types find it too "simplistic and message-laden."

| | OVERALL | ACTING | STORY | PROD. |

French Connection, The ✉   25 | 26 | 25 | 24

1971 | Directed by William Friedkin | With Gene Hackman, Roy Scheider, Fernando Rey | 104 minutes | Rated R

Famed for the "most harrowing car chase ever", this "seminal hard-boiled cop drama" is a "fast-paced" "exposé of the drug underworld" that's also "superbly acted", starting with Hackman's "explosive", Oscar-winning turn as the tough-talking 'Popeye' Doyle; it might seem "dated" to modernists, but that's "only because it's aped so frequently."

French Lieutenant's Woman, The   22 | 25 | 21 | 23

1981 | Directed by Karel Reisz | With Meryl Streep, Jeremy Irons, Hilton McRae | 127 minutes | Rated R

"Streep is fantastic" in this "original" romance detailing parallel relationships: one involving an upper-class gentleman and a lower-class lass in Victorian England, the other between the contemporary actors playing them; granted, Harold Pinter's scenario might be "a bit confusing at the get-go", but ultimately this "excellent" adaptation of John Fowles' novel is both "really cool and worthwhile."

Frenzy   20 | 20 | 22 | 21

1972 | Directed by Alfred Hitchcock | With Jon Finch, Barry Foster, Anna Massey, Billie Whitelaw | 116 minutes | Rated R

Alfred Hitchcock's "familiar obsession with mistaken identity" is the basis of this "violent" tale about a "necktie murderer" on the loose in London; "wonderful location settings" and renowned set pieces (the "stairway backtracking shot", the corpse in the sack of potatoes) draw applause, yet even though it's "more graphic than his earlier films", some moan the master is "well past his prime" here.

Frequency   19 | 20 | 22 | 19

2000 | Directed by Gregory Hoblit | With Dennis Quaid, James Caviezel | 118 minutes | Rated PG-13

Sure, it might be "unbelievable", but this "time-travel" tale generates lots of "surprise" with its "truly original story" about a young man who talks to his late father via ham radio; despite "metropolis-size plot holes", it's still "touching", with a baseball subplot that's "especially fun" for fans of NY's 1969 "Miracle Mets."

Freshman, The   21 | 22 | 21 | 20

1990 | Directed by Andrew Bergman | With Marlon Brando, Matthew Broderick, Penelope Ann Miller | 102 minutes | Rated PG

"Devotees of *The Godfather*" can't refuse this "lighthearted comedy", a "priceless" "Don Corleone send-up" with a "self-mocking" Brando playing a "straight-faced parody" of his signature role; the "screwball" plot about "boyish" student Broderick inadvertently "involved with the mob" is "silly", but even as a "one-gag" gig, this one's definitely "funny."

Frida   25 | 27 | 25 | 27

2002 | Directed by Julie Taymor | With Salma Hayek, Alfred Molina | 123 minutes | Rated R

"Fiery" Hayek "put her heart and soul" into this "underrated little" bio of "eccentric" Mexican artist Frida Kahlo, "and it shows"; she delivers her "finest performance", capturing the "pain, grief and personal tragedy that the painter expressed in her art" against a "visually stunning tapestry" of "color and texture" in which her "actual paintings come to life"; "wonderful" acting by Molina and an "amazing soundtrack" are more reasons "not to miss it."

Friday Night Lights
21 | 21 | 21 | 20

2004 | Directed by Peter Berg | With Billy Bob Thornton, Derek Luke, Jay Hernandez | 118 minutes | Rated PG-13

"Football fanatics" feel the "mojo" of this "gritty", "documentary-style" look at a Texas town's "bigger than life" devotion to high school gridiron; as an "embattled" coach preaching "love for the game", Thornton shows his "versatility", but some Monday morning quarterbacks are "unimpressed with the character development" and the "headache-inducing" camerawork.

Friday the 13th
16 | 9 | 15 | 13

1980 | Directed by Sean S. Cunningham | With Betsy Palmer, Adrienne King, Harry Crosby | 95 minutes | Rated R

The "granddaddy of modern-day horror films", this "cult slasher flick" "spawned an entire franchise" of "wretched sequels" that don't hold a candle to its "unrelenting creepiness"; set in a summer camp populated by "stupid, horny teenagers" who "scream a lot", it might "succeed more on a comedic level" today, but that "twist at the end" still "scares the hell" out of everybody.

Fried Green Tomatoes
23 | 25 | 23 | 22

1991 | Directed by Jon Avnet | With Kathy Bates, Jessica Tandy, Mary Stuart Masterson | 130 minutes | Rated PG-13

"Southern-fried memories" are the basis of this "heartwarming" dramedy detailing how a "pathetic excuse for a woman" transforms herself into a "take-charge wonder"; its "sweet story" might feature a dash of "male bashing", but it's "genuinely touching and involving" – no wonder many fried-food fans find this "feel-good" "tear-jerking" "chick flick" so gosh darn "yummy."

Friendly Persuasion
24 | 25 | 25 | 23

1956 | Directed by William Wyler | With Gary Cooper, Dorothy McGuire, Anthony Perkins | 140 minutes | Not Rated

"One for thy heart", this story of "Quakers during the Civil War" "trying to be pacifists" is an "all-around solid" picture thanks to a "strong storyline"; its "endearing characters" include the ultra-"believable" Cooper (the "Harrison Ford of his time") as well as a "moving" McGuire and Oscar-nominated Perkins.

Friends with Money
16 | 20 | 15 | 17

2006 | Directed by Nicole Holofcener | With Jennifer Aniston, Joan Cusack, Catherine Keener, Frances McDormand | 88 minutes | Rated R

Aniston goes "indie" in this "chick flick with a brain", a "moody" LA comedy featuring Jen as a singleton "doormat" who's "barely getting by", while her married pals cope with issues that "money can't cure"; maybe it's "underappreciated", but skeptics still see a "meandering character sketch" that amounts to a "whiny downer" for the "Sundance crowd."

Fritz the Cat
16 | - | 15 | 17

1972 | Directed by Ralph Bakshi | Animated | 78 minutes | Rated X

"Soft-core kitty porn" fans tout this "risqué" "stoner's delight", an "artifact of the underground comics scene" that's best remembered as the first X-rated animated feature; critical cats call it too "dumbed-down and diluted" ("Fritz's "creator, R. Crumb, supposedly disliked it"), but admit it "has its funny moments" provided your "drugs haven't worn off."

From Dusk Till Dawn
18 | 16 | 17 | 20

1996 | Directed by Robert Rodriguez | With Harvey Keitel, George Clooney, Quentin Tarantino, Juliette Lewis | 108 minutes | Rated R
"Awesome schlock" sucks "gorefest" fans into this "crass" crime/horror trip, a "lurid" tale of "gun-toting" baddies making a getaway to a Mexican roadhouse that's actually a "den of vampires"; it's a "roller-coaster" of "gratuitous exploitation" that lets "QT show off his acting" amid plenty of "cheap thrills", but buzz-killers yawn maybe the "title refers to the running time."

⊠ From Here to Eternity ⊠◑
26 | 27 | 24 | 24

1953 | Directed by Fred Zinnemann | With Burt Lancaster, Montgomery Clift, Deborah Kerr, Frank Sinatra, Donna Reed | 118 minutes | Not Rated
Based on James Jones' "powerful" novel, this "gold standard" of war dramas depicts military life in Honolulu's Pearl Harbor just before the Japanese attack; the "all-star cast" (including an Oscar-winning "Ol' Blue Eyes") and a "technically brilliant" production make this a "compelling classic" – though it's best remembered for Burt and Deborah's iconic "kissing-on-the-beach" scene.

From Russia With Love
23 | 21 | 23 | 23

1964 | Directed by Terence Young | With Sean Connery, Robert Shaw, Lotte Lenya, Daniela Bianchi | 115 minutes | Rated PG
Ride the "Orient Express from Istanbul to Venice" – with plenty of stops for "exotic locales", "scantily clad" gals and "great fight scenes" – in this early entrant in the James Bond series; the "formula never works better" thanks to an "incomparable" Connery pitted against "non-cartoon" villains, especially a very scary Lenya at her most "sadomasochistic."

Front, The
23 | 23 | 25 | 21

1976 | Directed by Martin Ritt | With Woody Allen, Zero Mostel, Andrea Marcovicci | 95 minutes | Rated PG
The "one great Woody movie" that he "didn't direct", this "dark comedy" is a "flashback" to "McCarthyism in the '50s" starring Allen as a "reluctant hero" shilling scripts penned by "blacklisted writers" (though "Mostel steals the show" as a comedian pressured into the "witch hunt"); suitably "sharp and cynical", it delivers a "powerful message" that "may still have resonance today."

Front Page, The ◑
24 | 24 | 25 | 20

1931 | Directed by Lewis Milestone | With Adolphe Menjou, Pat O'Brien, Edward Everett Horton | 101 minutes | Not Rated
Based on the timeless stage comedy from Ben Hecht and Charles MacArthur, this zany satire of tabloid journalism is propelled by a fast-moving plot delivered with rapid-fire, overlapping dialogue; since it's an early talkie, it hasn't aged well, but the story was well-regarded enough to inspire three remakes, including *His Girl Friday,* arguably the best of the bunch.

Fugitive, The
23 24 24 23

1993 | Directed by Andrew Davis | With Harrison Ford, Tommy Lee Jones, Sela Ward, Julianne Moore | 127 minutes | Rated PG-13

From the "ultimate adrenaline rush" of the opening "train wreck" to the "smashing grand finale", you'll be "on the edge of your seat" throughout this "thinking person's action flick", based on the "long-ago" TV series about a doctor unjustly accused of murder; the "cat-and-mouse" plot lends a "Hitchcockian" feel to the proceedings, while Ford and Jones deliver "pitch-perfect performances."

Full Metal Jacket
24 25 22 25

1987 | Directed by Stanley Kubrick | With Matthew Modine, Adam Baldwin, Vincent D'Onofrio | 116 minutes | Rated R

"Kubrick does Vietnam" in this "intense" war picture that's really "two amazing films in one": first up is the "disturbingly funny" depiction of "boot-camp" basic training, followed by an abrupt about-face to the "total hell" of the front-line war; "first-rate production and acting" keep things "compelling" throughout, even if peaceniks feel the "uneven" second half is a tad too "violent."

Full Monty, The
22 22 24 19

1997 | Directed by Peter Cattaneo | With Robert Carlyle, Mark Addy, Tom Wilkinson | 91 minutes | Rated R

Out-of-work, out-of-shape blokes put together a "Chippendale's-type" strip act as a "creative response to unemployment" in this "riotous" English comedy that mixes "bumps and grinds" with "serious social themes"; its "enthusiastic" if "unknown" ensemble cast shake their booties to a "terrific" pop soundtrack, though most prefer it "with subtitles" to decipher those "British accents."

Funny Face
24 24 21 25

1957 | Directed by Stanley Donen | With Audrey Hepburn, Fred Astaire, Kay Thompson | 103 minutes | Not Rated

"Cinderella" goes to Paris in this "fashion industry musical" wherein a "gracefully aging", "debonair" Astaire turns a "bookish" Hepburn into an "ethereal", "luminous" supermodel; despite "no story to speak of", it's "thoroughly enchanting" thanks to "magic" dancing and Gershwin's "s'wonderfully" "dreamy" score; best number: Thompson's "steal-the-movie" rendition of 'Think Pink.'

⏸ Funny Girl ✉
26 25 24 26

1968 | Directed by William Wyler | With Barbra Streisand, Omar Sharif, Walter Pidgeon | 151 minutes | Rated G

"Hello, gorgeous!"; Babs' "big movie debut" in one of the "last great traditional Hollywood musicals" made her the "greatest star" thanks to some "chutzpah", some "charm" and a voice "like buttah"; indeed, her Oscar-winning turn as comedienne Fanny Brice is so "socko" that it's easy to ignore the "schmaltzy" plot about the "man who got away."

Funny Lady
15 17 14 18

1975 | Directed by Herbert Ross | With Barbra Streisand, James Caan, Omar Sharif | 136 minutes | Rated PG

This "not-as-good follow-up to *Funny Girl*" (they should have "quit while they were ahead") strikes some as a Streisand "vanity production" trying to "milk the success" of the original, with "everything in excess – except the story and acting"; on the positive side, there are a couple of "sparkling Kander and Ebb" tunes.

	OVERALL	ACTING	STORY	PROD.

Funny Thing Happened on the Way to the Forum, A
22 | 22 | 21 | 20

1966 | Directed by Richard Lester | With Zero Mostel, Phil Silvers, Buster Keaton | 99 minutes | Not Rated

For "comedy tonight", try this "total farce" of a musical that depicts Ancient Rome as a freewheeling toga party; sure, "Zero's the greatest" at provoking "laugh after laugh", but fans of the "quite different" stage version find it "stupid" "schlock" with "a lot lost in the translation to the screen."

Fury ◑
▽ 25 | 25 | 25 | 23

1936 | Directed by Fritz Lang | With Spencer Tracy, Sylvia Sidney, Bruce Cabot | 90 minutes | Not Rated

"Paranoia master" Lang's first American film, this "chilling depiction of mob violence and collective hysteria" remains "as fresh today as it was in 1936" thanks to the director's "skillful manipulation of sympathies"; a "nice and bitter" Tracy is its lynchpin, playing a "morally ambiguous" everyman caught up in a "social tragedy."

F/X
21 | 19 | 23 | 21

1986 | Directed by Robert Mandel | With Bryan Brown, Brian Dennehy, Diane Venora | 109 minutes | Rated R

Go "behind the scenes" into the "world of effects masters" via this "fun romp" of a thriller about a movie-set special "F/X man" relying on some "imaginative tricks" after he's framed for murder and takes it on the run; though "somewhat implausible" and now "dated by CGI", it's "loaded" with enough "twists and turns" to "keep things moving" effectively.

Galaxy Quest
21 | 20 | 22 | 21

1999 | Directed by Dean Parisot | With Tim Allen, Sigourney Weaver, Alan Rickman | 102 minutes | Rated PG

Enjoyable for "lifelong Trekkies" and civilians alike, this "funny" sci-fi "send-up" follows "washed-up actors" from a canceled TV series who "make their living off conventions" – until they meet some "real aliens"; assets include Tim Allen "doing his best Shatner" and a smart script that "doesn't sacrifice the story for the sake of the gags."

Gallipoli
25 | 25 | 25 | 24

1981 | Directed by Peter Weir | With Mel Gibson, Mark Lee, Bill Kerr, David Argue | 110 minutes | Rated PG

A "fresh-faced" Gibson "comes of age" as an actor in this "oh-so-sad war movie" about a "disastrous WWI" battle in Turkey that points out the "pointlessness" of combat; "one of the best of the Australian New Wave" films, it winds up with a "10-hanky tragic ending" that "tugs at the heartstrings without being corny."

Game, The
22 | 22 | 24 | 22

1997 | Directed by David Fincher | With Michael Douglas, Sean Penn, Deborah Unger | 128 minutes | Rated R

"Fincher fans rejoice" at the director's "psych thriller follow-up" to *Seven*, a "gripping mind-bender" featuring Douglas as a "wealthy, overworked" broker who gets a "disturbing birthday present" from brother Penn: a ticket to a "twisted", real-life game; as an "unpredictable rush" it's "suspenseful to the last drop", but be prepared to play by "loopy" rules ("I'm still confused").

⚫ Gandhi ✉   27 | 28 | 27 | 27
1982 | Directed by Richard Attenborough | With Ben Kingsley, Candice Bergen, Edward Fox | 188 minutes | Rated PG
"Big Hollywood at its best", this "meticulously detailed" bio of the Indian leader is *The Ten Commandments* of the '80s", "long but riveting" and "emotionally wrenching"; Kingsley's "searing", Oscar-winning portrayal of the figure "who brought the British Empire to its knees" is the movie's "glorious centerpiece", and if a few find it "ponderous" and "overblown", there's no debate that it "captures the spiritual essence of the man perfectly."

Gangs of New York   21 | 23 | 20 | 25
2002 | Directed by Martin Scorsese | With Leonardo DiCaprio, Daniel Day-Lewis, Cameron Diaz | 166 minutes | Rated R
The "corrupt world" of "Civil War–era New York" is the backdrop for this "bloody good" "love and revenge" picture via Martin Scorsese that's "overwhelming visually" but "wholly uneven" plotwise; cynics skewer the "unnecessary violence", "moldy love story" and "way too long" running time, while fans counter Day-Lewis' "vivid" performance is the picture's "saving grace"; in sum, "flawed, but worth it."

Garden of the Finzi-Continis, The ✉🅵   25 | 24 | 27 | 25
1971 | Directed by Vittorio De Sica | With Dominique Sanda, Lino Capolicchio, Helmut Berger | 94 minutes | Rated R
"Complacency leads to disaster" in this "haunting" WWII drama about "upper-class Italian Jews" who "close their eyes to the looming evil" of fascism by believing that "money and position will insulate them"; "gripping and emotional", it also make the "beautiful" Sanda a star.

Garden State   22 | 23 | 21 | 20
2004 | Directed by Zach Braff | With Zach Braff, Natalie Portman, Peter Sarsgaard | 102 minutes | Rated R
Think of it as *The Graduate* for a new century": this "quirky" dramedy directed, written and starring Zach Braff is pitched to "disillusioned twentysomethings" with its depiction of the ultimate "quarter-life crisis sufferer"; despite mixed notices for the "enchanting" (or "annoying") Portman and catcalls for that "fake Hollywood ending", it's worth renting for the "kick-ass soundtrack" alone.

Gaslight ✉◑   26 | 27 | 26 | 24
1944 | Directed by George Cukor | With Ingrid Bergman, Charles Boyer, Joseph Cotten | 114 minutes | Not Rated
Anything but light, this "high-tension" thriller stars a "glowing", Oscar-winning Bergman as a newlywed who thinks she's "going insane – or is she?"; "mesmerized" fans say the "original" storyline "maintains the suspense to the end", helped by an atmospheric "Victorian setting" and a particularly "villainous villain" in Boyer.

Gattaca   20 | 20 | 23 | 22
1997 | Directed by Andrew Niccol | With Ethan Hawke, Uma Thurman, Jude Law | 101 minutes | Rated PG-13
Sci-fi spliced with "smarts", this "stylish" "dystopian vision" looks at a "scary future" where mere humans bargain with "co-conspirators" to

upgrade into the ranks of the "genetically engineered" elite; though "slow-moving", it's got the "philosophical" DNA to "make you think" and bears "rich moral implications" for the dawn of "designer babies."

Gauntlet, The | 17 | 17 | 18 | 18 |

1977 | Directed by Clint Eastwood | With Clint Eastwood, Sondra Locke | 109 minutes | Rated R

Catch the "pre-sensitive Clint" in a typical "clenched-jaw cop role" in this "not bad" action flick about a *"Dirty Harry*-ish" lawman with an uncharacteristically "weak" streak who's double-crossed after being assigned to "protect prostitute crime witness" Locke; it's a "watchable shoot 'em up" with a "savage climax", though both "credibility" and acting ability are "stretched thin" here.

Gay Divorcee, The ◐ | 25 | 23 | 20 | 25 |

1934 | Directed by Mark Sandrich | With Fred Astaire, Ginger Rogers, Edward Everett Horton | 107 minutes | Not Rated

"No one could dance like Fred and Ginger", and this footloose '30s musical "whirls" with production numbers "par excellence" as Rogers plays a spouse untying the knot in high style as Astaire duly falls into step; the "silly story" is trumped by the "dreamy" tunes and, of course, that terpsichorean team-up "can't be beat."

Z General, The ◐ | 28 | 27 | 26 | 27 |

1927 | Directed by Clyde Bruckman, Buster Keaton | With Buster Keaton, Marion Mack | 75 minutes | Not Rated

One of the "most remarkable" silent films, this pioneering effort "establishes gags still used today" in its story of a Civil War–era Southern engineer in relentless pursuit of a stolen locomotive; the "Great Stoneface's" most "ambitious" work, it also incorporates some "amazing physical comedy" – Keaton "does all his own stunts."

Z Gentleman's Agreement ✉◐ | 26 | 27 | 27 | 24 |

1947 | Directed by Elia Kazan | With Gregory Peck, Dorothy McGuire, Celeste Holm | 118 minutes | Not Rated

A once-"controversial exposé" of "American anti-Semitism", this "earnest" "message drama" offers Peck in a "wonderfully emotional" turn as an investigative reporter who passes himself off as Jewish and becomes a first-hand witness to "subtle prejudice"; if the final result seems a bit "dated" and "simplistic" today, it's still "interesting" as an early attempt at social criticism.

Gentlemen Prefer Blondes | 23 | 21 | 20 | 24 |

1953 | Directed by Howard Hawks | With Jane Russell, Marilyn Monroe, Charles Coburn | 91 minutes | Rated PG

You'll probably prefer Monroe's "ingenious, ingenuous" "dumb blonde" to the "nonexistent storyline" in this "guilty-pleasure" musical comedy, a "deliciously over-the-top" story of "gold diggers" made all the more vivid in "spectacular Technicolor"; it's "one for the time capsule", if only for Marilyn's "dazzling" rendition of 'Diamonds Are a Girl's Best Friend.'

George of the Jungle | 17 | 16 | 16 | 17 |

1997 | Directed by Sam Weisman | With Brendan Fraser, Leslie Mann, Thomas Haden Church | 91 minutes | Rated PG

Young chimps and big apes who "remember the cartoon" have "goofy fun" with this comedy featuring "Fraser in a loincloth" as a "moronic", secondhand Tarzan; cynics say Disney grabs for the vine and "falls short", but it is "surprisingly entertaining", even if the theme ditty will stay "in your head for days."

Georgy Girl ◗ 23 | 25 | 21 | 20

1966 | Directed by Silvio Narizzano | With Lynn Redgrave, James Mason, Alan Bates, Charlotte Rampling | 99 minutes | Not Rated

An "ever optimistic ugly duckling" takes on "London in the Swinging '60s" in this "poignant, bittersweet comedy" that makes you "laugh and cry" as you "root for the protagonist"; starring a "moving", "before-Weight-Watchers" Redgrave as the "odd person out", it "still holds up" over 40 years later, but beware: that "theme song will stick in your head for days."

Getaway, The 22 | 22 | 21 | 21

1972 | Directed by Sam Peckinpah | With Steve McQueen, Ali MacGraw, Ben Johnson | 122 minutes | Rated PG

"Steve and Ali sizzle" with their "on-screen (and off-screen) love affair" in this "essential" "crime spree road trip" flick about an ex-con and his missus "on the run from basically everyone they know"; McQueen is his "usual stoic yet likable self", MacGraw's deliciously "icy" and director Peckinpah provides enough "slo-mo" action to make for "exciting B-movie" thrills.

Get Shorty 20 | 22 | 21 | 20

1995 | Directed by Barry Sonnenfeld | With John Travolta, Gene Hackman, Rene Russo, Danny DeVito | 105 minutes | Rated R

Travolta brings his *Pulp Fiction* cool and charisma to this "zippy" crime farce about a "loan shark who comes to Hollywood" and goes native among "eccentric mobsters" and "movie business" types; with no shortage of "tongue-in-cheek satire" and casting coups, it proves that an Elmore Leonard story "done right" can be "more fun than a week in Vegas."

⊠ Gettysburg 25 | 24 | 25 | 27

1993 | Directed by Ronald F. Maxwell | With Tom Berenger, Jeff Daniels, Martin Sheen, Stephen Lang | 261 minutes | Rated PG

Perhaps the "definitive" depiction of the "ferocious" 1863 Civil War battle that "determined the course of American history", this "powerful" epic achieves full "factual accuracy" with authentic locations buttressed by an "excellent" cast enacting the "conflict's backstory" and commemorating the "bravery on both sides"; still, the four-hours-plus running time leaves even "history buffs" huffing "too long and drawn out."

Ghost ⊠ 21 | 21 | 22 | 21

1990 | Directed by Jerry Zucker | With Patrick Swayze, Demi Moore, Whoopi Goldberg | 128 minutes | Rated PG-13

There's "action for the boys and romance for the girls" in this comic "tearjerker" that's got "hot date movie" written all over it; sure, its story of a dead man watching over his surviving lover from above may be more than "improbable" (and "sappy and manipulative", according to cynics), yet somehow Moore and Swayze make it all seem so "sexy", while the "priceless", Oscar-winning Goldberg "delivers the laughs."

Ghost and Mrs. Muir, The ◑
24 | 25 | 25 | 22

1947 | Directed by Joseph L. Mankiewicz | With Rex Harrison, Gene
Tierney, George Sanders | 104 minutes | Not Rated
This "timeless" fantasy details the unlikely "love story" between a
widow and a "crusty old" sea captain who's "full of life" – even though
he's a ghost; the "otherworldly" romance that ensues avoids being
"sentimental goop" thanks to "superb performances" from Tierney,
Harrison and little "eight-year-old Natalie Wood."

Ghostbusters
21 | 18 | 21 | 23

1984 | Directed by Ivan Reitman | With Bill Murray, Dan Aykroyd,
Sigourney Weaver, Harold Ramis | 107 minutes | Rated PG
"Kooky, spooky" and flat-out "funny", this "classic '80s" "sci-fi comedy" about 'paranormal investigators' banishing ghosts from NYC is
"one of the best stupid movies ever", so "not much thinking is required"; "wonderful special effects" and a brilliantly "sarcastic
Murray" are its highlights, though its most lasting achievement is that
it "made the word 'slime' into a verb."

Ghost Rider
16 | 15 | 16 | 20

2007 | Directed by Mark Steven Sullivan | With Nicolas Cage, Eva
Mendes, Wes Bentley, Peter Fonda | 114 minutes | Rated PG-13
"Awesome visuals" (i.e. Cage "on a motorcycle with his skull on fire")
do the heavy lifting in this "popcorn" movie about a bounty hunter who
sells his soul to the devil, the latest in the seemingly "endless parade
of Marvel comics adaptations"; sure, Mendes is "totally hot", but otherwise the "story lacks punch", ditto the "lackluster" acting.

Ghost Story
21 | 22 | 22 | 21

1981 | Directed by John Irvin | With Fred Astaire, Melvyn Douglas,
Douglas Fairbanks Jr., John Houseman | 110 minutes | Rated R
Memorable for capturing the "final film performances" of Astaire and
Fairbanks, this "interesting" drama manages to scare up a "shudder or
two" with its "chilling" tale of four elderly gents sharing a dark secret
that "bleeds into the present"; the "marquee cast" delivers some
mighty "fine acting", though some say it "fails to deliver" fully on Peter
Straub's source novel.

Ghost World
23 | 26 | 22 | 21

2001 | Directed by Terry Zwigoff | With Thora Birch, Steve Buscemi,
Scarlett Johansson | 111 minutes | Rated R
A "witty" look at two "nonconformist" girls in a "homogenized" sub-
urb, this "random" comedy is a "nice departure from the typical teen
angst film"; the "quirky" characters sport "great thrift-store clothes",
while the "phenomenal Buscemi" is "pitch-perfect."

Giant ✉
24 | 23 | 24 | 24

1956 | Directed by George Stevens | With Elizabeth Taylor, Rock
Hudson, James Dean, Dennis Hopper | 201 minutes | Rated G
As "sprawling" as the Lone Star state itself, this "all-out wonderful"
Texas "epic" about money, love and oil "burns with star power", featuring some mighty "big names" – Liz, Rock and Jimmy (in his last
role) – "in their prime"; cynics say this "way too long" example of
"Hollywood bloat" is just "cornball hooey", but fans insist this "colossal '50s production" "holds your interest."

	OVERALL	ACTING	STORY	PROD.

Gigi ✉ 24 | 23 | 23 | 26

1958 | Directed by Vincente Minnelli | With Leslie Caron, Maurice Chevalier, Louis Jourdan | 119 minutes | Rated G

"Thank heaven" for this "fine rendering" of the Lerner and Loewe musical, an "unorthodox love story" about a "turn-of-the-century" Parisian courtesan and the client who wants to marry her; winner of nine Oscars, this "stunner" boasts a "radiant" Caron, suave Jourdan, "amusant" Chevalier and a "top-notch" production, so even if the end result might look like a "lavish" wad of "cotton candy", "just give in" and enjoy it.

Gilda ◑ 24 | 23 | 21 | 23

1946 | Directed by Charles Vidor | With Rita Hayworth, Glenn Ford, George Macready | 110 minutes | Not Rated

Noir was never more "delectable" than in this "solid" love triangle starring a "delicious" "Hayworth in her signature role" as the "glamorous", hair-tossing Gilda; though her "modified striptease" in the 'Put the Blame on Mame' number is the "only reason to see it" for some, others find enough "mystery and suspense" to make it "memorable."

Gimme Shelter 25 | - | 21 | 22

1970 | Directed by Albert Maysles, David Maysles, Charlotte Zwerin | Documentary | With The Rolling Stones | 91 minutes | Rated R

Originally commissioned by the Rolling Stones as a "simple concert" flick, this "rockumentary" took on a "darker side" after filmmakers inadvertently recorded a "real murder" at the group's infamous Altamont gig; the result is a "grim, gritty look" at the "turbulent '60s" "spiraling out of control", with a "complicated storyline" and "classic" soundtrack that put modern "music videos to shame"; hottest moment: the "amazing" Tina Turner at the mike.

Girl, Interrupted 18 | 22 | 18 | 18

1999 | Directed by James Mangold | With Winona Ryder, Angelina Jolie, Brittany Murphy | 127 minutes | Rated R

"Haunting if overwrought" drama providing a "hair-raising glimpse" inside a mental institution headlining a "convincing" Ryder as a "troubled" patient, though Jolie "steals the show" (and an Oscar) as the "sexiest crazy person" ever; fans insist it's a "compelling emotional trip", but others say it's so "soapy" that it "should have been a 'Cosmo' article."

Girl with a Pearl Earring 21 | 23 | 19 | 25

2003 | Directed by Peter Webber | With Colin Firth, Scarlett Johansson, Tom Wilkinson | 95 minutes | Rated PG-13

A "true art movie", this "beautifully photographed" period piece set in 17th-century "bourgeois Holland" is based on a Vermeer painting (and a recent novel) of the same name and explores the artist's "possible relationship" with a "lovely muse" played by Johansson, "who wows with her nearly wordless performance" as his "shy", "entrancing" servant; though the "slow" pacing is "like watching paint dry", enough "sexual tension abounds" to keep the interest level up.

ⓩ Gladiator ✉ 23 | 23 | 22 | 27

2000 | Directed by Ridley Scott | With Russell Crowe, Joaquin Phoenix, Oliver Reed, Richard Harris | 155 minutes | Rated R

"Everything a big Hollywood blockbuster should be", this "old-fashioned" "sword-and-sandal" extravaganza features lots of "action, adventure and backstabbing" in its story of a Roman general turned wretched slave; the "intense", Oscar-winning Crowe oozes plenty of "testosterone" and the "lavish re-creation of Ancient Rome" brings the "Coliseum to life", but thumbs-downers dismiss it as "bombastic beefcake."

Glengarry Glen Ross   23 | 27 | 22 | 20

1992 | Directed by James Foley | With Al Pacino, Jack Lemmon, Ed Harris, Alec Baldwin | 100 minutes | Rated R

"High-pressure" real-estate salesmen "with an axe about to fall on their jobs" get the David Mamet treatment in this "dark", "lacerating drama" about the "predatory world of business"; its "talky", expletive-laden scenario can be "intensely disturbing", but ultimately it "shows what can be done with a small cast, limited sets and Godzilla talent."

Gloria   22 | 26 | 22 | 20

1980 | Directed by John Cassavetes | With Gena Rowlands, John Adames, Buck Henry | 123 minutes | Rated PG

A "retired gun moll" and a six-year-old orphan go "on the run from the mob" in this "gritty" Cassavetes drama that manages to be both hard-boiled and "surprisingly moving" (with a "mystery ending" to boot); similarly, "tough cookie" Gena ranges from "fierce" to "maternal" in the "kick-butt" title turn; P.S. don't bother with Sharon Stone's "unfortunate" remake.

◪ Glory   25 | 26 | 26 | 26

1989 | Directed by Edward Zwick | With Matthew Broderick, Denzel Washington, Morgan Freeman | 122 minutes | Rated R

Based on the "true tale" about the "first black Civil War regiment and the white Union officer who led them", this "period piece" is a fine "evocation of a story few people know"; expect "great battle scenes", even if it "doesn't end the way you want it to."

Go   20 | 19 | 21 | 19

1999 | Directed by Doug Liman | With Sarah Polley, Desmond Askew, Jay Mohr, Scott Wolf, Katie Holmes, Timothy Olyphant | 103 minutes | Rated R

"Whip-smart and fast-paced", this "high-octane" crime thriller mashes up "multiple storylines" à la *Pulp Fiction* to tell its "disjointed" tale of a botched "drug deal" from three different points of view; director Liman's follow-up to *Swingers*, it's gaining "cult" momentum among "twentysomethings" thanks to its "unpredictable" scenario and that "great soundtrack."

◪ Godfather, The ✉   29 | 29 | 29 | 29

1972 | Directed by Francis Ford Coppola | With Marlon Brando, Al Pacino, Diane Keaton, Robert Duvall, James Caan, John Cazale | 175 minutes | Rated R

Perhaps the "best three hours you can spend sitting still", this "ultimate gangster film" and "cultural phenomenon" is ranked both Top Overall and Most Popular film in this Survey; an "absolutely flawless" "American epic", it recounts the "operatic" lives of the Corleone family via an "intricate" plot, "bravura photography" and "iconic performances" from Brando and Pacino; in fact, the end result is so "killer" that "nothing else comes close – except maybe the sequel"; favorite line: "leave the gun, take the cannoli."

	OVERALL	ACTING	STORY	PROD.

☒ Godfather Part II, The ✉ `29` `29` `28` `29`

1974 | Directed by Francis Ford Coppola | With Al Pacino, Robert Duvall, Diane Keaton, Robert De Niro, John Cazale | 200 minutes | Rated R

A "real rarity – a sequel as good as the original" – this "true masterpiece" "stands on its own laurels" as it "delves deeper into the Corleone family" saga; a "moody meditation on the emptiness of power", its "complex" plot "masterfully intercuts" two stories separated by a half-century into a "taut", "heartbreaking tale of innocence lost", and though "never overshadowing its big brother", it just might be "even more subtle and sublime"; most chilling moment: the "kiss between Michael and Fredo."

Godfather Part III, The `16` `18` `16` `21`

1990 | Directed by Francis Ford Coppola | With Al Pacino, Diane Keaton, Talia Shire, Andy Garcia | 161 minutes | Rated R

"Conspiracy, mayhem, opera, revenge": the "prime American" crime "saga" concludes with this "flawed" but "watchable" sequel as Pacino's don Michael aims to take the Corleones legit, despite beefs from both the old guard and his own clan; though it's a "must-see" for diehards, some say the "forced" plotting and "miscasting" ("two words: Sofia Coppola") are a "disgrace to the Family"; in short, it doesn't fill the "enormous shoes" of I and II.

Gods and Monsters ✉ `23` `27` `23` `22`

1998 | Directed by Bill Condon | With Ian McKellen, Brendan Fraser, Lynn Redgrave | 105 minutes | Rated R

McKellen's "brilliant" performance is the backbone of this "innovative biopic" detailing an "encounter between a hedge clipper and a has-been" moviemaker that's based on the life of 1930s "gay director" James Whale; partisans point to the Oscar-winning script as proof of why "indie films are such a delight."

Gods Must Be Crazy, The `22` `17` `23` `18`

1984 | Directed by Jamie Uys | With Marius Weyers, Sandra Prinsloo, N!xau | 109 minutes | Rated PG

"Consumerism meets primitive African bushmen" when a Coke bottle "falls out of the sky" in this "cult" "culture-clash" comedy that "proves you don't need a big Hollywood budget" to be "original and witty"; despite bare-bones production and middling acting, this "diamond in the rough" still exhibits "universal appeal" thanks to "creative" ideas.

Godzilla ◐ `16` `10` `16` `14`

1956 | Directed by Terry Morse, Ishiro Honda | With Raymond Burr, Takashi Shimura | 80 minutes | Not Rated

The menace of the atom age hovers over this sci-fi "classic" about a colossal, radiation-spawned lizard who rises up to become the "proto-typical city-destroying" beast, doing the "monster mash" through a model-train-gauge Tokyo; "laugh if you want" at the "camp-to-the-max" "Japanese footage" (with "Burr spliced in"), but the "bleak, creepy" A-bomb "echoes" throughout still have a "hold over our imaginations."

Going My Way ✉◐ `24` `23` `22` `21`

1944 | Directed by Leo McCarey | With Bing Crosby, Barry Fitzgerald, Risë Stevens | 126 minutes | Not Rated

"Sing along with Bing" in this "hokey but pleasant" musical drama showcasing Crosby "at his best" as a "popular priest" with heavenly pipes who converts a parish house choir to his feel-good philosophy; though multiple Oscars came its way, it looks "very dated" now since they "stopped making" this brand of "engaging schmaltz" "long ago."

Z Gold Diggers of 1933 ◑ | 25 | 19 | 16 | 26 |
1933 | Directed by Mervyn LeRoy | With Joan Blondell, Ruby Keeler, Dick Powell, Ginger Rogers | 96 minutes | Not Rated

An attempt to "cheer up" Depression-wracked America, this "wonderfully dated" "art deco musical" about down-and-out show people putting on a revue is best remembered for choreographer Busby Berkeley's "endlessly inventive" dance routines that evoke "joy and naughtiness" – along with a "bittersweet undercurrent of desperation"; don't-miss moment: "Ginger Rogers' pig latin version of 'We're in the Money.'"

Golden Child, The | 14 | 14 | 14 | 16 |
1986 | Directed by Michael Ritchie | With Eddie Murphy, Charlotte Lewis, Charles Dance | 94 minutes | Rated PG-13

Somewhere near the intersection of "*Beverly Hills Cop* and *Raiders of the Lost Ark*", this "weird blend of religion, action" and comedy stars Murphy as a social worker searching for a missing holy child; though it can be "stupidly funny" at times, most say this "throw-away" is hampered by "wooden acting" and a "leaden script."

Golden Compass, The | 17 | 18 | 18 | 23 |
2007 | Directed by Chris Weitz | With Dakota Blue Richards, Nicole Kidman, Daniel Craig, Eva Green | 113 minutes | Rated PG-13

"Talking polar bears", epic battles and "stunning visuals" keep things moving in this "interesting" fantasy set in a magical parallel universe where human souls walk beside their owners as animals; while some say it's a "defanged", "Cliff's Notes" version of Philip Pullman's source novels (and others sense an "anti-religious" tilt to the proceedings), there's agreement that Kidman's villainess is "deliciously evil."

GoldenEye | 19 | 19 | 19 | 23 |
1995 | Directed by Martin Campbell | With Pierce Brosnan, Sean Bean, Famke Janssen | 130 minutes | Rated PG-13

"Born to play the part" of the "never-fazed secret agent", Brosnan brings the 007 "franchise" "back from the dead" with a "suave" turn opposite Janssen's "great villainess" in this "modern Bond" flick; though the "convoluted storyline" about globe-busting weaponry in post-Soviet Russia is a "little clunky", overall it "gets the job done" with "outstanding action", "amazing special effects" and a "refreshing lack of hokeyness."

Z Goldfinger | 26 | 23 | 25 | 25 |
1964 | Directed by Guy Hamilton | With Sean Connery, Honor Blackman, Gert Frobe | 112 minutes | Rated PG

Rated the Top 007 picture in this Survey, this "classic" has it all: "formidable villains", the "coolest gadgets", an "out-of-this-world", "robbing-Fort-Knox" plot, a "fabulous theme song" "belted out by Shirley Bassey" and perhaps the "best-named" babe of them all, the one-and-only "Pussy Galore"; most memorable exchange: "do you expect me to talk? – no, Mr. Bond, I expect you to *die!*"

| | OVERALL | ACTING | STORY | PROD. |

☑ Gold Rush, The ◑
28 | 28 | 25 | 26

1925 | Directed by Charles Chaplin | With Charles Chaplin, Mack Swain | 82 minutes | Not Rated

Chaplin's "amazing talent" (as a writer, director and actor) is evident in this "brilliant" silent flicker, featuring the Little Tramp as a prospector "fighting the elements in the Klondike" and "overcoming all hurdles to get the girl" – and the gold; rife with "classic sequences" (the "bread-roll dance", the boiled "shoe for dinner", the cabin teetering on the edge of a cliff), it doesn't need dialogue "to evoke both laughter and pathos" – indeed, over 80 years later, many report a "lasting emotional impact."

Gone Baby Gone
24 | 26 | 23 | 23

2007 | Directed by Ben Affleck | With Casey Affleck, Michelle Monaghan, Morgan Freeman, Amy Ryan | 114 minutes | Rated R

The "Affleck brothers impress on both sides of the camera" in this "hard-driving" crime drama, with first-time director Ben flexing his "potential as a filmmaker" and sibling Casey delivering a "star-making performance" as a P.I. from "gritty" South Boston hired to "search for a missing girl"; rife with "moral quandaries", "surprising twists" and "spot-on" supporting turns ("authentic accents" included), it will "leave you thinking" "long after the lights go up."

Gone in Sixty Seconds
14 | 14 | 14 | 18

2000 | Directed by Dominic Sena | With Nicolas Cage, Angelina Jolie, Giovanni Ribisi, Robert Duvall | 117 minutes | Rated PG-13

"If you're a car person" revving for a "speed fix", this "flashy" action flick provides a "wild ride" as Cage and company get busy boosting 50 "hot" autos in a single night; but "slick chase scenes" aside (the "cars are the stars"), those who steer clear of "throwaways" with a "high cheese" factor just "wish it were over that fast."

☑ Gone with the Wind ✉
28 | 27 | 27 | 29

1939 | Directed by Victor Fleming | With Clark Gable, Vivien Leigh, Leslie Howard, Olivia de Havilland, Hattie McDaniel, Butterfly McQueen | 238 minutes | Rated G

A bona fide piece of "American pop culture", this Civil War melodrama based on Margaret Mitchell's "beloved" book is a "timeless", "sweeping" saga of love and loss in dwindling Dixieland; frankly, legions of admirers "do give a damn", rating it an "epic with a capital E" for its incredibly "beautiful production", "amazing" costumes and "perfect cast", especially Gable's "dashing" Rhett and Leigh's "performance of a lifetime" as the "feisty", "fiddle-dee-deeing" Scarlett; sure, it's a "long sit", yet in the end this "gorgeous triumph" "still thrills."

Goodbye, Columbus
19 | 19 | 20 | 19

1969 | Directed by Larry Peerce | With Richard Benjamin, Ali MacGraw, Jack Klugman | 102 minutes | Rated PG

Based on Philip Roth's once-provocative novella, this frank romantic comedy "might seem dated" now, but nostalgists remember its "good performances", especially MacGraw's tour-de-force turn as a "crush"-worthy "Jewish princess"; foes say that it "should have been better", considering the source material.

Goodbye Girl, The ✉ | 21 | 23 | 20 | 20 |

1977 | Directed by Herbert Ross | With Richard Dreyfuss, Marsha Mason, Paul Benedict | 110 minutes | Rated PG

"Exactly what a romantic comedy should be", this "feel-good movie" is about a "likable", lovelorn single mom forced to share an apartment with an unlikable, "lovable actor"; one of "Neil Simon's best" screenplays, this surprise hit garnered a clutch of Oscar nominations and won one for Dreyfuss' "charismatic" turn.

☑ Goodbye, Mr. Chips ✉◐ | 25 | 27 | 25 | 23 |

1939 | Directed by Sam Wood | With Robert Donat, Greer Garson, Paul Henreid | 114 minutes | Not Rated

More proof for the theory that "1939 was the best film year ever", this "touching" tale depicting 40 years in the life of everyone's "favorite" British schoolmaster is an unabashedly "sentimental story that will leave nary an eye dry"; credit "wonderful turns" from both Garson (in her screen debut) and Donat (who copped an Oscar) for making this "classic" "withstand the test of time."

☑ Goodfellas | 27 | 27 | 26 | 25 |

1990 | Directed by Martin Scorsese | With Robert De Niro, Ray Liotta, Joe Pesci | 146 minutes | Rated R

"Not for the faint of heart", "mob-master" Scorsese's "harrowing modern gangster" classic careens from "hysterically funny to terrifyingly violent" owing to an "electrifying" screenplay based on the true story of "'made' guys and greed" that reveals "mobsters as human beings" – albeit "vicious and heartless" ones; "beautiful lensing" and "stellar performances" make this one boil with "brutal power."

Good German, The ◐ | 16 | 19 | 16 | 19 |

2006 | Directed by Steven Soderbergh | With George Clooney, Cate Blanchett, Tobey Maguire | 105 minutes | Rated R

A "dark" tale of "intrigue" following an American journalist through post-WWII Germany, this "ambitious" drama mimics the "look and feel" of "classic noir" with glamorous stars, black-and-white lensing and a "hard-to-follow" plot; still, most say its "art piece" aspirations "fall flat" – it's hard to "make 'em like they used to."

Good Girl, The | 18 | 22 | 17 | 17 |

2002 | Directed by Miguel Arteta | With Jennifer Aniston, Jake Gyllenhaal, Zooey Deschanel, John C. Reilly | 93 minutes | Rated R

"Escaping the dreariness of real life" is the theme of this "downbeat" dramedy about a "disillusioned" shopgirl living in "Nowheresville" and "dreaming of better things"; it's "better than it had any right to be" thanks to Jake's "childish charm" and Jen's "nuanced", "low-key" work – there is "life after *Friends*" – even if foes find it "slow going" and saddled with an "oversupply of angst."

Good Morning, Vietnam | 22 | 24 | 22 | 22 |

1987 | Directed by Barry Levinson | With Robin Williams, Forest Whitaker, Bruno Kirby | 119 minutes | Rated R

Get a "different perspective on the Vietnam war" from this "bittersweet" tale of an army radio DJ in Saigon that "strikes just the right balance between comedy and drama", capturing the "reality" while still provoking beaucoup "laughs"; Williams "at his manic best" not only supplies the expected "hilarious ad-libbing" but shows off some "impressive acting skills" too.

Good Night, and Good Luck ◑   25 | 27 | 24 | 26

2005 | Directed by George Clooney | With David Strathairn, George Clooney, Robert Downey Jr. | 93 minutes | Rated PG

"History doesn't get much better" than George Clooney's recreation of the "tense", "smoke-filled" ambiance of CBS's 1950s-era newsroom, scene of an "intriguing showdown" between Senator Joseph McCarthy and broadcaster Edward R. Murrow ("they don't make journalists like that anymore"); crackling with "sharp dialogue" and blessed with a "sterling cast" headlined by the "phenomenal" Strathairn, it raises enough "thoughtful criticism" to incite "discussion about government censorship."

Good Shepherd, The   20 | 23 | 20 | 21

2006 | Directed by Robert De Niro | With Matt Damon, Angelina Jolie, Robert De Niro, William Hurt, Alec Baldwin | 167 minutes | Rated R

Witness the "birth of the CIA" through the eyes of a patriotic recruit who dutifully "sells his soul to the company" in this "compelling", "thinking-spy" thriller with a "killer cast" led by a "masterfully quiet" Damon; taking a "cerebral" approach to the "cloak-and-dagger business", it chooses "measured storytelling" over frenetic action and "demands your full attention."

Good, the Bad and the Ugly, The   24 | 21 | 23 | 23

1967 | Directed by Sergio Leone | With Clint Eastwood, Lee Van Cleef, Eli Wallach | 161 minutes | Rated R

A "delicious spaghetti Western" drenched in "tasty dramatic marinara sauce", this Clint-essential "Man-With-No-Name" oater about a trio of Civil War–era gunmen battling over Confederate treasure is a "true classic"; sure, Eastwood's "penetrating glare" is "hypnotic", but some say Wallach "steals the show" by injecting some "subtle comedy" into the mix, while composer Ennio Morricone's "memorable score" will "stick in your head for days."

⊠ Good Will Hunting ✉   24 | 25 | 24 | 22

1997 | Directed by Gus Van Sant | With Robin Williams, Matt Damon, Ben Affleck | 126 minutes | Rated R

Written by the "then-unknown" team of Damon and Affleck, this "intelligent" drama is built on an "uplifting", "powerful" screenplay about a "troubled petty criminal" who's coincidentally a "brilliant math genius"; its "searing yet subtle" performances include an Oscar-winning turn from Williams at his "most moving", and though the ill-willed badmouth it as "predictable", overall most folks "like them apples."

Good Year, A   16 | 18 | 17 | 19

2006 | Directed by Ridley Scott | With Russell Crowe, Marion Cotillard, Albert Finney, Abbie Cornish | 118 minutes | Rated PG-13

That old daydream about "quitting your job and moving to Provence" looks mighty "appealing" in this "pleasant" if "totally predictable" rom-com about an "arrogant" London bond trader who does just that; although it's "nice to see Russell Crowe not punching anyone out", his "flat" performance suggests he's a "better action hero than leading man."

	OVERALL	ACTING	STORY	PROD.

Goonies, The   23 | 19 | 23 | 21

1985 | Directed by Richard Donner | With Sean Astin, Josh Brolin, Corey Feldman | 114 minutes | Rated PG

One of the "best kids' adventures ever", this "smart, finely crafted" "family movie" about a gang of "pre-teen treasure hunters" who wield "go-go gadgets" and thwart bad guys is a fun "roller-coaster ride" "for all ages" (and a bona fide "nostalgia" trip for "Gen-Xers"); ok, it may have "some flaws", but at least it "doesn't take itself too seriously."

Gorillas in the Mist   19 | 21 | 20 | 21

1988 | Directed by Michael Apted | With Sigourney Weaver, Bryan Brown, Julie Harris | 129 minutes | Rated PG-13

"African jungles" supply the "beautiful setting" in this bio of primatologist Dian Fossey, the story of a complex woman who abandons humanity in favor of a group of endangered mountain gorillas; Weaver delivers a "great performance", the special effects blend real and artificial apes seamlessly and the "ending will stay with you."

Gorky Park   22 | 24 | 23 | 21

1983 | Directed by Michael Apted | With William Hurt, Lee Marvin, Brian Dennehy, Joanna Pacula | 128 minutes | Rated R

"One of the best results of the Cold War" is this "thoughtful thriller", a "taut mystery" following a "Muscovite policeman" investigating a "brutal murder" while encountering some "interesting twists" along the way; Hurt is "superb" as the fur-capped lead, while the bleak locations provide a "good peek" into the formerly off-limits USSR – even if it was "filmed in Finland."

Gosford Park ⊠   23 | 27 | 21 | 25

2001 | Directed by Robert Altman | With Clive Owen, Alan Bates, Maggie Smith, Helen Mirren, Kristin Scott Thomas | 137 minutes | Rated R

"Agatha Christie meets *Upstairs, Downstairs*" in this "jolly good show" of a "whodunit" that's an "insightful", "behind-the-scenes skewering of the British class system" set in a "'30s country estate"; "one of Altman's best", it boasts "rich atmosphere", "scintillating dialogue" and a "bloody great" ensemble cast all "acting up a storm", and if contrarians complain about its "convoluted", "hard-to-follow" plot, fans claim it "gets better every time you see it."

Gothika   17 | 19 | 17 | 19

2003 | Directed by Mathieu Kassovitz | With Halle Berry, Robert Downey Jr., Penélope Cruz | 98 minutes | Rated R

Surveyors split on this "supernatural thriller" in which a shrink in a psycho ward wakes up one day to find herself an inmate accused of murder: fans praise the "heebie-jeebie"-inducing cinematography and "keeps-you-guessing" plot, but foes find "very few scares" in this "standard" effort – even the "hot Halle can't heat it up."

⚡ Graduate, The ⊠   27 | 27 | 26 | 24

1967 | Directed by Mike Nichols | With Dustin Hoffman, Anne Bancroft, Katharine Ross | 105 minutes | Rated PG

The "benchmark coming-of-age comedy", this "knowing" look at a "confused young man" and his "older seductress" is the "definitive '60s alienation" flick and "somehow never ages"; credit its "witty script", Mike Nichols' "ahead-of-its-time direction", a "groovy"

Simon-and-Garfunkel soundtrack and "superb" turns from the "fab" Hoffman and the "unforgettable" Bancroft as – "koo-koo-ka-choo" – Mrs. Robinson; best word: "plastics."

Grand Canyon
	OVERALL	ACTING	STORY	PROD.
	18	21	18	18

1991 | Directed by Lawrence Kasdan | With Danny Glover, Kevin Kline, Steve Martin, Mary McDonnell | 134 minutes | Rated R

In this ambitious "meaning-of-life" drama, director Kasdan brings together a group of "average people leading average lives" to tell some "extraordinary stories" about "destiny and hope"; though some find the "fragmented", "confusing" result too "out there", most allow that this "surprisingly moving" moving picture "just misses being great."

Grand Hotel ✉◐
	25	26	24	25

1932 | Directed by Edmund Goulding | With Greta Garbo, John Barrymore, Joan Crawford, Lionel Barrymore | 112 minutes | Not Rated

"Intertwined lives" are the basis of this star-studded "early MGM talkie", one of the first multicharacter dramas set in a hotel; in addition to its "sumptuous" production and "literate" screenplay, it's endured thanks to a "brilliant" cast, particularly an "amazing Crawford", the "show-stealing" Barrymores and the "breathtaking Garbo", who utters her most famous line here: "I vant to be alone."

Grand Illusion ◐🄵
	28	28	27	26

1938 | Directed by Jean Renoir | With Jean Gabin, Erich von Stroheim, Pierre Fresnay | 114 minutes | Not Rated

"It's no illusion": this "compelling" WWI "masterpiece" has "inspired generations" with its "crushing portrayal of the futility of war" and is "still as powerful as ever"; director Renoir "shows how it should be done" in this "ahead-of-its-time" picture that's on "everyone's greatest list" simply because it "touches on every human emotion."

🄯 Grapes of Wrath, The ✉◐
	28	28	28	25

1940 | Directed by John Ford | With Henry Fonda, Jane Darwell, John Carradine | 128 minutes | Not Rated

"Every frame is a work of art" in this "faithful rendition" of Steinbeck's novel about dispossessed Depression-era farmers living in "desperate" times; possibly "Ford's best", it's a "classic for a reason" and "ranks high on the list of great American films" as an "important statement about life", the "depth of man's sorrow and the zenith of man's spirit."

🄯 Grease
	23	19	21	23

1978 | Directed by Randal Kleiser | With John Travolta, Olivia Newton-John, Stockard Channing | 110 minutes | Rated PG

"Fun" is the word for this "campy" comedy "classic", a "high-energy" "adaptation of the Broadway musical" that's a "'70s take on a "hokey '50s" story enacted by some of the "oldest high-school students ever"; still, the "hunky Travolta" and "stunning Newton-John" "light up the screen", and the "slick production" numbers are so "irresistible" that "cult followers" watch this "guilty pleasure" "over and over."

Great Debaters, The
	25	26	25	24

2007 | Directed by Denzel Washington | With Denzel Washington, Nate Parker, Jurnee Smollett, Forest Whitaker | 126 minutes | Rated PG-13

"It doesn't get any better than Washington and Whitaker" in this "earnest", "fact-based" tale of a "black college debate team" that "overcomes stacked odds" in the "racially tense", Depression-era South; though chances are "you can guess how it ends", the "extraordinary perspectives on African-American history" it offers are both "uplifting" and "inspirational."

ⓩ Great Dictator, The ◑
26 | 27 | 25 | 23

1940 | Directed by Charles Chaplin | With Charles Chaplin, Jack Oakie, Paulette Goddard | 124 minutes | Not Rated

The normally "silent Chaplin" "fearlessly" takes "aim at Hitler" in this rare talkie, a "scathing satire of fascist tyranny" in which he "plays two roles": a Jewish barber and "rabid" dictator Adenoid Hynkel, a "brilliant parody" of Der Führer; although "overly sentimental" and "preachy" to some, most find this "masterpiece of physical comedy" "thought-provoking and perpetually relevant."

ⓩ Great Escape, The
27 | 26 | 27 | 26

1963 | Directed by John Sturges | With Steve McQueen, James Garner, Richard Attenborough | 169 minutes | Not Rated

"Guy movies don't get any better" than this "absorbing" "prison break" flick "based on a true escape" from a World War II "German prisoner-of-war camp"; featuring McQueen backed up by an "all-star" ensemble, it also boasts "excellent writing", a "hummable score" and "flawless action" scenes, including the "best motorcycle scene ever filmed"; sure, it may be on the "long" side, it's "worth every minute."

ⓩ Great Expectations ◑
27 | 27 | 28 | 26

1947 | Directed by David Lean | With John Mills, Valerie Hobson, Alec Guinness, Jean Simmons | 118 minutes | Not Rated

A "pip of a movie", David Lean's "superb realization" of Dickens' novel about an orphan and his mysterious benefactor is a "masterpiece in every sense of the word"; it's "hauntingly shot" in "living black and white", and memorable moments include the "stunning graveyard sequence", Miss Havisham's "cobwebby wedding table" and "wonderful early performances by Simmons and Guinness"; in sum, "when they talk about a classic, this is what they mean."

Great Gatsby, The
22 | 22 | 24 | 23

1974 | Directed by Jack Clayton | With Robert Redford, Mia Farrow, Bruce Dern, Karen Black, Sam Waterston | 144 minutes | Rated PG

"Wealth doesn't buy happiness" in this "opulent" adaptation of Scott Fitzgerald's classic 1920s novel that's sure "gorgeous to look at" but otherwise splits surveyors: fans feel its "gangster-in-love" story is "wonderfully mounted" and the "hot blond" Redford and "luminous" Farrow are "superbly cast", but opponents say "overblown", "shallow" and distinctly "bottom drawer, old sport."

Great Race, The
20 | 18 | 20 | 20

1965 | Directed by Blake Edwards | With Jack Lemmon, Tony Curtis, Natalie Wood, Peter Falk | 150 minutes | Not Rated

Director Edwards revs up the engines in this "kitschy" "family" comedy about a turn-of-the-century auto race from NY to Paris, with plenty of "must-see" settings along the way; a tip-top cast supplies "over-the-top" performances, but the pièce de résistance is the "best pie fight in movie history"; in a word, it's a "hoot."

Great Santini, The

22 | 27 | 21 | 21

1979 | Directed by Lewis John Carlino | With Robert Duvall, Blythe Danner, Michael O'Keefe | 115 minutes | Rated PG

"Adapted from the painful Pat Conroy novel", this intense "dissection" of a "dysfunctional family" offers a "look inside the mind" of a "domineering" marine – "outstandingly" played by the "frighteningly good Duvall" – who treats his wife and kids like soldiers under his command; you'll "love him or hate him (or maybe both)", but in any event his "imperfect life" will "stay with you."

Great White Hope, The

25 | 27 | 25 | 23

1970 | Directed by Martin Ritt | With James Earl Jones, Jane Alexander | 103 minutes | Rated PG-13

"Way before Darth Vader", Jones is rematched with his "Broadway hit" role and delivers a "phenomenal" performance as a "Jack Johnson–esque heavyweight champion" whose devotion to Alexander is "doomed by racism and resentment"; in a unanimous decision, judges say this "riveting" drama "captures an era" with "tremendous emotion" and packs a "powerful punch."

Greed ❶∅

∇ 28 | 27 | 27 | 29

1925 | Directed by Erich von Stroheim | With Gibson Gowland, ZaSu Pitts, Jean Hersholt | 140 minutes | Not Rated

Originally "exceedingly long" (clocking in at 10 hours), this silent "tour de force" from Erich von Stroheim is famous for the studio's "hatchet job" to trim it to a commercially viable length; still, even in a "truncated" form, this "dark masterpiece" about a down-and-out dentist and his lottery-winning wife remains an exercise in "gritty realism", right down to that "stunning finale" in Death Valley.

Green Mile, The

23 | 25 | 23 | 24

1999 | Directed by Frank Darabont | With Tom Hanks, David Morse, Michael Clarke Duncan | 188 minutes | Rated R

Stephen King's "harrowing" serial novel is now "wonderfully translated to the screen" in this "disturbing drama" that "tugs at your emotions" with its "touching depiction" of "humanity at its best and worst"; despite "fine acting", this "very long" Mile makes some "wish it was an hour shorter."

Gremlins

19 | 14 | 20 | 20

1984 | Directed by Joe Dante | With Zach Galligan, Phoebe Cates, Hoyt Axton | 106 minutes | Rated PG

This "black comedy" features a "cuddly", "too-cute-for-words" pet who breeds "scary" offspring when exposed to bright light, water or being "fed after midnight"; although "lots of fun", some parents warn "proceed with caution": it has a "dark side", i.e. those "mean-spirited", "nightmare"-inducing gremlins who are much too violent for smaller fry.

Grey Gardens

25 | - | 23 | 22

1976 | Directed by Albert Maysles, David Maysles et al | Documentary | 100 minutes | Rated PG

Deserving its own "special place in the cult classic hall of fame", this "disturbing" documentary about "aristocrats sliding downward into poverty and neglect" captures the "bickering and bantering" between an "eccentric" mother and daughter living together in a "crumbling old mansion" (not incidentally, they happen to be "Jackie O's relatives"); all agree it's "totally engrossing", yet what's "hysterically amusing" for some is a "too sad" look at "mental illness" for others.

Greystoke: The Legend of Tarzan 15 | 14 | 17 | 19

1984 | Directed by Hugh Hudson | With Christopher Lambert, Andie MacDowell, Ian Holm | 130 minutes | Rated PG

Don't expect much monkey business in this "lush" drama, a "compelling retelling" of Edgar Rice Burroughs' ape-man tale that adds class-system critique and "animal welfare overtones" to the mix; there's plenty of "gorgeous" scenery as Lambert's jungle-bred hunk is introduced into English aristocracy, but even though it's "pretty to look at", many see an "overlong mess."

Gridiron Gang 19 | 18 | 22 | 19

2006 | Directed by Phil Joanou | With Dwayne Johnson, Xzibit | 125 minutes | Rated PG-13

Emotional "uplift" is the goal of this "enjoyable" if "unoriginal" sports flick about "troubled youths" incarcerated in a juvenile center who "learn valuable life lessons" and build self-esteem after forming a football team; star Johnson (aka 'The Rock') "pulls off his role pretty well", infusing the action with a manly dose of "inspirational" pep.

Grifters, The 22 | 26 | 23 | 21

1990 | Directed by Stephen Frears | With Anjelica Huston, John Cusack, Annette Bening | 119 minutes | Rated R

Despite "soulless characters" and a "cynical" theme, this very "adult" piece of "hard-core film noir" is a "first-class" study of "lowlife culture" (the "twisted" plot concerns a "mommy and her long-lost son who are reunited" only to "go down in flames"); while the "film gels" around the "powerhouse work of all three leads", some say the "real star" is Donald Westlake's "superb" script.

Grindhouse 21 | 19 | 18 | 23

2007 | Directed by Quentin Tarantino, Robert Rodriguez | With Kurt Russell, Rose McGowan, Freddy Rodriguez | 191 minutes | Rated R

This "clever homage" to the "spatter-and-gore" cinema of the 1970s ("campy" coming attractions and all) offers an "over-the-top" double feature: Rodriguez's "schlocky" zombie-fest, *Planet Terror,* and Tarantino's "talky" but still "awesome" car-stunt showcase, *Death Proof*; at three-plus hours running time, it "may be too much for one sitting", though appearances by a "gun-legged" McGowan and the "fantastic" Russell as a "cold-blooded serial killer" will keep the juices flowing.

Grosse Pointe Blank 22 | 21 | 22 | 19

1997 | Directed by George Armitage | With John Cusack, Minnie Driver, Alan Arkin, Dan Aykroyd | 107 minutes | Rated R

A "must-see" for Cusack fans, this "totally original" cult comedy finds the star "as charming as ever" playing a "nice-guy contract killer" who's returned to suburbia for his high school reunion only to be embroiled in a "showdown between competing assassins"; "dark premise" or not, it scores points with "every thirtysomething" for its snarky black humor" and "rockin' '80s soundtrack."

Groundhog Day

22 | 20 | 24 | 20

1993 | Directed by Harold Ramis | With Bill Murray, Andie MacDowell, Chris Elliott | 101 minutes | Rated PG

An "intelligent existential romp", this "literate comedy" has an "original concept": a "jerk" is forced to "live the same day over and over until he gets it right" and "becomes a lovable man"; ok, it's a "one-joke premise" that gets "tedious", but for most it "works like a charm" thanks to the "hilarious" Murray, who exchanges his "usual smart-ass" persona for something "surprisingly deep."

Grumpy Old Men

21 | 24 | 20 | 20

1993 | Directed by Donald Petrie | With Jack Lemmon, Walter Matthau, Ann-Margret | 103 minutes | Rated PG-13

Though "made for the *Murder, She Wrote*" set, this "lighthearted comedy" works for both "young and old", reuniting the "classic Matthau-and-Lemmon" team playing retired Minnesotans "vying for the affections" of a "comely" new neighbor (the "not-hard-to-watch Ann-Margret"); sure, "we've seen it all before", but these "well-loved icons" still provoke a "ton of laughs."

Guardian, The

18 | 18 | 19 | 21

2006 | Directed by Andrew Davis | With Kevin Costner, Ashton Kutcher, Sela Ward, Clancy Brown | 139 minutes | Rated PG-13

Saluting the "heroism of the Coast Guard", this "decent" action flick drops into an elite rescue divers' training camp where a "veteran" instructor and a "young Turk" collide to "familiar" dramatic effect (see the "*Top Gun*" and "*Officer and a Gentleman*" field manuals); "intense rescue scenes" enliven the otherwise "predictable" proceedings.

Guess Who

16 | 17 | 16 | 17

2005 | Directed by Kevin Rodney Sullivan | With Bernie Mac, Ashton Kutcher, Zoe Saldana, Judith Scott | 105 minutes | Rated PG-13

"Nowhere near the caliber" of the original, this "forgettable" remake of *Guess Who's Coming to Dinner* "reverses the races", this time sending a white man calling on his black fiancée's family; although some applaud the "surprisingly funny chemistry between Mac and Kutcher", the "uneven" script seems more like an "extended sitcom" borrowing heavily from "*Meet the Parents*."

∄ Guess Who's Coming to Dinner ⊠

25 | 27 | 25 | 22

1967 | Directed by Stanley Kramer | With Spencer Tracy, Sidney Poitier, Katharine Hepburn | 108 minutes | Not Rated

"Daring for its day", this '60s "commentary on race relations" is the "final film of Hollywood's finest couple", "class acts Hepburn and Tracy", at their most "powerful"; sure, its "controversial subject" of "interracial marriage" might seem a bit "stagy" and "dated" now, but its "poignant and charming" treatment assures that the "issues remain" relevant.

Guide to Recognizing Your Saints, A

18 | 22 | 17 | 16

2006 | Directed by Dito Montiel | With Robert Downey Jr., Shia LaBeouf, Chazz Palminteri, Dianne Wiest, Channing Tatum | 98 minutes | Rated R

"Powerful performances" from an "unusually good" ensemble lie at the heart of this coming-of-age story about a group of Queens teens "growing up poor in 1980s NYC"; determined to stay "true to its gritty subject", it comes equipped with the standard "indie"

trimmings – a "depressing" premise, lots of foul language and un-
steady, "camcorder"-style cinematography.

🅩 Gun Crazy ◑
(aka Deadly Is the Female)

OVERALL	ACTING	STORY	PROD.
27	24	27	22

1949 | Directed by Joseph H. Lewis | With Peggy Cummins, John Dall |
86 minutes | Not Rated

"Eat your heart out, *Bonnie and Clyde*" – this "tight little thriller" about
"gun-toting lovers on the run" is film noir at its most "brilliant" and
"economical", despite "B-list stars" and "zero budget"; there's plenty
of "subtly kinky" innuendo too, but it's best remembered for an "influential" robbery sequence, shot in one take from the backseat of a car.

Gunfight at the O.K. Corral

OVERALL	ACTING	STORY	PROD.
20	21	20	21

1957 | Directed by John Sturges | With Burt Lancaster, Kirk Douglas,
Rhonda Fleming | 122 minutes | Not Rated

Always "entertaining", this Western recounts the famed 19th-century
shoot-out between rival gangs in Tombstone, AZ; despite two
Hollywood icons "playing off each other wonderfully" – the rugged
Lancaster and the cleft-chinned Douglas – foes fume this "too-long"
production doesn't "move the way it should."

🅩 Gunga Din ◑

OVERALL	ACTING	STORY	PROD.
25	24	25	24

1939 | Directed by George Stevens | With Cary Grant, Victor McLaglen,
Douglas Fairbanks Jr | 117 minutes | Not Rated

This "rousing adventure flick" from "Hollywood's golden age" recounts the "golden age of the British Empire" via the "story of three
soldiers in imperial India" and the titular native lad who befriends
them; some snappy "byplay between Grant, McLaglen and Fairbanks"
makes it a "buddy film" prototype, though a few are troubled by the
"superior", "racist attitude" of the colonialists.

Gung Ho

OVERALL	ACTING	STORY	PROD.
17	16	18	15

1986 | Directed by Ron Howard | With Michael Keaton, Gedde Watanabe,
Mimi Rogers, George Wendt | 112 minutes | Rated PG-13

"Cultural clashes" drive this "light-hearted comedy" as Keaton engineers
a "Japanese firm's takeover" of an auto factory only to discover that
blue-collar "American spirit" gets fusty Far East execs to "loosen up"; it
"transports you back" to the "mid-'80s" for "a few laughs", but otherwise
this "heavy-handed" "archive of stereotypes" just "doesn't hold up."

Guns of Navarone, The

OVERALL	ACTING	STORY	PROD.
23	22	24	23

1961 | Directed by J. Lee Thompson | With Gregory Peck, David Niven,
Anthony Quinn | 158 minutes | Rated PG

"Even people who hate war movies love" this "star-studded" production about WWII Allied commandos plotting to destroy Nazi artillery;
"pounding" suspense and a "splendid cast" put this action-adventurer
"head-and-shoulders above" the rest – and that "climactic sequence"
will have you "holding your breath."

🅩 Guys and Dolls

OVERALL	ACTING	STORY	PROD.
24	21	24	24

1955 | Directed by Joseph L. Mankiewicz | With Marlon Brando, Jean
Simmons, Frank Sinatra | 150 minutes | Not Rated

"Brando sings!" in this "colorful" musical rendition of the "Damon
Runyon stories" about "gamblers, evangelists" and racehorses, all

dolled up into one "heavyweight" extravaganza set around Times Square, rife with "catchy tunes" and "showstopping" numbers; foes think Marlon's "miscast", pointing to his "bored", "sexually smug" rendition of 'Luck Be a Lady.'

Gypsy

| 20 | 21 | 22 | 22 |

1962 | Directed by Mervyn LeRoy | With Rosalind Russell, Natalie Wood, Karl Malden | 143 minutes | Not Rated

"Stripper Gypsy Rose Lee's life" is the basis of this "terrific" musical biography about the "original backstage mother" and her "passionate" efforts to mold her kids into stars; ok, it's "kind of windy" and Wood (in the title role) "doesn't really strip", while the "brilliant miscasting" of a "shrill" Russell leads many to say the part "should have gone to Ethel Merman", who delivered the "real goods" on Broadway.

Hair

| 20 | 18 | 21 | 21 |

1979 | Directed by Milos Forman | With John Savage, Treat Williams, Beverly D'Angelo | 121 minutes | Rated PG

The groovy "Broadway musical" that "defined the psychedelic '60s" gets a "terrific" big-screen transfer in this story of a draftee bound for Vietnam dallying with Central Park hippies; even though "Treat's a treat" in a role that "epitomizes the loving craziness" of the time, some say the "flower-child imagery" is "sadly faded."

Hairspray

| 19 | 17 | 18 | 18 |

1988 | Directed by John Waters | With Divine, Ricki Lake, Sonny Bono, Ruth Brown, Debbie Harry | 91 minutes | Rated PG

"Grab a can of Aquanet" and get ready to "shake a tailfeather": this "hilariously campy" story of a "fat girl who lives to dance" is underground director Waters' "mainstream" ode to his "beloved Baltimore" in the '60s and his "most family-friendly" flick (it even "unflinchingly looks at racism"); though "Divine's divine" and the "absolutely perfect" Lake wears her "big hair" well, "deviant" devotees hedge it's "kind of tame, but still fun."

Hairspray

| 21 | 22 | 21 | 24 |

2007 | Directed by Adam Shankman | With John Travolta, Christopher Walken, Nikki Blonsky, Michelle Pfeiffer | 117 minutes | Rated PG

John Waters' "subversive" cult classic becomes a "wholesome" musical in this "colorful" adaptation of the Broadway hit about 1960s Baltimore teens fighting for "civil rights" and a chubby chick's desire to dance in a "local TV bandstand program"; the music's "catchy", the energy level "high" and the "literally larger-than-life" Travolta is a "hoot" in "bad fat drag."

Halloween

| 22 | 16 | 20 | 19 |

1978 | Directed by John Carpenter | With Donald Pleasence, Jamie Lee Curtis | 91 minutes | Rated R

"Changing the face of horror movies forever", this "almost bloodless chiller shows that gore doesn't equal terror" as it depicts a "masked psycho stalker" who preys on "rowdy teens"; despite "zero-budget" production values and so-so acting (but mighty "great screaming by Jamie Lee"), this "influential" "slasher" flick spawned a slew of sequels and "still holds up."

⚡ Hamlet ✉◑   27 | 29 | 28 | 24

1948 | Directed by Laurence Olivier | With Laurence Olivier, Eileen Herlie, Basil Sydney, Jean Simmons | 153 minutes | Not Rated

"Probably the best Shakespeare film ever made with the greatest Shakespearean actor", this Oscar-winning epic is a "brilliantly visual" take on the Bard's "greatest drama"; director/producer/star Olivier does Hamlet as a blond "as only he can do it", and if the action scenes are less vivid than in other versions, overall it's considered "unfailingly great."

Hamlet   24 | 26 | 26 | 25

1996 | Directed by Kenneth Branagh | With Kenneth Branagh, Julie Christie, Derek Jacobi | 242 minutes | Rated PG-13

This oft-done (maybe "overdone") Shakespearean tragedy gets "expansive" treatment from "modern master" Branagh, who uses the Bard's full text, resulting in a "four-hour adaptation"; though "engrossing, suspenseful" and "beautifully reimagined" to fans, those who say "enough already" call it "*too much* of a good thing."

Hand That Rocks the Cradle, The   16 | 16 | 17 | 16

1992 | Directed by Curtis Hanson | With Annabella Sciorra, Rebecca De Mornay | 110 minutes | Rated R

It's De Mornay who "rocks" as the "world's most warped nanny" nursing a "psychopathic" grudge in this "well-done" thriller, a "real nailbiter" despite "huge plot holes" and "overwrought" situations; the ultimate in "working-mom paranoia", it delivers a "chilling" moral: "always check references!"

Hannah and Her Sisters ✉   24 | 25 | 23 | 23

1986 | Directed by Woody Allen | With Mia Farrow, Barbara Hershey, Dianne Wiest | 103 minutes | Rated PG-13

A "nice balance of jokes and philosophy", this "pertinent" romantic comedy about three sisters and their "struggle with the meaning of life" "brims with so much intelligence and heart" that many call it "Allen's most life-affirming" picture; featuring "all-around wonderful" acting, it's a "valentine" to "NYers in all their neurotic glory" that manages to "convey a message without tempering the laugh-out-loud humor."

Hannibal   15 | 21 | 14 | 19

2001 | Directed by Ridley Scott | With Anthony Hopkins, Julianne Moore, Ray Liotta, Gary Oldman | 131 minutes | Rated R

Sure, it's "not the same without Jodie", but this "grisly" *Silence of the Lambs* sequel lets the "fascinating" Hopkins chew the scenery as a refined psycho dreaded for his "wry comments" – "bon appétit!" – and unspeakable" cravings; buckets of "baroque gore" help distract from the "inferior story", yet many say it "crosses the line" into a "pointless ckfest" with a "tasteless (no pun intended)" climax better suited o "*Fear Factor*."

Happiness   23 | 25 | 22 | 20

1998 | Directed by Todd Solondz | With Jane Adams, Jon Lovitz, Philip eymour Hoffman | 134 minutes | Not Rated

orget the "truly ironic title": this extremely "dark" "feel-bad" comedy s "*American Beauty* with a lot more acid" and so "unrelentingly bleak" hat it's "not for the faint of heart"; given some "taboo subject matter", the unhappy call it a "sicko train wreck" that's "probably the worst first-date movie ever", but fans tout its "brave" if "perverted" take on the "middle classes."

Happy Feet
21 | - | 19 | 25

2006 | Directed by George Miller, Warren Coleman, Judy Morris | Animated | 108 minutes | Rated PG

The "penguins look so real, you almost forget they're animated" in this "warm and fuzzy" cartoon featuring "toe-tappin'" music and "large laughs" courtesy of "reliable" voice-veteran Robin Williams, who "of course steals the show" in multiple roles; as for the flick's "environmental message", surveyors stand at opposite poles: allies applaud the "valuable lessons" while detractors deem it too "heavy-handed."

Hard Day's Night, A ◐
24 | 19 | 19 | 24

1964 | Directed by Richard Lester | With The Beatles, Wilfrid Brambell | 87 minutes | Rated G

"Before there was MTV", there was this "best rock movie ever", an "ahead-of-its-time" "groundbreaker" shot with documentary-style "quick edits" that brilliantly convey the "lunacy" and the "pure joy of Beatlemania" in the "days of innocence"; it's "still a film of wonder", and, of course, there's that "incredible soundtrack" of "Fab Four" classics.

Harder They Come, The
▽ 25 | 19 | 21 | 20

1973 | Directed by Perry Henzell | With Jimmy Cliff, Carl Bradshaw, Janet Barkley | 98 minutes | Rated R

Get a "non-tourist view of Jamaica" via this "engrossing" drama, a "reggae-scored" Kingston import starring Cliff as a "wannabe singing star who turns to crime" under pressure of "racism and classism"; there's a "subtle message about power" in "post-colonial culture", but its cult appeal has to do with "one of the greatest soundtracks" ever.

Harold & Kumar Go to White Castle
19 | 17 | 17 | 16

2004 | Directed by Danny Leiner | With John Cho, Kal Penn, Paula Garcés | 88 minutes | Rated R

"Whoa, dude": "sophomoric stoner comedies" get a "whole new twist" (starting with the "long-overdue casting" of "Asians in the leads") in this "buddy" tale of "potheads" with the "munchies" on an "all-night journey" to score a "case of sliders"; the "gross-out humor", "pointless plot" and "cameo by Doogie Howser" are "so freakin' funny" that many are left "hungry for more."

Harold and Maude
25 | 25 | 25 | 21

1972 | Directed by Hal Ashby | With Ruth Gordon, Bud Cort, Vivian Pickles | 91 minutes | Rated PG

Ok, it "starts with a hanging", but this "counterculture cult classic gets funnier", managing to be both "morbid" and "absurdly wonderful" in its "May-December story" of a "death-obsessed" kid who finds love with a "free-spirited old lady"; while "not for everyone", this "original" features a "phenomenal" Gordon and a "gem" of a "Cat Stevens soundtrack."

Harper
21 | 23 | 20 | 21

1966 | Directed by Jack Smight | With Paul Newman, Lauren Bacall, Julie Harris, Arthur Hill, Janet Leigh, Pamela Tiffin, Robert Wagner, Shelley Winters | 121 minutes | Not Rated

Renowned for its all-star, scenery-shredding cast, this "fun" private dick flick features a "vintage Paul" hot on the trail of a missing hus band; if the "plot is entirely predictable", "none of the actors are", with special kudos to an "entertaining" Bacall as a witchy wife and a "classic" Winters as a blousy, boozy starlet.

Harry and the Hendersons

1987 | Directed by William Dear | With John Lithgow, Melinda Dillon | 110 minutes | Rated PG

"Good for the kids", this "silly" comedy about a family that inadvertently adopts "Bigfoot" is "mindless" "fluff" with plenty of "likable characters" and an underlying message of "compassion"; though "probably dated" for most modern youngsters, it is "endearing" for the soft-hearted.

☑ Harry Potter and the Chamber of Secrets

2002 | Directed by Chris Columbus | With Daniel Radcliffe, Rupert Grint, Emma Watson, Kenneth Branagh | 161 minutes | Rated PG

This "rare spectacular sequel" is "much darker and scarier than the first", but "fantastic fantasy fare for the family" nevertheless and an "excellent adaptation of the book" "within the limits of time"; the special effects are "amazing", of course, and "the young stars have grown into their roles and do an even better job" this time around, but fans who "can't wait for the next one" admit that "Dumbledore is going to be tough to replace."

☑ Harry Potter and the Goblet of Fire

2005 | Directed by Mike Newell | With Daniel Radcliffe, Rupert Grint, Emma Watson, Gary Oldman | 157 minutes | Rated PG-13

"Dragons", a giant "maze" and "puberty" spell trouble for Harry and the Hogwarts gang in this "fine addition" to a series that's "progressed beyond the kids movie" milieu and ventured into "darker" territory thanks to the maturing Potter's "increasing angst"; a "faithful compression" of Rowling's tome, it summons more "impressive" effects wizardry and "strong acting", keeping the franchise "on fire" as the wand passes to future episodes.

☑ Harry Potter and the Order of the Phoenix

2007 | Directed by David Yates | With Daniel Radcliffe, Rupert Grint, Emma Watson, Ralph Fiennes | 138 minutes | Rated PG-13

The *Potter* franchise "continues to soar" with this "fine" fifth entry, an "exciting" adventure that finds the "maturing" but ever "vulnerable" Harry spinning "out of control" just as the villainous Voldemort makes another bid for supremacy; overall, "consistency" reigns as acolytes applaud the scenarist for "keeping the story moving", the young cast for "getting better with age" and the "first-rate" production for its reliably "stellar" visuals.

☑ Harry Potter and the Prisoner of Azkaban

2004 | Directed by Alfonso Cuarón | With Daniel Radcliffe, Rupert Grint, Emma Watson | 141 minutes | Rated PG

Rowling's third installment in the "beloved" series of children's books about a triumvirate of young wizards is "as wonderful and fanciful as the others", with particularly "fabulous production values"; featuring just the "right touch of menace and darkness" to win over "older moviegoers", it has appeal for all ages, but since the "kids are growing up", some wonder "will Harry have a beard in the next one?"

⚡ Harry Potter and the Sorcerer's Stone   24 | 23 | 25 | 27

2001 | Directed by Chris Columbus | With Daniel Radcliffe, Rupert Grint, Emma Watson | 152 minutes | Rated PG

It's "Hogwarts brought to magic life": this "reverent" screen adaptation of the ultra-"popular children's book" about a school for young witches and wizards is simply "spellbinding" – nothing less than a "21st-century *Wizard of Oz*"; fans zero in on the "eye-popping special effects", "outstanding" ensemble cast and "perfect" scenario that "gets every character right", "just like you imagined them"; still, the "length and scariness factors" might mean it's "wasted on little kids."

Hart's War   16 | 18 | 17 | 18

2002 | Directed by Gregory Hoblit | With Bruce Willis, Colin Farrell, Terrence Howard, Cole Hauser | 125 minutes | Rated R

American GIs detained in a "Nazi prisoner-of-war camp" confront "racism" in their own ranks in this "old-style war movie" grafted onto a "courtroom drama"; "Colin crackles" and Bruce goes for "gritty glory", but overall this "plodding" picture is "not *Stalag 17* by any stretch."

Harvey   26 | 27 | 25 | 22

1950 | Directed by Henry Koster | With James Stewart, Josephine Hull, Peggy Dow | 104 minutes | Not Rated

"So sweet and genuine that it's never become dated", this ever "classic comedy" concerning an "adorable sot" and his "imaginary six-foot rabbit" is such an "enchanting, grown-up fairy tale" that the "word 'heartwarming' was coined for it"; "delightful performances" elevate this "feel-good" flick into the "can't-miss" category.

Hatari!   21 | 17 | 18 | 23

1962 | Directed by Howard Hawks | With John Wayne, Hardy Kruger, Elsa Martinelli | 157 minutes | Not Rated

"Great African location shots" and a "fab" Henry Mancini score make this "somewhat forgotten" action/adventurer "better than its reputation" (even if its rather "dull" plot about "wild animal" trappers lacks "political correctness"); though it's a "lesser" vehicle for the "bigger-than-life" Wayne, at least the "beautiful photography" supplies some real "entertainment value."

Heartbreak Kid, The   20 | 20 | 21 | 19

1972 | Directed by Elaine May | With Charles Grodin, Cybill Shepherd, Jeannie Berlin, Eddie Albert | 106 minutes | Rated PG

"Not your traditional romantic comedy", this "biting satire" tells the story of a "NY Jewish guy" who falls for a Midwestern "shiksa goddess" – while on his honeymoon; it's "hysterical" albeit "cringe-making" stuff, with Grodin appropriately "smarmy" in his "bulldoggish pursuit" of the "unobtainable" Shepherd, but the "fabulous" Berlin (director May's daughter) steals the picture, leaving many with a "complex about egg salad sandwiches."

Heartburn   19 | 24 | 19 | 19

1986 | Directed by Mike Nichols | With Meryl Streep, Jack Nicholson, Jeff Daniels, Maureen Stapleton | 108 minutes | Rated R

The "ups and downs of married life" are dissected in this "comedic" yet "acidic" story of "revenge" that's a "thinly veiled account" of writer Nora Ephron's relationship with "Watergate reporter" Carl Bernstein;

still, some say the "slight" story is "unworthy" of its "divine" stars, and outside of a memorable "Key lime pie", much of the movie is "tripe."

☑ Heart Is a Lonely Hunter, The ∅   25 | 27 | 24 | 22

1968 | Directed by Robert Ellis Miller | With Alan Arkin, Stacy Keach, Chuck McCann | 123 minutes | Not Rated

If you're in the mood for a "tearjerker", among the "best of its kind" is this "beautifully told" drama featuring Arkin "hitting all the right notes" as a "deaf-mute saint" who comes to a Southern town and alters "lonely" local lives; the cast is "incredible" at conveying "unspoken dialogue", and the poignant "parable" provides a "tug at the heartstrings" "you'll never forget."

Heat   22 | 25 | 19 | 22

1995 | Directed by Michael Mann | With Al Pacino, Robert De Niro, Val Kilmer, Jon Voight | 171 minutes | Rated R

"Both the cop and robber are heroes" in this "operatic" crime epic, a "star-studded killfest" that's cinematically historic, since "legends" Pacino and De Niro are "finally on-screen together" (their "face-to-face" "coffeehouse scene" is a "knockout"); yet "despite a captivating cast and storyline", "they could have done a better job in the editing room" – "there's a perfect two-hour movie" lurking in this sprawling, 171-minute marathon.

Heathers   21 | 19 | 22 | 18

1989 | Directed by Micheal Lehmann | With Winona Ryder, Christian Slater, Shannen Doherty | 102 minutes | Rated R

The "pinnacle of '80s dark humor" – maybe even "before its time" – this "out-there" "black comedy" is "twisted" and "proud of it" as it provides an important lesson in "teen peer pressure": "popularity can kill"; though "not for everyone" (especially the "lighthearted or light-stomached"), it did "launch Slater's and Ryder's careers", and the "deliciously biting dialogue is full of comebacks you wish you'd thought of."

Heaven Can Wait   24 | 24 | 24 | 22

1943 | Directed by Ernst Lubitsch | With Gene Tierney, Don Ameche, Charles Coburn | 112 minutes | Not Rated

The famed "Lubitsch touch" is rendered in Technicolor in this "witty, unsentimental" comedy about a deceased playboy at the gate of Hell hoping to be admitted by listing his many transgressions; it's a "clever" yet "charming" trifle about how "life doesn't meet up to one's expectations", with a "devilishly nice ending."

Heaven Can Wait   21 | 19 | 22 | 19

1978 | Directed by Warren Beatty, Buck Henry | With Warren Beatty, Julie Christie, Dyan Cannon | 101 minutes | Rated PG

An "enjoyable remake of *Here Comes Mr. Jordan*", this comedy-fantasy mix of true love and the afterlife is kind of "far-fetched, but it works"; sure, "Buck Henry's script is as good as the original" and Beatty's "likable", but the "hysterical" Charles Grodin "steals the show."

Heavenly Creatures   24 | 25 | 26 | 24

1994 | Directed by Peter Jackson | With Kate Winslet, Melanie Lynskey, Clive Merrison | 99 minutes | Rated R

One part "fantasy", one part "true crime", this "absolutely riveting" drama about two teens plotting "matricide" is a "surreal", "haunting descent into the imagination" as it details an "attachment that turns deadly"; Winslet's "career-launching" performance is so "astounding" that some say "*this* is the movie" that the *Titanic* star "should have gotten an Oscar nomination for."

Heaven's Gate

| | 14 | 15 | 14 | 19 |

1980 | Directed by Michael Cimino | With Kris Kristofferson, Christopher Walken, Sam Waterston, Isabelle Huppert | 219 minutes | Rated R

The "gorgeous fiasco" that nearly "bankrupted a studio", this infamously "overambitious" Western inflates the Johnson County War between homesteaders and rich cattlemen in 1890 Wyoming into a "beautifully filmed" but "plodding" epic with performances ranging from "wonderful" (Walken) to "wooden" (Kristofferson); in retrospect, it's "not as bad as its reputation", but heaven knows the gait is "interminable."

Heavy Metal

| 20 | - | - | 21 |

1981 | Directed by Gerald Potterton | Animated | 86 minutes | Rated R

"Based on the sci-fi comic book of the same name", this "cult" cartoon "classic" is a novel "departure for animation", given its "adult-oriented" content and "heavy metal" score; some shrug it "wavers between entertaining and dull", since this "strung-together anthology" of hard-rock-flavored "vignettes" is more than "a little choppy" (it "makes no sense without alcohol").

Hedwig and the Angry Inch

| 21 | 23 | 21 | 20 |

2001 | Directed by John Cameron Mitchell | With John Cameron Mitchell, Michael Pitt, Miriam Shor | 95 minutes | Rated R

Positively "not for the Pat Robertson crowd", this "offbeat indie musical" details the adventures of a "semi-transgendered wannabe rock star" – "yes, you read that right" – with "Farrah hair" and a "Ziggy Stardust"–esque stage act; based on the "off-off Broadway cult hit", it seems destined to become a "midnight movie" staple thanks to its "giddy, gritty" plot and "kick-ass music."

🇿 Heiress, The ✉◐

| 27 | 28 | 27 | 26 |

1949 | Directed by William Wyler | With Olivia de Havilland, Montgomery Clift, Miriam Hopkins | 115 minutes | Not Rated

There's "not a weak link" in this "haunting" "old-world" version of Henry James' *Washington Square*, with Oscar winner de Havilland leading an "aces" cast in a "multilayered" turn as a "plain-Jane heiress yearning to be loved" by "gold digger" Clift over the veto of her "stern" father; indeed, her "riveting" makeover "from wallflower to woman" generates "expertly crafted" drama.

Hellboy

| 16 | 16 | 16 | 21 |

2004 | Directed by Guillermo del Toro | With Ron Perlman, John Hurt, Selma Blair, Jeffrey Tambor | 122 minutes | Rated PG-13

"Yet another" comic-book adaptation, this "watchable" sci-fi flick features an "ugly", "angst-ridden" superhero (Perlman "under pounds of makeup"), who dispatches the "forces of evil" while simultaneously spouting "funny one-liners"; there's plenty of "rollicking" action and some "great" FX, but ultimately this "routine" exercise is only "mildly entertaining."

Hello, Dolly!

	20	19	20	23

1969 | Directed by Gene Kelly | With Barbra Streisand, Walter Matthau, Michael Crawford | 146 minutes | Rated G

This "big, over-the-top" musical concerning a turn-of-the-century matchmaker is a "colorful" romp with all the "beautiful music from the Broadway show"; but goodbye Charlies call it an "overblown spectacle", citing "one of the most unappealing romantic couplings imaginable": a "miscast" Streisand ("who knew Dolly Levi was 25 years old?") playing opposite an "embarrassing" Matthau.

Hellraiser

	19	15	20	20

1987 | Directed by Clive Barker | With Andrew Robinson, Clare Higgins, Ashley Laurence, Oliver Smith | 94 minutes | Rated R

"Sick, twisted and gory", this "squirm-inducing" "landmark" of horror history adds the "ugly side of sexual desire" to its "disturbing" story of an unfaithful wife mesmerized by her former lover – who's now a zombie; it's best remembered for the character "Pinhead", a "movie monster all-star" so "utterly creepy" that diehards "still have nightmares about him years later."

Hell's Angels ◑

	▽ 24	19	19	26

1930 | Directed by Howard Hughes | With Ben Lyon, James Hall, Jean Harlow | 127 minutes | Rated PG

"Howard Hughes' great aeronautic epic" set during WWI is worth seeing for its "amazing dogfight footage" as well as its "impressive", "big-budget" depiction of a Zeppelin raid over London; but some note that another "bombshell" – the "platinum blonde" Harlow in "her first major film role" – nearly "steals the show away from the brilliant camera work."

Help!

	19	16	15	20

1965 | Directed by Richard Lester | With The Beatles, Leo McKern, Eleanor Bron | 90 minutes | Rated G

"Sing along with the hits from 1965" that enliven this "zany musical comedy", a "perfectly enjoyable" if "silly John-Paul-George-and-Ringo romp" that's really not much more than a "platform to take advantage of the Beatles' popularity"; still, the "story's ok" ("at least there's a plot this time"), the international "locations are great" and, "of course, the soundtrack is terrific."

Henry & June

	20	22	20	21

1990 | Directed by Philip Kaufman | With Fred Ward, Uma Thurman, Maria de Medeiros | 136 minutes | Rated NC-17

"Not for the prudish", this "lushly produced" drama explores the libidinous "literary underbelly" of Paris in the '30s, where burgeoning bohemian scribe Henry Miller, his alluring wife June and their groupie Anaïs Nin indulge in a steamy triangle fueled by "curiosity and lust"; an ultra-"erotic lesbian love scene" helped tag this "perverse gem" with the "first NC-17 rating" ever.

⊿ Henry V

	26	28	27	26

1989 | Directed by Kenneth Branagh | With Kenneth Branagh, Derek Jacobi | 137 minutes | Rated PG-13

"Brush up on your Shakespeare" via this "revisionist" adaptation of the Bard's "difficult" history play about an English monarch at war with

France; "both spectacular and approachable", it makes the 17th-century dialogue "completely understandable to modern ears", and first-time director Branagh's "lavish, lusty" brio is so "brilliant" that many acolytes ask "Sir Laurence who?"

Hercules
17 | - | 17 | 21

1997 | Directed by Ron Clements, John Musker | Animated | 92 minutes | Rated G

To "Disney-fy" Greek mythology risks the wrath of Zeus, but this "witty", "well-told" animated saga is "elevated" Olympusward by a "strong voice cast", "great songs" and enough "jokes for adults" to make for "stylish family fun" with "an edge"; like its brawny hero fending off superhuman foes, it "stands up well" and marks a "departure from the usual formula."

Hero 🄵
25 | 22 | 23 | 27

2004 | Directed by Zhang Yimou | With Jet Li, Zhang Ziyi | 99 minutes | Rated PG-13

"Not your typical martial-arts movie", this Chinese "homage to *Rashomon*" told from multiple perspectives in "non-linear" format explodes with "luscious visuals", "chop-'em-up kung fu" fight scenes and even some "noble" performances ("Jet Li can act!"); still, while fans see a "thought-provoking" epic about "politics, loyalty and truth", a few Sinophobes can't help but read a "propaganda" message in the "nationalist storyline."

Hidalgo
20 | 21 | 21 | 23

2004 | Directed by Joe Johnston | With Viggo Mortensen, Omar Sharif | 136 minutes | Rated PG-13

"*The Little Engine That Could* meets *Lawrence of Arabia*" with "not quite epic" results in this "old-fashioned" story about an "underdog" cowboy undertaking a 3,000-mile horse race across the North African desert; while the scenery's "sumptuous" and Viggo's a "god" as the "handsome daredevil hero", neigh-sayers say the plot's "weak" and the running time "a little long."

High Anxiety
21 | 19 | 19 | 19

1977 | Directed by Mel Brooks | With Mel Brooks, Madeline Kahn, Cloris Leachman | 94 minutes | Rated PG

"Hitch would have laughed" at this "totally goofy" comic homage from the "totally insane" Mel Brooks that's a "send-up" of a number of films in the Hitchcockian oeuvre, particularly *Psycho* and *Vertigo*; only problem is, "you must know the material he's spoofing in order to get the jokes" or else this "silly" picture "doesn't really hang together."

High Crimes
16 | 19 | 17 | 17

2002 | Directed by Carl Franklin | With Ashley Judd, Morgan Freeman, Jim Caviezel | 115 minutes | Rated PG-13

Reunited *Kiss the Girls* co-stars Judd and Freeman "work well together again" in this "slick" if "average" military courtroom drama cut from the same story fatigues worn by "*A Few Good Men*"; though the story of a cover-up of a massacre in Salvador is fairly "predictable", it does "rush you along" and "keep you guessing" – maybe to divert attention from the "gaping plot holes."

	OVERALL	ACTING	STORY	PROD.

High Fidelity — 21 | 23 | 20 | 19

2000 | Directed by Stephen Frears | With John Cusack, Jack Black, Todd Louiso, Iben Hjejle | 113 minutes | Rated R

Cusack is "pitch perfect" as an "underachieving record-store owner who can't commit" in this "funny, biting" romantic comedy that "lives up to" its source material, the Nick Hornby novel; "people obsessed with list-making" tick off its virtues – an "excellent soundtrack", the spot-on "music-snob jokes", "Jack Black's breakout moment" as a "hilariously obnoxious clerk" – and rate this "rare straddle between a chick flick and a guy movie" as one of the "top five date movies" ever made.

Highlander — 19 | 15 | 21 | 19

1986 | Directed by Russell Mulcahy | With Christopher Lambert, Sean Connery, Roxanne Hart | 116 minutes | Rated R

A "cult following" favors this highly "original" fantasy flick, a "good vs. evil" face-off between "immortal warriors" settling "centuries-old" scores; though the acting's "adequate at best", the "awesome swordplay", "cool" effects and Queen's "rockin' soundtrack" make for an "entertaining" combo – just "don't bother" with the "subpar" sequels.

☑ High Noon ⊠◖ — 28 | 26 | 26 | 25

1952 | Directed by Fred Zinnemann | With Gary Cooper, Grace Kelly, Lloyd Bridges | 85 minutes | Not Rated

Voted the "best classic Western" in this Survey, this "tense drama" filmed in "real time" "breaks the mold" by combining all the "grit of the West" with a "strong comment on the McCarthyist '50s" and a touch of "Greek drama" to boot; as a "single-minded sheriff" with "principles", Cooper took home an Oscar, though many admit they're drawn to this timeless "allegory" for its "theme song" alone; in short, it's "absolutely tops" – nothing else "comes close."

High Plains Drifter — 18 | 19 | 20 | 19

1972 | Directed by Clint Eastwood | With Clint Eastwood, Verna Bloom, Marianna Hill | 105 minutes | Rated R

"Perennial badass" Eastwood plays a "violent" "avenging angel" in this "powerful" if by-the-numbers Western in which "everyone gets what they deserve"; connoisseurs say it's Clint's "defining moment", though the less enamored rate it an "acquired taste", "not up to the standard of some of his others."

High Sierra ◖ — 25 | 26 | 24 | 23

1941 | Directed by Raoul Walsh | With Humphrey Bogart, Ida Lupino, Alan Curtis | 100 minutes | Not Rated

Hard-boiled with a heart, this "gritty gangster pic" features a sneering Bogie in a "part made for him" as a "bad crook gone worse" who puts on a "tough" front to cover up the sentimental sap underneath; noir connoisseurs call it "dated but great", heaping high praise on Lupino's incredibly "hot" performance.

High Society — 23 | 22 | 22 | 23

1956 | Directed by Charles Walters | With Bing Crosby, Grace Kelly, Frank Sinatra, Celeste Holm | 107 minutes | Not Rated

"What a swell party" is this Cole Porter "musical rendition of *The Philadelphia Story*", a "sophisticated comedy of manners" set in a

"Newport mansion" inhabited by some "fantastic talent": a "gorgeous Grace", "swingin' Bing" and "delightful Sinatra"; sure, the original might be "far superior" plotwise, but fans dub this "softer" take the "Tiffany" of the singing-and-dancing genre.

Hilary and Jackie

| 21 | 26 | 22 | 21 |

1998 | Directed by Anand Tucker | With Emily Watson, Rachel Griffiths, David Morrissey | 121 minutes | Rated R

"Poignant and touching", this "overlooked" biodrama tells the true story of the prickly "relationship between two sisters", one a cellist who's "battling MS" as well as other "personal" demons; "outstanding lead performances from Watson and Griffiths" lend appeal to more than just "classical music fans", though some say it can be "difficult to watch", given the "tragic" storyline.

☒ Hiroshima, Mon Amour ◐𝔽

| 25 | 24 | 24 | 23 |

1960 | Directed by Alain Resnais | With Emmanuelle Riva, Eiji Okada | 90 minutes | Not Rated

Simultaneously "harrowing and beautiful", this "inventive", "intellectual" drama "explores the tragedies of war and the meaning of memory" by intercutting an "interracial love story" with "documentary footage" of the ruins of Hiroshima; though too "enigmatic" and "arty" for some ("I really want to like it, but . . ."), others tout the "cinematic importance" of this French New Wave "masterpiece."

☒ His Girl Friday ◐

| 26 | 28 | 24 | 22 |

1940 | Directed by Howard Hawks | With Cary Grant, Rosalind Russell, Ralph Bellamy | 92 minutes | Not Rated

"Pay attention" now: the "superfast-moving plot" "comes at you at 100 mph" in this "biting" screwball comedy that's a "wonderful adaptation" of *The Front Page*; Grant and Russell "snap and crackle" as a "newspaper editor and star reporter chasing the story of a lifetime – and each other" – and if the "breakneck speed" of this zippy "rollercoaster ride" can be "exhausting", the payoff is "absolute hilarity."

History Boys, The

| 22 | 24 | 22 | 21 |

2006 | Directed by Nicholas Hytner | With Richard Griffiths, Dominic Cooper, Samuel Barnett | 109 minutes | Rated R

Proving why the "English rarely disappoint" is this "jolly good" stage-to-screen transfer about eight "erudite" Ox-bridge hopefuls and their "idiosyncratic" instructors, with "beautiful" performances from the "original theatrical cast" ("Griffiths especially"); expect some "profound" insights into "teaching and learning", though even admirers admit the "quirky" spin on "child molestation" borders on "disturbing."

History of the World: Part I

| 22 | 19 | 21 | 20 |

1981 | Directed by Mel Brooks | With Mel Brooks, Gregory Hines, Madeline Kahn, Dom DeLuise, Harvey Korman | 92 minutes | Rated R

Mel's "in fine form" in this "raunchy" "romp through history", comprised of a "salacious" string of "winking" comedy sketches including a "Moses spoof", "standup at Julius Caesar's Palace" and a "musical version of the Inquisition"; if it's "dated (no pun intended)" and "not quite" Brooks' best, given all the "scattershot brilliance" it's "too bad there's no Part II."

History of Violence, A

| 22 | 25 | 22 | 22 |

2005 | Directed by David Cronenberg | With Viggo Mortensen, Maria Bello, Ed Harris, William Hurt | 96 minutes | Rated R

Examining the "brutal violence underlying a serene landscape", this "taut", "pitch-perfect" thriller from David Cronenberg asks the question "do you really know anyone?" in its story of a "quiet family man" who may be a "cold-blooded killer"; Viggo's "awesome" as the "ambiguous average Joe", "Hurt's a hoot" in a minor, "scene-stealing" turn and that "blatant" "stairway sex scene" is just plain "hot."

Hitch

| 21 | 21 | 20 | 20 |

2005 | Directed by Andy Tennant | With Will Smith, Eva Mendes, Kevin James | 118 minutes | Rated PG-13

A "charismatic" "date doctor" tutoring a "down-on-his-luck guy" on the "NYC singles scene" loses his cool in the face of true love in this "light" romantic comedy; while a tad "trite and silly" for those who disparage the "no-brainer" "Hollywood heart-tugger" ending, it's "no disappointment" for chuckleheads thanks to that "unforgettable dance scene."

Hitchhiker's Guide to the Galaxy, The

| 17 | 17 | 19 | 20 |

2005 | Directed by Garth Jennings | With Martin Freeman, Mos Def, Zooey Deschanel, Sam Rockwell | 109 minutes | Rated PG

The "crazy universe of Douglas Adams' cult smash novel" gets the big-screen treatment in this "wacky" comedy about an "Everyman" interacting with "weird" intergalactic characters; but despite the picture's "boffo effects" and "zany wit", the "grafted-on love story" gets a thumbs-down from the book's "disappointed" devotees and the "silly" shenanigans leave others "lost" ("should have taken the bus").

Hoax, The

| 21 | 23 | 22 | 21 |

2007 | Directed by Lasse Hallström | With Richard Gere, Alfred Molina, Marcia Gay Harden, Hope Davis | 116 minutes | Rated R

From the "amazing-but-true" department comes this "breezy" look at writer Clifford Irving's infamous "hoax biography" of Howard Hughes, a "publishing fraud" so elaborate that the "bashful billionaire" actually "came out of seclusion to expose it"; a "spot-on" Gere delivers the requisite "chutzpah", matched by equally "nimble" work from Molina as a nervous researcher.

Hoffa

| 19 | 23 | 20 | 19 |

1992 | Directed by Danny DeVito | With Jack Nicholson, Danny DeVito, Armand Assante | 140 minutes | Rated R

DeVito's laborious, "uneven" drama delivers a "real dose of reality" as it traces the rise and demise of notorious union boss Jimmy Hoffa, who uses rough justice and mob connections to win the Teamsters their due; though it's "very well-acted and photographed", critics call it an overlong, "flawed" piece of work.

Holes

| 23 | 23 | 24 | 22 |

2003 | Directed by Andrew Davis | With Sigourney Weaver, Jon Voight, Tim Blake Nelson | 117 minutes | Rated PG

The "wonderful children's book" about a boy punished for a crime he didn't commit has been "faithfully adapted" into this "excellent movie for the whole family"; a "creative, interesting story", "outstanding" performances by "old pros" and "young actors" alike and an "awesome soundtrack" that will keep "the kids singing all week" add up to a "highly entertaining" two hours.

❼ Holiday ◐ | 27 | 27 | 25 | 23 |

1938 | Directed by George Cukor | With Katharine Hepburn, Cary Grant, Doris Nolan, Lew Ayres | 95 minutes | Not Rated

"Nonconformity" and "high society" collide in this "glorious" romantic comedy about a "charming" average Joe on the verge of marrying into a wealthy family; "crisp" dialogue, "wonderful character actors" and "radiant" stars make this somewhat "overlooked" Kate-and-Cary vehicle the perfect choice when you "can't watch *Bringing Up Baby* or *The Philadelphia Story* one more time"; P.S. "who knew Grant could do such a good backflip?"

Holiday, The | 19 | 20 | 19 | 21 |

2006 | Directed by Nancy Meyers | With Cameron Diaz, Kate Winslet, Jude Law, Jack Black | 138 minutes | Rated PG-13

"Chick flick" fanatics "identify with the women" and "melt over the men" in this "sweet" romantic comedy starring an "adorable" A-list foursome, including a "surprisingly charming" Black; true, its "warm and fuzzy" story of single gals swapping houses at Christmastime is "fairly unbelievable", but "scenic" LA/London locales bolster the "escapist" appeal.

Holiday Inn ◐ | 23 | 20 | 20 | 23 |

1942 | Directed by Mark Sandrich | With Bing Crosby, Fred Astaire, Marjorie Reynolds | 100 minutes | Not Rated

"Crooner Bing" and "hoofer Astaire" are "rivals" in this "lively" "musical romance" that's chock-full of "Irving Berlin favorites" but most remembered for introducing 'White Christmas'; sure, the plot's pretty "lightweight", but at least the songs of this "holiday bonbon" will "stick in your brain well into the new year."

Hollywood Ending | 15 | 18 | 16 | 17 |

2002 | Directed by Woody Allen | With Woody Allen, Téa Leoni, George Hamilton, Debra Messing | 112 minutes | Rated PG-13

Ok, it has "a few memorable bon mots", but otherwise this "Woody-Allen-on-cruise-control" comedy about a has-been director who goes "hysterically blind" is "pretty bland" stuff; most say his shtick is "wearing a bit thin" (casting himself opposite "women a third of his age" is "unfunny") and feel he's "not having fun" anymore: "what happened?"

Hollywoodland | 16 | 20 | 18 | 18 |

2006 | Directed by Allen Coulter | With Adrien Brody, Diane Lane, Ben Affleck, Bob Hoskins | 126 minutes | Rated R

A "true Hollywood unsolved mystery" – the supposed "suicide" of George Reeves, "TV's original Superman" – is given a "noir" spin in this "moody", "flashback"-heavy detective piece; the "slow" pace and "convoluted" plot are offset by a "superb" cast, led by the "surprisingly impressive" Affleck.

Home Alone | 19 | 17 | 20 | 19 |

1990 | Directed by Chris Columbus | With Macaulay Culkin, Joe Pesci, Daniel Stern | 103 minutes | Rated PG

"Every parent's nightmare" – and "every child's fantasy" – this "ultimate sleepover movie" made Culkin a star as a "self-sufficient kid who defends himself against robbers" after his vacation-bound family accidentally "leaves him at home"; though its "loony premise" is "full of sight gags", some warn it can be too "violent" for smaller fry: "this is Bugs Bunny vs. Yosemite Sam for real."

Home at the End of the World, A   18 | 22 | 19 | 18

2004 | Directed by Michael Mayer | With Colin Farrell, Robin Wright Penn, Dallas Roberts, Sissy Spacek | 97 minutes | Rated R

Three "offbeat" characters – a gay man and a straight couple – make up the nontraditional family at the heart of this "touching" drama that "got little attention" on its theatrical release; Farrell's "brave" performance as a "boy-man who just wants everyone to love him" garners kudos even if some find the end result too "sentimental" and "disingenuous" – Michael Cunningham's "book is better than the movie."

Honey, I Shrunk the Kids   16 | 14 | 18 | 19

1989 | Directed by Joe Johnston | With Rick Moranis, Matt Frewer, Marcia Strassman | 101 minutes | Rated PG

A "cute", "creative idea" that "grows on you", this "wacky family" comedy concerns a "friendly mad scientist" dad whose "experiments go awry" when his kids are zapped down to sub-pint size; with "inventive" special effects to "overcome lame acting", it's "always good for some laughs", though most shrink from the "next two installments."

Honeymoon in Vegas   18 | 17 | 17 | 18

1992 | Directed by Andrew Bergman | With James Caan, Nicolas Cage, Sarah Jessica Parker | 96 minutes | Rated PG-13

Think a comedic take on "*Indecent Proposal*" to get the gist of this "cute" date movie wherein Cage and Caan vie for Parker's affections against scenic Sin City and Hawaiian backdrops; best remembered for the "flying Elvises" and "more cameo appearances than a Democratic fund-raiser", it's "lighthearted" "froth" – even if cynics "root for the wrong man to get the girl."

Hoodwinked   18 | - | 19 | 20

2005 | Directed by Cory Edwards, Todd Edwards, Tony Leech | Animated | 80 minutes | Rated PG

A winking look at the "underside of the fairy-tale world", this "computer-animated" flick is a "clever, *Rashomon*-like retelling of *Little Red Riding Hood*", jazzed up with a "whodunit" spin and "witty pop-culture references" that "work for adults as well as kids"; still, hard as it "tries to be *Shrek*", this "less-than-stellar" production is "not quite Pixar."

Hook   17 | 18 | 17 | 21

1991 | Directed by Steven Spielberg | With Robin Williams, Dustin Hoffman, Julia Roberts | 144 minutes | Rated PG

Presenting "Peter Pan if he grew up", this "clever" '90s "twist" on the adventure finds Williams' cynical adult Peter activating his "inner child" for a rematch with Hoffman's "memorable" Hook; if often a "pleasure to watch", it's also panned as a "bloated", "PC version" of the fairy tale and "one of Spielberg's rare mistakes."

☒ Hoop Dreams   26 | - | 26 | 23

1994 | Directed by Steve James | Documentary | 170 minutes | Rated PG-13

"Two young athletes who dream of NBA fame" as a way "to escape the inner city" are the subjects of this "gritty" documentary, a "slam-dunk exposé" of "naive boys" that's "quite moving" if a "tad long"; "superb editing" makes it feel more like a "drama" than a real-life story, but don't look for a "Hollywood ending": this one's so "devastatingly real", it just might "break your heart."

	OVERALL	ACTING	STORY	PROD.

Hoosiers
23 | 22 | 24 | 19

1986 | Directed by David Anspaugh | With Gene Hackman, Barbara Hershey, Dennis Hopper | 114 minutes | Rated PG

A modern-day "David and Goliath on the basketball court", this "inspirational" "classic of the small-town-team-rises-up genre" is a "corporate team builder" kind of flick; as the "motivational" but "down-and-out coach trying to make a comeback in the boonies", Hackman captures the spirit of "rural" hoops culture and supplies some "real heart."

☒ Hope and Glory
26 | 26 | 26 | 25

1987 | Directed by John Boorman | With Sarah Miles, Ian Bannen, Sebastian Rice-Edwards, Sammi Davis | 113 minutes | Rated PG-13

It's "chins way up" in Boorman's "nostalgic" drama set in WWII England, a "touching" tale told "through a boy's eyes" about a family escaping the London blitz to decamp in "small-town" Britannia; with "endearing honesty" that balances humor with the "heavy subject" of war, this "priceless gem" also boasts a "stellar" cast "mostly made up of unknowns."

Horse Feathers ◑
24 | 22 | 20 | 18

1932 | Directed by Norman Z. McLeod | With the Marx Brothers, Thelma Todd | 68 minutes | Not Rated

"One of the Marxes' zaniest comedies" showcases the boys in "peak form" in a college setting, in which Groucho is the incoming university president; expect the usual "breezy lunacy" "based on years of vaudeville antics" – especially the "hilarious" "French-farcical wooing of Todd" – and ignore that "abrupt ending."

Horse Whisperer, The
17 | 19 | 18 | 20

1998 | Directed by Robert Redford | With Robert Redford, Kristin Scott Thomas, Sam Neill | 169 minutes | Rated PG-13

"Redford and horses" are "so right" together in this "tearjerker" romance, with Bob taking a "real star turn" as a Montana cowpoke whose way with the "healing process" sweeps a city gal right out of her saddle; it's "uplifting" and "lovingly" shot, and if some bridle at the "boring", "interminable" pace, stay awake and you'll "learn a lot about horses."

Horton Hears a Who!
23 | - | 23 | 24

2008 | Directed by Jimmy Hayward, Steve Martino | Animated | 88 minutes | Rated G

Dr. Seuss' "classic" tale of an elephant protecting a dust-speck-size community receives the deluxe treatment in this "sweet" animated adaptation, taking on "added storylines" that "stick to the spirit" of the book and recruiting a who's-who of celeb voices led by Jim Carrey and Steve Carell; additional draws for the "family-entertainment" crowd include some "wonderful" CGI work and a pro-"tolerance" message.

Hostage
18 | 19 | 19 | 19

2005 | Directed by Florent Emilio Siri | With Bruce Willis, Kevin Pollak, Ben Foster, Michelle Horn | 113 minutes | Rated R

The "old Bruce is back" in this "action-packed" thriller, where he summons up "fraught emotion" – or at least "actual facial expressions" –

playing an ex-LAPD negotiator pressed back into service after hoodlums hijack a household; though "Willis can still pull it off", those less captivated by the "predictable patchwork" of "implausible" plot twists think the "audience is the real hostage."

🇿 Hotel Rwanda
28 | 28 | 28 | 26

2004 | Directed by Terry George | With Don Cheadle, Sophie Okonedo, Joaquin Phoenix, Nick Nolte | 121 minutes | Rated PG-13

A "heartwrenching" reminder of the "horrors" committed during the 1994 Rwandan genocide ("a modern-day Holocaust"), this "true story" of a hotel manager who "helped save 1,200 lives" eschews "preachy" moralizing and overt carnage in order to emphasize the "redemptive" notion that "courage can turn the tide"; the "magnificent" Cheadle and "brilliant" supporting cast "do a great service" to this "important piece of history", inspiring "much hope" that such an "appalling" tragedy "doesn't happen again."

Hot Fuzz
24 | 23 | 23 | 23

2007 | Directed by Edgar Wright | With Simon Pegg, Nick Frost, Timothy Dalton | 121 minutes | Rated R

The "brill" blokes behind *Shaun of the Dead* are back with this "way cool" spoof of "American buddy-cop movies", mixing "witty dialogue", "absurd" plot twists and "sick humor" (including "one of the most gruesome deaths ever shown in movies"); a "John Woo-worthy" gunfight and walk-ons by "favorite Brits" like Bill Nighy and Jim Broadbent add to the "nonstop" laughter.

Hound of the Baskervilles, The ◑
22 | 22 | 25 | 20

1939 | Directed by Sidney Lanfield | With Basil Rathbone, Nigel Bruce, Richard Greene | 80 minutes | Not Rated

Critics call this the "most successful" take on Arthur Conan Doyle's "classic" thriller, featuring Rathbone as Sherlock Holmes sleuthing around an English castle; it's "must" viewing for detective devotees, complete with "campy" ambiance and "over-the-top" emoting.

Hours, The ✉
25 | 28 | 24 | 25

2002 | Directed by Stephen Daldry | With Nicole Kidman, Julianne Moore, Meryl Streep, Ed Harris | 114 minutes | Rated PG-13

There's "no action, only acting" in this "intelligent, challenging" adaptation of the "brilliant" book about three women of different generations whose "not perfect" lives are linked by a Virginia Woolf novel – and the "acting by all three leading ladies" "deserved an Oscar" (Kidman "won by a nose"); "don't watch it if you're in a good mood", however, because it's "hopelessly depressing" and "so slow moving it should have been called *The Days*."

House of Flying Daggers 🇫
24 | 22 | 21 | 27

2004 | Directed by Zhang Yimou | With Takeshi Kaneshiro, Zhang Ziyi, Andy Lau | 119 minutes | Rated PG-13

"Exhilarating fight sequences" and "feast-for-the-eyes" scenery team up with a "tearjerker" story of "star-crossed lovers" in this "outstanding" Chinese epic from "virtuoso" director Zhang that kicks the martial arts genre to "new heights"; still, visual beauty aside, not everyone's flying high over the kung-fusing plot (with "more twists and turns than the Yangtze River"), ditto the seemingly "interminable" ending.

	OVERALL	ACTING	STORY	PROD.

☑ House of Games · 24 | 23 | 27 | 21

1987 | Directed by David Mamet | With Lindsay Crouse, Joe Mantegna, Lilia Skala | 102 minutes | Rated R

"Cold characters and clipped conversations" make this "mind-bending thriller" pure Mamet "at his most manipulative"; its "twisty" con-game plot (something like "*The Sting,* all grown-up") "keeps you guessing", and though the dialogue reminds some critics of "cartoons talking", it's "chilling on many levels", with a "head-spinning" ending.

House of Sand and Fog · 23 | 27 | 22 | 23

2003 | Directed by Vadim Perelman | With Jennifer Connelly, Ben Kingsley, Shoreh Aghdashloo | 126 minutes | Rated R

A "brilliant rendering" of the "moral stand-off" between a "slacker who loses her home" and a "desperate" Iranian who purchases it for his exiled family, this "taut", "heart-wrenching" drama explores "everything that the American dream is – and isn't"; "balanced directing" and "amazingly nuanced performances" by Kingsley, Connelly and Aghdashloo turn this inherently "dour material" into a "gripping", "haunting" tragedy.

House of Wax · 21 | 18 | 21 | 20

1953 | Directed by Andre de Toth | With Vincent Price, Frank Lovejoy, Phyllis Kirk | 90 minutes | Rated PG

"Look out for the giant vat of wax!": this "entertaining" "horror melo-drama" was one of the first flicks made in 3-D, but modern-day fans say it's "still fun" "even without the glasses"; featuring a "priceless Price", a "chiller"-diller story and "atmospheric", "gaslight-era" set-tings, it's ever the "stuff of nightmares" and always "spooky."

Howards End ✉ · 22 | 26 | 21 | 25

1992 | Directed by James Ivory | With Anthony Hopkins, Emma Thompson, Helena Bonham Carter | 140 minutes | Rated PG

"Another Merchant-Ivory masterpiece", this "period piece" adapta-tion of the E.M. Forster novel concerns a "snobby upper-class" British family scheming to cut an interloper out of their mother's will; though Anglophiles laud the lovely cinematography and appearances by "some of the best actors of our time" (including a "superb" Hopkins and Oscar-winning Thompson), phobes fret it's "way too slow."

☑ How Green Was My Valley ✉◐ · 27 | 26 | 26 | 26

1941 | Directed by John Ford | With Walter Pidgeon, Maureen O'Hara, Anna Lee, Donald Crisp | 118 minutes | Not Rated

Director Ford's "gentler side" is showcased in this "sentimental", "soulful" story of a Welsh mining family over the course of 50 years; renowned as the movie that "beat out *Citizen Kane*" for the year's Best Picture Oscar, it may seem a tad "corny" to modernists, but traditional types laud its "compassion, humanity" and "old-fashioned values."

Howling, The · 19 | 15 | 18 | 20

1981 | Directed by Joe Dante | With Dee Wallace, Dennis Dugan, Christopher Stone, Kevin McCarthy | 91 minutes | Rated R

Fangs to its "solid storyline" and "cool transformation" FX, this "were-wolf yarn" about a traumatized TV newscaster admitted to a secluded sanitarium remains "one of the better" relics of '80s horror; moony ad-mirers say "besides being scary, it's peppered with enough subtle hu-mor" to make for some "campy fun" – just be very afraid of the sequels.

Howl's Moving Castle

25 | **-** | **24** | **27**

2005 | Directed by Hayao Miyazaki | Animated | 119 minutes | Rated PG

An "escapist's dream", this "breathtaking" Japanese anime uses "complex", "jaw-dropping" visuals "that aren't pure CGI" to relate the "lyrical" tale of a young woman transformed into an old crone as she enters an "unreal world" of wizards and witches; devotees dub director Miyazaki a "true original", but fret that the "mind-trip" windup ("what???") is "totally unclear."

How the Grinch Stole Christmas

17 | **18** | **19** | **23**

2000 | Directed by Ron Howard | With Jim Carrey, Jeffrey Tambor, Christine Baranski | 105 minutes | Rated PG

Dr. Seuss gets the "grand production" treatment in this mighty "enjoyable" comedy featuring "great visuals" and a very "scary" Carrey as a "perfect Grinch" who's plotting Yuletide vengeance on the "über-commercialized" "world of the Whos"; while it's hailed as a "holiday keeper" that stands "heart to heart" with the "classic cartoon", some viewers see a "heavy-handed" effort that's a few sizes too "overinflated."

How the West Was Won ✉

23 | **21** | **22** | **25**

1963 | Directed by John Ford, Henry Hathaway, George Marshall | With Gregory Peck, Henry Fonda, James Stewart, George Peppard, Carroll Baker, Eli Wallach | 162 minutes | Rated G

A "true epic" that feels like "five films in one", this "sprawling Western" boasts an "all-star cast" hitting the trail to follow "compelling storylines" ranging from the Civil War to a prairie-schooner drive, all in blazing "Cinerama"; the "long overview" of the "taming" of the territories makes for a grand, "sweeping tale" that's "plenty entertaining", but see it in "wide-screen" or else "don't bother."

How to Lose a Guy in 10 Days

19 | **20** | **19** | **19**

2003 | Directed by Donald Petrie | With Kate Hudson, Matthew McConaughey | 116 minutes | Rated PG-13

"Cute" Kate "carries on her mother's legacy" in this high-concept romantic comedy, a kind of *"Losing Mr. Goodbar"* story about a journalist trying to get dumped so she can write about it; maybe it's a "total chick flick" with a "typical Hollywood ending", but both leads are so "likable" and "easy on the eyes" that it also works as a "surprisingly good" date movie.

How to Marry a Millionaire

22 | **20** | **19** | **22**

1953 | Directed by Jean Negulesco | With Betty Grable, Marilyn Monroe, Lauren Bacall | 95 minutes | Not Rated

"Fabulous gowns and mink coats are the stars" of this "rather entertaining" romantic comedy, a "guilty pleasure" about three gold diggers on the loose in Manhattan; "Lauren and Marilyn are charming in their own ways", while its "fascinating look" at women's roles in "'50s society" makes many feminists sigh "thank goodness for progress."

☑ Hud ✉◑

26 | **28** | **24** | **24**

1963 | Directed by Martin Ritt | With Paul Newman, Melvyn Douglas, Patricia Neal, Brandon De Wilde | 112 minutes | Not Rated

"Stud muffin" Newman is at his "bad boy best" playing an "alienated", "black-hearted" cowboy in this "truly adult" "modern Western" about

OVERALL ACTING STORY PROD.

a "struggle between a father and son"; sure, "Neal got the Oscar" (as did "heartbreaker Douglas" and that "gorgeous black-and-white cinematography"), but in the end, Paul's "heartbreakingly cool" anti-hero gets the most reaction.

Hudsucker Proxy, The — 22 | 22 | 21 | 23

1994 | Directed by Joel Coen | With Tim Robbins, Jennifer Jason Leigh, Paul Newman | 111 minutes | Rated PG

"Big business" and the "bootstrappy American dream" are satirized in this "sly satire" via the Coen brothers about a "plucky mailroom clerk" who "invents the hula hoop" ("ya know, for kids") and becomes president of the company; despite a "refreshingly cynical" script peppered with "dialogue so crisp you can hear the gum smacking", a few find it a bit "odd", though it's certainly "never dull."

Hulk — 12 | 13 | 12 | 18

2003 | Directed by Ang Lee | With Eric Bana, Jennifer Connelly, Sam Elliott, Nick Nolte | 138 minutes | Rated PG-13

Ang Lee's "darker, more serious" take on the superhero genre brings some "grown-up psychodrama" to this story of a genetic scientist whose experiments turn him into an "emerald behemoth" (think "Shrek on steroids") who's fraught with lingering "emotional" baggage; despite "ambitious" touches like "split screens to resemble a comic book", the "glacial pace", "Freudian moping" and "only ok" CGI effects have many sulking it's a "big dud."

Human Stain, The — 18 | 21 | 19 | 18

2003 | Directed by Robert Benton | With Anthony Hopkins, Nicole Kidman, Ed Harris, Gary Sinise | 106 minutes | Rated R

Based on Philip Roth's novel, this "absorbing" if "gloomy" drama features a "passionate" Hopkins playing a "black man passing for white" who's dubbed a "bigot" after a "misinterpreted comment" and further tarnished by a liaison with a "slutty janitor" (the "great-looking" Kidman); most maintain it's "well-acted" but "totally miscast", and ultimately "not convincing."

⊠ Hunchback of Notre Dame, The ◑ — 26 | 26 | 26 | 24

1939 | Directed by William Dieterle | With Charles Laughton, Cedric Hardwicke, Maureen O'Hara | 116 minutes | Not Rated

One of the more "remarkable" adaptations of the much-filmed Victor Hugo novel of 15th-century Paris, this "timeless" picture about a hunchback's love for a gypsy girl garners praise for its "terrific story and wonderful production"; in the flashy title role, the "spectacular" Laughton gives Lon Chaney's 1923 silent performance a run for its money; best word: "sanctuary!"

Hunchback of Notre Dame, The — 19 | - | 19 | 21

1996 | Directed by Gary Trousdale, Kirk Wise | Animated | 91 minutes | Rated G

"Disney does Victor Hugo" in this "underrated" bell-ringer that's "edgier than most animated fluff" and thus "more rewarding" for adults, given its "opera"-esque feel and "dark subtleties"; but cynics nix it as a bit "too sinister for children" and fear that the "forgettable songs" and "stupid talking gargoyles" must have the author "turning in his grave."

	OVERALL	ACTING	STORY	PROD.

Hunger, The
20 | **21** | **20** | **20**

1983 | Directed by Tony Scott | With Catherine Deneuve, David Bowie, Susan Sarandon | 100 minutes | Rated R

Deliciously "scary and erotic", this "stylish" "modern-day vampire film" "gets the blood moving" with a "to-die-for cast", including a "surprisingly effective Bowie" opposite Deneuve and Sarandon as two very "hot" vamps ("Buffy wouldn't stand a chance against them"); a pop Goth score by Bauhaus helps the atmospherics, but ultimately this one's best remembered for that notorious "lesbian" interlude.

Hunt for Red October, The
24 | **24** | **25** | **24**

1990 | Directed by John McTiernan | With Sean Connery, Alec Baldwin, Scott Glenn | 134 minutes | Rated PG

The "first and best Jack Ryan thriller", this "entertaining" "Cold War guy flick" about a "renegade Russian submarine captain" combines "heart-pounding" suspense with "characters you can root for" (i.e. the "powerhouse" Connery and "holding-his-own" Baldwin); the "twisting plot" supplies enough "white-knuckle" moments to make it every bit "as good as the book."

Hurricane, The
21 | **26** | **21** | **21**

1999 | Directed by Norman Jewison | With Denzel Washington, Liev Schreiber | 145 minutes | Rated R

Denzel's "excellent", "Oscar-worthy" performance is the glue in this true story about a hardscrabble middleweight boxer wrongly convicted of a triple murder; alternately "exciting and poignant", the script "really emphasizes human emotion", but it's Washington's "tremendous" performance that makes this miscarriage-of-justice movie so moving.

Husbands and Wives
22 | **24** | **21** | **20**

1992 | Directed by Woody Allen | With Woody Allen, Mia Farrow, Judy Davis, Sydney Pollack, Juliette Lewis | 108 minutes | Rated R

A "complex exploration of relationships", this "biting" dramedy examines two married couples breaking up "in a way that only Woody Allen can pull off"; expect the usual "fantastic ensemble cast" (notably the "glorious" Davis) and the usual "May/December romance" subplot, along with a twist: "jittery", hand-held camerawork that "takes some getting used to."

Hush . . . Hush, Sweet Charlotte ◐
24 | **26** | **23** | **23**

1964 | Directed by Robert Aldrich | With Bette Davis, Olivia de Havilland, Joseph Cotten, Agnes Moorehead | 133 minutes | Not Rated

Playing a "faded Dixie belle" with a "Lizzie Borden" rep, Davis "demonstrates the fine art of overacting" in this "Gothic horror classic" made as a follow-up (but not a sequel) to *Whatever Happened to Baby Jane?*; it's a "campy, creepy" ride revolving around a long-ago murder and its consequences that "holds your attention throughout."

Hustle & Flow
23 | **26** | **21** | **21**

2005 | Directed by Craig Brewer | With Terrence Howard, Anthony Anderson, Taryn Manning, Ludacris | 116 minutes | Rated R

This "gritty", "gutter-to-glory" story of a Southern "street hustler" chasing "rap star" dreams has a simple message: "it's tough out there for a pimp"; "emerging star" Howard turns in a "hard-to-the-bone" performance that morphs an "unlovable" character into "someone you root for", while his chief co-star – that "catchy soundtrack" – will "stick in your head for days."

Hustler, The ◑   25 | 26 | 24 | 22
1961 | Directed by Robert Rossen | With Paul Newman, Jackie Gleason, Piper Laurie | 134 minutes | Not Rated
"Dark, tense and beautifully delivered", this "ultimate movie about winning" is also a "love poem to the game of pool", featuring "Newman on a roll" opposite Gleason in a rare dramatic turn that nearly "steals the picture"; it's "convincing", "gripping" stuff, and though Paul reprised the character of Eddie Felson in *The Color of Money*, connoisseurs claim this first take is so "much better."

I Am Legend   19 | 22 | 18 | 23
2007 | Directed by Francis Lawrence | With Will Smith, Alice Braga, Dash Mihok | 101 minutes | Rated PG-13
As the last man left alive in an "eerily realistic", "post-apocalyptic" Manhattan, Smith staves off "solitary-existence"-induced "madness" in this "dark" sci-fi thriller focusing on his "relentless quest" to cure a virus that's morphed humanity into killer "zombies"; despite Will's "solid" acting and "scary" CGI creatures, many are "disappointed" by the "less-than-satisfying" ending.

I Am Sam   21 | 25 | 21 | 21
2001 | Directed by Jessie Nelson | With Sean Penn, Michelle Pfeiffer, Dakota Fanning | 132 minutes | Rated PG-13
Nary an emotion's left untouched in this "enjoyable, if predictable tearjerker" about a "mentally handicapped man's struggle to raise his child"; while it does "make one ponder the rights of the retarded", it's basically "a Barney movie for grown-ups" abetted by an "amazing soundtrack of Beatles remakes"; what saves it are the "luminous performances" from a "poignant" Penn and Fanning as "his darling daughter" ("I want one like her").

Ice Age   23 | - | 21 | 25
2002 | Directed by Chris Wedge, Carlos Saldanha | Animated | 81 minutes | Rated G
The "oddest combination" of ice-age mammals sets out to save a little girl in this "cute", "cross-generational animated flick" featuring a "perfectly chosen" "all-star" vocal cast (e.g. Ray Romano as a "whiney" woolly mammoth); although it's "not up to the current high animated film standards", the "laugh-out-loud-funny" script and "well-done graphics" certainly "won't leave you cold."

Ice Age: The Meltdown   21 | - | 19 | 24
2006 | Directed by Carlos Saldanha | Animated | 91 minutes | Rated PG
With a "cute" nod to "Noah's Ark", this "enjoyable", "family"-friendly animated sequel dishes out "lots of laughs" ("even for adults") as it sends a "mishmash" of "prehistoric animals" fleeing from the watery "doom" wrought by a "melting glacier"; if a few cynics smell a "warmed-over rehash" of the original, at least the "impressive visuals" help the adventure "stay fresh."

	OVERALL	ACTING	STORY	PROD.

Ice Storm, The
22 | 25 | 20 | 21

1997 | Directed by Ang Lee | With Kevin Kline, Joan Allen, Sigourney Weaver | 112 minutes | Rated R

Defrosting the "suburban '70s" with "dead-on insight", this "affecting drama" (from Rick Moody's novel) finds a "top-notch cast" acting out a "painful account" of "dysfunctional families" and "sexual awakening" among white-bread "upper-middle class" types; though certainly "chilling" ("brrr-r-r-r"), it's hailed as a "small masterpiece" that's "worth watching" so long as you don't mind things "dark and depressing."

Identity
18 | 20 | 19 | 20

2003 | Directed by James Mangold | With John Cusack, Ray Liotta, Amanda Peet, John Hawkes | 90 minutes | Rated R

"Ten strangers are stuck in a rained-out motel" – and "one of them is a killer" – in this "tricky", "twisty" thriller that owes a lot to "Agatha Christie's *10 Little Indians*"; though there's plenty of "razzle-dazzle" and an "amazing ensemble cast", the "surprise ending" is debatable: either "well thought out" or a "disappointing" "audience-cheater" that's "too clever for its own good."

Igby Goes Down
20 | 23 | 19 | 19

2002 | Directed by Burr Steers | With Kieran Culkin, Claire Danes, Jeff Goldblum, Amanda Peet, Ryan Phillippe | 97 minutes | Rated R

"Hints of *Catcher in the Rye*" permeate this "quirky" coming-of-ager featuring the "terrific" Culkin ("Macaulay, eat your heart out") as a Caulfield-esque "dispossessed teen" coping with his "rich, dysfunctional family" and other "messed-up" metropolitans; its "touching moments" and "fabulously dark" flourishes unfold at a "slow" pace that "loses energy" at times, so stay alert to "pick up where it's going."

I ♥ Huckabees
14 | 18 | 14 | 15

2004 | Directed by David O. Russell | With Jason Schwartzman, Dustin Hoffman, Lily Tomlin, Jude Law, Mark Wahlberg | 106 minutes | Rated R

This "nutty" "thinker's comedy", mixing mirth with metaphysics and "consumerism", features Hoffman and Tomlin as "wacky" "existential detectives" who get on the "philosophical" cases of Schwartzman and company; some tout its "challenging" ideas and "antiestablishment innuendos", but heartless sorts report it's "too esoteric for its own good."

Illusionist, The
23 | 24 | 24 | 25

2006 | Directed by Neil Burger | With Edward Norton, Paul Giamatti, Jessica Biel | 110 minutes | Rated PG-13

A "lush production" lit up by "gorgeous" cinematography reproduces the "old-world charm" of "fin de siècle" Vienna in this "clever", "lyrical musing on love and magic" starring the "brilliant" Norton as a "sly" soothsayer smitten by a nobleman's dame; the "intricate" plot "pleases and teases", with some appropriately "enchanting" contributions by Giamatti and Biel.

Il Postino 🄵
24 | 25 | 24 | 24

1995 | Directed by Michael Radford | With Massimo Troisi, Philippe Noiret | 108 minutes | Rated PG

A "charming" mix of "poetry and postal services", this "small treasure" "could only have been made in Italy", given its "lyrical", "humble" airs; the "sweet tale" of a "simple" postman "with the heart of a poet", it manages to be both a "great love story" and a "haunting" tale of "inspiration", with "bravura" acting and "beautiful scenery" that come together for "winning" moviemaking.

Imitation of Life

21 | 22 | 23 | 22

1959 | Directed by Douglas Sirk | With Lana Turner, John Gavin, Sandra Dee | 125 minutes | Not Rated

Bring "two boxes of Kleenex" before viewing this melodramatic Turner vehicle, a "classy" if "campy" "B movie" about a black woman who passes for white; a remake of the 1934 Claudette Colbert "tear-jerker", this time around it's "all gussied up in pretty color" with the "racial theme toned down", leading realists to rate it a "ridiculous", "sudsy" soap opera.

I'm No Angel ◑

23 | 22 | 21 | 21

1933 | Directed by Wesley Ruggles | With Mae West, Cary Grant | 87 minutes | Not Rated

Mae's a "hoot" in this "made-to-order vehicle" about a "brazen" sideshow performer and the many men in her life, including a hot millionaire whom she sues for breach of promise; the "risqué dialogue" showcases her sexy, "sassy sense of humor", though the picture's most famous line – "Beulah, peel me a grape" – isn't racy, just plain "hilarious."

I'm Not There

17 | 22 | 15 | 18

2007 | Directed by Todd Haynes | With Cate Blanchett, Richard Gere, Christian Bale, Heath Ledger, Ben Whishaw, Marcus Carl Franklin | 135 minutes | Rated R

Far from a straightforward biopic, this "esoteric" study of Bob Dylan's "many personas" is portrayed by six very different actors and filmed in "stream-of-conscious" style; despite some "wonderful" performances ("Blanchett does Dylan better than *he* does"), mixed response to the "abstract", "nonlinear" script echos the split reaction when the singer infamously went electric: "brilliant" vs. "mess."

Importance of Being Earnest

21 | 23 | 23 | 22

2002 | Directed by Oliver Parker | With Rupert Everett, Colin Firth, Frances O'Connor, Reese Witherspoon | 97 minutes | Rated PG

This "undemanding" production of Oscar Wilde's "comedy of mistaken identities, romance and your typical weekend at an English manor" scores with "gorgeous sets" and "wonderful" acting from a "cast that looks like they're enjoying themselves"; but purists who prefer the "perfect 1952 version" insist the "magically funny play didn't need 'opening up'" by the screenwriter.

☑ In America

26 | 27 | 25 | 24

2003 | Directed by Jim Sheridan | With Paddy Considine, Samantha Morton, Djimon Hounsou | 107 minutes | Rated PG-13

Sheridan's "beautiful" retelling of the "immigrants-come-to-NY" story is brought to life by an "exceptional ensemble" cast in this "small movie with a big heart"; while its "bittersweet" scenario of a poor Irish family trying to "rebuild after the tragic loss" of a child has many "crying like babies", it's executed so "brilliantly" that even the dry-eyed concur it's "without a single false moment."

In & Out

17 | 19 | 17 | 17

1997 | Directed by Frank Oz | With Kevin Kline, Joan Cusack, Matt Dillon, Tom Selleck | 90 minutes | Rated PG-13

"Is he gay or not?", that is the question: a Midwestern drama teacher protests too much after being outed at the Oscars in this "lighthearted" comedy that's like an extended *Saturday Night Live* skit"; though "well-acted" by an ace "ensemble cast", it's Kline's "inspired" lead – capped by a "scene-stealing boogie session" – that's the "very funny" payoff.

In Bruges

23 | 25 | 23 | 23

2008 | Directed by Martin McDonagh | With Colin Farrell, Brendan Gleeson, Ralph Fiennes | 107 minutes | Rated R

After a "bungled job", a pair of hit men "cool their heels" in the Belgian city of Bruges only to see their "moral quandary" deepen in ways both "tragic" and "hysterical" in this "well done" slice of "comic noir"; though the violence can be pretty "gruesome", it's tempered by "witty dialogue", "travelogue" photography and "top-notch" performances from an "especially fantastic" Farrell alongside fellow "pros" Gleeson and Fiennes.

☑ In Cold Blood ◑

25 | 26 | 26 | 22

1967 | Directed by Richard Brooks | With Robert Blake, Scott Wilson, John Forsythe | 134 minutes | Rated R

Brooks' "brilliant" adaptation of Truman Capote's "true-crime" "spellbinder" is "one of the most chilling films" about random murders ever made ("remember when not showing blood was more scary than showing it?"); shot "in almost documentary style" and all the more frightening thanks to Quincy Jones' evocative score, it "still works today" as "powerful" albeit "disturbing" moviemaking.

Inconvenient Truth, An

24 | - | 24 | 22

2006 | Directed by Davis Guggenheim | Documentary | 100 minutes | Rated PG

Self-described "Once Future President of the U.S." Al Gore sounds the alarm on the "global warming crisis" in this "informative" documentary that's "surprisingly entertaining" given that it's essentially a "glorified PowerPoint presentation" with a few "feel-good interludes" about the climate crusader's "life and career"; as polarizing as they get, it's either a "wake-up call" or a "real snooze", so if you "don't like the message or the messenger", "save your money" for something else.

☑ Incredibles, The

26 | - | 25 | 28

2004 | Directed by Brad Bird | Animated | 115 minutes | Rated PG

"Not everyone can be Batman", and this animated satire "with brains" depicts the everyday "humdrum" lives of "has-been superheroes" suddenly drawn into an "edge-of-your-seat" rescue; it's "not just for kids" what with its "existential take on superherodom", though its "stunning animation" and "witty" set pieces (the "Jack Jack attack", that "show-stealing costumer") appeal to "all ages"; in fact, its "old-fashioned" message – the "family comes first" – makes many "love cartoons again."

Indecent Proposal

15 | 16 | 17 | 17

1993 | Directed by Adrian Lyne | With Robert Redford, Demi Moore, Woody Harrelson | 117 minutes | Rated R

With a "provocative premise" that "spawned countless water-cooler debates", this drama features a "still-hot" Redford offering "down-on-

"their-luck" marrieds Harrelson and Moore an "improbable proposal": a "cool million" for a one-night dalliance with Demi; consensus calls it "much ado about not much" since many a missus "wouldn't even need the million" – or "two hours to think about it."

Independence Day

19 | 16 | 18 | 24

1996 | Directed by Roland Emmerich | With Will Smith, Bill Pullman, Jeff Goldblum | 145 minutes | Rated PG-13

"*E.T.* with an attitude", this "ultimate flying-saucer movie" might be a "remake of *War of the Worlds*" and "splashy trash" with a "plot as thin as a dime" that's "all noise and no substance", but at least it "doesn't take itself too seriously"; so grab some "popcorn" and hold on for a "helluva lot of fun."

Indiana Jones and the Kingdom of the Crystal Skull

20 | 20 | 16 | 25

2008 | Directed by Steven Spielberg | With Harrison Ford, Shia LaBeouf, Cate Blanchett, Karen Allen | 122 minutes | Rated PG-13

Though he's "grayer and wrinklier" since he last donned the fedora, Ford proves he can still "save the day" in this "rock 'em, sock 'em" adventure marking the Kingdom of Spielberg's fourth foray into Indy cinema; ok, the "sci-fi"-inflected premise verges on "ridiculous" ("*E.T.* in the Amazon?"), so just "accept it for what it is" and savor the "whip-smacking" action, Blanchett's "icy" villainess and the "nostalgia"-inducing return of *Raiders* romantic interest Karen Allen.

Indiana Jones and the Last Crusade

24 | 23 | 23 | 26

1989 | Directed by Steven Spielberg | With Harrison Ford, Sean Connery, Denholm Elliott | 127 minutes | Rated PG-13

"Almost as good as the first" installment, this third foray in the "Indy adventure" series is a "search-for-the-Holy-Grail" tale that alternates "lighthearted humor" with plenty of "gee-whiz", "close-call action sequences"; Ford is the "perfect hero", but Connery (as his dad) "takes the cake" in this fond salute to "old-fashioned Saturday afternoon movie serials" "brought up to date."

⊠ Indiana Jones and the Temple of Doom

22 | 21 | 21 | 25

1984 | Directed by Steven Spielberg | With Harrison Ford, Kate Capshaw, Quan Ke Huy | 118 minutes | Rated PG

"Ford rules the day and saves the world" – again – in this "take-me-away" action/adventure story, the "follow-up to *Raiders*" that "goes more for shock value than the original" (though as exhilaratingly "over the top" as ever); still, doomsayers say its "hooey"-heavy plot and "dark feel" can be "far too grisly for younger viewers", dismissing it as a "blip in the trilogy"; most indelible image: those "chilled monkey brains."

Indochine

23 | 25 | 23 | 25

1992 | Directed by Régis Wargnier | With Catherine Deneuve, Vincent Perez | 152 minutes | Rated PG-13

A "haunting", "epic" tale of French Indochina, this Foreign Language Oscar winner details an "enthralling romance" played out against the background of a country in turmoil; as a "beautiful" plantation owner, Deneuve "looks smashing in great clothes", though some say the end result is a "little too picture perfect."

	OVERALL	ACTING	STORY	PROD.

☑ I Never Sang for My Father ∅ `27 | 27 | 27 | 23`

1970 | Directed by Gilbert Cates | With Melvyn Douglas, Gene Hackman, Estelle Parsons | 92 minutes | Rated PG

Guys get their own "tearjerker" thanks to this stage drama adaptation that "hits home" with its "knowing depiction" of a "tortured son" forced to care for his widower father; the "excellent" Hackman's "controlled exasperation" in dealing with Douglas' "family patriarch" makes for a refrain that's manfully "maudlin" but rings "so true."

Infamous `21 | 24 | 21 | 21`

2006 | Directed by Douglas McGrath | With Toby Jones, Sandra Bullock, Daniel Craig, Sigourney Weaver | 110 minutes | Rated R

"Overshadowed by *Capote*" – which preceded it by a year – this "unfairly overlooked" biopic "covers the exact same period" when the writer was researching *In Cold Blood*; "more flamboyant, less dark" and "faster-paced" than its predecessor, this "second take" boasts star turns by the "surprising" Bullock, "excellent" Craig and "dead-on" Jones, who many report does "as good a job as Phillip Seymour Hoffman."

In Good Company `19 | 22 | 19 | 19`

2004 | Directed by Paul Weitz | With Dennis Quaid, Topher Grace, Scarlett Johansson | 109 minutes | Rated PG-13

Both a "comedy of manners" and a "timely" take on "corporate culture", this "warm" flick gives Grace his "breakout" role as a "young upstart" who becomes the boss of an "aging employee" – then further complicates matters by dating his underling's daughter; most relate to the "likable characters", though cynics nix the "disappointing" dénouement.

☑ Inherit the Wind ◑ `26 | 28 | 27 | 22`

1960 | Directed by Stanley Kramer | With Spencer Tracy, Fredric March, Gene Kelly | 128 minutes | Rated PG

"You'll go ape" for this "superb" "fictionalized account of the Scopes monkey trial", based on the true story of a teacher trying to bring Darwin into his Tennessee classroom; a "magnificent Tracy and March" are "at the top of their game" trying to "reconcile creationism with evolution" in this "relevant thought-provoker" that many call the "ultimate in intelligent courtroom drama."

In Her Shoes `18 | 20 | 19 | 18`

2005 | Directed by Curtis Hanson | With Cameron Diaz, Toni Collette, Shirley MacLaine | 130 minutes | Rated PG-13

Sibling "bonding" is the theme of this "sweet" dramedy built on the comic "chemistry" between careerist Collette and "ditzy" sis Diaz, who get "second chances" when their long-lost granny turns up; most stand by it as "lightweight" but "enjoyable" "rainy-day fare", but those who fall "out of step" cite a "sappy" scenario with "not enough sole."

In-Laws, The `24 | 24 | 24 | 20`

1979 | Directed by Arthur Hiller | With Peter Falk, Alan Arkin, Richard Libertini | 103 minutes | Rated PG-13

If you have any "weird" relatives-by-marriage, you'll "laugh out loud" at this "sidesplitting" comedy pitting a "chameleonic Falk" against a "befuddled Arkin" ("one of the great pairings of the cinema") as about-to-be in-laws; "totally unpredictable", it's "worth watching" if only to "find out where *Meet the Parents* came from."

In-Laws, The

2003 | Directed by Andrew Fleming | With Michael Douglas, Albert Brooks, Ryan Reynolds, Lindsay Sloane | 98 minutes | Rated PG-13

This "overall decent" redo of the '70s "classic comedy" delivers some "amusing twists" as Brooks' mild-mannered podiatrist becomes embroiled in "over-the-top" shenanigans with his future in-law, oddball CIA spook Douglas; the stars' "chemistry" can be "a hoot", but insiders seeking "real laughs" stick with the "far superior original."

Innerspace

15 | 15 | 18 | 17

1987 | Directed by Joe Dante | With Dennis Quaid, Martin Short, Meg Ryan, Kevin McCarthy | 120 minutes | Rated PG

Far-out FX and "likable" characters keep this "charming" entry in the "comedy sci-fi category" inneresting as Quaid's top-gun pilot is shrunken and inadvertently sent into the bloodstream of nerdy clerk Short, who's "never been better"; the "cute-as-always" Ryan rounds out the cast for an excursion that's lightweight but "quite funny" as crackpot "fantasy" goes.

Inside Man

23 | 25 | 23 | 23

2006 | Directed by Spike Lee | With Denzel Washington, Clive Owen, Jodie Foster | 129 minutes | Rated R

A "clever bank robber" undertakes an "elaborate" heist and tries to elude the "embattled cop" sent after him in this "intense" thriller driven by a "tight", "fast-paced" script that "keeps you guessing until the end"; featuring a "top-flight" cast led by the "sensational" duo of Denzel and Clive, it marks a "graceful" foray into "mainstream commercial" fare for Spike Lee.

Insider, The

25 | 28 | 25 | 23

1999 | Directed by Michael Mann | With Al Pacino, Russell Crowe, Christopher Plummer | 157 minutes | Rated R

Crowe turns in a "quietly intense" performance (while Pacino is intense but definitely not quiet), in this dramatic thriller about a tobacco company "whistle-blower" trying to "do the right thing no matter what the consequences"; although a "disillusioning behind-the-scenes look" at "big business, the media and public opinion", it's "absolutely riveting" and an "inspirational" profile in "courage."

Insomnia

18 | 22 | 18 | 19

2002 | Directed by Christopher Nolan | With Al Pacino, Robin Williams, Hilary Swank, Martin Donovan | 118 minutes | Rated R

There's "a lot of high-powered talent" on board this "above-average" "mainstream thriller" about a "wayward cop investigating a murder in Alaska", where the "round-the-clock sunshine" and "tense" goings-on keep him wide awake; as the "droopy-eyed" protagonist, Pacino sure looks "tired" and Williams is a "surprisingly good bad guy", yet those who "expected more" yawn it's so "forgettable" that they "had no trouble sleeping right through it."

Interiors

23 | 25 | 22 | 23

1978 | Directed by Woody Allen | With Geraldine Page, Diane Keaton, Mary Beth Hurt, Maureen Stapleton | 93 minutes | Rated PG

"Nuanced performances" and "brilliant cinematography" are the highlights of this Woody Allen "homage to Ingmar Bergman", a "thought ful" drama that examines "family dynamics" and "sibling rivalry" in the wake of a divorce; though some say the director should "stick to comedy", others counter this "wonderfully depressing" flick "didn't get its due when first released."

Internal Affairs
19 | 20 | 19 | 18
1990 | Directed by Mike Figgis | With Richard Gere, Andy Garcia, Laurie Metcalf, Nancy Travis | 115 minutes | Rated R

Gere "shows a different side" as a "natural sleazeball" in this "dark", "convoluted" police drama about a "dirty cop" under investigation by Internal Affairs detectives; advocates aver this "gripping" flick is "totally underrated", though others see a "standard-issue" thriller that's "entertaining but forgettable."

Interpreter, The
20 | 23 | 20 | 22
2005 | Directed by Sydney Pollack | With Nicole Kidman, Sean Penn | 128 minutes | Rated PG-13

A "United Nations interpreter overhears something she shouldn't and ends up under Secret Service protection" in this "promising" if "predictable" political thriller; while Kidman does the "classic movie heroine" thing well and Penn "gets better with age", the real star might be the "awe-inspiring" U.N. - this is the "first film shot inside the building."

Interview with the Vampire
19 | 19 | 20 | 22
1994 | Directed by Neil Jordan | With Tom Cruise, Brad Pitt, Antonio Banderas, Christian Slater | 123 minutes | Rated R

"Cover up your neck"; this "entertaining Gothic horror flick about a maladjusted trio of immortal vampires" is "almost as good" as Anne Rice's "overwrought" best-selling book; sure, it might be "too beautiful" for words and they "could have cut out some of the gore", but with "pretty boys" Brad, Tom and Antonio playing "yummy bloodsuckers", "what's not to like?"

In the Bedroom
22 | 26 | 20 | 21
2001 | Directed by Todd Field | With Sissy Spacek, Tom Wilkinson, Marisa Tomei | 130 minutes | Rated R

"Less is more" in this "intense" drama about murder, revenge and family "dysfunction" that's the kind of picture in which the "silences say more than any of the dialogue"; though "Spacek and Wilkinson are superb" and director Field "does an amazing job", critics sigh it's a "made-for-Lifetime movie" that's "dark, depressing and 20 minutes too long."

In the Company of Men
20 | 23 | 21 | 17
1997 | Directed by Neil LaBute | With Aaron Eckhart, Stacy Edwards, Matt Malloy | 95 minutes | Rated R

A "manipulative", "seriously despicable" loser abuses his "power over men and women alike" and "plays them for fools" in this "nasty little" drama that unflinchingly depicts the "evil that lurks in the hearts of men"; even those who "felt like they needed a shower" afterward admit being "strangely affected" by this "underwatched work."

In the Heat of the Night ✉
24 | 27 | 24 | 22
1967 | Directed by Norman Jewison | With Sidney Poitier, Rod Steiger, Warren Oates | 109 minutes | Rated PG

The "faint smell of honeysuckle hangs over" this "excellent" crime drama, a "brave statement on race relations" about a "black Yankee cop" suspected of murder in a small Southern town; it "generated a fair amount of controversy in its day" and was quite the Oscar magnet, taking home five statuettes including Best Picture and Best Actor for the "perfect Steiger."

In the Line of Fire

20 | 20 | 21 | 19

1993 | Directed by Wolfgang Petersen | With Clint Eastwood, John Malkovich, Rene Russo | 128 minutes | Rated R

"Eastwood is perfect" as an "aging but resourceful" Secret Service agent – "vulnerable, tough and world-weary" – battling a "would-be Presidential assassin" in this "solid action" thriller; throw in a "truly creepy" Malkovich as the "coldly reptilian" villain and you have a "completely engrossing" flick that's more than "effective", right up to the "suspenseful climax."

In the Name of the Father

23 | 25 | 24 | 21

1993 | Directed by Jim Sheridan | With Daniel Day-Lewis, Emma Thompson, Pete Postlethwaite | 133 minutes | Rated R

This "shattering" look at "desperate times" in Northern Ireland is a "riveting" true story about a "father and son jailed for a crime they did not commit"; "Day-Lewis is mesmerizing" and "totally believable" in this "troubling" account of "love and respect" amid a "terrible civil war."

In the Valley of Elah

22 | 27 | 23 | 21

2007 | Directed by Paul Haggis | With Tommy Lee Jones, Charlize Theron, Jason Patric | 121 minutes | Rated R

"Capturing the desperation of a parent" seeking answers about his son's disappearance after returning from overseas duty in Iraq, Jones "breaks your heart" with an "understated", "dead-on" performance in this "gripping, introspective" mystery; delineating the "emotional scars" incurred by modern soldiering, the film conveys a "powerful", "anti-any-war" message that's "thought-provoking" to some, "preachy" to others.

Intolerable Cruelty

15 | 18 | 15 | 17

2004 | Directed by Joel Coen | With George Clooney, Catherine Zeta-Jones, Geoffrey Rush, Billy Bob Thornton | 100 minutes | Rated PG-13

The Coen brothers go "mainstream" in this reworking of the "old war-between-the-sexes theme", a sporadically "snappy" screwball comedy involving a gold digger and a divorce attorney; critics complain "it's not Coen enough", citing a "rambling" story that "drags in parts", and even "gorgeous" George and "luscious" Catherine can't elevate its overall "tolerable" ratings.

Intolerance ◑

∇ 27 | 23 | 24 | 28

1918 | Directed by D.W. Griffith | With Lillian Gish, Mae Marsh, Constance Talmadge | 178 minutes | Not Rated

"D.W. Griffith's apology" for the racist subtext in his earlier film, *Birth of a Nation,* is this "monumental" silent "landmark", which intercuts four tales of intolerance set respectively in Babylon, Calvary, 15th-century France and contemporary California; the result is "grandiosity glorified" on a scale of "sheer staggering size" never seen before, and arguably the birth of "epic" filmmaking.

Into the Wild   23 | 25 | 24 | 24

2007 | Directed by Sean Penn | With Emile Hirsch, Marcia Gay Harden, Hal Holbrook, William Hurt | 148 minutes | Rated R

Penn's "fine" direction and Hirsch's "excellent" performance drive this "haunting", fact-based account of an idealistic youth whose quest to achieve "harmony with nature" led him to the "isolated wilds of Alaska" and an "inevitably sad" end; "breathtaking" shots of "wonderful scenery" make it "memorable", though cynics say it "romanticizes" the meanderings of a "spoiled kid."

Invasion of the Body Snatchers ◖   24 | 19 | 25 | 19

1956 | Directed by Don Siegel | With Kevin McCarthy, Dana Wynter, Larry Gates | 80 minutes | Not Rated

"Don't fall asleep!"; this '50s slice of "paranoid science fiction" posits that there are "alien pod people among us" "plotting to take over our hearts and minds"; alright, it's a "classic Red Scare parable", but "still perfectly effective today" despite "wooden acting" and that studio-enforced optimistic ending.

Invasion of the Body Snatchers   19 | 18 | 21 | 18

1978 | Directed by Philip Kaufman | With Donald Sutherland, Brooke Adams, Jeff Goldblum | 115 minutes | Rated PG

You'll be "looking for pods in the basement" after seeing this "thought-provoking", "very different" remake of the "classic" sci-fi thriller about an insidious alien invasion; this time around, the McCarthyist subtext has been replaced by 'Me Decade' pop psychobabble, and even if "less fun" than the original, it's still pretty darn "scary."

Invincible   21 | 21 | 23 | 20

2006 | Directed by Ericson Core | With Mark Wahlberg, Greg Kinnear, Elizabeth Banks, Kevin Conway | 105 minutes | Rated PG

Basically *Rocky* transposed to the gridiron, this "feel-good" football flick based on the "true story" of Vince Papale (a South Philly bartender who earned a spot with the Eagles in the '70s) "follows all the formulas" until you're "cheering for the underdog" on cue; "strong" performances by Kinnear and a "bicep"-baring Wahlberg score extra points.

Invisible Man, The ◖   22 | 20 | 21 | 20

1933 | Directed by James Whale | With Claude Rains, Gloria Stuart, William Harrigan | 71 minutes | Not Rated

"Fabulous effects" ("especially for its time") and some slyly "campy" moments make this "classic" creature feature worthy of "every movie lover's repertoire"; the tale of an inventor whose invisibility serum transforms him into a crazed killer, it stars an engrossing Rains in the "scary" title role, whose amazing acting has more to do with vocalizing than visibility.

Ipcress File, The   24 | 24 | 26 | 23

1965 | Directed by Sidney J. Furie | With Michael Caine, Nigel Green, Guy Doleman, Sue Lloyd | 109 minutes | Not Rated

"Caine rocks" in an "early" role as a distinctly non-Bond British agent in this "totally engaging" Cold War spy thriller, centering on a "heart-pounding" hunt for a top-secret file through a "bleak" underworld of brainwashing and betrayal; based on the Len Deighton novel, its "exciting" intelligence proves that "classic espionage never gets old."

Iris
24 | 28 | 22 | 22

2001 | Directed by Richard Eyre | With Judi Dench, Kate Winslet, Jim Broadbent | 90 minutes | Rated R

This "beautifully done" bio of English writer Iris Murdoch and her "spiral" into "frightening illness" shines with "amazing acting" and bookish wit; "flashbacks" follow her from a "sweet" Oxford courtship to later years when the "superb" Dench "realistically portrays" the onset of Alzheimer's in a "sad but finally uplifting" tribute to "true" fidelity.

Irma La Douce
21 | 23 | 20 | 21

1963 | Directed by Billy Wilder | With Shirley MacLaine, Jack Lemmon, Lou Jacobi | 147 minutes | Not Rated

A surprisingly "sweet" comedy from the acerbic Billy Wilder, this story of an honest Parisian cop who falls for a prostitute, becomes her unwilling pimp, then schemes to keep her off the streets is "funny and well done"; MacLaine plays the "hooker with a heart of gold" perfectly, while Lemmon mugs winningly in a dual role.

I, Robot
18 | 17 | 19 | 23

2004 | Directed by Alex Proyas | With Will Smith, Bridget Moynahan | 115 minutes | Rated PG-13

Sci-fi author Isaac Asimov's futuristic "classic" of "robots turning against man" gets a "blockbuster" buff-up in this "fast, fun" action flick full of "dazzling effects", "over-the-top" stunts and "cool set design"; Smith does his "typical" routine as a "wise-cracking" cop, though that glimpse of his "bare" ro-butt in the shower is definitely "worth the money."

Iron Giant, The
24 | - | 25 | 25

1999 | Directed by Brad Bird | Animated | 86 minutes | Rated PG

"Markedly different from other animated films", this story of a "quirky boy and an enormous robot from outer space" is both a "sly satire of the '50s" and a "message" flick about "tolerance and non-violence"; "criminally underrated" (it "slipped through the cracks due to poor marketing"), it's "entertaining and deserves to be seen."

☑ Iron Man
26 | 26 | 24 | 28

2008 | Directed by Jon Favreau | With Robert Downey Jr., Terrence Howard, Jeff Bridges, Gwyneth Paltrow | 126 minutes | Rated PG-13

Lending his signature "edge" to the role of "playboy arms dealer" turned metal-suited "crusader", the "gifted" Downey "excels" in this "top-notch" "thinking person's comic book movie", a "turbo charged" FX extravaganza that "sparkles" with "intelligence, humor" and "explosions galore"; enthusiasts are already "eagerly awaiting the sequel", flickers of which are screened in the "footage following the credits."

Island, The
16 | 16 | 17 | 20

2005 | Directed by Michael Bay | With Ewan McGregor, Scarlett Johansson, Djimon Hounsou | 136 minutes | Rated PG-13

Splicing director Bay's "trademark outlandish action" scenes into an "Orwellian future", this "slick" sci-fi flick stars McGregor and Johansson as "cool" clones on the lam from "Big Brother"-ish bad guys; no kidding, the actors are sure "nice to look at", but the "intriguing" premise soon spirals into "generic running and shooting" scenes that seem "cobbled together from the DNA of better movies."

	OVERALL	ACTING	STORY	PROD.

Italian Job, The — 22 19 21 24

2003 | Directed by F. Gary Gray | With Mark Wahlberg, Edward Norton, Charlize Theron | 111 minutes | Rated PG-13

The "Mini Cooper is the real star" of this "edge-of-your-seat" remake that "fires on most, if not all, cylinders", as a "fast-moving", "action-packed" "heist film" "filled with plot twists, maniacal car chases", "high-tech gadgets" and "timely pop-culture references"; while "not at all thought-provoking", it's "everything a summer movie should be."

◪ It Happened One Night ✉◑ — 28 28 26 25

1934 | Directed by Frank Capra | With Clark Gable, Claudette Colbert | 105 minutes | Not Rated

"Gable and Colbert are swell together" in this "great Depression spirit-lifter", the "mother of all screwball comedies" about a "wisecracking tabloid reporter" and a "snooty heiress" "on the run"; the first picture to "sweep all the major Oscars", it was also considered rather "racy for its time": indeed, Gable's baring of his chest in the "walls of Jericho" sequence sent the "undershirt industry" into a tizzy.

It's a Mad Mad Mad Mad World — 24 21 22 23

1963 | Directed by Stanley Kramer | With Spencer Tracy, Milton Berle, Sid Caesar, Buddy Hackett, Mickey Rooney, Ethel Merman, Edie Adams, Jonathan Winters | 192 minutes | Rated G

The ultimate "car comedy", this "sprawling gut-buster" features a "huge cast" of "crème de la crème" comedians in an "every-man-for-himself" "race to find a hidden fortune"; sure, it's a "long long long long movie", but it's "still terrifically entertaining" with plenty of "silly slapstick" and "great cameos" to keep things lively; best moment: "Jonathan Winters tearing up the gas station."

◪ It's a Wonderful Life ◑ — 27 27 27 25

1946 | Directed by Frank Capra | With James Stewart, Donna Reed, Henry Travers | 130 minutes | Not Rated

"Nobody tells a story like Capra", and this "inspirational" film "strikes a fundamental chord with lots of people" via its "small-town" tale about a "good guy" coping with "hard times" and proving "how one life can make a difference"; sure, it's a "little schmaltzy" and "surprisingly dark", but most say "it's a wonderful picture" and "Christmas wouldn't be Christmas without it" – even if you've seen it a "million times" on TV.

◪ I Want to Live! ✉◑ — 24 27 25 23

1958 | Directed by Robert Wise | With Susan Hayward, Simon Oakland, Theodore Bikel | 120 minutes | Not Rated

"Susan Hayward at her most Susan Hayward" gives a "scenery-chewing", Oscar-grabbing performance in this "gut-wrenching" true story about a "tough cookie" "party girl" headed for the gas chamber; though cynics hiss it's "extremely dated", more feel it's "not easily forgotten", particularly its still "effective" "anti–death penalty" theme.

I Was a Male War Bride ◑ — 21 24 20 20

1949 | Directed by Howard Hawks | With Cary Grant, Ann Sheridan | 103 minutes | Not Rated

Maybe it's "not in the pantheon of romantic comedies", but this "amusing little movie" is still "thoroughly watchable" thanks to the "debonair" Grant as a WWII French army captain who falls for an American lieutenant (the very "nice" Sheridan); it's best remembered for its sequences of "Cary in drag" – even in a skirt, he's as "irresistible" as ever.

	OVERALL	ACTING	STORY	PROD.

Jackass: The Movie

| 13 | 9 | 7 | 11 |

2002 | Directed by Jeff Tremaine | With Johnny Knoxville, Bam Margera, Steve-O, Chris Pontius | 87 minutes | Rated R

Fans of "sheer stupidity" fall for this "dumb", "title-says-it-all" flick based on the MTV series, in which a few "sick", "not-too-bright lads" perform "idiotic stunts" and "crude sight gags" for your amusement; while too "moronic" for highbrows and certainly not for those "squeamish about paper cuts and bodily fluids", it's "absolutely hilarious" to its "brainless" cult followers, who report that "alcohol helps" make it even funnier.

Jackie Brown

| 21 | 23 | 21 | 21 |

1997 | Directed by Quentin Tarantino | With Pam Grier, Robert Forster, Samuel L. Jackson, Bridget Fonda, Michael Keaton | 154 minutes | Rated R

There's "never a dull moment" in this Elmore Leonard–inspired "follow-up to *Pulp Fiction*" that oozes "pure cool" with the "still foxy" Grier and "perfectly cast" Forster in their "comeback performances", playing an aging pair caught in a trap between the Feds and a "sleazy" gun dealer; fans say that Tarantino's trademarked mix of "snappy dialogue" and "sassy soul" only "gets better with repeated viewings."

Jacob's Ladder

| 19 | 22 | 21 | 20 |

1990 | Directed by Adrian Lyne | With Tim Robbins, Elizabeth Pena, Danny Aiello | 115 minutes | Rated R

Step up for some "disturbing images that may stick around" "longer than you want" courtesy of this "unsettling" psychological thriller, featuring Robbins as a Vietnam vet back on the Brooklyn home front and afflicted with "paranoia" and "truly creepy" hallucinations; "cerebral" sorts salute the "mind-altering" scenario with a "haunting twist at the end", but for a few "all the unpleasantness" is just "not top rung."

Jagged Edge

| 22 | 22 | 22 | 20 |

1985 | Directed by Richard Marquand | With Glenn Close, Jeff Bridges, Peter Coyote | 108 minutes | Rated R

This "entertaining murder" thriller tells the tale of a "grisly homicide, a sensational trial and a forbidden love affair"; "great performances" from Close (as a lawyer with principles) and Bridges (as the "charming" client) keep it so "exciting" that you'll be "guessing to the very end."

Jailhouse Rock ◗

| 18 | 15 | 14 | 19 |

1957 | Directed by Richard Thorpe | With Elvis Presley, Judy Tyler, Mickey Shaughnessy | 96 minutes | Not Rated

The "only really good Elvis movie (and that's not saying much)", this "cheesy classic" about an ex-con turned crooner is "worth the price of admission alone" for its "big musical number" featuring chorus boys in prison stripes and the King in all his "hip-swiveling" glory; favorite lyric: "if you can't find a partner, use a wooden chair."

James and the Giant Peach

| 20 | - | 20 | 24 |

1996 | Directed by Henry Selick | Animated | 79 minutes | Rated PG

"Fantastic effects", a kinetic visual style and bushels of "charm" give this "quirky" cartoon a "different look from the typical animated movie"; the story of a boy and a house-size fruit, it blends "live-action" shots with animation, though the result is "too edgy" and "bizarre" for those who claim Roald Dahl's "book is much better."

⛶ Jane Eyre ◑   25 | 27 | 26 | 22

1944 | Directed by Robert Stevenson | With Orson Welles, Joan Fontaine, Margaret O'Brien | 97 minutes | Not Rated

A "moody rendition of the Brontë novel", this "damn good" Gothic romance concerns a "frail" governess, a rich landowner and a houseful of dark secrets; expect plenty of "gloom and doom" followed by atmospheric "shadows" and "Orson scowling" throughout – but as for that "disappointingly contrived ending", blame the author, not Hollywood.

Jarhead   17 | 20 | 17 | 20

2005 | Directed by Sam Mendes | With Jake Gyllenhaal, Jamie Foxx, Peter Sarsgaard | 123 minutes | Rated R

"War isn't fun" in this "troublingly accurate depiction of what Marines experienced on their tour of duty" during the first Gulf War – i.e. "waiting" and "boredom" (it's "not a good movie for action"); as a "gung-ho enlistee", Gyllenhaal is "believable", but the "labored pace" and "meandering" plot makes it "surprisingly uninvolving" for many: a "movie about soldiers doing nothing isn't that interesting to watch."

⛶ Jaws   26 | 22 | 25 | 26

1975 | Directed by Steven Spielberg | With Roy Scheider, Robert Shaw, Richard Dreyfuss | 124 minutes | Rated PG-13

"Sink your teeth" into this "classic summer" scarefest that "gets the adrenaline pumping", since it's got "everything": "horrifying shark attacks", "missing limbs", "crackling" John Williams music and even "fully developed characters"; it "launched the Spielberg juggernaut" by cleverly "making you fear what you don't see", and if the title character looks a bit dated today, the "seasick" wonder "will it ever be safe to go back in the water?"

⛶ Jean de Florette ᴳ   27 | 27 | 26 | 26

1987 | Directed by Claude Berri | With Yves Montand, Gérard Depardieu | 120 minutes | Rated PG

"As Balzacian as French cinema can get", this "epic" drama about farmers feuding over a natural spring in the "pastoral paradise of Provence" is "stunningly beautiful" and "compelling"; since it's only the "first half of a genuinely tragic tale", "make sure to see Manon of the Spring" (its sequel) to get the full scope of this truly "unforgettable story."

Jeremiah Johnson   23 | 21 | 23 | 22

1972 | Directed by Sydney Pollack | With Robert Redford, Will Geer, Stefan Gierasch | 108 minutes | Rated PG

"One of the earliest Westerns to change the movie stereotypes of Indian ways", this saga relates the story of an American soldier turned "mountain man" and his pitched, emotional battle with Crow Nation warriors; a precursor of Dances with Wolves, it showcases Redford "at his best" and is a "classic" to true believers.

Jerk, The   22 | 21 | 19 | 18

1979 | Directed by Carl Reiner | With Steve Martin, Bernadette Peters, Catlin Adams | 94 minutes | Rated R

Opening with "one of the best lines ever" – "I was born a poor black child" – this "absolutely hysterical" "rags-to-riches-to-rags" comedy captures the "wacky early Steve Martin" in all his "zany" glory (with ample support from Peters as his "sweetly naive love interest"); some say it's "silly", but "that's exactly the point."

Jerry Maguire
21 | 22 | 21 | 20

1996 | Directed by Cameron Crowe | With Tom Cruise, Cuba Gooding Jr., Renée Zellweger, Jonathan Lipnicki | 138 minutes | Rated R

A "gutsy sports agent" finally "sees the light" and "rediscovers his soul" in this "crowd-pleasing" dramedy that puts "football and love" together into an "honest", "better-than-average" brew; in the "tailor-made" title role, "Tom terrific" plays "Mr. Show Me the Money" with excellent backup from the Oscar-winning Gooding and a "little kid" who nearly "steals the movie"; most famous line: "you had me at hello."

Jesus Christ Superstar
21 | 18 | 22 | 21

1973 | Directed by Norman Jewison | With Ted Neeley, Carl Anderson, Yvonne Elliman | 108 minutes | Rated G

"Old flower children" find religion in this "visually arresting" "rock opera", a "fantastic" depiction of "Christ's humanity" featuring "hottie" Neeley in the title role and possibly the "best Andrew Lloyd Webber score" ever; heretics say it's "overindulgent" and "not as good as the stage show", speculating that the "cast was stoned the entire time" and thus it all "made sense to them."

Jewel of the Nile, The
19 | 19 | 19 | 20

1985 | Directed by Lewis Teague | With Michael Douglas, Kathleen Turner, Danny DeVito | 106 minutes | Rated PG

Alternately "rugged and romantic", this sequel to *Romancing the Stone* features Douglas, Turner and DeVito reprising their roles as "adventure-seekers" on a misguided Arabian treasure hunt who "end up toppling a government"; as a "tongue-in-cheek romp" it's a "fun rental", but those who miss the "excitement of the original" grade it "more paste than jewel."

Jezebel ✉◑
25 | 27 | 23 | 23

1938 | Directed by William Wyler | With Bette Davis, Henry Fonda, George Brent, Fay Bainter | 103 minutes | Not Rated

"Bette does *Gone with the Wind*" in this familiar-sounding "period piece" about an "obstinate Southern belle who defies a way of life about to be blown away"; granted, the "melodramatic" plot may be a bit "overbaked", but Davis' Oscar-winning performance as a "most delicious bitch" is sheer "perfection"; most "legendary" moment: the "red dress scene."

JFK
19 | 20 | 20 | 21

1991 | Directed by Oliver Stone | With Kevin Costner, Kevin Bacon, Tommy Lee Jones, Gary Oldman | 189 minutes | Rated R

This "riveting", "revisionist" "conspiracy-theory" drama about "what really happened on November 22, 1963" is, at the very least, a look at "what might have happened"; zealots swear it "makes a pretty good case" and delivers some "pull-out-all-the-stops" punches, but debunkers dub it "powerful paranoia" with "too many ifs, buts and maybes to be credible"; in the end, "whether truth or fiction", it remains as "controversial" as ever.

| | OVERALL | ACTING | STORY | PROD. |

Johnny Guitar ∅

19 | 20 | 18 | 19

1954 | Directed by Nicholas Ray | With Joan Crawford, Sterling Hayden, Mercedes McCambridge | 110 minutes | Not Rated

Think "Mildred Pierce in a cowboy hat" to get the gist of this "bizarre" Western rife with "sexual innuendo" and "Freudian overtones", courtesy of "tough-as-nails" saloonkeeper Crawford and her "tightly wound foil", land baron McCambridge; it may be the "strangest", "butchest" oater ever made, but for "camp" followers, it's "utterly fascinating" – and "unintentionally funny."

John Q

17 | 21 | 18 | 18

2002 | Directed by Nick Cassavetes | With Denzel Washington, Robert Duvall, James Woods, Anne Heche | 116 minutes | Rated PG-13

Distinctly "heart-wrenching", this "tearjerker" owes its "credibility" to Washington's "truly believable" performance as a "crazed dad" who holds a hospital emergency room hostage after his son is "refused a heart transplant" for lack of insurance; a few maintain the "movie-of-the-week" message about the "health-care crisis" is "too pat" and "predictable", but most agree it's "worth watching just for Denzel."

Journey to the Center of the Earth

19 | 16 | 21 | 18

1959 | Directed by Henry Levin | With James Mason, Pat Boone, Arlene Dahl, Diane Baker | 132 minutes | Rated G

"Bernard Herrmann's score lends enchantment" to this very "enjoyable" production based on "Jules Verne's fantastical tale" of underground exploration that's a "fun" sci-fi "romp" worth seeking out in a "widescreen" format; sure, it's a tad "hokey", but kids like its "Disney-esque" flavor and "superior special effects."

Joy Luck Club, The

25 | 25 | 26 | 24

1993 | Directed by Wayne Wang | With Ming-Na Wen, Tamlyn Tomita, Lauren Tom, Rosalind Chao | 139 minutes | Rated R

Both an "intergenerational" drama and a "class-A weeper", this "evocative" rendering of Amy Tan's best-seller traces the "interwoven stories" of four Chinese women and their daughters with "complex insight"; admirers who identify with this "real look at family dynamics" that "transcends all cultures" declare it "a joy to watch."

☒ Judgment at Nuremberg ⊠◑

26 | 27 | 25 | 22

1961 | Directed by Stanley Kramer | With Spencer Tracy, Burt Lancaster, Richard Widmark, Marlene Dietrich, Maximilian Schell, Judy Garland, Montgomery Clift | 178 minutes | Not Rated

Based on the "historic" 1948 Nazi war criminal trials, this "excellent courtroom drama" "asks some tough questions" and boasts "uniformly fine" players "often cast against type", as well as a "brilliant", Oscar-winning script; though the issues it raises are "unsettling", it remains a "relevant flick that everyone should see."

Jules and Jim ◑🅵

24 | 26 | 24 | 23

1962 | Directed by François Truffaut | With Jeanne Moreau, Oskar Werner, Henri Serre | 100 minutes | Not Rated

One of the "milestones of the French New Wave", this charming "Truffaut masterpiece" is the "ultimate" "love triangle", wherein Moreau's "enigmatic beauty" makes her the "elusive muse" of two best friends; the "chemistry" between the players is "haunting and lyrical", and though that "bad-dream" ending is mighty "sad", the "fascinating story" proves "how complicated life can be."

Julia ✉ | 25 | 27 | 25 | 24 |

1977 | Directed by Fred Zinnemann | With Jane Fonda, Vanessa Redgrave, Jason Robards | 118 minutes | Rated PG
"Fonda and Redgrave are radiant" in this "fascinating" drama, a "superb pairing of two actresses" cast as playwright Lillian Hellman and her "beloved childhood friend" Julia, a lefty resisting the Nazis in '30s Europe; fans applaud the "nervous" suspense and "moving" moments in this "frightening portrayal" of fraught times.

Juliet of the Spirits ▣ | 25 | 26 | 22 | 26 |

1965 | Directed by Federico Fellini | With Giulietta Masina, Mario Pisu, Sandra Milo | 142 minutes | Not Rated
"Fellini's first color feature", this "dreamlike" tale is the story of an unhappy housewife who escapes her "dreary marriage" and slides into "fantasy" after a séance; it "still haunts" fans who dub it a "vivid" look at the power of "imagination", thanks to the performance of the director's "likable" real-life wife Masina, along with a "surrealistic platter" of "fascinating" character actors.

Jumanji | 18 | 18 | 19 | 22 |

1995 | Directed by Joe Johnston | With Robin Williams, Bonnie Hunt, Kirsten Dunst | 104 minutes | Rated PG
"You'll see rolling dice in a whole different light" after a look at this "smartly done" adventure fantasy about a "mysterious board game" that swallows a young boy and coughs him up a quarter-century later – "along with a number of rampaging animals"; despite a "very cool concept" with "lots of action" and "loud CGI effects", it's "too scary for younger children" and ultimately might be a "better theme-park ride than movie."

Junebug | 21 | 25 | 19 | 19 |

2005 | Directed by Phil Morrison | With Embeth Davidtz, Alessandro Nivola, Amy Adams | 106 minutes | Rated R
A "rural" North Carolina family welcomes home the "son who got away" and his new "Blue State" bride in this "sleeper" dramedy whose "excellent" ensemble cast – notably the "sensational" Adams – manages to produce a "vivid", "lovingly" realized "slice of Southern life"; for most, the "non-formulaic" storyline is a "quirky delight", though a few fret it "rambles around with no discernible point."

Jungle Book, The | 24 | 21 | 25 | 24 |

1942 | Directed by Zoltan Korda | With Sabu, Joseph Calleia, Rosemary DeCamp | 109 minutes | Not Rated
Talk to the animals: this "great children's movie" is a picturesque take on the Kipling yarn of Mowgli, a lad reared by wolves who returns to village life only to face mercenary types hot on the scent of hidden riches; it's a wild eyeful of "classic" family fare that even outdoes "one of the best Disneys", the Mouse House's animated version made 25 years later.

Jungle Book, The | 23 | - | 23 | 24 |

1967 | Directed by Wolfgang Reitherman | Animated | 78 minutes | Rated G
Kipling's "Tarzan-like character and all his friends" pop up in this "charming" Disney cartoon that "makes an impression" with a "crowd-

pleasing" story full of "family fun"; it might not be the studio's "best animation", but its "enchanting" soundtrack has enough "delightful songs" to make for a thing of "pure joy."

Juno ✉   25 | 26 | 24 | 23

2007 | Directed by Jason Reitman | With Ellen Page, Michael Cera, Jennifer Garner | 96 minutes | Rated PG-13

A "feel-good film about teen pregnancy" may sound like an oxymoron, but this "savvy" take on a "controversial" subject "rings with authenticity" thanks to a "humane", Oscar-winning script and Page's "spirited" portrayal of a "wisecracking", knocked-up kid set on "giving her baby up for adoption"; maybe the "snappy" repartee is "occasionally over-cute", but the overall result is "refreshing", especially synched against that "great soundtrack."

Jurassic Park   22 | 16 | 22 | 27

1993 | Directed by Steven Spielberg | With Sam Neill, Laura Dern, Jeff Goldblum | 127 minutes | Rated PG-13

"Humans are upstaged by dinosaurs" in this sci-fi "thrill ride" from the "astounding" Spielberg set in an extinct-creatures-come-to-life theme park that's "every child's dream come true"; don't expect much from the "lame story" and "weak" actors (nothing more than "dinochow"), but hold on for "white-knuckle" pacing and "astounding special effects" so "truly frightening" that they "might scare younger viewers."

Just Like Heaven   19 | 20 | 19 | 19

2005 | Directed by Mark Waters | With Reese Witherspoon, Mark Ruffalo | 95 minutes | Rated PG-13

A slice of "date movie" heaven comes with this "fluffy" rom-com, provided "you're willing to ride along" with its "offbeat premise": a "cynical" San Fran man hooking up with the disembodied "spirit of a woman"; admirers ignore the "cutesy" script's "eye-rolling predictability."

Karate Kid, The   19 | 16 | 20 | 17

1984 | Directed by John G. Avildsen | With Ralph Macchio, Pat Morita, Elisabeth Shue | 126 minutes | Rated PG

"*Rocky* for teenagers", this "classic" "underdog-wins-the-day story" matches a "kid finding it hard to fit in" with a martial-arts "mentor" who teaches him control through "discipline and loyalty"; balancing "solid values" with "doses of action", this "not-typical teen movie" has the "coming-of-age" thing down pat and is "inspiring" to boot.

Kate & Leopold   16 | 17 | 16 | 18

2001 | Directed by James Mangold | With Meg Ryan, Hugh Jackman, Liev Schreiber | 118 minutes | Rated PG-13

"Boy meets girl with a historical twist" in this "romantic fantasy"–cum–"time travel yarn" that casts Jackman as a "sexy" nobleman from the 1800s transported to modern-day NYC, where he meets the "feisty" Meg; overall, it's a "far-fetched", "feel-good chick flick", but despite the presence of "two charming actors", some find "no charm" here.

Keeping Up with the Steins   17 | 18 | 18 | 17

2006 | Directed by Scott Marshall | With Jeremy Piven, Jami Gertz, Daryl Hannah, Garry Marshall | 99 minutes | Rated PG-13

This "harmless" comedy "strikes a chord" with social climbers via its "on-target send-up" of a "lavish", "over-the-top" bar mitzvah; although the "first half is hilarious" and Piven is "funny" playing the "same character" he portrays on *Entourage,* its "preachy" second-act depiction of "grandpa/grandson love" skews "slightly sappy."

☒ Key Largo ◑   26 26 23 23
1948 | Directed by John Huston | With Humphrey Bogart, Edward G. Robinson, Lauren Bacall | 101 minutes | Not Rated

"Tough guys and dolls bring back the golden Warner Brothers days" in this "hard-hitting" noir showcase about a group held hostage by a "super-rat" of a gangster – until "anti-hero" Bogart shows up; near the "top of Huston's body of work", it features a "highly suspenseful" plot, "stellar performances" and some "vintage" Bogie and Bacall moments – "'nuff said."

Kid Stays in the Picture, The   21 - 22 20
2002 | Directed by Nanette Burstein, Brett Morgen | Documentary | 93 minutes | Rated R

The "rise and fall" of legendary producer/studio head Robert Evans (*Chinatown, The Godfather, Rosemary's Baby*) gets the big-screen treatment in this "stylish documentary", an "only-in-America story" that's "narrated by the subject himself"; although "self-congratulatory propaganda" to some, most find it a "fascinating", "inside" look at moviemaking – "if you can get past Evans' enormous ego", that is.

Kill Bill Vol. 1   23 22 21 25
2003 | Directed by Quentin Tarantino | With Uma Thurman, Lucy Liu, Vivica A. Fox, Sonny Chiba | 111 minutes | Rated R

"Violence and gore abound" in this "over-the-top", "occasionally ridiculous" first installment of Quentin Tarantino's two-part salute to "comic strips", "spaghetti westerns" and "grindhouse kung fu flicks"; starring a "butt-kicking" Uma as a "revenge"-seeking "killing machine", it's "not for everyone" what with all the "spurting blood", "flying limbs" and "gross sound effects", but thrill freaks purr its "adrenaline" rush is simply "cool as heck" – provided you "check your brains at the door" before viewing.

Kill Bill Vol. 2   25 24 24 26
2004 | Directed by Quentin Tarantino | With Uma Thurman, David Carradine, Michael Madsen, Daryl Hannah | 136 minutes | Rated R

A continuation that "improves upon the original", this "gentler cousin" of the "obscenely graphic" *Vol. 1* features "less red food coloring" and more "character development", while remaining a "wickedly referential" homage to martial arts movies; as the ever-vengeful assassin, Thurman still "burns bright" and despite "trademark" Tarantino dialogue that gets a bit "long-winded", fans say there's a "true heart beating at the center of all the fighting" that lends "emotional heft" to both parts.

Killers, The ◑   25 25 25 23
1946 | Directed by Robert Siodmak | With Burt Lancaster, Ava Gardner, Edmond O'Brien | 105 minutes | Not Rated

"Lancaster makes a powerful film debut" backed up by an "outstanding" Gardner in this "riveting" flick "expanded from the Hemingway short story" about a mysterious small-town murder and its aftermath; it gets to the "core of film noir" through a burbling mix of "moral ambiguity, sexual tension and crime."

	OVERALL	ACTING	STORY	PROD.

Killing, The ◐
`25` `24` `25` `24`

1956 | Directed by Stanley Kubrick | With Sterling Hayden, Coleen Gray, Elisha Cook Jr. | 85 minutes | Not Rated

"Long before Quentin Tarantino", this "hardened noir" from the "early Kubrick" elevated a "B-list cast" and "run-of-the-mill" racetrack robbery story into a "nail-biting knockout" that typifies "taut" pacing and "tough-guy" attitude; an "overlooked" but "influential" effort with a diced-up structure that's "ahead of its time", it's a killer calling card from "one of the masters."

☑ Killing Fields, The
`26` `26` `27` `25`

1984 | Directed by Roland Joffé | With Sam Waterston, Haing S. Ngor, John Malkovich | 141 minutes | Rated R

"Friendship is tested by war" in this "harrowing" true story "told through the eyes of a journalist" relating the "atrocities in Cambodia" and the "horrors of the Khmer Rouge" following the U.S. pullout from Vietnam; "worthy Oscar-winner Ngor" (a real-life survivor of this "holocaust") turns in an "honest" performance that "will move you to tears" and "make you think" a lot.

☑ Kind Hearts and Coronets ◐
`26` `28` `26` `24`

1950 | Directed by Robert Hamer | With Alec Guinness, Dennis Price, Valerie Hobson | 106 minutes | Not Rated

For "quintessential" "English humor" that "gets better with each viewing", check out this "matchless black comedy" about the disinherited scion of a noble family who tries to achieve dukedom through serial murder; in an inspired twist, his victims – all eight of them – are played by the one-and-only Alec Guinness, whose spot-on performance squarely places this one on the "forever best list."

☑ King and I, The ✉
`27` `26` `25` `27`

1956 | Directed by Walter Lang | With Yul Brynner, Deborah Kerr, Rita Moreno | 133 minutes | Rated G

The "'Shall We Dance' scene" alone is "worth the price of admission" to this regally "sumptuous" version of Rodgers and Hammerstein's "terrific, old-fashioned" Broadway musical; though it may be "historically inaccurate", "who cares?" given the "stunning production", "gorgeous score" and "totally engaging" team of the "lovely Kerr" "getting to know" Oscar-winner Brynner.

King Arthur
`15` `16` `16` `20`

2004 | Directed by Antoine Fuqua | With Clive Owen, Ioan Gruffudd, Keira Knightley | 126 minutes | Rated PG-13

Camelot gets a "revisionist" makeover in this "gritty" epic recounting "how Arthur became a legend" via an "elaborate re-creation" of "Roman times in Britain"; unfortunately, the focus on "sword action" and "insanely violent" battle scenes bypasses all of the "mythology magic", making for a "long", "muddled" rehashing that "not even Merlin can save."

Kingdom of Heaven
`18` `19` `18` `25`

2005 | Directed by Ridley Scott | With Orlando Bloom, Liam Neeson, Jeremy Irons, Eva Green | 145 minutes | Rated R

Ridley Scott's "beautifully filmed" epic gives the Crusades a "fairly accurate" treatment with a "sullen" Bloom as a 12th-century Frenchman en route to Jerusalem only to find "unbelievable parallels to today's relationships in the Middle East"; the "top-notch" production values and "incredible battle scenes" carry the day even if the "long-winded" "yawner" of a script comes up decidedly "short of *Gladiator*" – "where is Russell Crowe when you need him?"

☒ King Kong ◑
25 | 15 | 24 | 24

1933 | Directed by Merian C. Cooper, Ernest B. Schoedsack | With Fay Wray, Robert Armstrong, Bruce Cabot | 100 minutes | Rated PG

This "granddaddy of all monster flicks" "still rules the roost" as an "essential piece of cinema history" and the inspiration for "countless" imitators; ok, the "stop-motion" special effects are "Stone Age stuff by today's standards", but this "warped beauty-and-the-beast saga" remains memorable for its "indelible" imagery, that iconic "climax atop the Empire State Building" and most of all for the "irreplaceable" Fay Wray, "filmdom's finest screamer."

King Kong
20 | 18 | 19 | 26

2005 | Directed by Peter Jackson | With Naomi Watts, Jack Black, Adrien Brody | 187 minutes | Rated PG-13

"Less would have been more" in this "bloated remake" of the '30s classic about a "big monkey coerced into show business" that many dub more "video game" than movie; though fans can't help but "love the big furball" and are awed by the "mega-bucks" production, "slow pacing" and endless "monkeying around before the inevitable climb up the Empire State Building" add up to one "way-too-long" flick; in sum, director Jackson should either "hire an editor" or "stick to Middle-Earth."

King of Comedy, The
23 | 26 | 23 | 21

1983 | Directed by Martin Scorsese | With Robert De Niro, Jerry Lewis, Sandra Bernhard | 101 minutes | Rated PG

"Sharp, insightful and totally original", this pitch-black comedy about a wannabe comedian and the talk-show host he stalks is a different kind of "De Niro psycho flick" that's "complex and unsettling, but kind of fun"; as the stalkee, Lewis is both "funny and sad" ("maybe the French do know something"), and the picture itself is the "most underrated of Scorsese's career."

☒ King of Hearts ☐
26 | 26 | 26 | 24

1967 | Directed by Philippe de Broca | With Alan Bates, Geneviève Bujold, Pierre Brasseur, Adolfo Celi | 100 minutes | Not Rated

One of the "best anti-war flicks", this "satiric" allegory tells of a WWI soldier's attempt to dismantle a bomb set in a village solely inhabited by "insane asylum inmates"; while some snort its "pacifist" message is too "simplistic" and "heavy-handed", more say this "cult classic" is a "thought-provoking" indictment of the "madness of war."

Kingpin
18 | 18 | 18 | 17

1996 | Directed by Bobby Farrelly, Peter Farrelly | With Woody Harrelson, Randy Quaid, Vanessa Angel | 113 minutes | Rated PG-13

The Farrelly brothers roll out their "usual gross-out humor" in this "harmless" comedy framed around a former bowling champion mentoring his latest prodigy (sort of an "inane version of *The Color of Money*"); while there's "no thinking required" and "no redeeming social values" lurking in this "slobfest", it "helps to have a sick sense of humor."

King Solomon's Mines

20 | 18 | 20 | 22

1950 | Directed by Compton Bennett, Andrew Marton | With Stewart Granger, Deborah Kerr | 103 minutes | Not Rated

"Location filming on the beautiful African continent" is the raison d'être of this H. Rider Haggard "chestnut" that's "hardly the most realistic" action flick, but a "good enough rendition" for most; it delivers some "romance" (via its "matinee idol" marquee names) and some "camp" (that "noble savages" subtext), but whether it's truly "Indiana Jones *before* Indiana Jones" is your call.

Kings Row ◐

22 | 20 | 22 | 21

1942 | Directed by Sam Wood | With Ann Sheridan, Robert Cummings, Ronald Reagan, Betty Field | 125 minutes | Not Rated

A "curiosity" that proves "Reagan could really act", this "dark" drama follows the "trials and tribulations" of folks in "small-town America" via a "predictable but well-done" chronicle of sundry amorous entanglements; even foes admit that the "soap opera" plot "keeps you interested", though for many the "only memorable thing" is the Great Communicator's most unforgettable line: "where's the rest of me?"

Kinky Boots

23 | 24 | 22 | 23

2006 | Directed by Julian Jarrold | With Joel Edgerton, Chiwetel Ejiofor | 107 minutes | Rated PG-13

There's "off-kilter British comedy" afoot in this "sweet, funny" story of a failing shoe manufacturer that hires a design-savvy transvestite to lift it up by the bootstraps; with a "little moralizing" about "tolerance" and a lot of "charming fluff", it delivers "quirky", "feel-good" fare "in the same vein as *The Full Monty*."

Kinsey

22 | 26 | 22 | 22

2004 | Directed by Bill Condon | With Liam Neeson, Laura Linney, Chris O'Donnell, Peter Sarsgaard | 118 minutes | Rated R

"Kinky", "controversial" sex therapist Alfred Kinsey is the subject of this "racy", "pulls-no-punches" biopic that details "how the sexual revolution started" as well as "how far we've progressed and how far we have to go"; Neeson is "arousing" and Linney ever the "acting goddess", but overall what's "provocative and poignant" to some is "sterile and congratulatory" to others; P.S. "don't watch it with your parents."

Kissing Jessica Stein

21 | 20 | 21 | 19

2001 | Directed by Charles Herman-Wurmfeld | With Jennifer Westfeldt, Heather Juergensen, Tovah Feldshuh | 97 minutes | Rated R

"Single women relate" to this "new-age chick flick", a "quirky romantic comedy" about a "funny, likable" gal "discouraged by the dating scene" who embarks on a lesbian affair; it's rendered in such a "sensitive" way that it "transcends moral objections" (i.e. it "won't offend your mother"), and even if "not profound", it's sure "sweet and solid."

Kiss Kiss Bang Bang

20 | 22 | 20 | 20

2005 | Directed by Shane Black | With Robert Downey Jr., Val Kilmer, Michelle Monaghan | 102 minutes | Rated R

This "tongue-in-cheek" film noir "send-up" is "fast, slick and darkly funny" thanks to a "twisted", "*Pulp Fiction*"-esque plot played at full tilt by an "on-the-money" cast, starting with the "superb" Downey as a thief-turned-thespian-turned-private eye on the loose in LA; loyalists lament "nobody saw this movie", while critics contend the whole enterprise is a bit "too impressed with itself."

Kiss Me Deadly ◑

	OVERALL	ACTING	STORY	PROD.
	24	20	23	21

1955 | Directed by Robert Aldrich | With Ralph Meeker, Albert Dekker, Paul Stewart, Marian Carr | 104 minutes | Not Rated

"Cold War propaganda has never been more frightening" than in this "mesmerizing" example of "classic film noir" rife with girls, guns and "cynicism", topped off with some "nuclear paranoia"; based on Mickey Spillane's lurid best-seller, it "bears repeat viewing" thanks to Aldrich's "superb direction", a "memorable ending" and that famous "suitcase", later "paid homage to in *Pulp Fiction.*"

Kiss Me Kate

24	21	24	25

1953 | Directed by George Sidney | With Howard Keel, Kathryn Grayson, Ann Miller | 109 minutes | Not Rated

"Cole Porter's Broadway smash" gets the "Hollywood treatment" in this "sparkling film version" that's a reworking of "*The Taming of the Shrew*"; even though the "principals lack star power", you can still "brush up on your Shakespeare" nicely with "great musical numbers" and "exciting dancing", which come together famously in Miller's "knock-'em-dead" turn in 'Too Darn Hot.'

Kiss of Death ◑

23	24	22	22

1947 | Directed by Henry Hathaway | With Victor Mature, Brian Donlevy, Richard Widmark, Coleen Gray | 98 minutes | Not Rated

A "decent ex-con" hoping to lead a straight life fends off a "very bad man" from his criminal past in this "classic" noir best remembered for Widmark's Oscar-nominated, big-screen debut as "chilling" hit man Tommy Udo ("you'll remember his cackle forever"); creepiest scene: when the "old lady in the wheelchair" meets her fate.

Kiss of the Spider Woman ✉

22	25	22	21

1985 | Directed by Hector Babenco | With William Hurt, Raul Julia, Sonia Braga | 120 minutes | Rated R

An "odd couple" – a political activist and a gay pederast – inhabit the same prison cell in this "intense drama" based on the Manuel Puig novel that deals with "love, corruption and redemption"; though "worth seeing" for its "moving" script and Hurt's Oscar-winning turn, it may be "too much" for mainstream audiences.

Kiss the Girls

20	22	22	20

1997 | Directed by Gary Fleder | With Morgan Freeman, Ashley Judd, Cary Elwes | 111 minutes | Rated R

"Chilling" and "quite true" to James Patterson's best-seller, this "suspenseful" thriller features Freeman as a forensic expert tracking a serial killer along with "hotter-than-a-racecar" Judd, an escaped victim who joins the pursuit; still, cynics say this "airplane movie" is "engrossing enough while watching" but totally "forgettable" the minute it's over.

Kite Runner, The ▣

24	24	25	24

2007 | Directed by Marc Forster | With Khalid Abdalla, Atossa Leoni, Shaun Toub | 128 minutes | Rated PG-13

Novelist Khaled Hosseini's "gripping" tale of two friends in conflict-torn Afghanistan is "tastefully" transferred to the big screen in this "simplified" adaptation, sparing many "background details" while still conveying the narrative's "moralistic" core – i.e. "how childhood events determine the course of an entire life"; enriched by a "vivid" production and some "wonderful kid actors", it packs a "powerful" punch.

Klute ✉   20 | 23 | 21 | 19

1971 | Directed by Alan J. Pakula | With Jane Fonda, Donald Sutherland, Roy Scheider | 114 minutes | Rated R

Oscar-winner Fonda stars as an "unhappy hooker" in this "heart-pounding" thriller, where she's "stalked by a killer" but protected by an "excellent" Sutherland as the cop who humanizes her; it "avoids all the clichés" of the genre via a chillingly matter-of-fact script, and if a bit "forgotten", at least Jane's shag "hairdo" is memorable.

Knife in the Water ❶🅵   24 | 23 | 24 | 22

1963 | Directed by Roman Polanski | With Leon Niemczyk, Jolanta Umecka, Zygmunt Malanowicz | 94 minutes | Not Rated

Polanski's "breakthrough" movie achieves "suspense in a boat" via its story of a married couple who invite a hitchhiker along on their sailing expedition; despite a "small cast" and "obvious low budget", the "mesmerizing" result achieves "Hitchcock-level tension", no mean feat considering that it was the director's first feature.

Knight's Tale, A   18 | 17 | 17 | 20

2001 | Directed by Brian Helgeland | With Heath Ledger, Rufus Sewell, Shannyn Sossamon, Paul Bettany | 132 minutes | Rated PG-13

A "man of humble birth" yearning to lance a lot schemes to become a tournament knight in this "inoffensive" medieval action comedy loosely based on Chaucer's *Canterbury Tales*; expect some boldly "modern" twists – namely that "'70s rock music" soundtrack – though what's "purposeful anachronism" to some strikes others as joust "a bit silly."

K-19: The Widowmaker   16 | 16 | 18 | 19

2002 | Directed by Kathryn Bigelow | With Harrison Ford, Liam Neeson, Peter Sarsgaard | 138 minutes | Rated PG-13

A "tribute to heroism" – with the "Soviets as the good guys" – this "taut" Cold War thriller told from the Russian point of view stars Ford as the skipper of a nuclear sub crippled by a "near-fatal" mishap that threatens to spark World War III; it's "thoughtful" enough, yet *nyet*-sayers cite Harrison's "laughable" accent and a "dull" narrative that's too "predictable."

Knocked Up   19 | 18 | 18 | 18

2007 | Directed by Judd Apatow | With Seth Rogen, Katherine Heigl, Paul Rudd, Leslie Mann | 129 minutes | Rated R

"Unplanned pregnancy" is played for laffs in this comedy of "drunken sex and its aftermath" that pairs a "smoking hot" gal with a "slacker schlub"; bluenoses aren't knocked out by the "offensive title", "pass-the-bong" jokes and "unnecessarily graphic language", but grudgingly admit "it has heart", "likable characters" and an "unexpectedly sweet" ending.

K-Pax   16 | 21 | 18 | 17

2001 | Directed by Iain Softley | With Kevin Spacey, Jeff Bridges | 120 minutes | Rated PG-13

"Alien or human?" is the "perplexing" question at the heart of this sci-fi-inflected drama starring the "stellar" K-Spacey as a psych patient who claims to be an E.T. and "keeps you guessing" whether he's for real or "really mad"; sure, it "starts off with potential", but the ultimate diagnosis is "could have been more interesting."

Kramer vs. Kramer ✉

23 | 26 | 23 | 21

1979 | Directed by Robert Benton | With Dustin Hoffman, Meryl Streep, Justin Henry | 105 minutes | Rated PG

"All about the acting", this "riveting drama" won Oscars for Hoffman and Streep as a married couple undergoing the "trauma of divorce and child custody"; overturning the "gender-biased view of parenting", its depiction of a growing "father-son" bond is the core of the story, though its "heart-wrenching" theme "hits you hard" – "there are no winners" in this split-up.

Kung Fu Hustle ▣

23 | 20 | 21 | 24

2005 | Directed by Stephen Chow | With Stephen Chow, Yuen Wah, Qiu Yuen | 95 minutes | Rated R

"Move over Jackie Chan!": this "wildly imaginative" piece of "chop-socky" merges "mind-boggling fight choreography" with "genre-blending" aplomb in its tale of "unlikely heroes" facing off against mobsters; its "spaghetti-western-meets-*Crouching-Tiger*"approach is equal parts "Bruce Lee, Wile E. Coyote and Quentin Tarantino", with a dash of "Bob Fosse" thrown in for good measure.

La Bamba

20 | 21 | 21 | 19

1987 | Directed by Luis Valdez | With Lou Diamond Phillips, Esai Morales, Rosanna DeSoto | 108 minutes | Rated PG-13

The "passionate" spirit of '50s Chicano rocker Ritchie Valens, whose "brief life" was "cut too short" by a tragic plane crash, "comes through strongly" in this "haunting" biopic; fronted by a "spot-on" Phillips, it also draws applause for exploring "immigrant family" themes, but ultimately it's the "fantastic" *música* that will "touch your heart."

Labyrinth

22 | 19 | 22 | 23

1986 | Directed by Jim Henson | With David Bowie, Jennifer Connelly | 101 minutes | Rated PG

This "trippy" fairy tale from the "weird" mind of Muppetmaster Henson uses both puppets and live actors to tell its story of a young girl trying to rescue her kidnapped brother from an "evil" Goblin King; credit the "whimsical" blend of "out-there" visuals and "catchy" tunes for its longstanding rep as one of the "most rewatchable movies" ever.

La Cage aux Folles ▣

24 | 26 | 25 | 22

1979 | Directed by Edouard Molinaro | With Michel Serrault, Ugo Tognazzi, Remy Laurent | 100 minutes | Rated R

"Funnier than the American remake", the "Broadway musical" and the "two sequels", this "absurd" French farce is "light-years ahead of its time" telling the story of two gay blades forced to "play it straight" in order to impress prospective in-laws; "overacted to perfection" by an "unbeatable" cast, it defines flaming "frivolity", even if a few cluck it's become "a bit faded" with time.

▨ L.A. Confidential ✉

26 | 27 | 25 | 26

1997 | Directed by Curtis Hanson | With Kevin Spacey, Russell Crowe, Guy Pearce, Kim Basinger | 138 minutes | Rated R

"Every nuance is perfect" in this "steamy" period crime drama, an "explosive exposé" about "crooks, hookers" and "police corruption" in

'50s LA that's "sharp", "detailed" and "violent as hell"; though it "made a star of Crowe", the overall "dead-on casting" advances the "case for an ensemble acting award", while the "smart", Oscar-winning script has "all the grit" of a "film noir" classic, boosted by "21st-century production values."

Ladder 49

	OVERALL	ACTING	STORY	PROD.
	19	21	19	22

2004 | Directed by Jay Russell | With Joaquin Phoenix, John Travolta | 115 minutes | Rated PG-13

"Hunky" Phoenix and Travolta suit up to battle blazes in this "stirring tribute to firefighters", which impresses with "frightening" inferno scenes and "tugs at the heartstrings" with its "introspective" looks at "camaraderie" and "sacrifice"; most feel its themes carry special "poignancy in post-9/11" times, though a few hose it for being a bit "predictable and corny."

⊠ La Dolce Vita ❶🅕

25	25	23	25

1961 | Directed by Federico Fellini | With Marcello Mastroianni, Anita Ekberg, Anouk Aimée | 167 minutes | Not Rated

"Celebrity-obsessed culture" goes under the microscope in this "scandalous" study of "decadence", "damnation and redemption" as seen in '60s Rome through the eyes of a jaded gossip columnist (Mastroianni "at his best") fed up with the "sweet life"; arguably "Fellini's most famous" film, it's a "decidedly unglamorous look at glamour" that "introduced the word 'paparazzi'" into the world lexicon; most iconic scene: "Ekberg in the Trevi Fountain."

Lady and the Tramp

26	-	24	25

1955 | Directed by Wilfred Jackson, Hamilton Luske, Clyde Geronimi | Animated | 75 minutes | Rated G

Puppy love gets a "gorgeous vintage Disney" spin in this "cute" canine romance awash in "lush animation" and lensed in "beautiful" CinemaScope; doggy devotees adore its fetching characters, "endearing story" and "great songs" ("highlighted by Peggy Lee's" sultry rendition of 'He's a Tramp'), though the most unforgettable moment has to be its "famous spaghetti kiss."

⊠ Lady Eve, The ❶

28	28	27	26

1941 | Directed by Preston Sturges | With Barbara Stanwyck, Henry Fonda, Charles Coburn | 97 minutes | Not Rated

"Steamy innuendo" and "wacky pratfalls" coexist in this "smart" Preston Sturges "romp" about a "scheming con artist" out to snare an "unsuspecting" "wealthy geek", aided by an "outstanding supporting cast" of "cardsharps"; a "sassy", "shameless" Stanwyck does "that sultry thing" so well that Fonda's "bumbling rube" "doesn't stand a chance" in this "slyly amusing" screwball comedy that many pronounce "perfect."

Lady from Shanghai, The ❶

25	23	22	26

1948 | Directed by Orson Welles | With Orson Welles, Rita Hayworth, Everett Sloane | 87 minutes | Not Rated

"Another Orson Welles achievement", this "bravura" "B movie" is "completely enjoyable" for many, thanks to some memorable "standout scenes": the "shootout in the hall of mirrors", "Rita Hayworth speaking Chinese"; still, skeptics shrug the plot is a "confusing mess" that "looks like it's been cut to death."

	OVERALL	ACTING	STORY	PROD.

Ladyhawke
21 20 22 21

1985 | Directed by Richard Donner | With Matthew Broderick, Rutger Hauer, Michelle Pfeiffer | 121 minutes | Rated PG-13

"Hauer was never more noble" and "Pfeiffer never looked better" than in this "mystical medieval fantasy" about the "unrequited love" of a "star-crossed" pair destined to remain apart since "one's a wolf by night, the other a hawk by day"; it's "well-crafted", "well-acted" stuff, even if the "dated synthesizer soundtrack" ruffles some feathers.

Lady in the Water
14 17 14 17

2006 | Directed by M. Night Shyamalan | With Paul Giamatti, Bryce Dallas Howard, Bob Balaban | 110 minutes | Rated PG-13

"Shyamalan strikes again" with this "scary fairy tale" about an apartment superintendent who enters a "reality beneath our reality" after discovering a sea-sprite living in his building's swimming pool; less enchantingly, consensus says a "good cast is wasted" on a "waterlogged" premise and a lot of "mystic mumbo-jumbo" that could stand a "life preserver."

Ladykillers, The
21 23 21 20

1956 | Directed by Alexander Mackendrick | With Alec Guinness, Cecil Parker, Peter Sellers, Katie Johnson | 97 minutes | Not Rated

"Inspired lunacy" from Britain's Ealing Studios, this "really funny" black comedy tells the story of a band of "incompetent" con artists planning a heist but "done in by a sweet little old lady"; the "marvelous" cast includes a "first-rate" Guinness and a "just-starting-out" Sellers, but many say the picture's "stolen" by Katie Johnson, who's a "brilliant foil" as the elderly dowager.

Ladykillers, The
15 19 16 18

2004 | Directed by Ethan Coen, Joel Coen | With Tom Hanks, Irma P. Hall, Marlon Wayans | 104 minutes | Rated R

"Trying to recapture the magic of *O Brother, Where Art Thou?*", the Coen brothers again head to the Deep South for this "flat" remake of the British black comedy that has some "good single laughs" but ultimately seems "another lame attempt by Hollywood to co-opt a classic film"; playing a "witty" if "uncharacteristically evil" con man, the "over-the-top" Hanks doesn't fare well either: despite a "great set of false teeth", he's "no Alec Guinness."

Lady Sings the Blues
22 23 23 23

1972 | Directed by Sidney J. Furie | With Diana Ross, Billy Dee Williams, Richard Pryor | 144 minutes | Rated R

"Sad yet real", this biography of songbird Billie Holiday moves to the tempo of the "commanding" Miss Ross' body-and-soul performance; following Lady Day from hard times to the big time to her "strung-out" decline, it "holds you from beginning to end", though for diva devotees it's Diana who's the "best part."

Lady Vanishes, The ◑
25 24 26 23

1938 | Directed by Alfred Hitchcock | With Margaret Lockwood, Michael Redgrave, Dame May Whitty | 97 minutes | Not Rated

A first-class ticket to "intrigue", this "crackerjack Hitchcock classic" finds the master at his "most fleet" and "fascinating", cooking up a "sublime combination" of the comic and the thrilling; its story of a strange disappearance on a train full of "memorable characters" is such "sheer entertainment" that even those who "know the ending" "never tire" of jumping back aboard.

La Femme Nikita 🅕

	OVERALL	ACTING	STORY	PROD.
	23	22	24	23

1991 | Directed by Luc Besson | With Anne Parillaud, Jean-Hugues Anglade, Jeanne Moreau | 115 minutes | Rated R
The "intelligent foreign film" gets a "violent jolt of adrenaline" in this "fast-paced" but "thought-provoking" "tough chick" flick about a punk junkie turned professional assassin; as the "kick-ass" lead, the "mesmerizing" Parillaud performs "spectacular stunts" that "hold your attention" so completely that it's more than "worth the effort to read the subtitles."

Lake House, The

16	18	17	18

2006 | Directed by Alejandro Agresti | With Keanu Reeves, Sandra Bullock, Christopher Plummer | 105 minutes | Rated PG
Reeves and Bullock "pair up again" sans "runaway bus" in this "rainy-day romance" about "would-be lovers" who "share the same home" – only in "two different time periods" – and thus are obliged to "correspond through a magical mailbox"; takers term it a "sweet contrivance" despite the "far-fetched premise", "gauzy", "chick-flick" cinematography and iffy thesping ("Keanu's more wooden than the house").

Land Before Time, The

20	-	20	21

1988 | Directed by Don Bluth | Animated | 70 minutes | Rated G
A "must-watch" for the "five-and-under set", this "timeless" animated feature tells the "heartfelt" tale of an orphaned brontosaurus who embarks on an "incredible" Jurassic journey that "teaches lessons without lecturing"; it lands on the list of "childhood favorites", though the "umpteen" straight-to-video sequels "don't hold a candle to the original."

Lara Croft: Tomb Raider

13	13	12	19

2001 | Directed by Simon West | With Angelina Jolie, Jon Voight, Iain Glen, Daniel Craig | 100 minutes | Rated PG-13
A "popular video game" character akin to a "female Indiana Jones" bungees onto the silver screen via this "slick" but "mindless" action vehicle for "eye-candy" queen Jolie; with "cool gadgets", "beautiful locales" and Angie's "great bodysuit" making up the "deluxe" visuals, seekers of "guilty viewing pleasure" shrug "who cares about story?"

Lara Croft Tomb Raider: The Cradle of Life

14	15	14	19

2003 | Directed by Jan de Bont | With Angelina Jolie, Gerard Butler, Ciarán Hinds | 117 minutes | Rated PG-13
Jolie returns as the "strong and sexy" archeologist with a penchant for "skintight outfits" in this "titillating" sequel to the video game–derived action flick, a "fast-paced" escapade involving Pandora's box, a sunken sanctuary and Hong Kong mobsters that's a little bit "better than the first one"; though foes fret the "only thing worse than Angie's acting is the plot", die-hard fans would gladly "watch her butter toast."

Lars and the Real Girl

22	26	23	21

2007 | Directed by Craig Gillespie | With Ryan Gosling, Emily Mortimer, Paul Schneider | 106 minutes | Rated PG-13
"Thoroughly offbeat" and "unexpectedly endearing", this "feel-good" fable tells the story of a loner in love with a life-size blow-up "sex doll"

and the "tolerant" community that "comes together to support him"; though the "production isn't fancy", the "exceptional ensemble" led by the "talented" Gosling ably delivers the "laughter and tears", and if nothing else, it sure is an "original concept."

Last Detail, The

22 | 26 | 22 | 19

1973 | Directed by Hal Ashby | With Jack Nicholson, Randy Quaid, Otis Young | 103 minutes | Rated R

"Pull up your socks" – this "accurate depiction of Navy life" (that includes plenty of "poetic cursing") details a young sailor's trip to a military prison, escorted by two enlisted men who decide to show him one last good time along the way; though certainly "not a happy story", it's "well worth seeing" for a glimpse of an "early Jack" at "his most free-form."

☑ Last Emperor, The ✉

26 | 24 | 25 | 28

1987 | Directed by Bernardo Bertolucci | With John Lone, Joan Chen, Peter O'Toole | 160 minutes | Rated PG-13

"Truly an epic, and a darned good one" at that, this "sweeping", "large-scale" bio tells the story of China's "final monarch" from his ascent to the throne at age three through war, occupation and "revolutionary changes" in his kingdom; credit "lavish" sets, "spectacular scenery" and "outstanding" acting by Lone and O'Toole for its winning an impressive "nine Academy Awards"; P.S. several versions exist, but all are on the "long" side.

Last Holiday

19 | 19 | 18 | 19

2006 | Directed by Wayne Wang | With Queen Latifah, LL Cool J, Timothy Hutton, Gérard Depardieu | 112 minutes | Rated PG-13

"Joie de vivre" brightens this "lighthearted" dramedy, a "retelling" of a '50s British flick with Latifah as a "play-it-safe type who breaks out of her shell" once she "believes she's dying"; even though "you know what's going to happen, you'll enjoy the ride anyway", and Queenie's "last fling" in Europe includes some "spectacular" gourmet repasts that will titillate "foodies."

☑ Last King of Scotland, The ✉

25 | 29 | 24 | 25

2006 | Directed by Kevin Macdonald | With Forest Whitaker, James McAvoy, Kerry Washington, Gillian Anderson | 123 minutes | Rated R

"Perfectly capturing the charisma and paranoia" of Ugandan dictator Idi Amin, Whitaker's "transcendental", Oscar-winning performance is an "indelible achievement" that brings a "barbarous" chapter in African history to light; told from the perspective of a "fictionalized" doctor, it features several depictions of "gruesome" violence, including "one of the most horrific torture scenes ever."

Last Metro, The ▤

24 | 25 | 23 | 23

1981 | Directed by François Truffaut | With Catherine Deneuve, Gérard Depardieu, Jean Poiret | 131 minutes | Rated PG

"Love and loyalty" are the underlying themes of this "wistful" tale of a French theatrical troupe staging a play in Nazi-occupied Paris; it's "vintage Truffaut" with "beautiful" work from the "haunting" Deneuve, and might work best as a "double bill with *Day For Night*", the same director's "tribute to movies and movie folk."

	OVERALL	ACTING	STORY	PROD.

Last Mimzy, The
`21` `20` `21` `22`

2007 | Directed by Robert Shaye | With Joely Richardson, Timothy Hutton, Rhiannon Leigh Wryn, Chris O'Neil | 90 minutes | Rated PG

"Not just for nerds", this "neat" sci-fi "kid flick" tells the "imaginative" story of a brother and sister who find a horde of toys (including the titular rabbit doll) that are charged with paranormal powers; ok, this "offbeat parable" may be a bit "New Agey", but overall this "pleasant surprise" works well for the "whole family."

Last of the Mohicans, The
`22` `22` `22` `25`

1992 | Directed by Michael Mann | With Daniel Day-Lewis, Madeleine Stowe, Russell Means | 122 minutes | Rated R

For a "realistic portrayal of the French and Indian War", this "historical adventure set in the battle-torn American colonies" doesn't stint on the "barbarism", though it's tempered by "beautiful scenery" and an "incredible score"; "truly evil villains and larger-than-life heroes" make this "wonderful realization of James Fenimore Cooper's book" "top-notch filmmaking."

L.A. Story
`20` `20` `20` `19`

1991 | Directed by Mick Jackson | With Steve Martin, Victoria Tennant, Sarah Jessica Parker | 95 minutes | Rated PG-13

"Every LA stereotype is played for laughs" in this "on-point" romantic comedy that's a "biting" if "loving put-down" of the "outrageous city" where people "really do drive down the road to get the mail"; Martin's "effortlessly intelligent" script throws "wacky" curves – and foretells the Starbucks invasion with its priceless "half-caff-triple-shot-no-foam-cappuccino" scene.

Last Picture Show, The ◑
`23` `23` `23` `22`

1971 | Directed by Peter Bogdanovich | With Timothy Bottoms, Jeff Bridges, Cybill Shepherd, Ben Johnson | 118 minutes | Rated R

This "gritty portrait of a small Texas town on the brink of extinction" is "stunningly realized" in Bogdanovich's "masterpiece" that captures the loss so well "you can practically hear the death rattle"; the "birthplace of many new stars", it features some mighty "raw performances" from its "marvelous ensemble", a "strong script" and ultra-"realistic production values"; in short, it's a "lovely" if "sad" tribute to "something intrinsically American."

☒ La Strada ✉◗⏺
`27` `28` `26` `25`

1956 | Directed by Federico Fellini | With Giulietta Masina, Anthony Quinn, Richard Basehart | 108 minutes | Not Rated

Set in a "traveling circus", Fellini's "parable of goodness thwarted by cruelty" pairs a "strongman who's all muscle and no heart" with a "peasant girl who's nothing but heart"; the "waiflike" Masina is "luminous" opposite a "surprisingly good" Quinn, and combined with "beautiful imagery" and "sad" "music that will stay with you", it's plain to see why this "masterwork" won the very first Best Foreign Film Oscar.

Last Samurai, The
`23` `23` `22` `27`

2003 | Directed by Edward Zwick | With Tom Cruise, Ken Watanabe, Tony Goldwyn | 154 minutes | Rated R

"Shogun" meets "Dances with Wolves" in this "rousing" epic, wherein a haunted, "drunken Civil War vet" goes to feudal Japan to fight the samurai and is instead taken hostage by their "honor and spirit"; while Cruise garners an equivocal appraisal ("bang-up job" vs. "doesn't cut it"), "Watanabe wildly outshines him" as the "noble, betrayed" samurai leader; despite "slow pacing" and way "too much blood", this "clash of cultures" still swells with "sweeping vistas", "beautiful cinematography" and "amazing fight scenes."

Last Seduction, The

22 | 24 | 22 | 20

1994 | Directed by John Dahl | With Linda Fiorentino, Peter Berg, Bill Pullman | 110 minutes | Rated R

"Fiorentino sizzles" as a "bad"-to-the-bone "femme fatale" in this "deliciously wicked" neo-noir crime thriller about a "very sexy" gal who rips off her husband and takes cover with a love-struck doofus; sure, it's "low budget" and there may be more than a few "holes in the plot", but "man, what a ride!"

Last Tango in Paris

17 | 20 | 15 | 19

1973 | Directed by Bernardo Bertolucci | With Marlon Brando, Maria Schneider | 129 minutes | Rated NC-17

Definitely not about dance lessons, this "evocative blend" of the "romantic" and the "erotic" presents a "graphically sexual" Parisian pas de deux between a "compelling" Brando and a limber Schneider; scenes that "seemed steamy then" may come off as "pointless" now, but Marlon's "at his best" "mumbling in two languages" and dreaming up "risqué" ways to "use butter."

Last Temptation of Christ, The

22 | 23 | 25 | 22

1988 | Directed by Martin Scorsese | With Willem Dafoe, Harvey Keitel, Barbara Hershey | 164 minutes | Rated R

"Controversial" with a big C, this "intriguing" drama "reexamines Christian faith" by portraying "one of the most humanizing perspectives on Jesus" ever filmed; of course, those "rigid on the Scriptures" consider it blasphemous (and it's still not available in certain video chains to this day), but believers say this "absorbing", "important" Scorsese drama must "be seen to be criticized."

☒ Last Waltz, The

26 | - | 20 | 26

1978 | Directed by Martin Scorsese | Documentary | With The Band | 117 minutes | Rated PG

In the running for "best concert movie of all time", this renowned documentary "captures the end of a rock 'n' roll era" in its recording of The Band's last gasp, abetted by a musical "dream team" that includes, among others, Bob Dylan, Eric Clapton, Joni Mitchell, Muddy Waters, Neil Young and Van Morrison; it's "clearly a labor of love from Scorsese" that "shouldn't be this good, but it is."

☒ Laura ◑

27 | 25 | 27 | 26

1944 | Directed by Otto Preminger | With Gene Tierney, Dana Andrews, Clifton Webb | 88 minutes | Not Rated

A "suspenseful, elegant whodunit with a twist" – the "detective falls in love with the murder victim" – this "chic" take on film noir provides plenty of "romantic goose bumps" owing to the simmering "chemistry" between the "brooding" Andrews and "exquisite" Tierney; throw in some "haunting music" and a "nicely paced" if somewhat "silly plot", and the result is "Preminger's best flick."

| | OVERALL | ACTING | STORY | PROD. |

Laurel Canyon

18 | 24 | 17 | 20

2003 | Directed by Lisa Cholodenko | With Frances McDormand, Christian Bale, Kate Beckinsale | 103 minutes | Rated R

A "dysfunctional family" is dissected in this "quirky" drama pitting an "aging hippie" record producer against her "conservative" son, who's moved back in with her; the "radiant" McDormand "carries the film" as the "hot, smart" mama, though she's up against a "predictable", "unfulfilling" story that "doesn't quite come together."

☑ Lavender Hill Mob, The ✉◗

25 | 26 | 23 | 22

1951 | Directed by Charles Crichton | With Alec Guinness, Stanley Holloway | 78 minutes | Not Rated

"Wittily whimsical", this British comic "gem" helped introduce Alec Guinness – an "actor's actor with the most expressive raised eyebrow in film" – to America; the caper-gone-awry story involving a milquetoast bank clerk who dreams up the "perfect crime" is "delightfully funny" thanks to its "wonderful" script.

☑ La Vie en Rose ✉🇫

25 | 28 | 23 | 25

2007 | Directed by Olivier Dahan | With Marion Cotillard, Sylvie Testud, Emmanuelle Seigner, Gérard Depardieu | 140 minutes | Rated PG-13

The "tumultuous life" of "tragic" French chanteuse Édith Piaf is revealed in this "engrossing" biopic that's rather "ironically titled" given "a rose whose life was all thorns"; while the "hard-to-follow" story unfolds via "constant flashbacks" and "confusing time shifts", Cotillard's "*magnifique*", Oscar-winning performance has "not a false note" and manages to "redefine the phrase 'soul music'" along the way.

L'Avventura ◗🇫

24 | 23 | 22 | 25

1961 | Directed by Michelangelo Antonioni | With Gabriele Ferzetti, Monica Vitti, Lea Massari | 145 minutes | Not Rated

A real art-house "landmark" and one of "Antonioni's most accessible" films, this "minimalist masterwork" follows a jaded playboy as he hunts for his missing mistress on a Mediterranean isle; its "stark visual and intellectual" values are hailed as "revolutionary", though literalists wading through the "ennui" come up "baffled and confused."

☑ Lawrence of Arabia ✉

29 | 28 | 27 | 29

1962 | Directed by David Lean | With Peter O'Toole, Omar Sharif, Alec Guinness | 222 minutes | Rated PG

The "biggest epic of them all", this bio of WWI British soldier T.E. Lawrence "sets the standard for large-scale filmmaking" with its "stunning" desert cinematography, "suspense by the duneful" and "stupendous cast", led by the "perfect" O'Toole; thanks to Lean's "painterly techniques", the "background is as consistently amazing as the foreground" in this "gold standard" of an Oscar magnet that "demands to be seen on the big screen."

League of Extraordinary Gentlemen, The

12 | 15 | 13 | 18

2003 | Directed by Stephen Norrington | With Sean Connery, Peta Wilson, Stuart Townsend, Shane West | 110 minutes | Rated PG-13

"Victorian literary characters" – everyone from Tom Sawyer to Captain Nemo – join forces to fight evil in this alt-universe action flick adapted from the graphic novel; although it musters enough "nifty gadgets" and "inventive" effects to make for a "typical popcorn movie", foes say the "ho-hum" "hodgepodge of heroes" is a "waste of extraordinary talent."

League of Their Own, A   20 | 20 | 22 | 20

1992 | Directed by Penny Marshall | With Geena Davis, Tom Hanks, Madonna, Lori Petty, Rosie O'Donnell | 128 minutes | Rated PG
"There's no crying in baseball", though this "nostalgic gem" about a WWII women's team has fans praising its "fantastic" ensemble cast ("even Madonna is good"); "bringing back the innocence" of simpler times, this "piece of history" might have a "sentimental epilogue", but its "feel-good" aura makes it "highly rewatchable."

Leatherheads   17 | 19 | 16 | 19

2008 | Directed by George Clooney | With George Clooney, Renée Zellweger, John Krasinski | 114 minutes | Rated PG-13
This "amusing" comedy set against the backdrop of 1920s-era pro football invites you to "lose yourself" in "throwback" period details and the screwball antics of Clooney and Zellweger, who "play well off each other" in the "Tracy/Hepburn" style; still, "pretty" eye candy isn't enough to save the "weak storyline", "overlong" running time and overall "unentertaining" result.

Leaving Las Vegas ✉   20 | 24 | 18 | 18

1995 | Directed by Mike Figgis | With Nicolas Cage, Elisabeth Shue, Julian Sands | 111 minutes | Rated R
"Disturbing", "depressing" and "painful to watch", this "tragic love story" between a "suicidal alcoholic" and a "burned-out prostitute" is still "brilliant in all aspects", leaving viewers "emotionally drained"; while giddy fans agree the "damn good" Cage "deservedly won the Oscar" for his "best work thus far", soberer sorts call this "feel-bad" flick the "ultimate downer."

Legal Eagles   17 | 19 | 18 | 18

1985 | Directed by Ivan Reitman | With Robert Redford, Debra Winger, Daryl Hannah | 116 minutes | Rated PG
Many make the case for this "whodunit romantic comedy", a "decent" enough pairing of Redford and Winger at the "top of their game" playing NYC attorneys investigating an art-world insurance scam; tougher judges rule the proceedings rather "flimsy", citing dated references ("big shoulder pads", "Daryl Hannah") that "couldn't be more '80s."

Legally Blonde   19 | 20 | 17 | 19

2001 | Directed by Robert Luketic | With Reese Witherspoon, Luke Wilson, Selma Blair, Victor Garber | 96 minutes | Rated PG-13
The near-unanimous verdict on this *Clueless*-goes-to-law-school" comedy: "cute-as-a-button" Witherspoon is "irresistible" as a "Valley Girl" "bursting the stereotype" and proving that "anyone can achieve their dream"; though most jurors decree that "even an intellectual can like" this "pink puffball of a movie", some say "there ought to be a law" against such "derivative piffle."

Legally Blonde 2: Red, White & Blonde   13 | 15 | 11 | 15

2003 | Directed by Charles Herman-Wurmfeld | With Reese Witherspoon, Sally Field, Luke Wilson | 95 minutes | Rated PG-13
The "blonde is back" with a "political agenda" in this "light" comedy sequel transposed to Capitol Hill (think *Barbie Goes to Washington*")

where Reese reprises her role as a "ditzy" young thing with a penchant for "pink accessories"; most feel that this "take-the-money-and-run rehash" is "not as cute as the first one" – "they should have quit while they were ahead."

Legend

1986 | Directed by Ridley Scott | With Tom Cruise, Mia Sara, Tim Curry, David Bennent | 94 minutes | Rated PG

"Fantasy" fanatics adore this "mythical" tale of a quest to rescue an "innocent princess" and free the "last remaining unicorn" by a group of "bumbling elves" and a "forest boy"; while it's atmospheric enough to be a "guilty pleasure" for some, "dippy" dialogue makes it a "winner in the unintentional humor" department for others.

Legends of the Fall

1994 | Directed by Edward Zwick | With Brad Pitt, Anthony Hopkins, Aidan Quinn, Julia Ormond | 133 minutes | Rated R

This "sweeping epic" set in "untamed 19th-century America" chronicles "one family's struggle in times of political turmoil" and the "moving" story of a woman "tragically passed between three brothers"; sure, a few label it "pretentious" and "no threat to the best Westerns", but there are no complaints about the "fantastic scenery" – and "nothing beats Pitt riding in on that horse!"

Lemony Snicket's
A Series of Unfortunate Events

2004 | Directed by Brad Siberling | With Jim Carrey, Liam Aiken, Emily Browning | 107 minutes | Rated PG

Brimming with "visually pleasing" sets and costumes à la "Tim Burton", this "dark yet heartwarming" orphan tale is distilled from the popular children's book series; while the kid actors fit their parts "to a tee", super-"ham" Carrey's "scenery-devouring" turn as villainous Count Olaf splits surveyors: supporters say it's "overacting at its best" but foes fume it "drags the movie down."

Lenny ◐

1974 | Directed by Bob Fosse | With Dustin Hoffman, Valerie Perrine | 111 minutes | Rated R

"Blue comic" Lenny Bruce gets the Bob Fosse scrutiny in this "knockout", "ahead-of-its-time" biopic that's alternately "depressing and funny"; the amused applaud the "virtuoso" Hoffman, "excellent" Perrine ("who knew?") and "gritty" black-and-white cinematography that perfectly "captures the kind of seedy clubs" where the "self-destructive" comedian got his start.

Leopard, The 🄵

1963 | Directed by Luchino Visconti | With Burt Lancaster, Claudia Cardinale, Alain Delon | 187 minutes | Rated PG

"Historical sweep", "stunning visuals" and "personal reverie" combine in this "magnificent period piece" from Luchino Visconti, a "sumptuous" epic set in 19th-century Italy detailing the rise of Garibaldi and subsequent "decline of the aristocracy"; despite a "sluggish pace" and mixed marks for Lancaster's title turn as an Italian prince, "awesome" production values and the finale's "lauded" ballroom sequence make this one a "must-see" for cineasts.

| | OVERALL | ACTING | STORY | PROD. |

Les Misérables
21 | 22 | 24 | 21

1998 | Directed by Bille August | With Liam Neeson, Geoffrey Rush, Uma Thurman, Claire Danes | 134 minutes | Rated PG-13

It "isn't a musical", rather a "wonderful adaptation" of the Victor Hugo "classic" about an ex-con in 19th-century France who "rises above adversity" while being pursued by a *gendarme* "bent on revenge"; "*joyeux*" admirers praise the "relatable" acting and "pretty" scenery, though stage-struck types hiss it was "better on Broadway."

Lethal Weapon
21 | 19 | 20 | 21

1987 | Directed by Richard Donner | With Mel Gibson, Danny Glover, Gary Busey | 112 minutes | Rated R

"Top-notch" action peppered with "plenty of laughs" establishes this "classic buddy" flick as the "first and best of the franchise" (three sequels and counting); as "hard-bitten, job-weary" LA detectives, Gibson and Glover are "at the top of their form" with such "tremendous chemistry" that the picture became the "model for '80s cop movies", a "classic" of the genre.

Letter, The ◑
▽ 25 | 28 | 26 | 25

1940 | Directed by William Wyler | With Bette Davis, Herbert Marshall, Gale Sondergaard | 95 minutes | Not Rated

"Bette shines" as a cool customer in torrid British Malaya in this "superb" drama based on Somerset Maugham's story of a planter's wife who goes postal on her paramour; replete with "tinkling chimes and clouded full moons", the "exotic ambiance" lends "scary impact" to the proceedings, while Davis' "incredible" chops set the "standard for judging acting to this day."

❷ Letters from Iwo Jima 🇫
27 | 27 | 26 | 28

2006 | Directed by Clint Eastwood | With Ken Watanabe, Kazunari Ninomiya, Tsuyoshi Ihara | 141 minutes | Rated R

The "incomparable" Eastwood "brilliantly" bookends *Flags of Our Fathers* with this "eloquent" foreign-language epic, dubbed "one of the best WWII films ever" for its "humane" and ultimately "heartbreaking" depiction of the Japanese during their "doomed" final days on Iwo Jima; with the "fabulous" Watanabe leading an "outstanding" cast through "beautifully filmed" but "gruesome" battle scenes, this "remarkable achievement" dares to suggest that "we are all the same."

Letter to Three Wives, A ✉◑
24 | 23 | 25 | 23

1949 | Directed by Joseph L. Mankiewicz | With Jeanne Crain, Linda Darnell, Ann Sothern, Kirk Douglas | 103 minutes | Not Rated

Three "country-club-set" women stuck on a boat trip "have an entire day to figure out" which one of their husbands "will be leaving town with the local seductress" in this "golden oldie" chick flick that "really takes you back"; Mankiewicz's "solid" script and direction both nabbed Academy Awards, leading some to label it the "witty precursor" to his later Oscar-winner, *All About Eve*.

Liar Liar
16 | 17 | 16 | 16

1997 | Directed by Tom Shadyac | With Jim Carrey, Maura Tierney, Justin Cooper | 87 minutes | Rated PG-13

Critics quibble over this "Carrey vehicle" about a lawyer compelled to tell the truth for 24 hours for the sake of his child; while some laud the star's "hilarious", "effective" performance shaded with some "poignant, non-hammy" moments, cynics nix the "not believable" (verging on "boring") story.

License to Kill

| 14 | 13 | 13 | 17 |

1989 | Directed by John Glen | With Timothy Dalton, Carey Lowell, Robert Davi, Talisa Soto | 133 minutes | Rated PG-13
Dalton's second turn as 007 is also "thankfully his last" as this "grim" Bonder bucks the franchise formula to show the normally suave spy "losing his cool" and going on a mission to "get even" with a drug lord; the violence is "too graphic" and the tone overly "mean spirited" gripe critics who lament "there's no fun in this one."

Life Aquatic with Steve Zissou, The

| 16 | 19 | 14 | 19 |

2004 | Directed by Wes Anderson | With Bill Murray, Owen Wilson, Cate Blanchett, Anjelica Huston | 119 minutes | Rated R
"Quirk"-meister Anderson captains this "esoteric" undersea "parody of Jacques Cousteau" (and *Moby Dick*) that's awash in "droll" humor, "visual candy" and "great actors", chiefly the "brilliant" Murray; all told, what's "imaginative filmmaking" to some feels like "flat" "self-indulgence" to a majority who can't fathom "what all the fuss is about."

Lifeboat ◑

| 25 | 26 | 25 | 22 |

1944 | Directed by Alfred Hitchcock | With Tallulah Bankhead, William Bendix, Walter Slezak | 96 minutes | Not Rated
"Can a one-set movie hold your attention?": this "fascinating Hitchcock" war-era thriller does, providing "more drama per square inch", since the "entire picture takes place in a small lifeboat"; among the "bickering crew of castaways", Bankhead is "superb, dahling", but blink and you'll miss the director's "inspired" cameo.

☑ Life Is Beautiful ✉ 🄵

| 27 | 27 | 27 | 25 |

1998 | Directed by Roberto Benigni | With Roberto Benigni, Nicoletta Braschi | 118 minutes | Rated PG-13
Simultaneously "heart-wrenching" and "uplifting", this story about an Italian family's attempt to shelter their son from the Holocaust is a "bittersweet fable about the triumph of the human spirit"; Oscar-winner Benigni provides an "emotional roller-coaster ride" with some "inspired comedic" touches, and though some "uncomfortable" viewers suggest a "trivialization" of a very serious subject, most agree "if you don't shed a tear, you're not human."

Life of Brian

| 23 | 21 | 23 | 20 |

1979 | Directed by Terry Jones | With Monty Python | 94 minutes | Rated R
"Profane, sacrilegious and really funny", this "hysterical" "cult classic" about a Holy Land sad sack mistaken for the Messiah is "as bitingly original a spoof as has ever been made" and "probably one of God's favorites"; only "Monty Python at their finest" could "get away with" the final scene that "sends you off singing 'Always Look on the Bright Side of Life.'"

Life of David Gale

| 21 | 24 | 22 | 20 |

2003 | Directed by Alan Parker | With Kevin Spacey, Kate Winslet, Laura Linney | 130 minutes | Rated R
Expect a "great shocker at the end" of this "compelling" capital punishment drama, "but getting there has some pretty dull moments";

"surprised" surveyors "love the twists and turns", while those who "figured things out ahead of time" find the story "predictable" and "contrived", but "interesting nonetheless."

Like Water for Chocolate 🇫

`25` `24` `25` `25`

1993 | Directed by Alfonso Arau | With Lumi Cavazos, Marco Leonardi | 123 minutes | Rated R

"Ahh, food and sex" make a "lip-smacking" combination in this "mouth-watering" Mexican "foodie classic" that serves up an "eccentric" love story that's "as pleasing to the eye as it is to the palate"; "deliciously true to the novel", it offers "magical realism at its best" and, "like a warm dessert", leaves one feeling so "content and hopeful" that many show up for "another helping."

Lili ⊘

`24` `24` `23` `24`

1953 | Directed by Charles Walters | With Leslie Caron, Mel Ferrer, Jean-Pierre Aumont | 81 minutes | Rated G

Walking a tightrope between "deep whimsy" and "endearing" drama, this ringside look at an "innocent" orphan follows "ultimate waif" Caron as she joins the circus; enlivened by "one song" and some occasional dancing, the story is almost "too cute", but an "outstanding" cast ensures it will "turn on the tears every time."

Z Lilies of the Field ✉◗

`25` `26` `24` `23`

1963 | Directed by Ralph Nelson | With Sidney Poitier, Lilia Skala, Stanley Adams | 94 minutes | Not Rated

With his "flawless" performance in this "simple" tale about a handyman who helps refugee nuns build a chapel, Poitier became the first African-American to win a lead-role Oscar and also helped "open up racial dialogue" in the Civil Rights era; admirers hail it as a "sweet story" told with "heart and charm" that delivers a "lesson in dignity and trust."

Lilo & Stitch

`23` `-` `22` `24`

2002 | Directed by Chris Sanders, Dean DeBlois | Animated | 85 minutes | Rated PG

"Different from the usual Disney stuff", this "adorable" animated tale features a "spunky" orphaned Hawaiian girl who adopts a "lovable" blue 'dog' that turns out to be a space alien; it's a "heartwarming story" with "great life lessons" about "finding your place in the world", as well as "laughs from beginning to end" and an Elvis-infused soundtrack; "beautiful watercolor backdrops" give the film its "distinctive look."

Limelight ◗

`24` `25` `22` `23`

1952 | Directed by Charles Chaplin | With Charles Chaplin, Claire Bloom, Buster Keaton, Nigel Bruce | 137 minutes | Rated G

"Chaplin's last great film", this "poignant" look at a British ballerina and a music hall clown draws mixed responses; foes call it "dated corn" and protest its "overstated" "self-indulgence", but fans counter it's "sensitive" stuff, and certainly worth watching to see "two giants of the silent film era [Charlie and Buster Keaton] on-screen together."

Z Lion in Winter, The ✉

`28` `29` `27` `26`

1968 | Directed by Anthony Harvey | With Peter O'Toole, Katharine Hepburn | 134 minutes | Rated PG

Hepburn and O'Toole give "performances so brilliant your eyes will hurt" as "two titans battling each other and history" in this "intelligent, delicious" drama that reigns as "one of the best historical films ever made"; indeed, this "masterful" look at Henry II and Eleanor of Aquitaine (the original "dysfunctional royal family") is so "superb" that it earned Kate her third Oscar, as well as statuettes for its "sparkling" screenplay and score.

☑ Lion King, The   25 | - | 25 | 27

1994 | Directed by Roger Allers, Rob Minkoff | Animated | 89 minutes | Rated G
Hakuna Matata!: this "crowning achievement" garners roars of approval as one of "Disney's best" thanks to its "breakthrough animation techniques", "toe-tapping" music and "exceptional voice characterizations by Matthew Broderick and Jeremy Irons"; though this "heartwarming" tale about an exiled lion cub (sort of the "same story as *Bambi*") is "touching" and often "comedic", the film has some bona fide "scary moments" and "may be too intense" for smaller fry.

Little Big Man   24 | 25 | 24 | 23

1970 | Directed by Arthur Penn | With Dustin Hoffman, Faye Dunaway, Chief Dan George | 147 minutes | Rated PG
A "rousing" Wild West "saga", this "memorable period piece" concerns a "Forrest Gump-like" character with a knack for popping up at "famous historical moments"; plaudits go to its "engrossing blend of humor and drama" and "great" performances by George and Hoffman ("truly the man of 1,000 faces") - indeed, it's "one of the best looks at Native Americans" ever portrayed in moviedom.

Little Caesar ◑   24 | 26 | 23 | 22

1931 | Directed by Mervyn LeRoy | With Edward G. Robinson, Douglas Fairbanks Jr., Glenda Farrell | 79 minutes | Not Rated
"Crime doesn't pay" in this "seminal" gangster flicker, a "fictionalized" version of the Al Capone story starring "true Hollywood tough guy" Robinson, who brings some "Greek tragedy" to the role of a "moiderous bum"; it's a "gritty", "fast-paced" ride that's best remembered for its immortal last line: "mother of mercy, is this the end of Rico?"

Little Children   24 | 27 | 23 | 23

2006 | Directed by Todd Field | With Kate Winslet, Patrick Wilson, Jennifer Connelly, Jackie Earle Haley | 130 minutes | Rated R
"Brilliant" Winslet and "easy-on-the-eyes" Wilson play "desperate" stay-at-home parents consumed by "forbidden attraction" in this "*American Beauty*"-esque study of suburban "infidelity" and "discontent"; though a "pedophilia" subplot adds a decidedly "dark" touch, Haley's "standout" supporting turn as a "creepy sex offender you actually feel bad for" drives home the picture's "powerful message about the consequences of your actions."

☑ Little Foxes, The ◑   26 | 28 | 26 | 25

1941 | Directed by William Wyler | With Bette Davis, Herbert Marshall, Teresa Wright, Dan Duryea | 116 minutes | Not Rated
All the "power" of Lillian Hellman's "bitter little" stage drama is apparent in this "excellent" film adaptation via William Wyler, a showcase for "Bette at her bitchy best" as the mercenary missus in a shifty Southern family; the sly scheming and deadly betrayal make for such a bang-up "lesson in acting" that many wonder "why don't they make movies like this anymore."

Little Mermaid, The   24 | - | 23 | 25

1989 | Directed by Ron Clements, John Musker | Animated |
82 minutes | Rated G

This "first of the great second wave of Disney classics" manages to "hold its own against *Cinderella* and *Snow White*", what with its delightful cartoon "critters", "witty dialogue" and "upbeat", Oscar-winning music that "made animation sing again"; sure, feminists discern a "sexist message" ("why does the woman have to change for the man?"), but in the end "how could you not love this adorable redheaded mermaid?"

Little Miss Sunshine ✉   24 | 26 | 24 | 23

2006 | Directed by Jonathan Dayton, Valerie Faris | With Abigail Breslin, Greg Kinnear, Steve Carell, Toni Collette, Alan Arkin | 101 minutes | Rated R

"Wackiness" abounds when a "totally dysfunctional family" hops aboard a sputtering VW van en route to a beauty pageant in this "hilarious" but "dark"-edged road-trip comedy that's akin to an "indie version of *National Lampoon's Vacation*"; harnessing the talents of a "fine" ensemble cast – Carell is "fabulous", Breslin a "real find" and Arkin a "foul-mouthed treasure" – it's topped off with a "memorable" dance sequence that will "leave you squirming in your seat."

Little Princess, A   24 | 22 | 25 | 25

1995 | Directed by Alfonso Cuarón | With Liesel Matthews, Eleanor Bron | 97 minutes | Rated G

"Shirley Temple's version has nothing on" this "sumptuous", "perfectly played" family fable of a "pampered" boarding-school lass with "mystical" leanings who goes from "riches to rags and back" after her dragoon dad is declared dead during WWI; though it attracts less than the "attention it deserves", loyalists label it a "top-flight tearjerker."

Little Shop of Horrors   19 | 19 | 20 | 21

1986 | Directed by Frank Oz | With Rick Moranis, Ellen Greene, Steve Martin | 94 minutes | Rated PG-13

If "campy" "sci-fi musicals" ring your bell, this "twisted" tale about a boy, a girl and a "smart-ass, man-eating plant" (based on an old Roger Corman B-movie) "ranks right up there with *The Rocky Horror Picture Show* as a cult classic"; credit the "great cast" and "humorously dark score" for the ensuing "goofy fun"; most "priceless" moment: Martin's "sadistic dentist" treating "masochist patient" Bill Murray.

Little Women   21 | 23 | 24 | 21

1994 | Directed by Gillian Armstrong | With Winona Ryder, Susan Sarandon | 115 minutes | Rated PG

Surveyors split on this "feminist" adaptation of Louisa May Alcott's classic novel about a Civil War–era family: partisans of George Cukor's 1933 version dismiss this remake as "unnecessary", harrumphing that "Ryder can't compare to Katharine Hepburn", yet others swear it's "worth watching" for Sarandon's performance alone; still its "great message" – about a "family loving each other no matter what" – is "well done."

Live and Let Die   19 | 17 | 20 | 21

1973 | Directed by Guy Hamilton | With Roger Moore, Jane Seymour, Yaphet Kotto | 119 minutes | Rated PG

Expect "beautiful women, fast cars", "snakes, voodoo and Yaphet Kotto" in this "exotic" James Bond caper set in the Caribbean and the

| | OVERALL | ACTING | STORY | PROD. |

"sultry South"; "nonstop" action sequences ("particularly the bayou boat chase"), "humor that's shaken (not stirred)" and Moore's first 007 impersonation make it worth watching – even if Sean Connery loyalists label it the "beginning of the decline."

Live Free or Die Hard
20 | **18** | **18** | **23**

2007 | Directed by Len Wiseman | With Bruce Willis, Timothy Olyphant, Justin Long, Maggie Q | 130 minutes | Rated PG-13

"Gun fights, car chases" and "pithy one-liners" whiz by in rapid-fire succession in this "loud", "fast-paced" fourth installment of the *Die Hard* franchise; Bruce may be "older and balder" this time, but still can dodge "thousands of bullets" at a clip while taking on whole "platoons of cyber-terrorists" bent on bringing on the "apocalypse"; be prepared to "suspend your belief in reality."

Ⓩ Lives of Others, The ✉Ⓕ
28 | **28** | **28** | **27**

2007 | Directed by Florian Henckel von Donnersmarck | With Ulrich Mühe, Martina Gedeck, Sebastian Koch | 137 minutes | Rated R

A "fascinating yet chilling" peek "behind the Iron Curtain", this "near-perfect" drama exhibits the "stifling of artistic expression" in "pre-glasnost" East Germany, a "real-life police state" where "Big Brother" is always "listening in"; winner of the Oscar for Best Foreign Language Film, it features a "universally excellent" cast and its "suspenseful" script, highlighting the "best and worst of humanity", "keeps you guessing until the last scene."

Living Daylights, The
14 | **14** | **14** | **18**

1987 | Directed by John Glen | With Timothy Dalton, Maryam d'Abo, Jeroen Krabbé, Joe Don Baker | 130 minutes | Rated PG

There's heated debate about Timothy Dalton's first stab at James Bond, with fans saying his "underrated", "hard-edged" performance is "very true to Ian Fleming", while foes fume his "brooding", "gritty" take does the character a "disservice" (007 "doesn't have to be politically correct"); as for the plot, it's the usual over-the-top thrill ride involving a defecting Russian general, an American arms dealer and a drop-dead gorgeous cellist/assassin.

Ⓩ Local Hero
26 | **24** | **26** | **23**

1983 | Directed by Bill Forsyth | With Burt Lancaster, Peter Riegert, Peter Capaldi | 111 minutes | Rated PG

"The little people triumph over the money people" in this "understated but brilliant" comedy contrasting the differences between a "quaint Scottish town" and the "corporate world"; its "engaging characters", "quirky" storyline and "great soundtrack" make for such "bighearted", "whimsical" fun that many argue it "deserves a larger following."

Lock, Stock and Two Smoking Barrels
23 | **22** | **25** | **23**

1999 | Directed by Guy Ritchie | With Jason Flemyng, Dexter Fletcher, Nick Moran | 105 minutes | Rated R

"First-time director" Ritchie does a "brilliant job co-opting every gangster flick cliché" in this "violent but riveting" thriller that's a "Cockney" take on *Pulp Fiction*; agreed, it's "hard to understand the accents", but the "acting, setting and soundtrack are dead-on" and "super plot surprises" abound; all in all, this "fun romp with guns" is "lean", mean and "wonderfully produced."

Lolita ◐

24 | 24 | 24 | 23

1962 | Directed by Stanley Kubrick | With James Mason, Sue Lyon, Shelley Winters, Peter Sellers | 152 minutes | Not Rated

Though this "fine adaptation of the Nabokov classic" might be somewhat "sanitized" ("it was made in 1962, after all"), it's still "slyly dirty" enough for its very adult subject, a middle-aged man's obsession with a barely teenaged girl; though ageists argue Lyon is "too old" for the title role, there still are plenty of "choice moments" supplied by an "extremely funny" Sellers and Winters, who "gives the performance of her life."

⚡ Lone Star

25 | 25 | 25 | 22

1996 | Directed by John Sayles | With Kris Kristofferson, Matthew McConaughey, Chris Cooper | 135 minutes | Rated R

Director Sayles' "overlooked masterpiece" is a "flawless murder mystery that digs deep into the American psyche" and "takes a hard look at race relations"; following the discovery of a buried skeleton in a small Texas town, the plot goes through "more twists and turns than the Rio Grande" but still "works on multiple levels" as it "seamlessly interweaves multiple characters" – and that "ending will make your jaw drop."

Longest Day, The ◐

24 | 20 | 25 | 26

1962 | Directed by Ken Annakin, Andrew Marton et al | With John Wayne, Rod Steiger | 180 minutes | Rated G

As far as "war-as-spectacle" epics go, this "sweeping" saga of the Normandy invasion sets the "standard by which all others are measured"; D-day devotees dig the "superb dedication to detail" and "all-star cast" that "really gets into their characters" thanks to a script that "includes the point of view of everyone involved"; still, foes snipe "too many cameos" turn it into a "cattle call."

Longest Yard, The

17 | 15 | 18 | 16

1974 | Directed by Robert Aldrich | With Burt Reynolds, Eddie Albert, Michael Conrad | 121 minutes | Rated R

A "guy's movie" Hall of Famer, this "prison football comedy" stars Reynolds as a pro quarterback sent to the big house only to "lead a Heisman-quality cast" of roughneck convicts in a game against the guards; scoring many "memorable lines", it has "Mean Machine" mavens ruling it "arguably the best" pigskin pic ever.

Longest Yard, The

17 | 16 | 17 | 18

2005 | Directed by Peter Segal | With Adam Sandler, Chris Rock, Burt Reynolds, Nelly | 113 minutes | Rated PG-13

A "decent remake of an already good film", this "mildly amusing" sports comedy about a prison football team "rehashes" the original, adding a "more modern soundtrack" and "cameos galore"; still, foes fret this "formulaic" flick "fumbles on every level", starting with Sandler, who's "unbelievable as a quarterback" – "once a waterboy, always a waterboy."

Long Kiss Goodnight, The

19 | 19 | 19 | 20

1996 | Directed by Renny Harlin | With Geena Davis, Samuel L. Jackson, Craig Bierko | 120 minutes | Rated R

"Entertaining" intrigue with a "female lead" propels this "underrated" spy thriller starring Davis as an "amnesiac assassin" who takes it on the lam with private eye Jackson when her memory begins to return;

"yup, the storyline's far-fetched" and the dialogue "weak", but no one cares given the abundant "badass" action sequences.

Longtime Companion
23 | 25 | 25 | 21

1990 | Directed by Norman René | With Campbell Scott, Mary-Louise Parker, Bruce Davison | 100 minutes | Rated R

"Love and heartbreak" are the themes of this "groundbreaking" film that follows seven gay men throughout a "specific time and place": '80s Manhattan during the "first wave of AIDS"; "just as devastating today as when first released", it "gives legitimacy" to a former "forbidden subject" but "doesn't pander or trivialize the issues" thanks to "heartfelt" acting, notably the "standout" Davison and "up-and-coming" Parker.

Looking for Mr. Goodbar ∅
18 | 21 | 19 | 18

1977 | Directed by Richard Brooks | With Diane Keaton, Tuesday Weld, Richard Gere | 135 minutes | Rated R

Powered by Keaton's "brilliant" turn as a "sexually repressed" teacher by day who "trolls the bars by night", this "sobering tale of '70s promiscuity" is a "dark primer for single women" that "sends chills down your spine" – with a "gruesome ending" delivered "like a sledgehammer upside the head."

Look Who's Talking
16 | 15 | 17 | 16

1989 | Directed by Amy Heckerling | With John Travolta, Kirstie Alley, George Segal, Olympia Dukakis | 93 minutes | Rated PG-13

This "cutesy" comedy is tied to a "corny gimmick", a "smart-aleck baby" delivering "witty comments" on life "from fetushood to toddler" (voiced by Bruce Willis); while would-be parents Travolta and Alley make for a fairly "engaging" match, fans of this "guilty pleasure" disown the "unfunny" franchise it gave birth to.

Lord of the Flies ❶
23 | 21 | 25 | 20

1963 | Directed by Peter Brook | With James Aubrey, Tom Chapin, Hugh Edwards | 90 minutes | Not Rated

The last word in youth gone wild, this "powerful" take on novelist William Golding's "modern classic" finds a pack of marooned British schoolboys slipping into "disturbing" behavior as barbarity overtakes breeding; the "realistic" style makes for an "unsettling" drama with bonus "social commentary buried within", though some savage the "incompetent acting" and sniff "read the book instead."

Lord of the Rings, The
15 | - | 22 | 16

1978 | Directed by Ralph Bakshi | Animated | 132 minutes | Rated PG

Graphics guru Bakshi's animated take on Tolkien is no "Fritz the Hobbit": it's "true to the books" in presenting the elfin Frodo's "epic" face-off with the forces of evil (even if it's "too bad" the "truncated storyline" "breaks off halfway" into the trilogy); but others say that this "muddled" "travesty" often "looks ridiculous" – "thank God for Peter Jackson."

⊠ Lord of the Rings: The Fellowship of the Ring
27 | 25 | 27 | 29

2001 | Directed by Peter Jackson | With Elijah Wood, Ian McKellen, Viggo Mortensen, Sean Astin, Liv Tyler | 178 minutes | Rated PG-13

This "enthralling", "true-to-the-book" retelling of Tolkien's classic epic "transcends the genre" and "sets the benchmark for fantasy films to come" with its "lovingly crafted" visualization of Middle Earth; despite a somewhat "slow beginning", "three hours of brilliant bliss" ensue that are "exhilaratingly" perfect, "right down to the hairy Hobbit feet."

☒ Lord of the Rings: The Return of the King ✉

28 26 27 29

2003 | Directed by Peter Jackson | With Elijah Wood, Ian McKellen, Viggo Mortensen, Sean Astin, Liv Tyler | 201 minutes | Rated PG-13

Jackson "should be knighted" for this "history-making", Oscar-grabbing finale to the "superlative trilogy", a "paean to the goodness of good" in the Fellowship's "united allegiance against evil"; it "lives up to the hoopla" from its two "faithfully rendered" predecessors thanks to "mythic sweep and grandeur" and a "cast obviously devoted to the picture"; in sum, this "masterpiece" is a "cinematic monument" to Tolkien's original fantasy, capped by a "long ending" that nonetheless draws a "big round of applause."

☒ Lord of the Rings: The Two Towers

27 25 26 29

2002 | Directed by Peter Jackson | With Elijah Wood, Ian McKellen, Viggo Mortensen, Sean Astin, Liv Tyler | 179 minutes | Rated PG-13

There's "much less exposition" and much "more testosterone" in the second "gripping" installment of the Tolkien trilogy, which "starts right where the last one ended"; grab a "comfortable chair" and brace yourself for three hours of "flawless special effects" ("Gollum rocks"), "wonderful" acting by "hot guys", "epic battles the likes of which have never before been captured on celluloid" and an "amazing storyline" that really "does justice" to the book.

Lord of War

18 21 19 20

2005 | Directed by Andrew Niccol | With Nicolas Cage, Jared Leto, Ethan Hawke, Bridget Moynahan | 122 minutes | Rated R

"Timely" and "all too true", this "sobering" drama–cum–"modern-day morality tale" delineates the "underworld arms trade" as seen through the eyes of an "international gun dealer" consumed by "callousness" (the "pitch-perfect" Cage); Nic's "voice-over narration" underscores the filmmakers' "strong viewpoint", though a few take aim at the "preachy", "totally depressing" windup; P.S. don't-miss moment: the "awesome", history-of-a-bullet opening sequence.

Lost Boys, The

21 18 20 20

1987 | Directed by Joel Schumacher | With Jason Patric, Corey Haim, Kiefer Sutherland, Corey Feldman | 97 minutes | Rated R

"Vamp it up" with yesteryear's "tween heartthrobs" in this "hip horror flick" grafted onto a "teen comedy", featuring "bad-boy Keifer" and the Coreys "during their heyday" playing undead "children of the night" "running amok" in a California hamlet; with its "unexpected humor" and "killer" '80s soundtrack, it's the "cult classic" that "made vampire flicks cool."

Lost Highway

16 18 15 19

1997 | Directed by David Lynch | With Bill Pullman, Patricia Arquette, Balthazar Getty | 135 minutes | Rated R

"Something different with a capital D", this "stylish nightmare" from David Lynch relates the "surreal" story of a husband's "journey into madness and jealousy"; hard-core fans find it "beautifully shot" and "totally addictive", but most everyone else says the "convoluted", "weird-with-a-side-dish-of-weird" plot "doesn't make a damn bit of sense."

Lost Horizon ◑ | 25 | 24 | 26 | 22

1937 | Directed by Frank Capra | With Ronald Colman, Jane Wyatt, Margo, Sam Jaffe | 138 minutes | Not Rated

A "nostalgic reminder of Hollywood's Golden Age", this "moving" adaptation of James Hilton's best-seller still "casts a spell" thanks to an "irresistible" conceit, the utopia known as "Shangri-la"; sure, this "fairy tale" of a picture may seem rather "quaint" and "dated" now, but Colman's performance is "as contemporary as if it were made today."

Lost in America | 20 | 20 | 21 | 17

1985 | Directed by Albert Brooks | With Albert Brooks, Julie Hagerty, Garry Marshall | 91 minutes | Rated R

Brooks' "seriously underrated" satire about a yuppie couple who chuck it all and hit the road is dryly "hilarious" filmmaking boasting what may be the "funniest first 45 minutes in movie history"; though a few lost souls protest the "premise doesn't quite get there", the majority reports the "situations, characters and jokes are all in sync."

Lost in Translation ✉ | 21 | 24 | 19 | 21

2003 | Directed by Sofia Coppola | With Bill Murray, Scarlett Johansson | 102 minutes | Rated R

"Not much happens" in this "poignant" look at a young woman and a "has-been" movie star who meet out of "boredom and insomnia" in a Tokyo hotel; admirers say it's "eminently watchable" thanks to "talented" writer/director Coppola (it must "run in the family") as well as the "surprising chemistry" between the "world-weary" Murray and "enigmatic" Johansson; still, "baffled" viewers want to know "what the hoopla is all about" – and especially "what he whispers at the end"; best scene: the "Suntory commercial."

Lost Weekend, The ✉◑ | 25 | 27 | 24 | 22

1945 | Directed by Billy Wilder | With Ray Milland, Jane Wyman, Phillip Terry | 101 minutes | Not Rated

"Strong" stuff served neat, this "smart", sobering drama depicts the "terrifying inner world" of an alcoholic who "lives only" for the bottle, starring Milland in a "top-shelf", Oscar-winning turn as a barfly on a bender careening from double bourbons to detox to the d.t.'s; some maintain it "should be required viewing" at AA meetings – it's the "scariest movie of all time if you drink."

Love Actually | 22 | 23 | 21 | 22

2003 | Directed by Richard Curtis | With Hugh Grant, Liam Neeson, Colin Firth, Laura Linney, Emma Thompson, Alan Rickman, Keira Knightley, Bill Nighy | 135 minutes | Rated R

"Intertwining" vignettes of lovesick Londoners meeting up "cute" and breaking up "sad" form the core of this "walk-away-smiling" romantic comedy; while Brit chick flick fans are "delighted" by the "great ensemble" with a special nod to the habitually "charming" Grant, those finding it "not that good actually" zap its "saccharine", "scattershot" script as barely "tolerable fluff."

Love Bug, The
18 | 15 | 16 | 17

1969 | Directed by Robert Stevenson | With Dean Jones, Michele Lee, Buddy Hackett | 107 minutes | Rated G

"They don't get much sillier" than this "imaginative" Disney "oldie" about Herbie, a "sweet"-talking VW bug that supplies boomers with plenty of "fond memories"; it still "stands the test of time" well enough for it to be a perennial "rainy-afternoon" rental.

Love in the Afternoon
24 | 25 | 21 | 22

1957 | Directed by Billy Wilder | With Gary Cooper, Audrey Hepburn, Maurice Chevalier | 130 minutes | Not Rated

An "old-fashioned" romance set in "misty" Paree, this "witty" Wilder "treat" stars Coop as an "American playboy" who goes "mad with desire" for the much-younger Hepburn; if the "age difference" between the "odd couple" might seem "unspannable", the "bright cast" shows lots of "chemistry" – "isn't love grand?"

Love Is a Many-Splendored Thing
22 | 23 | 22 | 21

1955 | Directed by Henry King | With Jennifer Jones, William Holden | 102 minutes | Not Rated

"What drama! what heartbreak!" sigh admirers of this "classic" romantic "tearjerker", an "ahead-of-its-time" tale about an affair between a "liberated" Eurasian woman and a conflicted American war correspondent; ok, it's a little "soppy" and "Jones isn't believable as a Eurasian", but the "breathtaking" Hong Kong scenery and "memorable", Oscar-winning theme song "make the whole thing worth it."

Love Song for Bobby Long, A
19 | 23 | 19 | 19

2004 | Directed by Shainee Gabel | With John Travolta, Scarlett Johansson, Gabriel Macht | 119 minutes | Rated R

Travolta pours all he's got into his "fearless" performance as an "unlikable", "aging drunk" forced to live with a teen "misfit" in this "soapy" drama set in N'Awlins; filmed at a "slow" tempo that intensifies the overall "depressing vibe", the picture ultimately splits surveyors: it's either a "lovable sleeper" or a "tedious" soporific.

Love Story
19 | 18 | 20 | 18

1970 | Directed by Arthur Hiller | With Ali MacGraw, Ryan O'Neal, Ray Milland | 99 minutes | Rated PG

"Get out the Kleenex" – this "three-hanky chick flick" about a "rich boy, a poor girl" and an incurable disease is applauded for its "adorable" leads, the "cute" O'Neal and "divine" MacGraw; critics of this "shameless" "schmaltz"-fest sneer that "love means having to say you're sorry every five minutes", but even they admit "35 years of soggy-eyed females can't be wrong."

Love! Valour! Compassion!
21 | 24 | 23 | 22

1997 | Directed by Joe Mantello | With Jason Alexander, Stephen Spinella, John Glover | 108 minutes | Rated R

Adapted from Terrence McNally's "Broadway smash", this "well-acted" dramedy follows eight gay men over three weekends in the country; alternately "funny, touching and sad", it's a "social commentary about the early years of the AIDS epidemic", but the compassionate claim it's "only peripherally about homosexuality" and really more about "the power of the human heart."

Lucky Number Slevin
21 | 22 | 22 | 21

2006 | Directed by Paul McGuigan | With Josh Hartnett, Morgan Freeman, Ben Kingsley, Lucy Liu, Bruce Willis | 109 minutes | Rated R

Tapping a "pulp vein" rich in "snappy dialogue" and "body bag"-stuffing violence, this "enjoyable" gangster thriller features a roster of "top-shelf" talents playing "juicy roles"; factor in a "cerebral", mistaken-identity storyline with "lots of twists and turns", and there's lots to "hold your interest" – even if the payoff reminds some of *The Usual Suspects*."

Lust for Life
23 | 25 | 23 | 23

1956 | Directed by Vincente Minnelli | With Kirk Douglas, Anthony Quinn, James Donald | 122 minutes | Rated PG

Kirk's "at his most tormented" as "revolutionary painter" Vincent van Gogh in this "powerful" biopic canvassing the "disturbed" Dutchman's "complex" life, along with his stormy friendship with Paul Gauguin (the Oscar-winning Quinn); a "colorful, vibrant" production filmed at many of the "original locations" where the master worked, it immortalizes a "genius" who was "never appreciated in his lifetime."

⚡ M ⊙🅵
26 | 26 | 26 | 23

1933 | Directed by Fritz Lang | With Peter Lorre, Ellen Widmann, Gustaf Gründgens | 99 minutes | Not Rated

Still "frightening seven decades later", this crime thriller features Lorre as a "nervous, sweaty little child killer" in a "riveting" performance that evokes "horror and pity at the same time"; set in "'30s Berlin" "plunging headlong into fascism", it's known for its "expressionistic" camerawork and montage sequences that "set the benchmark for film editing."

MacArthur
21 | 24 | 22 | 21

1977 | Directed by Joseph Sargent | With Gregory Peck, Dan O'Herlihy, Ed Flanders | 130 minutes | Rated PG

"You really believe he's the General" claim fans of Peck's "superb" work in this profile of Douglas MacArthur, the soldier/politician whose "extraordinary career" and famously "imperious manner" made him "one of the most iconic – and flawed – figures of the 20th century"; though a "10-hour miniseries" might better serve the subject, this "solid" effort remains an "insightful" window into a "fascinating" life.

Machinist, The
20 | 25 | 20 | 19

2004 | Directed by Brad Anderson | With Christian Bale, Jennifer Jason Leigh | 102 minutes | Rated R

The "phenomenal" Bale "lost 60 pounds" to play a "troubled blue-collar worker" in this "disturbing" drama about a "skeletal" amnesiac whose "eerie" hallucinations and "repressed memories" make for really "creepy" viewing; the "bleak" atmospherics and "unnerving physical transformation" leave many "chilled to the bone", though skeptics cite "more mood than substance" here.

Madagascar
21 | - | 19 | 24

2005 | Directed by Eric Darnell, Tom McGrath | Animated | 86 minutes | Rated PG

"NYC zoo animals" fly the coop and end up "in the wilds of Africa" in this "wholesome" animated feature rendered in "eye-popping colors", and with enough "zaniness for kids" (and "'in' jokes" for adults) to keep viewers of all ages happy; sure, its "uneven" storyline eventually gets "tangled" in its own nets, so it's a good thing those "penguins steal the show."

⚡ Mad Hot Ballroom
27 | - | 25 | 25

2005 | Directed by Marilyn Agrelo | Documentary | 105 minutes | Rated PG
"If you're not moved, you might need an EKG" declare enthusiasts hot on this "sweet 'n' sassy documentary" about the NYC public schools' "annual ballroom dance contest", an "uplifting" "*Spellbound*-meets-*Fame*" account of "winsome" fifth graders of diverse backgrounds training to "swing and tango"; besides "making you laugh and cheer", it also pounds the parquet for "arts in the schools."

Mad Max
20 | 17 | 19 | 19

1980 | Directed by George Miller | With Mel Gibson, Joanne Samuel, Hugh Keays-Byrne | 93 minutes | Rated R
"Raw" and thrillingly "underproduced", this "seminal" tale of "post-apocalyptic", "Darwinian doom" is one of the "all-time great low-budget fantasies", done with "conviction and style"; it pits a "fabulous Mel in tight black leather" against some "truly bad bad guys" and is so "ultimately effective" that it spawned two sequels (though connoisseurs claim the first is "the best").

Mad Max Beyond Thunderdome
17 | 16 | 17 | 21

1985 | Directed by George Miller, George Ogilvie | With Mel Gibson, Tina Turner, Bruce Spence | 107 minutes | Rated R
For "early Mel Gibson" ("before he went nuts"), check out this final installment in the Mad Max trilogy about a "post-apocalyptic world" where the survivors are entertained in Thunderdome, a latter-day blood-and-circuses arena; sure, the pace is "fast", the mayhem "inventive", the villains "inspired" and Tina simply "the best", yet many still say "like most Part Threes", this one's "disappointing."

Madness of King George, The
22 | 26 | 23 | 24

1994 | Directed by Nicholas Hytner | With Nigel Hawthorne, Helen Mirren, Ian Holm | 107 minutes | Rated PG-13
"Insightful" bio of the "mad, irascible" British monarch who, among other things, lost the American colonies; though "history buffs" declare the "accuracy is debatable", there's no debate about Hawthorne's "superb" performance (that "almost makes George III sympathetic"), not that it's "visually stunning", with an Art Direction Oscar as proof.

Magdalene Sisters, The
25 | 26 | 26 | 23

2003 | Directed by Peter Mullan | With Anne-Marie Duff, Dorothy Duffy, Eileen Walsh, Nora-Jane Noone | 119 minutes | Rated R
"Quite an eye-opener", this Irish "exposé" tells the true story of young women "deemed immoral" and committed to asylums to "pay for their sins" "in the name of religion"; its "documentary-like style" and strong cast of "little-known actors" make for "raw" filmmaking that "stays in your mind."

⚡ Magnificent Ambersons, The ❶∅
25 | 26 | 22 | 24

1942 | Directed by Orson Welles | With Joseph Cotten, Dolores Costello, Anne Baxter, Agnes Moorehead | 88 minutes | Not Rated
"In the shadow of *Citizen Kane*" stands Welles' "visually brilliant" but oft-"overlooked" follow-up, this "turn-of-the-century" drama detailing

the "downfall of an Indiana family" whose spoiled scion can't "keep up with the times"; some magnificence is lost due to the "damage done by the studio's re-editing", but admirers say this "90% masterpiece" is still "brilliant filmmaking."

Magnificent Obsession
22 | 22 | 21 | 22

1954 | Directed by Douglas Sirk | With Jane Wyman, Rock Hudson, Barbara Rush, Agnes Moorehead | 108 minutes | Not Rated

"Tissue anyone?" – those yearning to "drown in suds" tout this "ultimate soap opera", the "twisted" story of a jaded playboy's attempts to win the heart of a blind woman whom he's wronged; while the "florid acting", "melodramatic" goings-on and "eye-popping color" lead cynics to dub it *Magnificent Hokum*, analytical types say its "value lies in what it tells us about the times in which it was filmed."

Z Magnificent Seven, The
26 | 22 | 25 | 23

1960 | Directed by John Sturges | With Yul Brynner, Steve McQueen, Eli Wallach, Charles Bronson | 128 minutes | Not Rated

"Gunfighter cool" is alive and well in this "magnificent remake" of *The Seven Samurai* that "stands on its own" despite being "translated into a Western" and cast with "big stars of the '60s"; those who "never tire of watching it" "enjoy the adventure", "love the score" and attempt to "memorize the dialogue" that's become "fodder for countless movie trivia questions."

Magnolia
20 | 23 | 18 | 21

1999 | Directed by Paul Thomas Anderson | With Tom Cruise, Julianne Moore, Philip Seymour Hoffman, Jason Robards Jr., John C. Reilly | 188 minutes | Rated R

"Love-it-or-hate-it" filmmaking from auteur Anderson that's either a "compelling" study of "intersecting lives" in the San Fernando Valley or a "never-ending" "letdown" about a "bunch of dysfunctional people"; still, the direction is "energetic" and "Cruise actually acts", though some ask "what's up with the frogs?"

Magnum Force
22 | 21 | 20 | 21

1973 | Directed by Ted Post | With Clint Eastwood, Hal Holbrook, Felton Perry | 124 minutes | Rated R

"Clint's the man" and he's "stepped up his game" in this "key Dirty Harry" outing, the first sequel in the "classic" crime series that places Detective Callahan in a "magnum" showdown with some vigilante "motorcycle cops" right out of "central casting"; diehards claim "it just doesn't get any better" than this, citing "good action" and an "interesting plot."

Maid in Manhattan
14 | 14 | 13 | 16

2002 | Directed by Wayne Wang | With Jennifer Lopez, Ralph Fiennes, Natasha Richardson | 105 minutes | Rated PG-13

"Warm and fuzzy" says it all about this "modern day Cinderella" story, a romantic comedy about a hotel chambermaid with a "great booty" who lands a "JFK Jr.-esque bachelor" (wags tag it *Pretty Cleaning Woman*); while it's certainly "harmless" enough "airline entertainment", cynics say "sappy", citing "no chemistry" between the leads, the "all-glammed-up-but-nowhere-to-go" J. Lo and "uncomfortable-looking" Fiennes.

Major League

21 **17** **20** **19**

1989 | Directed by David S. Ward | With Tom Berenger, Charlie Sheen, Corbin Bernsen, Wesley Snipes | 107 minutes | Rated R

Aka "*The Bad News Bears Grow Up*", this "irreverent" baseball farce "leads the league" in "rough-edged" humor as a squad of error-prone Cleveland Indian "underdogs" pursue the pennant in spite of their team's owner, who's hoping to relocate the franchise to Miami; though it spawned several sequels, athletic supporters say the "original is the best."

Malcolm X

23 **26** **23** **23**

1992 | Directed by Spike Lee | With Denzel Washington, Angela Bassett, Al Freeman Jr | 194 minutes | Rated PG-13

In this "galvanizing", "probing" bio, the "transformation" of Malcolm X from "young hustler" to "outspoken" Civil Rights leader is portrayed by an "emotional" Washington in such a "bravura", "sympathetic" way that many say he was "robbed of an Oscar"; still, this "profound" film is a "time capsule of black American style" that "captivates and educates."

Mallrats

18 **16** **18** **15**

1995 | Directed by Kevin Smith | With Shannen Doherty, Jeremy London, Jason Lee, Claire Forlani, Ben Affleck | 94 minutes | Rated R

Director Smith's "sound" follow-up to *Clerks* mines the mall for "silly", "low-budget amusement", capturing a generation of "bored losers" who mouth "memorable", "profanity-laced" dialogue in between comic "pratfalls"; though "not as good" as its predecessor (there's "not much of a storyline"), it's got enough "Jedi mind tricks" up its sleeve to touch the "'90s child in us all."

☒ Maltese Falcon, The ◐

28 **27** **27** **25**

1941 | Directed by John Huston | With Humphrey Bogart, Mary Astor, Peter Lorre | 101 minutes | Not Rated

The "stuff movies should be made of", this "vintage noir gem" boasts an "unforgettable Bogie" as the "hard-boiled detective" Sam Spade, plus a "blue-ribbon" supporting cast of "creeps and crooks", all searching for a mysterious "rara avis"; although its "taut script" that "runs like a Swiss watch" and "keeps you guessing to the end" is "often imitated", this "perfect rendering" of Dashiell Hammett's novel has been "never duplicated."

Mambo Kings, The

20 **21** **20** **20**

1992 | Directed by Arne Glimcher | With Armand Assante, Antonio Banderas, Cathy Moriarty | 104 minutes | Rated R

Aficionados of this "sexy" chronicle of two Cuban musicians' "rollicking" immigrant experience in '50s NY simply "don't know whom to love more": Antonio or Armand – two equally "talented", "gorgeous" specimens; not just a "pleasure to watch", however, the film also drums up enough "incredible" Latin tunes to spice up the already "well-done" proceedings.

☒ Man and a Woman, A ✉🅵

24 **24** **24** **24**

1966 | Directed by Claude Lelouch | With Anouk Aimée, Jean-Louis Trintignant | 102 minutes | Not Rated

For "romance par excellence", this "touching", "very French" '60s "classic" is served with "panache" and is "still worth seeing" today – indeed, the "music alone can make you fall in love"; detailing an affair

subscribe to ZAGAT.com

between a widow and widower, it stars a "beautiful Aimée" opposite "Trintignant at his best"; "see it with someone special" and you may produce your own little sequel.

Man Called Horse, A 　　　22 | 23 | 22 | 22

1970 | Directed by Elliot Silverstein | With Richard Harris, Judith Anderson | 114 minutes | Rated R

An "English aristocrat is captured by Sioux Indians and becomes one of them" in this "moving" Western made two decades before *Dances with Wolves* and featuring the "intense" Harris in one of his "greatest roles"; a warning for "weak stomachs": be prepared for some "pretty gruesome moments", i.e. the "sadomasochistic", "purple nipple" initiation scene.

☑ Manchurian Candidate, The ◐ 　　　27 | 26 | 28 | 25

1962 | Directed by John Frankenheimer | With Frank Sinatra, Laurence Harvey, Angela Lansbury | 126 minutes | Rated PG-13

As "perfectly paranoid" "Cold War" filmmaking, this provocative "conspiracy thriller" about Korean War–era "brainwashing" still packs a "wallop" due to a "twist"-laden script and a "take-your-breath-away" ending; Sinatra and Harvey are "electrifying", but the real revelation is Lansbury as an "evil", solitaire-playing mommy.

Manchurian Candidate, The 　　　18 | 21 | 19 | 19

2004 | Directed by Jonathan Demme | With Denzel Washington, Meryl Streep, Liev Schreiber | 129 minutes | Rated R

"Cleverly updated" by substituting "corporate conspiracies" for "Cold War paranoia", this remake of the "classic" '60s political thriller is "different enough to be interesting", yet ultimately many wonder "why mess with perfection?"; even if Denzel "does his best" and Meryl "gives Angela Lansbury a run for her money", this "unnecessary" effort "doesn't hold a candle to the original."

☑ Man for All Seasons, A ✉ 　　　28 | 28 | 27 | 27

1966 | Directed by Fred Zinnemann | With Paul Scofield, Wendy Hiller, Robert Shaw | 120 minutes | Rated G

"Intelligent and riveting in a quiet way", this "literate" historical drama about the "conflict between conscience and convenience" between Henry VIII and Sir Thomas More garnered six Oscars, including Best Actor for the "magnificent Scofield"; a "rare film about integrity", "loyalty and betrayal", it serves as a "reminder of the days when the movies enlightened."

Man from Elysian Fields, The 　　　21 | 23 | 21 | 21

2002 | Directed by George Hickenlooper | With Andy Garcia, Mick Jagger, Julianna Margulies | 106 minutes | Rated R

A "struggling writer" turns gigolo to make ends meet in this "sexy, stylish" variation on the "Faust legend"; although Garcia is a bit "one-note" and the "story falls off at the end", the big "surprise" here is Jagger, who "makes the whole thing worthwhile" portraying a "dapper", high-end pimp.

☑ Manhattan ◐ 　　　26 | 24 | 23 | 24

1979 | Directed by Woody Allen | With Woody Allen, Diane Keaton, Michael Murphy, Mariel Hemingway | 96 minutes | Rated R

"Even NYers get all mushy" about this "love letter to the Big Apple" filmed in "fantastic black and white" and set to a thrilling "Gershwin soundtrack"; a romance laced with "angst", it appeals to those who like their "philosophy mixed with a little comedy" and is "more fully realized than *Annie Hall*"; in a nutshell, "it can be fun to be depressing."

Manhattan Murder Mystery

1993 | Directed by Woody Allen | With Woody Allen, Diane Keaton, Anjelica Huston, Alan Alda | 104 minutes | Rated PG

It's "*Rear Window*, Woody-style" as Allen and Keaton "reprise their neurotic couple shtick", this time as bored Manhattanites who get in over their heads as they investigate a murder "that may or may not have happened"; it's "talky" but "likable", "more crimedy than crime."

Manhunter `21` `21` `25` `20`

1986 | Directed by Michael Mann | With William Petersen, Kim Greist, Brian Cox, Joan Allen | Rated R

As the "first filmed version" of Thomas Harris' novel *Red Dragon*, this "scary" prequel to *The Silence of the Lambs* is "relatively unknown" but may be "better" than its 2002 remake thanks to a "slick" production showcasing director Mann's "brilliant visuals"; nope, "Anthony Hopkins isn't in it", but Cox's "different" spin on Hannibal Lecter makes this picture "well worth a look."

Man of the Year `16` `19` `17` `17`

2006 | Directed by Barry Levinson | With Robin Williams, Laura Linney, Christopher Walken | 115 minutes | Rated PG-13

A "Williams vehicle" with a "timely twist", this satiric "send-up of the presidential election system" casts the funnyman as a talk-show host who's unexpectedly swept into the White House; some voters find it simultaneously "madcap and sobering", but the majority contends that this "blah" outing "loses momentum" and is "not one of Robin's best."

Man on Fire `21` `25` `21` `22`

2004 | Directed by Tony Scott | With Denzel Washington, Dakota Fanning, Christopher Walken | 146 minutes | Rated R

"Revenge" is the emotion driving this "intense" thriller starring a "prime Denzel" as "one bad mother" bodyguard who turns "vigilante" after his charge is kidnapped; critics find the beginning "compelling" enough, but say the second half disintegrates into a "mindless shoot-'em-up" further muddied by "hyperactive" camerawork; "no lasting impact" is the final verdict.

Man on the Moon `16` `22` `15` `17`

1999 | Directed by Milos Forman | With Jim Carrey, Danny DeVito, Courtney Love | 118 minutes | Rated R

Carrey is "better as Andy than Andy himself" in this "affecting" bio of spaced-out '70s comic Andy Kaufman, whose "funny but strange" routines conclude with an early curtain after he succumbs to cancer; though it's heckled as a "disappointing, disjointed" portrait that "doesn't shed much light" on its "complicated" subject, it's still "entertaining" for Dada comedy fans.

◪ Man Who Came to Dinner, The ◑ `26` `27` `26` `24`

1942 | Directed by William Keighley | With Bette Davis, Ann Sheridan, Monty Woolley | 112 minutes | Not Rated

Fans of "smart, hilarious" comedy relish the "unforgettable feast" in this screen treatment of Kaufman and Hart's stage play à clef, with

Woolley "stealing the movie" as a "pompous radio personality" who visits a Midwestern household and "won't go home" after becoming wheelchair-bound; mixing "acid wit" with "fast-paced" dialogue, it's a "not-to-be-missed" "scream" from the "old school."

Man Who Fell to Earth, The

18 18 20 17

1976 | Directed by Nicolas Roeg | With David Bowie, Rip Torn, Candy Clark | 140 minutes | Rated R

Followers of this "way-ahead-of-its-time" sci-fi fantasy about an extraterrestrial "searching for water" to save his planet say it's "still relevant", citing its "inventive" storyline and "perfect casting" ("Bowie has no trouble playing a trippy alien"); however, some dismiss it as an "incoherent", "unwatchable mess" that's too "creepy and weird."

Man Who Knew Too Much, The

24 24 25 24

1956 | Directed by Alfred Hitchcock | With James Stewart, Doris Day, Brenda de Banzie | 120 minutes | Rated PG

A "Hitchcock remake of an earlier Hitchcock" thriller, this "more commercial" version plays up the "amazing ordinariness" of its "everyman" stars as they desperately seek their kidnapped son; for most, it's "very exciting" – especially the "unbearably suspenseful" "scene in Royal Albert Hall" – though a few "could do without" Day's "cornball" rendition of 'Que Sera, Sera' (which still snagged a Best Song Oscar).

◪ Man Who Shot Liberty Valance, The ◑

25 24 25 23

1962 | Directed by John Ford | With John Wayne, James Stewart, Vera Miles, Lee Marvin, Edmond O'Brien | 123 minutes | Not Rated

The formidable Ford's "darkest Western" is illuminated by a "star-studded" cast featuring "all-time bad guy" Lee Marvin in his "finest performance", with "dynamic" backup from Wayne and Stewart; though a bit "claustrophobic" (it was filmed "mostly on Hollywood soundstages"), this is still "mythic" moviemaking that "works like a huge, sprawling novel"; biggest surprise: "Wayne loses the girl."

Man Who Wasn't There, The ◑

21 25 19 25

2001 | Directed by Joel Coen | With Billy Bob Thornton, Frances McDormand, James Gandolfini | 116 minutes | Rated R

This "quirky, haunting" take on vintage film noir ("as only the Coen brothers can re-create it") charts the last days of a "hapless" small-town barber whose "decline is a metaphor" for nothing less than "modern alienation"; the "stylistically incredible" cinematography is "so colorful you forget it's filmed in black and white", while Thornton's titular turn nearly manages to "out-Bogart Bogart."

◪ Man Who Would Be King, The

25 26 26 25

1975 | Directed by John Huston | With Sean Connery, Michael Caine, Christopher Plummer | 129 minutes | Rated PG

Based on Rudyard Kipling's "epic tale of friendship and heroism", this "classic adaptation" is a "ripsnorting", "good-time adventure" chronicling the perils of a pair of "opportunistic" "British rogues" on a "grand lark" in 19th-century colonial India; the combination of "sweeping vistas", "incandescent chemistry" between Connery and Caine and a "haunting ending" make for a "buddy flick that rises way above the genre."

Man with the Golden Arm, The ◑   24 | 26 | 25 | 22

1955 | Directed by Otto Preminger | With Frank Sinatra, Eleanor Parker, Kim Novak | 119 minutes | Not Rated

Proof that "Sinatra was as good an actor as he was a singer", this "grim" look at one man's "drug problem" stars an "excellent" (Oscar-nominated) Frankie as a professional card dealer/"recovering heroin addict" who falls into a "downward spiral" after being discharged from rehab; some users find it rather "dated", but most warn it's a "harrowing", "fasten-your-seatbelts" ride.

Man with the Golden Gun, The   18 | 17 | 17 | 20

1974 | Directed by Guy Hamilton | With Roger Moore, Christopher Lee, Britt Ekland | 125 minutes | Rated PG

"Moore almost redeems himself" in his second stab at 007 ("much better than his debut"), though Lee steals the show as a "droll" assassin boasting "three nipples" as well as a golden gun; still, despite the sizzle supplied by Ekland and some "great Asian scenery", foes dismiss it as a "disjointed, inferior" misfire in the Bond canon.

Marathon Man   24 | 27 | 24 | 22

1976 | Directed by John Schlesinger | With Dustin Hoffman, Laurence Olivier, Roy Scheider | 125 minutes | Rated R

"Just when you thought it was safe to go back to the dentist" comes this "nasty" little thriller about a "totally mad", "tooth-drilling" "Nazi on the loose" hell-bent on retrieving ill-gotten loot; the "huffing, puffing" Hoffman is "superlative" as a man "drawn into something way beyond his control", while set pieces like the "whining drill" scene and the "diamond-swallowing" finale raise enough "goose bumps" to make most "swear off checkups for life."

☑ March of the Penguins   26 | - | 25 | 28

2005 | Directed by Luc Jacquet | Documentary | 85 minutes | Rated G

The "majestic" emperor penguins who "struggle to survive and procreate" in the "hostile", "frigid ice fields" of Antarctica will "melt your heart" in this "superlative" documentary, an "entertaining, educational" dramatization of the "tuxedo-clad" critters' life cycle; mixing "breathtaking" footage with Freeman's "perfectly voiced" narration, it may paint an overly "anthropomorphized" picture – "they're just birds" – but somehow it manages to make "human problems seem petty" by comparison.

Maria Full of Grace ⑤   25 | 26 | 25 | 22

2004 | Directed by Joshua Marston | With Catalina Sandino Moreno, Yenny Paola Vega | 101 minutes | Rated R

The "horrific plight" of women desperate to "wean themselves from poverty" by becoming "pawns in the drug trade" is the "untold story" brought to light by this "raw", "impactful" indie; newcomer Moreno shows she's "full of talent" in the role of a Colombian cocaine mule, and while her near-"suicidal" mission "puts you through a wringer", it's worth it for the film's "unbleached message of hope."

Marie Antoinette   17 | 17 | 16 | 24

2006 | Directed by Sofia Coppola | With Kirsten Dunst, Jason Schwartzman, Judy Davis, Rip Torn | 123 minutes | Rated PG-13

"Versailles rocks" in this "amusingly modernized", "visually stunning" bio of the "reluctant" French queen, an "18th-century pop star" whose "vacuous" lifestyle is delineated via "lavish sets", "delicious dresses" and beaucoup de "shoes"; still, some guillotine the "shaky history", "jarring" '80s new-wave soundtrack and an overall sensibility that's "more Paris Hilton than Paris, France."

Mark of Zorro, The ◑

| 22 | 19 | 22 | 19 |

1940 | Directed by Rouben Mamoulian | With Tyrone Power, Linda Darnell, Basil Rathbone | 94 minutes | Not Rated

This "rousing adventure" tale of "double identity and romance" has "hardly dated" thanks to the "dashing", buckle-swashing Power's "sexy swordfighting"; "lady-in-distress" Darnell is "unbelievably lovely", "fop" Rathbone "as dastardly as ever" and a "marvelous" Alfred Newman score provides the cinematic coup de grace.

Marnie

| 21 | 21 | 22 | 21 |

1964 | Directed by Alfred Hitchcock | With Tippi Hedren, Sean Connery, Diane Baker | 130 minutes | Rated PG

A "rich man falls for a compulsive thief" in this "tense" psychological Hitchcock thriller starring a "young", "yummy" Sean opposite a very "blonde" Tippi (the last-minute "Grace Kelly replacement"); still, critics call this "second-rate" effort the master of suspense's "last gasp", citing "murky, pseudo-Freudian goings-on" and a "bored-looking" cast.

Marriage of Maria Braun, The 🇫

| 25 | 25 | 24 | 23 |

1979 | Directed by Rainer Werner Fassbinder | With Hanna Schygulla, Klaus Löwitsch, Ivan Desny | 120 minutes | Rated R

This "scathing portrait" of "survival in postwar Germany" traces its gritty heroine's determined climb the economic ladder with some "bitingly funny" scenes that prove "you can't bury the past", no matter how hard you try to disguise it; "extraordinary" work from director Fassbinder and the "brilliant" Schygulla make up for that "letdown of an ending."

Married to the Mob

| 17 | 17 | 16 | 16 |

1988 | Directed by Jonathan Demme | With Michelle Pfeiffer, Matthew Modine, Dean Stockwell | 103 minutes | Rated R

'Family' fare à la Jonathan Demme, this "quirky" comedy stars a "gorgeous" Pfeiffer playing a "small-time mobster's wife" parting with The Life after a dishonored don rubs out her hubby; "silly" but "easy to watch", it features a "fine" ensemble cast "having a great time" as well as a "don't-miss-it" cameo from "Alec Baldwin's chest hair."

Marty ✉◑

| 25 | 27 | 24 | 21 |

1955 | Directed by Delbert Mann | With Ernest Borgnine, Betsy Blair, Esther Minciotti | 91 minutes | Not Rated

Ok, the story of a "sloppy butcher" who finds love with a "mousy clerk" might "never play", but this "poignant" Paddy Chayefsky drama proved naysayers wrong, garnering four Oscars (including Best Actor for Borgnine, who's "perfect" as an ordinary Brooklyn schmo); shot in black and white, its "realistic style" "never gets old" – but be prepared for a feeling of "hopelessness" throughout.

🆉 Mary Poppins ✉

| 27 | 24 | 25 | 27 |

1964 | Directed by Robert Stevenson | With Julie Andrews, Dick Van Dyke, David Tomlinson | 140 minutes | Rated G

Mix a "perky" Andrews (as an "odd" nanny with "magical powers") with a "cheeky" Van Dyke, "fantastic animation" and "catchy tunes", add a "spoonful of sugar" and the result is a "super-duper" Disney "treat"; a "technical marvel of its time", this "jolly" production "makes you feel good at any age" and serves as a dandy "introduction to musicals for kids."

⚡ MASH ✉   `26` `25` `26` `24`
1970 | Directed by Robert Altman | With Donald Sutherland, Elliott Gould, Sally Kellerman | 116 minutes | Rated PG

"War is hell (and funny)" in this "groundbreaking" "black" satire about a dysfunctional Korean War medical unit that still "holds up" as "one of the smartest comedies ever written" – "once you get past all the blood", that is; maybe the "last third" goes "downhill" during the "lame" football game, but there's no doubt this is "Altman's breakthrough."

Mask   `21` `24` `23` `19`
1985 | Directed by Peter Bogdanovich | With Cher, Sam Elliott, Eric Stoltz | 120 minutes | Rated PG-13

Proof that "Cher can act", this "touching tearjerker" showcases the diva in "top form" as a single biker mom "in a tough situation with a challenged kid" who's horribly disfigured; as the "grotesque" teen who just "wants to be treated normally", an "amazing" Stoltz radiates enough "inner beauty" to remind the rest of us "how lucky we are."

Mask, The   `17` `18` `15` `20`
1994 | Directed by Chuck Russell | With Jim Carrey, Cameron Diaz, Peter Riegert | 101 minutes | Rated PG-13

A bedraggled schmo finds a magical mask that transforms him into a swinging, macho hero in this "entertaining" comedy that might hinge on a "ridiculous concept" but nevertheless "works" (thanks to Carrey's "funny" performance); though "kinda stupid" to brainiacs, fans are wowed by the "dazzling effects", including the "luminous Diaz", who makes her "delightful" screen debut here.

Mask of Zorro, The   `18` `17` `18` `21`
1998 | Directed by Martin Campbell | With Antonio Banderas, Catherine Zeta-Jones | 136 minutes | Rated PG-13

This "big-budget" spin on the "Zorro legend" provokes dueling opinions: zealots admire its "old-school movie style" ("great swordfights", "breathtaking" production values) and ask "is there a better-looking cast ever assembled?"; but critics parry it's "lightweight fluff" that might work well with "popcorn" but "doesn't hold a candle to the 1940 version."

Master and Commander: `23` `24` `22` `27`
The Far Side of the World
2003 | Directed by Peter Weir | With Russell Crowe, Paul Bettany | 138 minutes | Rated PG-13

For "textbook adventure filmmaking" sailing over the "bounding main", set your sights on this "visually extraordinary" nautical epic depicting "cat-and-mouse" high-sea games during the Napoleonic War; the all-male cast includes the "great-as-usual" Crowe backed up by a "strong" Bettany, but despite "incredible battle scenes", "magnificent storms" and "stellar" special effects, mutineers say the "thin" storyline and "endless frigate jargon" simply "don't hold water"; other seafarers, however, "look forward to another installment."

Matador, The
20 | 22 | 20 | 19

2005 | Directed by Richard Shepard | With Pierce Brosnan, Greg Kinnear, Hope Davis | 96 minutes | Rated R

A "gone-to-seed" Brosnan earns *olés* playing "against type" as a "foul-mouthed" hitman "who wants to quit the game" in this "dark", "offbeat" comedy about a midlife crisis; Kinnear is a "perfect foil" as the "push-over" pulled into the assassin biz, making for a "surprisingly touching" buddy picture that puts a "new slant" on the "odd-couple" scenario.

Match Point
22 | 23 | 22 | 22

2005 | Directed by Woody Allen | With Jonathan Rhys Meyers, Scarlett Johansson, Matthew Goode | 124 minutes | Rated R

Breaking from his usual "silly slapstick", Woody Allen channels both "Hitchcock" and "Theodore Dreiser" to serve up this "mesmerizing", "keeps-you-guessing" London thriller whose "chilling portrait of a so-cial climber" examines "the role of luck in life"; further assuring the film's place in the sun are the "outstanding" Rhys Meyers and "sump-tuous" Scarlett, who simmer with "intense chemistry."

Matchstick Men
20 | 24 | 21 | 19

2003 | Directed by Ridley Scott | With Nicolas Cage, Sam Rockwell, Alison Lohman | 116 minutes | Rated PG-13

A "neurotic" con artist "with more tics than a time bomb" shows his "soft" side when he plays dad to a "junior swindler" in this "smart", "dark"-edged comic caper featuring "excellent" performances from Cage and the "stardom"-bound Lohman; it "takes a while" to get go-ing, but don't fret – the "surprise twist" at the end will "hook you."

▣ Matrix, The
25 | 19 | 25 | 28

1999 | Directed by Andy Wachowski, Larry Wachowski | With Keanu Reeves, Laurence Fishburne, Carrie-Anne Moss | 136 minutes | Rated R

"Move over, *Star Wars*"; not even Reeves' "leaden" acting can sink this "mind-bending, reality-rocking" movie that "raised the bar on special effects" and "revolutionized hand-to-hand combat in filmmaking"; even if its "intricate" plot (something about a computer hacker turned "humanity's last hope") verges on "incoherence", this "sci-fi shoot-'em-up for people with brains" just "gets better every time you see it."

Matrix Reloaded, The
21 | 17 | 18 | 26

2003 | Directed by Andy Wachowski, Larry Wachowski | With Keanu Reeves, Carrie-Anne Moss, Laurence Fishburne, Hugo Weaving | 138 minutes | Rated R

The "conceptual novelty's gone", the "story is not as compelling as the original" and it "could have benefited from some editing", yet the "sex-ier" second installment of the "groundbreaking" sci-fi trilogy is still "worth a watch" for its "eye candy galore" – "off-the-charts special ef-fects", "take-your-breath-away fight scenes" and a "car-chase scene that just blows your mind"; now if only there were "a *Matrix for Dummies* to explain what happened."

Matrix Revolutions, The
15 | 14 | 13 | 23

2003 | Directed by Andy Wachowski, Larry Wachowski | With Keanu Reeves, Laurence Fishburne, Carrie-Ann Moss | 129 minutes | Rated R

This "less than stellar end" to the martial-arts/sci-fi trilogy features the same "over-the-top CGI effects" and "garbled-but-intriguing philosophy" as the preceding installments, but this time out there's "too much action and not enough thought"; in fact, it's such a "letdown" to a series that "started with so much potential" that many think "they should have stopped after the first one."

Maverick
18 | 20 | 17 | 19

1994 | Directed by Richard Donner | With Mel Gibson, Jodie Foster, James Garner | 127 minutes | Rated PG

As TV shows morphed into movies go, this "laid-back Western" based on ABC's '50s series "works well" by loading the deck with "escapism", "modern twists" and Gibson as a "tall, dark stranger" who's "having more fun than the audience"; but it's the "effortless style" of Garner (the original Maverick) that wins big.

McCabe & Mrs. Miller
23 | 23 | 23 | 24

1971 | Directed by Robert Altman | With Warren Beatty, Julie Christie, Shelley Duvall | 120 minutes | Rated R

Decidedly "not for conventional Western" fans, this "brilliantly directed", "postmodern deconstruction" of the genre "eliminates the clichés" and "faithfully re-creates what the West was really like": namely, "harsh, cruel and lacking true heroes"; despite one major drawback – "you can't understand what anyone is saying" – it's more than evident that the leads are "impossibly in love."

Mean Girls
20 | 19 | 20 | 19

2004 | Directed by Mark Waters | With Lindsay Lohan, Rachel McAdams, Tina Fey | 97 minutes | Rated PG-13

The "*Heathers* of the new millennium", this "smart teen comedy" brings back "painful high school memories" of the "trauma of trying to fit in" at a time when "social status seems so important"; as the new kid on the block, "goddess" Lohan demonstrates she's definitely "going places" and Tina Fey's "witty" script "hits the nail on the head" – even if the "sappy" finale is a tad too "preachy" for many.

Meaning of Life, The
24 | 22 | 20 | 20

1983 | Directed by Terry Jones, Terry Gilliam | With Monty Python | 107 minutes | Rated R

"Lunacy abounds" in this "wonderfully outrageous" Monty Python flick rolling "music, comedy and philosophy" vignettes that attempt to answer life's big questions into one "screamingly funny" (if sometimes "retch-covered") package; marking the British troupe's "last spurt" of cinematic collaboration, it suffers the occasional "second-rate" segment but endures as a "classic" that "shines in comparison to what else is out there."

Mean Streets
24 | 27 | 23 | 22

1973 | Directed by Martin Scorsese | With Harvey Keitel, Robert De Niro | 110 minutes | Rated R

"Gritty and graphic before that became the norm", Martin Scorsese's breakout drama of hoods in the 'hood "rings with truth" as a "definitive slice of New York", with Keitel out to "make it in the mob" in spite of "Catholic guilt" and ties to De Niro's "unforgettable" loose-cannon "loser"; it's a "grim" but "passionate" study of streetwise style, including some "pioneering" use of "oldies but goodies" on the soundtrack.

| | OVERALL | ACTING | STORY | PROD. |

Meatballs

18 | 15 | 17 | 14

1979 | Directed by Ivan Reitman | With Bill Murray, Harvey Atkin, Kate Lynch | 99 minutes | Rated PG

A pre-"*Caddyshack*" Murray plays a wisecracking "summer camp counselor everyone would love to have" in this "underrated", lowbrow "comedy staple", later "ruined" by three sequels; ok, it might be a "little dated" and "poor production quality" detracts, but overall it conveys the "experience every camper hopes for."

Mediterraneo

21 | 21 | 20 | 23

1992 | Directed by Gabriele Salvatores | With Diego Abatantuono, Claudio Bigagli | 96 minutes | Rated R

Sure, this "sweet" comedy about a group of WWII Italian soldiers "stranded" on a Greek isle is a "trifle", but the "beautiful cinematography" and "sweep-you-away" soundtrack nicely complement its assortment of "cute characters"; some report the story "drags in some parts" (resulting in "awkward" scenes), but it offers enough "great escapism" to make for a primo "date flick."

Meet Joe Black

17 | 19 | 18 | 19

1998 | Directed by Martin Brest | With Brad Pitt, Anthony Hopkins, Claire Forlani, Marcia Gay Harden | 178 minutes | Rated PG-13

This "ethereal" romance, a remake of the "classic *Death Takes a Holiday*", stars "cutie pie" Pitt as the Grim Reaper who "comes to collect Hopkins' soul" but "sticks around" awhile to dally with his daughter; sure, the "drawn-out" script "could have been edited more tightly" (all that "endless longing" is a "snooze"), but soft-hearted sorts insist that this "poignant" flick "speaks to your soul."

Meet John Doe ◑

24 | 26 | 23 | 22

1941 | Directed by Frank Capra | With Gary Cooper, Barbara Stanwyck, Edward Arnold, Walter Brennan | 123 minutes | Not Rated

Cooper and Stanwyck are a "joy to watch" in this "classic" Capra fanfare for the "common man" that mixes some "social commentary" into its tale of an "honest" hobo who's recruited by a newspaper to "threaten suicide" in the name of America's "lost ideals" – and ends up capturing the nation's "attention and hearts"; despite the film's "heroic" intentions, "politics are still corrupt", but the "warm, fuzzy dream" that "things can be better" never looked so "convincing."

☑ Meet Me in St. Louis

26 | 24 | 23 | 26

1944 | Directed by Vincente Minnelli | With Judy Garland, Margaret O'Brien, Mary Astor | 113 minutes | Not Rated

Clang, clang, clang, here comes Garland "at her radiant finest" as a girl who "adores the boy next door" in this musical "treasure" about a "turn-of-the-century" American family; fans laud its "sumptuous" Technicolor production and "unforgettable" tunes, while brainiacs hint it's "darker and deeper than its rep suggests."

Meet the Fockers

18 | 21 | 17 | 19

2004 | Directed by Jay Roach | With Robert De Niro, Ben Stiller, Dustin Hoffman, Barbra Streisand | 115 minutes | Rated PG-13

There's "major star wattage" on display in this *Meet the Parents* sequel, starting with the "oy vey" pairing of "big names" Dusty and Babs, who "steal the show" along with a can of "whipped cream";

otherwise, this "crude" comedy about in-laws interacting for the first time earns mixed marks: it's either a "one-trick movie" with "too many potty jokes" or else "hilarious", "verging on ridiculous – what's wrong with that?"

Meet the Parents

| 19 | 21 | 19 | 19 |

2000 | Directed by Jay Roach | With Robert De Niro, Ben Stiller, Blythe Danner | 108 minutes | Rated PG-13

"Every guy's worst nightmare" about being introduced to his "prospective in-laws" comes true in this very "watchable" comedy that succeeds mainly because of the "brilliant pairing of Stiller and De Niro"; though the unamused frown it "relies too much on slapstick" and repeats the "same joke for two hours straight", most say it "pinpoints" an "all-too-real" situation.

Meet the Robinsons

| 22 | - | 21 | 25 |

2007 | Directed by Stephen J. Anderson | Animated | 102 minutes | Rated G

A "brainy orphan's search for his parents" takes a "deliriously zany" turn into *Back-to-the-Future* territory in this "clever" Disney 'toon featuring a "heartwarming" moral about the "meaning of family" and some "great" visuals (the "T-Rex scene is worth the price of admission" alone); while "not the best" animated flick you'll ever meet, it's good enough to "keep the kids from killing each other for 90 minutes."

Melinda and Melinda

| 17 | 21 | 18 | 18 |

2005 | Directed by Woody Allen | With Radha Mitchell, Will Ferrell, Chloë Sevigny | 100 minutes | Rated PG-13

"Two versions of the same tale – one comic, one tragic – form the framework for this "intriguing" Woody Allen flicker about a "nervous" adulteress adrift in "ultrasophisticated Manhattan"; fans feel the Woodman "flits between the two stories with ease", but those who retitle it *Monotonous and Monotonous* advise he "join the 21st century" ("who can afford those apartments?") or else "retire."

Melvin and Howard ✉

| 22 | 23 | 22 | 19 |

1980 | Directed by Jonathan Demme | With Paul Le Mat, Mary Steenburgen, Jason Robards | 95 minutes | Rated R

A "small movie that landed in a big way", this "wacky" riff on the "Howard Hughes myth" tells the tale of a milkman who befriends a bum, who's really a gazillionaire, who wills the milkman a fortune; it's "funny", "off-the-wall" stuff that's "uplifting without being preachy or schmaltzy" and might be best enjoyed "as a companion piece to *The Aviator*."

⊠ Member of the Wedding, The ◑

| 25 | 27 | 26 | 25 |

1952 | Directed by Fred Zinnemann | With Ethel Waters, Julie Harris, Brandon De Wilde | 93 minutes | Not Rated

"One of the most touching films ever", this "sweet" slice of Americana adapted from (and "capturing the essence of") Carson McCullers' play delineates a Southern household's "moving dynamic" between an alienated youngster, her black housekeeper and her soon-to-be-married brother; fans sing the praises of its "remarkable" cast, singling out the "soaring" Harris and the "remarkable" Waters, whose on-screen rendition of the hymn 'His Eye Is on the Sparrow' is "thankfully preserved forever."

| | OVERALL | ACTING | STORY | PROD. |

⚡ Memento   26 | 25 | 27 | 25

2000 | Directed by Christopher Nolan | With Guy Pearce, Carrie-Anne Moss | 113 minutes | Rated R

"Bring your brain to the theater, you'll need it" for this "exquisitely existential" "mind-bender" about a man who loses his "short-term memory" following his wife's murder; it "turns traditional narrative on its head" by telling the story "in reverse" – so it may "require several viewings to get it all straight"; though there's applause for the "stunning" Pearce, befuddled folks "still trying to figure it out" wail it's too "gnisufnoc."

Memoirs of a Geisha   21 | 23 | 21 | 26

2005 | Directed by Rob Marshall | With Zhang Ziyi, Ken Watanabe, Gong Li, Michelle Yeoh | 145 minutes | Rated PG-13

"Beautiful costumes" and "breathtaking" cinematography ("every shot feels like a painting") shine in this "poignant", "rags-to-silks" period drama that offers a rare glimpse inside the "closed society" of Japan's geishas; despite some grumbling that "Chinese actors playing Japanese" characters may be "politically incorrect", overall most find the experience "transporting", albeit at a "slow" clip.

Men in Black   21 | 20 | 21 | 24

1997 | Directed by Barry Sonnenfeld | With Tommy Lee Jones, Will Smith, Linda Fiorentino | 98 minutes | Rated PG-13

"Wisecracking" Smith and "deadpan" Jones show "great chemistry" as they battle "slime, aliens and explosions" in this "action-packed" sci-fi flick that's "delicious fun"; a "kids' movie for adults", it's a "hugely enjoyable spoof" that some find "silly" and may be a "little gross."

Men in Black II   14 | 16 | 12 | 20

2002 | Directed by Barry Sonnenfeld | With Tommy Lee Jones, Will Smith, Rip Torn, Lara Flynn Boyle | 88 minutes | Rated PG-13

An "overload of special effects", a "cast on autopilot" and "no real storyline" are the classic symptoms of "sequel syndrome" afflicting this "mediocre" encore to the hit sci-fi comedy; fortunately, a "few amusing sight gags" (i.e. the "worth-a-laugh Michael Jackson cameo") and the "short" running time "make it bearable."

Merchant of Venice, The   23 | 25 | 25 | 25

2004 | Directed by Michael Radford | With Al Pacino, Jeremy Irons, Joseph Fiennes, Lynn Collins | 138 minutes | Rated R

Pacino "owns the screen" with his "multifaceted", "take-no-prisoners" portrayal of the moneylender Shylock in this "exemplary" rendering of the Bard's "most problematic" comedy; the "stellar cast", "beautiful" photography and "splendid" production design (with "actual scenes shot in Venice") "bring Shakespeare to life" with, appropriately, "much ado."

⚡ Metropolis ◑   27 | 22 | 24 | 28

1927 | Directed by Fritz Lang | With Alfred Abel, Gustav Froelich, Brigitte Helm | 153 minutes | Not Rated

A "visionary" film of "magnitude, imagination and depth", this "sci-fi social commentary" about "oppression and uprising" set in a "futuristic city" "still retains its visual impact" seven decades later; indeed, Lang's "man-versus-machine" story (embodied by a "fetishized woman robot") remains "revolutionary in every sense of the word" – this is a "movie everybody should watch at least once."

| | OVERALL | ACTING | STORY | PROD. |

Metropolitan
20 | 19 | 20 | 17

1990 | Directed by Whit Stillman | With Carolyn Farina, Edward Clements, Christopher Eigeman | 99 minutes | Rated PG-13

The "young and the privileged" in "present-day NY" get the Jane Austen treatment in this "charming" "coming-of-age" comedy with an "exciting young cast" spouting "intensely dry", "droll" dialogue; those fascinated by "rich kids and their problems" say it's one part "Woody Allen", one part "George Plimpton."

Michael Clayton
24 | 26 | 23 | 23

2007 | Directed by Tony Gilroy | With George Clooney, Tom Wilkinson, Tilda Swinton, Sydney Pollack | 119 minutes | Rated R

Clooney's "at his smoothest" playing a "law firm fixer" who's "expert at cleaning up messes" in this "thinking person's" legal thriller delineating the "world of corporate greed" and the extreme lengths taken to "kill a class-action lawsuit"; Swinton's Oscar-winning turn as an "ice queen" chief counsel is as "intense" as the rest of this "tight", "complex" film, but "pay close attention" – you "might not understand it all on the first viewing."

Michael Collins
21 | 24 | 22 | 21

1996 | Directed by Neil Jordan | With Liam Neeson, Aidan Quinn, Stephen Rea, Alan Rickman, Julia Roberts | 133 minutes | Rated R

Built around Neeson's "terrific" turn as a "true hero" of the Irish rebellion against British rule, this "powerful" biopic not only "tells the story of Michael Collins", but "makes you believe in his cause"; maybe the "miscast" Roberts and "contrived romantic angle" strike a somewhat "sour note", but otherwise this "heartfelt" flick makes some "want to march on St. Patrick's Day."

⛁ Midnight Cowboy ✉
26 | 28 | 24 | 24

1969 | Directed by John Schlesinger | With Dustin Hoffman, Jon Voight, Sylvia Miles | 113 minutes | Rated R

"Still as gritty as ever", this "unvarnished look at NYC street life" is a "touching" if "depressing" depiction of a pair of "down-and-out" losers "spiraling downward" that turns the "buddy-flick concept" on its ear; the first "X-rated" film to take Best Picture honors (and since re-rated), it continues to wow with "inner beauty", "haunting music" and "brilliant" turns from Hoffman and Voight – and that "ending on the bus is unforgettable."

Midnight Express ✉
24 | 24 | 25 | 22

1978 | Directed by Alan Parker | With Brad Davis, Randy Quaid, John Hurt | 120 minutes | Rated R

This "frighteningly realistic" drama about a not-so-innocent American abroad imprisoned for smuggling hash "should be required viewing for teens and travelers", even though this "eye-opener" might "induce nightmares for years to come"; it probably "did more to stop kids from doing drugs" than all of "Nancy Reagan's efforts" combined.

Midnight in the Garden of Good and Evil
20 | 23 | 22 | 21

1997 | Directed by Clint Eastwood | With Kevin Spacey, John Cusack, Jude Law, Lady Chablis | 155 minutes | Rated R

"Beautiful Savannah" is a major character in this "twisty" Dixie murder mystery rife with enough "Southern eccentrics", uptight "Yankees" and "hot rough trade" to "keep you guessing until the end"; Spacey delivers his usual "stellar" work, though many say the picture is stolen by drag queen Lady Chablis, "playing herself."

Midnight Run

23 | 25 | 23 | 21

1988 | Directed by Martin Brest | With Robert De Niro, Charles Grodin, Yaphet Kotto | 126 minutes | Rated R

For a "quintessential" buddy flick, try this "wild", "witty" action comedy about a "white-collar crook" and the bounty hunter who "tries to bring him in alive" that runs strong on the "great chemistry" of "old pros" De Niro and Grodin, the "funniest odd couple since Oscar and Felix"; add in some "quirky" supporting players (a "fleet of FBI agents", "inept mobsters" and other "eccentrics"), and there's "never a dull moment."

Midsummer Night's Sex Comedy, A

18 | 20 | 19 | 19

1982 | Directed by Woody Allen | With Woody Allen, Mia Farrow, Julie Hagerty, José Ferrer | 88 minutes | Rated PG

"Funny" albeit "fairly forgettable", this "romantic Woody Allen romp" follows three turn-of-the-century couples over a weekend in the country; one part "Shakespeare" satire, one part ode to Bergman's *Smiles of a Summer Night*, it's altogether "silly" stuff and if "far from the director's best", it's "pleasant enough for a Saturday afternoon."

Mighty Aphrodite

18 | 21 | 18 | 18

1995 | Directed by Woody Allen | With Woody Allen, Mira Sorvino, Michael Rapaport | 98 minutes | Rated R

Maybe "not as incisive" as Allen's "best", this "minor Woody" work still exudes "inventive charm" in its story of a man seeking the biological mother of his adopted child; throw in an "inspired Greek chorus" providing commentary and Sorvino's Oscar-winning turn as a "ditzy hooker", and the result is "painless fun."

Mighty Ducks, The

18 | 16 | 19 | 18

1992 | Directed by Stephen Herek | With Emilio Estevez, Joshua Jackson, Lane Smith | 100 minutes | Rated PG

"So good they named an NHL team after it", this "heartwarming" family flick takes the "typical underdog story" and puts it "on ice" via a hockey squad of pee-wee "misfits" led by an "unwilling coach"; "inspirational" if mighty "formulaic" (and requiring "no thinking on the audience's part" whatsoever), it's "perfect for kids" and hatched two so-so sequels.

Mighty Heart, A

21 | 24 | 23 | 21

2007 | Directed by Michael Winterbottom | With Angelina Jolie, Dan Futterman | 108 minutes | Rated R

Jolie delivers a "heartbreaking" performance as a "frantic wife" whose husband has vanished in this "excellent dramatization" of the events surrounding the 2002 kidnapping of journalist Daniel Pearl by Islamic extremists; while the "realistic" presentation can be "tough to watch" – since many already "know the outcome" – it's a "fitting tribute" to one woman's "grace and courage."

Mighty Wind, A

23 | 26 | 21 | 23

2003 | Directed by Christopher Guest | With Bob Balaban, Christopher Guest, John Michael Higgins, Eugene Levy | 91 minutes | Rated PG-13

"You'll have almost as much fun as the cast" watching this "hysterical mockumentary" about the "'60s folk music scene" full of "priceless material", a "hilarious cast of characters" and "lots of hidden humor"; while "not as good as *Best in Show*", "anything by Guest is better than most everyone else's work."

ⓩ Mildred Pierce ✉◑ | 26 | 25 | 25 | 24 |

1945 | Directed by Michael Curtiz | With Joan Crawford, Jack Carson, Ann Blyth, Eve Arden, Zachary Scott | 111 minutes | Not Rated

Oscar-winner Crawford is in "full weeper bloom" (with "shoulder pads for days" and "star lighting to make sure you get the point") in this noir "sudser" based on the James M. Cain novel about a "mother who sacrifices everything for her daughter"; "camp" followers crack up over Arden's "witty repartee" (which "would put any drag queen to shame") and "rent it as a double feature with *Mommie Dearest* for full impact."

Miller's Crossing | 22 | 23 | 22 | 22 |

1990 | Directed by Joel Coen | With Gabriel Byrne, Albert Finney, Marcia Gay Harden | 115 minutes | Rated R

"Don't give the high hat" to this "subtle", "criminally underrated" early Coen brothers "gem" about a gangland war between Irish and Italian mobsters that proves "betrayal can come back to haunt you"; devotees declare it "deserves to be up there with *Goodfellas*", given the worthiness of the "broody" Byrne, "knockout Finney" and "deliciously tangled" plot "larded with obscure underworld slang."

ⓩ Million Dollar Baby ✉ | 27 | 28 | 25 | 26 |

2004 | Directed by Clint Eastwood | With Clint Eastwood, Hilary Swank, Morgan Freeman | 132 minutes | Rated PG-13

What begins as a boxing "Cinderella story" about a "guilt-racked coach" mentoring a "determined female fighter" takes a "sharp turn" and becomes a "profound" meditation on "significant moral dilemmas" in this "knockout" Oscar magnet from "powerhouse" actor/director Eastwood; a "flawless Swank" and "quietly brilliant" Freeman round out the cast in this "simple", "less-is-more" production, with a "surprise" ending that "leaves you breathless."

Minority Report | 21 | 20 | 22 | 25 |

2002 | Directed by Steven Spielberg | With Tom Cruise, Colin Farrell, Samantha Morton, Max von Sydow | 145 minutes | Rated PG-13

"Cruise and Spielberg are a great combo" in this "intelligent, exciting" sci-fi thriller with "stunning visual effects" and "a mind-bending premise" – catching murderers before they commit the actual crime; though the "original, chilling storyline" "moves at lightning speed", it's "hard to follow at times", making it more difficult to detect the "holes in the plot"; bottom line: "better than the box office would indicate."

Miracle | 24 | 23 | 26 | 24 |

2004 | Directed by Gavin O'Connor | With Kurt Russell, Patricia Clarkson | 135 minutes | Rated PG

Although most already "know the ending", this "feel-good" "insider's look" at the U.S. hockey team's quest for gold at the 1980 Olympics keeps athletic supporters "riveted" with its taut "they-shoot-they-score" script; indeed, Kurt's "commanding performance" and the "realistic moments on and off the ice" keep its "inspirational" themes resonating long afterwards – "way to go, team."

Miracle of Morgan's Creek, The ◑   23 | 22 | 25 | 21

1944 | Directed by Preston Sturges | With Eddie Bracken, Betty Hutton, William Demarest | 99 minutes | Not Rated

From the "fabulous" Preston Sturges comes this "raucous farce" starring Betty Hutton as Trudy Kockenlocker, an "unwed mother-to-be who can't remember who the father is" ("they're still debating how the story got past the Hollywood production code"); admirers say this "crackerjack comedy" is all about the "tremendous dialogue" and only "grows richer with age" – capped by an "ending that should be enshrined in the Movie Hall of Fame."

⊠ Miracle on 34th Street ✉◑   25 | 23 | 26 | 23

1947 | Directed by George Seaton | With Maureen O'Hara, Natalie Wood, Edmund Gwenn | 96 minutes | Not Rated

It "can't be Christmas" without a screening of this "schmaltzy", "charming fantasy" that embodies a "child's belief in Santa Claus" so well that it's become an enduring "seasonal favorite" for "every generation"; true believers say the Oscar-winning screenplay is the key behind this "perfect" "holiday classic" that puts the remakes to shame.

Miracle Worker, The ✉◑   25 | 28 | 24 | 22

1962 | Directed by Arthur Penn | With Anne Bancroft, Patty Duke, Victor Jory, Inga Swenson | 106 minutes | Not Rated

"Beautifully transferred from stage to screen" by director Penn, this "moving" account of deaf-and-blind Helen Keller and her teacher Annie Sullivan garnered Oscars for both leads (who reprised their Broadway roles); while Duke is undeniably "superb", it's Bancroft who "dominates" this "fiercely acted", "exceptional" film; most memorable moment: at the water pump.

Misery ✉   21 | 24 | 23 | 19

1990 | Directed by Rob Reiner | With James Caan, Kathy Bates, Richard Farnsworth | 107 minutes | Rated R

This "freaky" yarn about an injured writer "rescued" from a snowstorm by a "seriously deranged" fan is a "crackling-with-tension" experience that really "packs a wallop"; Oscar-winner Bates is beyond "mesmerizing" as the seriously "obsessed" captor opposite Caan's "excellent", hapless hostage, though diehards say the real credit goes to Reiner's "great hand when it comes to directing Stephen King stories."

Misfits, The ◑   21 | 24 | 21 | 22

1961 | Directed by John Huston | With Clark Gable, Marilyn Monroe, Montgomery Clift, Thelma Ritter, Eli Wallach | 124 minutes | Not Rated

The "swan song of Gable and Monroe" (and the "last movie" for both), this "bittersweet" romance between a divorcée and an aging cowboy has a big theme at its heart, the demise of the Old West; while Arthur Miller's script is "thought-provoking", some say this "famously troubled production" ("were they all as dead tired as they appeared?") has "taken on an aura it doesn't deserve."

Miss Congeniality   15 | 16 | 15 | 16

2000 | Directed by Donald Petrie | With Sandra Bullock, Michael Caine, Benjamin Bratt | 109 minutes | Rated PG-13

Action comedy meets "chick flick" in this "lighthearted send-up" of beauty-contest culture starring Bullock at her most "adorable" as a "tomboy FBI agent" who goes undercover as cheesecake in a national pageant; ok, it's "slight" and "sophomoric", but in the eyes of most beholders it's "endearing fun" – despite the absence of "Bert Parks."

Missing ✉   24 | 26 | 25 | 22

1982 | Directed by Costa-Gavras | With Jack Lemmon, Sissy Spacek, John Shea | 122 minutes | Rated PG

Based on "actual events in South America", this fictionalized account of a U.S.-sanctioned military coup and its bloody aftermath is a "riveting" yet "moving" political thriller with a "devastating" message: "governments lie"; given "strong" performances by Lemmon and Spacek that "save it from being too preachy", many wonder why this Best Picture nominee is so "unheralded" and "overlooked" 25 years later.

Missing, The   18 | 22 | 18 | 19

2003 | Directed by Ron Howard | With Tommy Lee Jones, Cate Blanchett | 137 minutes | Rated R

Helmer Howard goes for grit in this "entertaining" if "somewhat disturbing" Western that adds a "supernatural" slant to a "familiar" abducted-child storyline ("isn't this *The Searchers* in disguise?"); in spite of "great acting on all parts" and some "gorgeous scenery", those with reservations claim the "slow pace" sends things "a little off the mark."

Mission, The   24 | 24 | 22 | 25

1986 | Directed by Roland Joffé | With Robert De Niro, Jeremy Irons, Liam Neeson | 126 minutes | Rated PG

"Beautifully shot", Oscar-winning cinematography nearly steals the show in this "intriguing drama" about an 18th-century struggle between missionaries and mercenaries over the riches of South America; even though evangelist Irons and reformed slave trader De Niro turn out their usual "amazing" work, unfazed foes feel Ennio Morricone's "soundtrack is far better" than the picture itself.

Mission: Impossible   16 | 15 | 15 | 21

1996 | Directed by Brian De Palma | With Tom Cruise, Jon Voight, Ving Rhames | 110 minutes | Rated PG-13

Many "convoluted" plot "twists" make this "tense", "James Bond–ish" action/adventurer a "watchable" if "highly confusing" picture; while diehards "drool" over the "never-looking-better" Tom in an "all-black DKNY-ish outfit" performing "amazing stunts", purists pronounce it "not as good as the TV show" and bawl "bring back Peter Graves."

Mission: Impossible II   15 | 14 | 15 | 21

2000 | Directed by John Woo | With Tom Cruise, Dougray Scott, Thandie Newton, Ving Rhames | 123 minutes | Rated PG-13

There's "lots of flash but not much else" in this "slick" second installment of the franchise pairing "wannabe tough guy" Cruise ("before his freak-out") with Woo's directorial "bravado" for a "fast-paced" Ethan Hunt spy adventure; while "easier to follow" than the original, most still maul the "dull, Bond retread" plot and those "unrealistic" action scenes.

Mission: Impossible III   18 | 17 | 16 | 23

2006 | Directed by J.J. Abrams | With Tom Cruise, Philip Seymour Hoffman, Michelle Monaghan | 126 minutes | Rated PG-13

There's "never a dull moment" in this "whiz-bang", "megabucks" sequel that's voted the "best of the trilogy" given its "nonstop action", "believable love interest" subplot and Hoffman's "steal-the-show" performance as the "ultimate bad guy"; though critics complain about "not enough story" (adding "there's no such thing as a good movie with a colon in the title"), at least "Cruise appears saner here than in real life", performing "lots of jumping around" stunts but thankfully "none off couches."

Mississippi Burning
23 | 24 | 23 | 22

1988 | Directed by Alan Parker | With Gene Hackman, Willem Dafoe, Frances McDormand | 128 minutes | Rated R

A "story that needed to be told", this "powerful" depiction of '60s "racial unrest" focuses on an investigation of the murder of three Civil Rights workers; yet despite an "all-too-real glimpse of life in the Deep South", critics say it overemphasizes "white hate" to the point that there are few "speaking parts for black actors."

Missouri Breaks, The
16 | 20 | 17 | 18

1976 | Directed by Arthur Penn | With Marlon Brando, Jack Nicholson, Randy Quaid, Harry Dean Stanton | 126 minutes | Rated PG

Set in central Montana's river-carved badlands (aka the Missouri Breaks), this "unusual" Western about a gang of horse thieves features "excellent work by Nicholson" but is nearly "overacted" to oblivion by – "yikes!" – a very "bloated" Brando in "one of the weirdest performances ever put on celluoid"; ultimately, the flick "isn't for all tastes", though some aficionados find its "off-kilter" approach rather "fascinating."

Miss Pettigrew Lives for a Day
21 | 24 | 21 | 23

2008 | Directed by Bharat Nalluri | With Frances McDormand, Amy Adams | 92 minutes | Rated PG-13

An "unattractive, out-of-work nanny" hired by a "beautiful, ditzy" actress with "too many beaux" make for a "perfect mismatch" in this "pleasant" screwball comedy burnished by a "trip-back-in-time" recreation of 1930s London; though its window into the "lives of the idle rich" runs "light" on substance, the "winning performances" make it "worth watching."

Miss Potter
21 | 23 | 20 | 23

2006 | Directed by Chris Noonan | With Renée Zellweger, Ewan McGregor, Emily Watson | 92 minutes | Rated PG

A "delightful" look at the life of writer/illustrator Beatrix Potter, this "quality" biopic features Zellweger as the "slightly off-kilter" gal who "created Peter Rabbit and other children's tales" while "breaking societal boundaries" in Victorian England; escapists exult in the "stunning views of the Lake District" and the "clever incorporation of animation" that "fits the mood perfectly."

☒ Mister Roberts
27 | 27 | 24 | 23

1955 | Directed by John Ford, Mervyn LeRoy | With Henry Fonda, James Cagney, Jack Lemmon | 123 minutes | Not Rated

A Broadway hit transposed to the big screen, this "heartfelt" story about the misadventures of a WWII supply ship crew delivers "wonderful acting all around", from the "unforgettable" Cagney to the "perfect" Fonda and "no-slouch" Lemmon; a "great wartime comedy with a serious side", it leaves even tough guys with a "lump in their throat."

Modern Times 28 | 26 | 26 | 25

1936 | Directed by Charles Chaplin | With Charles Chaplin, Paulette Goddard | 87 minutes | Not Rated

"Timelessly funny and resonant", this "man-vs.-machine" story runs on a "blend of slapstick and pathos" guaranteed to make you "smile . . . though your heart is breaking"; there's "little dialogue" (save for Chaplin's "singing waiter" "gibberish number"), but his "heartwarming" performance and sharp "swipes at the age of technology" transcend words; in short, this one's a "must-see in *these* times."

Mommie Dearest 17 | 19 | 16 | 17

1981 | Directed by Frank Perry | With Faye Dunaway, Diana Scarwid, Steve Forrest | 129 minutes | Rated PG

Right up there in the "camp classic" pantheon is this look at "ice lady" Joan Crawford and her adopted daughter Christina that's notorious for Dunaway's "uncanny", "over-the-top" title performance, a truly "scary" imagining of the "horror of being a fading star"; though some call it "exploitive", "bitter stuff", others insist it's "absorbing" and sometimes "terribly funny"; most quoted line: *"no more wire hangers!"*

Mona Lisa Smile 16 | 19 | 16 | 18

2003 | Directed by Mike Newell | With Julia Roberts, Kirsten Dunst, Julia Stiles, Maggie Gyllenhaal | 117 minutes | Rated PG-13

Set "in the days before women's lib", this "female version of *Dead Poets Society*" tells the story of a "strong-willed", 1950s college professor hoping to inspire her Stepford-esque students; though some call it "superficial", "watered-down feminism for the masses", side benefits include "authentic period touches", "beautiful costumes" and a "who's who of top young actresses stealing scenes from Queen Julia."

Money Pit, The 16 | 17 | 17 | 16

1986 | Directed by Richard Benjamin | With Tom Hanks, Shelley Long, Alexander Godunov, Maureen Stapleton | 91 minutes | Rated PG

Hanks and Long find themselves "in over their heads" as spouses saddled with the "fixer-upper from hell" in this "silly" comedy taking "what every homeowner experiences" to levels of "frustrating insanity"; but those who feel it liens toward "lackluster" recommend you hold out for the "original version, *Mr. Blandings Builds His Dream House.*"

☑ Monkey Business ◑ 26 | 24 | 21 | 22

1931 | Directed by Norman Z. McLeod | With the Marx Brothers, Thelma Todd | 77 minutes | Not Rated

This "early" Marx Brothers' "Hollywood vehicle" is both "solidly entertaining" and "suitably anarchic" as the sibs stow away on a luxury liner and much "hilarious" "shipboard mayhem" ensues; though maybe "not quite their best" work, this "could be their looniest" of all – especially Harpo's "Punch and Judy" riff.

☑ Mon Oncle ✉◨ 26 | 25 | 22 | 23

1958 | Directed by Jacques Tati | With Jacques Tati, Jean-Pierre Zola | 110 minutes | Not Rated

A trove of "very French" folly to "tickle your brain" and "set you giggling", this "delightful" comedy has Tati reprising his "sad-sack" Hulot act as he "bumbles through life" in a series of "superb gags and set pieces"; his "everyman-as-a-buffoon" shtick is a trusty "chuckle producer", while the underlying "commentary on modernity gone awry" is "really funny" too.

Monsieur Verdoux ◑   ▽ 25 | 25 | 23 | 22

1947 | Directed by Charles Chaplin | With Charles Chaplin, Martha Raye, Isobel Elsom | 124 minutes | Not Rated

Cynics who say "Chaplin's little tramp is too sentimental" relish this "wicked" comedy of murders, a "dark, dark, dark" tale in which Charlie plays a "serial-killing", modern-day "bluebeard"; admirers say it's way "ahead of its time", some find it "too preachy at the end", but most agree this "overlooked" work is still "very moving."

Monsoon Wedding 🇫   24 | 23 | 23 | 23

2002 | Directed by Mira Nair | With Naseeruddin Shah, Lillete Dubey, Shefali Shetty, Vasundhara Das, Parvin Dabas | 114 minutes | Rated R

A "feast for the funny bone, eyes and mind", this "charming" dramedy about a "dysfunctional" Indian family and the wedding of their daughter "proves that all families are the same no matter the ethnicity"; it's "a bit slow", but the "colorful cinematography" and "fantastic music" will make you "want to see it again."

Monster ✉   24 | 29 | 24 | 22

2003 | Directed by Patty Jenkins | With Charlize Theron, Christina Ricci | 109 minutes | Rated R

"Frighteningly believable" and thus "tough to watch", this bio of serial murderess Aileen Wuornos "pushes all the emotional buttons" thanks to a "complete immersion" in the role by the Oscar-winning, "makeup"-slathered Theron (with ample backup from the "unsung" Ricci as her girlfriend); though "not as gruesome as it could have been", this "downer" does deliver enough imagery so "violent" that many vow to "never pick up a hitchhiker again."

Monster House   20 | - | 20 | 23

2006 | Directed by Gil Kenan | Animated | 91 minutes | Rated PG

"Great creepy fun" that "makes you laugh", this animated "original" pits "kids against a haunted house" as Halloween approaches and the titular residence whets its appetite for trick-or-treaters; the "sparky" characters, "unsyrupy" story and "dark" CGI work make for "compelling" moviemaking, though given the "surprisingly scary" effects it may be "best for slightly older" viewers.

Monster-in-Law   15 | 17 | 15 | 17

2005 | Directed by Robert Luketic | With Jennifer Lopez, Jane Fonda, Michael Vartan | 101 minutes | Rated PG-13

Ending her 15-year "retirement" from the silver screen, J-Fo meets J-Lo in this "by-the-numbers" comedy about a "Barbara Walters type" who "channels all her energies" into squashing her son's engagement; if the "story holes" and "flat jokes" aren't scary enough, you can count on it to "put the ever-living fear of weddings into you."

Monster's Ball ✉   22 | 26 | 21 | 21

2001 | Directed by Marc Forster | With Billy Bob Thornton, Halle Berry | 111 minutes | Rated R

A "redneck" prison guard and the widow of an inmate he helped execute fall in love in this "disturbingly good" drama, a "gritty depiction" of "two lost souls"; the "slow-moving" story sometimes seems "strained", but is redeemed by the acting" of a deglamorized, Oscar-winning Berry and a "solid" Thornton, who display "great chemistry" during that "steamy sex scene."

⚡ Monsters, Inc.　　26 | - | 25 | 28
2001 | Directed by Peter Docter, David Silverman, Lee Unkrich | Animated | 92 minutes | Rated G

"Pixar does it again" with this "innovative" "animation gem" that "shows kids that the monsters in their closets are really harmless"; this time around, the *Toy Story* tech team alloy an "original" plot, "amazing attention to detail" and "ugly" but "cute" characters to create an "endearing" entertainment that works "for adults" too; P.S. the "blow-you-away" "flying door" sequence has got "theme-park ride" written all over it.

⚡ Monty Python & the Holy Grail　　26 | 22 | 23 | 21
1975 | Directed by Terry Gilliam, Terry Jones | With Monty Python | 91 minutes | Rated PG

By dint of "sheer tasteless genius", this "absurdly wacky" "burlesque of the King Arthur legend" turns "historic reverence" on its ear and rules among "true" Pythonettes as the "movie of a thousand quotes" ("bring out your dead!"); granted, it may be comprised of a series of "strung-together skits" involving "killer bunnies" and "knights who say 'ni'", but the array of "knee-slapping" characters provides enough "lunacy to last the ages."

Moonlight Mile　　17 | 22 | 17 | 18
2002 | Directed by Brad Silberling | With Jake Gyllenhaal, Dustin Hoffman, Susan Sarandon | 117 minutes | Rated PG-13

A "young man makes peace" with his murdered fiancée's "grieving family" and "falls in love" again in this "touching" drama based on the writer-director's "real-life" experience; though there's ample praise for the "three super leads" who milk the "tough" material's "every dysfunctional second", critics contend that the "wanting script" drags down what "could have been spectacular."

Moonraker　　16 | 14 | 15 | 20
1979 | Directed by Lewis Gilbert | With Roger Moore, Lois Chiles, Richard Kiel | 126 minutes | Rated PG

A "stiff" Roger Moore pursues the usual mad villain in this 007 picture that has a hard time living up to its "dynamite credits sequence"; most agree the "silly" scenario is "quite a stretch", what with metal-mouth "Jaws finding love" and a "laughable space battle" that "tries to cash in on *Star Wars*" but "plays more like a Bond spoof."

Moonstruck ✉　　24 | 25 | 24 | 22
1987 | Directed by Norman Jewison | With Cher, Nicolas Cage, Olympia Dukakis | 102 minutes | Rated PG

Both "Italians and wannabe Italians" fall for this "totally charming" "romp" that shows how "love can be found in the least likely places" – even Brooklyn; a "phenomenal" Cher and Cage (making *amore* at such "full throttle" that the "heat between them could peel wallpaper") combine with a "dead-on", "star-studded" ensemble to keep this "romance classic" shining bright; fave scene: the "snap-out-of-it" slap.

| | OVERALL | ACTING | STORY | PROD. |

Moscow on the Hudson
19 | 20 | 20 | 18

1984 | Directed by Paul Mazursky | With Robin Williams, Maria Conchita Alonso | 115 minutes | Rated R

A "Soviet circus performer" bids the Motherland goodbye and "defects to NYC" in this "patriotic" Reagan-era comedy that doubles as a "tender tribute to the immigrant experience"; if post–Cold War audiences find the "need-for-freedom" shtick a bit "corny", at least Williams' "fine" performance supplies some "soul."

Mosquito Coast, The
16 | 19 | 18 | 18

1986 | Directed by Peter Weir | With Harrison Ford, Helen Mirren, River Phoenix | 117 minutes | Rated PG

A "refreshingly different" Ford stars in this "intriguing" adaptation of the Paul Theroux novel in which a utopian inventor "forsakes American civilization" to live with his family in the jungle, only to descend into "fanaticism" and beyond; while the "awesome" Phoenix is a bonus, skeptics swat the flick as "boring" and gnat very memorable.

Mothman Prophecies, The
15 | 16 | 16 | 16

2002 | Directed by Mark Pellington | With Richard Gere, Laura Linney, Debra Messing, Will Patton | 119 minutes | Rated PG-13

"Loosely based on real events", this "psychological ghost story" plays to the "*X-Files* crowd" with its "spooky" tale of a West Virginia town visited by an "eerie" apparition that can "predict tragedy"; some see "potential" given the "solid" cast and "creepy" ambiance, but the "confusing" plot and "slow" pacing ultimately make for a "murky", "incoherent" film.

Motorcycle Diaries, The 🄵
23 | 25 | 23 | 24

2004 | Directed by Walter Salles | With Gael García Bernal, Rodrigo de la Serna | 128 minutes | Rated R

Witness the "seeds of social conscience" sprouting in "young Che Guevara" in this "poetic" road picture set amid "breathtaking South American scenery"; "ogle"-icious Bernal's "marvelous" turn as the future "legendary figure" stokes the revolutionary fire despite hitting a raw nerve with a few *capitalistas* who claim this "saintly" depiction fosters too much "undeserved attention."

Moulin Rouge
21 | 22 | 20 | 26

1952 | Directed by John Huston | With José Ferrer, Zsa Zsa Gabor, Colette Marchand | 119 minutes | Not Rated

"Drenched in color and the excitement of belle epoque Paris", this "original" look at the tortured life of artist Toulouse-Lautrec is the "lush" product of an era when "movies were movies"; Ferrer's "completely entertaining" performance as the "completely odd" painter is the glue here, even if his gloomy portrayal might be at odds with the "eye-candy" production values.

Moulin Rouge!
23 | 23 | 20 | 27

2001 | Directed by Baz Luhrmann | With Nicole Kidman, Ewan McGregor, Jim Broadbent | 127 minutes | Rated PG-13

This "dizzying, decadent" "fever dream of a musical" set in "bohemian Paris" earned a clutch of Oscar nominations and may have "single-handedly revived and re-created the genre" for the "new millennium"; the ever-"ravishing" Kidman "sheds her icy image" in a "kaleidoscopic" turn as a notorious "shady lady" smitten by a "naive poet", and it turns out "McGregor can sing", but naysayers call it a "confusing", "overedited" "mishmash" that's "all glitter, no substance."

Mouse That Roared, The
23 | 23 | 24 | 19

1959 | Directed by Jack Arnold | With Peter Sellers, Jean Seberg, David Kossoff | 83 minutes | Not Rated

"British humor has never been better" than in this "priceless" Cold War–era import about an impoverished nation that declares war on America, planning to lose in exchange for foreign aid; an "ingenious" satire that "pokes lots of holes" in a lot of targets, it's "worth seeing" for "Sellers' expert multiple performances alone."

Mr. & Mrs. Smith
16 | 17 | 15 | 19

2005 | Directed by Doug Liman | With Brad Pitt, Angelina Jolie, Vince Vaughn | 120 minutes | Rated PG-13

"Über-sexy" stars Pitt and Jolie make "one hell of an explosive couple" onscreen in this "over-the-top" action comedy made "infamous" by the leads' "headline"-hogging offscreen antics; but beyond the "Brangelina hype", it's mostly a "mindless" merger of *The War of the Roses* and *Prizzi's Honor* gussied up with standard "tongue-in-cheek" repartee and "nonstop" mayhem.

Mr. Blandings Builds His Dream House ◗
23 | 24 | 23 | 21

1948 | Directed by H.C. Potter | With Cary Grant, Myrna Loy, Melvyn Douglas | 94 minutes | Not Rated

"If you're thinking of building or remodeling your home", "there's no funnier movie" than this "timeless" "cautionary tale" that proves the "perils haven't changed in the last 50 years"; "fixer-uppers" laugh along with this amusing view of the "suburban dream gone askew", most notably "Myrna's painting-the-living-room" scene.

Mr. Deeds Goes to Town ✉◗
25 | 26 | 24 | 23

1936 | Directed by Frank Capra | With Gary Cooper, Jean Arthur, George Bancroft, Lionel Stander | 115 minutes | Not Rated

With "all the heart and soul" (and "schmaltz") that you expect from director "Capra-corn", this "sweet" tale of a "pixilated" eccentric who inherits a fortune and then tries to give it away is one of the "great populist films" of the '30s; thanks to the "feel-good" mood, "heartwarming ending" and Cooper's "trademark underplaying", it's become a "standard" and is "much superior" to the Adam Sandler remake, *Mr. Deeds.*

Mr. Holland's Opus
21 | 22 | 21 | 19

1995 | Directed by Stephen Herek | With Richard Dreyfuss, Glenne Headly | 143 minutes | Rated PG

"Sweet, funny and insightful", this "uplifting" opus chronicles the career of a "reluctant" high-school music teacher "who makes a difference in the lives of his students" while "struggling to come to terms with his own deaf son"; though the hard-hearted fuss it's too "preachy", most swear this "inspirational" story is worth seeing for Dreyfuss' "superb" performance alone.

Mr. Hulot's Holiday ◗🅕
25 | 25 | 22 | 22

1954 | Directed by Jacques Tati | With Jacques Tati, Nathalie Pascaud | 86 minutes | Not Rated

Right "up there with Keaton and Chaplin", Tati's "irresistible" "comic masterpiece" is bound to "take away the worst blues" with some of the "best sight gags" delivered in "almost pure mime"; when its "hilariously" maladroit title character goes to a vacation retreat, whatever "could possibly go wrong does" and the payoff's a "quirky", "low-key" "laugh riot."

Mr. Mom ✉   18 | 18 | 20 | 17

1983 | Directed by Stan Dragoti | With Michael Keaton, Teri Garr, Martin Mull | 91 minutes | Rated PG

Mom and pop "switch roles" in this "fish-out-of-water" comedy detailing the misadventures of a "stay-at-home dad" reduced to "ironing grilled-cheese sandwiches" and "playing poker" with housewives for "shopping coupons"; but even though Keaton is a "likable" enough "slob" in the title role, rewinders report this "guilty pleasure" "doesn't hold up" to repeated viewings.

Mrs. Brown   22 | 28 | 23 | 23

1997 | Directed by John Madden | With Judi Dench, Billy Connolly, Geoffrey Palmer | 103 minutes | Rated PG

"Not widely seen", this "intelligent" drama detailing the platonic relationship between Queen Victoria and her groomsman shows that "even the most hardened heart can be changed by love"; naturally, many say that the "amazing" Dench is "the reason to see it", given her "poignant" performance, though the "intriguing" plot and "subtle" work from Connolly are equally "wonderful."

Mrs. Doubtfire   20 | 23 | 20 | 20

1993 | Directed by Chris Columbus | With Robin Williams, Sally Field, Pierce Brosnan | 125 minutes | Rated PG-13

This "laugh-out-loud" story of a man attempting to "win back his ex and kids" by impersonating a "nanny" manages to be "over-the-top", "subversive" and "endearing" all at once; sure, doubters snipe the "far-fetched" screenplay "can't decide if it's a farce or a tear-jerker", but it's agreed that "riot" Williams is "at his manic best" when in "drag."

Mrs. Henderson Presents   23 | 27 | 22 | 23

2005 | Directed by Stephen Frears | With Judi Dench, Bob Hoskins, Kelly Reilly, Christopher Guest | 103 minutes | Rated R

"Dench didn't earn her reputation for nothing", as demonstrated by her "marvelous" performance in this British comedy about an "eccentric" theater owner whose "nude cuties" revue helps stiffen public resolve during WWII; co-star Hoskins is equally "wonderful" in support, and the pairing of "top-notch humor" with "poignant" meditations on "love and loss" strikes a "crowd-pleasing" balance.

Mrs. Miniver ✉◑   25 | 27 | 24 | 24

1942 | Directed by William Wyler | With Greer Garson, Walter Pidgeon, Teresa Wright | 134 minutes | Not Rated

For "WWII without the combat scenes", check out the "civilian side" in this "stirring" saga of Britain during the Blitz, starring Garson as a "stiff-upper-lipped" homemaker who stoically endures everything from "harrowing air raids" to "Nazi paratroopers" in the kitchen; while cynics say it seems "more propaganda than entertainment", the film was an Oscar magnet, taking home six statuettes, including Best Picture and Best Actress.

	OVERALL	ACTING	STORY	PROD.

☑ Mr. Smith Goes to Washington ◑ — 26 27 25 22

1939 | Directed by Frank Capra | With James Stewart, Jean Arthur, Claude Rains | 125 minutes | Not Rated

"As American as two slices of apple pie", Frank Capra's "rousing" "political fairy tale" about "one man's belief in goodness" and his eventual "triumph" "appeals to the idealist in each of us"; "corny", perhaps, but "you can't help but be moved" by Stewart waging the "filibuster to beat all filibusters" – and proving "you *can* beat City Hall."

Mulan — 23 – 23 24

1998 | Directed by Tony Bancroft, Barry Cook | Animated | 88 minutes | Rated G

An "underrated" rarity, this "gorgeously realized" animated "Chinese folk tale" features a Disney heroine "who can carry a movie on her own"; its mix of "family honor" and "women power" make it "good for a girl's self-esteem", while "just the right balance of seriousness and humor" "sends its message without preaching."

Mulholland Dr. — 20 22 19 22

2001 | Directed by David Lynch | With Naomi Watts, Laura Harring, Justin Theroux | 145 minutes | Rated R

"Another confusing but consuming Lynch production", this "intriguing", "utterly disquieting" "portrait of Hollywood losers" "requires contemplation" since it's particularly "hard to follow"; sure, fans say its "smoldering" leads are so "beautiful" that their presence alone makes the film "visually worth it", but cynics feel "totally ripped off" by this "weird" "nonsense."

Mummy, The ◑ — 24 20 22 23

1932 | Directed by Karl Freund | With Boris Karloff, Zita Johann | 72 minutes | Not Rated

Fresh out of his Frankenstein boots, "master" of fear Karloff wraps himself around the role of an ancient Egyptian priest who's revived when foolhardy explorers open his crypt in this "standout" horror flick; indeed, Boris is "so very creepy" that many say this "original" version of the oft-filmed tale is still the "best."

Mummy, The — 19 16 18 24

1999 | Directed by Stephen Sommers | With Brendan Fraser, Rachel Weisz | 124 minutes | Rated PG-13

Archeologists ravage Egyptian tombs to disastrous results in this "cornball" "modern B movie" featuring lots of "fancy CGI effects" and a plot that lurches somewhere between "scary and funny"; but foes who dis its "ridiculous" premise suggest you "rent the original – *Raiders of the Lost Ark.*"

Mummy Returns, The — 18 17 18 23

2001 | Directed by Stephen Sommers | With Brendan Fraser, Rachel Weisz, The Rock | 130 minutes | Rated PG-13

Wrapped in even more "neat FX" and "tongue-in-cheek" nods to "monster movies" than before, this "fast-paced" sequel sees the return of *The Mummy*'s "dependable" cast for another "old-fashioned" adventure" in "pop" Egyptology by way of Indiana Jones; alright, it's "not an award-winner by any means", but for "brainless" fare, "you can't go wrong."

	OVERALL	ACTING	STORY	PROD.

Munich
23 24 23 24

2005 | Directed by Steven Spielberg | With Eric Bana, Daniel Craig, Geoffrey Rush | 164 minutes | Rated R

The "spiritually corrosive effects of revenge" come under Steven Spielberg's "soul-searching" lens in this "provocative", "action-packed" thriller modeled on the "real events" that followed the 1972 "massacre of Israeli Olympic athletes" by Palestinian terrorists; treating the "very sensitive issue" of the Middle East conflict in a "balanced" manner, it suggests there are "no easy answers", frustrating foes who prefer a less "muddy" moral message.

Muppet Movie, The
24 23 23 25

1979 | Directed by James Frawley | With Charles Durning, Austin Pendleton | 97 minutes | Rated G

"You're never too old" to enjoy this "goofy" but "utterly delightful" romp that might unleash your "inner kid" thanks to some "wonderful puppetry" abetted by an array of star-studded cameos from everyone from Milton Berle to Steve Martin; fans say it's the "best" of the Muppet oeuvre, crediting the "genius" of "national treasure" Jim Henson for the "successful transition" of *Sesame Street*'s denizens to the big screen.

Murderball
25 - 25 22

2005 | Directed by Henry Alex Rubin, Dana Adam Shapiro | Documentary | 88 minutes | Rated PG-13

"Leave your pity at the door" and hold tight for this "hard-hitting" documentary profiling the "fierce competitors" of "quadriplegic rugby", a "rough" wheelchair sport with a rep for "demolition derby" intensity; smashing the conventional "clichés about the disabled", it's a "non-sentimental" glimpse at a "seldom seen" group whose "guts, strength and love of life" are an "inspiration" to all.

Murder by Death
21 21 22 19

1976 | Directed by Robert Moore | With Peter Falk, Peter Sellers, Maggie Smith, Alec Guinness | 94 minutes | Rated PG

A "kooky lampoon that hits the spot", this Neil Simon–penned whodunit "spoof" places a "diverse" group of private eyes in a castle where murder ensues; given the efforts of a Charlie Chan–esque Sellers and a Bogart-channeling Falk, this "madcap" exercise is a "must-see satire for mystery lovers", even if some turn up evidence of too many "good actors playing useless parts."

Murder, My Sweet ◑
24 24 24 22

1944 | Directed by Edward Dmytryk | With Dick Powell, Claire Trevor, Anne Shirley, Otto Kruger | 95 minutes | Not Rated

For "Dick Powell without Ruby Keeler", check out his "breakout" role as the "tough" private dick Philip Marlowe in this adaptation of Raymond Chandler's *Farewell, My Lovely*; it's a "quintessential" piece of "early noir", replete with a "perfect femme fatale", "unsurpassed" dialogue and a world-weary, "wisecracking" outlook on life.

Murder on the Orient Express
23 23 26 24

1974 | Directed by Sidney Lumet | With Albert Finney, Lauren Bacall, Ingrid Bergman | 128 minutes | Rated PG

"Agatha Christie hasn't been done better" than in this "complex, lushly produced" Hercule Poirot mystery set onboard the Orient Express;

boasting a "crisply directed" "all-star" ensemble cast that "looks like they're having the time of their lives", this "luxuriously funny" "perfect thriller" certainly "won't bore you" – and "you'll never guess whodunit."

Muriel's Wedding

| 22 | 24 | 22 | 20 |

1995 | Directed by P.J. Hogan | With Toni Collette, Rachel Griffiths, Bill Hunter | 106 minutes | Rated R

Mating Aussie "quirkiness" to a "big heart", this "unique" romantic comedy gives the "dynamite" Collette her "breakthrough role" as a "nuptial-obsessed" small-town "wallflower" who "comes of age" with spirited support from gal-pal Griffiths; from the exuberant "ABBA-licious" soundtrack to its "poignant" undercurrent, devotees are wholly engaged and "left wanting more."

Music and Lyrics

| 17 | 19 | 17 | 18 |

2007 | Directed by Marc Lawrence | With Hugh Grant, Drew Barrymore, Haley Bennett | 96 minutes | Rated PG-13

Hugh and Drew make a "catchy" couple in this "brain-free" romantic comedy starring Grant as a "has-been" '80s singer who enlists the "ever-adorable" Barrymore to help him pen a tune for "one last shot at fame"; despite a few "clichéd" notes, it's "fun and frivolous" stuff – "like a pop song" – and worth checking out for the "mock music video" alone.

Music Man, The

| 25 | 24 | 25 | 26 |

1962 | Directed by Morton DaCosta | With Robert Preston, Shirley Jones, Buddy Hackett | 151 minutes | Rated G

Making an "exquisite, seamless transition from Broadway to the silver screen", this slice of "pure Americana" about a "traveling con man" let loose in River City, Iowa, hits "classic" notes with its "catchy" Meredith Willson score; thanks to a "tour-de-force" turn by a "mesmerizing" Preston, this "family treat" "never grows old."

Must Love Dogs

| 16 | 18 | 15 | 16 |

2005 | Directed by Gary David Goldberg | With Diane Lane, John Cusack, Elizabeth Perkins | 98 minutes | Rated PG-13

Taking a "lighthearted" look at the "horrors of dating after divorce", this "run-of-the-mill" chick flick boasts a "wonderful" cast led by two "rock stars of romantic comedy", the "charming" Lane and "endearing" Cusack; problem is, there's absolutely "no chemistry between them", and a "slow-paced", "dog-tired" script to boot.

⚡ Mutiny on the Bounty ✉◑

| 25 | 25 | 25 | 23 |

1935 | Directed by Frank Lloyd | With Charles Laughton, Clark Gable, Franchot Tone | 132 minutes | Not Rated

Despite being "a bit creaky" after all these years, this original version of a legendary clash of egos on the high seas remains "the one and only" simply because "you don't get acting like this anymore": Laughton is darn "grand" as "definitive villain" Captain Bligh, and "Gable is, well, Gable" as Mr. Christian, his second-in-command.

Mutiny on the Bounty

| 22 | 24 | 24 | 22 |

1962 | Directed by Lewis Milestone | With Marlon Brando, Trevor Howard, Richard Harris | 178 minutes | Not Rated

Ultra-"fabulous scenery" that will surely make you "want to move to Tahiti" and a "cast of thousands" collide in this "big-budget" MGM remake about an uprising at sea; Brando turns in "one of his most controversial roles" as a "foppish" Fletcher Christian, even if foes harrumph "I'll take Gable."

My Beautiful Laundrette   23 | 24 | 23 | 19

1986 | Directed by Stephen Frears | With Daniel Day-Lewis, Gordon Warnecke | 98 minutes | Rated R

This "highly original" drama of "modern London" puts race and assimilation through a "wonderfully up-front" spin cycle in its story of "smart", "entrepreneurial" immigrants vs. the nativist "lower classes"; amid the many "honest" moments that come out in the wash is the "daring" bond between Warnecke's go-getting Pakistani and Day-Lewis' tough hooligan, resulting in some "steamy gay kissing."

My Best Friend's Wedding   19 | 19 | 19 | 19

1997 | Directed by P.J. Hogan | With Julia Roberts, Dermot Mulroney, Rupert Everett | 105 minutes | Rated PG-13

There's "no thinking required" in this "enjoyable if predictable" "chick flick" about a single gal bent on preventing her best male friend from getting hitched; while a "surprisingly funny Roberts" and "yummy Everett" "chew up the scenery" entertainingly, those through with love find this "anti-romance" "contrived" and "obvious" – except for the "'Say a Little Prayer'" sing-along.

My Big Fat Greek Wedding   23 | 22 | 23 | 21

2002 | Directed by Joel Zwick | With Nia Vardalos, John Corbett, Lainie Kazan | 96 minutes | Rated PG

It "doesn't matter whether you are Greek, Jewish, Italian or Albanian" – "we all see our crazy relatives up on the screen" in this "absolutely hilarious" "feel-good" look at Hellenic matrimony featuring a "likable cast of characters that you grow to love despite all their quirks"; critics claim "too much big fat hype", but they're outvoted by fans who "will never look at Windex the same way again."

My Bodyguard   18 | 18 | 19 | 16

1980 | Directed by Tony Bill | With Chris Makepeace, Adam Baldwin, Matt Dillon | 96 minutes | Rated PG

The "ultimate teenage revenge fantasy", this "feel-good" flick about an "underdog" high-schooler who hires a tough classmate to protect him from a bully "rings true" with "anyone who was ever picked on"; sure, there's a "silly, irrelevant" subplot about "eccentric grown-ups", but overall this "endearing" "coming-of-age saga" is "well done."

My Brilliant Career   25 | 28 | 25 | 23

1980 | Directed by Gillian Armstrong | With Judy Davis, Sam Neill, Wendy Hughes | 100 minutes | Rated G

A "headstrong young woman" coming of age in 19th-century Australia must choose between a man or a career in this "wonderful" drama that's a "feminist favorite" ("it changed my life"); in the "brilliant performance" that made her a star, "Davis rules", and abetted by "lovely photography and scenery", the film's an "absorbing" testimony to "girl power."

My Cousin Vinny   22 | 24 | 21 | 19

1992 | Directed by Jonathan Lynn | With Joe Pesci, Ralph Macchio, Marisa Tomei | 120 minutes | Rated R

"Fuhgeddaboudit": this "laugh-out-loud", "quotable" "courtroom classic" about a novice "Noo Yawk lawyer" representing his cousin in an

Alabama murder trial is a "cleverly written" comic look at "Southern justice"; a "perfect" Pesci "carries the show", amply assisted by Tomei, who earned a "well-deserved Oscar" just by "making a Brooklyn accent the sexiest sound around"; P.S. it works best with "ordered-in pizza."

ⓩ My Darling Clementine ◖ | 25 | 27 | 23 | 24 |

1946 | Directed by John Ford | With Henry Fonda, Linda Darnell, Victor Mature, Walter Brennan | 97 minutes | Not Rated

"One of the all-time great Westerns", this "wonderfully humane" Ford oater strays from the "real history" behind the "shootout at the O.K. Corral" to pose an "idealized" Wyatt Earp against a "rich" backdrop of a frontier "on the verge of change"; fortified with "romance", "moody characters" (Doc Holliday "reciting Shakespeare") and, you bet, lots of "gunplay", it's a "rewarding" ride that exemplifies the "definition of 'classic.'"

My Dinner with Andre | 21 | 21 | 18 | 19 |

1981 | Directed by Louis Malle | With Wallace Shawn, Andre Gregory | 110 minutes | Not Rated

Who'd have thought a movie that "consists entirely of a dinner conversation" between two acquaintances could keep you entertained for two hours?; although with talk "spanning every philosophical topic" that "captures the magic in the ordinary", Shawn and Gregory do just that; "remarkable for how little it works with", this "simple, unpretentious" art-house hit is "oddly fascinating" to those who wish their own dining companions "could be as interesting."

ⓩ My Fair Lady ✉ | 27 | 27 | 27 | 27 |

1964 | Directed by George Cukor | With Audrey Hepburn, Rex Harrison, Stanley Holloway | 170 minutes | Rated G

"Hollywood couldn't have done a better job" than this "grand, classy" version of Broadway's Lerner and Loewe musical "based on *Pygmalion*"; a "breathtaking" (but "dubbed") Hepburn is "incomparable" as the Cockney "guttersnipe turned into a lady", while Oscar-winner Harrison "at his tweedy best" plays her "superior yet vulnerable" teacher; "infectious" tunes and costumes that "leave you weak-kneed" ("those hats!") make this "luscious production" all the more "loverly."

My Favorite Year | 22 | 25 | 22 | 20 |

1982 | Directed by Richard Benjamin | With Peter O'Toole, Mark Linn-Baker, Jessica Harper | 92 minutes | Rated PG

This "winning comedy" about the "early days of TV" involves a boozy matinee idol's appearance on a program that's a "great riff on the old Sid Caesar show"; although "O'Toole playing a drunk might not be a stretch", he "nails every nuance", turning this "affectionate period piece" into "one of the funniest movies no one has ever seen."

My Girl | 20 | 18 | 19 | 18 |

1991 | Directed by Howard Zieff | With Dan Aykroyd, Jamie Lee Curtis, Anna Chlumsky | 102 minutes | Rated PG

Get out your handkerchiefs: this "make-you-cry" dramedy pulls out all the stops in its depiction of a motherless girl dealing with emotional awakening (and her father's new girlfriend); Chlumsky's "sweet", "heart-wrenching" turn nails the "innocence and complexity of childhood" so well that many would like to "have her as a daughter."

	OVERALL	ACTING	STORY	PROD.

My Left Foot ✉   25 | 28 | 25 | 23

1989 | Directed by Jim Sheridan | With Daniel Day-Lewis, Brenda Fricker, Hugh O'Conor | 98 minutes | Rated R

It "could have been sappy and overly sentimental", but this "stereotype-smashing" true account of an Irish man born with cerebral palsy is "handled with unvarnished dignity" thanks to the Oscar-winning Day-Lewis, who "maintains the contorted body and emotional scars" of his condition so adeptly that "you forget you're watching an actor"; "very moving", this film's a "beacon of light for all."

My Life As a Dog 🇫   25 | 24 | 25 | 22

1987 | Directed by Lasse Hallström | With Anton Glanzelius, Melinda Kinnaman | 101 minutes | Rated PG-13

"For once, an adult really gets into a child's head" in this "enchanting" Swedish "coming-of-age" drama that devotees deem director "Hallström's best"; the "puckish" lead is both "complex" and "cute", his fellow villagers "wacky" and the story "heart-tugging" without a "single false note" – no wonder many say it's "goose bump-worthy."

My Little Chickadee ◑   23 | 23 | 18 | 19

1940 | Directed by Edward F. Cline | With Mae West, W.C. Fields | 83 minutes | Not Rated

"Two comic pros" take on the Old West in this screwball oater about a fallen woman run out of town and the con man she weds; Mae's "priceless line delivery" works well against W.C.'s "vaudeville-era" gags – but since they "share very little screen time together" (interrupted by lengthy "pedestrian melodramatics"), some say the pairing of these screen legends "isn't as effective as one might hope."

Ⓩ My Man Godfrey ◑   25 | 25 | 23 | 21

1936 | Directed by Gregory La Cava | With William Powell, Carole Lombard, Eugene Pallette | 94 minutes | Not Rated

As an "unconventional love-struck heiress", Lombard displays "impeccable timing" opposite the "masterful" Powell as the "hobo hired to be the family butler" in this "ultimate screwball comedy", the standard by which "all others are measured"; of course, the "fast-paced", fast-talking "plot is absurd" (that's "precisely the point"), but the "charming" principals "make it look convincing."

My Night at Maud's ◑🇫   ▽ 26 | 26 | 23 | 23

1970 | Directed by Eric Rohmer | With Jean-Louis Trintignant, Françoise Fabian, Marie-Christine Barrault | 105 minutes | Rated PG

A "movie about grown-ups for grown-ups", this "rewarding philosophical" drama examines the "concept of morality" in its story of a man attracted to two very different women; it's "mostly an extended conversation" with *beaucoup* "talk, talk and more talk", but intellectuals insist "all of it is worth listening to" (or reading about in the subtitles).

My Own Private Idaho   19 | 21 | 19 | 19

1991 | Directed by Gus Van Sant | With River Phoenix, Keanu Reeves, William Richert | 102 minutes | Rated R

"Beautiful boys" work the streets of Portland in this "original modern romance" about a "narcoleptic hustler" (Phoenix, in a "heartbreaking" turn) who falls for a "man he can never have"; once the plot drifts off into a "pretentious" takeoff of *Henry IV*", some say it becomes "over-reaching" and downright "depressing", but still there are "enough good moments to make it worthwhile."

Mystic Pizza

17 | 18 | 17 | 15

1988 | Directed by Donald Petrie | With Annabeth Gish, Julia Roberts, Lili Taylor | 104 minutes | Rated R

"Female friendships" and young romance are examined in this "coming-of-age charmer" set in a New England pizza parlor, an "authentic slice of life" that's also a "great Sunday afternoon chick flick"; notable for being "Julia's first major movie", it's "very fluffy", though its "sweetness" is very "winning."

☑ Mystic River ✉

26 | 28 | 25 | 25

2003 | Directed by Clint Eastwood | With Sean Penn, Tim Robbins, Kevin Bacon, Laurence Fishburne, Marcia Gay Harden, Laura Linney | 137 minutes | Rated R

"Lots of angst and anger" lie beneath this "bleak" tale of childhood buddies reunited as adults in the aftermath of a murder; it really "packs a wallop" thanks to a "pitch-perfect", "all-star" ensemble (with special kudos to Oscar winners Penn and Robbins for their "kick-in-the-gut" performances), not to mention Clint's "compelling" direction and "haunting score"; the only dissonant note is that "slightly off-the-mark" ending.

Nacho Libre

12 | 13 | 11 | 13

2006 | Directed by Jared Hess | With Jack Black, Héctor Jiménez, Ana de la Reguera | 100 minutes | Rated PG

Jack Black's a "sight in tights" playing a "Mexican monk turned wrestler" in this "goofy" "physical comedy" that mixes "slapstick" and "sight gags" with *mucho* "junior high-level humor"; the "demented premise" provides some "cheap laughs", but most maintain there's "too much cheese on this nacho", an "overlong sketch" that spreads itself too thin and ultimately "falls flat."

Naked Gun, The

20 | 17 | 17 | 18

1988 | Directed by David Zucker | With Leslie Nielsen, Priscilla Presley, George Kennedy | 85 minutes | Rated PG-13

This "laugh-a-minute" "cop spoof" from the minds behind *Airplane!* stars a "deadpan" Nielsen, who "raises the bar for satirical comedy" with his "terrific" performance; granted, the "brilliantly dumb characters" and "loopy overlapping dialogue" are equally "riotous", but in the end "you definitely have to be a guy to enjoy this much stupidity"; P.S. some surveyors find it "discomfortingly amusing" when O.J. Simpson appears.

Naked Lunch

17 | 19 | 17 | 18

1991 | Directed by David Cronenberg | With Peter Weller, Judy Davis, Ian Holm, Roy Scheider | 115 minutes | Rated R

Cronenberg's "well-meaning" adaptation of William Burroughs' iconic chronicle of "heroin-induced hallucinations" endured in a North African "expat community" injects a blend of the author's "bio and fiction" into a nightmarish hash of "mind-bending" imagery; "not for the faint of heart", it could "freak out" the uninitiated as well as bug beatniks who insist "this book can't be filmed."

	OVERALL	ACTING	STORY	PROD.

Name of the Rose, The
22 | 24 | 24 | 23

1986 | Directed by Jean-Jacques Annaud | With Sean Connery, Christian Slater, F. Murray Abraham | 130 minutes | Rated R

The "cold, scary world" of the Middle Ages comes to life in this "excellent period mystery" drawn from Umberto Eco's "intricate" novel about a "monk who visits a monastery plagued by unexplained murders"; blessed by Connery's "top-notch" turn as a kind of "14th-century 007", it's an "entertaining" take on "religious conspiracy" that many find "superior to *The Da Vinci Code.*"

Nanny McPhee
21 | 22 | 21 | 23

2006 | Directed by Kirk Jones | With Emma Thompson, Colin Firth, Angela Lansbury | 97 minutes | Rated PG

A "lonely" widower saddled with an "awful bunch" of "misbehaving children" dials "nanny 9-1-1" and receives "magical", "Mary Poppins"-esque relief in this "charming" fairy tale; Thompson is "fabulous" in the title role (her "makeup's unbelievable" too), and if the McPlot veers toward "formulaic", know that small fry are "sure to enjoy" it.

☑ Napoléon ①∅
28 | 24 | 26 | 28

1929 | Directed by Abel Gance | With Albert Dieudonné, Antonin Artaud | 235 minutes | Rated G

"Eye-popping even today", this bio of Napoléon Bonaparte from "audacious" director Gance is a "sweeping epic" from the silent era that had been truncated over time but then restored to its former glory; its "unsurpassed" camerawork includes shots made "from horseback" and on a "pendulum", but its "final triptych", predating widescreen photography, makes for a particularly "rousing" windup.

Napoleon Dynamite
19 | 20 | 17 | 17

2004 | Directed by Jared Hess | With Jon Heder, Jon Gries | 82 minutes | Rated PG

"Gosh", the road to "cult classic" status was short for this "flippin' sweet" underdog comedy whose "deadpan" depiction of a carrot-topped, "tater tot"-chomping "born loser" pays "honest" homage to that "nerdy kid you went to school with"; voters "love it or hate it": lovers like its "quotable lines" ("vote for Pedro") and the "best dance scene ever", though foes fret it "goes nowhere and does nothing."

Nashville
23 | 23 | 22 | 24

1975 | Directed by Robert Altman | With Ronee Blakley, Keith Carradine, Lily Tomlin, Geraldine Chaplin, Karen Black, Shelley Duvall, Henry Gibson, Scott Glenn | 159 minutes | Rated R

It's the "wonderful ensemble" cast that makes this comic "portrait of '70s America" set in Nashville "richer and funnier with every viewing"; though some find it "frustrating" ("too many people talking at once"), "black humor" fans dub it "Altman's best", with enough "interesting characters" and "smart observations" to make it the "country cousin of *Gosford Park.*"

National Lampoon's Vacation
22 | 17 | 20 | 17

1983 | Directed by Harold Ramis | With Chevy Chase, Beverly D'Angelo, Randy Quaid | 98 minutes | Rated R

"Bad taste has never been funnier" than in this "vacation-from-hell" comedy recounting a "dysfunctional family's" cross-country road trip;

as the beleaguered dad, Chase is at the "pinnacle of his career", though many say he's upstaged by fleeting glimpses of white-"hot" "Christie Brinkley in a red sports car."

National Treasure

2004 | Directed by John Turteltaub | With Nicolas Cage, Jon Voight | 131 minutes | Rated PG

"Indiana Jones meets *The Da Vinci Code*" in this "helluva roller-coaster ride" hinged around a treasure map discovered "on the back of the Declaration of Independence" ("seriously") and other "far-fetched" clues geared toward "American history buffs"; granted, Nic may be "no Harrison Ford" and the flick an "utterly disposable" "no-brainer", but it's more than "ok for a little escapism" and works best with a "large bag of popcorn."

National Treasure: Book of Secrets

20 | 19 | 19 | 23

2007 | Directed by Jon Turteltaub | With Nicolas Cage, Justin Bartha, Diane Kruger, Jon Voight | 124 minutes | Rated PG

"Same plot, different treasure" is the open secret of this "enjoyable" sequel catapulting its "likable cast" through another "rush of action and scenery changes" in service of an "interesting" albeit "improbable" historical mystery (something to do with Abe Lincoln's assassination and a "secret book" meant only for the eyes of U.S. presidents); so long as the franchise creators "don't run out of ideas", expect the hunt for more "blockbuster" follow-ups to continue.

National Velvet

24 | 24 | 24 | 22

1945 | Directed by Clarence Brown | With Elizabeth Taylor, Mickey Rooney, Anne Revere | 123 minutes | Rated G

The movie equivalent of "comfort food", this "classic" "coming-of-age story" about a "girl and her horse" stars a "dazzlingly young Taylor" and a "scene-stealing" Rooney in a "feel-good" parable of "surmounting obstacles to make dreams come true"; maybe it's "corny", but any young lady "who ever dreamed of having a pony" can't help but "gush" over that climatic steeplechase race.

Natural, The

23 | 21 | 23 | 22

1984 | Directed by Barry Levinson | With Robert Redford, Robert Duvall, Glenn Close | 134 minutes | Rated PG

"Every Little Leaguer's favorite flick", this mix of "magic" and "major league baseball" stars a "rugged Redford" as a "middle-aged rookie" who hits a "chill"-inducing "home run into the lights"; though some sigh it's too "sentimental", fans cheer this "solid period drama" (and Randy Newman's "unforgettable score").

Natural Born Killers

14 | 16 | 14 | 17

1994 | Directed by Oliver Stone | With Woody Harrelson, Juliette Lewis, Robert Downey Jr., Tommy Lee Jones | 118 minutes | Rated R

Ok, it's director Stone's "most controversial work", but otherwise this "raw" (as in "bloody") look at how "mass murderers" are portrayed by the "mass media" galvanizes surveyors: admirers call it a "blistering social commentary" that's both "visionary" and "visually stunning", but sinkers say its "violence-as-a-cartoon" ethos is "gratuitous", "pointless" and ultimately "more stupid than thrilling."

| | OVERALL | ACTING | STORY | PROD. |

Negotiator, The
20 | 22 | 20 | 20

1998 | Directed by F. Gary Gray | With Samuel L. Jackson, Kevin Spacey, J.T. Walsh, Paul Giamatti | 139 minutes | Rated R

Suckers for "suspense" get what they bargained for from this "smart", "tight-paced" thriller featuring a "riveting performance" by Jackson as a hostage negotiator trying to clear himself of a murder via a "gripping standoff" with counterpart Spacey; the "tension between the two men" gives the otherwise "standard-issue" setup a "wow"-inducing jolt.

Net, The
16 | 17 | 18 | 16

1995 | Directed by Irwin Winkler | With Sandra Bullock, Jeremy Northam, Dennis Miller | 114 minutes | Rated PG-13

"Before anyone ever heard of identity theft", there was this "fast-paced" "popcorn thriller" featuring Bullock as a "computer geek" who has her personal data "completely erased" after she stumbles upon online government secrets; the "fear-of-technology" theme may be somewhat "dated" and "overbaked", but it's still worth logging on for the random "cheap thrills."

Network ⊠
24 | 25 | 24 | 22

1976 | Directed by Sidney Lumet | With Faye Dunaway, William Holden, Peter Finch, Beatrice Straight | 120 minutes | Rated R

Even 30 years later, newscaster Howard Beale's "fateful cry, 'I'm mad as hell, and I'm not going to take it anymore'" is still "relevant" to proponents of this "prophetic" dramedy about television's "battle between news and entertainment"; "expertly written" by Paddy Chayefsky and "brilliantly acted" by Finch, Dunaway and Straight (who all won Oscars), this "biting" dark comedy has surveyors citing "*Jerry Springer*" and sighing "it's all true now."

Neverending Story, The
23 | 19 | 24 | 24

1984 | Directed by Wolfgang Petersen | With Barret Oliver, Gerald McRaney, Noah Hathaway, Tami Stronach | 102 minutes | Rated PG

A "pre-*Harry Potter*" "escape from the mundane", this "visionary" fantasy combining live actors and animated creatures is an "enthralling" rendering of a "beautiful children's tale" about a lad who's "magically transported" by a storybook and finds he has the "power to save a far-off land"; despite "weak acting" and "'80s special effects", it still "holds up for family viewing after all these years"; P.S. "skip the sequels."

Never on Sunday ◑
24 | 26 | 23 | 21

1960 | Directed by Jules Dassin | With Melina Mercouri, Jules Dassin | 91 minutes | Not Rated

A "sensuous" Mercouri became an international star after illuminating the screen in this "delightful" drama about an "earthy" Greek prostitute and an uptight American (played by director Dassin) who tries to pull a Pygmalion on her; although once "shocking" and now "delightfully dated", every-nighters could "watch it anytime – even on a Sunday."

Never Say Never Again
18 | 20 | 17 | 19

1983 | Directed by Irvin Kershner | With Sean Connery, Klaus Maria Brandauer, Barbara Carrera | 134 minutes | Rated PG

Live-and-let-diehards declare it's "fun to see Connery reprise the role that made him famous (and rich)" in this "rehash of *Thunderball*" featuring an "older" though "still studly" 007 who's "stunningly" teamed with Carrera; but foes say this "disappointing" picture "shouldn't be considered a Bond film", since it lacks the "appropriate music" and panache of producer Albert Broccoli.

New World, The

16 | 17 | 15 | 23

2005 | Directed by Terrence Malick | With Colin Farrell, Q'Orianka Kilcher, Christopher Plummer | 135 minutes | Rated PG-13

"Visual poet" Malick stays "true to form" with this "contemplative, brooding" look at the "life of Pocahontas" as a metaphor for the "broken love affair" between Native Americans and Virginia's first British colonists; but while fans faun over the "lush", "put-a-frame-around-it" imagery and 14-year-old Kilcher's "particularly good" performance, just as many malign the film's "slow" pace and "pretentious" airs.

New York, New York

19 | 21 | 18 | 22

1977 | Directed by Martin Scorsese | With Liza Minnelli, Robert De Niro, Mary Kay Place | 164 minutes | Rated PG

Minnelli's "perfectly cast" and in "flawless voice" in this "postmodern musical from Martin Scorsese" about married musicians yearning for "fame in the 1940s"; still, many moan "De Niro's character is so unlikable" that the "picture never works", resulting in a "forgettable muddle" – "except for a certain song."

Niagara

21 | 22 | 20 | 22

1953 | Directed by Henry Hathaway | With Marilyn Monroe, Joseph Cotten, Jean Peters | 92 minutes | Not Rated

The movie that "made Monroe a star", this "twisted" Technicolor thriller is set back in the day when Niagara Falls was a "hot destination" for honeymooners; its "double-cross", "soap opera"–esque plot involves a "treacherous wife", a frustrated husband and a pair of naive newlyweds, but its most "unforgettable" moment is Marilyn's "famous walk" through a parking lot, which totally "overshadows" everything else in the picture.

Nicholas Nickleby

22 | 23 | 24 | 22

2002 | Directed by Douglas McGrath | With Christopher Plummer, Jim Broadbent, Charlie Hunnam, Anne Hathaway | 132 minutes | Rated PG

"Escape to another era" and follow the "wholesome" adventures of a "down-on-his-luck" bloke who "rises to the top" in this "rich", "intelligently pared-down" rendering of Dickens' "very long novel"; "outstanding performances" by the "wonderfully odious" Plummer and fellow "fine talents" contribute to an overall "solid" production, leaving fans to ponder why "nobody saw it."

Night at the Museum

19 | 18 | 21 | 24

2006 | Directed by Shawn Levy | With Ben Stiller, Robin Williams, Carla Gugino, Dick Van Dyke | 108 minutes | Rated PG

Exhibiting "appeal to all ages", this family flick stars Stiller as a "guard at the Museum of Natural History" who discovers the displays "come to life at night" (the parade of "incredible effects" is nearly stolen by Williams' "bully" channeling of Teddy Roosevelt); despite the "slight story" and "blatant thievery from *Jumanji*", the production values are "brilliant" and it sure is "great to see Dick Van Dyke again."

	OVERALL	ACTING	STORY	PROD.

Z Night at the Opera, A ◑
26 | 25 | 22 | 22

1935 | Directed by Sam Wood | With the Marx Brothers, Kitty Carlisle, Margaret Dumont | 96 minutes | Not Rated

"Inspired insanity" meets "Marxist lunacy" in this "nutty" comedy (the "origin of the term 'laugh riot'") from the brothers Marx, wherein Groucho persuades a social-climbing Dumont to invest in an opera production; fans fast-forward through the "saccharine musical moments" in favor of the "verbal dazzle" of the "contract routine", the "baseball-in-the-orchestra-pit" bit and, of course, that "not-to-be-believed stateroom scene."

Nightmare Alley ◑
▽ 22 | 23 | 21 | 21

1947 | Directed by Edmund Goulding | With Tyrone Power, Joan Blondell, Coleen Gray | 110 minutes | Not Rated

"Talk about a downer" – this "creepy" film noir flick depicts the "moral disintegration" of a "true charlatan", a carnival roustabout turned "phony nightclub spiritualist" who "goes too far to reach his dream"; Power "fearlessly proves he's not just another pretty face" with a "scary yet appealing" performance that's "stunning for its time."

Nightmare Before Christmas, The
24 | - | 22 | 28

1993 | Directed by Henry Selick | Animated | 76 minutes | Rated PG

The "perfect antidote to the holidays" may well be this "magical", "macabre masterpiece" of stop-motion animation that ideally epitomizes the "bizarre genius" of producer Tim Burton; with a "cool story" – Halloween meets Christmas – "interesting characters" and "Danny Elfman's great score", it's a "must-see for kids of all ages."

Nightmare on Elm Street, A
19 | 14 | 19 | 18

1984 | Directed by Wes Craven | With John Saxon, Ronee Blakley, Johnny Depp | 91 minutes | Rated R

Built around the "idea that your nightmares are real", this "original splatter" flick "did for sleeping what *Jaws* did for swimming" thanks to Freddy Krueger, its "pizza-faced" villain with "knives for fingers"; 25 years later, this "darn scary" picture is recognized as a "modern horror classic."

Z Night of the Hunter, The ◑
27 | 28 | 25 | 26

1955 | Directed by Charles Laughton | With Robert Mitchum, Shelley Winters, Lillian Gish | 93 minutes | Not Rated

Playing a "semi-psychotic preacher" "personifying pure evil", the "mesmerizing" Mitchum "terrorizes a bunch of kids" (and "invents tattooed knuckles") in this "strange" film noir frightfest; it's a "pity this was Laughton's only directorial" effort, given the "exquisite cinematography" and "unforgettable" performances that add up to "stunningly innovative cinema."

Night of the Iguana, The ◑
23 | 26 | 22 | 22

1964 | Directed by John Huston | With Richard Burton, Ava Gardner, Deborah Kerr, Sue Lyon | 125 minutes | Not Rated

This "beautiful rendering" of Tennessee Williams' play concerns a defrocked clergyman turned south-of-the-border tour guide who lusts after three women, but is probably better known as the "movie that put Puerto Vallarta on the map as a tourist destination"; fans say the script is so "sultry" that you can almost "see the heat coming off the screen" – check out "Ava Gardner and those beach boys."

Night of the Living Dead ◗

22 | 13 | 19 | 16

1968 | Directed by George A. Romero | With Duane Jones, Judith O'Dea, Russ Streiner | 96 minutes | Not Rated

Director Romero "does zombies right" in this "zero-budget" indie "landmark" that proves that even "schlocky" special effects, a "shabby storyline" and "bad acting" can produce what living dead–heads call the "scariest movie ever made"; the "grainy black-and-white film used adds to the creepy aura", right down to the "freak-you-out", "pj-wetting" finale.

Night Shift

19 | 20 | 19 | 17

1982 | Directed by Ron Howard | With Henry Winkler, Michael Keaton, Shelley Long | 105 minutes | Rated R

A prostitution ring setting up shop in a NYC morgue is the "goofy concept" servicing this "sleeper" buddy comedy best remembered for Keaton's "hysterical", "star-making" debut as the "nutty" sidekick to Winkler's "stuck-in-a-rut" shlub; P.S. "look fast" for Kevin Costner appearing in a "bit part."

Nights of Cabiria ✉◗🅵

27 | 28 | 25 | 24

1957 | Directed by Federico Fellini | With Giulietta Masina, François Périer | 117 minutes | Not Rated

"Post-WWII Italy" as seen "through the eyes of a streetwalker" is the premise of this "simple, heartfelt" drama that's one of Fellini's "most moving" (and least "bizarre") films; as the "lovable girl of the streets", the "radiant" Masina is nothing less than a "female Charlie Chaplin", rendering an "amazing" performance that "ranges from tragedy to transcendence to flat-out comedy."

9½ Weeks

15 | 15 | 15 | 16

1986 | Directed by Adrian Lyne | With Mickey Rourke, Kim Basinger | 113 minutes | Rated R

"Groundbreaking for its time", this "steamy" rendering of an "obsessive relationship" remains a definite "third-date movie", what with the "twisted" Rourke and "hot! hot! hot!" Basinger engaged in "kinky sex" via blindfolds, "ice cubes" and peanut shells; still, bluenoses find it "dreary, numbing" "softcore porn" that's nowhere near "as sexy as *An Officer and a Gentleman.*"

1941

14 | 15 | 14 | 18

1979 | Directed by Steven Spielberg | With John Belushi, Dan Aykroyd, Tim Matheson, Robert Stack, Warren Oates | 118 minutes | Rated PG

An unlikely pair –"Spielberg and Belushi?!" – collide in this "frenetic" WWII comedy about a "feared Japanese attack on LA" in the uncertain days after Pearl Harbor; while supporters say this "overlooked" "guilty pleasure" rolls out a "great cast" and a "fun" John Williams score, sinkers strafe it as "overlong", "unfunny" and, ahem, "not good history."

1900 🅵

22 | 25 | 21 | 25

1977 | Directed by Bernardo Bertolucci | With Robert De Niro, Gérard Depardieu, Burt Lancaster | 243 minutes | Rated R

This "sweeping epic" from Bernardo Bertolucci is a "sumptuous", "fascinating study of Italian society and politics in the first half of the 20th century"; "finely acted" by De Niro (playing an aristocrat) and

Depardieu (as a proletariat labor leader), it might be "a bit long and self-indulgent", but most find its "operatic form" and "meticulous" camerawork completely "involving."

9 to 5

	OVERALL	ACTING	STORY	PROD.
	18	18	19	17

1980 | Directed by Colin Higgins | With Jane Fonda, Lily Tomlin, Dolly Parton, Dabney Coleman | 110 minutes | Rated PG

"Every secretary's dream" of "getting even with the boss" comes true in this "silly comedy", a "feminist classic" with a "relevant message" (though chauvinists snicker it's "proof that women's lib can be sexist too"); still, its "strong" protagonists exhibit "amazing chemistry" and Parton's theme song sure is "catchy."

Ninotchka ◐

25	27	24	23

1939 | Directed by Ernst Lubitsch | With Greta Garbo, Melvyn Douglas, Ina Claire | 110 minutes | Not Rated

This "great American comedy" depicts Soviet comrades seduced by capitalism, but is best known as the picture in which "Garbo laughs" for the first time on-screen; playing a "woman who follows her heart rather than the Communist manifesto", she's "smooth and sexy" spouting "incredibly funny dialogue" courtesy of a group of ace scenarists including Billy Wilder.

No Country for Old Men ✉

24	27	22	25

2007 | Directed by Joel Coen, Ethan Coen | With Tommy Lee Jones, Javier Bardem, Josh Brolin, Woody Harrelson | 122 minutes | Rated R

"Bone-chilling" is the word for this "bleak" "nightmare-maker" from the Coen brothers, a "Western horror film" about a "suitcase full of money" and the "bounty hunter" from hell out to get it (Bardem, who copped an Oscar as a "stone-faced" sociopath with a "scary" hairdo); provided "you can stomach the high body count" and "maddening ending", this "challenging" exercise in "pure nihilism" is "must-see" moviemaking, with a Best Picture statuette to prove it.

Noises Off

21	23	24	20

1992 | Directed by Peter Bogdanovich | With Michael Caine, Carol Burnett, Julie Hagerty, John Ritter, Nicollette Sheridan, Christopher Reeve, Marilu Henner, Mark Linn-Baker | 101 minutes | Rated PG-13

A "must-see" for "theater geeks" and "screwball" buffs, this "high-energy" adaptation of the "riotous stage farce" is the "funny" chronicle of the "chaos behind the scenes" of a "badly jinxed" British play touring the Midwest; even if it's a "little less sparkling as a movie" than it was on Broadway, this rather "overlooked" comedy does boast a "fast pace" and a "terrific" ensemble cast.

No Reservations

16	17	16	17

2007 | Directed by Scott Hicks | With Catherine Zeta-Jones, Aaron Eckhart, Abigail Breslin | 104 minutes | Rated PG

Think "the Food Channel with romance" to get the gist of this "culinary romantic comedy" about a top chef trying to "juggle her career, love life" and recently orphaned niece, who's come to live with her; no surprise, the "buttery" Zeta-Jones is "pretty tasty" and "Eckhart can visit my kitchen any time", though nonpartisans pan a plot "as predictable as a Big Mac" and a "little heavy on the sugar" to boot.

Norma Rae ✉

24 | 27 | 24 | 21

1979 | Directed by Martin Ritt | With Sally Field, Beau Bridges, Ron Leibman, Pat Hingle | 110 minutes | Rated PG

A "stirring tale about ordinary people", this "uplifting" drama "based on a true story" is a "painfully accurate look" at a "courageous" mill worker's "fight for justice" when caught between "unions and management"; in the title role, the "superb" Field really "earned her Oscar", and the "image of her holding up that sign" has become iconically "indelible."

ⓩ North by Northwest

28 | 26 | 27 | 27

1959 | Directed by Alfred Hitchcock | With Cary Grant, Eva Marie Saint, James Mason, Martin Landau | 136 minutes | Not Rated

"James Bond, eat your heart out" – "no one is cooler than Cary Grant" in this "incredibly stylish" Hitchcock thriller, a "twisting story of mistaken identity" set "all over the country" involving a "cool blonde", a "smooth villain" and a "malevolent crop duster"; despite some "holes in the script", there's distraction via that "exhilarating" climb down Mount Rushmore and the "double entendre" scenario (e.g. the "train entering a tunnel" at the climax).

North Country

22 | 26 | 22 | 21

2005 | Directed by Niki Caro | With Charlize Theron, Frances McDormand, Woody Harrelson, Sissy Spacek | 126 minutes | Rated R

"Boy, can Theron act" declare devotees of her "fine performance" as a miner fighting "sexual harassment in the Minnesota iron range" in this "powerful" drama inspired by "real events"; highlighting a "piece of history few know about", this "message film" risks "heavy-handedness" to stand as a "harsh reminder" of "how hard it is for women to earn a living."

North Dallas Forty

19 | 18 | 20 | 18

1979 | Directed by Ted Kotcheff | With Nick Nolte, Mac Davis, Charles Durning, Dayle Haddon | 119 minutes | Rated R

"Way before the steroids controversy" was this "ahead-of-its-time" depiction of the "dirty underside of pro football", a "pre-ESPN" flick starring Nolte as an "aging", "medicated" player ("boy, those needles look like they hurt"); the "tell-it-like-it-is" script "doesn't have a storybook ending", and many are convinced the team is a "thinly disguised version of the Dallas Cowboys" in their '70s heyday.

Nosferatu ◑

26 | 22 | 24 | 24

1922 | Directed by F.W. Murnau | With Max Schreck, Gustav von Wangenheim, Greta Schroeder | 84 minutes | Not Rated

"Still creepy after all these years", this "important German horror film" (an "unauthorized version of *Dracula*") is "one spooky" silent flick that can "evoke terror" thanks to the "genuinely scary Schreck"; it's the "most poetic of vampire films" and the "standard that others are measured against – and usually found lacking."

Nosferatu the Vampyre 🄵

22 | 24 | 22 | 25

1979 | Directed by Werner Herzog | With Klaus Kinski, Isabelle Adjani, Bruno Ganz | 107 minutes | Rated PG

A "stylish retelling" of the "familiar" Dracula story, this "great remake" via Werner Herzog owes a lot to the "mesmerizing", "out-there" Kinski who "stakes his claim" on the title role; "visually stunning" and imbued with a "strong political subtext", it's "reasonably creepy", but paced at such a "hypnotic crawl" that purists insist the Murnau original is "still the gold standard."

Notebook, The | 23 | 24 | 24 | 23 |

2004 | Directed by Nick Cassavetes | With Ryan Gosling, Rachel McAdams, James Garner, Gena Rowlands | 123 minutes | Rated PG-13

Sweet enough to "dissolve a tooth", this "hauntingly beautiful" sob-o-rama based on the Nicholas Sparks best-seller might be the "ultimate chick flick", a "testament to the awesome power of love" as it endures "through the ages"; naturally, the dry-eyed cry "corny", but even they credit the "genuinely sad Alzheimer's storyline" for addressing an issue that's "not often given attention."

☒ Notes on a Scandal | 24 | 28 | 23 | 23 |

2006 | Directed by Richard Eyre | With Judi Dench, Cate Blanchett, Bill Nighy | 92 minutes | Rated R

A "sad tale of obsessive love", this "disturbing" picture details "quite the touchy subject", a "pathetic spinster teacher" (Dench) enamored with a younger colleague (Blanchett) who "has a full life without her" – not to mention a "tawdry" secret of her own; it's "unsettling", "creepy" stuff that's "adult in the best way", with "wonderful" performances that will "scare the hell out of you."

Nothing Sacred | ▽ 23 | 23 | 20 | 20 |

1937 | Directed by William Wellman | With Carole Lombard, Fredric March | 75 minutes | Not Rated

The "notion of celebrity is lampooned" in this nutty screwball comedy, the story of a woman diagnosed with a terminal disease who's feted by a newspaper in exchange for her exclusive story – only to find out that she's been misdiagnosed; it's way "ahead of its time" in its arch analysis of the fame game alone.

No Time for Sergeants ⓞⵁ | 23 | 22 | 22 | 19 |

1958 | Directed by Mervyn LeRoy | With Andy Griffith, Myron McCornick, Nick Adams | 119 minutes | Not Rated

Managing to be "endearing without being annoying", Griffith "delivers the goods" in this "hilarious" comedy about a "dim hayseed who nearly destroys the U.S. Air Force", aided by "perfect foil" Don Knotts; the "toilet-seat scene" is a "display of American ingenuity" at its finest.

☒ Notorious ◑ | 27 | 27 | 26 | 26 |

1946 | Directed by Alfred Hitchcock | With Cary Grant, Ingrid Bergman, Claude Rains | 101 minutes | Not Rated

"Fetching" Ingrid Bergman "goes under the sheets for her country and gets Cary Grant as a reward" in this "brilliantly subversive" Hitchcock spy thriller featuring equal parts of "suspense", "suspicion", "hurt pride" and "Nazis too"; best remembered for the leads' "lingering, smoldering love scene", it also boasts "top-notch" supporting work from Rains, who has the best line: "mother, I'm married to an American agent."

Notting Hill | 19 | 19 | 18 | 19 |

1999 | Directed by Roger Michell | With Julia Roberts, Hugh Grant, Rhys Ifans | 124 minutes | Rated PG-13

"Straight-up chick flick" about a "hair-flicking" movie star who finds love with an "endearing" bookseller; though rotters relate it's "formulaic" (with "Roberts playing herself" and Grant in his "stammering in-génue" mode), at least the supporting cast is "brilliantly funny"; the London scenery provides the "charm."

No Way Out

OVERALL	ACTING	STORY	PROD.
20	19	23	19

1987 | Directed by Roger Donaldson | With Kevin Costner, Gene Hackman, Sean Young | 114 minutes | Rated R

Perhaps "Costner's finest hour", this "entirely enjoyable military thriller" offers "wonderful intrigue" in its way-out plot, something to do with the KGB, the Pentagon, the backseat of a limousine and a classy call girl (the "very hot" Young); while coolly "tense" throughout, the "unexpected", "twisty" ending is still a "shocker."

Z Now, Voyager ◑

27	28	26	25

1942 | Directed by Irving Rapper | With Bette Davis, Paul Henreid, Claude Rains | 117 minutes | Not Rated

"Break out the hankies" – this "chick flick extraordinaire" features "the moon, the stars and Bette Davis", who effects an "appealing transfor-mation" as an "old maid" defecting from a "demanding mother" to find kismet with a "perfect" Henreid; though the "two-cigarette scene" is decidedly un-PC today, it's become a "sacred" (and paradoxically "life-affirming") moment in this "classy" "mature love story."

Nurse Betty

15	18	15	15

2000 | Directed by Neil LaBute | With Renée Zellweger, Morgan Freeman, Chris Rock | 108 minutes | Rated R

"Entertaining" but "unconventional", this "quirky black comedy" top-lines Zellweger as a "clueless blonde" soap opera buff pursued by vicious hitmen; foes find the mix of comedy and gore too "unnecessarily violent" ("what planet did the screenwriter come from?"), and even fans admit it's "not for everyone" – just those who dig "inventive" filmmaking.

Nutty Professor, The

21	19	18	18

1963 | Directed by Jerry Lewis | With Jerry Lewis, Stella Stevens, Del Moore | 107 minutes | Not Rated

Jerry's "finest hour", this "can't-be-improved-upon" "wacky" comedy concerns a nerdy college prof who is transformed from Dr. Jerk-yll into Mr. Hyde after guzzling an exotic tonic; fans find it "sweet", foes shrug "typical Lewis shtick" and deep thinkers deem it a "metaphor for the monsters inside the greatest comedians."

Nutty Professor, The

15	18	14	18

1996 | Directed by Tom Shadyac | With Eddie Murphy, Jada Pinkett, James Coburn | 95 minutes | Rated PG-13

This "competent remake" of the Jerry Lewis comedy features Murphy in "amazingly versatile" mode, playing a seriously overweight profes-sor (in a "great fat suit") in addition to six other minor characters; it may be "more sentimental and less sharp" than the original – and "probably not appreciated by the French" – but those "dinner table scenes" are "wet-your-pants funny."

O Brother, Where Art Thou?

22	23	22	24

2000 | Directed by Joel Coen | With George Clooney, John Turturro, Tim Blake Nelson, John Goodman | 106 minutes | Rated PG-13

"Who else but the Coen brothers could mix Greek mythology, blue-grass and George Clooney?" ask fans of this picaresque, "perversely funny" satire "based on Homer's *Odyssey*" that details the adventures of three Depression-era "hayseeds" who bust out of prison; though a bit too "highbrow" for some, the "beautiful period detail" and "best roots music soundtrack ever" keep this "sweet" if "strange" genre-bender accessible.

Ocean's Eleven

OVERALL	ACTING	STORY	PROD.
16	15	19	18

1960 | Directed by Lewis Milestone | With Frank Sinatra, Dean Martin, Sammy Davis, Jr., Peter Lawford | 127 minutes | Not Rated

A "guilty pleasure to be sure", this "original version" of the casino heist caper features the "Rat Pack at their best" in a fab "1960 Las Vegas" setting ("when all the buildings were one story"); sure, it may be a bit "slow" in the beginning, but the look is "so stylish", the cast "so cool" and the ending so "clever" that it's always "entertaining."

Ocean's Eleven

19	19	19	22

2001 | Directed by Steven Soderbergh | With George Clooney, Brad Pitt, Andy Garcia | 116 minutes | Rated PG-13

"Fluffy fun" that "goes down smooth like a good martini", this "breezy caper" flick is "more lively than the original" version with its "great shots of Vegas", "never-a-dull-moment" plot and "lots of eye candy for the ladies"; ok, it might be "really silly", but the "slick", "all-star cast" and "genius director du jour Soderbergh" serve up something "wonderfully entertaining."

Ocean's Twelve

14	17	13	18

2004 | Directed by Steven Soderbergh | With George Clooney, Brad Pitt, Catherine Zeta-Jones | 125 minutes | Rated PG-13

An impressive conclave of "fabulously cool" A-listers is the "expensive excuse" for this "throwaway" sequel dispatching "Clooney and pals" to "beautiful" European hot spots in service of a "convoluted" heist plot; no doubt, "it looks like they had a great time making it", but in the end, the numbers lie: "*Twelve* is less than *Eleven*."

Ocean's Thirteen

17	19	16	20

2007 | Directed by Steven Soderbergh | With George Clooney, Brad Pitt, Matt Damon | 122 minutes | Rated PG-13

The "boys are back in Vegas" to "knock off a new casino" in this "hokey", "mildly entertaining" threequel; odds are you'll detect a "been-there-robbed-that" vibe, but as luck would have it, the "big-name" cast (including newly recruited stars Al Pacino and Ellen Barkin) and "glitzy" production pay off for "eye-candy" enthusiasts.

Octopussy

17	15	16	19

1983 | Directed by John Glen | With Roger Moore, Maud Adams, Louis Jourdan | 130 minutes | Rated PG

James Bond goes to India in this "over-the-top" feature whose "name lets you know how silly it is"; it might have a rather "basic", "assembly-line" formula, a "hokey" script and a star "getting too old for the part", but fans say it's worth seeing just for a look at 007 masquerading "as a clown."

Odd Couple, The

25	27	25	21

1968 | Directed by Gene Saks | With Jack Lemmon, Walter Matthau, John Fiedler | 105 minutes | Rated G

Lemmon and Matthau are "brilliant" in this "timeless" Neil Simon "classic" (which spawned a sequel and a TV series) that poses the question 'can two divorced men share an apartment without driving each other crazy?'; the ensuing dilemma makes for "unbeatable" comedy that'll make your "sides hurt from laughter."

Officer and a Gentleman, An
22 | 21 | 21 | 20

1982 | Directed by Taylor Hackford | With Richard Gere, Debra Winger, David Keith | 122 minutes | Rated R

"What gal doesn't dream" of Richard Gere "sweeping" her into his arms and lifting her up where she belongs?; this "quintessential" '80s "date movie" provides plenty of fodder for "guilty-pleasure" fantasizing with its love story between a "young enlisted man" and a "poor" working girl, even if foes pan it as "a bit lame" and advise "fast-forward to the last scene that makes the rest worthwhile."

Office Space
25 | 21 | 24 | 20

1999 | Directed by Mike Judge | With Ron Livingston, Jennifer Aniston, Gary Cole | 89 minutes | Rated R

"Required viewing for any cubicle dweller", this "instant classic" delivers a "spot-on skewering" of the "daily grind" in corporate America, "winning the hearts of the working class" with its "freaking hilarious" depiction of "disgruntled" desk jockeys; fans say there are "too many good lines to pick a favorite" in this "subversive" comedy, but "I think you have my stapler" and "it sounds like someone's got a case of the Mondays" are definite front runners.

☑ Of Mice and Men ◑
26 | 27 | 27 | 23

1939 | Directed by Lewis Milestone | With Burgess Meredith, Lon Chaney Jr., Betty Field | 106 minutes | Not Rated

The "first and best screen adaptation" of John Steinbeck's acclaimed novel, this "moving" Depression-era portrait of two wandering farmhands – the diminutive George and his giant, feeble-minded companion Lenny – "sticks with you" thanks to the "fine performances of" Meredith and Chaney; an all-around "marvelous" production featuring an Oscar-nominated Aaron Copland score, it's an essential "classic" – and another reason why "1939 was the greatest year ever" in American film.

Oh, God!
17 | 17 | 18 | 16

1977 | Directed by Carl Reiner | With George Burns, John Denver, Teri Garr, Paul Sorvino | 104 minutes | Rated PG

For pure "entertainment value", it's tough to top this "irresistible" comedy about an average Joe chosen by God to spread His word; believers say Burns is "perfectly cast" in the title role ("he's old enough to be God") and Denver as his disciple is "surprisingly effective", but even though this "humanist" picture is "worth a watch", it "didn't deserve to launch a series of follow-ups."

Oklahoma!
24 | 22 | 23 | 25

1955 | Directed by Fred Zinnemann | With Gordon MacRae, Shirley Jones, Gloria Grahame | 145 minutes | Rated G

"Every song" in this "sprawling" Rodgers and Hammerstein musical/ Western "makes you want to sing along" with the "lovely" voices of Jones and MacRae, plus there are "rousing dance numbers"; though modernists malign it as a "little dated", for most it's a whole lot "more than O-K", it's a pure "C-L-A-S-S-I-C."

Old School · 20 | 19 | 18 | 17

2003 | Directed by Todd Phillips | With Luke Wilson, Will Ferrell, Vince Vaughn | 91 minutes | Rated R

"Ninth-grade cafeteria humor" underlies this "sophomoric" albeit "pee-your-pants-funny" comedy of "old frat guys who relive their youth" by opening an "adult fraternity"; sure, it's plenty "stupid" ("don't bring your brain") with a "derivative" plot that "couldn't exist without *Animal House*", but its "good-natured doofiness" and Ferrell's "manic performance" are both pretty "classic."

Old Yeller · 24 | 20 | 24 | 20

1957 | Directed by Robert Stevenson | With Dorothy McGuire, Fess Parker, Tommy Kirk | 83 minutes | Rated G

"You can't help but cry your eyes out" after watching this "outstanding" Disney "tearjerker" about a "boy and his big yellow dog"; if a few find the acting "formulaic" and the plot "sappy", most agree it's an "all-time" children's "standard" that even adults "never tire of watching" – despite that gosh-darned "sad ending."

Oliver! 24 | 23 | 24 | 26

1968 | Directed by Carol Reed | With Mark Lester, Ron Moody, Shani Wallis, Oliver Reed | 153 minutes | Rated G

Dickens' "bleak yet hopeful" novel is "lovingly brought to the screen" in this Oscar-winning adaptation of the "classic" stage musical; given the "incredible" production numbers, "wonderful" score and "just-about-perfect" cast, many "English orphan" wannabes beg 'please, sir can we watch it again?'

Oliver Twist ◐ · 25 | 26 | 26 | 24

1951 | Directed by David Lean | With Robert Newton, Alec Guinness, John Howard Davies | 116 minutes | Not Rated

David Lean's "classic" take on Dickens' ageless novel "stands up over time" so well that many consider it the "best version of the book" put onto celluloid (indeed, it's "almost as good as *Great Expectations*"); admirers applaud Newton's "stunning", "tug-at-the-heartstrings" title turn and the "jolly good" Guinness, whose "controversial" performance as Fagin (deemed anti-Semitic by some) delayed the film's U.S. release.

Oliver Twist · 20 | 22 | 24 | 23

2005 | Directed by Roman Polanski | With Barney Clark, Ben Kingsley, Jamie Foreman | 130 minutes | Rated PG-13

"Master" director Polanski re-creates the "bleakness" of Victorian London to stay "true to Dickens" in this "well-done" if "underappreciated" interpretation of the "classic" orphan opus; maybe it's "not up to the David Lean version" in quality, but the casting of "superb child actors" and the "mesmerizing" Kingsley (as Fagin) keep it "involving."

Omen, The · 21 | 21 | 22 | 20

1976 | Directed by Richard Donner | With Gregory Peck, Lee Remick, David Warner | 111 minutes | Rated R

This "genuinely spooky" thriller has a "brilliant premise" – a couple unwittingly adopts the devil's child – and features an appropriately "satanic" storyline, "eerie" music and a frightening turn by the "scariest kid ever to be in a horror movie" (Harvey Stephens); thrill-seekers report its "terrifying" special effects make the "unbelievable believable."

On a Clear Day You Can See Forever

20 | 21 | 19 | 21

1970 | Directed by Vincente Minnelli | With Barbra Streisand, Yves Montand, Jack Nicholson | 129 minutes | Rated G

There's plenty of "star power" to behold in this film version of the Broadway musical, pitting a "classic" Babs opposite an über-"Gallic" Yves (though many say it's "most interesting" to see the "early Jack" in action); despite an appealingly "offbeat" plot – something about a "Regency-era femme fatale" reincarnated as a "psychic" New Yorker – some seers say it "never simmers like it should."

Once

25 | 23 | 24 | 21

2007 | Directed by John Carney | With Glen Hansard, Markéta Irglová | 85 minutes | Rated R

"Love is the leitmotif" and "longing is the lyric" of this "sweet", "uplifting" little picture about two lonely souls connecting through the "joy of making music"; "great chemistry" between the leads, an Oscar-winning song and enough "sincere charm" to "melt an icy heart" is all "testament" to the "potential brilliance of low-budget filmmaking."

Once Upon a Time in America

24 | 26 | 24 | 24

1984 | Directed by Sergio Leone | With Robert De Niro, James Woods, Elizabeth McGovern | 227 minutes | Rated R

Some of De Niro's "most subtle and effective" acting is on display in this "unfairly neglected" crime epic spanning four decades, which hard-core cineasts hail as "truly remarkable" when "seen in the long [227-minute] director's cut"; but despite a "top-drawer cast" and "magnificent" direction, others are less enthused about the "flawed" end result that's awash in "too much blood."

Once Upon a Time in Mexico

15 | 18 | 14 | 18

2003 | Directed by Robert Rodriguez | With Antonio Banderas, Salma Hayek, Johnny Depp | 102 minutes | Rated R

A diet "light on plot, heavy on action" helps pulp director Rodriguez cap his Mariachi trilogy with a "bang bang", but this "lackluster" series finale shoots its way through a "muddled" revenge storyline rendered by mere "moments of visual brilliance"; muchas gracias go to Depp for his "outrageous" performance, even if his "scene-stealing" antics can't save this "disappointment."

Once Upon a Time in the West

25 | 24 | 23 | 25

1969 | Directed by Sergio Leone | With Henry Fonda, Claudia Cardinale, Charles Bronson | 165 minutes | Rated PG-13

This "ultimate Western" is "epic in every way", starting with its "big-name" cast, "long, long" running time and operatic plot about the desperate struggle for a piece of land; throw in Fonda as an "amazingly evil" villain, Ennio Morricone's "magical score" and "one of the coolest opening scenes ever", and it's easy to see why many consider this "high-water mark" to be director Leone's "definitive" work.

☑ One Flew Over the Cuckoo's Nest ✉

27 | 29 | 27 | 25

1975 | Directed by Milos Forman | With Jack Nicholson, Louise Fletcher, Will Sampson | 133 minutes | Rated R

"Life in a mental ward" gets the "stand-up-for-your-rights" treatment in this "disturbing", "influential" drama starring "national treasure" Nicholson at his "ornery best", backed up by an "amazing" ensemble cast; no surprise, it took five major Oscars, made Nurse Ratched a household name and is "hard to top" – folks are just plain "nuts about it."

One Hour Photo · 18 | 23 | 18 | 18

2002 | Directed by Mark Romanek | With Robin Williams, Connie Nielsen, Michael Vartan | 96 minutes | Rated R

Williams "sheds his funny-man image" and "gives good villain" in this "super-creepy" psychological thriller-cum-"stalker movie" about "Sy the photo guy", a "mega-mart" lab technician obsessed by a picture-perfect, all-American family whose photos he processes; despite a "slow" pace and "out-of-focus" script that "needed more time in the darkroom", the movie's ultimately "disturbing" enough for some to consider "switching to Polaroids" or "digital cameras."

101 Dalmatians · 24 | - | 22 | 24

1961 | Directed by Wolfgang Reitherman, Clyde Geronimi, Hamilton Luske | Animated | 79 minutes | Rated G

Puppy proponents put their paws together for Pongo, Perdita and their prolific progeny when watching this "fast, funny" piece of Disney animation; its "hugely entertaining" tale of a klatch of "cute" canines outrunning über-villainess Cruella De Vil appeals to the "little kid in everyone" and makes this one an "enduring winner."

101 Dalmatians · 18 | 19 | 19 | 22

1996 | Directed by Stephen Herek | With Glenn Close, Jeff Daniels, Joely Richardson | 103 minutes | Rated G

"*The* reason" to see Disney's "cute" live-action "update" of their earlier animated feature is the "over-the-top" Close as the "truly wicked" Cruella De Vil (though there's also "dry humor" courtesy of the largely British supporting cast); still, cynics nix this "wholly unnecessary remake" as "not as good as the original."

One, Two, Three ◑ · 23 | 23 | 22 | 22

1961 | Directed by Billy Wilder | With James Cagney, Horst Buchholz, Pamela Tiffin | 108 minutes | Not Rated

"Billy Wilder scores in this Cold War comedy" set in Berlin, a "fast and furious farce" about a "harried Coca-Cola executive" whose "world is collapsing around him"; Cagney's "machine-gun delivery is a scream", though diehards say the picture's "underrated" and "overshadowed" by the director's better-known films.

On Golden Pond ✉ · 24 | 27 | 23 | 23

1981 | Directed by Mark Rydell | With Katharine Hepburn, Henry Fonda, Jane Fonda | 109 minutes | Rated PG

A "beautiful tale of growing old and looking back on life", this "brilliant" drama features the "stunning", Oscar-winning Hank and Kate "pulling out all the stops" as an elderly couple coming to terms with their child and each other; the "real-life tension" between the real-life father-and-daughter Fondas supplies some "electric" moments, while its timeless theme about the "strength of the human spirit" "will appeal to all."

On Her Majesty's Secret Service · 19 | 15 | 21 | 20

1969 | Directed by Peter R. Hunt | With George Lazenby, Diana Rigg, Telly Savalas | 140 minutes | Rated PG

"James Bond gets married" in this "respectable" flick featuring "astonishing ski chases", "Swiss Alp views" and a "believable love story" for a change; still, opinion splits on Lazenby's one-time-only turn as 007 ("wooden" vs. "formidable"), and as for the end result, it's either "underrated" or "the worst" in the series.

Onion Field, The

| | 24 | 26 | 25 | 23 |

1979 | Directed by Harold Becker | With John Savage, James Woods, Ted Danson, Franklyn Seales | 122 minutes | Rated R

A "disturbing" look at the "sad" side of police work, this "gritty crime drama" delineates a cop's gangland-style execution and its "depressing" aftermath; adapted from the Joseph Wambaugh book (itself based on an actual case), it's "more true to life than we want to believe" and features fine work from the "chilling" Woods and a "serious Danson."

Only Angels Have Wings ◑

| | 21 | 21 | 20 | 19 |

1939 | Directed by Howard Hawks | With Cary Grant, Jean Arthur, Rita Hayworth | 121 minutes | Not Rated

It's "not your typical" Grant in this Hawks melodrama starring the debonair dame-magnet as a "roughneck pilot" tempted by a "wonderful" Arthur and "breathtaking" Hayworth on an Andean outpost – where "you prove your manhood by gritting your teeth when a friend's plane goes down in flames"; but in the end, this "classic" flies high enough to further fuel the theory that "1939 was the greatest year in American film."

☒ On the Beach ◑

| | 26 | 26 | 27 | 23 |

1959 | Directed by Stanley Kramer | With Gregory Peck, Ava Gardner, Fred Astaire, Anthony Perkins | 134 minutes | Not Rated

"Now dated, but still riveting", this "chilling" Cold War-era message picture details the "aftermath of a nuclear war", where the earth's sole survivors struggle to stay alive in Australia; it's an "intense" look at "how people spend their last days" that "isn't about explosions, but emotions", and many report "never listening to 'Waltzing Matilda' the same way again" after seeing it.

On the Town

| | 23 | 23 | 21 | 25 |

1949 | Directed by Stanley Donen, Gene Kelly | With Gene Kelly, Frank Sinatra, Jules Munshin | 98 minutes | Not Rated

Despite "wonderful dancing by Kelly" and some "funny" bits from the ensemble cast, "NYC is the real star" of this "exuberant" musical "celebrating the American spirit in the '40s"; "filmed partially on location" and juiced up by a "great Leonard Bernstein score", it follows three sailors at liberty on the town, and although rather "silly", it effortlessly radiates the "pure joy" of simpler times.

☒ On the Waterfront ✉◑

| | 28 | 29 | 26 | 26 |

1954 | Directed by Elia Kazan | With Marlon Brando, Karl Malden, Eva Marie Saint, Rod Steiger | 108 minutes | Not Rated

Most decidedly a "candidate for all-time greatest" film, this "gritty tale of corruption on the NJ docks" is a "movie to turn you onto movies", with Oscar wins by the "phenomenal Brando" (as a "washed-up", "Palookaville"-bound boxer) and a "knockout" Saint (in her screen debut); indeed, this "gutsy", "brutal masterwork" "rings so true" and is so "emotionally satisfying" that it's "nothing less than brilliant"; best line: "I coulda been a contender."

| | OVERALL | ACTING | STORY | PROD. |

⊘ Open City ◑🅵

▽ 28 | 29 | 28 | 25

1946 | Directed by Roberto Rossellini | With Aldo Fabrizi, Anna Magnani | 105 minutes | Not Rated

One of the major works of Italian neorealism, this "devastating" look at occupied '40s Rome shows the "devastation that war produces and how people pick up the pieces that are left"; the "unforgettable" Magnani's performance "burns in one's memory", while the picture itself is credited for reawakening American interest in modern international films.

Open Range

21 | 23 | 20 | 23

2003 | Directed by Kevin Costner | With Robert Duvall, Kevin Costner, Annette Bening | 139 minutes | Rated R

A "top-notch" oater with "no added sugar", this "old-fashioned" Western with an "updated feel" features the "perfectly cast" Costner and Duvall playing small-time cattlemen pitted against a ruthless rancher; maybe the "pace plods" a bit, but it earns its spurs with a "credible" story and "stunning" cinematography – not to mention a "blow-your-hat-off" climactic shootout.

Open Season

18 | - | 18 | 20

2006 | Directed by Roger Allers, Jill Culton, Anthony Stacchi | Animated | 86 minutes | Rated PG

This "feel-good" animated flick gets "great mileage" out of "surprisingly funny" voiceover work led by Martin Lawrence and Ashton Kutcher as bear-and-deer buddies on the run from gun-toting hunters; though "kids are engrossed" and it delivers "enough laughs" to keep adults happy, a few find the "bland content" too "boring and predictable."

Open Water

15 | 15 | 18 | 15

2004 | Directed by Chris Kentis | With Blanchard Ryan, Daniel Travis | 79 minutes | Rated R

"If you liked *Jaws*, there are more fish in the sea" thanks to this "low-budget" "video verité" thriller, a "pulse-pounding" "true story" of a scuba-diving couple "abandoned in the ocean" and "surrounded by sharks"; the "too-real" attack scenes are "intense" enough to make you "rethink vacation excursions", though the "porn-quality acting" and "disappointing ending" tend to "water down the thrills."

Operation Petticoat

19 | 19 | 18 | 19

1959 | Directed by Blake Edwards | With Cary Grant, Tony Curtis, Joan O'Brien, Dina Merrill | 124 minutes | Not Rated

"Feel-good" WWII comedy having to do with a Navy captain's "emergency" efforts to keep a gaggle of army nurses and a "pink submarine" afloat; despite smooth "chemistry" between Grant and Curtis resulting in some pretty "funny" situations (i.e. lots of tight-quarters gags), the unamused torpedo it as "contrived."

Opposite of Sex, The

19 | 23 | 19 | 19

1998 | Directed by Don Roos | With Christina Ricci, Martin Donovan, Lisa Kudrow, Lyle Lovett | 105 minutes | Rated R

"Venomous humor" drips from the "dark" comedic fangs of this "sharply observed character study" centering on the "fabulous" Ricci's "amoral" teen runaway, a "wicked" sort who "lives to torment everyone she encounters", mainly her gay half-brother; factor in "witty dialogue" and the use of *Friends*-ter Kudrow playing against type (i.e. "someone who's not a complete idiot") and it's clear why this flick's the "opposite of bad."

Ordinary People ✉

25 | 27 | 25 | 23

1980 | Directed by Robert Redford | With Donald Sutherland, Mary Tyler Moore, Timothy Hutton | 124 minutes | Rated R

"Every parent's nightmare" – the death of a child – is dissected in this "devastating" drama that goes below the "veneer of an upper-middle-class family" to plumb the "dysfunction" below; Redford's directorial debut copped a Best Picture Oscar, but it's Moore's "playing-against-type" role as a "classy" but "coldhearted" mom that "steals the movie."

Other Boleyn Girl, The

19 | 21 | 20 | 23

2008 | Directed by Justin Chadwick | With Natalie Portman, Scarlett Johansson, Eric Bana | 115 minutes | Rated PG-13

Feed your "fascination for the Tudors" with this "lush" period piece offering a "behind-the-scenes" glimpse at the "naked ambition" that foisted Boleyn sisters Anne and Mary into the thick of Henry VIII's quest for a male heir; there's agreement on the "rich" imagery and "amazing costumes", but surveyors split on the acting: "outstanding" vs. "one-dimensional."

Others, The

23 | 25 | 23 | 24

2001 | Directed by Alejandro Amenábar | With Nicole Kidman, Fionnula Flanagan | 101 minutes | Rated PG-13

A "dynamic" Kidman delivers an "old-school movie star turn" in this "grand ghost story" about a mother protecting her children who suffer from a rare "photosensitive" condition (an "excellent excuse to keep the house dark and murky"); "wonderfully atmospheric" and "deliciously scary", it's "highbrow horror" with a "jeepers-creepers" ending that's a "real shocker."

Our Man Flint

19 | 16 | 16 | 17

1966 | Directed by Daniel Mann | With James Coburn, Lee J. Cobb, Gila Golan | 108 minutes | Not Rated

A "time-capsule spoof of James Bond", this "fun period piece" stars Coburn as a smooth secret agent in a performance that's "one continuous wink" at the "spy movie" genre ("*Austin Powers* cribbed from it, among others"); but in spite of its "groovy" '60s scenery and "cool satire of male prowess", cynics call it "dated", "passably entertaining" stuff that's a "poor substitution" for the real 007.

Outbreak

16 | 18 | 17 | 18

1995 | Directed by Wolfgang Petersen | With Dustin Hoffman, Rene Russo, Morgan Freeman | 127 minutes | Rated R

"Cheer the hero and hiss the villain" in this "entertaining bio-thriller" where "time's running out" in a California community threatened by "wayward monkeys" and "airborne viruses"; in his first "action hero" role, Hoffman is "realistic" enough, but foes say the upshot is "silly" – "more bad science" – and suggest you "read *The Hot Zone* instead."

Outlaw Josey Wales, The

25 | 23 | 24 | 23

1976 | Directed by Clint Eastwood | With Clint Eastwood, Sondra Locke, Chief Dan George | 135 minutes | Rated PG

Playing a renegade Confederate soldier seeking revenge after his wife and children are murdered, Eastwood is his "usual unreadable self" (though you "feel for his plight") in this "quirky" Western that's a "rural version of *Death Wish*"; fans rate it "better-than-usual Clint", given its "classic lines" and "profound issues."

Out of Africa ✉

1985 | Directed by Sydney Pollack | With Meryl Streep, Robert Redford, Klaus Maria Brandauer | 150 minutes | Rated PG

Supporters are "spellbound" by this "splendiferous" "love story played out against the mysterious continent" starring a "radiant" Streep as Danish writer Karen Blixen (aka Isak Dinesen) and a "great-looking" Redford as her paramour; the "beauty" of Africa and "soaring score" "amplify the emotion", and even though it's a "real tearjerker", most eat up this "treat" "again and again."

Out of Sight 21 21 21 22

1998 | Directed by Steven Soderbergh | With George Clooney, Jennifer Lopez, Ving Rhames | 123 minutes | Rated R

"Clooney and Lopez generate electricity aplenty" in this "smart caper" flick that "oozes cool" in its depiction of a "cocksure" con artist, his "eye-candy police pursuer" and "one of the sexiest love scenes" ever; a "crackling" story (via Elmore Leonard's novel) and "brilliant" direction from Soderbergh make this one an "overlooked gem."

☑ Out of the Past ◐ 26 26 25 25

1947 | Directed by Jacques Tourneur | With Robert Mitchum, Jane Greer, Kirk Douglas | 97 minutes | Not Rated

The "*Citizen Kane* of film noir", this "fabled" picture "sets the standard" for the genre by pitting a "classic antihero" ("Mitchum at his laconic best") against the "ultimate femme fatale" (the "beautiful but deadly" Greer); the "insanely labyrinthine plot" with "twists in all directions" is equally "note perfect", and perfumed with a "whiff of French existentialism."

Out-of-Towners, The 20 22 22 18

1970 | Directed by Arthur Hiller | With Jack Lemmon, Sandy Dennis, Sandy Baron | 98 minutes | Rated G

"They don't make comedies" like this Neil Simon–scripted "classic" anymore, the saga of an Ohio couple visiting "Fun City" only to discover that it's their "worst nightmare" as they endure one "hilariously miserable" mishap after another; "Lemmon and Dennis are perfection as the tortured tourists", leading many to wonder "why they remade this movie" at all.

Outrageous Fortune 15 14 14 13

1987 | Directed by Arthur Hiller | With Shelley Long, Bette Midler, Peter Coyote | 100 minutes | Rated R

"Midler and Long make a funny team" in this buddy comedy about two struggling actresses tracking down a mutual boyfriend turned espionage agent; though too "strident" and "formulaic" for some, it's "guilty pleasure" time for those in the mood for something "silly."

Outsiders, The 22 21 22 19

1983 | Directed by Francis Ford Coppola | With C. Thomas Howell, Matt Dillon, Ralph Macchio | 91 minutes | Rated PG

Coppola "paints a great picture" of "teen angst" in this "coming-of-age story" that limns the "problems" between adolescent gangs in a '50s

Oklahoma hamlet; what seems like the "entire Brat Pack" delivers such "outstanding" work that the end result is "almost as good" as S.E. Hinton's enduring novel.

Over the Hedge

 `23 | - | 22 | 25`

2006 | Directed by Tim Johnson, Karey Kirkpatrick | Animated | 83 minutes | Rated PG

Their habitat "dwindling as suburbia spreads", a gang of animals "tries to get food from humans" in this "clever" cartoon powered by "fantastic" animation and "excellent" celeb voicings ("Steve Carell's squirrel steals the show"); a "real crowd-pleaser", it boasts an "easy-to-follow" story for small fry plus "commentary about society" that goes over well with adults.

Owl and the Pussycat, The

`17 | 19 | 16 | 18`

1970 | Directed by Herbert Ross | With Barbra Streisand, George Segal | 95 minutes | Rated PG

A truly odd couple – a struggling writer and an "outrageous hooker" – hook up in this "wacky" comedy pitting a "nonsinging" Streisand against a "very funny" Segal; but even though the leads' "chemistry is terrific", some find the proceedings "dated" and "overrated"; Babs' best line: "who gave you permission to read my panties?"

❷ Ox-Bow Incident, The ◑

`27 | 27 | 26 | 23`

1943 | Directed by William Wellman | With Henry Fonda, Dana Andrews | 75 minutes | Not Rated

"Decent, law-abiding folk never looked more pathetic" than in this message Western, a "gripping story of mob violence gone mad" that's a chilling indictment of American justice; there are no heroes in this dark "morality tale", though the "excellent ensemble" makes this "adaptation of the classic novel" come alive.

Painted Veil, The

`23 | 25 | 23 | 26`

2006 | Directed by John Curran | With Naomi Watts, Edward Norton, Liev Schreiber, Toby Jones | 125 minutes | Rated PG-13

Strains of "*The English Patient*" infect this "emotionally charged" W. Somerset Maugham adaptation starring Watts and Norton as "flawed" spouses who try to salvage their "fragile marriage" in the testy "political climate of 1920s China"; productionwise, the "gorgeous" cinematography shows off some "magnificent" Far East scenery – a "picturesque" palliative for what some call a "languid" drama.

Paint Your Wagon

`18 | 18 | 19 | 21`

1969 | Directed by Joshua Logan | With Lee Marvin, Clint Eastwood, Jean Seberg | 166 minutes | Rated PG-13

"See Clint sing" in this tuneful Lerner and Loewe Western that cynics say is the "reason why musicals have had a hard time succeeding since the '60s"; but champions claim this story of bigamous Wild West gold miners "pokes fun at many cultures" and believe that the "non-singer" cast "does a surprisingly good job."

Palm Beach Story, The ◑

`25 | 25 | 25 | 24`

1942 | Directed by Preston Sturges | With Claudette Colbert, Joel McCrea, Mary Astor, Rudy Vallee | 88 minutes | Not Rated

Screwball comedies "don't get much better" than this "zany romp" about a married couple who separate over money troubles; the

	OVERALL	ACTING	STORY	PROD.

"smart" dialogue, "fast" pacing and "ridiculous" plot showcase director Sturges "at his wittiest and loopiest", and then there's the "irresistible" Colbert and "perfect" Rudy Vallee – "they don't write 'em like this anymore."

Panic Room

| 18 | 21 | 18 | 20 |

2002 | Directed by David Fincher | With Jodie Foster, Kristen Stewart, Forest Whitaker, Jared Leto | 112 minutes | Rated R

The "Hitchcockian opening credits" echo the "innovative camerawork" in this "state-of-the-art thriller" from "style-freak" director Fincher about a "resourceful" mother and daughter fending off burglars in their townhouse's "bulletproof safe room"; though the plot elicits mixed notices – a "real nail-biter" vs. "disappointingly predictable" – Jodie's her usual "terrific" self as the "smart-thinking, anti-Buffy heroine."

Z Pan's Labyrinth F

| 27 | 26 | 26 | 28 |

2006 | Directed by Guillermo del Toro | With Ivana Baquero, Sergi López, Maribel Verdú | 120 minutes | Rated R

Fantasy film fans faun over this "ethereal", "adult"-themed fairy tale – think a "grim" *Alice in Wonderland* – from "master" helmer del Toro, who corrals some "wild" visuals to depict the "nightmarish" imaginings of a "brilliant child" and the "harsh realities of Franco-era fascism" that spawn them; "enchanting" performances and spurts of "graphic violence" that "stay with you" should placate even the most "subtitle-leery" of onlookers.

Paper Chase, The

| 23 | 25 | 24 | 20 |

1973 | Directed by James Bridges | With Timothy Bottoms, Lindsay Wagner, John Houseman | 111 minutes | Rated PG

The "terrors and rigors of the first year of Harvard Law School" are revealed in this "seminal" '70s movie that re-creates the student "rat race" in an "entertaining" way; despite "outstanding performances by all", the Oscar-winning Houseman (as a "crusty professor") is the "main reason to see it."

Paper Moon ◖

| 22 | 23 | 21 | 22 |

1973 | Directed by Peter Bogdanovich | With Ryan O'Neal, Tatum O'Neal, Madeline Kahn | 102 minutes | Rated PG

Have "fun watching Ryan and Tatum acting together" in this "delightful" "father/daughter bonding flick", the "charming" story of a Depression-era con man and his equally manipulative offspring who "drift" through the Midwest in glorious black and white; though some say this "sweet little comedy" was "stolen by Madeline Kahn", it was the younger O'Neal who copped the Oscar.

Z Papillon

| 26 | 27 | 26 | 24 |

1973 | Directed by Franklin J. Schaffner | With Steve McQueen, Dustin Hoffman | 150 minutes | Rated R

It's hard to escape from this "powerful" tale of prisoners scheming to break out of Devil's Island, the French Guiana penal colony that makes "HBO's *Oz* look like Club Med"; a "consistently cool McQueen" and "heavyweight Hoffman" play "mistreated-but-not-defeated" inmates "determined to be free" in this "tight", taut drama that's all the more "scary" since it's "based on a true story."

Parallax View, The

24 | 23 | 25 | 21

1974 | Directed by Alan J. Pakula | With Warren Beatty, Paula Prentiss, William Daniels | 102 minutes | Rated R

"Conspiracy theorists" dig this "paranoid thriller" made in the "post-Kennedy assassination era" that's as "taut" and "frightening" as they come; playing a hotheaded young reporter who blunders into a perilous web of intrigue, a "young" Beatty "shows he can excel with serious material" and keep viewers on the "edge of their seats."

Parenthood

22 | 22 | 22 | 20

1989 | Directed by Ron Howard | With Steve Martin, Mary Steenburgen, Dianne Wiest | 124 minutes | Rated PG-13

"Modern family life" gets "compelling" treatment in this "harrowing if affectionate look at being a parent", a "feel-good" dramedy that confirms "you need a sense of humor" when you have kids; "smart, insightful" and briskly paced thanks to "multiple plotlines", it features "one of Martin's better performances."

Parent Trap, The

23 | 21 | 23 | 21

1961 | Directed by David Swift | With Hayley Mills, Maureen O'Hara, Brian Keith | 129 minutes | Rated G

"Hayley Mills and Hayley Mills" star as "twins separated at birth plotting to bring their estranged parents together" in this "non-animated Disney classic", an "entertaining romp" that serves up "warmhearted family fare"; one of the "most remembered" movies in boomerdom, it boasts such a "timeless story" that most "stick to the original", having "no need for the remake."

Paris is Burning

24 | - | 25 | 20

1990 | Directed by Jennie Livingston | Documentary | 71 minutes | Rated R

"Spotlighting a cultural scene not often on view", this "bang-up" documentary focuses on cross-dressing black and Latino men, a "marginalized" subculture who live for drag balls and "voguing" contests; it's a "moving" portrait of people "being true to themselves despite formidable obstacles" that's "at times funny, at times tragic", but always "compelling."

Paris, Texas

22 | 24 | 21 | 20

1984 | Directed by Wim Wenders | With Harry Dean Stanton, Nastassja Kinski, Dean Stockwell | 147 minutes | Rated R

"Haunting landscapes" and "outstanding performances" are the hallmarks of this "unconventional" (verging on "totally bizarre") road movie about a lost soul rediscovering his wife and child; while there's praise for writer Sam Shepard's "spare dialogue" and composer Ry Cooder's "perfect soundtrack", many say the "drawn-out", "slow-moving" pace makes for "awfully strange" filmmaking.

Passage to India, A

25 | 26 | 23 | 26

1984 | Directed by David Lean | With Judy Davis, Victor Banerjee, Peggy Ashcroft, James Fox, Alec Guinness | 163 minutes | Rated PG

Lean's final opus, this "well-done epic" adapted from the E.M. Forster novel showcases the legendary director "at his very best", working as one part "exotic travelogue" to "gorgeous" Indian locales and one part "gripping history piece" exploring the "tensions" between Britain and its colonial subjects in the 1920s; "expertly acted" performances from

Davis and Ashcroft heighten the "ethereal" "sensory experience", even if a few travelers report a rather "slow-moving" journey.

Passion of the Christ, The 🄵   22 | 23 | 21 | 23

2004 | Directed by Mel Gibson | With James Caviezel, Monica Bellucci, Maia Morgenstern | 127 minutes | Rated R

Echoing the "overblown controversy" surrounding its release, Gibson's "brutal portrayal" of the last 12 hours of Christ's life similarly "polarizes" surveyors: proponents praise its "lengthy torture scenes" as "necessary to make the point" of "what Jesus went through", but "traumatized" viewers see a "slasher film" full of "prejudice and propaganda" that "preaches to the converted"; both sides concur it's "not for kids" (nor for subtitle-phobes, given the all-Aramaic/Latin/Hebrew dialogue).

Patch Adams   16 | 18 | 17 | 15

1998 | Directed by Tom Shadyac | With Robin Williams, Daniel London, Monica Potter | 115 minutes | Rated PG-13

Laughter's the best medicine in this tale of a doctor who tries to heal patients with humor, an "inspiring" story that's both "funny and sad" but ultimately "uplifting"; eye-rollers counter that Williams "needs to get back to his roots" and avoid such "sappy" material.

🄩 Paths of Glory ◑   28 | 27 | 28 | 26

1957 | Directed by Stanley Kubrick | With Kirk Douglas, Ralph Meeker, George Macready | 86 minutes | Not Rated

"All the hopelessness, folly and stupidity" of WWI is "dramatically" shown in Kubrick's "devastating" "anti-war" picture that "ruthlessly" depicts "corrupt" officers deploying "scapegoated enlisted men" as "cannon fodder"; even though this "grim" yet "moving" film is in black and white, the "story is full color", and it "really makes its point" and "stands the test of time."

Patriot, The   21 | 21 | 21 | 23

2000 | Directed by Roland Emmerich | With Mel Gibson, Heath Ledger, Joely Richardson | 164 minutes | Rated R

Present-day patriots salute this "epic in the Gibson tradition" as an "inspiring portrait" of a reluctant American "hero" enmeshed in "gruesome Revolutionary War battles"; though turncoats dismiss it as typical "Hollywood good guy/bad guy nonsense" ("Lethal Musket"), they're outvoted by partisans who "feel liberated" by this "heartfelt" history jazzed up with some "entertainment value."

Patriot Games   21 | 21 | 22 | 21

1992 | Directed by Phillip Noyce | With Harrison Ford, Anne Archer, Patrick Bergin | 117 minutes | Rated R

"Harrison gets cool again" as a "humble hero whose life is turned upside down by an IRA terrorist" in this "slick" action-adventurer known for its "mind-spinning chase across oceans and freeways"; though it's as "thrilling on the screen as on the written page", foes say it's "cookie-cutter espionage" and say that Alec Baldwin is the "more believable Jack Ryan."

🄩 Patton ✉   27 | 28 | 26 | 27

1970 | Directed by Franklin J. Schaffner | With George C. Scott, Karl Malden | 170 minutes | Rated PG

Legions salute "one of the best biopics ever made", this "hauntingly mounted character study" of fabled WWII General Patton, who's "superbly fleshed out" as both "monstrous and human"; though there's "lots of drama" throughout, it "doesn't get much better than that opening speech" by "Old Blood and Guts", probably the most "memorable" scene; P.S. the "convincing" portrayal won Scott an Oscar, which he famously rejected.

Z Pawnbroker, The   26 | 28 | 24 | 22
1965 | Directed by Sidney Lumet | With Rod Steiger, Geraldine Fitzgerald | 116 minutes | Not Rated
This "disturbing", "depressing message picture", expertly rendered in "chilling black and white", shows the "horrors of the Holocaust" by focusing on one survivor, the owner of a Harlem pawnshop; in "one of the all-time great screen performances", Steiger is nothing short of "mesmerizing" in the title role – too bad it's been so "sadly neglected" over the years.

Pearl Harbor   14 | 14 | 13 | 21
2001 | Directed by Michael Bay | With Ben Affleck, Josh Hartnett, Kate Beckinsale, Cuba Gooding Jr. | 183 minutes | Rated PG-13
"*Titanic* meets *Saving Private Ryan*" in this "predictable", "heavy-handed" epic that juxtaposes a "romantic subplot" against a historic backdrop, the "horrific attack" that led the U.S. into WWII; most agree the "dumb", "cardboard-charactered" love story is completely "unnecessary", blown away by "breathtaking action" and "superior special effects", so for best results, "skip the first hour-and-a-half" and fast-forward to the "battle scenes only."

Pee-wee's Big Adventure   19 | 17 | 17 | 20
1985 | Directed by Tim Burton | With Paul Reubens, Elizabeth Daily, Diane Salinger | 90 minutes | Rated PG
"Wacky", "campy", maybe even "inspired", this comic "cult classic" is a "work of the sublime from the ridiculous" team of "twisted" director Burton and "genius" performer Reubens; though ostensibly aimed at small fry, "adults love it" too, yet the pleasure is bittersweet for those who "miss Pee-wee" and "wish for another" installment; P.S. "Large Marge is worth the price of admission."

Peggy Sue Got Married   19 | 20 | 21 | 18
1986 | Directed by Francis Ford Coppola | With Kathleen Turner, Nicolas Cage | 104 minutes | Rated PG-13
Unhappily married Peggy Sue "magically enters her teenage self's world" in this "timeless", "back-in-time" comedy from Francis Ford Coppola "with a heart and a brain"; though ageists say Turner is "too old" for the role, the "original premise" and "nostalgic" mood provide ample distraction.

Pelican Brief, The   16 | 18 | 18 | 16
1993 | Directed by Alan J. Pakula | With Julia Roberts, Denzel Washington, Sam Shepard | 141 minutes | Rated PG-13
In this "fast-paced" adaptation of John Grisham's best-seller, an inventive law student posits a dangerously compelling conspiracy theory after two Supreme Court justices are murdered; while "terminally predictable" for "suspense-thriller" seekers, it has a "great team" in Julia and Denzel – even if their characters' book romance didn't make it to the silver screen.

Pennies from Heaven | 17 | 19 | 18 | 20 |

1981 | Directed by Herbert Ross | With Steve Martin, Bernadette Peters, Christopher Walken | 108 minutes | Rated R

"Not your typical Steve Martin movie", this "high-concept" musical based on the British TV miniseries concerns a "Depression-era sheet music salesman and his fantasies" (with characters lip-synching period songs to escape their troubles); it's definitely "something original", but most find the plot's "unrelieved grimness" way too "dark" – with the exception of Walken's "knockout" dance routine.

People vs. Larry Flynt, The | 18 | 21 | 18 | 18 |

1996 | Directed by Milos Forman | With Woody Harrelson, Courtney Love, Edward Norton | 129 minutes | Rated R

Forman's "daring movie" creates an unlikely "hero" out of a "less than excellent subject", "pornographer" Larry Flynt, whose "rags-to-riches-to-ruin story" is rendered in such "heartbreaking" but "inspiring" terms that you wind up "loving the bad guy"; Harrelson is "first-rate" in the title role, Love "really can act" and you might just come away with a "whole new outlook" on smut.

Perfect Murder, A | 19 | 20 | 20 | 19 |

1998 | Directed by Andrew Davis | With Michael Douglas, Gwyneth Paltrow, Viggo Mortensen | 108 minutes | Rated R

A "slick", "updated" remake of *Dial M for Murder,* this "edge-of-your-chair" thriller about a wronged husband scheming to murder his wandering wife boasts a "wonderful cast" and "stylish" production values; but many cite "endless implausibilities" – starting with the "dopey" pairing of the "wrinkle-free" Paltrow and the "chicken-necked" Douglas – and note that "remaking Hitchcock is generally not a good idea."

Perfect Storm, The | 16 | 16 | 18 | 22 |

2000 | Directed by Wolfgang Petersen | With George Clooney, Mark Wahlberg, John C. Reilly | 129 minutes | Rated PG-13

There's "never a dull moment" in this "compelling" tale of an "ill-fated fishing boat crew" swept up in 1991's 'storm of the century'; no question, the deep-sea FX are "stunning", but the "unconvincing script" strikes some as "surprisingly shallow", "pulling the heartstrings" in a "dumbed-down", "big-budget Hollywood" way.

⨀ Persona ⦿🅵 | 27 | 28 | 25 | 26 |

1967 | Directed by Ingmar Bergman | With Bibi Andersson, Liv Ullmann | 81 minutes | Not Rated

Bergman's "plunge into the mysteries of the self" beguiles surveyors who say this "intense, very moving" film is the director's "best synthesis of symbolism and reality"; the story of a nurse and her patient (an actress who has gone mute) is "not rational but psychologically satisfying" as the two characters' identities "blend" together to make a "stunning" whole.

Personal Best | 15 | 17 | 18 | 16 |

1982 | Directed by Robert Towne | With Mariel Hemingway, Scott Glenn, Patrice Donnelly | 124 minutes | Rated R

This "pioneering" flick – "one of the earliest with a lesbian storyline" – depicts two track and field stars enmeshed in a love affair while competing for the same Olympics berth; while an "honest" – and maybe even "historically important" – attempt at depicting "realistic female athletes", many find it rather "boring."

Peter Pan

OVERALL	ACTING	STORY	PROD.
25	-	25	25

1953 | Directed by Clyde Geronimi, Wilfred Jackson, Hamilton Luske | Animated | 76 minutes | Rated G

Lost boys and girls who "never want to grow up" fly to this pixie dust-peppered tale concerning the eternally youthful Peter's adventures in Neverland; a "true classic" of Disney animation from the days when "Walt was running the show", it's an "important" enough childhood film for latter-day critics to ask "why did they bother with a remake?"

Peter Pan

OVERALL	ACTING	STORY	PROD.
20	19	21	23

2003 | Directed by P.J. Hogan | With Jeremy Sumpter, Jason Isaacs, Rachel Hurd-Wood, Lynn Redgrave | 113 minutes | Rated PG

"Move over, Disney": J.M. Barrie's oft-filmed children's classic gets a "beautiful live-action" retelling in this "well-done" movie that "really captures what it feels like to grow up"; a "seductive undertone" and some "darker aspects" make it a "bit more adult than previous versions", and if this puts off traditionalists ("after Mary Martin, why bother?"), most find it "thoroughly enjoyable."

Pete's Dragon

OVERALL	ACTING	STORY	PROD.
20	-	20	21

1977 | Directed by Don Chaffey | Animated | With Helen Reddy, Jim Dale, Mickey Rooney | 128 minutes | Rated G

Surveyors slayed by this "Disney classic" combining both animation and live action cheer its "heartwarming" story of a runaway orphan and his sometimes-invisible dragon companion; though fire-breathers blast it as "overlong" and "unmemorable", most agree the "kids will dig it", which is all that matters.

Peyton Place

OVERALL	ACTING	STORY	PROD.
20	20	21	21

1957 | Directed by Mark Robson | With Lana Turner, Hope Lange, Diane Varsi, Arthur Kennedy | 162 minutes | Not Rated

"Ninety-nine and 44/100 percent melodrama", this campy "mother of all soap operas" based on Grace Metalious' "trashy" mega-seller is set in a "small New England town" rife with "secrets and scandals" – or at least "what passed for scandalous in the 1950s"; in fact, most say what was "shocking" and "racy" then seems rather "timid" and "schmaltzy" now.

Phantom of the Opera, The

OVERALL	ACTING	STORY	PROD.
21	20	23	26

2004 | Directed by Joel Schumacher | With Gerard Butler, Emmy Rossum, Patrick Wilson | 143 minutes | Rated PG-13

Towing along its "lavish sets" and "to-die-for" tunes, Andrew Lloyd Webber's "Gothic romance" hit musical leaps onto the silver screen in this "faithful adaptation" courtesy of "over-the-top" director Schumacher; castwise, Phantom fandom is "swept away" by Rossum's "starmaking performance" as the "angelic" ingénue, though some purists wince at "hunk" Butler's "rock 'n' roll" rendition of the titular masked marauder.

Phenomenon

OVERALL	ACTING	STORY	PROD.
18	18	19	17

1996 | Directed by John Turteltaub | With John Travolta, Kyra Sedgwick, Forest Whitaker | 124 minutes | Rated PG

This "inspirational" "tearjerker" "pulls at the heartstrings" and "makes you want to live a better, fuller life" by showcasing a "convincing" Travolta as a small-town schmo who acquires supernatural powers and becomes a benevolent hero; though the dubious dub it "new-age hooey", for many the "message is touching" and the "beautiful images" leave a "good feeling."

Philadelphia ✉   24 | 27 | 25 | 23
1993 | Directed by Jonathan Demme | With Tom Hanks, Denzel Washington | 125 minutes | Rated PG-13

"Hollywood takes on AIDS" in this "extraordinarily powerful and poignant" drama that "puts a human face" on a "depressing" subject thanks to Hanks' "brave", Oscar-winning portrayal of a gay lawyer battling the "double-edged sword of discrimination and physical deterioration"; the final result resonates with "thought-provoking" issues, but don't forget to "bring the tissues – it's painful to watch."

⨂ Philadelphia Story, The ✉◗   27 | 28 | 26 | 25
1940 | Directed by George Cukor | With Cary Grant, Katharine Hepburn, James Stewart | 112 minutes | Not Rated

For the "sheer joy" of "listening to fast, furious dialogue" that "doesn't insult your intelligence", this "laugh-out-loud" screwball "comedy of manners" provides a "wild ride"; "you'll need a scorecard to keep up" with the "banter and spark" between the "classy" Kate, "acerbic" Grant and "underplaying" Stewart, uttered in settings so "perfectly frothy" that many wish that "life was really like that."

Phone Booth   18 | 20 | 18 | 18
2003 | Directed by Joel Schumacher | With Colin Farrell, Kiefer Sutherland, Forest Whitaker | 81 minutes | Rated R

You "don't see many original ideas anymore", so there's applause for this "implausible but diverting" thriller, a "tightly woven", high-concept "doozy" about a man trapped in a phone booth by a "really creepy" sniper; Farrell's "raw", "one-man-show" performance keeps most from hanging up, despite a script that "starts promisingly but runs out of steam toward the end."

⨂ Pianist, The ✉   28 | 29 | 27 | 28
2002 | Directed by Roman Polanski | With Adrien Brody, Thomas Kretschmann | 150 minutes | Rated R

"Agonizing and beautiful all at once", this "haunting" true story about a concert pianist's struggle to survive in Nazi-occupied Warsaw receives raves as "Polanski's historic achievement", a "masterpiece of filmmaking" that "will stay in your mind"; Brody's "brilliant", "subdued performance" "conveys so much without hardly saying a word", while the "depiction of the horror" is "accurate and harrowing in its detail"; in sum, both the director and star "deserved to win those Oscars."

Piano, The ✉   21 | 24 | 19 | 22
1993 | Directed by Jane Campion | With Holly Hunter, Harvey Keitel, Sam Neill | 121 minutes | Rated R

"Each frame could be a painting" in this "exquisitely shot" drama set in 19th-century New Zealand concerning a "mute woman" and her "search for fulfillment"; though Hunter delivers an "expressive", Oscar-winning performance (despite very "limited dialogue") opposite Keitel at his "sensual", "full-frontal" best, critics contend the "contrived" plot strikes flat notes.

Pickup on South Street `23` `24` `24` `22`

1953 | Directed by Samuel Fuller | With Richard Widmark, Jean Peters, Thelma Ritter, Richard Kiley | 80 minutes | Not Rated

For "film noir at its best", check out this "knockout" flick about a pickpocket and a prostitute inadvertently mixed up with a "Communist spy" ring; it's an "old-school", Red-menace ride with fine work from the "consummate" Widmark and the overripe Peters, and if that's not enough for you, "there's Thelma Ritter too."

Picnic `24` `24` `24` `24`

1955 | Directed by Joshua Logan | With William Holden, Kim Novak, Rosalind Russell, Arthur O'Connell | 115 minutes | Not Rated

Darn "sexy for its time", this "star-crossed", "moonglow"-drenched romance relates the havoc that a "handsome drifter" wreaks upon a group of "small-town" gals; fans say it "retains its charm", since it "epitomizes the lush storytelling of the '50s", but admit it may be a "little too theatrical to appeal to today's audiences"; hottest scene, no contest: Novak and Holden's "sizzling dance on the bridge."

Picnic at Hanging Rock `24` `23` `24` `24`

1979 | Directed by Peter Weir | With Rachel Roberts, Anne-Louise Lambert, Helen Morse | 107 minutes | Rated PG

You "never really know what's going on" in this "enigmatic" drama from the "innovative" Peter Weir recounting the disappearance of three students from a "repressive girls' boarding school" in "Victorian Australia"; granted, the "slow" pacing is "not for short attention spans", but admirers say its "unrelentingly atmospheric" cinematography and "unresolved ending" make for "hypnotic", "discussion"-worthy moviemaking.

Pieces of April `21` `24` `21` `19`

2003 | Directed by Peter Hedges | With Katie Holmes, Patricia Clarkson, Derek Luke | 80 minutes | Rated PG-13

A Thanksgiving dinner rife with "family dysfunction" is the setting of this "hysterical yet heartbreaking" dramedy that's "touching without being overly sentimental"; while Holmes gives a "winning performance" as the estranged title character and an "off-the-wall" cast keeps pace, the "stunning" Clarkson as her cynical, cancer-stricken mother steals this "little film with a big heart."

Pillow Talk ✉ `20` `20` `17` `19`

1959 | Directed by Michael Gordon | With Doris Day, Rock Hudson, Tony Randall, Thelma Ritter | 103 minutes | Not Rated

The "first – and best – of the Rock-Doris bedroom farces", this "gloriously goofy" romantic comedy about an "unlikely" pair who share a telephone party line is "good clean fun" with "no laugh track needed"; alright, the "setup is a bit dated" (verging on "insipid"), but more than a few fess up it's a "true guilty pleasure" that they "never tire of watching."

Pink Flamingos `18` `13` `15` `13`

1972 | Directed by John Waters | With Divine, David Lochary, Mink Stole, Edith Massey | 95 minutes | Rated NC-17

Watch it "at your own risk": this "cult favorite from John Waters" is the rare flick with "something to offend absolutely everyone", with a plot incorporating a "demented" drag queen, a "filthy" motor home, a "gross" half-dead chicken and topped off by an "extreme" ending too "disgusting" to relate; it's "lowbrow" and ultra "low-budget", but "mondo trasho" mavens maintain it's the "best worst movie ever made."

Pink Floyd The Wall 23 | 17 | 18 | 24

1982 | Directed by Alan Parker | With Bob Geldof, Bob Hoskins | 95 minutes | Rated R

"Provocative and disturbing", this "psychedelic rock opera" about a musician's "all-encompassing depression" is "one crazy movie" but a "classic" just the same thanks to its "masterful blend" of "out-of-this-world" imagery combined with Pink Floyd's "incredible" soundtrack; "required viewing for stoned high school students", it's altogether an "awesome" cinematic "head trip" – "even when viewed sober."

Pink Panther, The 24 | 24 | 21 | 21

1964 | Directed by Blake Edwards | With Peter Sellers, David Niven, Robert Wagner | 113 minutes | Not Rated

"Hilarity abounds" – "starting with the opening credits" – in this "out-landish" caper, the first production by the "comedy dream team" of director Edwards and actor Sellers (in his "brilliant" debut as "bumbling Jacques Clouseau"); "funny to this day", it marked the start of a "sequel brigade" that marched along for years afterward.

◪ Pinocchio 26 | - | 26 | 26

1940 | Directed by Hamilton Luske, Ben Sharpsteen | Animated | 88 minutes | Rated G

"Forget the wooden kid with the schnoz" (who's a bit "dull" anyway) – this "wonderful" animated fantasy is more memorable for its introduction of the "classic" character of Jiminy Cricket and its Oscar-winning song, 'When You Wish Upon a Star'; otherwise, this story of a puppet transformed into a boy still "combines some of the sweetest and scariest scenes" in all of Disneydom.

Pirates of the Caribbean: At World's End 21 | 23 | 18 | 26

2007 | Directed by Gore Verbinski | With Johnny Depp, Geoffrey Rush, Orlando Bloom, Keira Knightley | 168 minutes | Rated PG-13

A "bum-aching" 168-minute "maelstrom" of "rip-roarin'" action, "scenery chewing" by Depp and Rush and "twisty-turny" plot maneuvers so complex "you need a flow chart to follow them", this "rollicking" but "bloated" trilogy topper "ties up the loose ends" and leaves "a little hanging" for future voyages; P.S. the "cameo by Keith Richards" and the "extra scene after the credits" provide extra "bang for your doubloon."

Pirates of the Caribbean: Dead Man's Chest 20 | 22 | 17 | 26

2006 | Directed by Gore Verbinski | With Johnny Depp, Orlando Bloom, Keira Knightley, Bill Nighy | 150 minutes | Rated PG-13

Depp sets sail again as "flamboyant" buccaneer Jack Sparrow in this "amusing" but "overlong" middle-passage sequel setting up the franchise third act (At World's End) with a boatload of "cannibals, sea creatures" and "elaborate" stunt gags, including a "sword fight on a giant hamster wheel"; aye, the "confusing" yarn is just yo-"ho-hum", but ye must remember: "this is a pirate movie, not a David Lean epic."

Pirates of the Caribbean: The Curse of the Black Pearl

24 25 22 27

2003 | Directed by Gore Verbinski | With Johnny Depp, Geoffrey Rush, Orlando Bloom, Keira Knightley | 143 minutes | Rated PG-13

"Eat your heart out, Errol Flynn" – Johnny Depp's a real "hoot" in this Disney high seas adventure, turning in an "over-the-top" performance as a pirate captain who's half "swashbuckling", half "swish" (think "Keith Richards with a cutlass"); though it "could have been fluff" given its "audio-animatronic", "theme-park-ride" origins, this "rollicking" romp keeps the violence "stylized" and rolls out enough "impressive" FX to provide lots of "salty fun."

Pit and the Pendulum, The

22 21 22 20

1961 | Directed by Roger Corman | With Vincent Price, John Kerr, Barbara Steele | 80 minutes | Not Rated

"Vincent Price does Edgar Allen Poe" in this low-budget "B movie" that might bear little resemblance to the source material (save the climax), but is "scary" throughout; part of a series based on Poe stories, this one's the "all-time favorite" of dyed-in-the-wool Roger Corman fans.

Pitch Black

19 15 19 21

2000 | Directed by David Twohy | With Vin Diesel, Radha Mitchell, Cole Hauser | 110 minutes | Rated R

"You'll leave the lights on" after weathering the "jolts" in this "well-executed" sci-fi flick in which a "crew of misfits" crash-lands on a "barren planet" only to tussle with some "scary monsters"; the first Diesel-powered action vehicle, it propelled the buff "badass" to stardom – mysteriously so, as his "detached" performance is "not much to see."

☢ Place in the Sun, A ✉◗

27 27 27 24

1951 | Directed by George Stevens | With Montgomery Clift, Elizabeth Taylor, Shelley Winters | 122 minutes | Not Rated

This "classic American" love triangle from Oscar-winning director Stevens might be a "glamorized version of the Dreiser novel" but was still rather daring for its time given the unwed-mother subplot; while it's hard to miss the "radiant Clift and Taylor" (thanks to some swoon-worthy giant close-ups), "poor Shelley Winters'" role as the third wheel may well be the best performance; most famous line: Liz's smoldering "'tell mama all.'"

Places in the Heart ✉

20 22 20 18

1984 | Directed by Robert Benton | With Sally Field, Lindsay Crouse, Ed Harris, Danny Glover | 112 minutes | Rated PG

Softhearted souls really, really like this "moving Depression-era tale" of a Texas "woman alone with kids, a farm, a mortgage" and, thankfully, plenty of "courage"; though both Field and screenwriter Benton snagged Oscars for this "heartwarming" study, the hard-hearted nix it as too "depressing."

Planes, Trains and Automobiles

22 23 21 20

1987 | Directed by John Hughes | With Steve Martin, John Candy | 93 minutes | Rated R

The "road movie" that "does for traveling what *Jaws* did to swimming", this "sweet" comedy pairs "frazzled" "straight man" Martin with "obnoxious" "sad sack" Candy as strange bedfellows "trying to get home" in time for Thanksgiving in the face of "numerous mishaps"; although it's "super-funny", many note it also has "more heart than Jarvik's research lab"; most quoted line: "those aren't pillows!"

Planet of the Apes
23 | 20 | 25 | 23

1968 | Directed by Franklin J. Schaffner | With Charlton Heston, Roddy McDowall, Kim Hunter | 112 minutes | Rated G

"Darwin would have loved" this "thought-provoking" stew of "science fiction and pop culture" about an American astronaut who crashes on a simian-ruled planet; Heston's "brawny" turn brings equal parts "paranoid power" and "Republican campiness" to the leading role, while that "wallop" of an ending remains one of the "most talked-about ever."

Platoon
25 | 25 | 24 | 26

1986 | Directed by Oliver Stone | With Tom Berenger, Willem Dafoe, Charlie Sheen | 120 minutes | Rated R

"Disturbing" yet "unforgettable", this "almost-too-real" war picture offers a "raw" view of the Vietnam conflict as seen "through the eyes of a recruit just arrived in the jungle"; granted, it "fails to offer the slightest glimmer of hope", but it "captures the desperation" of battle "better than any other movie", with a clutch of Oscars (including Best Picture and Best Director) to prove it.

Player, The
23 | 23 | 23 | 22

1992 | Directed by Robert Altman | With Tim Robbins, Greta Scacchi, Fred Ward | 124 minutes | Rated R

"People who love movies about movies" love this "scathing satire" of "cutthroat" Hollywood, "perfectly directed" by "genius" Altman; cineasts cite the "excellent opening shot" (eight minutes "without a cut") and the "wonderful all-star cameo" appearances peppered throughout, but zero in on Robbins' "marvelous" portrayal of a "ne'er-do-well producer" as the real standout.

Play It Again, Sam
22 | 21 | 23 | 20

1972 | Directed by Herbert Ross | With Woody Allen, Diane Keaton, Tony Roberts | 85 minutes | Rated PG

Woody's "wonderful" in this "fine early comedy" adapted from his Broadway hit about a lovelorn film critic so enamored with *Casablanca* that he conjures up an imaginary Bogie for advice; though this spoof "works on every level" for "hard-core" Allen fans, purists protest there's one major problem: "he didn't direct it."

Play Misty for Me
22 | 20 | 23 | 19

1971 | Directed by Clint Eastwood | With Clint Eastwood, Jessica Walter, Donna Mills | 102 minutes | Rated R

The "original, much creepier" version of "*Fatal Attraction*", this "scary", "suspenseful" erotic thriller concerns a 'Misty'-spinning DJ "stalked by a deranged radio listener" (who supplies the "jump-out-at-you" moments); fans "get a thrill" out of Clint playing the "hunted instead of the hunter" for a change and dub his directorial debut "must-see" material.

Pleasantville
20 | 21 | 22 | 23

1998 | Directed by Gary Ross | With Tobey Maguire, Jeff Daniels, Joan Allen, Reese Witherspoon | 124 minutes | Rated PG-13

"Two modern teens" are magically transported into the "world of a '50s sitcom" in this "totally disarming" parable about "American fam-

| | OVERALL | ACTING | STORY | PROD. |

ily" life that's enlivened by some "high-tech tricks" (notably the "imaginative" use of "color vs. black and white"); though a bit "heavy-handed" for some, its "clever premise" and "memorable Randy Newman score" make for "unique" moviemaking.

Pocahontas
17 | - | 16 | 20

1995 | Directed by Mike Gabriel, Eric Goldberg | Animated | 82 minutes | Rated G

"Disney does it again" with this "subtly beautiful" animated feature about American Indians and English invaders in the Virginia colonies that might be "not historically accurate" but does offer a "great message" vis-à-vis tolerance and true love; if too "bland and preachy" for some, at least the "music's exceptional."

Point Blank
21 | 21 | 20 | 20

1967 | Directed by John Boorman | With Lee Marvin, Angie Dickinson, Keenan Wynn, Carroll O'Connor | 92 minutes | Not Rated

"Marvin sets the standard for antiheroes" in this "gritty" yet "stylized" example of modern noir, playing an "unstoppable killing machine" bent on collecting his $93,000 share of a robbery; it's an "extremely effective revenge" saga, with "fantastic cinematography", a "hallucinogenic plot" and the "wow"-inducing Angie as The Girl, even if soft-hearted sorts say it's too "vicious."

Polar Express, The
21 | - | 21 | 25

2004 | Directed by Robert Zemeckis | Animated | With Tom Hanks | 99 minutes | Rated G

Showcasing an "impressive" new filming technique that drops a "CGI"-enhanced Hanks into "five roles", this "good-spirited" animated adaptation of the "classic" children's book about a little boy who "doesn't believe in Santa" is "destined to become a holiday classic"; still, concerned parents caution that while the "choo-choo magic" is "pretty to look at", there are a "few scary spots" that might creep out the "preschooler set."

Pollock
22 | 26 | 21 | 22

2000 | Directed by Ed Harris | With Ed Harris, Marcia Gay Harden, Amy Madigan, Jennifer Connelly | 122 minutes | Rated R

Harris is absolutely "uncanny" capturing the "essence of dark genius" Jackson Pollock, the "misunderstood" 20th-century artist/"self-destructive" individual who's the eponymous subject of this "unflashy" biopic; as his mate and fellow painter, "Harden matches him every step of the way" in a "deservedly Oscar-winning" performance that further helps to transform this "amazing life" story into a "real work of art."

Poltergeist
22 | 20 | 23 | 24

1982 | Directed by Tobe Hooper | With JoBeth Williams, Craig T. Nelson, Beatrice Straight | 114 minutes | Rated PG

"Half social satire, half haunted-house tale", this "vivid" "roller-coaster ride" of a horror flick has a "pure Spielberg" premise: "affluent parents and cute children" living in a home "built over a graveyard" that's chock-full of "pesky ghosts"; the "strong story", "ahead-of-its-time special effects" and that "little voice" squeaking "they're he-ere" still resonate with boo-mers over "25 years later."

Polyester

	OVERALL	ACTING	STORY	PROD.
	19	16	17	16

1981 | Directed by John Waters | With Divine, Tab Hunter, Edith Massey, David Samson | 86 minutes | Rated R

From "prince of prurience" John Waters comes this "rude" black comedy featuring the "cross-dressing diva" Divine opposite "sex symbol of yore" Tab Hunter; the only picture ever shot in "Odorama" (a "gimmick" involving "scratch-and-sniff cards"), it tells the "silly" story of a put-upon housewife and is ultimately "so over the top, you wind up back down at the bottom."

Popeye

	OVERALL	ACTING	STORY	PROD.
	13	15	12	16

1980 | Directed by Robert Altman | With Robin Williams, Shelley Duvall, Paul Dooley, Paul L. Smith | 114 minutes | Rated PG

Fans fret about its "unjust bad rap", but this "quirky", "universally panned" musical comedy about a "spinach-eating" sailor may feature the "most perfect casting of a cartoon character ever": Duvall's "blow-me-down" version of Olive Oyl; true, Williams "never finds his sea legs" and there's too much "mumbling", but when the dialogue can be understood, it's "wonderful" – i.e. "I ain't no physicist but I know what matters."

Porky's

	OVERALL	ACTING	STORY	PROD.
	14	11	13	12

1982 | Directed by Bob Clark | With Dan Monahan, Kaki Hunter, Kim Cattrall, Scott Colomby | 94 minutes | Rated R

The "gold standard" of "horny teen movies", this "lewd, crude" comedy is a "classic of the genre", an "*Animal-House*-goes-to-high-school" story of "raunchy" 1950s dudes trying to lose their virginity; the "precursor of *American Pie*", it's pretty "sophomoric" stuff, somewhat redeemed by the "best shower scene in movie history – at least for 15-year-old boys."

Portrait of a Lady, The

	OVERALL	ACTING	STORY	PROD.
	16	21	19	21

1996 | Directed by Jane Campion | With Nicole Kidman, Barbara Hershey, John Malkovich | 142 minutes | Rated PG-13

Fans of novelist Henry James say this interpretation of his 1881 opus concerning an American heiress in Europe is "not to be missed" even though it does "leave out some major elements of the story"; but many others – even Nicole buffs – claim sitting through this "strange, sad" portrait is a lot "like watching paint dry."

Poseidon Adventure, The

	OVERALL	ACTING	STORY	PROD.
	19	18	20	22

1972 | Directed by Ronald Neame | With Gene Hackman, Ernest Borgnine, Red Buttons, Stella Stevens, Shelley Winters | 117 minutes | Rated PG

A "boat flips over" and the "actors flip out" in this "topsy-turvy" "granddaddy of Hollywood all-star disaster flicks" that's "more fun in a campy way than you'd expect"; sure, the "phenomenal underwater footage" and "unforgettable (if not completely subtle) performances" are "entertaining" enough, but foes sneer this "kitschy" "sinking ship" defines the "true meaning of 'all wet.'"

Possession

	OVERALL	ACTING	STORY	PROD.
	17	19	19	18

2002 | Directed by Neil LaBute | With Gwyneth Paltrow, Aaron Eckhart, Jeremy Northam, Jennifer Ehle | 102 minutes | Rated PG-13

A "good but not great" adaptation of A.S. Byatt's "complex" book, this romance packs "two love stories in one", spanning the centuries to chronicle a pair of "present-day researchers" (Paltrow and Eckhart) and the "Victorian poets" (Ehle and Northam) that they're studying; while most agree there's "no charisma between the modern couple", there's debate about whether it's more *Masterpiece Theatre* or "trashy romance novel" overall.

Postcards from the Edge | 18 | 23 | 19 | 18 |

1990 | Directed by Mike Nichols | With Meryl Streep, Shirley MacLaine, Dennis Quaid, Annette Bening | 101 minutes | Rated R

Edgy types tout this "Hollywood insider story" as a "terrifically funny" look at the relationship between a "recovering-druggie" movie star and her scenery-chewing movie-star mom; though both the "biting" MacLaine and "brilliant" Streep "shine", fans say that the "sharp" script is as acidly "amusing" as they come.

Postman Always Rings Twice, The ◑ | 25 | 25 | 25 | 24 |

1946 | Directed by Tay Garnett | With John Garfield, Lana Turner, Cecil Kellaway | 113 minutes | Not Rated

Garfield and Turner "set off the smoke alarms" in this "steamy" slice of film noir, a "deliciously sinful" saga about a "married femme fatale", a "streetwise vagabond" and their simmering affair that "boils over into murderous passion"; though this "twisting" tale of "love, betrayal" and "homicide" is pretty "wonderful", one question remains: "didn't people know about divorce in those days?"

Postman Always Rings Twice, The | 20 | 23 | 22 | 19 |

1981 | Directed by Bob Rafelson | With Jack Nicholson, Jessica Lange, John Colicos | 122 minutes | Rated R

Maybe it's "not as good as the original", but this "decent" enough remake of the film noir classic features "real sex" scenes instead of "implied" ones, most notably that display of "countertop love" that inspired many to install "butcher blocks in their kitchens"; "Jack is as creepy as ever" and Jessica's "good" as well, though purists pout "there's too much emphasis on sex at the expense of characterization" here.

☒ Potemkin ◑ | 27 | 22 | 25 | 27 |

1926 | Directed by Sergei Eisenstein | With Aleksandr Antonov, Viadimir Barsky | 75 minutes | Not Rated

Over 80 years later, cineasts are still electrified by director Eisenstein's "influential" "triumph" that "put 'montage' into the filmmaking lexicon" and "forever set the standards for camerawork"; detailing the failed 1905 uprising against the Czar, it's best known for its "often copied baby-carriage-on-the-Odessa-steps sequence" that "paved the way for edit-happy MTV directors"; indeed, it's so "exciting" that many insist it "should be mandatory moviegoing."

Prairie Home Companion, A | 18 | 22 | 15 | 20 |

2006 | Directed by Robert Altman | With Meryl Streep, Lily Tomlin, Kevin Kline, Lindsay Lohan, Woody Harrelson, John C. Reilly, Tommy Lee Jones, Virginia Madsen | 105 minutes | Rated PG-13

Loosely based on Garrison Keillor's NPR radio program, this "touching" depiction of "one night backstage" at a failing variety show is enacted by an "all-star" ensemble alternately singing and "trading jibes"; fans feel that Altman's "swan song" is "fittingly bittersweet", though foes fault a "slow-moving" plot that gets "lost in its own metaphoric cleverness."

| | OVERALL | ACTING | STORY | PROD. |

Predator
20 14 20 23

1987 | Directed by John McTiernan | With Arnold Schwarzenegger, Carl Weathers, Jesse Ventura, Bill Duke | 107 minutes | Rated R

An army commando squad in the Latin American jungle falls prey to the "universe's baddest killer" in this sci-fi "guy flick" that takes the "alien gorefest" concept to "action-packed" extremes; best known as the "movie that spawned two governors" (Arnold and Jesse) and a "video game", it's "suspenseful", "campy" and "very rewatchable" – just "beware of the sequel."

Prelude to a Kiss
16 16 17 15

1992 | Directed by Norman René | With Alec Baldwin, Meg Ryan, Kathy Bates | 105 minutes | Rated PG-13

A stage-to-screen transfer of Craig Lucas' play, this "quirky" love story involving a bride's "weird" body-swap with an elderly stranger sheds some "poetic" perspective on "interesting themes" like "identity and acceptance"; it may be "nothing to write home about", but count on the "charming" Ryan to add some "sweet" notes to the "sentimental" script.

Prestige, The
22 24 23 24

2006 | Directed by Christopher Nolan | With Hugh Jackman, Christian Bale, Michael Caine, Scarlett Johansson | 130 minutes | Rated PG-13

Portraying "rival magicians" who "go to extremes" to win over audiences, Bale and Jackman "keep you enthralled" throughout this "dark" Victorian meditation on "pride", "obsession" and "love"; given a plot full of "twists and turns" that some find sleight-ly "tough to follow", "repeated viewings" are recommended, if only to savor David Bowie's "notable cameo" again and again.

Presumed Innocent
20 21 22 18

1990 | Directed by Alan J. Pakula | With Harrison Ford, Brian Dennehy, Raul Julia | 127 minutes | Rated R

Based on Scott Turow's best-seller, this "darkly powerful courtroom thriller" concerns a Philadelphia prosecutor whose life takes a "rollercoaster" turn after he's accused of murder; jurists say its "cliffhanger" storyline boasts a "perfect surprise ending" that "keeps you guessing up till the last frame."

Pretty Baby
17 18 17 18

1978 | Directed by Louis Malle | With Brooke Shields, Keith Carradine, Susan Sarandon | 109 minutes | Rated R

Despite the "iffy" subject matter – "child prostitution in WWI-era New Orleans" – this "controversial" drama is "presented so matter-of-factly" that jaded folks "may find it a bit dull"; starring a "very young Brooke" (who's "just fine" in the title role), it's "beautifully filmed" in "soft focus" and "not exploitative", though a few "shocked" sorts say it "could never be made today."

Pretty in Pink
19 18 19 18

1986 | Directed by Howard Deutch | With Molly Ringwald, Harry Dean Stanton, Jon Cryer | 96 minutes | Rated PG-13

For a most "entertaining" "glimpse into the horrors of teenage dating", try this "Brat Pack" comedy "classic" starring Ringwald (at her late-'80s "poutiest") as an "angst"-ridden gal from the "wrong side of the tracks" who falls for a "rich preppie"; ok, it's "sappy" and "not too original", but given all the "cute touches" and that "killer soundtrack", many call it a "guilty pleasure to the nth degree."

Ⓩ Pretty Woman

23 | 22 | 22 | 22

1990 | Directed by Garry Marshall | With Richard Gere, Julia Roberts, Jason Alexander | 119 minutes | Rated R

Despite a premise somewhere between "Cinderella" and "Eliza Doolittle", this story of a "hooker with a heart of gold" who bags "Prince Charming" is a "happily-ever-after" romance that "put Julia (and her smile) on the map"; credit the "dizzying charisma" and "palpable chemistry between its stars" for its "believability", and though the "glamorization-of-prostitution" angle turns off bluenoses, "hopeless romantics" insist it will "steal your heart."

Pride and Prejudice ◑

25 | 25 | 26 | 23

1940 | Directed by Robert Z. Leonard | With Greer Garson, Laurence Olivier, Mary Boland | 118 minutes | Not Rated

A "lovely, headstrong heroine and a handsome haughty hero" make "sparks fly" in this "lush", "true-to-the-book" adaptation of the Jane Austen classic; "fabulous period costumes and sets" in high MGM style contribute to the "splendid" feel, while "Garson and Olivier play off each other wonderfully" – now, "that's style."

Pride & Prejudice

23 | 24 | 25 | 25

2005 | Directed by Joe Wright | With Keira Knightley, Matthew Macfadyen, Donald Sutherland | 127 minutes | Rated PG

"New insights into an old classic" flow from this "pared-down" translation of Jane Austen's novel featuring a "radiant" Knightley as the "headstrong" heroine who finds a "sparring partner and true love" in "brooding English Lord" Mr. Darcy; a "lavish production" featuring "breathtaking scenery", "intelligent" dialogue and an "alluring soundtrack", it maintains a modern "freshness" that tickles "silly romantic" types.

Pride of the Yankees, The ◑

22 | 22 | 23 | 20

1942 | Directed by Sam Wood | With Gary Cooper, Teresa Wright, Walter Brennan | 127 minutes | Not Rated

A "must" for both "baseball and Yankee fans", this "best sports" biopic virtually guarantees a "lump in the throat" as it delineates the life story of the "great Lou Gehrig" and his courage in the face of death; in the title role, Cooper is so effectively "self-effacing" that repeat viewers "cry every time" they hear his "farewell speech."

Primal Fear

22 | 25 | 23 | 21

1996 | Directed by Gregory Hoblit | With Richard Gere, Laura Linney, Edward Norton | 129 minutes | Rated R

The verdict's in: an "amazing" Norton "hits a home run" in his "stunning debut" as a "timid, stuttering" altar boy accused of killing an archbishop in this "unsettling" murder mystery/courtroom drama; otherwise, the "acting is on-point all around", though the performances are nearly "blown away" by that "knock-you-for-a-loop" "surprise ending."

Primary Colors

16 | 19 | 17 | 17

1998 | Directed by Mike Nichols | With John Travolta, Emma Thompson, Kathy Bates | 143 minutes | Rated R

An "uncomfortable peek" into the '92 Presidential campaign, this "tight" political comedy stars a "right-on" Travolta as a "thinly disguised" Bill

| | OVERALL | ACTING | STORY | PROD. |

Clinton in all his "lovably infuriating" grandeur; though hindered by "unnecessary melodrama", this "underrated" picture is a "good insider's view" of the "way things probably were – and you wish they weren't."

Prime
17 | 20 | 17 | 17

2005 | Directed by Ben Younger | With Meryl Streep, Uma Thurman, Bryan Greenberg | 105 minutes | Rated PG-13

A "Jewish therapist's son falls for her non-Jewish patient" ("oy vey!") in this "offbeat" rom-com starring the "magic" Meryl opposite "stunning" Uma and "endearing" newcomer Greenberg; it's a "funny" enough "dissection of love and maturity", though those hoping for a "Hollywood ending" are rather "disappointed" by its "true-to-life" windup.

Prime of Miss Jean Brodie, The ✉
25 | 28 | 24 | 23

1969 | Directed by Ronald Neame | With Maggie Smith, Robert Stephens, Pamela Franklin, Jane Carr | 116 minutes | Rated PG

Transposing "Dead Poets Society" to a '30s-era Scottish boarding school, this portrait of a "free-thinking teacher" is "worth revisiting" for Dame Maggie's "towering", Oscar-grabbing turn (which "does for Jean Brodie what Roz Russell did for Auntie Mame"); it's a "coming-of-age classic" crafted with "impressionable girls" in mind, despite its "heartbreaker" message: "idealism can be bad for you."

Prince of Egypt, The
19 | - | 19 | 23

1998 | Directed by Simon Wells, Brenda Chapman, Steve Hickner | Animated | 99 minutes | Rated PG

Respondents part like the Red Sea over this "history/cartoon combo": fans insist it's a "fascinating modern Bible retelling" of the story of Moses' exodus with the Jews from Egypt, with "terrific animation" and "beautiful songs", but foes say it's an "overwrought" derivation of the "Disney formula" that "lacks" in all areas "except special effects."

Prince of Tides, The
19 | 21 | 21 | 20

1991 | Directed by Barbra Streisand | With Barbra Streisand, Nick Nolte, Blythe Danner | 132 minutes | Rated R

In this "interesting story" about a "Southern football coach, his dysfunctional family" and the "New York City psychiatrist who sorts it all out", the "convincing Nolte really gives his all"; yet despite the "lyricism" and "stunning scenery", some say the "self-important" Babs "never should have directed herself" in this "vanity" production.

☑ Princess Bride, The
27 | 23 | 27 | 24

1987 | Directed by Rob Reiner | With Cary Elwes, Mandy Patinkin, Robin Wright | 98 minutes | Rated PG

Despite the "chick-flick title", this "lighthearted" but "fractured fairy tale" defies any easy "categorization" and is admired by "even the most macho" guys for its "swordfights" and "verbal jousting"; thanks to an "intelligent" William Goldman script, "masterful" direction by Reiner and an "incredibly talented" cast, "finding a better movie is inconceivable" – "plus, it's got André the Giant."

Princess Diaries, The
18 | 19 | 17 | 18

2001 | Directed by Garry Marshall | With Julie Andrews, Anne Hathaway, Hector Elizondo | 114 minutes | Rated G

It's "every girl's dream" – to discover she's "actually a princess" (albeit of "some little country you've never heard of") – and this "wholesome"

"mom-and-daughter" comedy follows newcomer Hathaway's transformation from "high-school dork" to crowned head amusingly enough; but even though this "feel-good" flick appeals to the "teenager inside us all", critics complain it's a "little flat for older audiences."

Princess Diaries 2: Royal Engagement, The

2004 | Directed by Garry Marshall | With Julie Andrews, Anne Hathaway, Hector Elizondo, Chris Pine | 113 minutes | Rated G

Set "in a castle instead of a high school", this "sugar-coated", family-appropriate sequel courts the "younger set" as it continues the story of a "charming" American teen who wears the crown in a pint-sized kingdom; it's "worth seeing" just to "hear Julie sing again", even if many consider the "predictable" plot and "phoned-in" performances a "royal snore."

Prisoner of Second Avenue, The `22` `25` `21` `20`

1975 | Directed by Melvin Frank | With Jack Lemmon, Anne Bancroft, Gene Saks | 98 minutes | Rated PG

There's "a lot of hollering out the window" going on in this Neil Simon comedy about a frustrated worker who loses his job and has a "classic breakdown" in circa-1970 New York; it's a "quintessential" Lemmon role (with Bancroft equally "awesome" as his put-upon wife), and if some dismiss it as a "not funny enough" "sitcom", at least it's a "well-acted one"; P.S. watch for a "fun cameo" from the then-unknown Sylvester Stallone.

Private Benjamin `17` `19` `17` `16`

1980 | Directed by Howard Zieff | With Goldie Hawn, Eileen Brennan, Armand Assante | 100 minutes | Rated R

"Goldie's golden" in this "funny, inspirational" comedy about a newly widowed Jewish princess who comes into her own after unwittingly enlisting in the army; a "lighthearted twist on women's liberation", it "shines" with "punchy" dialogue and a "charming" cast, particularly an acerbic Brennan and a "what-a-hunk" Assante as the romantic interest.

Prize Winner of Defiance, Ohio, The `22` `24` `23` `22`

2005 | Directed by Jane Anderson | With Julianne Moore, Woody Harrelson, Laura Dern | 99 minutes | Rated PG-13

"Based on a true story", this "nostalgic" drama stars the "amazing" Moore as a "saintly" '50s housewife who supports "10 kids and an alcoholic husband" by "winning jingle-writing contests"; given its "brilliant evocation" of a "time when you were somebody only if you were a man", many feel this entry "deserved more attention than it got."

Prizzi's Honor `21` `24` `21` `19`

1985 | Directed by John Huston | With Jack Nicholson, Kathleen Turner, Anjelica Huston | 130 minutes | Rated R

This "terrific black comedy about a dysfunctional mob family" anticipates The Sopranos with "cynical", "give-and-take" dialogue delivered by the "perfect cast" (a "bright" Jack and a "stellar", Oscar-copping Anjelica); one of John Huston's "last masterpieces", this "whacked-out gangster farce" wrings laughs via a "play-it-straight" script peppered with "in-jokes"; biggest conundrum: "do I ice her? do I marry her?"

| | OVERALL | ACTING | STORY | PROD. |

Producers, The ✉
26 26 26 23

1968 | Directed by Mel Brooks | With Zero Mostel, Gene Wilder, Kenneth Mars | 88 minutes | Rated PG

Flaunting "silly and shocking originality" long before the "Broadway hoopla", this "anarchic", "appallingly funny" comedy boasts Mostel and Wilder "at their best" as perps of a "Ponzi scheme" to produce an "unbelievably over-the-top" musical winningly titled *Springtime for Hitler* and cash in on its failure; it earns a standing ovation as "unrelenting", "inspired lunacy" from the "warped mind" of Mel Brooks that still "holds up" as a manic "masterpiece."

Producers, The
18 20 21 21

2005 | Directed by Susan Stroman | With Nathan Lane, Matthew Broderick, Uma Thurman, Will Ferrell | 134 minutes | Rated PG-13

Alright, there were "huge expectations" for this "movie musical based on a stage show based on a film comedy", but surveyors' reactions are mixed: "once-was-enough" types fret it "doesn't capture the charm of the original" picture (the "ghost of Zero Mostel hovers over every scene"), though fans say there are enough "catchy tunes" and big, "old-fashioned production numbers" (like the "old-ladies-and-the-walkers" routine) to make it a "lasting souvenir of a great Broadway show."

Professional, The
25 25 24 23

(aka Leon - The Professional)

1994 | Directed by Luc Besson | With Jean Reno, Gary Oldman, Natalie Portman | 110 minutes | Rated R

A "rare" example of a "well-executed" action flick, this "compelling" portrait of a hit man "with a heart of gold" who takes an orphan "under his wing" soars with its "unconventional" coupling of the "terrific" Reno with a "luminous" young Portman (in her feature film debut); count on "scary" Gary's "hyped-up bad cop" and some "wonderfully filmed" gunfight sequences to heighten the already "intense" mood.

Proof
18 22 20 18

2005 | Directed by John Madden | With Gwyneth Paltrow, Anthony Hopkins, Jake Gyllenhaal | 99 minutes | Rated PG-13

The thin line between "genius" and "madness" bisects this "intelligent" stage-to-screen adaptation starring Paltrow at her most "compassionate" as a "tortured" soul "suffering in the shadow" of her "brilliant" but "crazy" mathematician father; Hopkins is "mesmerizing as usual" in support of the "top-notch" script, though some suggest the "lethargic" pacing proves why this "treat for the intellect" is often "overlooked."

⊠ Psycho ◐
28 26 27 27

1960 | Directed by Alfred Hitchcock | With Anthony Perkins, Vera Miles, John Gavin, Janet Leigh | 109 minutes | Rated R

"Generations of moviegoers started double-locking their bathroom doors" after one look at the "famous shower scene" in this "classic Hitchcock" "psycho-logical thriller" that was "quite a shocker in its day" and "still packs a wallop" – "without the gross violence of modern flicks"; standouts include Bernard Herrmann's "scariest film score ever" and Perkins' "twitchy", "tour-de-force" performance as the ultimate "mama's boy."

Psycho

14 | 14 | 18 | 14

1998 | Directed by Gus Van Sant | With Vince Vaughn, Anne Heche, Julianne Moore, Viggo Mortensen | 105 minutes | Rated R

Gus Van Sant's "shot for shot" remake of Hitchcock's "homage to the dysfunctional son" strikes many as "blasphemy", a "cut-and-paste" exercise that surely must have "Alfred twirling in his grave"; sure, Vaughn is "creepily seductive" in the title role, but many say there was "absolutely no need for a new version" – "wouldn't it have been cheaper to colorize the original?"

Public Enemy ◑

25 | 25 | 22 | 22

1931 | Directed by William Wellman | With James Cagney, Jean Harlow, Edward Woods, Mae Clarke | 84 minutes | Not Rated

"Cagney's spectacular" in this "classic '30s gangster flick" that made him a star in the role of a petty crook who evolves into a "dangerous" crime czar; the picture still delivers quite a punch, brimming with "energy", especially the famous scene in which the girlfriend gets it in the kisser with a grapefruit.

ⓩ Pulp Fiction ✉

26 | 26 | 25 | 25

1994 | Directed by Quentin Tarantino | With John Travolta, Samuel L. Jackson, Uma Thurman, Bruce Willis, Amanda Plummer, Tim Roth, Ving Rhames, Harvey Keitel | 154 minutes | Rated R

A "pioneer of plot shuffling" and "twisty chronology", this "propulsive", "in-your-face" thriller is a "true original" with an "unpredictable storyline" and "dialogue that's like a punch in the face"; recounting the affairs of some "charming hit men", it stars a "rogues' gallery of actors" in memorable bits ("Travolta's dancing", Uma's overdose, Plummer's "psychotic rant") played out with "dark humor", "intense violence" and "foul language"; not only did it "put Tarantino on the map", it's in a "genre all by itself."

Pumping Iron

17 | - | 18 | 15

1977 | Directed by George Butler, Robert Fiore | Documentary | With Arnold Schwarzenegger, Lou Ferrigno | 85 minutes | Rated PG

An "enlightening" look into the "world of competitive bodybuilding", this "muscle-bound" documentary "put working out on the map" but is better known for "introducing Arnold to the world" in all his "cocky", "competitive" glory, full of the "charisma" and "ambition" that led to his "running the state of California" – "talk about foreshadowing!"

Pump Up the Volume

18 | 18 | 18 | 16

1990 | Directed by Allan Moyle | With Christian Slater, Samantha Mathis | 102 minutes | Rated R

This "antiestablishment" drama "tunes out the drivel" as Slater "comes into his own" playing a "nebbishy" dude with a "secret life" as a "pirate radio DJ"; it's a "better-than-average anthem" to "teen angst", and advocates are still pumped on its "rebellious" undercurrent and primo "period soundtrack."

Punch-Drunk Love

17 | 20 | 16 | 17

2002 | Directed by Paul Thomas Anderson | With Adam Sandler, Emily Watson, Philip Seymour Hoffman | 95 minutes | Rated R

"Not for everyone", this "quirky" "love story for losers" stars a "zombified" Sandler as an "angry, passive-aggressive type" who falls for an "adorable" if somewhat "weird" gal; foes find "more potential than payoff" here and say it's "about as self-important as movies get", while even fans admit it will "leave you scratching your head a little . . . kind of the way life does"; best line: "I beat up the bathroom."

Purple Rain
14 | 10 | 11 | 16

1984 | Directed by Albert Magnoli | With Prince, Appolonia Kotero, Morris Day | 111 minutes | Rated R

Acknowledged as the flick that "catapulted an unknown into a super-star", this "modern musical" relates the travails of a struggling singer, played by the one-and-only Prince; purple-xed types say this "two-hour music video" "hasn't aged well" (too much "bad acting" and "'80s fash-ion"), but most agree its "amazing", Oscar-winning soundtrack reigns.

Purple Rose of Cairo, The
21 | 21 | 24 | 21

1985 | Directed by Woody Allen | With Mia Farrow, Jeff Daniels, Danny Aiello | 84 minutes | Rated PG

The Woodman rises to the occasion with this "clever", "not-self-absorbed" comedy, a "bittersweet tale" featuring "Farrow's best" work as a Depression-era moviegoer whose "fantasy world" merges with "real life" when an RKO star walks off the screen into her life; the "imaginative" plot takes an "inside-out" look at "love of the movies", with a last reel calculated to "break your heart."

Pursuit of Happyness, The
23 | 25 | 24 | 22

2006 | Directed by Gabriele Muccino | With Will Smith, Jaden Smith, Thandie Newton | 117 minutes | Rated PG-13

Open up and say "awww": this "heartstring-pulling" paean to the "American dream" will "grab you" with its "Alger"-esque plot and Will's "phenomenal" performance as a "dedicated father" who "never gives up" despite "life's hardships"; sure, "you know where it's going right from the beginning", but the fact that it's "based on a true story" keeps the "sappyness" in check.

Z Queen, The ✉
26 | 29 | 23 | 25

2006 | Directed by Stephen Frears | With Helen Mirren, Michael Sheen, Helen McCrory, James Cromwell | 103 minutes | Rated PG-13

The "private side" of the British monarchy gets a public airing in this "wholly absorbing" look at the "royal response to the death of Diana", Princess of Wales; in the title role, Oscar-winner Mirren gives a "beautifully restrained" performance that goes "beyond the icy veneer" to "humanize" the "insulated" Queen and almost single-handedly crafts an "immensely entertaining" picture from "seemingly bland subject matter."

Quest for Fire
17 | 16 | 17 | 19

1981 | Directed by Jean-Jacques Annaud | With Everett McGill, Ron Perlman, Rae Dawn Chong | 100 minutes | Rated R

An "ambitious attempt" to dramatize the daily life of "prehistoric man", from the "frightening" (think "cannibalism and warfare") to the "erotic and even funny", this "unique" saga follows "three brave warriors" as they traverse "untamed land" on a mission to save their tribe from extinction; despite the "lush production", however, some have a bone to pick with the "sedate pace" and non-subtitled, "grunt-and-groan" dialogue.

Quiet American, The   24 | 26 | 24 | 24

2002 | Directed by Phillip Noyce | With Michael Caine, Brendan Fraser | 101 minutes | Rated R

Delivering a "powerful performance", Caine demonstrates why he's "legendary" in this "highly underrated" adaptation of the Graham Greene novel about "America's involvement in the early stages of the Vietnam War"; a "terrific" Fraser, a "wonderful story" and a "lavish" re-creation of 1950s Saigon are more reasons why many say "it's a shame" this "sleeper wasn't promoted enough."

∅ Quiet Man, The ✉   27 | 25 | 25 | 27

1952 | Directed by John Ford | With John Wayne, Maureen O'Hara, Barry Fitzgerald | 129 minutes | Not Rated

"Every Irish cliché" is "alive and well" in this "romanticized" drama, starring the Duke as an American boxer who hangs up his gloves and settles in his Hibernian "ancestral home" only to be smitten by the "beautiful", "feisty" O'Hara; presenting a "postcard" Ireland populated by "enchanting townspeople", it's "witty" and – despite a wee bit o' "blarney" – judged "worthy of a yearly viewing."

Quills   22 | 25 | 20 | 23

2000 | Directed by Philip Kaufman | With Geoffrey Rush, Kate Winslet, Joaquin Phoenix, Michael Caine | 124 minutes | Rated R

"Don't bring the kids" ("or the narrow-minded") to this "provocative" drama delineating the "imprisonment of the Marquis de Sade" in a Napoleonic insane asylum; while director Kaufman's "sexy, twisted" style is "compelling" if "disturbing" and the cast "excellent" (particularly the "magnificent" Rush), crueler critics contend this "perverted period piece" is "too icky for words."

Quiz Show   21 | 23 | 21 | 20

1994 | Directed by Robert Redford | With Ralph Fiennes, John Turturro, Rob Morrow | 133 minutes | Rated PG-13

"America's loss of innocence" is the subtext for this "intelligent" drama chronicling the '50s TV quiz-show scandals, a "blistering" commentary on the "mania for celebrity and money"; Turturro is the cast's "bright spot" as a bought-off contestant in a rigged highbrow showdown, and nostalgists prize the "vivid picture of the era", long before *Millionaire* – the "kicker is it really happened."

∅ Rabbit-Proof Fence   26 | 25 | 26 | 24

2002 | Directed by Phillip Noyce | With Everlyn Sampi, Tianna Sansbury, Laura Monaghan, Kenneth Branagh | 94 minutes | Rated PG

Young Aboriginal girls "escape forced slavery" and trek 1,500 miles across the Australian outback to return home in this "heart-wrenching true story" "acted wonderfully" by "three unknowns"; "don't expect special effects", and make sure to "watch the credits and you'll see the real children, now in their 80s."

Racing Stripes   18 | 18 | 18 | 19

2005 | Directed by Frederik Du Chau | With Hayden Panettiere, Bruce Greenwood | 102 minutes | Rated PG

"Talking animals" voiced by a star-studded crew (including Dustin Hoffman and Frankie Muniz) gives some zip to this "harmless" family feature about a father-daughter team training an "outcast" zebra who wants to be a racehorse; but even with "jokes galore" and a "message about appearance and fitting in", the "after school special-ish" approach leaves "not much for anyone over 12."

Radio
22 | 25 | 23 | 22

2003 | Directed by Michael Tollin | With Cuba Gooding Jr., Ed Harris | 109 minutes | Rated PG

"Small-scale" and proud of it, this "inspiring" sports drama recounts the true story of a "friendly football coach" who molds a "less fortunate", mentally disabled man into a popular mascot-cum-cheerleader (played by the "outstanding" Gooding, who "loses himself in the character"); parents say its "old-fashioned, feel-good" scenario teaches "great life lessons for kids."

Radio Days
23 | 23 | 23 | 23

1987 | Directed by Woody Allen | With Mia Farrow, Julie Kavner, Dianne Wiest | 85 minutes | Rated PG

Tune in for "fond memories" to this "charming" "family comedy", an "affectionate period piece" set in late-'30s Rockaway Beach, where "childhood innocence, neurotic relatives" and golden-age radio fill the airwaves in a series of "warm vignettes"; touted for "top-to-bottom acting excellence", it's a "funny", "free-form" sampler of "Allen at his sunniest" and "most enjoyable."

☑ Raging Bull ✉◐
26 | 28 | 24 | 26

1980 | Directed by Martin Scorsese | With Robert De Niro, Cathy Moriarty, Joe Pesci | 129 minutes | Rated R

Perhaps the "best boxing movie of all time", this "riveting" biopic charts the "rise and fall" of former middleweight champion Jake LaMotta, whose toughest opponents were his own "self-destructive tendencies"; shot in "beautiful black and white", it features a "primo De Niro", and though it can be "as painful as an open wound" to watch, most feel this is "knockout" filmmaking.

Ragtime
21 | 23 | 23 | 23

1981 | Directed by Milos Forman | With Howard Rollins Jr., Elizabeth McGovern, Mandy Patinkin, James Cagney, Mary Steenburgen, Brad Dourif, Mandy Patinkin | 155 minutes | Rated PG

Based on "E.L. Doctorow's bravura novel", this "big production" takes on nothing less than the "Victorian era" with a "big storyline" that places fictional characters alongside such real-life figures as Stanford White, Evelyn Nesbit, Harry Houdini and Booker T. Washington; while some find it all "fascinating" and the cast "outstanding", others sigh it's too "longwinded" and "not as good as the book."

☑ Raiders of the Lost Ark
28 | 24 | 27 | 28

1981 | Directed by Steven Spielberg | With Harrison Ford, Karen Allen, Paul Freeman, Denholm Elliott | 115 minutes | Rated PG

It doesn't get "more exciting" than this "benchmark" of "nonstop pulp-fiction action", Spielberg's "roller-coaster" homage to "Saturday matinee" serials that introduces the "rakish" Indiana Jones, a tweedy archaeologist with a "strapping-hero" alter ego who scraps with the Nazis over an "all-powerful artifact"; chock-full of "retro" delights like "tongue-in-cheek" humor, "improbable cliff-hanger escapes" and a "love interest" amid the "snakes, whips and guns", it's a "rousing blockbuster" that proves the "'80s weren't all bad."

Rainmaker, The

21 | 22 | 22 | 20

1997 | Directed by Francis Ford Coppola | With Matt Damon, Danny DeVito, Claire Danes, Jon Voight | 135 minutes | Rated PG-13

Proving again why he's one of the "best in the business", Coppola molds a "clichéd" John Grisham novel into a "moving" courtroom drama detailing the "seamy side of law practice"; a "fine" Damon and "hysterical" DeVito play "ambulance chasers" targeting a heartless insurance company opposite Voight, a "perfectly menacing" shark who enlivens the "excellent trial scenes."

Rain Man ✉

25 | 27 | 24 | 23

1988 | Directed by Barry Levinson | With Dustin Hoffman, Tom Cruise, Valeria Golino | 133 minutes | Rated R

This Best Picture winner is an unconventional "brothers bonding" drama driven by an Oscar-winning performance from Hoffman, who's "nothing short of incredible" as a full-grown "autistic savant" blessed with an endless supply of "quirky mannerisms" and "memorable lines"; Cruise shows off his own "acting chops" as the "scheming" sibling angling for half his inheritance, bringing on showers of "insight" that clear up to let a "feel-good" resolution shine through.

Raising Arizona

23 | 23 | 23 | 21

1987 | Directed by Joel Coen | With Nicolas Cage, Holly Hunter, John Goodman | 94 minutes | Rated PG-13

For a "completely original" and truly "bizarre" screwball comedy, check out this "hilarious white-trash" "cult classic" about a "childless", "criminal-class" couple (a policewoman married to a "failed convenience-store thief") that kidnaps a kid; Cage and Hunter are drolly "deadpan" delivering "dialogue that can't be beat", while the plot is typical Coen brothers: "goofy", "quirky" and gosh "darn funny."

Ⓩ Raisin in the Sun, A ◑

26 | 28 | 26 | 23

1961 | Directed by Daniel Petrie | With Sidney Poitier, Claudia McNeil, Ruby Dee, Diana Sands | 128 minutes | Not Rated

"Equal to" Lorraine Hansberry's award-winning Broadway play, this "groundbreaking" adaptation tells the story of a poor black family coping with a modest financial windfall; there's "emotional conflict" aplenty in its "dueling themes" of "racism, motherhood and manhood" and the "strong" cast is up to the challenge (particularly the "poignant Poitier"); pessimists say it's "sadly as applicable today as it was in the '60s."

Ⓩ Ran Ⓕ

27 | 25 | 27 | 29

1985 | Directed by Akira Kurosawa | With Tatsuya Nakadai, Mieko Harada, Daisuke Ryu | 160 minutes | Rated R

"Big, bold and beautiful", Kurosawa's "swan song" shows his "deft touch" intact in this "expansive retelling of *King Lear*" transformed into a "riveting" samurai "epic" involving a Shogun warlord whose decision to sheath his sword leads to intra-clan "betrayals"; suitably "Shakespearean" in scale, with "stunning" depictions of "feudal society" and "incredible battle scenes", it's "slow"-running pacewise but most hail it as "brilliant almost beyond belief."

| | OVERALL | ACTING | STORY | PROD. |

Ransom
16 18 17 17

1996 | Directed by Ron Howard | With Mel Gibson, Rene Russo, Gary Sinise, Lili Taylor | 120 minutes | Rated R

"Gripping" suspense is tempered with "much emotion" in this "dark" tale of a kidnapped child, starring "Mel in a suit" as a "conflicted" dad; though some bluff-callers deem it "overblown" and "formulaic", others swear by its "realistic" tension that's "scary to every parent out there."

Z Rashomon ◑F
29 27 29 25

1951 | Directed by Akira Kurosawa | With Toshiro Mifune, Machiko Kyo, Masayuki Mori | 88 minutes | Not Rated

Surely "truth is in the eye of the beholder", but most agree that Akira Kurosawa's "superb head-twister" of a Japanese drama should be "required viewing"; aided by "exquisite" camerawork and "fine medieval embellishments", it's a "simple story" about an ambush in the forest told from "four different points of view", proving that "self-interest" amounts to "nine-tenths of everything"; in sum, this "seminal" tale has been tirelessly "copied but never equaled."

Z Ratatouille
26 – 25 27

2007 | Directed by Brad Bird, Jan Pinkava | Animated | 111 minutes | Rated G

In this animated "valentine to Paris and the art of cooking", an "unusual alliance" between a bus boy and a rodent "obsessed with haute cuisine" equals "another masterpiece cooked up by Pixar"; a "perfect recipe" for "broad audience appeal", it blends "visually stunning" animation with "loads of charm", adds "silly antics" for the kids and folds in some "smart dialogue" for adults; in sum, "c'est magnifique!"

Z Ray ✉
26 29 25 26

2004 | Directed by Taylor Hackford | With Jamie Foxx, Kerry Washington, Regina King | 152 minutes | Rated PG-13

"Foxx almost disappears into the person of Ray Charles" in this "phenomenal" bio-"tribute" to the "legendary musician", nabbing a "well-deserved" Oscar for his "foot-stomping", "heartrending" portrayal of the superstar that's so convincing you'll "forget who you're really watching"; fans agree the "uncompromising" look at the soul man's "boozing, drugs and womanizing" is right on key, with additional hoo-rays going out to that "marvelous soundtrack."

Reality Bites
19 18 18 17

1994 | Directed by Ben Stiller | With Winona Ryder, Ethan Hawke, Janeane Garofalo | 99 minutes | Rated PG-13

"Escape with the losers" in this romantic comedy of "post-college" Gen-X existence as Winona and company find themselves "going nowhere" but obliged to deal when faced with "job woes", tainted love and "utter annoyance with life"; vets of the day say as a "portrayal of MTV and other pop-culture" touchstones, "nothing represents the '90s more accurately."

Real Women Have Curves
21 22 21 19

2002 | Directed by Patricia Cardoso | With America Ferrera, Lupe Ontiveros, Ingrid Oliu, George Lopez | 90 minutes | Rated PG-13

Those with "less-than-supermodel bodies" – "which is about 99 percent of the population" – will especially enjoy this "inspirational" coming-of-age story about a "courageous" Latina teen "who isn't a size eight" "caught between family traditions and modern mores"; "there needs to be more movies" like this "celebration of women."

☒ Rear Window — 28 | 27 | 28 | 27

1954 | Directed by Alfred Hitchcock | With James Stewart, Grace Kelly, Thelma Ritter, Raymond Burr | 112 minutes | Rated PG

"Voyeurism" meets "suspense" in this "snooper's dream" about a "wheelchair-bound" photographer "spying on his neighbors" and trying to "trap a killer" while fending off his girlfriend, who's tempting him into "another trap – marriage"; while the "crisp script" and "great NY set" draw huzzahs, fans tout its "perfectly cast" leads, the "solid" Stewart and "deeelicious" Kelly; so many find it "unsurpassed" that it was voted the top Hitchcock flick in this Survey.

☒ Rebecca ✉◑ — 27 | 27 | 27 | 25

1940 | Directed by Alfred Hitchcock | With Laurence Olivier, Joan Fontaine, Judith Anderson | 130 minutes | Not Rated

Based on Daphne du Maurier's "ultimate romance novel", "Hitchcock's first American film" is a "dark, moody" tale of a woman living in the shadow of her new husband's old wife; "haunting" and "eerily captivating", it showcases an "excellent" Olivier and a "gorgeous" Fontaine, but it's the "over-the-top" Anderson who's the real "hoot" here.

Rebel Without a Cause — 24 | 24 | 21 | 22

1955 | Directed by Nicholas Ray | With James Dean, Natalie Wood, Sal Mineo | 111 minutes | Not Rated

A "lost generation lives on" in this "terse drama" of "disaffected youth" and "family conflict", which elevated Dean to "icon" status as a "rebellious" juvenile delinquent who leads a "great cast" as they cope with "hope, fear and love" in the "inchoate LA" of the '50s; if all that acting out is a bit "dated", most maintain it "lives up to its rep" as the "ultimate" ode to "teen alienation."

Recruit, The — 17 | 20 | 18 | 19

2003 | Directed by Roger Donaldson | With Al Pacino, Colin Farrell, Bridget Moynahan | 115 minutes | Rated PG-13

"Nothing is what it seems" in this "keeps-you-guessing" spy thriller wherein a "secretive CIA" man attempts to enlist a promising recruit; though Farrell "holds his own" as the protégé, some say Pacino's "patented screaming mentor role" is "starting to sound the same in every movie", and despite all the "twists and turns", the "ending's weak."

Red Dawn — 17 | 15 | 19 | 18

1984 | Directed by John Milius | With Patrick Swayze, C. Thomas Howell, Lea Thompson, Charlie Sheen | 114 minutes | Rated PG-13

This "Cold War fantasy" delivers "plenty of action" as the "young Swayze" leads high-school "freedom fighters" in "guerilla warfare" after Russian and Cuban troops invade their tiny town; its "patriotic" zeal makes some want to "wave the flag", but foes say such "heavy-handed" "right-wing propaganda" was "implausible even when it was released."

Red Dragon — 19 | 22 | 20 | 20

2002 | Directed by Brett Ratner | With Anthony Hopkins, Edward Norton, Ralph Fiennes, Harvey Keitel | 124 minutes | Rated R

"Better than *Hannibal*" but "not as good as *Silence of the Lambs*" is this "engaging" "prequel" wind-up of the "Lecter trilogy", a "suspenseful" thriller pitting a "stoic" G-man against a "disturbed murderer", and featuring the obligatory "mental chess match" with Hopkins' "good doctor" (albeit in a "minor role"); P.S. compare it with 1986's *Manhunter*, based on the same novel and often considered the "superior" version.

Red Eye

	OVERALL	ACTING	STORY	PROD.
	16	18	16	17

2005 | Directed by Wes Craven | With Rachel McAdams, Cillian Murphy, Brian Cox | 85 minutes | Rated PG-13

"Hold on to your seat" – this "adrenaline-filled" thriller ramps up some airborne intrigue as the "downright creepy" Murphy "insinuates his way" into the life of a "wide-eyed ingénue" aboard a late-night flight; the "good-looking leads" display enough "winning charisma" to compensate for an "implausible" plot and an "anticlimactic", "bumpy landing" of an ending.

⚡ Red River ◐

	26	25	25	27

1948 | Directed by Howard Hawks | With John Wayne, Montgomery Clift, Joanne Dru | 133 minutes | Not Rated

"Perhaps the grandest" Western of all, this cowpuncher "classic" breaks into a gallop when "lots of hunky men" saddle up for a dangerous cattle drive along the Chisholm Trail; Wayne "excels in an unsympathetic role" as a "stolid" rancher who turns against Monty, who "holds his own" as a buckaroo of "brooding sensitivity"; the result is a horn-lock that fans brand a grade-A prime "rewatcher."

Reds ✉

	21	21	20	22

1981 | Directed by Warren Beatty | With Warren Beatty, Diane Keaton, Jack Nicholson | 194 minutes | Rated PG

Agitprop meets "epic romance" in this "impressive" bio of writers John Reed and Louise Bryant that chronicles their courtship and activities as bolshie sympathizers during the Russian Revolution; "Beatty's labor of love" celebrating "American radicalism", it's an "excellent re-creation" of the time, framed by "remembrances" of "largely forgotten men and women", but "major themes" or no, critics say this "big production" is "too long to keep you interested."

⚡ Red Shoes, The

	26	24	24	26

1948 | Directed by Michael Powell, Emeric Pressburger | With Anton Walbrook, Moira Shearer | 133 minutes | Not Rated

With a tip of the slipper to Hans Christian Andersen, this "ageless" drama of "romance and ballet" "takes a fairy tale and creates magic" around the story of a young dancer who joins a celebrated troupe only to enter into a pas de deux with a composer; "sumptuous" staging and "dreamy choreography" make it a terpsichorean "benchmark", and fans "love every bit of it."

Red Violin, The ▣

	24	23	24	24

1999 | Directed by François Girard | With Samuel L. Jackson, Greta Scacchi | 131 minutes | Rated R

A "symphony" recounting the "many tales of a violin's life", this "intricate" drama "follows the path" of a "fabulous instrument" from its creation in Renaissance Italy though various owners, countries and epochs, up to Jackson's encounter as a present-day appraiser; in spite of "art-house" airs, boosters bow to a "twisting" story that "keeps you guessing" – backed by a really "stunning" soundtrack featuring "real music by a real composer."

Regarding Henry | 20 | 23 | 21 | 19 |

1991 | Directed by Mike Nichols | With Harrison Ford, Annette Bening | 108 minutes | Rated PG-13

"Ford does an admirable job" with a "non-action" role in this "touching" "adult drama", a "well-cast" parable about a heartless corporate lawyer who is transformed into a "vulnerable" family man in the "aftermath of a brain injury"; it's well regarded for its "insightful" "moral lesson" about "what's important in life", though naysayers dismiss it as a "movie-of-the-week" "tearjerker."

Reign Over Me | 20 | 24 | 21 | 21 |

2007 | Directed by Mike Binder | With Adam Sandler, Don Cheadle, Jada Pinkett Smith, Liv Tyler | 124 minutes | Rated R

"Surprisingly touching", this "underappreciated" drama of "life after 9/11" demonstrates that Sandler can "shine in a serious role", playing a victim of post-traumatic stress who's supported by an old friend, the "superb" Cheadle; the "heartfelt acting" really "draws you in", and despite a few "improbabilities", most find its blend of "sorrow and inspiration" to be genuinely "rewarding."

Remains of the Day, The | 24 | 27 | 23 | 25 |

1993 | Directed by James Ivory | With Anthony Hopkins, Emma Thompson, Christopher Reeve | 138 minutes | Rated PG

"If you loved *Howards End*", you'll dig this "complex and entertaining" drama of "two fragile souls" on a British estate in the late '30s; "repressed" head butler Hopkins "puts duty above all else", even his yen for housekeeper Thompson, and both give "precise, controlled performances" filled with "gripping silences" to suit its "nuanced" story of "unfulfilled love", "class-system" bias and the "obtuseness of the upper crust" – just "don't expect action."

Remember the Titans | 20 | 21 | 21 | 19 |

2000 | Directed by Boaz Yakin | With Denzel Washington, Will Patton, Wood Harris | 113 minutes | Rated PG

"Denzel is the man" to knock a ball team into shape while tackling "racial fault lines" in this "inspirational" family drama about a black high-school coach taking over a newly integrated football squad; if the "feel-good" theme of "tolerance and social understanding" on and off the field plays out as rather "hokey" and "about as deep as astroturf", supporters "cheer anyway" for a "sleeper" that never fumbles its underlying "hope."

Rent | 19 | 20 | 20 | 20 |

2005 | Directed by Chris Columbus | With Anthony Rapp, Adam Pascal, Rosario Dawson, Jesse L. Martin | 135 minutes | Rated PG-13

Of course, there's "nothing like the live Broadway show", but this stage-to-screen transfer of Jonathan Larson's "groundbreaking" musical actually "holds its own" thanks to the casting of "most of the original" players (albeit "aged" some years) for an "energetic" reprise of those "rousing" song-and-dance numbers; if a few critics charge the AIDS-themed storyline "loses its punch" in translation, most feel it's still as "poignant as ever."

	OVERALL	ACTING	STORY	PROD.

Replacement Killers, The
16 | 15 | 17 | 18

1998 | Directed by Antoine Fuqua | With Chow Yun-Fat, Mira Sorvino | 87 minutes | Rated R

For a "good time" – "without too much stress on the ol' gray cells" – check out this "underrated" thriller about a conscience-stricken hit man unable to complete his latest hit; the picture was supposed to be "Hong Kong superstar" Yun-Fat's "ticket to American stardom", but unfortunately a "slim", "not exactly believable" scenario tricked up with lots of "generic action" makes it play like "John Woo lite."

Repo Man
17 | 15 | 17 | 16

1984 | Directed by Alex Cox | With Harry Dean Stanton, Emilio Estevez | 92 minutes | Rated R

A "cult classic with a serious following", this "wacko" comedy "captures the nihilism of the '80s punk scene" in its story of lowlifes repossessing cars and chasing after UFOs; with lots of "throwaway gags", "quotable lines" and an "overlooked soundtrack", this "silly delight" is proudly "over the edge" and "hard to resist."

Repulsion ◑
▽ 25 | 27 | 24 | 23

1965 | Directed by Roman Polanski | With Catherine Deneuve, Ian Hendry | 105 minutes | Not Rated

Polanski's first English-language feature, this "disturbing" psychological thriller top bills an "unbeatable" Deneuve as an unstable young woman slowly descending into madness; although made on a shoe-string budget, it's still really "frightening" in its "depiction of insanity from the inside out" and is already showing "definite cult potential."

Requiem for a Dream
25 | 27 | 24 | 25

2000 | Directed by Darren Aronofsky | With Ellen Burstyn, Jared Leto, Jennifer Connelly | 102 minutes | Not Rated

"Heavy" and "altogether devastating", this "bleak" "druggy" drama "spirals into the depths of hell" on the back of some "scary", strung-out imagery and Burstyn's "amazing" turn as a magenta-maned diet-pill popper with a none-too-swift junkie son; a "stomach-churning" depiction of "major drug use" that pushes Aronofsky to the "cutting edge" of "directing talents", it's "not subtle" but lingers like a "brilliant", "unnerving nightmare" – "be prepared" for some "grueling" going.

⚡ Requiem for a Heavyweight ◑
26 | 28 | 26 | 23

1962 | Directed by Ralph Nelson | With Anthony Quinn, Jackie Gleason, Mickey Rooney, Julie Harris | 95 minutes | Not Rated

Adapted from Rod Serling's Emmy-winning television play, this "knock-out" drama is "one of the best fight films around", detailing a punch-drunk boxer's "gut-wrenching" decline; maybe it's turned "dated" and "preachy" over time, but for diversion there's always that "superb" ensemble cast, especially the "amazing" Quinn; N.B. look for cameos from real-life heavyweights Jack Dempsey and Muhammad Ali (billed here as Cassius Clay).

Rescuers, The
23 | - | 23 | 23

1977 | Directed by Wolfgang Reitherman, John Lounsbery, Art Stevens | Animated | 76 minutes | Rated G

A "must-see for every child", this animated Disney feature stars a pair of "adorable" mice bent on rescuing a kidnapped little girl; although maybe not at the top of the Mouse House pantheon, it's still "fun" with memorable voicework from Bob Newhart, Eva Gabor and Geraldine Page.

Reservoir Dogs

OVERALL	ACTING	STORY	PROD.
24	25	24	22

1992 | Directed by Quentin Tarantino | With Harvey Keitel, Tim Roth, Michael Madsen, Steve Buscemi | 99 minutes | Rated R
The Tarantino "template" for a "new" style of crime thriller splices "hip" dialogue with "hard-core violence" as a "dream cast" turns a jewel heist into a "riveting" "bloody spectacle"; the "clever" script relies on diced chronology, "sly riffs" on pop culture and "psychological twists" to lend heart to the "vicious" gang, though many howl the "nasty" bits ("ear removal", anyone?) are still "painful to watch."

Revenge of the Nerds

19	16	19	16

1984 | Directed by Jeff Kanew | With Robert Carradine, Anthony Edwards, Timothy Busfield, Curtis Armstrong | 90 minutes | Rated R
"Geeky guys unite" in this collegiate "comedy classic", which finds a "lovable bunch of nerds" banding together as frat brothers to "fight back against the jocks"; "goofy", "irreverent" and maybe even "inspirational" (i.e. those "completely gratuitous nude scenes"), it's all "stupid fun", although the follow-ups are "not as original as the original."

Reversal of Fortune ⊠

23	26	23	21

1990 | Directed by Barbet Schroeder | With Jeremy Irons, Glenn Close, Ron Silver | 120 minutes | Rated R
"You can't make this stuff up" – Oscar-winner Irons is "totally mesmerizing" in his "smarmy" take on the real-life Claus von Bulow, the high-society ladies' man accused of sending his heiress wife into an irreversible coma; Close and Silver also deliver the goods in this "solid" picture whose only drawback is "not having the ending that you want."

☑ Rififi ◑🎬

26	24	27	24

1956 | Directed by Jules Dassin | With Jean Servais, Carl Mohner, Robert Manuel | 115 minutes | Not Rated
Arguably the "first modern caper film", this "original" French take on film noir is loaded with "intrigue, gangsters and great scenes of Paris" as it details the plans to burgle a jewelry store; its "stunning" heist sequence – "totally silent for half an hour" – assures its "classic" status, and even if the "production quality seems dated now", ultimately it "still holds up after 50 years."

☑ Right Stuff, The

26	24	26	26

1983 | Directed by Philip Kaufman | With Sam Shepard, Scott Glenn, Ed Harris | 193 minutes | Rated PG
"Exuberant", "involving" and "proud to be American", this "triumphant" drama "never flags" in launching Tom Wolfe's "snarky yet sincere" "epic of the space age" onto the big screen; a "retelling of true events" surrounding the evolution of test pilots into astronauts in the Mercury program, it takes "historical" stuff and pushes the envelope with "adventure, humor" and a cast that's "A-ok in every way."

Ring, The

19	18	20	21

2002 | Directed by Gore Verbinski | With Naomi Watts, Martin Henderson, David Dorfman, Brian Cox | 115 minutes | Rated PG-13
Viewers of a "mysterious videotape" receive a "spooky" call and "die seven days later" in this "genuinely scary" ghost story that delivers its

"spine-tingling" chills without the "gross-out effects" common to the genre; cynical cinephiles say the "convoluted" story "falls apart" toward the end (*Ringu,* the "original Japanese version, is better"), but most are still "clutching their armrests" and vowing "never to answer the phone again."

Rio Bravo
24 | 22 | 21 | 22

1959 | Directed by Howard Hawks | With John Wayne, Dean Martin, Ricky Nelson | 141 minutes | Not Rated

"As Westerns go", this "entertaining" oater from the Hawks/Wayne team is an "expert reshuffling" of the plot elements of "*High Noon*", the story of a sheriff trying to hold a prisoner against a threatening mob virtually alone; though the picture was remade as *El Dorado* (and later as *Rio Lobo*), aficionados say the original is the "best version."

Risky Business
20 | 18 | 19 | 18

1983 | Directed by Paul Brickman | With Tom Cruise, Rebecca De Mornay, Bronson Pinchot | 98 minutes | Rated R

"Every boy's dream" comes true in this "smart, sexy" "coming-of-age" comedy, with Cruise as the high-schooler who turns chez suburbia into party central when his parents leave town – only to fall into "the arms of a beautiful hooker" and venture into the brothel business; it's a "funny" jibe at "upper-middle-class teenage life" with some "raging hormones" thrown in, and that celebrated scene of "Tom dancing in his Jockeys" is nothing short of "starmaking."

River Runs Through It, A
22 | 23 | 21 | 25

1992 | Directed by Robert Redford | With Brad Pitt, Craig Sheffer, Tom Skerritt | 123 minutes | Rated PG

Sounding "deep" waters with a "pastoral" tale of "life as we no longer know it", Redford's "elegiac" drama of "family bonds" takes a "moving", "candid" look at the sibling rivalry between two small-town minister's sons; the "smooth" pace is set by the stars' "subtle emotion" and "striking" cinematography that captures the "Montana wilderness" in all of its full "majesty", though some clock-watchers find the running time a bit "too slow."

Road to Perdition
23 | 26 | 22 | 25

2002 | Directed by Sam Mendes | With Tom Hanks, Paul Newman, Daniel Craig, Jude Law | 117 minutes | Rated R

"Hanks proves his versatility" in this "evocative period piece", playing a "cold-blooded hit man" for the Irish mafia during the Depression; the "intense journey" is "impeccably done", with Newman in "stellar form", Oscar-winning cinematography that will "take your breath away" (notably that "tommy gun scene in the rain") and "top-notch screenwriting" that "stays true to the novel."

Road Warrior, The
22 | 18 | 21 | 20

1982 | Directed by George Miller | With Mel Gibson, Bruce Spence, Mike Preston | 94 minutes | Rated R

"Road rage" kicks into overdrive in this "raw Aussie action flick", with "lean, mean" Gibson "at his baddest" as Mad Max, a "lone, reluctant cowboy" cruising a "post-apocalyptic" wasteland and upholding his "own brand of justice"; set in a "nihilistic" near-future when barbaric gangs comb the desert pestering decent folk for petrol, its combo of an "intriguing" setup and "incredible car stunts" makes it a "visceral" "cult favorite"; gas up.

Robe, The

22 | 20 | 21 | 24

1953 | Directed by Henry Koster | With Richard Burton, Jean Simmons, Victor Mature | 135 minutes | Not Rated

"Burton reigns" as a Roman centurion who oversees the crucifixion, then wins Christ's robe in a dice game in this '50s "religious movie" that inspired a slew of biblical flicks; most memorable for being the first feature shot in CinemaScope, it's "big" in every way, though some ask "can it really be an epic without Charlton Heston?"

Robin and Marian
20 | 23 | 20 | 21

1976 | Directed by Richard Lester | With Sean Connery, Audrey Hepburn, Robert Shaw | 106 minutes | Rated PG

In "Robin Hood's later years" he resumes his affair with Maid Marian in this "wistful wisp" of a tale worth seeing for the "casting" alone; the "sadness of time passing is palpable" (right down to that "darkly romantic ending"), and if it's mainly a "woman's film", there's still "enough swordplay" to keep the guys happy.

Robin Hood: Prince of Thieves
16 | 14 | 17 | 18

1991 | Directed by Kevin Reynolds | With Kevin Costner, Morgan Freeman, Alan Rickman | 138 minutes | Rated PG-13

This retelling of the spurned-lord-turned-benevolent-thief legend is "surprisingly original", with a "super villain" and enough "tongue-in-cheek" antics to "keep it moving"; but Costner's "now-you-hear-it, now-you-don't English accent" and other "inaccuracies" make hold-outs hold out for "Errol Flynn."

RoboCop
16 | 13 | 17 | 19

1987 | Directed by Paul Verhoeven | With Peter Weller, Nancy Allen, Ronny Cox | 103 minutes | Rated R

"Ruthlessly smart and satirical", this "novel" sci-fi adventure flick tells the story of a cop killed in the line of duty then brought back to life as a bio-mechanical robot; alternately "violent and hilarious", this "live-action comic book" is a "thought-provoking look" at a "techno vigilante" and a heck of a lot "better than it should have been."

Robots
20 | - | 19 | 24

2005 | Directed by Chris Wedge, Carlos Saldanha | Animated | 91 minutes | Not Rated

"Dazzling", "Rube Goldberg-esque" animation "keeps the whole family entertained" in this "simple", "heartfelt" 'toon about a young 'droid who "leaves home to chase a dream" in the big city; ok, the "ho-hum" "fish-out-of-water" plotline is "as mechanical as the characters", 'bot at least it's got an "uplifting", "you-can-do-anything-you-put-your-mind-to" message for the kids.

Rock, The
20 | 21 | 20 | 22

1996 | Directed by Michael Bay | With Sean Connery, Nicolas Cage, Ed Harris | 136 minutes | Rated R

Find out who's got the biggest "fireballs" in this very "noisy testosterone fix", bringing "slick", "edge-of-your-seat action" to Alcatraz as "crusty" ex-spy Connery and "bumbling" weapons-expert Cage penetrate the prison walls to stop a mad general from blitzing the Bay Area with nerve gas; fans find the pair "amazing together", and despite the highly "not-likely" scenario, the "awesome locale" and "great FX" ensure a "kick-ass" good time.

Rocketeer, The | 18 | 16 | 19 | 21 |

1991 | Directed by Joe Johnston | With Bill Campbell, Jennifer Connelly, Alan Arkin, Timothy Dalton | 108 minutes | Rated PG

Like a souped-up "Saturday afternoon serial", this "swashbuckling" adventure set in 1930s Los Angeles has "idealized hero" Campbell strapping on a portable "rocket pack" and taking to the air against some "nasty Nazis"; despite "hokey" acting and a "melodramatic feel", it's loaded with "old-fashioned patriotic pride" and "suitable for the whole family."

⏁ Rocky ✉ | 25 | 20 | 25 | 21 |

1976 | Directed by John G. Avildsen | With Sylvester Stallone, Talia Shire, Burt Young | 119 minutes | Rated PG

This "red-blooded" ring drama (and Oscar champ) "goes the distance" with an "underdog-makes-good" theme as "two-bit" boxer Sly "wins over everyone's heart" when he "gets his shot" at the title, works up "lots of sweat" and "finds true love" along the way; though part "hokey" "Hollywood fantasy", it's also a "stirring confidence-booster" that packs an everlasting "wallop."

Rocky Balboa | 18 | 17 | 18 | 18 |

2006 | Directed by Sylvester Stallone | With Sylvester Stallone, Burt Young, Antonio Tarver, Geraldine Hughes | 102 minutes | Rated PG

An "aging pugilist from South Philly" gets back into the ring for a "nostalgic final bout" with the reigning champ in this "better-than-expected" drama that brings the fistic "saga" to a "worthy finish"; fans say the "emotionally satisfying" tone ("reminiscent of the first installment") redeems the franchise so the Rock can "retire in peace" – "hopefully."

Rocky Horror Picture Show, The | 21 | 18 | 19 | 22 |

1975 | Directed by Jim Sharman | With Tim Curry, Susan Sarandon, Barry Bostwick | 100 minutes | Rated R

"Beyond weird" to the uninitiated, this "camp classic" rock 'n' roll musical is famed for the "floor show" put on at "midnight screenings" by costumed carousers who pronounce it the "best trash ever"; a "pure B-movie" spoof involving a pair of innocents who stumble into the lair of a "sweet transvestite", it's "silly" but "entertaining on its own bizarre level", so "get out your toast, rice and lighter" and "sing along" with this "legendary mess."

Roger & Me | 24 | - | 24 | 20 |

1989 | Directed by Michael Moore | Documentary | 91 minutes | Rated R

"Laugh and cringe" at this salvo of "guerrilla filmmaking", an "eye-opening" documentary chronicling both the "disintegration" of a Michigan town after its GM plant pulls up stakes and "squeaky wheel" Moore's "quest to confront" the corporation's CEO; the "too-real" footage is "drop-dead funny" yet "sobering" ("rabbit lovers beware"), and if a few find the "irreverent" tone "annoying", progressives everywhere hail it as a "vital exposé" of the "new global economy" and a "stirring" fanfare for the "common man."

	OVERALL	ACTING	STORY	PROD.

Roger Dodger

| | 18 | 22 | 18 | 16 |

2002 | Directed by Dylan Kidd | With Campbell Scott, Jesse Eisenberg, Isabella Rossellini | 104 minutes | Rated R

Playing the "biggest cad since Alfie", the "underappreciated" Scott is "socko" in this "sharp little indie" that ventures into "Neil LaBute" territory in its story of a "smarmy", "lecherous adman" instructing his "wide-eyed teenage nephew" in the "art of seduction"; despite "lots of talk", it's "never dull", though some find this "bitter, mean-spirited rant" "hard to watch."

Rollerball

| | 19 | 18 | 21 | 20 |

1975 | Directed by Norman Jewison | With James Caan, John Houseman, John Beck, Maud Adams | 129 minutes | Rated R

A "dark vision" of a "future that's almost here", this "fierce" sci-fi flick set in 2018 rolls out Caan as an avatar of "individualism" in a "corporate-run" world, a champion player of an ultraviolent sport that's a bone-crushing mashup of motocross and roller derby; "dated" but "still gritty", it's "tight and tough" and "so much better than the remake."

Romancing the Stone

| | 20 | 19 | 21 | 20 |

1984 | Directed by Robert Zemeckis | With Michael Douglas, Kathleen Turner, Danny DeVito | 105 minutes | Rated PG-13

This "poor man's *Raiders of the Lost Ark*" turns a "lighthearted" adventure into a "fast-paced crowd-pleaser", with Turner cast as a "nerdy" romance novelist who hooks up with "tongue-in-cheek hero" Douglas down South America way; the two are "quite the duo", and some "humorous action sequences" with archrival DeVito "trying to keep up" make for "durable escapism."

☑ Roman Holiday ✉◐

| | 27 | 26 | 25 | 25 |

1953 | Directed by William Wyler | With Gregory Peck, Audrey Hepburn, Eddie Albert | 118 minutes | Not Rated

A "date movie without equal", this "frothy", "witty romance" presents a "radiant" Hepburn as the "rebellious" "gamine princess" with a "pixie cut" who plays hooky in the Eternal City, escorted by "charming", "not-so-hard-boiled reporter" Peck; helped along by "wondrous Roman scenery", their "coy" exchanges lead things on their natural "exhilarating" course, making for a "captivating fantasy" that draws to a "bittersweet", "refreshingly realistic" ending ("awww!").

☑ Romeo and Juliet

| | 26 | 24 | 27 | 26 |

1968 | Directed by Franco Zeffirelli | With Olivia Hussey, Leonard Whiting | 138 minutes | Rated PG

"Achingly beautiful" and played with "youthful vigor", this "faithful Zeffirelli" reading renders the "grand" romance of star-crossed love so "accessible" that "even boys cry" during the tragic last act; the "classic" production stays "true to the Bard" with "so-cute" teenage actors and "gorgeous" sets, and is the odds-on favorite to be the Shakespeare everyone's "made to watch in school."

Romeo + Juliet

| | 19 | 17 | 22 | 23 |

1996 | Directed by Baz Luhrmann | With Leonardo DiCaprio, Claire Danes, John Leguizamo | 120 minutes | Rated PG-13

Flash master Luhrmann presents the ageless romance "in a different light" in this "daring updating", a "kinetic visual feast" that aims to please the "MTV generation" with "pop music" and "creative" modern-day staging; Leo and Claire lend the lovers "teen-idol" allure, and if some sniff at "style over substance" and say the "acting seriously lacks", those who are "ok with extravagance" find it "effective" and "really cool."

Romy and Michele's High School Reunion | 14 | 15 | 15 | 14 |

1997 | Directed by David Mirkin | With Mira Sorvino, Lisa Kudrow, Janeane Garofalo | 92 minutes | Rated R

Sorvino and Kudrow star as "airheads with hearts of gold" who dream of "impressing former classmates" at their high school reunion in this "silly" comic "tribute to nerds and outsiders" everywhere; it's definitely "not to be taken seriously", but for "brainless fun" synchronized to a "great" '80s soundtrack, this "trifle" is, like, quite the "guilty pleasure."

Ronin | 20 | 22 | 19 | 21 |

1998 | Directed by John Frankenheimer | With Robert De Niro, Jean Reno, Natascha McElhone, Jonathan Pryce | 121 minutes | Rated R

"It's all about the car chases" in this "gritty", "grown-up" thriller revved up by an "excellent ensemble" cast (led by the "subtly powerful Reno") and an "interesting" heist plot that "twists and turns" against "great European backdrops"; one of the "last hurrahs" from action genre pioneer Frankenheimer, it's "not a thinking person's film" – so don't fret over "what's in that suitcase."

Rookie, The | 22 | 22 | 23 | 20 |

2002 | Directed by John Lee Hancock | With Dennis Quaid, Rachel Griffiths, Brian Cox | 127 minutes | Rated G

Quaid "hits a grand slam" as an over-the-hill major-league baseball rookie in this "feel-good movie for the whole family to enjoy" and "learn from"; it's a true story (with a "little Disney sprinkled on it") "that shows the importance of following your dreams" "even when it seems too late"; critics have just one quibble: it "drags on longer than a low-scoring doubleheader."

Room at the Top ✉◑ | 24 | 27 | 24 | 23 |

1959 | Directed by Jack Clayton | With Simone Signoret, Laurence Harvey, Heather Sears | 115 minutes | Not Rated

Britain's "class struggle" is the subject of this "powerful" "drama of ambition" starring an "excellent" Harvey as an angry young man bent on improving his lot in life by wooing a naive heiress; along the way, he has some "provocative" moments with the "smoky" Signoret, who steals the picture (and copped a Best Actress Oscar) as his "sultry, world-weary" playmate.

⊠ Room with a View, A ✉ | 26 | 26 | 24 | 27 |

1986 | Directed by James Ivory | With Maggie Smith, Helena Bonham Carter, Denholm Elliott | 117 minutes | Not Rated

"Florence looks like heaven" in this "crisp" costume drama about a "proper Victorian girl's" sightseeing tour that's considerably perked up by "friendships that form in a pensione", leading to her "romantic awakening"; the "brilliant acting" brings "wit and energy" to a "sunny" "study of class and character" that finds all kinds of room for "superb fin de siècle" touches and "seductive" shots of the Italian landscape.

Rope

22 | 21 | 23 | 22

1948 | Directed by Alfred Hitchcock | With Farley Granger, James Stewart, John Dall | 80 minutes | Rated PG

"One word – Hitchcock" – draws film buffs to this "chilling" reworking of the Leopold and Loeb murder case that's told with a "compelling gimmick": it was "shot entirely on one set" and "runs in real time"; though a few snore "slow and stagy", at least the master's "eye to detail" makes it an "interesting curiosity."

Rose, The

19 | 23 | 18 | 18

1979 | Directed by Mark Rydell | With Bette Midler, Alan Bates, Frederic Forrest | 125 minutes | Rated R

The "mesmerizing" Miss M makes the "most stunning movie debut since Streisand" in this rock-chanteuse drama, a "homage" to the wild-at-heart chronicling the life and times of a "self-destructive Janis Joplin type" as she barrels down the road to ruin; groupies who insist Midler's "strong performance" should have "won the Oscar" find consolation in that "great title song."

Rosemary's Baby

24 | 25 | 25 | 22

1968 | Directed by Roman Polanski | With Mia Farrow, John Cassavetes, Ruth Gordon | 136 minutes | Rated R

A "glamorous horror" flick about a "naive" housewife duped into bearing "Satan's child", this "gut-wrenching classic" still "scares the hell out" of nearly everybody; "pro-choice" types tout Farrow's "amazing" turn (and "faaabulous haircut") as well as Polanski's "very faithful adaptation" of Ira Levin's novel, but everyone says that the "devilishly good", Oscar-winning Gordon "steals the show."

Roxanne

21 | 21 | 21 | 19

1987 | Directed by Fred Schepisi | With Steve Martin, Daryl Hannah, Rick Rossovich | 107 minutes | Rated PG

Schnoz aficionados consider this "amusing" romance the "quintessential Martin vehicle": a "modernization" of *Cyrano de Bergerac* concerning a fire chief cursed with a prodigious proboscis but blessed with a "grab bag of comic devices" with which he helps a surrogate court the highly "watchable" Hannah; though some find it too "cute", "God nose" it's a "good-natured" yarn with a "ton of heart."

Royal Tenenbaums, The

20 | 24 | 18 | 21

2001 | Directed by Wes Anderson | With Gene Hackman, Anjelica Huston, Ben Stiller, Gwyneth Paltrow | 109 minutes | Rated R

This "very black" yet colorful "character-driven" comedy delineates the "humorous side of dysfunctionality" within a "wacky family of overachievers"; while the "Oscar-worthy" script and "stellar ensemble cast" draw applause, some shrug it's a "movie about nothing" that's "too clever" and "cynical" – the "reviewers liked it more than I did."

Rudy

23 | 22 | 25 | 21

1993 | Directed by David Anspaugh | With Sean Astin, Jon Favreau, Ned Beatty | 116 minutes | Rated PG

"What *Hoosiers* is to basketball", this "inspiring" flick is to college football, "bringing grown men to tears" with its "sentimental" celebration of true-life "ultimate underdog" Rudy Ruettiger, an "undersized kid with an oversized heart" who famously tackled his "lifelong dream to play for Notre Dame"; fielding a stellar cast led by the "excellent" Astin, it will "have you chanting with the crowd" during the "feel-good" finale.

☑ Rules of the Game, The ◐🄵   ▽ 27 | 24 | 25 | 26

1939 | Directed by Jean Renoir | With Marcel Dalio, Nora Gregor, Mila Parély | 110 minutes | Not Rated

"Always on the short list of the greatest films ever made" is this "scathing indictment of the French upper class" from "master" filmmaker Renoir, which "takes place at a weekend retreat in the country" and contrasts the romantic entanglements of both rich and poor alike; although "perfectly written, filmed and acted", it was not a hit in its initial release, and only garnered its rep after resurfacing at a film festival 20 years later.

Ruling Class, The   23 | 26 | 22 | 21

1972 | Directed by Peter Medak | With Peter O'Toole, Alastair Sim, Arthur Lowe, Harry Andrews | 154 minutes | Rated PG

Alternately "funny and disturbing", this black "social satire" takes on "the British upper class" in its story of a "delusional" fellow who becomes "the 14th Earl of Gurney" after the death of his father; the "bizarre" plot includes some "absurd song-and-dance routines" but "moves like lightning", and as the "bonkers" nobleman, O'Toole's "totally over the top."

Rumor Has It   14 | 17 | 15 | 16

2005 | Directed by Rob Reiner | With Jennifer Aniston, Kevin Costner, Shirley MacLaine, Mark Ruffalo | 96 minutes | Rated PG-13

This comedy's "playful" premise posits Jen as a "cutesy" thirtysomething who learns that her family history is the "true story" behind *The Graduate* (with "MacLaine stealing the show" as the erstwhile model for Mrs. Robinson); still, most want to "put this rumor to rest", citing "hammy" acting, "slow pacing" and "slight" scripting.

Runaway Jury   20 | 22 | 21 | 20

2003 | Directed by Gary Fleder | With John Cusack, Gene Hackman, Dustin Hoffman | 127 minutes | Rated PG-13

"Liberal Hollywood goes after the gun industry" in this courtroom drama pitting a "jury-stacking lawyer" against a "righteous underdog"; ok, it "doesn't follow the storyline" of its John Grisham origins, but devotees dig watching "old pros Hackman and Hoffman square off" just the same – even if they appear together on-screen in "just one scene."

Runaway Train   21 | 22 | 20 | 21

1985 | Directed by Andrei Konchalovsky | With Jon Voight, Eric Roberts, Rebecca de Mornay | 111 minutes | Rated R

"Surprisingly" stimulating despite "cheapish production values", this "stark", "existential actioner" keeps onlookers "enthralled" with a "twist on the prison-break" scenario as a freight train carrying a pair of fugitive cons careens through the Alaskan wild ("bring a parka") while the law looks on; though "over the top" enough to nearly hop the rails, this "bleak masterwork" also offers "powerful" acting and "dark" themes.

Rundown, The   17 | 16 | 16 | 18

2003 | Directed by Peter Berg | With Dwayne Johnson, Seann William Scott, Christopher Walken, Rosario Dawson | 104 minutes | Rated PG

"Wrestler turned actor" Johnson shows equal parts of "granite and gumption" as he shoots for "action stardom" in this "entertaining" treasure hunt tale set in the "Brazilian jungle"; sure, there's "nothing thought-provoking" going on in this "typical guy flick", though seers see the "torch being passed" from "Arnold" to Dwayne.

Run Lola Run 🗗

23 | 21 | 24 | 24

1999 | Directed by Tom Tykwer | With Franka Potente, Moritz Bleibtreu, Herbert Knaup | 81 minutes | Rated R

There's "never a dull moment" in this "amped-up" German import involving the "sweat-dripping" effort of a fleet-footed fräulein to hustle a big pile of cash to save her boyfriend from a nasty mobster; "strongly driven" by an "adrenaline"-pumping "techno soundtrack" and "video-game" vibe, the "breathless" "nonlinear" narrative forges "different perspectives" and "time repeats" into a "pulse-pounding" "original" that's as "ultra-watchable" as it is "quirky."

Running Man, The

17 | 13 | 19 | 18

1987 | Directed by Paul Michael Glaser | With Arnold Schwarzenegger, Maria Conchita Alonso, Yaphet Kotto | 101 minutes | Rated R

"Required viewing for anyone who wants to be on reality TV", this "cartoon-esque" action picture stars Ahnold as a contestant in a "futuristic" game show that "allows criminals to compete for their freedom" (think *Family Feud* gone horribly wrong); sure, it's a "guilty pleasure", but our survey says "Richard Dawson steals it as the host from hell."

Rush Hour

19 | 17 | 16 | 20

1998 | Directed by Brett Ratner | With Jackie Chan, Chris Tucker, Tom Wilkinson | 97 minutes | Rated PG-13

Formula "fluff" with "all the right moves", this actioner finds time for "comic relief" as a crime-fighting pair of "exact opposites" teams up to rescue a kidnapped kid; "high-kicking" Chan breaks out with some "inventive chop-socky sequences" and "exhilarating" stunts while playing it straight alongside outspoken "wild man" Tucker, so even if the "plot's not much", the "buddy pairing" offers enough crowd-pleasing "chemistry" to translate into "loads of fun."

Rush Hour 2

17 | 16 | 16 | 19

2001 | Directed by Brett Ratner | With Jackie Chan, Chris Tucker, Zhang Ziyi | 90 minutes | Rated PG-13

The lucrative recipe of "great martial arts" seasoned with "goofball" shtick skewering East-West "cultural differences" plates this second helping of "entertaining" action-comedy; true, there are "no surprises" as the reunited Chan and Tucker once again "kick butt" and deliver "laughs" playing a "mismatched pair" of crimestoppers, but most agree it's "not so bad" for an "overdone Hollywood ride."

Rushmore

23 | 25 | 22 | 22

1998 | Directed by Wes Anderson | With Jason Schwartzman, Olivia Williams, Bill Murray | 93 minutes | Rated R

A monument of "quality quirkiness", this "unabashedly unusual" comedy stars Schwartzman as an "arrogant and clever" but "dysfunctional" scholarship student at an elite prep school whose "coming of age" takes many a "droll" twist when he befriends a rich alumnus and falls for a teacher; the "smart", "character-driven" script is "expertly acted", leading to high marks for a "winning gem" with "real heart" "beneath the smarminess" – and how about that "killer soundtrack"?

	OVERALL	ACTING	STORY	PROD.

Russians Are Coming, The Russians Are Coming, The
21 21 22 20

1966 | Directed by Norman Jewison | With Alan Arkin, John Phillip Law, Jonathan Winters | 120 minutes | Not Rated

Da, comrades, this "classic '60s" "Cold War satire" offers a "sweet take" on a paranoid period as a Red Navy sub goes aground off the Massachusetts coast and Soviet swabbie Arkin is recruited to find a rescue boat, setting off rumors of an invasion; *Strangelove* it ain't, but the "very funny" situations are still "worth the time."

Ruthless People
20 19 19 17

1986 | Directed by David Zucker, Jerry Zucker, Jim Abrahams | With Danny DeVito, Bette Midler | 93 minutes | Rated R

Echt '80s in its send-up of "pure greed", this pretty "crass" but "side-splitting" black comedy gets going when a couple of "inept kidnappers" snatch Midler (carrying on at her "bitchy best") and demand ransom from DeVito, a "standout" as the "crude", double-dealing "spandex king" husband scheming to rid himself of a despised spouse; "lots of plot twists" ensue in a "silly", "hilarious" caper that anyone with a cynical side shouldn't overlook.

Ryan's Daughter
22 23 22 24

1970 | Directed by David Lean | With Robert Mitchum, Trevor Howard, Sarah Miles, John Mills | 176 minutes | Rated PG

"Love and infidelity" are played out against a "magnificent Irish seacoast setting" in this "epic tearjerker" via David Lean, a "weak-in-the-knees romance" that's "gorgeously filmed" and set to "haunting music"; its "bracing scenery" and "powerful" story – depicting "love as steadfastness rather than a cheap emotion" – lead many to call it "underrated."

Saboteur ❶
23 21 24 23

1942 | Directed by Alfred Hitchcock | With Robert Cummings, Priscilla Lane, Otto Kruger, Norman Lloyd | 108 minutes | Not Rated

"Cross-country intrigue" underlies this "effective" Hitchcock "romp across America", wherein an "innocent man" is "unwittingly involved in an espionage plot"; maybe it's a bit "cheesy by today's standards", but even "Bob Cummings' wooden performance" is blown away by that "unforgettable finale" atop the "torch of the Statue of Liberty."

Sabrina ❶
25 25 25 23

1954 | Directed by Billy Wilder | With Humphrey Bogart, Audrey Hepburn, William Holden | 113 minutes | Not Rated

Like an order of "first-class everything", this "delicious" "rags-to-riches" romance sparkles with "wit and couture" as an "ethereal" Hepburn plays a "beguiling", love-struck chauffeur's daughter in a "little black dress"; the "modern Cinderella" scenario finds Bogie in a "comedic role" as an all-business heir determined to beat out his "younger playboy brother" for Audrey's affections; as for Harrison Ford's 1995 remake, loyalists "consider it blasphemy."

Sahara
17 16 16 20

2005 | Directed by Breck Eisner | With Matthew McConaughey, Penélope Cruz, Steve Zahn | 124 minutes | Rated PG-13

An "amusing" if "minor-league Indiana Jones rip-off", this "carefree" adventure yarn based on Clive Cussler's best-seller grafts the search for a "Civil War battleship in Africa" onto an "enviro-sensitive" story of a catastrophic plague threatening the worlds' oceans; though Matthew, Penélope and the "exotic locales" make for "beautiful scenery", the end result is "pretty to look at, but not much else."

Salvador

21 | 24 | 21 | 20

1986 | Directed by Oliver Stone | With James Woods, James Belushi, John Savage | 123 minutes | Rated R

Oliver Stone keeps it fairly "lucid" in this early drama, a "worthwhile" character study starring the Oscar-nominated Woods, who proves he "can flat-out act" playing a burnt-out photojournalist desperate to score freelance work in war-torn Central America; though *Platoon* (from the same director) took Best Picture honors that year, a few feel this one's the "better movie."

Same Time, Next Year

22 | 24 | 25 | 21

1978 | Directed by Robert Mulligan | With Ellen Burstyn, Alan Alda, Ivan Bonar | 119 minutes | Rated PG

Expect to go from "laughter to tears and back again" in this "decade-spanning romance", featuring "convincing" turns from Alda and Burstyn as a couple of "married lovers who meet once a year"; adapted from the stage, the "annual adultery" device tracks the two as they "change with the times", making for "sweet", "warm" entertainment – even if it does "promote affairs."

Sand Pebbles, The

24 | 26 | 25 | 24

1966 | Directed by Robert Wise | With Steve McQueen, Richard Crenna, Richard Attenborough, Candice Bergen | 179 minutes | Rated PG-13

An "epic of China" told from the point of view of Yank sailors knee-deep in the revolutionary turmoil of 1926, this "powerful, pertinent" war drama features "authentic hero" McQueen "smoldering in top form" as a "tough-guy" Navy mechanic "with a heart of gold", manning an American patrol boat; if the tale "meanders like the Yellow River", it's still a "must-see" for History Channel addicts.

Santa Clause, The

19 | 17 | 19 | 19

1994 | Directed by John Pasquin | With Tim Allen, Judge Reinhold, Wendy Crewson | 97 minutes | Rated PG

"Corny in a good way", this holiday comedy packages the "fantastic" with the "real world" when exec Allen takes over the reins from an abruptly retired Kris Kringle, mysteriously begins "fattening" and meets with complications in the custody of his young son; though it sleds along on a "sappy story", consensus calls it rather "original" as far as Yuletide yarns go.

Sarah Silverman: Jesus Is Magic

18 | 17 | 14 | 14

2005 | Directed by Liam Lynch | With Sarah Silverman | 72 minutes | Not Rated

"Edgy" comic Silverman ratchets up the "shock value" in this "filmed stand-up concert", a "rudely hilarious" string of "profane riffs" on "third-rail topics" that are "sometimes grating, often funny" and "not for the faint of heart"; her "subversive" routine is "anything but demure", but be warned that the sketches and musical numbers inserted for the sake of variety can "fall flat."

	OVERALL	ACTING	STORY	PROD.

Saturday Night Fever
22 | 19 | 20 | 22

1977 | Directed by John Badham | With John Travolta, Karen Lynn Gorney | 118 minutes | Rated R

A paean to "polyester", this romance defines the "days of disco" with an "electric" Travolta as the blow-dried mook who lives to "look good" and "shake his groove thing" but has to boogie to "improve his life" when love comes to town; iconic "dance scenes" accentuate an "affecting" story with "dark" undercurrents that "perfectly evokes" "real life in Brooklyn" circa '77, even if some survivors of those "cheesy times" "feel embarrassed" about it now.

Satyricon ☒
20 | 17 | 17 | 24

1970 | Directed by Federico Fellini | With Martin Potter, Hiram Keller, Capucine, Alain Cuny | 129 minutes | Rated R

"Nothing's sacred" in this "out-there" "hymn to decadence", a "provocative", "surreal" trip through Nero's Rome that's based on incomplete remnants of a satire by Petronius, which might explain its "oddly fragmented" structure ("can someone please tell me what it's about?"); definitely "not for everyone" (especially kids), this is "disturbing", ultra-"kinky" stuff – either "Fellini at his indulgent worst" or "awe-inspiring in its sheer extravagance."

Savages, The
23 | 28 | 22 | 22

2007 | Directed by Tamara Jenkins | With Laura Linney, Philip Seymour Hoffman, Philip Bosco | 113 minutes | Rated R

"Watching a parent's decline" is the "tough" theme of this "compassionate" indie flick about two "dysfunctional" siblings "dealing with their dad's dementia" while "still grappling with their own childhood issues"; though it's oftentimes "too real for comfort", "highly nuanced acting" and a "savagely smart script" make the "tricky subject matter" work.

Save the Last Dance
17 | 17 | 17 | 17

2001 | Directed by Thomas Carter | With Julia Stiles, Sean Patrick Thomas, Kerry Washington | 112 minutes | Rated PG-13

This "modern star-crossed-lovers" saga stars Stiles as a suburban teen transferred to an inner-city school where she falls into an interracial "across-the-tracks romance"; though the "textbook" set-ups "could have been more inventive", the picture imparts a "good message", abetted by a "great soundtrack", some "fancy footwork" and a climactic "hip-hop 'n' classical ballet."

Save the Tiger ✉
22 | 26 | 22 | 20

1973 | Directed by John G. Avildsen | With Jack Lemmon, Jack Gilford, Thayer David | 100 minutes | Rated R

"One of Lemmon's greatest performances" – an "Oscar winner", in fact – is the lynchpin of this "well-done" portrait of a struggling businessman who considers arson as a means to "survive in the fashion industry"; also notable for Gilford's "strong" supporting work, this one is a "pleasure to see", so long as you can abide its "grim look at the travails of middle age."

☒ Saving Private Ryan ✉
26 | 26 | 24 | 28

1998 | Directed by Steven Spielberg | With Tom Hanks, Tom Sizemore, Edward Burns | 170 minutes | Rated R

"As intense as it gets", Steven Spielberg's "celluloid monument" to WWII evokes the fear of war with "in-your-face" footage like the "dev-

astating" opening, a "masterful" montage of "graphic" death and mayhem on a D-day beachhead; thereafter Hanks leads a "superbly" cast
unit through no-man's-land on a "compelling" quest for a missing
grunt, and despite sniping that "the story bogs down", it's a "wrenching" oh-"so-real" reminder that "war is hell."

Saw

18 | 17 | 22 | 19

2004 | Directed by James Wan | With Leigh Whannell, Cary Elwes,
Danny Glover | 100 minutes | Rated R

"Graphic" and "gruesome", this "edge-of-your-seat thriller" is definitely "not for the squeamish" ("don't eat beforehand") in its story
of two men chained in a lavatory with a hacksaw – for sawing off
their own legs – their only means of escape; while hard-core aficionados dis the "lousy acting" and a *Seven* rip-off" plot, many more praise
its "real scares" and that "absolutely stunning ending" – "you won't
see it coming."

Saw II

19 | 16 | 19 | 19

2005 | Directed by Darren Lynn Bousman | With Tobin Bell, Shawnee
Smith, Donnie Wahlberg | 93 minutes | Rated R

This "gory-as-it-gets" sequel features a "whole new gang" of human
guinea pigs forced to "play a psychopath's games" in a "sick" house of
horrors ("if this doesn't make your skin crawl, you must be dead");
maybe it's "not as, um, cutting edge" as the original, but devotees still
dub it a "doozy" and "can't wait" for more.

Saw III

17 | 16 | 17 | 19

2006 | Directed by Darren Lynn Bousman | With Tobin Bell, Shawnee
Smith, Angus Macfadyen | 113 minutes | Rated R

Aficionados of "all-out horror" get a "gruesome adrenaline rush" from
this "gorefest" sequel wherein a demented serial killer and his sidekick
concoct "ingenious" "new traps" to elicit maximum "blood and
screams"; the "nasty plot twists" still "keep you guessing", but foes of
the "played-out" series say this one doesn't make the cut – "two was
more than enough."

Say Anything

23 | 22 | 22 | 20

1989 | Directed by Cameron Crowe | With John Cusack, Ione Skye,
John Mahoney | 100 minutes | Rated PG-13

"Teenage love is beautiful" in this "quintessential" '80s romance
that had a "serious impact on Gen-X women" by making them "fall in
love with Cusack", the "geek who gets the popular girl" from a "different class of society"; though naysayers suggest the "dad drama"
subplot "slows things down", overall this "youth-in-angst" story
has become the "touchstone of a generation"; most memorable prop
the "boom box."

Scanner Darkly, A

17 | 18 | 18 | 23

2006 | Directed by Richard Linklater | With Keanu Reeves, Robert
Downey Jr., Woody Harrelson, Winona Ryder | 100 minutes | Rated R

"Definitely something different", this "trippy" sci-fi feature applies a
"super-cool" rotoscoping technique to its "Gen-X-revisited cast" in
this adaptation of Philip K. Dick's "twisted story" of a narc in a "dystopian future"; it's "visually stunning" stuff, but "disoriented" types find
this "attempt to film the unfilmable" a tad "too confusing."

Scarface
22 | 23 | 22 | 22

1983 | Directed by Brian De Palma | With Al Pacino, Steven Bauer, Michelle Pfeiffer | 170 minutes | Rated R

"Raw and fun all at once", this "benchmark" crime thriller about a Miami-based "Latin drug ring" is ultra-"intense" and "extravagantly bloody" ("close your eyes when they bring out that chainsaw!"); addicts attest that it's worth seeing for Pacino's "over-the-top" turn as the "kind of bad guy you could really like", but the unmoved sneer it's "ultimately unredeeming" – and too "profane" to boot ("how many times can you say the F-word?").

Scarlet Empress, The ◑
▽ 24 | 23 | 22 | 27

1934 | Directed by Josef von Sternberg | With Marlene Dietrich, John Lodge, Sam Jaffe, Louise Dresser | 104 minutes | Not Rated

"Spectacularly bizarre", this over-the-top take on the life of Catherine the Great is a "masterpiece of fantasy pretending to be biography" that's worth watching for its "dazzling" production values, period; La Dietrich enacts the title role in a "series of poses" lovingly lit by director von Sternberg, and even if it's "not *The Blue Angel*", this "delirious mess" is certainly "like nothing else you've ever seen."

Scarlet Street ◑
▽ 25 | 26 | 24 | 23

1945 | Directed by Fritz Lang | With Edward G. Robinson, Joan Bennett, Dan Duryea | 103 minutes | Not Rated

A "pathetic old man is caught in a sticky web of sex and murder" when he meets the ultimate femme fatale in Fritz Lang's "creepy" but "painfully brilliant" entry in the film noir canon; the pulpy goings-on may be "entertaining on a trashy level", but even if "you think you've remembered every plot twist" of the genre, this picture "really surprises."

Scenes from a Marriage ⊞
25 | 27 | 23 | 23

1974 | Directed by Ingmar Bergman | With Liv Ullmann, Erland Josephson, Bibi Andersson | 168 minutes | Rated PG

Originally a six-hour TV miniseries pared down to feature length, this still "powerful" portrayal of a "marriage breaking down" via Ingmar Bergman is a "real, poignant" tale told with such "rich execution" that it might "scare off all but the bravest from the altar"; though "hard to take for its intensity", this "talkathon" is worth seeing for its simply "astonishing performances."

Scent of a Woman ✉
21 | 25 | 21 | 21

1992 | Directed by Martin Brest | With Al Pacino, Chris O'Donnell, Philip Seymour Hoffman | 157 minutes | Rated R

Pacino's "bravura" Best Actor bit has him cast as a retired military man compensating for his visual impairment with an "abrasive personality" and "foghorn" pipes as he drags his "meek" preppy babysitter along for a wild weekend in the Naked City; where cynics see "hokum" that "tends to drag", fans of the "too-fabulous" Al find it worthwhile "for the tango scene" alone.

⋥ Schindler's List ✉◑
29 | 29 | 28 | 29

1993 | Directed by Steven Spielberg | With Liam Neeson, Ben Kingsley, Ralph Fiennes | 197 minutes | Rated R

Embarking on a "tour-de-force" "journey through a dark period", Spielberg's "direct", "painful" wartime drama "crystallizes the real-life horror" of the Holocaust in "stunning quasi-documentary" black-and-white, with Neeson as the man of "moral conscience" dealing with the Nazis in "shattering" circumstances; "beyond moving" and "tough to watch" in spite of its "understatement" and "touches of grace", it's a top Oscar honoree that's all-but-unanimously cited as "unforgettable required viewing."

School for Scoundrels

16 | 18 | 17 | 17

2006 | Directed by Todd Phillips | With Billy Bob Thornton, Jon Heder, Jacinda Barrett, Sarah Silverman | 100 minutes | Rated PG-13

This "easygoing" update of the old-school British comedy casts Heder as a "hapless schmo" who takes self-improvement lessons from a narcissistic "creep" in the hope of attracting the opposite sex; while it may be "good for a couple of laughs", most label it a "sophomoric", "unnecessarily crude" enterprise.

School of Rock

20 | 20 | 20 | 19

2003 | Directed by Richard Linklater | With Jack Black, Joan Cusack | 108 minutes | Rated PG-13

"Jack Black's manic zeal" takes center stage in this comedy about a "selfish wannabe" pop star who learns "selflessness" and turns a "bunch of buttoned-up prep schoolers" into "rock monsters"; it's "cute" and "sappy" in a "predictable", "family-friendly" way, but the "infectious energy" embodies the "irreverent spirit of classic rock" well enough to appeal to "young and old alike."

Science of Sleep, The

18 | 21 | 16 | 22

2006 | Directed by Michel Gondry | With Gael García Bernal, Charlotte Gainsbourg, Alain Chabat, Miou-Miou | 105 minutes | Rated R

"Original" if nothing else, this "surrealistic" fantasy tells the story of a shy, "ultravulnerable" fellow whose dream-world "flights of fancy" merge with his "befuddled" reality when he falls in love; director Gondry's "unique vision" and all that "beautiful imagery" are well worth staying awake for, though a minority sees an exercise in "style over substance."

Scoop

18 | 20 | 18 | 19

2006 | Directed by Woody Allen | With Scarlett Johansson, Hugh Jackman, Woody Allen, Ian McShane | 96 minutes | Rated PG-13

"One of the better late Woodys" is the scoop on this "screwball mystery caper", a "lighthearted" comedy starring the "lovely Scarlett" as a London-based journalist investigating and romancing "hunky" murder suspect Jackman; loyalists report plenty of "brainy chuckles", but ultimately it's a "trifle" compared to "vintage Allen" pictures.

Score, The

17 | 21 | 18 | 18

2001 | Directed by Frank Oz | With Robert De Niro, Edward Norton, Marlon Brando, Angela Bassett | 124 minutes | Rated R

"Three generations of great method actors" – Norton, De Niro and an "over-the-top" Brando in his final film appearance – play criminals bent on burglarizing the Montreal Customs House in this "enjoyable" albeit "boilerplate" caper; though fans praise the "top-drawer" casting and that "really cool ending", it scores lower for its "slow" pace and "seen-it-all-before" storyline.

Scream

20 | 16 | 21 | 19

1996 | Directed by Wes Craven | With David Arquette, Neve Campbell, Courteney Cox | 111 minutes | Rated R

In an "aptly titled" entry, *Nightmare on Elm Street*'s Wes Craven "revives" the horror genre by aiming "clever potshots" at a host of hackneyed "slasher-film" clichés, lending a "humorously self-aware twist" to a "fast-paced" story of a "slice-and-dice" psycho at large among suburban teens; sure, the picture "makes fun of itself", but it's still "scary stuff" that sets a "bloody and gross" precedent for a "slew of imitators."

Scrooged

19 | 19 | 20 | 20

1988 | Directed by Richard Donner | With Bill Murray, Karen Allen, Carol Kane, Bobcat Goldthwait | 101 minutes | Rated PG-13

Dickens' *A Christmas Carol* gets a "modern" makeover complete with "dark" comedic notes via this "inspired" parody led by Murray ("at his deadpan best") playing a "cruel TV exec" in desperate need of a "morality lesson"; further boosted by an "excellent" supporting cast, "it's become a tradition" to include it in the annual "holiday movie marathon."

Seabiscuit

25 | 25 | 25 | 26

2003 | Directed by Gary Ross | With Tobey Maguire, Jeff Bridges, Chris Cooper | 141 minutes | Rated PG-13

Set against the "backdrop of the Great Depression", this "winning" adaptation of Laura Hillenbrand's best-selling pony tale trots out an "old-fashioned" story about a "little horse that could"; "moving" turns from Maguire, Bridges and Cooper (as jockey, owner and trainer) and "beautifully photographed", "suspenseful" racing sequences evoke cheers, even if a few find this gelding's gait a tad "slow", saying "it misses greatness by a nose."

Sea Inside, The ✉🅵

25 | 28 | 24 | 24

2004 | Directed by Alejandro Amenábar | With Javier Bardem, Belén Rueda, Mabel Rivera | 125 minutes | Rated PG-13

A "beautiful movie about a sad subject", this "deeply felt" Spanish drama stars a "luminous", "beyond convincing" Bardem as a "quadriplegic fighting for his right to assisted suicide"; sure, the "downer" theme can be "difficult" to take, but the "poetic subtlety and grace" of its handling make for a "moving", "thought-provoking" experience.

Sea of Love

20 | 23 | 21 | 19

1989 | Directed by Harold Becker | With Al Pacino, Ellen Barkin, John Goodman | 113 minutes | Rated R

"Pacino and Barkin sizzle like ham and eggs" in this "intense", "atmospheric" thriller about a "tortured cop" on the trail of a serial killer who becomes enmeshed in a "steamy" affair with a "hot" "temptress/suspect"; dancing around the old "did-she-or-didn't-she?" question, the "taut" script plants enough "seeds of doubt" along the way to keep things "interesting" till the windup.

🅴 Searchers, The

27 | 25 | 27 | 27

1956 | Directed by John Ford | With John Wayne, Jeffrey Hunter, Vera Miles | 120 minutes | Not Rated

Not just a shoot-'em-up", this "thinking person's" Western boasts "peak" work from Wayne, who delivers a "gripping" portrayal of a "brooding" Civil War vet obsessed with tracking down his niece, abducted by Comanches; with its "spectacular" backdrops and "contro-versial" handling of "kinship and racism", it's much praised as "Ford's masterpiece", "perhaps the finest in the genre."

Searching for Bobby Fischer

24 | 23 | 24 | 21

1993 | Directed by Steven Zaillian | With Max Pomeranc, Joe Mantegna, Ben Kingsley, Joan Allen | 110 minutes | Rated PG

The fraught dynamics between "parents and gifted children" underlie this "all-ages" drama featuring the "wonderful" Pomeranc as a chess-board "prodigy" who "learns about fair play" from a caring parent and a cutthroat grandmaster; even "without a lot of flash", it's "compel-ling" moviemaking – "who knew chess was this interesting?"

Secondhand Lions

22 | 25 | 22 | 22

2003 | Directed by Tim McCanlies | With Michael Caine, Robert Duvall, Haley Joel Osment | 109 minutes | Rated PG

A young boy spends the summer in the "middle of nowhere" with his "eccentric uncles" in this "family-friendly", "feel-good" flicker that teaches "moral lessons about integrity and honor", yet is still "fun to watch"; as two "grumpy old men" weaving "tall tales from truth", Caine and Duvall exhibit "perfect timing", despite a somewhat "corny", "predictable" premise.

Secretary

21 | 24 | 20 | 19

2002 | Directed by Steven Shainberg | With James Spader, Maggie Gyllenhaal | 104 minutes | Rated R

A "repressed" attorney "takes out his do-as-I-say delights on his all-too-willing secretary" in this "brilliant black comedy" (or is it a "kinky love story"?) that "makes you realize there's someone for everyone"; "hilarious characters", "interesting plot twists" and "superb acting" add up to an "ass-spanking good time."

Secret of NIMH, The

24 | - | 25 | 24

1982 | Directed by Don Bluth | Animated | 82 minutes | Rated G

From the all-pro pens of "former Disney artists" comes this "freaky", oft-"forgotten" "alternative to sugar-coated" animation, a "beautifully drawn gem" of a barnyard yarn about a mama mouse desperately seeking a new nest for her brood; the "captivating" depiction of farm life comes with "character development" and an "interesting" story designed to appeal to the "adult" in everyone.

Secrets & Lies

24 | 27 | 24 | 22

1996 | Directed by Mike Leigh | With Brenda Blethyn, Marianne Jean-Baptiste | 136 minutes | Rated R

Bad boy Leigh turns "accessible" in this "smart", "solid British drama" of "long-lost" family ties about a young black Londoner who "searches out her biological mother" only to find out that mum may be a working-class white woman; led by Blethyn's "pure, honest performance", the actors do a "terrific job" of making this tale "involving" and "heartbreaking."

Seduction of Joe Tynan, The

▽ 22 | 25 | 22 | 19

1979 | Directed by Jerry Schatzberg | With Alan Alda, Barbara Harris, Meryl Streep, Melvyn Douglas | 107 minutes | Rated R

Along with *The Candidate*, this "well-done" portrait of a "hard-charging" "Ted Kennedy–esque" Senator whose extramarital exploits roil both his private life and his public "ambitions" is required viewing for "anyone thinking of a career in politics"; scripted by and starring the "awesome" Alda, it also features an "incandescent" Streep.

☑ Sense and Sensibility ✉

26 | 27 | 26 | 26

1995 | Directed by Ang Lee | With Emma Thompson, Alan Rickman, Kate Winslet, Hugh Grant | 136 minutes | Rated PG

"Jane Austen would have liked" this "bittersweet" story of two husband-hunting sisters that "captures the true flavor" of her novel "with wit and honesty" largely due to a "strong", Oscar-winning script from the "so-fine" Emma Thompson; sensitive types tout the "beautiful" scenery, director Lee's "brilliant" job and an ensemble cast that "rises to the occasion" – "this is what moviemaking should be."

Sentinel, The

17 | 19 | 18 | 19

2006 | Directed by Clark Johnson | With Michael Douglas, Kiefer Sutherland, Eva Longoria, Kim Basinger | 108 minutes | Rated PG-13

Patterned after an "old-fashioned thriller", this "entertaining" effort casts Douglas as a Secret Service agent framed for murder and hunted by "by-the-book" Fed Sutherland; though wags tag it "24: The Movie" (even though it "takes place over a few days"), it's "worthwhile" enough for die-hard "fans of the genre."

Serenity

23 | 22 | 23 | 24

2005 | Directed by Joss Whedon | With Nathan Fillion, Gina Torres, Alan Tudyk | 119 minutes | Rated PG-13

A big-screen adaptation of the "short-lived" "cult" TV series *Firefly*, this "enjoyable" sci-fi/Western spins an "innovative" outer-space adventure enlivened by "solid" FX and a "memorable" cast of "relative unknowns" armed with a payload of "witty lines"; advice to the "uninitiated": viewing the original show "isn't mandatory", but it might make the "convoluted" story less "confusing."

Sergeant York ✉◑

25 | 25 | 24 | 22

1941 | Directed by Howard Hawks | With Gary Cooper, Walter Brennan, Joan Leslie | 134 minutes | Not Rated

A "true story that needs no amplification", this "satisfying" biopic stars an Oscar-winning Cooper as the pacifist who became WWI's most decorated soldier after single-handedly dismantling an enemy regiment; a "complex" piece of pro-war propaganda, it's also a "great depiction" of a man of "quiet inner strength."

Serpico

23 | 26 | 24 | 21

1973 | Directed by Sidney Lumet | With Al Pacino, John Randolph, Tony Roberts | 129 minutes | Rated R

Honesty "doesn't pay" in this "gritty" true story starring a "superb" Pacino as a whistle-blowing NYPD do-gooder who becomes a "man alone" after his exposure of "cop corruption"; if all the "raw emotion" can grow "frustrating" and the milieu seems "a bit dated", it remains arresting as a "compelling commentary on the times."

Servant, The ◑

25 | 27 | 25 | 23

1963 | Directed by Joseph Losey | With Dirk Bogarde, James Fox, Sarah Miles, Wendy Craig | 112 minutes | Not Rated

The "British class structure" gets the Harold Pinter treatment in this "dark", "nasty piece of work" detailing the "power struggle" between a "menacing butler" and his "decadent", weak-willed master; in the title role, the "peerless" Bogarde is so "appropriately creepy" that some consider "giving up their household staff."

Seven

23 | 23 | 24 | 23

1995 | Directed by David Fincher | With Brad Pitt, Morgan Freeman, Kevin Spacey | 123 minutes | Rated R

All the "elegant nastiness" of a "guided tour through hell" surfaces in this "macabre psychological thriller" about two big-city detectives on the trail of an "ingenious" serial killer who dreams up "genuinely disturbing" torments "based on the seven deadly sins"; an "unrelenting" dose of "creepy modern noir" at its "darkest", it's wickedly "riveting" and "impressive" but "hard-to-take" and "gruesome" – with "no happy ending."

☑ Seven Beauties ☐

26 | 26 | 25 | 24

1976 | Directed by Lina Wertmüller | With Giancarlo Giannini, Fernando Rey, Shirley Stoler | 115 minutes | Rated R

Wertmüller's "extraordinary" exploration of "survival in WWII" stars Giannini as a Chaplin-esque romeo trying to stay alive in a German concentration camp; a "brilliant" "amalgam of comedy and drama", it's a "powerful introduction to foreign filmmaking."

Seven Brides for Seven Brothers

24 | 20 | 21 | 25

1954 | Directed by Stanley Donen | With Howard Keel, Jane Powell, Russ Tamblyn | 103 minutes | Rated G

Ok, it's "low on feasibility", but this "down-home" musical of "seven eligible backwoodsmen looking for love" with a septet of hillbilly "Sabine women" strikes "pure gold" with its "great Johnny Mercer" tunes and "extraordinary" choreography; fans dig its "exuberant" production numbers so "athletic" that they "make dance macho."

☑ Seven Days in May ◐

26 | 24 | 28 | 22

1964 | Directed by John Frankenheimer | With Burt Lancaster, Kirk Douglas, Fredric March | 118 minutes | Not Rated

"It could happen here", or so says this "scary" Cold War story about disgruntled Pentagon brass who lay plans for a "military takeover"; soldiering along with "well-plotted" plausibility and "Douglas and Lancaster turning up the star heat", it's a "powerful nail-biter" that "political junkies" consider – gulp – "as timely today as ever."

☑ Seven Samurai, The ◐☐

29 | 27 | 28 | 27

1956 | Directed by Akira Kurosawa | With Toshiro Mifune, Takashi Shimura | 203 minutes | Not Rated

Credited with "defining its own genre", Kurosawa's "awesome", "pivotal" Japanese adventure introduces the "original magnificent seven" as old-time samurai "warrior-heroes" who rise to the defense of a village menaced by a "vicious band of marauders"; the "epic running time melts away" before the "exciting" display of "honor", "courage" and "classic swordplay", and though there are "countless" reworkings, connoisseurs claim this "way-cool prototype" is "far superior."

1776

22 | 22 | 24 | 23

1972 | Directed by Peter H. Hunt | With William Daniels, Howard da Silva, Blythe Danner | 142 minutes | Rated G

Put away the books and take an "entertaining shortcut" to U.S. history via this "faithful" rendering of the Broadway musical, a "patriotic pageant" wherein periwigged radicals assemble in Philly and wrangle over the Declaration of Independence, backed up by "wonderful music and lyrics"; it's a "smart" way to "put a face" on "those lovable founding fathers", and they turn out to be "such great singers" – "who knew?"

☑ Seventh Seal, The ❶🄵   27 | 27 | 26 | 26

1958 | Directed by Ingmar Bergman | With Max von Sydow, Gunnar Björnstrand, Nils Poppe | 96 minutes | Not Rated

An utterly foreign flick and staple of "college days", Bergman's "challenging" drama is a "dark allegory" with von Sydow as a "knight returning from the Crusades to plague-swept Europe" only to hunker down for a high-stakes "chess game with Death"; as a "cerebral" meditation on the "meaning of existence", it seals the deal with "some of the greatest visuals ever" and a "symbolic story" that "makes everything else look like a game of checkers."

7th Voyage of Sinbad, The   20 | 12 | 20 | 22

1958 | Directed by Nathan Juran | With Kerwin Mathews, Kathryn Grant, Torin Thatcher | 88 minutes | Rated G

"Amazing for its time", this "delightful" adventure "throwback" "makes myth real without computers" using '50s-era FX to summon up a host of "lovingly created monsters"; ok, the "Saturday-matinee" storyline is "standard cheese", but it's a "fondly remembered fantasy" for fans who happily "take it for what it is."

Seven Year Itch, The   23 | 23 | 20 | 20

1955 | Directed by Billy Wilder | With Marilyn Monroe, Tom Ewell, Evelyn Keyes | 105 minutes | Not Rated

Marilyn's billowing-dress "subway-grate scene" is the iconic moment in this "enjoyable" comedy, which finds "ordinary guy" Ewell "on his own" when the wife and kiddies split for summer vacation simultaneously with the arrival of his new neighbor, a most "memorable" Monroe in full "innocent-sexpot" mode, who brings on a major "midlife crisis"; sure, the repartee seems "dated and stagy", but it can still tickle the "funny" bone.

Sex and the City   22 | 22 | 21 | 25

2008 | Directed by Michael Patrick King | With Sarah Jessica Parker, Kim Cattrall, Kristin Davis, Cynthia Nixon | 148 minutes | Rated R

The "cosmo"-chugging "fab four" are back in this big-screen adaptation of the hit HBO series, a "chick flick par excellence" about the pursuit of "labels and love" in the big city; fans say it's a "perfect sendoff" for "our girls" ("like a reunion with friends you haven't seen in years"), fanatics "can't wait for the sequel" and foes yawn "too long", with too much "clothing porn" and "product placement"; all agree that the "men don't really matter" when there are so many "nice shoes" to look at.

Sex, Lies and Videotape   19 | 20 | 20 | 18

1989 | Directed by Steven Soderbergh | With James Spader, Andie MacDowell, Peter Gallagher | 98 minutes | Rated R

Wounded libidos fight the "battles of the sexes" in this "fresh take" on the "deterioration of relationships", a "simple", "well-crafted" drama about a college chum visiting an unhappily married couple and getting some spicy tell-all on tape; it's an "intelligent" look at the "permissive age" heated up by erotic "suspense" more than "actual" on-screen whoopee, though some find it "hard to care about."

| | OVERALL | ACTING | STORY | PROD. |

⚡ Shadow of a Doubt ◐   `26` `26` `26` `25`

1943 | Directed by Alfred Hitchcock | With Teresa Wright, Joseph Cotten, Macdonald Carey | 108 minutes | Not Rated

Hitchcock's "first truly American film" (and his "personal favorite"), this "dark" thriller is set in a "sunny", "Norman Rockwell"-esque town that's home to a "young girl and her mysterious yet appealing uncle" who's suspected of murder; the "is-he-or-isn't-he" plot works thanks to the "spot-on" Cotten, whose performance is "chilling" enough for you to consider "background checks on your own family."

Shadow of the Vampire   `20` `25` `20` `23`

2000 | Directed by E. Elias Merhige | With John Malkovich, Willem Dafoe, Cary Elwes | 92 minutes | Rated R

Maybe it's "not scary", but this "unusual", "behind-the-scenes" drama does apply a few shadowy "touches of horror" as it chronicles the "legendary production" of the fiendish '20s masterwork *Nosferatu*; Dafoe does a "great job" vamping as an undead actor, but foes call it a "disappointing" "art-house mess" that's "not sharp" enough to draw blood.

Shaft   ▽ `17` `16` `18` `15`

1971 | Directed by Gordon Parks | With Richard Roundtree, Moses Gunn, Charles Cioffi | 100 minutes | Rated R

With its pimped-out portrayal of "'70s Harlem" – "Afros" and all – plus Roundtree's star turn as a "bad mother" private eye, this unabashedly "cheesy" action thriller is hailed as a pioneering entry in the "blaxploitation" genre; no question, it looks "outdated", but no one cares once Isaac Hayes' Oscar-winning title tune starts to play – can you dig it?

Shakespeare in Love ✉   `24` `25` `24` `26`

1998 | Directed by John Madden | With Gwyneth Paltrow, Geoffrey Rush, Joseph Fiennes, Judi Dench | 122 minutes | Rated R

"Whether it be true or not", this "lush, literate" romance is a "good-humored confection" that "lights up the screen" with "adorable" performances from Fiennes (an "ink-stained" Elizabethan scribe) whose "writer's block" is cleared by the "exquisitely attired" Paltrow (his not-so-secret admirer); a "rich" depiction of the age "laced with dialogue" from the plays, it's a "rip-roaring" ride that's "accessible at any level."

Shall We Dance ◐   `25` `22` `20` `25`

1937 | Directed by Mark Sandrich | With Fred Astaire, Ginger Rogers, Edward Everett Horton | 109 minutes | Not Rated

"Fred and Ginger" meet "George and Ira" (Gershwin) in this "champagne-bubbly" romance between a Russian ballet star and an American hoofer; maybe the "weak plot" is just another "variation on the same storyline" from the series, but "who cares?" what with that "iconic" choreography and "great chemistry" between its "elegant" stars.

Shall We Dance?   `17` `17` `17` `18`

2004 | Directed by Peter Chelsom | With Richard Gere, Jennifer Lopez, Susan Sarandon | 106 minutes | Rated PG-13

A married "everyman" caught in the grip of an "innocent midlife crisis" takes ballroom dancing lessons to "spruce up his daily grind" in this "light" romantic comedy; ok, it's "nothing deep" and the original "Japanese version is better", but Gere and J-Lo "burn up the screen" with their two-steps, bringing some needed "sizzle" to this "piece of fluff."

	OVERALL	ACTING	STORY	PROD.

Shampoo
16 | 16 | 15 | 16

1975 | Directed by Hal Ashby | With Warren Beatty, Julie Christie, Goldie Hawn, Lee Grant, Carrie Fisher | 109 minutes | Rated R

Starring a "state-of-the-art Warren Beatty at his prettiest", this bedroom farce unfolds over election day, 1968, and follows the "hysterical" ups and downs of a randy hairdresser bouncing around Beverly Hills; both Christie and Hawn are a "blast", the premise is "very funny" and the "bittersweet" ending is a "touching" surprise.

⚡ Shane
26 | 25 | 25 | 25

1953 | Directed by George Stevens | With Alan Ladd, Jean Arthur, Van Heflin | 118 minutes | Not Rated

There's "always a nuance to savor" in this "towering", "classic" Western, telling the "mythical American" tale of a "world-weary gunslinger forced out of retirement" when he sides with a homesteader family menaced by "ruthless cattle ranchers"; the "poignant" setup pays off with a "great finale" as Ladd walks tall in a showdown with "no-good" varmint Jack Palance, leading many oater voters to name it "best" in the West.

Shanghai Knights
16 | 16 | 14 | 19

2003 | Directed by David Dobkin | With Jackie Chan, Owen Wilson, Aidan Gillen | 114 minutes | Rated PG-13

"Faster and funnier than the original", this "good-humored" follow-up to *Shanghai Noon* brings the "tongue-in-cheek" action-comedy formula to Victorian London where our heroes arrive to avenge a murder; Chan's "creative" kung-fu choreography and "fine chemistry" with Wilson deliver the expected kicks, even if spoilsports shrug "great stunts, weak everything else."

Shark Tale
19 | - | 18 | 23

2004 | Directed by Bibo Bergeron, Vicky Jenson, Rob Letterman | Animated | 90 minutes | Rated PG

A "whale-size list of celeb voices" (Robert De Niro, Renée Zellweger, Angelina Jolie) adds buoyancy to this aquatic-themed animated feature that desperately "wants to be *Finding Nemo*" but just "isn't in the same league"; still, it "tries hard" with a positive, "be-yourself" message for the kiddies and "cute sight gags" for their parents (e.g. the "characters' resemblance to the actors voicing them").

Shattered Glass
21 | 23 | 24 | 19

2003 | Directed by Billy Ray | With Hayden Christensen, Peter Sarsgaard, Chloë Sevigny | 95 minutes | Rated PG-13

A "smart surprise" reminiscent of "*All the President's Men*", this true story about a "gifted journalist who self-destructs" after "making up articles for the *New Republic*" is an "engrossing", behind-the-scenes look at "how the media manipulates what the public sees"; though it "drags a tad", Christensen delivers a "surprisingly mature performance" – "why couldn't he do that in *Star Wars?*"

Shaun of the Dead
22 | 19 | 22 | 20

2004 | Directed by Edgar Wright | With Simon Pegg, Kate Ashfield, Nick Frost | 99 minutes | Rated R

Leave it to "those crazy Brits" to concoct this "groovy" "send-up of zombie movies" combining equal doses of "campy fun" and "all-out horror bloodbath" to give you "giggles with your chills"; geeks advise watching some "George Romero flicks" first to "get all the references", but if that's not doable, "a few pints of ale" should be sufficient to prime your "brainnnnssss."

☑ Shawshank Redemption, The 28 | 28 | 28 | 27

1994 | Directed by Frank Darabont | With Tim Robbins, Morgan Freeman, Bob Gunton | 142 minutes | Rated R

Finding the "stirring" in the stir and big hearts in the big house, this "first-rate" "gripper" of a prison drama goes behind the walls of a "dismal" state pen to follow fellow lifers Robbins and Freeman on a "long, dark journey" that pits "friendship", "ingenuity and inner strength" against a "brutal, corrupt system"; besides the "marvelous acting", there's a last-reel "surprise" to add a "feel-good factor" and even some "hope."

She Done Him Wrong ◑ 22 | 22 | 18 | 19

1933 | Directed by Lowell Sherman | With Mae West, Cary Grant | 66 minutes | Not Rated

From the early days "when Hollywood still told it like it was", this "racy, pre-code" comedy is based on *Diamond Lil,* West's stage play about shady cabaret owners in the Gay Nineties; it's best remembered for Mae's immortal line – 'why don't you come up some time and see me?' – delivered to Cary Grant, who "looks like he's about 10 years old" here.

Sheltering Sky, The 16 | 19 | 15 | 21

1990 | Directed by Bernardo Bertolucci | With Debra Winger, John Malkovich, Campbell Scott | 138 minutes | Rated R

"Morocco never looked so beautiful" as in this "gorgeously filmed" adaptation of Paul Bowles' existential novel about a couple's aimless roaming around North Africa in the hope of rekindling their romance; many report it's "rambling" and "pretentious", with too much "sand" and not enough plot, so "to avoid disappointment, see the movie first and then read the book."

Sherrybaby 18 | 25 | 18 | 17

2006 | Directed by Laurie Collyer | With Maggie Gyllenhaal, Brad William Henke, Danny Trejo | 96 minutes | Rated R

Though "not a pretty picture", this "real, raw" indie drama "stays with you" on the strength of Gyllenhaal's "brave", "no-holds-barred" performance as an "ex-con and recovering addict" attempting to go straight and "raise her daughter"; an "accurate depiction" of "low-life" heartbreak, it's "hard to watch, but for the right reasons."

She's Gotta Have It ◑ 21 | 19 | 20 | 17

1986 | Directed by Spike Lee | With Tracy Camilla Johns, Tommy Redmond Hicks, John Canada Terrell, Spike Lee | 84 minutes | Rated R

Spike's first feature, this "interesting" relationships comedy set in Brooklyn "keeps it real" with a "fresh" take on the age-old battle between "Mars and Venus", in this case, a woman with three beaus; true, this "seminal" indie production "has the feel of a student film" (it was shot in two weeks for $160,000), yet fans say it's a "brilliant" moviemaker's "great debut."

| | OVERALL | ACTING | STORY | PROD. |

She Wore a Yellow Ribbon
24 | 22 | 23 | 25

1949 | Directed by John Ford | With John Wayne, Joanne Dru, John Agar, Ben Johnson | 103 minutes | Not Rated

Ford's second bugle blast in his "cavalry trilogy" finds the director "at his best" in a tribute to the "honor and tradition" of horse soldiers posted to the ever-fleeting frontier; the Duke is typically "bigger than life" as a stiff-brimmed but sympathetic old man about to hang up his hat after a career in Injun territory, all portrayed against boundlessly "beautiful" big-sky scenery – "what else does a Western need?"

Shine ✉
22 | 25 | 21 | 21

1996 | Directed by Scott Hicks | With Geoffrey Rush, Armin Mueller-Stahl, Lynn Redgrave | 105 minutes | Rated PG-13

"Mad musician makes good" in this "enlightening", "uplifting true story" about a gifted Australian pianist who succeeds in the shadow of an inflexible father but succumbs to a "harrowing" bout with schizophrenia – only to return to the bench for a midlife comeback; Rush's "compelling" turn keeps things uptempo, and if some dub it an "overrated curiosity", more offer bravos for a portrait that "shines" from first movement to last.

Shining, The
25 | 26 | 25 | 25

1980 | Directed by Stanley Kubrick | With Jack Nicholson, Shelley Duvall, Scatman Crothers | 146 minutes | Rated R

The "supernatural and psychotic" collide in this "revolutionary horror film", a "downright scary" story from the Stephen King novel about a "snowbound caretaker of an old hotel" running amok; though voters agree that the "elevator scene", "Diane Arbus twin girls" and "gloriously unhinged Nicholson" all shine, Duvall gets mixed marks: "intensely annoying" vs. "profoundly brilliant"; best line, no contest: "heeere's Johnny!"

Ship of Fools ◑
23 | 25 | 24 | 23

1965 | Directed by Stanley Kramer | With Vivien Leigh, Simone Signoret, José Ferrer, Lee Marvin, Oskar Werner, Elizabeth Ashley, George Segal, Michael Dunn | 149 minutes | Not Rated

A "touching but loaded adaptation" of the Katherine Anne Porter novel, this "clever" drama follows a clutch of characters "aboard an ocean liner" traveling from Mexico to Germany "on the eve of WWII"; while sinkers shrug it off as "hammy", "soap operatic" stuff (think *Grand Hotel* at sea), far more feel the "all-star" international cast is worth watching, notably the "memorable" Signoret, "standout" Werner and "heartbreaking" Leigh, who's "too convincing as a faded beauty."

Shipping News, The
18 | 21 | 17 | 21

2001 | Directed by Lasse Hallström | With Kevin Spacey, Julianne Moore, Judi Dench | 111 minutes | Rated R

Based on the best-selling book, this drama tells the "strange story" of a "hopeless mope" doing drudge work at a small-town gazette who gets a "second chance" when his wife dies and he ships out to the Newfoundland coast; though it's praised as "ultimately optimistic", foes torpedo the "overblown", "contrived" production as a "lackluster" Miramax bid for the Oscar race.

Shirley Valentine   24 | 24 | 23 | 20

1989 | Directed by Lewis Gilbert | With Pauline Collins, Tom Conti, Alison Steadman | 108 minutes | Rated R

A real "charmer" with a "Liverpudlian accent", this "spirited" comedy sends a "terrific message" with its "sweet midlife fantasy" of a "bored English housewife" who flees to the Aegean "looking for love"; adapted from the "superb" stage show, it "loses nothing in the translation" as a "wise" celebration of "independence and self-respect."

☒ Shoah 🄵   28 | - | 28 | 26

1985 | Directed by Claude Lanzmann | Documentary | 563 minutes | Not Rated

"Not a film to watch casually", this documentary addresses the "horror of the Holocaust" through "first-hand accounts" as a "necessary antidote" to "one of the worst episodes in human history"; Lanzmann uses witnesses from both sides of the "barbed-wire fence" to record their "intense", "shattering" memories of an entire society's "complicity", and "emotions pour out" over "eight hours of painful viewing" that are "impossibly sad and difficult" – but "worth all of it."

Shooter   20 | 20 | 19 | 21

2007 | Directed by Antoine Fuqua | With Mark Wahlberg, Michael Peña, Danny Glover | 124 minutes | Rated R

A "bull's-eye" for aficionados of "guns and tough talk", this "solid action" pic is loaded with "conspiracy-type twists" as an ex-Marine sniper gets "played as a patsy for an assassination" only to target the "government characters" who set him up; while skeptics take aim at the "far-fetched" scenario, the "nonstop" excitement makes it "worth seeing."

Shoot the Piano Player ◑🄵   25 | 24 | 23 | 22

1962 | Directed by François Truffaut | With Charles Aznavour, Marie Dubois, Nicole Berger | 84 minutes | Not Rated

Beside the "great title", Truffaut's "stylized" sophomore effort is a "slightly weird" combination of Gallic satire and American gangster picture that features a "not-so-romantic view of Paris"; its "unusual" story of a former concert pianist (the "sexy" Aznavour) mixed up with hooligans may be "for movie lovers only", but cineasts advise "see it with small expectations and you'll be rewarded."

Shop Around the Corner, The ◑   24 | 25 | 25 | 23

1940 | Directed by Ernst Lubitsch | With Margaret Sullavan, James Stewart, Frank Morgan | 99 minutes | Not Rated

Lubitsch plies his signature touch to a "classic" romantic comedy template – "two people who don't like each other" falling in love – and cooks up this "tasteful but funny" production starring Stewart and Sullavan as "colleagues who spar at work" while sharing a passionate but "anonymous" postal correspondence on the side; like many "good old-fashioned" flicks, this one's been "remade and remade" (try "*You've Got Mail*"), but as usual, the imitators "can't beat" the original.

Shopgirl   18 | 21 | 18 | 18

2005 | Directed by Anand Tucker | With Steve Martin, Claire Danes, Jason Schwartzman | 104 minutes | Rated R

A "refreshing change from Hollywood's usual date movies", this "thinking person's romance" based on the Steve Martin novella delineates a bittersweet love triangle involving a shy, "Cinderella-like salesgirl" and "two Prince Charmings": a "scruffy slacker" and a "suave, middle-aged" millionaire; Danes is a "revelation" and the story "subtly nuanced", but some find it "uninvolving" and "rather bleak", noting that it "takes less time to read the better book."

☑ Shop on Main Street, The ✉◐▣ | 27 | 27 | 26 | 24 |

1966 | Directed by Ján Kadár, Elmar Klos | With Ida Kaminska, Jozef Kroner | 125 minutes | Not Rated

A "classic" Czech import, this "delicate, heartrending" drama of "one man's moral struggle" is centered around an "elderly shopkeeper caught up in the beginning of the Holocaust"; winner of the Best Foreign Film Oscar, its "slow but powerful" narrative leaves one with the "long-lasting impression" reserved for "real art."

Shortbus | 18 | 16 | 16 | 17 |

2006 | Directed by John Cameron Mitchell | With Sook-Yin Lee, Paul Dawson, Lindsay Beamish, PJ DeBoy | 101 minutes | Not Rated

Gird your loins for busloads of "graphic, hard-core" sex in this "very adult", "very human" drama about everyday folks undergoing erotic "confusion" in "polysexual" NYC; while "short of dazzling" and cast with unknowns, it still manages to "push boundaries" by mixing "explicit", "steamy" action with "oddly compelling charm."

Short Cuts | 22 | 24 | 21 | 20 |

1993 | Directed by Robert Altman | With Julianne Moore, Jack Lemmon, Lily Tomlin, Jennifer Jason Leigh, Andie MacDowell, Robert Downey Jr. | 187 minutes | Rated R

A "must-see for anyone who loves storytelling", this "intelligent" Robert Altman drama is a patchwork of "several Raymond Carver short stories" woven into a "delightful film that really draws you in"; ok, it's "lengthy" and the story "doesn't really go anywhere" – maybe "that's the point" – but it's "essential viewing for LA residents" and for everyone else, it's worth seeing for its "star-studded" ensemble cast.

Shot in the Dark, A | 23 | 22 | 20 | 20 |

1964 | Directed by Blake Edwards | With Peter Sellers, Elke Sommer, George Sanders | 102 minutes | Rated PG

Sort of a cub *Pink Panther,* this "laugh-aloud funny" comedy features a "brilliant" Sellers as the clueless Inspector Clouseau, bumbling his way through a "delicious red-herring salad" of a plot that finds him assigned to solve a murder pinned on a Parisian chambermaid; if the "charmingly quirky" setup has its "slow" moments, the "master" makes it watchable "for his accent alone."

Show Boat | 23 | 20 | 24 | 25 |

1951 | Directed by George Sidney | With Kathryn Grayson, Ava Gardner, Howard Keel | 107 minutes | Not Rated

The "schmaltzy" but "fabulous" hit from the Broadway boards gets the "brightest Technicolor" treatment in this "sterling MGM musical" about a showgirl's "sentimental" entanglement with a riverboat gambler; the big wheel paddles along to "unforgettable" songs, "solid production numbers" and hoofers who "dance up a storm", and if purists prefer 1936's "glory-days" version, most can't help lovin' dat "beautiful, melodic" spectacle.

| | OVERALL | ACTING | STORY | PROD. |

Showgirls   5 | 4 | 4 | 10
1995 | Directed by Paul Verhoeven | With Elizabeth Berkley, Kyle MacLachlan, Gina Gershon | 131 minutes | Rated NC-17

Alright already, "nobody expected Shakespeare", but this "sorry" saga of a stripper hell-bent on becoming a Vegas showgirl is one truly "tacky", "pointless" enterprise, with "absolutely no redeeming value" and an NC-17 rating to boot; for "camp" followers, however, it's "unintentionally funny" (sort of a "nudie" version of *All About Eve*) and "so awful it's wonderful"; biggest howler: the "swimming pool sex scene."

⚡ Shrek   26 | – | 25 | 28
2001 | Directed by Andrew Adamson, Vicky Jenson | Animated | 90 minutes | Rated PG

They "added a category" on Oscar night to honor this "playfully creative original" that uses "exceptional" CGI animation and "great voicing" to rework a "hoary storyline" about an ogre saving a princess into "highly entertaining" fare; it challenges the "Disney fairy-tale formula" with adult-level "parody" and "inside jokes" underscored with a "positive message" for all.

⚡ Shrek 2   26 | – | 24 | 28
2004 | Directed by Andrew Adamson, Kelly Asbury, Conrad Vernon | Animated | 92 minutes | Rated PG

"Another ogre-achiever", this "worthy sequel" once again features "incredible animation so lifelike you forget it's animation", "star voice actors" (Mike Myers, Eddie Murphy, Cameron Diaz) and a "laugh-out-loud" love story that sends up classic fairy-tale films; the "sly" satire and "clever" dialogue are "as much fun for adults as for the kids", and new addition Antonio Banderas – "purrfect as Puss 'n' Boots" – nearly "steals the movie."

Shrek the Third   20 | – | 18 | 25
2007 | Directed by Chris Miller, Raman Hui | Animated | 92 minutes | Rated PG

Staunch shrekkies report "satisfying" viewing via this "fun" three-peat by Hollywood's profitably "adorable" ogre, who returns with an "excellent cast and animation (as always)" in tow for more "hilarious" misadventures; but some are less than enchanted, claiming the "hokey storyline" and excessively "crude" humor prove that the "third time's not always the charm."

Sicko   23 | – | 23 | 20
2007 | Directed by Michael Moore | Documentary | 123 minutes | Rated PG-13

A "tamer" Moore sets aside "his usual broad brush" to administer a "healthy dose of reality" to this "persuasive documentary" about America's "lamentable" health care system, allowing others to "speak to the issues" and build a case for "free universal coverage"; ok, that "excursion to Cuba" is a bit "over the top", but the overall message – "even with its bias" – remains "vitally important."

Sid & Nancy   18 | 20 | 18 | 16
1986 | Directed by Alex Cox | With Gary Oldman, Chloe Webb, David Hayman | 112 minutes | Rated R

An "absolutely demented but totally compelling love story", this "gripping" slice of "rock history" details the rise and fall of the "Sex Pistols' wildest member", featuring a "convincing Oldman" as Sid Vicious and the "scarily real" Webb as his "crazy girlfriend"; though the story of their downward, drug-laden spiral is not for the faint-hearted, groupies dig it 'cause it's "dark, ugly and vibrant all at once."

Sideways
23 | 26 | 22 | 22

2004 | Directed by Alexander Payne | With Paul Giamatti, Thomas Haden Church, Virginia Madsen, Sandra Oh | 123 minutes | Rated R

Oenophiles toast this "intoxicatingly hilarious" road tripper pitting Giamatti's "shlub" against Church's "crack-up" for a Bacchian weekend of "middle-aged angst"–inspired "debauchery" in "scenic California wine country"; the "literate", Oscar-winning script uncorks some "wonderfully painful" scenes that are "so real" it's "like watching a train wreck", though a few whine it's just a "mundane soaper" with as much depth as a "glass of merlot."

Siege, The
19 | 21 | 20 | 20

1998 | Directed by Edward Zwick | With Denzel Washington, Annette Bening, Bruce Willis, Tony Shalhoub | 116 minutes | Rated R

Primed with a "spookily prescient" premise, this "too-believable" action flick presents a "worst-case scenario" as a campaign of terrorist bombings in NYC draws an FBI guy and a "blowhard" general into a "paranoid" cycle of internment and counter-ops; given the "parallels" in a "post-9/11" world, many shudder it "hits way too close to home."

Signs
18 | 20 | 18 | 20

2002 | Directed by M. Night Shyamalan | With Mel Gibson, Joaquin Phoenix, Rory Culkin | 106 minutes | Rated PG-13

Farmer Mel Gibson finds weird "crop circles" in his cornfields in this "paranormal" thriller from M. Night Shyamalan that delivers a "good number of jump-out-of-your-seat moments"; some say it's a really a "religious movie disguised as science fiction" ("I've coughed up scarier things"), yet there's a "creepy realness" about it that keeps the mood "tense."

☑ Silence of the Lambs, The ✉
27 | 28 | 27 | 26

1991 | Directed by Jonathan Demme | With Jodie Foster, Anthony Hopkins, Scott Glenn | 118 minutes | Rated R

Every subsequent "psych-profiling" flick owes something to this "masterful", "profoundly creepy" thriller that combines "heart-thumping suspense" with "premier" performances as Foster, an FBI greenhorn on a serial-killer hunt, is drawn into "intense mind games" with the "soft-spoken" madman Hopkins; its "well-deserved Oscars" speak for its "twisted", "truly terrifying" achievement, though some say it "gives fava beans a bad name."

Silent Movie
20 | 20 | 19 | 20

1976 | Directed by Mel Brooks | With Mel Brooks, Marty Feldman, Dom DeLuise, Sid Caesar | 87 minutes | Rated PG

"Kudos" to Brooks for ditching dialogue and scoring "audience roars" with "clever" sight gags in this "entertaining" send-up of silent films; expect a parade of "star" cameos (Burt Reynolds, Liza Minnelli, Paul Newman), though the "best moment" belongs to mime Marcel Marceau, who utters the picture's "only spoken word."

Silkwood

22 | 26 | 25 | 21

1983 | Directed by Mike Nichols | With Meryl Streep, Kurt Russell, Cher, Craig T. Nelson | 131 minutes | Rated R

This "somewhat forgotten" drama generates a "great deal of tension" telling the fact-based story of a whistle-blowing nuclear plant worker who comes to a "mysterious end" when she tries to go public with hazardous goings-on at the facility; lit up by "terrific acting" from "marvelous" Meryl and "eye-opener" Cher, it's a "moving" picture of blue-collar good guys vs. white-collar baddies.

Silverado

24 | 24 | 23 | 24

1985 | Directed by Lawrence Kasdan | With Kevin Kline, Scott Glenn, Kevin Costner | 127 minutes | Rated PG-13

Boys, the "fun Western" rides again in this "well-made" "modern horse opera", a "true homage" that "throws in all the clichés" and delivers some "slick sequences" and "great one-liners" of its own; a "tremendous" cast "manages to upstage the glorious scenery", though it's best appreciated on the "biggest screen you can find."

Silver Streak

19 | 19 | 18 | 19

1976 | Directed by Arthur Hiller | With Gene Wilder, Richard Pryor, Jill Clayburgh | 114 minutes | Rated PG

"One of the best comedy teams on film" gets its "first pairing" in this "slick takeoff" on Hitchcock-style "train capers", featuring Wilder in the "amusing" role of an innocent railroaded in an art-world murder only to find himself on the run along with the "beyond-funny" Pryor; devotees call it "enjoyable" and "underappreciated."

Simple Plan, A

19 | 22 | 22 | 19

1998 | Directed by Sam Raimi | With Bill Paxton, Bridget Fonda, Billy Bob Thornton | 121 minutes | Rated R

B-movie maestro Raimi's "entry into respectable filmdom" is a "well-paced thriller" with a "convincing" scenario about a rustic threesome in the backwoods who stumble upon a wrecked plane and a bag of cash; "plot-twisting" and "suspense" ensue as lives "unravel" in a "tragic" parable of the "evils of ill-gotten gain" that makes it the *Treasure of the Sierra Madre* for the "*Fargo*" crowd.

Simpsons Movie, The

19 | - | 17 | 21

2007 | Directed by David Silverman | Animated | 87 minutes | Rated PG-13

A "long time coming", "America's favorite cartoon family" finally hits the big screen in this "admirable" comedy that's basically an "extended episode" (in which a toxic Springfield is enclosed under a glass dome); d'oh, it's "nothing earth-shattering", but diehards dig the trademarked "silliness" and "iconoclastic humor."

Sin City

22 | 21 | 20 | 26

2005 | Directed by Frank Miller, Robert Rodriguez, Quentin Tarantino | With Bruce Willis, Mickey Rourke, Jessica Alba | 124 minutes | Rated R

This "sin-tillating" noir take on a pulp comic book series is "gritty" and "ultra-violent", with a "meandering", three-part storyline played out in mix of black-and-white live action as well as blood-red and gut-yellow "comic animation"; Willis is "compelling", a "'roided-up Rourke" makes his "comeback", Elijah Wood does "Frodo-turned-psycho" and a "scantily clad" Alba does tricks with a "lasso."

	OVERALL	ACTING	STORY	PROD.

⚡ Singin' in the Rain
28 | 26 | 25 | 28

1952 | Directed by Stanley Donen, Gene Kelly | With Gene Kelly, Donald O'Connor, Debbie Reynolds | 103 minutes | Rated G

"Giddy", "wet and wonderful", this "timeless" musical brightens the worst day with an "exuberant" "something-for-everyone" blend of "quintessential" song and dance, "satire" and a "sappy, funny love story"; the "flawless" Kelly plays a silent movie star in a "sweet send-up" of Hollywood's early talkie days and effortlessly executes the puddle-hopping "title number", leaving fans "awed."

Single White Female
16 | 18 | 17 | 15

1992 | Directed by Barbet Schroeder | With Bridget Fonda, Jennifer Jason Leigh, Steven Weber | 107 minutes | Rated R

"Watch your back!": this "roommate-from-hell thriller" "keeps you on edge" with its "sick vulgarity" and mounting "suspense"; though the trading-identities storyline might be "derivative", the picture's still "full of surprises" and "done well" enough to "make you think it could actually happen"; P.S. brace yourself for a particularly "nasty ending."

Sister Act
18 | 18 | 17 | 17

1992 | Directed by Emile Ardolino | With Whoopi Goldberg, Maggie Smith, Kathy Najimy | 100 minutes | Rated PG

Whoopi gets a witness protection program in this "engaging" "fish-out-of-water comedy" about a lounge diva who sings for the cops after her beau commits homicide, only to find herself stashed in "nun other than" a convent; the verdict: a "guilty pleasure" that rises above the "run of the mill" with "cool" musical interludes.

Sisterhood of the Traveling Pants, The
19 | 19 | 20 | 19

2005 | Directed by Ken Kwapis | With Amber Tamblyn, Alexis Bledel, America Ferrera, Blake Lively | 119 minutes | Rated PG

The "angst"-ridden "summer adventures" of four "very different" teen girls are sewn together by a "pair of magical pants" in this "charming" coming-of-ager featuring an "adorable" cast of young actresses; sure, it's a "tear-jerking" "chick flick if there ever was one", but its one-size-fits-all spirit means "even males" may be reaching for a "hanky."

Sisters
▽ 22 | 21 | 23 | 20

1973 | Directed by Brian De Palma | With Margot Kidder, Jennifer Salt, Charles Durning | 92 minutes | Rated R

"De Palma does Hitchcock" ("again") in this "tense", "really scary" thriller about a pair of "warped" Siamese twins, recently separated; filmed on Staten Island for what looks like a "$2.50" budget, it's most "memorable" for Bernard Herrmann's "excellent score" and some "great acting" from a "pre–Lois Lane" Kidder.

Six Degrees of Separation
21 | 24 | 23 | 20

1993 | Directed by Fred Schepisi | With Will Smith, Stockard Channing, Donald Sutherland | 112 minutes | Rated R

"Great performances" ensure this "intriguing" "stage-to-screen" drama "adjusts quite nicely" to celluloid as a "sublime" Channing offers an encore of her theatrical role opposite a "young" Smith in the "challenging" part of a "charming hustler" posing as Sidney Poitier's son; it draws applause as a "clever" critique of "moneyed values" that's "surprisingly strong."

16 Blocks
17 | 19 | 18 | 19

2006 | Directed by Richard Donner | With Bruce Willis, Mos Def, David Morse | 102 minutes | Rated PG-13

A pair of "strong performances" primes this "slick" action flick, starring an "older" Willis as a "boozy", "wrung-out" detective who kindles a "spark of decency" while escorting state's witness Mos Def (a "rapper who can act") through a "cop vs. cop" gauntlet; it's "well-filmed" and "suspenseful" (if "nothing profound"), though stretches of "implausible", "formula-driven" plotting can mean "16 blocks never felt so long."

Sixteen Candles
22 | 18 | 21 | 19

1984 | Directed by John Hughes | With Molly Ringwald, Justin Henry, Anthony Michael Hall | 93 minutes | Rated PG

"Ringwald will steal your heart" in this "sweet coming-of-age classic", a "day-in-the-life" comedy that conveys the "teen angst" of high school, "first love and puberty" as seen through the eyes of a 16-year-old "birthday girl whom everyone forgot"; though its "damn funny" "Brat Pack" cast "characterizes the '80s to a tee", modernists who love this "brilliant" send-up "can still relate to it."

⚡ Sixth Sense, The
26 | 25 | 27 | 25

1999 | Directed by M. Night Shyamalan | With Bruce Willis, Haley Joel Osment, Toni Collette | 107 minutes | Rated PG-13

A "tricky" one, this mega-hit thriller "surprises even the most astute" with its "perfectly crafted story" of a troubled boy with an "unwelcome gift" who finds a friend in Willis, leading to "really spooky" plot developments; it's hailed as an "unpredictable" sensation that rewards with "white-knuckle jolts" and a "stunning" "O. Henry"–esque ending.

Skeleton Key, The
17 | 19 | 18 | 18

2005 | Directed by Iain Softley | With Kate Hudson, Gena Rowlands, John Hurt, Peter Sarsgaard | 104 minutes | Rated PG-13

"Hoodoo practices and rituals" are the bare bones of this "haunting" flick that keys up "Gothic" horror as NoLa-based caregiver Hudson goes to work for "freaky" oldsters in a "house of evil"; while the overall story is "strong on atmospherics" but "small on scares", the final "twist" will "leave you speechless – if you understand it."

Sky Captain and the World of Tomorrow
15 | 14 | 14 | 22

2004 | Directed by Kerry Conran | With Gwyneth Paltrow, Jude Law, Angelina Jolie, Giovanni Ribisi | 106 minutes | Rated PG

An attempt to re-create the "classic episodic cliffhangers" of yesteryear, this *Buck Rogers*–type adventure boasts a "high-gloss" production replete with "techno-gadgets" galore, all courtesy of "green-screen" CGI; too bad the "stiff" acting and "silly story" (ace reporter Paltrow and aviator Law out to save the world) makes it all seem so "plodding."

Sky High
16 | 15 | 18 | 19

2005 | Directed by Mike Mitchell | With Kurt Russell, Kelly Preston, Michael Angarano | 100 minutes | Rated PG

"Nice with popcorn", this "watchable family flick" follows the "comical rites of passage" of a "pubescent superhero entering high school" who's obliged to "live up to the reputation of his famous superhero parents"; it's "corny" but "winning" fare for "kids and early teens", though cynics say this "retread of The Incredibles" "lacks zing.

| | OVERALL | ACTING | STORY | PROD. |

Slap Shot
22 | 18 | 19 | 17

1977 | Directed by George Roy Hill | With Paul Newman, Michael Ontkean, Strother Martin | 122 minutes | Rated R

Right up there with the "funniest sports flicks", this puckish comedy finds "Newman on skates" as the "foul-mouthed coach" of a "dark horse" minor-league hockey team with a "strange way" of turning every face-off into a riot on ice; it "epitomizes the goonery" of the high-sticking '70s, resulting in "crazy", "profane" and "fairly violent" fare that hardcore fans "cannot live without."

Slaughterhouse-Five
22 | 20 | 25 | 20

1972 | Directed by George Roy Hill | With Michael Sacks, Valerie Perrine, Ron Leibman | 104 minutes | Rated R

Countering the conventional wisdom that Kurt Vonnegut's "classic" novel is "impossible to translate to film", this "well-done adaptation" preserves the "powerful" punch of the book and is "worth watching for the curiosity factor alone"; recounting the "strange" adventures of one Billy Pilgrim, an everyman who becomes 'unstuck in time', it's a "wildly original" blend of "funny" fantasy and "heart-tugging reality."

Sleeper
23 | 19 | 23 | 20

1973 | Directed by Woody Allen | With Woody Allen, Diane Keaton, John Beck | 89 minutes | Rated PG

Orwell's wake-up call has nothing on this "inspired sci-fi spoof", a "hilarious" comedy of a nebbishy NYer who's cryogenically preserved then "defrosted in the future"; "laced with fast-paced verbal" cracks, it's "vintage" Allen at his "goofiest" and "most slapsticky" in a romp that generates "nonstop laughs" – the "orgasmatron alone is worth the price of admission."

Sleepers
22 | 25 | 23 | 22

1996 | Directed by Barry Levinson | With Kevin Bacon, Jason Patric, Robert De Niro, Brad Pitt | 147 minutes | Rated R

Years after a "terrible mistake" landed them in a "tough juvenile detention center" (where "abuse" was a staff specialty), four best friends exact "revenge" on their former tormentors in this "very dark" Levinson drama; though there's debate at to whether it's actually "based on actual events", most find the story "moving" enough and credit the "stellar" ensemble for conferring a "psychological" authenticity to the proceedings.

Sleeping Beauty
25 | - | 23 | 25

1959 | Directed by Clyde Geronimi | Animated | 75 minutes | Rated G

No snooze among the "old Disney greats", this "lushly animated" "princess movie" has a trio of good fairies protecting the titular knockout from an evil spell by zapping her into a sound nap, interrupted only after her true love battles it out with filmdom's most fearsome dragon lady; the very wicked witch may be "too scary for the little ones", but most say this "classic" only "gets better with age."

Sleeping with the Enemy
17 | 18 | 18 | 17

1991 | Directed by Joseph Ruben | With Julia Roberts, Patrick Bergin, Kevin Anderson | 99 minutes | Rated R

"Harrowing scenes of spousal abuse" supply the "scary edge" in this "Julia Roberts vehicle" about a "murderous husband and the wife determined to get away from him"; though it strikes a few as "over-wrought and cartoonish", this thriller makes others "think long and hard" about a problem that could be "more common than we think."

Sleepless in Seattle

21 | 22 | 22 | 21

1993 | Directed by Nora Ephron | With Tom Hanks, Meg Ryan, Rosie O'Donnell | 105 minutes | Rated PG

Although pretty "predictable", this Ephron romance "works", renewing faith in the "soul-mate concept" as the "perfectly cast", "totally lovable" Hanks and Ryan make "a great match" in the story of a woman who pursues a lonely-hearts stranger cross country; sure, this "toothache-sweet trifle" is "a bit far-fetched" ("at least Harry *met* Sally"), but it's also a "funny", "male-tolerable chick flick" that's likely to spring eternal for "hopeless romantics."

Sleepy Hollow

17 | 18 | 17 | 23

1999 | Directed by Tim Burton | With Johnny Depp, Christina Ricci, Miranda Richardson | 105 minutes | Rated R

All your "decapitation entertainment needs will be fulfilled" in this "engrossing" rendition of Washington Irving's "headless horseman fable", a "funny but gory" ride from Tim Burton that's a "wonderful update of the Hammer horror films"; Depp is "daringly unconventional", and the "eye-popping" cinematography is "visually splendid" – so it's alright to nod off during that "big Hollywood action finale."

Sleuth

25 | 28 | 26 | 23

1972 | Directed by Joseph L. Mankiewicz | With Laurence Olivier, Michael Caine | 138 minutes | Rated PG

It's no mystery why this suspense thriller based on the Broadway smash adapts "wonderfully to film": "masters-at-work" Olivier and Caine offer "witty", "subtle" work as a cuckolded writer and his rival engaged in a calculated confrontation in an English country manor; the "creative" story builds "numerous plot twists" that cross and double-cross, and "two of the greatest" muster up some of the liveliest back-and-forth volleys ever seen "outside of Wimbledon."

Sliding Doors

21 | 21 | 24 | 20

1998 | Directed by Peter Howitt | With Gwyneth Paltrow, John Hannah, John Lynch | 99 minutes | Rated R

If you've ever "wondered what your life would be like if one detail had been slightly altered", this "quirky" but "poignant" romance offers a "clever" side-by-side examination of a woman's "parallel worlds" that offers "lots to think about" and will "keep you hooked"; a "fab", "pre-Coldplay" Gwyneth shines in "dual" lead roles, while the "completely lovable" Hannah adds some "charm" to the mix.

Sling Blade ✉

25 | 27 | 25 | 22

1996 | Directed by Billy Bob Thornton | With Billy Bob Thornton, Dwight Yoakam, J.T. Walsh | 135 minutes | Rated R

"Too convincing" in the role that lands him "on the map", "creepy Billy Bob" is "brilliantly believable" in this "tragedy from the real world" playing a slow-witted country boy who's sprung from the state booby hatch and taken in by a single mom; a "unique, touching" drama of man trouble, it "earns every accolade" with "excellent acting" and an "unforgettable punch" at the climax.

| | OVERALL | ACTING | STORY | PROD. |

☑ Smiles of a Summer Night ◑ ◪
26 | 26 | 25 | 26

1957 | Directed by Ingmar Bergman | With Ulla Jacobsson, Eva Dahlbeck, Gunnar Björnstrand | 108 minutes | Not Rated

For "Bergman without the angst", check out his "rare venture" into romantic comedy, this "sumptuous" tale of love, desire and "what it means to be human" set in fin de siècle Sweden; probably the director's "lightest, most approachable" film, it was "most influential" to a generation of artists, and best known today as the inspiration for Sondheim's *A Little Night Music*.

Smokey and the Bandit
16 | 13 | 15 | 15

1977 | Directed by Hal Needham | With Burt Reynolds, Sally Field, Jackie Gleason | 96 minutes | Rated PG

This "good ol' boys car chase" comedy is a rootin' tootin' good "road movie" about a cross-country "race against time"; sure, it's "corny", "cheaply made" stuff based on what appears to be a completely improvised script, but in the end, it's plain that "everyone's having fun", particularly the "dynamite duo" of Reynolds and Field.

Snake Pit, The ◑
25 | 28 | 25 | 24

1948 | Directed by Anatole Litvak | With Olivia de Havilland, Mark Stevens, Leo Genn, Celeste Holm | 108 minutes | Not Rated

"Daring for its time", this "hair-raising" depiction of conditions inside a mental institution was made during the postwar "heyday of psychoanalytic films" and is "still frightening" today; in addition to de Havilland's "sensitive", Oscar-nominated performance, many say it's most "memorable" for that "bird's-eye view" of the asylum's psycho ward.

Snakes on a Plane
11 | 11 | 10 | 14

2006 | Directed by David R. Ellis | With Samuel L. Jackson, Julianna Margulies, Rachel Blanchard, Lin Shaye | 105 minutes | Rated R

Best known for the advance "Internet hype" inspired by that "perfect title", this "schlock" action flick pits an FBI agent against a "fanged menace" after a nest of serpents is released aboard a flight and "havoc fills the skies"; though some insist the "cheese factor" and "stupid thrills" are "enjoyably bad", the majority hisses it's "just plain bad."

Snatch
21 | 23 | 22 | 22

2000 | Directed by Guy Ritchie | With Benicio Del Toro, Dennis Farina, Brad Pitt | 104 minutes | Rated R

Fittingly "splashy" fare from Mr. Madonna, director Ritchie's sophomore effort is a "relentless crime comedy" with a substantial cast of "wild" London gangsters who follow "interacting storylines" in a "quick-witted" "mix-'em-up heist" caper centered around a stolen diamond; the results are "bloody hilarious", and though you might need "subtitles" to decipher Pitt's "crazy-man accent", at least it's "never boring."

☑ Snow White & the Seven Dwarfs
27 | - | 26 | 27

1937 | Directed by David Hand | Animated | 83 minutes | Rated G

The "one that started it all", this "true classic" is the *Citizen Kane* of animation, the "first full-length feature" from the Disney drawing boards and "still the finest" of them all; this tale of a fair maiden hiding in the forest with a band of "cute little guys" to escape a "terrifying wicked queen" is a "masterpiece" of "charm, simplicity and beauty" that continues to "entertain generations" and leave 'em humming "hi ho, hi ho!"

☒ Soldier's Story, A

26 | 26 | 25 | 22

1984 | Directed by Norman Jewison | With Howard E. Rollins Jr., Adolph Caesar, Denzel Washington | 101 minutes | Rated PG

Partially a "mystery" chronicling an "investigation into the murder of an African-American soldier on an army base" in the segregated South, this "powerful" drama also functions as an "important morality play" dealing with the "class issues facing black men" under white rule; enhanced by the "riveting performances" of Rollins, Caesar and a "then-young" Denzel, it's a "gripping" exercise building up to a "great twist at the end."

☒ Some Like It Hot ◖

28 | 27 | 26 | 26

1959 | Directed by Billy Wilder | With Marilyn Monroe, Tony Curtis, Jack Lemmon, Joe E. Brown | 120 minutes | Rated PG

"Cross-dressing was never so hilarious" as in this "legendary" "laff riot" about "two patsies on the run from the mob" who don dresses and join an all-girl band as part of their escape plan; thanks to Wilder's "sure touch" and the "sidesplitting" script's "countless priceless scenes" ("Lemmon with the maracas", "Curtis' riff on Cary Grant", Monroe "running wild"), this is one hot contender for the "greatest comedy ever made" – with the "best closing line" in moviedom: "nobody's perfect."

Something's Gotta Give

23 | 26 | 22 | 23

2003 | Directed by Nancy Meyers | With Jack Nicholson, Diane Keaton, Keanu Reeves | 128 minutes | Rated PG-13

"People over 50 having sex" is the novel premise of this "middle-aged" romantic comedy positing that "growing old can be fun"; cynics nix the "lousy title" and "predictable", "sitcom-lite" plot, but the "*Architectural Digest*–worthy" settings and mighty "excellent chemistry" between Jack and Diane make it go down easy for "mature audiences"; just ignore the "lame", "too-bad-she-wound-up-with-the-wrong-guy" ending.

Something Wild

20 | 20 | 20 | 19

1986 | Directed by Jonathan Demme | With Jeff Daniels, Melanie Griffith, Ray Liotta | 113 minutes | Rated R

"You're never quite sure what's going on" when a "funky gal" meets a "conservative guy" in this "wild road movie", a "fast-paced", "fasten-your-seatbelt" ride that "starts funny", "ends tragically" and "constantly surprises at every turn"; the "pre-plastic surgery" Griffith "sizzles" as the "new wave femme fatale", Daniels "shines" as the good-natured chump and Liotta is just plain "scary as hell"; ultimately, the "title says it all" about this one.

Song of Bernadette, The ✉◖

22 | 24 | 22 | 21

1943 | Directed by Henry King | With Jennifer Jones, Charles Bickford, Gladys Cooper, Anne Revere | 156 minutes | Not Rated

This "uplifting", "inspirational" tale of a French peasant girl who claims to have seen a vision of the Virgin Mary features a "sympathetic", Oscar-winning performance by Jones that will make you "believe her, even if no one else in the film does"; overall, the picture's a relic of "less cynical" times and may be too "syrupy" for modern audiences, but "it can still touch your heart, if you let it."

| | OVERALL | ACTING | STORY | PROD. |

Song of the South ∅
23 | - | 22 | 26
1946 | Directed by Wilfred Jackson, Harve Foster | Animated | With Ruth Warrick, James Baskett | 94 minutes | Rated G

Yup, it's "corny and dated", but "Disney's version of the Uncle Remus stories" is also "one of the earliest" to offer an "animation–live action mix" as a young boy encounters Brers Rabbit, Fox and Bear; its "controversial" stereotyping of plantation life means it's currently "missing in action" on DVD, but music lovers say it will always be "tough to top 'Zip-A-Dee-Doo-Dah.'"

☒ Sophie's Choice ⊠
26 | 28 | 26 | 24
1982 | Directed by Alan J. Pakula | With Meryl Streep, Kevin Kline, Peter MacNicol | 150 minutes | Rated R

A "luminous" Streep with a "faint Polish accent" "shows her stuff" in this "haunting", highly "emotional" drama, which draws its "powerful story" from William Styron's novel about an Auschwitz survivor; though "wrenching" at points, it's a "compelling tour de force" that many see as Oscar-winner Meryl's "finest" hour.

☒ Sorrow and the Pity, The ◑ⓕ
29 | - | 28 | 25
1972 | Directed by Marcel Ophüls | Documentary | 251 minutes | Rated PG

The "truth about the Nazi occupation of France" is revealed in this "devastating" but "essential" documentary that shows how "even civilized countries can fall victim to fascism"; *bien sûr*, it's "a bit long" (clocking in at just over four hours) and its "chilling depiction of neighbor against neighbor" is "not easy to take", but it's "required viewing for historical revisionists everywhere" thanks to its "relentlessly tenacious" director.

Sorry, Wrong Number ◑
25 | 25 | 25 | 23
1948 | Directed by Anatole Litvak | With Barbara Stanwyck, Burt Lancaster | 89 minutes | Not Rated

This "real thriller" adapted from a famed radio play stars Stanwyck as an "invalid heiress" who overhears a murder plot over crossed telephone wires; it's "pretty much a one-woman show" that relies on flashbacks to keep in motion, and if some say the "static" story is "stretched too thin", more report "enough twists" to keep your "spine tingling."

☒ Sounder
26 | 27 | 26 | 25
1972 | Directed by Martin Ritt | With Cicely Tyson, Paul Winfield, Kevin Hooks | 105 minutes | Rated G

The "sadness and dignity" of life as a black sharecropper in the Depression-era South "still resonate" with those who grew up watching this "classic with a heart", a "beautifully crafted" story of "strength" over suffering highlighted by a boy's "poignant" odyssey to locate his imprisoned father; featuring the "wonderful", Oscar-nominated Winfield and Tyson – not to mention that "heartbreaking" dog – "it might be one of the best family films ever."

☒ Sound of Music, The ⊠
28 | 25 | 27 | 28
1965 | Directed by Robert Wise | With Julie Andrews, Christopher Plummer, Eleanor Parker | 174 minutes | Rated G

Everyone has an Alp-size "soft spot" for this "schmaltzy" Rodgers and Hammerstein musical, wherein a "charming" governess marries into a "do-re-mi" singing family and "stands on principle" after the Huns invade; the only Best Picture winner to feature "nuns, Nazis" and "kids

| | OVERALL | ACTING | STORY | PROD. |

in lederhosen", it's "shamelessly saccharine" but loved for its "uplifting" story, "fantastic" songs and "lush" scenery.

South Pacific   24 | 22 | 24 | 25

1958 | Directed by Joshua Logan | With Mitzi Gaynor, Rossano Brazzi, John Kerr | 151 minutes | Not Rated

"Incomparable music" washes up in a "tropical paradise" in this Rodgers and Hammerstein songfest, which finds American sea dogs and dames singing along to "beautiful orchestrations" on a WWII Pacific atoll; though a huge hit in its day owing to those "eternal" tunes, some say it "doesn't hold up" anymore, pointing to the "filtered camera gels" that drown meaningful moments in "gaudy Technicolor" tints.

South Park   20 | - | 19 | 16

1999 | Directed by Trey Parker | Animated | 81 minutes | Rated R

Don't "blame Canada" for this "tasteless" full-length treatment of the "rude, crude" TV series, a "very un-PC" "equal-opportunity offender" with a "raunchy" mix of "lowbrow" laffs and "catchy" musical interludes; "rated R for a reason", it's "unbelievably funny" but "not for the kiddies" or "faint-of-heart" adults.

Spaceballs   18 | 15 | 17 | 17

1987 | Directed by Mel Brooks | With Mel Brooks, John Candy, Rick Moranis | 96 minutes | Rated PG

"Brooks strikes again" in this "goofy takeoff on *Star Wars*" that skewers sci-fi as a couple of space cowboys rocket to the rescue of a princess, setting up "cornball" gags that are the "hysterical" stuff of Mel's genre parodies; though hard-core fans find it "gets funnier every time", those unamused by the "tired", "obvious" humor contend it's "hard to believe" this is the work of a "genius."

Space Jam   16 | - | 14 | 19

1996 | Directed by Joe Pytka | Animated | With Michael Jordan, Wayne Knight, Charles Barkley | 87 minutes | Rated PG

The "Looney Tunes get their own movie" in this "fun fantasy" in which Bugs and crew play b-ball with über-hoopster Jordan and other stars to free themselves from alien kidnappers; despite "so-so" acting and storytelling, the "surprisingly good" matching of animation and live action makes this one "fun for the whole family."

Spanglish   19 | 20 | 18 | 18

2004 | Directed by James L. Brooks | With Adam Sandler, Téa Leoni, Paz Vega, Cloris Leachman | 131 minutes | Rated PG-13

Cultures clash in this "more-serious"-than-you'd-expect film from James L. Brooks about a privileged, "dysfunctional" family turned upside down when a "beautiful" Latina becomes their housekeeper; though there's applause for Sandler's "serious acting chops", critics say Téa's "too over the top" as the "control-freak wife" and "aren't sure about the ending", nor the "after-school-special" script.

⧉ Spartacus   26 | 24 | 25 | 26

1960 | Directed by Stanley Kubrick | With Kirk Douglas, Laurence Olivier, Jean Simmons | 184 minutes | Rated PG-13

"Elevated" by its "sweeping vision" and "superb all-star cast", Kubrick's "impressive" epic headlines Douglas as the "virile" leader of a "slave revolt against Rome"; pairing a "psychologically complex" story with plenty of "gory but good" action, it's an "exciting" box-office big-timer that's "matched by few" in the "classic" spectacle sweeps.

Speed
18 | 14 | 19 | 20

1994 | Directed by Jan de Bont | With Keanu Reeves, Dennis Hopper, Sandra Bullock | 116 minutes | Rated R

"*Die Hard* on a bus" is the "inanely simple" premise behind this "fast-moving" "high-concept actioner", with "sweetheart" Bullock and "studly SWAT boy" Reeves making a "cute and feisty" twosome as they find themselves "trapped" on a "tense", "nonstop" "thrill ride" aboard a "runaway bus" wired to "go boom"; though it's dismissed as "lightweight bubblegum" with "wooden" line readings from "Mr. Whoa", at least there's "no letup."

Spellbound ◑
24 | 25 | 23 | 24

1945 | Directed by Alfred Hitchcock | With Gregory Peck, Ingrid Bergman, Leo G. Carroll | 111 minutes | Not Rated

One of the first mainstream movies to tackle psychiatry, this "outstanding" Hitchcock thriller deals with unlocking a "repressed memory", and the "perfect Bergman" and "gorgeous Peck" are a "good match" as doctor and patient; but despite touches like the "ahead-of-its-time dream sequences" designed by Salvador Dali, some analysts dismiss it as "dated Freudian nonsense."

☑ Spellbound
28 | - | 27 | 26

2003 | Directed by Jeffrey Blitz | Documentary | 97 minutes | Rated G

A "fascinating commentary on American education", this "charming" documentary profiles eight grammar-school contestants bound for the National Spelling Bee in Washington, DC; most surveyors are "a-m-a-z-e-d" that such subject matter can be so much "fun to watch", but the word is this "letter perfect" picture is alternately "poignant", "uplifting" and "completely riveting."

Spider-Man
21 | 19 | 20 | 25

2002 | Directed by Sam Raimi | With Tobey Maguire, Kirsten Dunst, Willem Dafoe, James Franco | 121 minutes | Rated PG-13

Comic-book mavens marvel at how well this "adaptation captures the spirit of the original" – a literally "loopy tale" of "spider bites boy" (Maguire), who sprouts superpowers and "spins around town on threads", battling "campy, cackling nemesis" Dafoe and kissing "hot" honey Dunst upside down; heroes hail the "CGI effects seamlessly woven" into the "action-packed visuals" but hiss the "wooden acting and predictable plot"; overall, it's caught most folks "in its web."

Spider-Man 2
22 | 20 | 21 | 26

2004 | Directed by Sam Raimi | With Tobey Maguire, Kirsten Dunst, Alfred Molina, James Franco | 127 minutes | Rated PG-13

"Spidey tries to hang up his tights" and "live his own life" only to be bugged by "super villain" Doc Ock in this comic-book movie follow-up that's "as good as the original"; expect the usual "jaw-dropping" FX plus a "deeper" exploration of the webslinger's struggles with "guilt, sacrifice" and "love", and get ready for "further sequels" 'cause this franchise has legs.

| | OVERALL | ACTING | STORY | PROD. |

Spider-Man 3
19 | 17 | 16 | 25

2007 | Directed by Sam Raimi | With Tobey Maguire, Kirsten Dunst, James Franco, Thomas Haden Church | 140 minutes | Rated PG-13

World-saving wallcrawler Spider-Man dabbles with the "dark side" while facing down "three villains for the price of one" in this "shiny" but ultimately "thin" threequel "crammed" with "fancy effects" (i.e. Sandman), "tangled plots" and a "kinda corny" dance interlude featuring an "emo" Peter Parker; at a "lonnng" two-plus hours, not even the "Bruce Campbell cameo" eases fans' "disappointment."

Spies Like Us
16 | 16 | 15 | 15

1985 | Directed by John Landis | With Chevy Chase, Dan Aykroyd, Donna Dixon | 102 minutes | Rated PG

If you "love Chevy and Dan", this "Cold War comedy" offers a "fun screen pairing" with the duo mugging it up as "loser" CIA spooks engaged in "goofball" espionage against the Soviets; a "homage to the Crosby-Hope road movies", it's still "good for a chuckle" even if critics charge its "self-indulgent" antics "have not aged well."

Spirit: Stallion of the Cimarron
21 | - | 21 | 23

2002 | Directed by Kelly Asbury, Lorna Cook | Animated | 83 minutes | Rated G

A "gorgeous" combination of hand-drawn and computer animation "elevates" this "charming tearjerker" about a "spirited wild stallion and man's hapless efforts to tame him"; it's "great for kids and adults who grew up watching old Westerns", with "endearing characters" and a "sad" but "beautiful storyline."

☑ Spirited Away
27 | - | 25 | 28

2002 | Directed by Hayao Miyazaki | Animated | 125 minutes | Rated PG

"Master storyteller" Miyazaki's "inventive", "visually stunning" Japanese version of *The Wizard of Oz*" meets *Alice in Wonderland* "transcends the animation genre", bringing viewers to an "enchanted" "spirit world" filled with "bizarre characters", "unexpected sights" and "fantastic artwork"; it's "a tad long" and "has some pretty scary moments in it", so it may be best for "those 10 and up" – "unless you want to spend money on therapy" for the kids later.

Splash
19 | 18 | 19 | 20

1984 | Directed by Ron Howard | With Tom Hanks, Daryl Hannah, John Candy | 111 minutes | Rated PG

More "sweet" than salty yet "not too mushy", this "fish-out-of-water love story" is an "engaging" comedy shored up by Hannah's starmaking splash as a "sexy mermaid" whom Hanks courts and transports to NYC; the fantasy is buoyed by a cast of "charming" characters "you can't help but like", including some "sterling support" from a "scene-stealing" Candy – so dive in and "enjoy."

Splendor in the Grass ✉
25 | 25 | 24 | 22

1961 | Directed by Elia Kazan | With Natalie Wood, Warren Beatty, Zohra Lampert | 124 minutes | Not Rated

There's "heartbreak" in the heartland as "yearning" breeds "teen angst" in this "bittersweet" romance set in pre-Depression Kansas; the very "young" and very "gorgeous" Wood and Beatty supply some "real acting" as a "modern Romeo and Juliet" driven to "wrenching" extremes in this drama of "stolen dreams" and "lost love" that makes some sob sisters "cry just thinking about it."

SpongeBob SquarePants Movie, The 16 | - | 15 | 18

2004 | Directed by Stephen Hillenburg | Animated | 90 minutes | Rated PG

Cable TV's favorite "little yellow sea creature" soaks up the silver-screen spotlight in this "cheerfully cheesy" cartoon, wherein the hero and a "starfish pal" set out on a "humorous" underwater "road trip"; though guaranteed to make the kiddies "happy as a clam", it fares less swimmingly with grown-ups, in spite of a "cute cameo" by David Hasselhoff.

Spy Game 19 | 21 | 19 | 19

2001 | Directed by Tony Scott | With Robert Redford, Brad Pitt | 126 minutes | Rated R

With a "creative" but "complicated" plot that flashes "backward, forward and sideways" in its pursuit of "clever cat-and-mouse" action, this "solid" espionage thriller maintains a "hypnotic" grip on you "until the last fulfilling bit"; Redford and Pitt "shine" as a CIA mentor-protégé team – "plus they're easy on the eyes, which never hurts."

Spy Kids 19 | 17 | 19 | 21

2001 | Directed by Robert Rodriguez | With Antonio Banderas, Carla Gugino, Alexa Vega, Daryl Sabara | 88 minutes | Rated PG

Look for "good clean spy fun" in this "appealing" family adventure that's "empowering for kids" in its story of a bungling parental pair of agents "called back into duty", leaving it up to their "cute" tykes to "save the world"; there are plenty of "cool gadgets", so grown-ups might not want to "check their brain" after all.

Spy Kids 2: Island of Lost Dreams 16 | 15 | 16 | 20

2002 | Directed by Robert Rodriguez | With Antonio Banderas, Carla Gugino, Alexa Vega, Daryl Sabara | 100 minutes | Rated PG

An eye-popping parade of "dazzling effects" and "great gizmos" heralds the return of pint-size secret agent sibs Carmen and Juni as they once again try to save the world" in this "longer, louder" sci-fi sequel; if the consensus is it's "not nearly as good as the first", some still spy a "decent way to keep the kids quiet."

Spy Who Came in from the Cold, The ● 25 | 26 | 25 | 22

1965 | Directed by Martin Ritt | With Richard Burton, Claire Bloom, Oskar Werner | 112 minutes | Not Rated

Spying isn't pretty" in this "very cold look at the Cold War" adapted from John Le Carré's "first major success"; Burton's "at his peak" as a "brooding" British secret agent who defects to East Germany, and his "brilliant" work is backed up by "taut direction" and a "stark", "realistic" screenplay – "James Bond, this is not."

Spy Who Loved Me, The 21 | 17 | 20 | 22

1977 | Directed by Lewis Gilbert | With Roger Moore, Barbara Bach, Richard Kiel | 125 minutes | Rated PG

When it comes to "popcorn" action fare, "nobody does it better" than Mr. Bond, and this is "one of Moore's better outings" as 007 pursues a nuclear blackmailer and fights off the "awesome", metal-mouthed nemesis Jaws; if by now the scripts are "superfluous", it's still the leading franchise for "fast cars, fast women" in "clingy clothes" ("oh, James!") and "lots of things that blow up."

Squid and the Whale, The
21 | 25 | 20 | 20

2005 | Directed by Noah Baumbach | With Jeff Daniels, Laura Linney, Jessie Eisenberg, Owen Kline | 81 minutes | Rated R

"Ultra-real" performances (led by Daniels' "brilliant" turn as a "pompous", has-been writer) propel this "sharply observed" study of a "dysfunctional", "not completely likable" family "riven by divorce"; though "often very funny" in its take on "self-involved parenting" and its "effects on the kids", it's painted with "uncomfortably realistic" strokes – some outright "bizarre" – that "ring so true."

Stage Beauty
20 | 24 | 21 | 22

2004 | Directed by Richard Eyre | With Billy Crudup, Claire Danes, Rupert Everett | 106 minutes | Rated R

"Exploring gender role reversal" among 17th-century "Shakespearean actors", this "potent" period drama recounts a "fascinating era in theater history" when men traditionally played women onstage – until a wardrobe lass inadvertently becomes the "first English actress"; "beautifully produced" but "sadly overlooked", it's gaining a cult reputation as the "new *Shakespeare in Love*."

☒ Stagecoach ◐
27 | 24 | 26 | 25

1939 | Directed by John Ford | With John Wayne, Claire Trevor, John Carradine | 96 minutes | Not Rated

"Wayne's grand entrance" alone immortalizes this "archetypal" Ford Western about a group of stock frontier types "traversing hostile Indian territory" by rickety stage; featuring the young Duke in his "breakthrough role" as a fugitive convict, it rolls along on "great dialogue" and "well-acted" ensemble work interrupted by "viscerally exciting" action scenes, making it the "classic source" of countless tumbleweed "clichés."

Stage Door ◐
25 | 26 | 23 | 22

1937 | Directed by Gregory La Cava | With Katharine Hepburn, Ginger Rogers, Gail Patrick, Lucille Ball | 92 minutes | Not Rated

A "chick flick for the old guard", this "witty" dramedy is set in a boarding house occupied by "scrappy wannabe actresses" who "live and die for the theatuh"; its "nearly all-female" cast (a "who's who of stars" of the time) is "unusually cohesive", helped along by a "multifaceted screenplay" peppered with plenty of "snappy" patter; most legendary line: Kate's "the calla lilies are in bloom again . . ."

☒ Stalag 17 ✉◐
27 | 26 | 27 | 24

1953 | Directed by Billy Wilder | With William Holden, Don Taylor, Otto Preminger | 120 minutes | Not Rated

Wilder's "wonderful" adaptation of the stage drama supplies the "intrigue" of a "psychological thriller" with some comic relief in this story starring the "properly Oscarized" Holden as a "cynical prisoner" in a WWII POW camp who's "suspected of being a German spy"; thanks to "tremendous acting" and "tense" plotting that "keeps you guessing until the end", this study of military "camaraderie" and "mob judgment" is "not to be missed."

	OVERALL	ACTING	STORY	PROD.

Stand and Deliver
20 22 22 17

1988 | Directed by Ramon Menendez | With Edward James Olmos, Lou Diamond Phillips | 102 minutes | Rated PG

Giving credit to the "common man", this "inspirational" drama presents Olmos as the real-life Jaime Escalante, a "math teacher who makes a difference" in a tough East LA school by tutoring a class of bad-attitude kids; tough graders say this "good fun flick" also scores as an "underrated" self-esteem booster.

Stand by Me
24 23 25 23

1986 | Directed by Rob Reiner | With Wil Wheaton, River Phoenix, Corey Feldman | 89 minutes | Rated R

This "wholesome" "coming-of-ager" focuses on preadolescent "best buddies" in '50s Oregon who set out "in search of a missing boy", bonding in the face of various perils and learning about the "real stuff" along the way; a platform for "young talent", it carries a "strong message" about the "struggle to grow up."

Stardust
22 21 22 23

2007 | Directed by Matthew Vaughn | With Charlie Cox, Sienna Miller, Claire Danes, Michelle Pfeiffer, Robert De Niro | 127 minutes | Rated PG-13

A "grown-up fairy tale" in *The Princess Bride* vein, this "well-done" sci-fi/fantasy about a hero's journey to a "magical land" to "prove his love for a woman" mixes "irreverent humor" with a "stunning" production to make for "entertaining" moviegoing; there are lots of "great actors" aboard, but the biggest "hoot" is De Niro's "cross-dressing pirate."

Stardust Memories ◗
19 20 18 19

1980 | Directed by Woody Allen | With Woody Allen, Charlotte Rampling, Jessica Harper | 91 minutes | Rated PG

In what could be "his most autobiographical role ever", Allen plays a film director at a weekend retreat badgered by fans "who miss his early, funny pictures" and dismiss his later, more serious work; maybe it's "not his best by a long shot" – antis call it an "explosion of bile aimed at the audience" – although his "tribute to his idols" Bergman and Fellini is "sweet" enough.

Star 80
16 16 16 15

1983 | Directed by Bob Fosse | With Mariel Hemingway, Eric Roberts, Cliff Robertson | 100 minutes | Rated R

Bob Fosse's last film depicts the "tragic true story" of *Playboy* centerfold Dorothy Stratten, an "angelic beauty" bound for "superstardom" whose growing popularity leaves her "boorish husband stewing with resentment"; it's a "sad, gruesome" look at one man's "obsession", but ultimately such an "emotional drain" that many find it too "disturbing" to watch.

Stargate
18 17 20 22

1994 | Directed by Roland Emmerich | With Kurt Russell, James Spader, Jaye Davidson | 121 minutes | Rated PG-13

"Egypt" meets "outer space" in this "interesting" sci-fi flicker about a "portal" discovered in the desert that's an intergalactic wormhole to a "distant world" enslaved by the "powerful" Egyptian god Ra; the ensuing "face-off" is long on "thoughtless action" and "terrific" pyrotechnics but "never delivers" on the "great premise."

⚡ Star Is Born, A | 25 | 26 | 26 | 26 |

1954 | Directed by George Cukor | With Judy Garland, James Mason, Jack Carson | 181 minutes | Rated PG

"Forget the other versions": this "heartbreaking" musical drama revisits the Tinseltown parable of fickle celebrity fortunes with the "best Judy ever", showcasing her "true range" as the nobody whose rise to fame is paralleled by her big-name hubby's descent; whether laughing, singing or "turning on the waterworks", the "mesmerizing" Garland gives the "performance of her life", leaving loyalists to lament the Oscar "that got away."

Starman | 19 | 20 | 21 | 17 |

1984 | Directed by John Carpenter | With Jeff Bridges, Karen Allen, Richard Jaeckel | 115 minutes | Rated PG-13

A spacecraft falls to Earth and an "alien and earthling fall for each other" in this "overlooked date movie"; a "first-rate" Bridges plays an "E.T. in human form" who inhabits the bod of Allen's recently deceased husband, leading to "sentimental" getting-to-know-you sessions and a "romantic" road trip that draws to a "sweet" if "predictable" conclusion.

Starship Troopers | 15 | 9 | 15 | 21 |

1997 | Directed by Paul Verhoeven | With Casper Van Dien, Dina Meyer, Denise Richards | 129 minutes | Rated R

"Robert A. Heinlein's classic yarn" about an invasion of "big bad bugs" gets a "campy" rendering in this "full-throttle sci-fi" flick loaded with "amazing" big-budget F/X; while cynics nix the "appallingly cheesy acting", "trite" plot and "pointless violence", "nonstop action" fans counter that this "critique of militarism" isn't "meant to be taken seriously."

Starsky & Hutch | 14 | 15 | 12 | 16 |

2004 | Directed by Todd Phillips | With Ben Stiller, Owen Wilson, Snoop Dogg | 101 minutes | Rated PG-13

Proving yet again that it can't "leave the original alone", Hollywood un-retires Bay City's "metrosexual" five-o's (and their "fun-to-look-at" Ford Torino) and sends them after a white-collar criminal in this "schlocky" spoof of the '70s TV series; P.S. forget Stiller and Wilson – Snoop Dogg as Huggy Bear is the "best casting" choice.

Starting Over | 20 | 20 | 20 | 20 |

1979 | Directed by Alan J. Pakula | With Burt Reynolds, Jill Clayburgh, Candice Bergen | 105 minutes | Rated R

An "appealing" Reynolds "proves he can act" in this "enjoyable" romantic comedy depicting a middle-aged divorcé's misadventures in born-again bachelorhood ("valium", anyone?); the "good casting" extends to both Clayburgh and Bergen, while the picture's overarching optimism "convinces you there's someone out there for everyone."

Star Trek: The Motion Picture | 14 | 13 | 13 | 19 |

1979 | Directed by Robert Wise | With William Shatner, Leonard Nimoy, DeForest Kelley, Stephen Collins | 132 minutes | Rated PG

With the original cast aboard, this sci-fi spin-off marks the TV series' "transition to the big screen", giving "die-hard Trekkies" "lots to think about" as the *Enterprise* crew copes with a mysterious cloud of cosmic energy; foes find the going so "slow" it "should be retitled" the "motionless picture", even if it "paved the way" for more successful treks.

	OVERALL	ACTING	STORY	PROD.

Star Trek II: The Wrath of Khan

23 | 19 | 24 | 24

1982 | Directed by Nicholas Meyer | With William Shatner, Leonard Nimoy, DeForest Kelley, Ricardo Montalban | 113 minutes | Rated PG

"Best villain + best story" = "best *Trek*": so say supporters of this "ripping" sci-fi sequel that hits warp speed when "scenery-chewing" outer-space outlaw Khan hijacks a starship and goes gunning for Admiral Kirk, back for yet one more mission with his familiar Starfleet crew; it offers all the "overblown acting" and "heart of the original", and the windup with Spock on the spot has enough "emotional punch" to "make a Trekkie out of anyone."

Star Trek IV: The Voyage Home

21 | 17 | 21 | 23

1986 | Directed by Leonard Nimoy | With William Shatner, Leonard Nimoy, DeForest Kelley | 119 minutes | Rated PG

The final frontiersmen send us a "message from the future" in this "easygoing", "most accessible" of the sci-fi spin-offs, with Kirk and company "letting their hair down" to indulge in "tongue-in-cheek" inter-play as they travel backward through the centuries to join a modern-day "scientific babe" in a mission to "save the whales"; it's a little "light-weight" despite the "timely ecological" theme, but as with the other "even-numbered" entries in the series, the voyaging is "not at all bad."

⊘ Star Wars

28 | 22 | 28 | 29

(aka Star Wars Episode IV: A New Hope)

1977 | Directed by George Lucas | With Mark Hamill, Harrison Ford, Carrie Fisher | 121 minutes | Rated PG

Lucas' "Force is strong" in this "visionary" blockbuster, the "quantum leap" that "redefined sci-fi" and established a "dynasty" by locating the "universal" in a "galaxy far, far away", where "original" "critters" and "futuristic samurais" side with a put-upon princess against an evil Empire; building to a "black hats/white hats" showdown, it's an "entertaining" mix of "modern myth" and "thrill-and-a-half" FX; subsequent space operas "can't touch" it.

Star Wars Episode I: The Phantom Menace

18 | 16 | 18 | 26

1999 | Directed by George Lucas | With Liam Neeson, Ewan McGregor, Natalie Portman | 133 minutes | Rated PG

"After all the hype", here's the "good-looking" sci-fi prequel, which finds an earlier Jedi generation aiding a "planet under blockade" while setting some backstories straight as Obi-Wan and Skywalker père are groomed for knighthood; though denounced as a "giant misstep" that makes do with "so-so" storytelling while "pandering to the kiddies" with CGI "overkill" and "irritating" cast members ("why Jar Jar?"), "it's still *Star Wars*", and many "escapists" welcome it as a "worthy addition."

Star Wars Episode II: Attack of the Clones

17 | 13 | 16 | 24

2002 | Directed by George Lucas | With Hayden Christensen, Ewan McGregor, Natalie Portman | 143 minutes | Rated PG

Unmoved by thunderous legions jeering the "magic is missing", franchise faithfuls stand by this "impressive" second act of the prequel trilogy, lauding its "mesmerizing visuals", "foreboding" moods and "many-questions-answered" plotlines; of course, even diehards don't deny Anakin and Padmé's courtship is a "cardboard"-acted, "dire attempt at romance", yet it's all "worthwhile" for the "showstopping" scene when Yoda fights.

Star Wars Episode III: Revenge of the Sith | 23 | 16 | 23 | 28 |

2005 | Directed by George Lucas | With Hayden Christensen, Ewan McGregor, Ian McDiarmid | 140 minutes | Rated PG-13

"Even though you know" how it wraps up, seeing the "missing pieces of the puzzle" fall into place brings "closure" to a generation of fans who've waited "20-plus years" to learn how Jedi "badass" Anakin Skywalker falls from grace and "becomes Darth Vader" in this "very dark", "epic conclusion" to the beloved space saga; piling on more "dazzling" FX and "campy acting" than ever, it's the "stronger story" this time 'round ("it took Lucas three tries") that explains why it's widely considered "the best of the prequels."

☑ Star Wars Episode V: The Empire Strikes Back | 26 | 21 | 26 | 28 |

1980 | Directed by Irvin Kershner | With Mark Hamill, Harrison Ford, Carrie Fisher, Billy Dee Williams | 124 minutes | Rated PG

The "darkest of the Star Wars series", this "worthy" first sequel features more "depth" in its characterizations and the "best storyline so far", "revealing many important secrets" as the "cosmic struggle continues"; "blissfully free of wooden dialogue", it might be the "most adult" of the "original trilogy", while that open-ended "cliff-hanger" of a finale makes for a suitably "spectacular" windup.

Star Wars Episode VI: Return of the Jedi | 24 | 20 | 23 | 28 |

1983 | Directed by Richard Marquand | With Mark Hamill, Harrison Ford, Carrie Fisher, Billy Dee Williams | 134 minutes | Rated PG

Either a "worthy sequel" or "leftovers", this "wrap-up" episode of the Star Wars original trilogy finds the now-classic cast "comfortable in their roles", mugging their way through a "patented good-wins-over-evil storyline" with ample space for "cool special effects" and an "amazing final battle"; loyalists say the force is with it, but skeptics see a "weak entry" overrun with "cute, furry Ewoks", foreshadowing "toy tie-ins" and the "beginnings of Jar Jar."

Station Agent, The | 25 | 27 | 23 | 23 |

2003 | Directed by Thomas McCarthy | With Peter Dinklage, Patricia Clarkson, Bobby Cannavale | 88 minutes | Rated R

"Putting the Q in quirky and the S in subtle", this "quiet little film" also puts the I in indie with its "arty" but "restrained" portrayal of the unlikely friendship between three "eccentrics" in rural New Jersey; while "not much happens" in this "meandering character study", a "great ensemble performance" (especially little person Dinklage's "charisma"-laden turn as a train enthusiast) makes for a "funny", "poignant" flick that "never falls off the track."

Steel Magnolias | 24 | 25 | 24 | 23 |

1989 | Directed by Herbert Ross | With Sally Field, Dolly Parton, Shirley MacLaine, Daryl Hannah | 117 minutes | Rated PG

Break out the "Kleenex" for this "estrogen"-soaked drama, a "major tearjerker" smothered in "Southern-fried flavor", dashed with "laughs" and played "to the hilt and then some" by a "talented" bunch of "adorable" all-star "belles"; the story of "best girlfriends" in a Looziana beauty parlor bonding through "thick and thin", it's "captivating", "well-made" and "weepy" enough to qualify as the "ultimate chick flick."

St. Elmo's Fire | 17 | 17 | 17 | 17 |

1985 | Directed by Joel Schumacher | With Rob Lowe, Demi Moore, Andrew McCarthy, Judd Nelson | 110 minutes | Rated R
This "nostalgic" '80s "cult classic" starring the "Brat Pack at its finest" addresses "issues faced in life just after college"; sure, there are some "weak spots" and a few moments that are now "unintentionally hilarious", but overall, it remains a "favorite" "coming-of-age flick", like *The Big Chill* for Generation X.

Stepford Wives, The | 12 | 15 | 12 | 15 |

2004 | Directed by Frank Oz | With Nicole Kidman, Matthew Broderick, Bette Midler, Glenn Close | 93 minutes | Rated PG-13
Expect "all kitsch and no fright" in this "high-camp" rendition of Ira Levin's "grim" horror/sci-fi novel about an "idyllic" town whose "June Cleaver"-esque housewives are in fact "creepy" robots; no match for the "much better" 1975 version, it's altogether a "waste of a great cast" and, "like the suburbs, bland, bland, bland."

Stepmom | 19 | 22 | 19 | 19 |

1998 | Directed by Chris Columbus | With Julia Roberts, Susan Sarandon, Ed Harris | 124 minutes | Rated PG-13
"Get out the tissues" – "you'll need 'em" – for this "emotional" family drama tackling the "real-life" challenges posed by "divorce, illness and forgiveness"; examining the "complex" relationship between a "Stella Dallas–like mother" and the "pretty young thing" who "snagged her husband", it "jerks those tears" by depicting the "worst fear" for a parent in splitsville: "that someone else will raise the children."

◿ Sting, The ✉ | 27 | 26 | 27 | 26 |

1973 | Directed by George Roy Hill | With Paul Newman, Robert Redford, Robert Shaw | 129 minutes | Rated PG
"Deftly" charming its way to Best Picture honors, this "classy" comedy "caper" "succeeds in spades" as a "likable", "fast-paced" vehicle for Newman and Redford, radiating "great rapport" as a pair of grifters playing a gangster for a sucker in Depression-era Chicago; a "funny, intriguing" "period piece" set to "elegant" Joplin rags, it raises the "suspense" stakes with "masterful" plotting and a final "zinger" that saves the sharpest sting for last.

Stir Crazy | 20 | 21 | 19 | 18 |

1980 | Directed by Sidney Poitier | With Gene Wilder, Richard Pryor, JoBeth Williams | 111 minutes | Rated R
The second "outing from the estimable team of Pryor and Wilder" (after the successful *Silver Streak*), this buddy comedy concerns two wrongly imprisoned jokers out to clear their names; though some consider it somewhat downhill from the comedians' first matchup, it was popular enough to spawn a TV sitcom.

Stop Making Sense | 25 | - | 14 | 24 |

1984 | Directed by Jonathan Demme | Documentary | With Talking Heads | 88 minutes | Not Rated
"Turn up the sound", because Demme's "alterna-rockumentary" presents a "superior" show from new wave faves the Talking Heads in

their "heyday", burning down the house with "energetic music"; the flick proves the "exception to the rule that concerts don't translate" to the big screen and finds bandleader "David Byrne in top form", "swaying" in his trademark "enormous suit."

Story of Adele H., The 🄵

24 | 26 | 24 | 24

1975 | Directed by François Truffaut | With Isabelle Adjani, Bruce Robinson | 96 minutes | Rated PG

"Unrequited love" turns into "single-minded obsession" and then to flat-out "stalking" in this "intense" psychological drama from François Truffaut, the story of a 19th-century woman (based on "Victor Hugo's actual daughter") infatuated with one "cruelly oblivious man"; in the Oscar-nominated performance that made her an international star, Adjani is "near perfect", alternately "radiant, commanding and heartbreaking."

Straight Story, The

24 | 27 | 22 | 21

1999 | Directed by David Lynch | With Richard Farnsworth, Sissy Spacek, Jane Galloway | 111 minutes | Rated G

The "only G-rated" effort from malaise-meister Lynch goes straight for the heart in this "odd" but "compelling" drama of a septuagenarian "who rides his John Deere" power mower cross country to mend fences with his infirm brother; this "interesting" "character study" is polished into an "absolute gem" by "brilliant performances" and a "lovely" meditation on the "ending of the life cycle", but be warned that "travel by tractor" can be a "slow" ride.

Strange Days

17 | 18 | 19 | 19

1995 | Directed by Kathryn Bigelow | With Ralph Fiennes, Angela Bassett, Juliette Lewis | 145 minutes | Rated R

"Virtual reality devices" containing people's "recorded memories and emotions" take "voyeurism" to "intense" extremes in this "original" if "overlooked" sci-fi thriller set in the "frightening future"; led by an "angst-ridden" Fiennes as an ex-cop "trying to solve a murder", it's a "pretty cool" trip that touches upon some "interesting themes", including "drugs, love and loss."

🆉 Strangers on a Train ◑

26 | 24 | 27 | 24

1951 | Directed by Alfred Hitchcock | With Farley Granger, Robert Walker, Ruth Roman | 101 minutes | Rated PG

Be careful "what you wish for" is the underlying theme of this "fascinating", "forward-thinking" Hitchcock thriller wherein a flippant "promise to exchange murders" spirals out of control into a "dark tale of unwanted bedfellows"; "spine-tingler" aficionados single out Walker's "chilling" turn as a "wacko" mama's boy, and among many "tense moments", the "carousel finale still amazes."

Stranger Than Fiction

21 | 23 | 23 | 21

2006 | Directed by Marc Forster | With Will Ferrell, Emma Thompson, Maggie Gyllenhaal, Dustin Hoffman | 113 minutes | Rated PG-13

The "last thing you'd expect" from Ferrell, this "sharp", "surprisingly affecting" dramedy demonstrates the comic's "serious acting chops" ("who knew?") in its "postmodern" story of a man who discovers that he's really a character in a novel; seeing Will "hold his own" "minus the usual stupidity" is as "eye-opening" as the strangely "engaging" premise.

Straw Dogs
21 | 25 | 21 | 21

1971 | Directed by Sam Peckinpah | With Dustin Hoffman, Susan George, David Warner | 113 minutes | Rated R

Expect "unsettling" carnage, Sam Peckinpah–style, in this "nightmare" thriller, a "beautifully acted" demonstration of "man's inhumanity to man" with Hoffman as a math professor in small-town Britain whose "entire character changes" after he's "pushed to the edge" by local thugs; it's hailed as "gut-wrenching" but "great", though many are hounded by the "almost unwatchable violence."

☑ Streetcar Named Desire, A ✉◑
27 | 28 | 26 | 25

1951 | Directed by Elia Kazan | With Vivien Leigh, Marlon Brando, Kim Hunter, Karl Malden | 125 minutes | Rated PG

Destined to "hold great forever", this "brilliant interpretation" of Tennessee Williams' "overwrought classic" showcases the "amazing" Brando "exploding onto the scene" ("hey, *Stella!*") in the "legendary" role of a "rugged" slob who engages in "shattering" "psychological warfare" with his delicate sister-in-law (the "wonderful", "so-sad" Leigh); fans say it's worth watching if only for a look at the "virile" Marlon when he was "still acting."

Strictly Ballroom
23 | 21 | 23 | 22

1993 | Directed by Baz Luhrmann | With Paul Mercurio, Tara Morice, Bill Hunter | 94 minutes | Rated PG

This "quirky" dose of "flash and flamenco" is a surprise charmer of a romantic comedy pairing a "hot" Aussie hoofer with an "ugly duckling", who proceed to shake up a dance championship; a "delightful send-up" of the "viciousness of the competitive ballroom circuit", it amuses with "well-executed" moves, even if onlookers "kinda know" how the strictly by-the-numbers story will turn out.

Stripes
21 | 18 | 18 | 18

1981 | Directed by Ivan Reitman | With Bill Murray, Harold Ramis, Warren Oates | 101 minutes | Rated R

"Red-blooded guys" are quick to salute this "service comedy" starring "cynical" Murray as a goldbricking civilian who joins the Army and endures basic training with the idea that it's "all about laughs"; with a "strong comic cast" and gags ranging from the truly "hilarious" to the sublimely "ridiculous", it ranks as "one of the funniest" in its class, though deserters say it "bogs down" midway and caution it's "no *Caddyshack*" – and "that's a fact, Jack."

Stuart Little
19 | 18 | 19 | 21

1999 | Directed by Rob Minkoff | With Geena Davis, Hugh Laurie, Jonathan Lipnicki | 84 minutes | Rated PG

Adapted from E.B. White's "sweet" children's classic, this "cute production" craftily combines "amazing animation" and live action to tell the tale of an "adorable" "talking mouse" who's adopted by humans only to be claimed by a couple of rodents posing as his "birth parents"; most can't help "lovin'" its "warm" "poignancy", though a few whiskers twitch at the "piffle"-ridden plot that "mangles the original" into a flick "only a little kid could like."

Stuart Little 2

19 | 18 | 18 | 22

2002 | Directed by Rob Minkoff | With Geena Davis, Hugh Laurie, Jonathan Lipnicki | 78 minutes | Rated PG

From the continuing chronicles of mice and men comes this "winner" of a sequel to E.B. White's classic tale, marking a respectable reprise for the "adorable" and "wonderfully animated" titular rodent as he teams up with a feathered friend and "tackles a new adventure"; though it's probably better suited for "grandkids" than grown-ups, keep a hawk's eye peeled for the "adult humor tucked in the dialogue."

Stunt Man, The

22 | 25 | 22 | 21

1980 | Directed by Richard Rush | With Peter O'Toole, Steve Railsback, Barbara Hershey | 131 minutes | Rated R

"Expect the unexpected" in this "entirely original" "Hollywood insider" story about an escaped convict who "strikes a devil's bargain" with a "manipulative" film director to masquerade as a stunt man on a movie shoot; given the "satirical", "red herring"–filled script and an "over-the-top", "eat-the-scenery" turn by O'Toole, many marvel at the picture's "overlooked", "underrated" status.

Sudden Impact

20 | 19 | 18 | 20

1983 | Directed by Clint Eastwood | With Clint Eastwood, Sondra Locke, Pat Hingle | 117 minutes | Rated R

"Go ahead, make my sequel" growl Dirty Harry devotees as the series' fourth outing brings the "usual sadism, sexism and action" to a California coastal town, now with a "revenge angle" as Eastwood and ladylove Locke pay back the "punks" who traumatized her; sure, it boasts the "film line of the decade" – "make my day" – but otherwise its impact is merely "standard."

Suddenly, Last Summer ◑

24 | 26 | 23 | 22

1959 | Directed by Joseph L. Mankiewicz | With Elizabeth Taylor, Katharine Hepburn, Montgomery Clift | 114 minutes | Not Rated

Alright, this "sensational" Tennessee Williams "stunner" about a wealthy woman scheming to have her niece lobotomized in order to "silence her" is "a bit much" – and a little too "murky", "talky" and "icky" for the squeamish; but fans flip for its "baroque excess", Liz's "tight white bathing suit", the cast's "fine chewing of the scenery" and, most of all, that truly "shocking ending."

Sugarland Express, The

18 | 20 | 18 | 18

1974 | Directed by Steven Spielberg | With Goldie Hawn, William Atherton, Ben Johnson, Michael Sacks | 110 minutes | Rated PG

"Spielberg's first movie" ("before he went CGI mad") is this "little-seen" true story that "concentrates on characters instead of effects" and even has a "downer ending"; it stars a "young" Goldie, who "runs away with the picture" as a "not-so-nice" gal who springs her hubby from prison in order to "reclaim their baby from foster care."

⛏ Sullivan's Travels ◑

27 | 25 | 26 | 25

1941 | Directed by Preston Sturges | With Joel McCrea, Veronica Lake, William Demarest | 90 minutes | Not Rated

A Depression-era movie director suffering from a "mid-career crisis" "develops a conscience" and decides to shoot a truly "serious film" in this "profound comedy" from Preston Sturges; the result is a delight fully "inspirational" flick that not only has "something important to say about America", but also is one of the "best pictures ever made about Hollywood – even though it hardly takes place there."

Summer of '42

	OVERALL	ACTING	STORY	PROD.
	21	19	23	19

1971 | Directed by Robert Mulligan | With Jennifer O'Neill, Gary Grimes, Jerry Houser | 103 minutes | Rated R

Sentimental yearning and raging hormones drive this "coming-of-age" romance, which finds a trio of "pubescent boys" spending the first summer after Pearl Harbor goofing off until one of them hooks up with a young soldier's widow; the combination of "humor" and "heartbreak" is also a "moving" remembrance of a "time of war", while the Oscar-winning score alone is "worth the price of admission."

Summertime

	23	26	23	24

1955 | Directed by David Lean | With Katharine Hepburn, Rossano Brazzi | 100 minutes | Not Rated

"Venice is the star" of this "bittersweet" love story about an "aging spinster" who "experiences *amore*" while on holiday in "timeless" Italy; there's "not a false note" in Kate's "delicious" performance (though holdouts insist she's "too dynamic" to be an old maid), played against "stunning locales" and a "swooningly romantic score."

Sum of All Fears, The

	16	15	18	19

2002 | Directed by Phil Alden Robinson | With Ben Affleck, Morgan Freeman, James Cromwell | 124 minutes | Rated PG-13

"Neo-Nazis" seize a nuclear warhead and restart the Cold War in this "average" suspense thriller that boasts "good production values" but is certainly "not the best of the series" based on the Tom Clancy bestsellers; Affleck's "laughable" as Jack Ryan ("Harrison Ford he ain't"), and the "goodbye-Baltimore" finale "so implausible" that many advise "read the book, it's much better."

Sunday Bloody Sunday

	24	26	24	22

1971 | Directed by John Schlesinger | With Peter Finch, Glenda Jackson, Murray Head | 110 minutes | Rated R

"Very adult for its time", this "complex" film about "a man, a woman and their shared male lover" is "still very adult", starting with its "unflinching look at homosexuality"; Oscar nominees Jackson and Finch are "unforgettable" as "lost souls in the modern world" on the opposite sides of this "love triangle", while a "literate" script and "flawless" direction make this "groundbreaking" work "as relevant today as it was then."

☑ Sunset Boulevard ⊠◑

	28	28	27	27

1950 | Directed by Billy Wilder | With William Holden, Gloria Swanson, Erich Von Stroheim | 110 minutes | Not Rated

"Some of the greatest dialogue ever" (most famously, "I'm ready for my close-up, Mr. DeMille") graces this hybrid of "Gothic" and "film noir", a "scabrous take on Hollywood" from the standpoint of a "struggling screenwriter" trying to "resurrect the career of a silent movie star" who's "not exactly in touch with reality"; given Wilder's "acerbic" direction, an "'in'-joke"-laced script and "pitch-perfect" performances from a "larger-than-life Swanson" and "hunky Holden", "who needs a musical version?"

Sunshine Boys, The

1975 | Directed by Herbert Ross | With Walter Matthau, George Burns, Richard Benjamin | 111 minutes | Rated PG

The radiant screen rendition of Neil Simon's Broadway comedy presents Matthau and Burns (who reappears after decades offscreen and snags an Oscar) as a couple of crusty "vaudeville greats who must work together" on a TV reunion show, even though they're given to much bickering; the "funny story" makes for surefire yuks, but razzers report the act as a whole is "not so bright."

Sunshine State

2002 | Directed by John Sayles | With Edie Falco, Jane Alexander, Ralph Waite, Angela Bassett | 141 minutes | Rated PG-13

A "great ensemble cast" (notably the "terrific" Falco) is the bright ray of sunshine in this "thought provoking" "social drama" set in a moribund Florida community; devotees delight in the "ambitious script" that spins "lots of subplots" and leaves behind "untied loose ends", but detractors yawn "boring" and insist it's "not the best" effort from indie auteur Sayles.

Superbad

2007 | Directed by Greg Mottola | With Jonah Hill, Michael Cera, Christopher Mintz-Plasse, Seth Rogen | 114 minutes | Rated R

"Horny teen" comedies don't get much "raunchier" than this "out-there" flick following the adventures of "three high school nerds" out to score booze armed with a "fake ID"; fans dub it a "fall-down funny" "coming-of-age story for the 21st century" (comparisons to *Animal House* and *American Pie* abound), though cynics shrug "the title says it all"; P.S. Mintz-Plasse's portrayal of über-"geek" McLovin "steals the show."

Superman

1978 | Directed by Richard Donner | With Christopher Reeve, Margot Kidder, Gene Hackman | 143 minutes | Rated PG

"You'll really believe a man can fly" after a look at this "ahead-of-its-time" superhero fantasy, the "delightful", "campy" saga of a survivor from a doomed planet who grows up to be a "man of steel"; even if the "comic-book sensibility" is "a little silly" and the line readings "stiff", a super "heart shines through" as Reeve turns in the "definitive", "true-blue portrayal" of "all things good" – when he's not "sizing up telephone booths", that is.

Superman Returns

2006 | Directed by Bryan Singer | With Brandon Routh, Kate Bosworth, Kevin Spacey | 154 minutes | Rated PG-13

"New guy" Brandon Routh "fills the tights" in this "welcome" entry in the superhero series that recounts the "caped wonder's" long-delayed return to Metropolis; with "some amazing FX" and "nods to the earlier films", it's "not a bad reboot", even if the "wooden acting" and a story that "never really soars" make many "long for Christopher Reeve."

Super Size Me

2004 | Directed by Morgan Spurlock | Documentary | 96 minutes | Rated G

Near-"suicide by gluttony" is both "disturbing" and "funny" in this "crowd-pleasing documentary" wherein director/star Spurlock submits himself to an all-McDonald's diet for a full month; although "not the most researched study of fast food" and perhaps "lacking in nutritional substance", this "eye-opening, stomach-churning" "wake-up call" still might send you running for a "piece of fruit."

Suspect
20 | 21 | 22 | 19

1987 | Directed by Peter Yates | With Cher, Dennis Quaid, Liam Neeson | 121 minutes | Rated R

Cher's an ambitious public defender in this "courtroom thriller" about a high-level conspiracy involving a slick lobbyist, a dead Supreme Court justice and a deaf-and-dumb homeless man; though "predictable" and only "relatively involving" to the suspicious, others say it "keeps you wondering" until the "surprise ending."

Suspicion
25 | 26 | 25 | 25

1941 | Directed by Alfred Hitchcock | With Joan Fontaine, Cary Grant, Cedric Hardwicke, Nigel Bruce | 99 minutes | Not Rated

A "poor little rich girl" hooks up with a "potential murderer" in this "top Hitchcock" thriller starring an appropriately "menacing" Grant and a "wimpy" (but Oscar-winning) Fontaine; if some find the picture "a bit tentative" for the master of suspense (who was famously forced to "change the ending"), everyone agrees on its most unforgettable prop, the "scariest looking glass of milk in cinema history."

S.W.A.T.
15 | 15 | 15 | 18

2003 | Directed by Clark Johnson | With Samuel L. Jackson, Colin Farrell, Michelle Rodriguez, LL Cool J | 117 minutes | Rated PG-13

Hollywood's ever-profitable pairing of "guns and testosterone" is the trigger for this "muscle"-bound "peek into the life of a SWAT agent", a "generic" "guy flick" bulging with "badass" coppers and the usual "through-the-roof" action; factor in the plot's "telegraphed twists" and most prefer their "fond memories of the original TV series" over this "tired revival."

Sweeney Todd: The Demon Barber of Fleet Street
23 | 26 | 23 | 26

2007 | Directed by Tim Burton | With Johnny Depp, Helena Bonham Carter, Alan Rickman, Sacha Baron Cohen | 116 minutes | Rated R

"Johnny sings" in this "bloody good" musical that "goes for the jugular" in its "gruesome" story of a "homicidal" Victorian-era barber whose victims are ground into "yummy meat pies"; Depp is "superb as always", Bonham Carter less so, and their singing is "good-enough-but-don't-quit-your-day-job" quality, while Burton gives a "Gothic-excess" spin to Sondheim's "Broadway classic"; still, hair-splitters say all that "blood flowing by the gallon" can be "difficult to digest."

Sweet and Lowdown
21 | 24 | 20 | 21

1999 | Directed by Woody Allen | With Sean Penn, Uma Thurman, Anthony LaPaglia, Samantha Morton | 95 minutes | Rated PG-13

"Allen's love of jazz shines through" this "sweet-natured" dramedy, a "tribute to the great Django Reinhardt" with Penn giving his "usual intense performance" as a '30s-era "genius" guitarist leading a caddish offstage life; though it's "often overlooked", fans say this "nearly pitch-perfect" character study is "better than most" of Woody's recent opuses.

| | OVERALL | ACTING | STORY | PROD. |

Sweet Bird of Youth
24 | 28 | 24 | 23

1962 | Directed by Richard Brooks | With Paul Newman, Geraldine Page, Ed Begley, Shirley Knight | 120 minutes | Not Rated

A "young, gorgeous" Newman and "brilliant" Page ("what a combo!") reprise their stage roles in this cinematic adaptation of Tennessee Williams' play about a wannabe actor/gigolo and a faded, *Sunset Boulevard*–esque movie queen; sure, the story has been somewhat sanitized for the big screen, but most birdies still tweet "how sweet it is . . ."

Sweet Charity
20 | 21 | 19 | 23

1969 | Directed by Bob Fosse | With Shirley MacLaine, John McMartin, Chita Rivera | 149 minutes | Rated G

"Fosse's directorial debut" adapts a boffo Broadway show into an "exciting" musical featuring "MacLaine at her best" as a honey of a dance-hall damsel; look for "over-the-top production numbers" (especially Chita's raucous 'Big Spender') with "memorable staging" and "great tunes", and if the "quirky" story "drifts" when the music stops, charitable types cheer the players for "trying with all their might."

Sweet Hereafter, The
24 | 25 | 23 | 23

1997 | Directed by Atom Egoyan | With Ian Holm, Sarah Polley, Bruce Greenwood | 112 minutes | Rated R

"Haunting" in a "somber" way, this adaptation of Russell Banks' novel is a "beautifully shot", "terribly moving" drama about the "aftermath of a small-town tragedy" and the "dysfunction" it lays bare; the "terrific cast" led by Holm and Polley sees the burg's "delicate balance" upset when a group of children die in a bus crash, and the camera lends a "hypnotic" feel to material that's "smart" but "shrouded in sadness."

Sweet Home Alabama
17 | 18 | 16 | 18

2002 | Directed by Andy Tennant | With Reese Witherspoon, Josh Lucas, Patrick Dempsey | 108 minutes | Rated PG-13

A "country girl turned NYC fashionista" choosing between two suitors "returns to her roots" to make a decision in this "pass-me-the-popcorn" rom-com that's "good for a girls' night out"; while "America's Sweetheart" Reese just "couldn't be cuter", the "no-surprises", "by-the-book" script and "stereotypical", "culture-clash humor" aren't as sweet.

✦ Sweet Smell of Success, The ◐
27 | 28 | 26 | 26

1957 | Directed by Alexander Mackendrick | With Burt Lancaster, Tony Curtis, Martin Milner, Susan Harrison | 96 minutes | Not Rated

A "cookie full of arsenic" soaked in "hydrochloric acid", this extra-"tasty" morsel of "moody noir" unearths the "seamy side" of showbiz with its "cynical" "character study" of the "slimy" sorts working the "publicity end": a "superb" Lancaster as a "brutal", Winchell-esque columnist and the "unctuous Curtis" as his publicist toady; brace yourself for "crackling dialogue" and some "beyond beautiful" NYC "nighttime shots" in this "timeless" but never "more timely" picture.

Swept Away 🄵
24 | 24 | 24 | 24

1975 | Directed by Lina Wertmüller | With Mariangela Melato, Giancarlo Giannini | 116 minutes | Rated R

Stranding strangers on a "sunbaked isle" long "before the arrival of *Survivor*", Wertmüller's "unforgettable" Italian comedy "steams up the screen" as a snobbish socialite and a coarsely "expressive" boatman develop a "passionate" "love/hate relationship" alone on a Mediterranean cay; the satire "speaks volumes" as a "comment on class" and the "battle of the sexes", though there's a strong undercurrent of "violence" running beneath the beautiful "scenery."

Swimming Pool

	OVERALL	ACTING	STORY	PROD.
	20	23	20	20

2003 | Directed by François Ozon | With Charlotte Rampling, Ludivine Sagnier, Charles Dance | 103 minutes | Rated R

A burnt-out "older British woman" and a "slutty French girl" share a house in the south of France in this "plenty sexy" psychological thriller revealing "wonderfully uncomfortable" "generational differences"; while the "cryptic" climax leaves cynics perplexed – "could someone please explain the ending?" – boobs say it's "worth renting for the nudity" alone.

Swingers

23	22	23	20

1996 | Directed by Doug Liman | With Jon Favreau, Vince Vaughn, Heather Graham | 96 minutes | Rated R

"Hooking up in the '90s" gets a "hilarious" but "realistic" spin in this "hip, kinetic" buddy comedy-cum-"cultural phenomenon" about two single guys "finding their mojo" on the "Los Angeles dating scene"; it's "immensely funny", universally "accurate in defining a generation" and "'so money' that it spawned its very own vernacular."

☑ Swing Time ◑

26	23	20	26

1936 | Directed by George Stevens | With Fred Astaire, Ginger Rogers, Helen Broderick, Victor Moore | 103 minutes | Not Rated

The "easy grace" (and "winged feet") of Astaire and Rogers make for one "magical musical" in this "superb offering" that's voted "the best" of their pairings in this Survey; as usual, "there's not much of a story", but compensations include Fred's "sublime" 'Bojangles of Harlem' number and an "outstanding" Jerome Kern score, highlighted by the Oscar-winning 'The Way You Look Tonight.'

Swiss Family Robinson

23	20	24	23

1960 | Directed by Ken Annakin | With John Mills, Dorothy McGuire, James MacArthur, Tommy Kirk | 126 minutes | Rated G

"Action, romance, adventure and comedy" coexist amiably in this "absolute classic" from Walt Disney, a story of castaways shipwrecked on a tropical isle that "bears little resemblance to the novel"; an exercise in "good, clean fun", it's everything a "family movie should be", and that "terrific" treehouse set "still fascinates" smaller fry.

Swordfish

15	15	16	18

2001 | Directed by Dominic Sena | With John Travolta, Hugh Jackman, Halle Berry, Don Cheadle | 99 minutes | Rated R

A mother lode of "government secrets and money" tempts "swaggerin'" Travolta and his assembled "team of computer hackers" in this techno-thriller whose "explosive" opening quickly yields to more "predictable" fare; don't bother trying to figure out "who's a white hat or a black hat" and just savor the "highlight" of this flick: "Halle's topless scene."

Sylvia

16	20	16	19

2003 | Directed by Christine Jeffs | With Gwyneth Paltrow, Daniel Craig, Jared Harris, Blythe Danner | 110 minutes | Rated R

"Troubled writer" Sylvia Plath is the subject of this "relentlessly morose" biopic that gets somewhat of a lift from Paltrow's "strong yet fragile" title turn; although it's an "even-handed treatment of an uneven marriage", many find the story too "depressing and pointless", wondering if "her life is interesting enough" to "deserve its own movie."

Syriana
21 | 24 | 20 | 22

2005 | Directed by Stephen Gaghan | With Jeffrey Wright, George Clooney, Matt Damon | 126 minutes | Rated R

Holding up a "mirror to current events", this "tough-minded" drama about "the Middle East", "Big Oil" and the "dirty tricks" that bind them together weaves a "complex" (if at times "confusing") tapestry of "intersecting plotlines" loaded with "twists"; Clooney's "fabulous" performance as a "disillusioned CIA agent" is one good reason why this political "wake-up call" rewards "multiple viewings."

Tadpole
19 | 21 | 19 | 17

2002 | Directed by Gary Winick | With Aaron Stanford, Sigourney Weaver, Bebe Neuwirth, John Ritter | 78 minutes | Rated PG-13

"Quirky" characters found "only in New York" populate this "witty" indie comedy about a "precocious" prep-schooler who "has a thing for his stepmother"; cynics nix the rather "creepy" premise and the low-budget, "film-school-project" vibe, but agree that Neuwirth's turn as a 40-year-old "guilt-free seductress" is a "most memorable" bonus.

Take the Money and Run
21 | 18 | 21 | 17

1969 | Directed by Woody Allen | With Woody Allen, Janet Margolin, Marcel Hillaire | 85 minutes | Rated R

Woody's "first full-fledged feature" wings it with "pure slapstick" and "typical" self-deprecating shtick, depicting the escapades of a "hopeless nerd bank robber" into a phony documentary that's "basically a series of blackouts and sketches"; though a bit "threadbare" in between the "patches of brilliance", it packs in enough "anarchy and whimsy" to foretell things to come.

Talented Mr. Ripley, The
18 | 21 | 19 | 21

1999 | Directed by Anthony Minghella | With Matt Damon, Jude Law, Gwyneth Paltrow, Cate Blanchett | 139 minutes | Rated R

A "lush thriller of mistaken identity" set in '50s Europe, this "unsettling", "underrated" study of a murderous "schmuck-turned-socialite" stars Damon as the "slippery" title character (in a performance that's either "unnervingly good" or totally "botched"); while the "disturbing storyline" played out against "spectacular scenery" enthralls many, critics see little talent in its "lack of warmth" and way-"too-long" running time.

☑ Talk to Her ✉ 🄵
26 | 26 | 26 | 25

2002 | Directed by Pedro Almodóvar | With Javier Cámara, Darío Grandinetti, Leonor Watling | 112 minutes | Rated R

"Don't think about it too much and it will captivate you" advise fans of this "brilliant piece of art" by the "risk-taking" Almodóvar, a "haunting", "highly original" drama, comedy and mystery all in one" about "two women who have fallen into comas and the men who love them"; a "wonderful cast" tackles a "provocative" "multilayered storyline" that "allows fantasy to play with reality" – "finally, a film for mature audiences!"

Talladega Nights: The Ballad of Ricky Bobby | 15 | 16 | 14 | 17 |

2006 | Directed by Adam McKay | With Will Ferrell, John C. Reilly, Sacha Baron Cohen | 108 minutes | Rated PG-13

NASCAR and all the "stereotypes of redneck Middle America" get a "dopey" send-up in this "lowbrow comedy" as "Ferrell brings on the laughs" playing an American racer challenged by a "French Grand Prix driver"; friends of Will lap up the "mindless hilarity", but others sigh the "infantile shtick" "drags on and on."

Taps | 20 | 22 | 21 | 19 |

1981 | Directed by Harold Becker | With George C. Scott, Timothy Hutton, Ronny Cox, Sean Penn, Tom Cruise | 126 minutes | Rated PG

"*Lord of the Flies* meets *Dead Poets Society*" in this "powerful" feature dubbed the "ultimate military academy drama" for its "plausible" depiction of a soon-to-close school's armed takeover by a platoon of "punchy" cadets; a "who's-who" roster of "before-they-were-famous stars" (like Cruise, Penn and Hutton) fills the ranks of the "sensational young cast", while the more mature Scott lends some "*Patton*"-esque gravitas.

Tarzan | 22 | - | 21 | 24 |

1999 | Directed by Chris Buck, Kevin Lima | Animated | 88 minutes | Rated G

Some of "Disney's best work" "re-creates the magic" of a "classic" in this tale of man and monkey swinging through life via "phenomenally innovative" animation; a "fast-paced adventure" that takes time out for "character" but "keeps things relatively lighthearted", it adds some "thoughtful modern" angles and a "great score", including an Oscar-winning song from Phil Collins.

Tarzan and His Mate ◑ | 21 | 16 | 19 | 20 |

1934 | Directed by Cedric Gibbons | With Johnny Weissmuller, Maureen O'Sullivan, Neil Hamilton | 104 minutes | Not Rated

See "what movies were like before the censors" in this rather racy sequel to *Tarzan the Ape Man* flaunting barely there costumes, "nude underwater" frolicking and title characters living together sans holy matrimony; despite some "racist" undertones and acting that "leaves a lot to be desired", some consider it the "best" of the Weissmuller Tarzans.

Tarzan the Ape Man ◑ | 21 | 16 | 21 | 18 |

1932 | Directed by W.S. Van Dyke | With Johnny Weissmuller, Maureen O'Sullivan, Neil Hamilton | 99 minutes | Not Rated

An "old-fashioned" fave among the "first real adventure films", this "memorable" intersection of Hollywood and vine finds a Brit lady Jane abducted by the ape-bred hero only to civilize him (and catch a bit of jungle fever herself); Olympic swimmer Weissmuller brings "definitive" bravura to the title role, and thus this "campy" but "trendsetting original" "holds up better" than all the sequels you can shake a banana at.

☑ Taxi Driver | 27 | 29 | 25 | 25 |

1976 | Directed by Martin Scorsese | With Robert De Niro, Jodie Foster, Harvey Keitel, Cybill Shepherd | 113 minutes | Rated R

Confirming "non-NYers' greatest fears" about the "brutal underbelly" of "modern urban life", Scorsese's vividly "cerebral" thriller rolls through "sleazy" streets and "neon" nights charged by De Niro's "monumental performance" as a "creepy", insomniac hack – "you talking to me?" – whose live-wire issues build to "harrowing" magnum

	OVERALL	ACTING	STORY	PROD.

force in the "steam-filled" city; overall, its depiction of "urban decay, rage and alienation" is "top-class" but "lurid" and very "intense."

Team America: World Police
18 | - | 17 | 21

2004 | Directed by Trey Parker | Animated | 98 minutes | Rated R

The "*South Park* dudes" are back with this "incredibly un-PC" comedy, an "action movie parody" played by puppets that takes "equal-opportunity potshots" at "U.S. military policy *and* Hollywood activism"; it's "laugh-out-loud offensive", but "hide the children" – the "potty-mouth humor" and "eye-popping puppet porn" can be "a little much."

Tears of the Sun
18 | 18 | 18 | 21

2003 | Directed by Antoine Fuqua | With Bruce Willis, Monica Bellucci, Cole Hauser | 121 minutes | Rated R

"Blood, guts and guns" combine with a "meaningful" message in this "worthwhile" action picture featuring Willis as a U.S. soldier escorting a medic and a group of refugees to safety across war-torn Africa; though the drama is "strong in parts", some critics say this "typical white-man's-burden" saga "in PC clothing" "falls woefully short."

Teen Wolf
15 | 15 | 15 | 15

1985 | Directed by Rod Daniel | With Michael J. Fox, James Hampton, Jerry Levine | 91 minutes | Rated PG

Putting a "hokey '80s" spin on the "teenage werewolf" trope, this "cute" comedy is "carried by Fox's charm" as it relates the story of a high-school loser whose puberty entails sprouting fangs and a pelt; though "howlingly cheesy" and "farfetched", it's "still fun junk food" for the "teenybopper" set.

10
17 | 16 | 16 | 17

1979 | Directed by Blake Edwards | With Dudley Moore, Julie Andrews, Bo Derek, Robert Webber | 122 minutes | Rated R

This "midlife crisis movie for men" might be "silly" and "rather dated", but will always be a "time capsule of the American dream, circa 1979" thanks to the iconic image of "Derek in cornrows" bouncing on the beach in "slow motion"; sure, it has about as much depth as the "*Sports Illustrated* swimsuit issue", but it's "still funny" and proves that "short guys can be sexy."

⊠ Ten Commandments, The
24 | 21 | 25 | 27

1956 | Directed by Cecil B. DeMille | With Charlton Heston, Yul Brynner, Anne Baxter, Edward G. Robinson | 220 minutes | Rated G

"Let it be written" that DeMille's "over-the-top" biblical blockbuster is the "epic of all epics", a "Cliffs Notes" account of Exodus built on "Heston's finest" role as the "one and only Moses", performer of "monumental" miracles on land and Red Sea; though "fantastic sets" and Brynner's "badass" Egyptian king distract from the "kitschy" script and "overblown" production, it's "entertaining" enough to keep a "cast of thousands" in "constant circulation."

Tender Mercies ⊠
24 | 26 | 22 | 22

1983 | Directed by Bruce Beresford | With Robert Duvall, Tess Harper, Betty Buckley, Ellen Barkin | 92 minutes | Rated PG

"Proving that less is more", Duvall delivers a "quiet yet unforgettable" portrait of a "has-been country singer" hiding out in a Texas motel, and

| | OVERALL | ACTING | STORY | PROD. |

transforms a "simple story" into something "truly great"; winner of two Oscars (for Best Actor and Screenplay), it also boasts a "rather good" soundtrack that lends the film its "haunting" air.

Tequila Sunrise
17 | 18 | 17 | 18

1988 | Directed by Robert Towne | With Mel Gibson, Michelle Pfeiffer, Kurt Russell | 115 minutes | Rated R

"Unusually beautiful people" make up a "classic love triangle" – and "what a perfect triangle it is" – in this "decent" drama about a restaurateur involved with a cop and a drug dealer; some say the "usual story line" features too much "froth" and "dead dialogue", but all agree it's worth a look to gaze upon Michelle and Kurt "in their prime" – not to mention Mel "before he found God."

Terminal, The
18 | 22 | 18 | 20

2004 | Directed by Steven Spielberg | With Tom Hanks, Catherine Zeta-Jones, Stanley Tucci | 128 minutes | Rated PG-13

"Every traveler's nightmare" comes true in this story of an "Eastern European stranded for months at JFK" that divides viewers, with fans praising the "truly original" idea, "spare-no-expense" production and Tom's "gold-standard" performance; but those who say it "just doesn't fly" find it "terminally dull", given the "strained", *Castaway*-in-an-airport" story, "unsatisfying", "Capra-esque ending" and "zero chemistry" between the "not sexy" Hanks and "wasted" Zeta-Jones.

Terminator, The
24 | 18 | 24 | 24

1984 | Directed by James Cameron | With Arnold Schwarzenegger, Michael Biehn, Linda Hamilton | 108 minutes | Rated R

Buckle up for Cameron's "unstoppable breakthrough", this sci-fi/action "genre-maker" about an "evil cyborg sent from the future" to wreak havoc on the past via Ah-nuld's "seriously scary presence" alone; it "doesn't disappoint" in dispensing "awesome" "violent" mayhem all over '80s LA, and its most famous line – "I'll be back" – was a harbinger of the sequels to come.

Terminator 2: Judgment Day
23 | 17 | 22 | 26

1991 | Directed by James Cameron | With Arnold Schwarzenegger, Linda Hamilton, Edward Furlong | 137 minutes | Rated R

The Terminator's "baaack" as a "kinder, gentler" cyborg in this "outsize thrill ride" that deftly embellishes the initial premise of murderous, "time-traveling" robots; fans say it's a "rare sequel that fulfills the promise of the original", citing the "whiz-bang", "ahead-of-their-time" FX, Hamilton's "buff", "kick-butt" heroine and the one-and-only Arnold, whose "mechanical" performance makes him the "perfect choice to play an android."

Terminator 3: Rise of the Machines
16 | 13 | 15 | 22

2003 | Directed by Jonathan Mostow | With Arnold Schwarzenegger, Nick Stahl, Claire Danes | 109 minutes | Rated R

"Staying true" to its origins, this third entry in the long-unfolding sci-fi series features the usual "bang-up" pyrotechnics and "breezy" plotting, along with a "twist": a fembot Terminatrix villainess; still, foes fret the "franchise has run out of steam", citing "retread special effects", "phoned-in" work from Arnold and that "downer" of an ending; in the final analysis, "they should have stopped at 2."

Terms of Endearment ✉

25 | 26 | 24 | 22

1983 | Directed by James L. Brooks | With Shirley MacLaine, Debra Winger, Jack Nicholson, Jeff Daniels | 132 minutes | Rated PG

A "four-hanky tearjerker" "worth its weight in Kleenex", this "engrossing" "weepie with a spine" starts off comically enough depicting a "tangled mother-daughter relationship" but takes a "serious" turn in the second act when "life-and-death" issues arise; quite the Oscar magnet, it took home Best Picture honors as well as statuettes for the "amazing" MacLaine and Nicholson, who's a "hoot" as the former astronaut who lives next door.

Tess

21 | 22 | 21 | 22

1980 | Directed by Roman Polanski | With Nastassja Kinski, Peter Firth, Leigh Lawson | 172 minutes | Rated PG

"Spectacularly beautiful", this "faithful rendition" of Thomas Hardy's "melancholy" classic Tess of the D'Urbervilles stars a "simply luminous" Kinski as a peasant girl trying to improve her station in life; some say it's "schmaltzy" and "overly long", but most praise Polanski's "really fine adaptation" and promise you'll "never look at strawberries the same way" after seeing it.

Texas Chainsaw Massacre, The

17 | 13 | 17 | 15

1974 | Directed by Tobe Hooper | With Marilyn Burns, Allen Danziger, Paul A. Partain | 83 minutes | Rated R

Something "like a car wreck", this "alternately repulsive and fascinating" "slashfest" is the "nightmarish" story of innocent folk "falling prey to a cannibalistic family" and is "creepy beyond belief" despite "surprisingly little overt gore"; aficionados call it the "Casablanca of horror films" notwithstanding the "low-budget" looks and "bad acting" – but "truly amazing screaming."

Thank You for Smoking

23 | 23 | 23 | 21

2006 | Directed by Jason Reitman | With Aaron Eckhart, Maria Bello, Rob Lowe, Robert Duvall, William H. Macy, Katie Holmes | 92 minutes | Rated R

Eckhart's "killer" portrayal of a "smug" but "lovable" cigarette industry spin doctor has you "rooting for the bad guy" in this "hysterically sarcastic" send-up of "Big Tobacco" and the "art of lobbying"; packed with "intelligent commentary" and featuring a star-studded cast, it "throws moral curveballs" that leave "plenty to talk about after the credits roll."

That's Entertainment!

25 | - | - | 25

1974 | Directed by Jack Haley Jr | Documentary | With Gene Kelly, Fred Astaire | 127 minutes | Rated G

This "remarkable survey of MGM musicals" lays out a "delicious", "crème-de-la-crème" buffet of glorious "old clips" set up with "narration by some mighty big stars"; showcasing the likes of Kelly and Astaire at their "thrilling" peak, this compilation is "desert-island" viewing and an "entertaining introduction" to the bygone days of "real talent."

Thelma & Louise ✉

23 | 25 | 23 | 21

1991 | Directed by Ridley Scott | With Susan Sarandon, Geena Davis, Brad Pitt, Harvey Keitel | 129 minutes | Rated R

A "high-powered" "girl-power" flick focusing on a "feminist crime spree", this "groundbreaking" display of "female macho" "rocks" as two everyday gals "finally get back" at the men who've wronged them by becoming "devil-may-care outlaws" on the lam; the "superb storyline" and "stellar performances" keep things "involving" right up to the "heartbreaking", *Butch Cassidy*–esque "bad ending."

There's Something About Mary

	OVERALL	ACTING	STORY	PROD.
	21	19	20	19

1998 | Directed by Bobby Farrelly, Peter Farrelly | With Cameron Diaz, Matt Dillon, Ben Stiller | 119 minutes | Rated R

Proceed "at your own risk" as the "ultra-crude" Farrelly brothers "push the limits" of "gross-out comedy" in this "tacky laugh riot" about a "loser with a heart of gold" and the "good-sport" girl he loves that's an "oh-my-gosh" compendium of "high-school humor" and "vulgar" "sight gags" (the "dog", the "zipper", the "hair gel"); but foes moan this movie "made by morons for morons" is "even dumber than *Dumb and Dumber.*"

There Will Be Blood ✉

23	28	21	26

2007 | Directed by Paul Thomas Anderson | With Daniel Day-Lewis, Paul Dano, Kevin J. O'Connor, Ciarán Hinds | 158 minutes | Rated R

A "compelling portrait of a repellant man", this "booming, expansive epic" loosely based on an Upton Sinclair novel depicts the "rise of industrialization" and "everything that's wrong about capitalism" in its story of "greed, malice" and a "dark-as-coal" petroleum baron on the loose in turn-of-the-century California oilfields; Day-Lewis' "otherworldly" "gusher of a performance" deservedly won the Oscar, and despite "unlikable characters" and a "long" running time, this "companion piece to *Citizen Kane*" is widely considered an "instant classic"; already legendary line: "I drink your milkshake."

They Shoot Horses, Don't They?

21	24	22	21

1969 | Directed by Sydney Pollack | With Jane Fonda, Michael Sarrazin, Susannah York, Gig Young | 120 minutes | Rated PG

"Jane Fonda at her world-weariest" provides the glue in this "classic" Depression drama about "desperate" marathon dancers frantically trying to make a buck; though the story's "small" and the sentiments grim, its ensemble cast is "unforgettable" – particularly the "superlative" Gig Young, who copped an Oscar for the role of the slimy emcee.

Thief of Bagdad, The ◐

24	22	23	23

1924 | Directed by Raoul Walsh | With Douglas Fairbanks, Snitz Edwards, Julanne Johnston | 155 minutes | Not Rated

This Arabian Nights fantasy is a "definitive swashbuckler", featuring an "athletic" Fairbanks "at his best" as a charming rogue seeking a princess' hand; one of the most expensive silent movies ever made, it's a "lavish" spectacle with sets by William Cameron Menzies that are "still amazing by today's standards"; in short, it's simply "great."

Thing, The ◐
(aka The Thing from Another World)

23	19	25	19

1951 | Directed by Christian Nyby | With Kenneth Tobey, Margaret Sheridan | 87 minutes | Not Rated

This "serious" '50s sci-fi suspenser "still holds up" as a "smart" "flying-saucer" shocker about scientists driven to "creepy" extremes in a "claustrophobic, paranoid" encounter with a murderous alien found frozen in the Arctic ice; despite "skimpy" special effects, the "tight script" builds enough "tension" to frighten the "daylights" out of fans, who spurn the "gory remake" – there's nothing like "the real *Thing.*"

Thing, The
23 | 19 | 23 | 23

1982 | Directed by John Carpenter | With Kurt Russell, Wilford Brimley, David Clennon | 109 minutes | Rated R

"Chills" abound in Carpenter's "excellent remake of the '51 classic", wherein the Antarctic's most "frigid science outpost" is beset by a "horrible alien" capable of disguising itself in human form; an "imaginative" contribution to the "sci-fi/horror pantheon", it supplies enough "true suspense" to keep the audience "guessing" as the "paranoia" mounts.

Ⓩ Thin Man, The ◑
26 | 25 | 23 | 23

1934 | Directed by W.S. Van Dyke | With William Powell, Myrna Loy, Maureen O'Sullivan | 93 minutes | Not Rated

"Break out the martini glasses": "mystery meets screwball comedy" in this "snazzy" flicker featuring "cool detective" Nick Charles and his "classy wife", Nora, "drinking like fish" and "fluidly" spouting "snappy dialogue" ("double entendre, anyone?") as they investigate a murder; the "suave, sexy fun" is so "cosmopolitan" and "wonderfully evocative of the '30s" that it seems unsporting to point out that the "whodunit" plot is a bit thin.

Thin Red Line, The
19 | 21 | 17 | 22

1998 | Directed by Terrence Malick | With Sean Penn, George Clooney, John Cusack, Woody Harrelson | 170 minutes | Rated R

Malick's "experimental war epic" is made for those who "enjoy thinking about big questions", with Penn exuding "gravity" as a sarge facing the front lines at Guadalcanal with a "star-studded" company of "common soldiers"; "stunning visuals" "attempt to poeticize" the "horror and beauty" of battle and warfare's "emotional effects", though detractors grunt it's "incoherent."

Ⓩ Third Man, The ◑
28 | 28 | 27 | 28

1949 | Directed by Carol Reed | With Joseph Cotten, Alida Valli, Orson Welles, Trevor Howard | 104 minutes | Not Rated

"Oh, that zither!"; this "masterful" piece of "postwar" noir simmers with shadowy "intrigue" as an "alienated" Cotten encounters "romance" and "betrayal" while searching "bombed-out" Vienna for a "mysterious" black marketeer (played by Welles, who makes the most of a "small" role with an "arresting" entrance); graced with "expressionist" lensing, Graham Greene's "clever, dark script" and a "memorable" final fade, it's hailed as "all-around perfect."

Thirteen
21 | 26 | 22 | 19

2003 | Directed by Catherine Hardwicke | With Holly Hunter, Evan Rachel Wood, Nikki Reed | 100 minutes | Rated R

"You won't want to let your kids out of the house" after a gander at this "disturbing" cautionary tale about a pair of "troubled" 13-year-olds who are "harder to control than Mike Tyson"; while critics hiss the "clichéd", "after-school-special" script and "weak ending", far more applaud this "wake-up call" for telling it like it is "without sugar coating."

Thirteen Days
22 | 22 | 23 | 21

2000 | Directed by Roger Donaldson | With Kevin Costner, Bruce Greenwood, Steven Culp, Dylan Baker | 145 minutes | Rated PG-13

This "gripping" "real-life drama" revisits the "Cuban missile crisis", with "exceptional" work from an ensemble cast playing the Kennedy cabinet at the tense moment in history when WWIII seemed likely; politicos plug an "underrated" effort that yields "fascinating insights" and "keeps up the suspense", even if "everyone knows how it ends."

13 Going on 30

	OVERALL	ACTING	STORY	PROD.
	19	21	17	19

2004 | Directed by Gary Winick | With Jennifer Garner, Mark Ruffalo | 98 minutes | Rated PG-13

"Look out Julia Roberts": the adorably "dimpled" Garner lunges for the "America's Sweetheart" crown in this "giggle"-worthy chick flick about a young teen fast-forwarded into adulthood; a remix of "*Big* and *The Devil Wears Prada*", it may be on the "fluffy" side, but "teenyboppers" and "'80s music" fans don't care.

☒ 39 Steps, The ◑

27	25	27	24

1935 | Directed by Alfred Hitchcock | With Robert Donat, Madeleine Carroll, Lucie Mannheim | 86 minutes | Not Rated

"You can't go wrong" with this "classic" "British period" Hitchcock nail-biter, a "virtuoso" "thriller diller" wherein an "innocent man wrongly accused" of murder tries to clear his name amid "chase scenes, foreign spy intrigue and romance" (with a woman he winds up "handcuffed" to); sure, the "dated" special effects are on the low-tech side, but this "tense mystery" delivers enough suspense to "keep you on the edge of your seat."

This Boy's Life

21	25	22	21

1993 | Directed by Michael Caton-Jones | With Robert De Niro, Ellen Barkin, Leonardo DiCaprio | 115 minutes | Rated R

Author Tobias Wolff's "autobiographical" sketch of troubled boyhood comes to life via this "poignant" drama starring an "incredible" young DiCaprio, "before he started acting like a movie star"; factor in Barkin's "excellent" portrayal of a struggling mom and a "scary" De Niro (who takes the "evil" stepfather role "to a new low") and there's plenty of "pain and abuse" to digest – a challenge that some find "tough" to handle.

☒ This Is Spinal Tap

26	24	25	22

1984 | Directed by Rob Reiner | With Christopher Guest, Michael McKean, Rob Reiner | 82 minutes | Rated R

"VH1's *Behind the Music*" pales before this "hysterical" "rock mockumentary", an "unbelievably authentic-feeling send-up" of the music industry and superstar "pretensions" that follows an "aging heavy-metal band" taking its act on the road; the "stellar cast" plays an "unforgettable" group of clueless musicians, simulating a "sidesplitting insider's view" that's alarmingly "like the real thing" – except "every single second is funny."

Thomas Crown Affair, The

23	23	24	22

1968 | Directed by Norman Jewison | With Steve McQueen, Faye Dunaway, Paul Burke | 102 minutes | Rated R

This "slick", "grown-up romance" offers a "cat-and-mouse" plot as millionaire McQueen engineers a bank heist for kicks until he encounters Dunaway, a "knockout" insurance sleuth in mad pursuit; their "smoldering", "high-tension" affair is a "stylish" standoff down to the final "checkmate" in that famed chess match, and as for the remake, "do not accept imitations."

Thoroughly Modern Millie

	OVERALL	ACTING	STORY	PROD.
	18	19	16	21

1967 | Directed by George Roy Hill | With Julie Andrews, Mary Tyler Moore, Carol Channing | 138 minutes | Rated G

"Roaring '20s" razzle-dazzle makes this musical comedy an "absolute hoot", with "Andrews at her peak" as a big-city rookie trying to land a man; it's played as a "slapstick farce set to song and dance" that alternates new tunes with "flapper-era" standards, and if "silly fluff", all that "jazzy fun" is "entertaining nonetheless."

Thousand Clowns, A ◑∅

	OVERALL	ACTING	STORY	PROD.
	25	26	24	21

1965 | Directed by Fred Coe | With Jason Robards, Barbara Harris, Barry Gordon, Martin Balsam | 118 minutes | Not Rated

A "wonderful" cast including the "brilliant" Robards and Harris (and Oscar-winning Balsam) drives this "touching" but "unusual" comedy about a "nonconformist" whose disdain for the "daily grind" jeopardizes his guardianship of a beloved nephew; based on the Herb Gardner play, it's a "classic" example of the '60s "do-your-own-thing" ethic that nonetheless "has a lot of truth" in it.

Three Amigos

	OVERALL	ACTING	STORY	PROD.
	16	17	14	16

1986 | Directed by John Landis | With Chevy Chase, Steve Martin, Martin Short | 104 minutes | Rated PG

"Magnificent Seven, move over" for an "all-star" trio of *Saturday Night Live* alums" who "make the most of" this "completely silly" yet "infectious" comedy about "washed-up" silent-screen actors who don "studded mariachi costumes" to "save a Mexican village"; it will "never be confused with high art", but fans of "goofy fun" are in for "guaranteed laughs."

Three Burials of Melquiades Estrada, The

	OVERALL	ACTING	STORY	PROD.
	22	25	22	22

2005 | Directed by Tommy Lee Jones | With Tommy Lee Jones, Julio César Cedillo, Barry Pepper, January Jones | 121 minutes | Rated R

"Truly fresh and original", this "offbeat" contemporary Western concerns a "cowboy who does it his way" by abducting a border patrol cop who's gunned down the title character; as a "relevant" take on "immigration issues", it's "totally satisfying" (albeit funereally "slow"), though all agree on Jones' "impressive directorial debut."

Three Coins in the Fountain

	OVERALL	ACTING	STORY	PROD.
	21	21	21	22

1954 | Directed by Jean Negulesco | With Clifton Webb, Dorothy McGuire, Jean Peters, Louis Jourdan | 102 minutes | Not Rated

"Rome at its best" is the real "star" of this "good old-fashioned love story" about three husband-hunters making coin-tossing wishes in the Trevi Fountain; it's every 1950s "female's dream" and still "so much emotional fun" that it's easy to ignore the correspondingly overripe 1950s "sentimentality."

Three Days of the Condor

	OVERALL	ACTING	STORY	PROD.
	24	24	25	22

1975 | Directed by Sydney Pollack | With Robert Redford, Faye Dunaway, Cliff Robertson | 117 minutes | Rated R

Filmed during the Watergate era, this "paranoid thriller" "still flies" today thanks to Redford's "absorbing" work as an "enigmatic", low-level CIA researcher "caught up in a conspiracy" and dodging an "impersonal assassin"; it's "absorbing", "expertly crafted" stuff, with a "twisty" plot that "puts the intelligence back into, um, intelligence."

Three Faces of Eve, The | 24 | 27 | 24 | 20 |

1957 | Directed by Nunnally Johnson | With Joanne Woodward, David Wayne, Lee J. Cobb | 91 minutes | Not Rated

"Incredible" Oscar-winner Woodward delivers a "tour-de-force" turn in this "multiple-personality genre film", an "interesting drama" about a "woman tormented" by triple identities; switching from subdued homemaker to brazen party girl, Woodward does a "stellar" job of "bringing all three characters to life."

300 | 22 | 20 | 22 | 27 |

2007 | Directed by Zack Snyder | With Gerard Butler, Lena Headey, Dominic West, David Wenham | 117 minutes | Rated R

"Hunky" Hellenic he-men "wearing next to nothing" duke it out with the Persians at the Battle of Thermopylae in this "cool, stylish" and ultra-"gory" sword 'n' sandal epic adapted from Frank Miller's graphic novel; no question, the "balletic" action sequences and "top-notch" effects are a "treat for the eyes", but a phalanx of fence-sitters fret it's "all bang and no substance."

Three Kings | 20 | 21 | 21 | 22 |

1999 | Directed by David O. Russell | With George Clooney, Mark Wahlberg, Ice Cube | 114 minutes | Rated R

Opening at the close of Desert Storm, this "bold and different" war flick offers a combo of "crackerjack action" and "surprisingly good" acting as "irreverent army guy" Clooney launches a "chase for stolen Kuwaiti gold" that morphs into a "morality tale" midway through; the "insightful" scenario and "creative" visuals make it royally "enjoyable on many levels", though a few are "not impressed" by the "chaotic storyline" and "preachy dialogue."

Three Men and a Baby | 16 | 15 | 17 | 16 |

1987 | Directed by Leonard Nimoy | With Tom Selleck, Steve Guttenberg, Ted Danson | 102 minutes | Rated PG

Like the title implies, "three men care for a baby girl" in this "big-hearted" comedy with a "charming ensemble" cast that makes most viewers "laugh and feel good"; the unamused suggest you "bring insulin" or hold out for the "much better" original French film on which it's based: *Three Men and a Cradle.*

Three Musketeers, The | 22 | 22 | 22 | 23 |

1974 | Directed by Richard Lester | With Oliver Reed, Richard Chamberlain, Michael York | 105 minutes | Rated PG

A "rollicking rendition" of the Dumas classic, this "rousing" "old-fashioned" adventure "stays faithful" to the original tale but spices up the swordplay with "slapstick" and "bawdy" humor as a brave band of swashbucklers defends the queen's honor against that crooked cardinal; the "lavish" 17th-century sets and all-for-one "charm" of the "great cast" ensure its place as the "quintessential" version by which all others "shall be judged."

3:10 to Yuma | 23 | 25 | 22 | 24 |

2007 | Directed by James Mangold | With Russell Crowe, Christian Bale, Ben Foster, Peter Fonda | 122 minutes | Rated R

"John Wayne would have loved" this "solid" remake of the "classic oater" that "stands up well on its own" thanks to more than "solid"

production values and "pitch-perfect performances" by Bale and
Crowe, respectively playing a rancher and an outlaw going head-
to-head in an epic "battle of wits"; yee-haw, there's also "plenty of
gun-fighting and explosions" occurring along the way to its much-
debated "surprise ending."

3 Women
25 | 26 | 21 | 23

1977 | Directed by Robert Altman | With Shelley Duvall, Sissy Spacek,
Janice Rule | 124 minutes | Rated PG

Altman is "at his trickiest" in this "dreamlike" drama about a down-
wardly mobile desert-town gal and her "ripe-for-the-picking" room-
mate who form an "eerie" triangle with a wronged spouse; though the
"cryptic narrative" can be "easily dismissed as weird", it's still a "fascinating" exercise in feminine psychology with "super" acting – think
Single White Female for the arty set."

Thunderball
22 | 21 | 21 | 23

1965 | Directed by Terence Young | With Sean Connery, Claudine
Auger, Adolfo Celi | 130 minutes | Rated PG

Bringing the "basic Bond formula" to the Bahamas, this swimming entry in the superspy series has Connery breaking out his arsenal of
"gadgets" and dry wisecracks against the "very real threat" of stolen
nukes held for ransom; the "nonstop action" and "incredible underwater fight sequences" made it a thunderous success in its day, and if
now "underappreciated", connoisseurs nevertheless rank it "near the
top" of the 007 oeuvre.

Tie Me Up! Tie Me Down! 🇫
20 | 21 | 20 | 20

1990 | Directed by Pedro Almodóvar | With Victoria Abril, Antonio
Banderas, Loles Leon | 111 minutes | Rated NC-17

"Madcap" director Almodóvar strikes again in this naughty knotty
comedy about a kidnapped, trussed-up B-movie star that's a cross between "*The Collector*" and a soft-core bondage flick; its "sexy", "vivid
characters" and "nice" Ennio Morricone soundtrack further spice up a
storyline that's already "hysterically funny."

Time After Time
23 | 23 | 25 | 21

1979 | Directed by Nicholas Meyer | With Malcolm McDowell, Mary
Steenburgen, David Warner | 112 minutes | Rated PG

A "clever" bit of "brainy entertainment", this "charming" sci-fi thriller
recounts "H.G. Wells chasing Jack the Ripper to modern-day San
Francisco" via a "functioning time machine"; a "witty" romp expertly
blending "romantic" interludes between McDowell and Steenburgen
with "suspenseful" sequencing, it's "well worth seeing" for Warner's
"helluva performance" alone.

Time Bandits
21 | 19 | 23 | 22

1981 | Directed by Terry Gilliam | With John Cleese, Sean Connery,
Shelley Duvall | 116 minutes | Rated PG

Gilliam's "warped-mind" "genius" shines in this "bittersweet" time-
travel fantasy about the "classic struggle between good and evil", with
a sprawling cast that includes a "band of midgets", a "fantastic villain"
and a parade of "delightful" cameos; though the visual effects may be
showing their age, there are still enough "juicy moments" to justify its
"cult-classic" status.

| | OVERALL | ACTING | STORY | PROD. |

Time Machine, The
22 | 17 | 26 | 23

1960 | Directed by George Pal | With Rod Taylor, Alan Young, Yvette Mimieux | 103 minutes | Rated G

"Faithful to both the letter and spirit of H.G. Wells' novel", this "grand-daddy of time-travel movies" concerning a 19th-century scientist flabbergasted by the future is "nicely paced" and "fondly remembered" for its "thought-provoking storyline" and "good special effects for the era" (which won an Oscar); though the "remake isn't bad", the "much-better" original is the real "gem."

Time to Kill, A
18 | 18 | 22 | 19

1996 | Directed by Joel Schumacher | With Matthew McConaughey, Sandra Bullock, Samuel L. Jackson | 149 minutes | Rated R

"Very adult" and "suspenseful to the end", this "hard-hitting" Mississippi courtroom drama about racist violence and retribution is a "solid adaptation of the John Grisham novel"; despite the very "Hollywood ending", it's "captivating" thanks to "intelligent" turns from Bullock and McConaughey ("his best role").

Tin Cup
18 | 17 | 17 | 18

1996 | Directed by Ron Shelton | With Kevin Costner, Rene Russo, Don Johnson, Cheech Marin | 135 minutes | Rated R

Even those with "no interest in golf" admit it's "fun to watch" this "lighthearted" links comedy casting Costner as a "small-time" driving range owner who meets the "glamorous" Russo and signs up for the "PGA tour to win her affections"; foes say *Caddyshack* is better" than this "below par" *Bull Durham* wannabe, but praise the "cameos by real-life pros."

Tin Drum, The ✉🅵
23 | 23 | 24 | 23

1980 | Directed by Volker Schlöndorff | With David Bennent, Mario Adorf, Angela Winkler | 142 minutes | Rated R

A "fine social commentary" about apathy and "life in Nazi Germany", this "disturbing" allegorical drama about a young boy who refuses to grow old "preserves the spirit of Günter Grass' novel" while charting the rise and fall of the Third Reich; the "well-deserved winner of the Best Foreign Film Oscar", it's a "surreal" work that remains "vivid and haunting" a generation later.

Titanic ✉
19 | 16 | 18 | 26

1997 | Directed by James Cameron | With Leonardo DiCaprio, Kate Winslet, Billy Zane, Gloria Stuart | 194 minutes | Rated PG-13

Ok, it's "not highbrow stuff", but this "over-the-top spectacular" detailing a "doomed love story" aboard a "doomed ocean liner" thrills with "dazzling" special effects, including a "fantastic" "re-creation of the original ship" and icebergs so real "you can almost touch them"; some torpedo the "shallow" "cardboard characters", "soap opera"-esque script and "weak acting" as "all wet", and whether it's "deserving of its Oscars" – all 11 of them – is still hotly debated.

To Be or Not to Be ◐
24 | 24 | 25 | 23

1942 | Directed by Ernst Lubitsch | With Carole Lombard, Jack Benny, Robert Stack | 99 minutes | Not Rated

"Life in Nazi-occupied Europe" becomes "exhilarating comedy" in this "funny but poignant" war story, an "oft-overlooked gem" via the ever

| | OVERALL | ACTING | STORY | PROD. |

"clever" Ernst Lubitsch; playing married actors, Benny and Lombard supply "barrels of laughs" – particularly when Jack "does to Shakespeare what the Germans are doing to Poland."

To Catch a Thief
25 | 25 | 24 | 25

1955 | Directed by Alfred Hitchcock | With Grace Kelly, Cary Grant, Jesse Royce Landis, Brigitte Auber | 106 minutes | Not Rated
"Slick, sophisticated and oh-so-cool", this romantic thriller may be "Hitchcock lite", but Grant and Kelly provide plenty of "dazzle" in an amusing trifle about a cat burglar prowling the south of France; maybe the "plot is secondary" to the "enjoyable scenery" and "fab clothes", but there's snappy patter aplenty, notably Grace's classic picnic query "would you prefer a leg or a breast?"

To Die For
18 | 21 | 19 | 18

1995 | Directed by Gus Van Sant | With Nicole Kidman, Matt Dillon, Joaquin Phoenix, Illeana Douglas | 106 minutes | Rated R
A "true tabloid story" becomes "cuttingly observed satire" in this drama about "America's obsession with fame", a "wicked black comedy" due to "Buck Henry's brilliant script" and Van Sant's "incisive" direction; in her "most original role", Kidman "positively shines" as an "ambitious" TV weathergirl "trying to get ahead in her job and out of her marriage" – many say her performance alone is the "reason to see it."

❷ To Have and Have Not ◑
26 | 27 | 24 | 24

1944 | Directed by Howard Hawks | With Humphrey Bogart, Lauren Bacall, Walter Brennan, Hoagy Carmichael | 100 minutes | Not Rated
Bacall (in her screen debut) teams with future real-life hubby Bogart to "define star chemistry" in this dramatization of the Hemingway novel about WWII resistance runners; Martinique supplies a sultry backdrop for the two stars to "smolder", especially when Lauren "steams up the screen" with her legendary question "you know how to whistle, don't you?"

❷ To Kill a Mockingbird ✉◑
29 | 29 | 29 | 26

1962 | Directed by Robert Mulligan | With Gregory Peck, Mary Badham, Robert Duvall | 129 minutes | Not Rated
"After all these years", this Southern courtroom drama about racism and prejudice "told from the point of view of a young girl" "still packs the same emotional punch"; kudos go to Oscar-winning screenwriter Horton Foote "for not having strayed" from Harper Lee's "original text", and to an "im-peck-able" Peck at his "peak" as the "dad we wish we had"; in short, "Hollywood got this one right."

To Live and Die in L.A.
20 | 21 | 21 | 20

1985 | Directed by William Friedkin | With William L. Petersen, Willem Dafoe, John Pankow | 116 minutes | Rated R
With its "bleak" Southern California setting, "morally devoid" characters and atmospheric Wang Chung soundtrack, this "taut", "violent" crime thriller earns a slot in the "quintessential '80s" canon with its "noir"-ish tale of a cop crusading against a counterfeiter; while "no major classic", it's certainly worth fast-forwarding to that "amazing car chase."

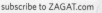

| | OVERALL | ACTING | STORY | PROD. |

Tombstone
21 | 22 | 21 | 21

1993 | Directed by George P. Cosmatos | With Kurt Russell, Val Kilmer, Sam Elliott, Bill Paxton | 130 minutes | Rated R

More than an ok rendition of the "O.K. Corral story", this "slick retelling" brings legends Wyatt Earp and Doc Holliday up to date with plenty of good old "modern-day violence"; starring a pistol-packing Russell and "fun-to-watch" Kilmer, it's a "worthy" enough stab at pure "entertainment" – "even if you don't like Westerns."

Tom Jones ✉
25 | 24 | 24 | 25

1963 | Directed by Tony Richardson | With Albert Finney, Susannah York, Hugh Griffith | 121 minutes | Not Rated

"Richly crafted and craftily acted" – with four Oscars to prove it – this hilariously "bawdy" "period piece par excellence" might be set in 18th-century England but moodwise is more like a "snapshot of the Swinging '60s"; devotees are ever smitten with its "clever script", "lively direction" and Finney's "lusty" title turn, while gourmands eat up that "sexy food-seduction scene."

Tommy
16 | 14 | 16 | 20

1975 | Directed by Ken Russell | With Roger Daltrey, Ann-Margret, Oliver Reed, Elton John | 111 minutes | Rated PG

The Who's "seminal rock opera" goes Hollywood in this "over-the-top feast for the senses" that divides voters: ravers revel in the "great score", "Tina Turner as the Acid Queen" and that "scene with Ann-Margret and the baked beans", but bashers bawl it's a "disservice to both musicals and rock 'n' roll."

Tomorrow Never Dies
20 | 20 | 17 | 21

1997 | Directed by Roger Spottiswoode | With Pierce Brosnan, Jonathan Pryce, Michelle Yeoh | 119 minutes | Rated PG-13

". . . and neither does James" joke 007 junkies of the juggernaut's 18th entry, wherein "Brosnan fills Connery's" custom-made shoes and "brings back" the secret agent's "cruel streak"; the "thoughtful plot" (something about a mad "media magnate" bent on starting WWIII) is buoyed by "high-tech special effects", though Bond-girl watchers say the picture belongs to the "fabulous" Yeoh.

Tootsie
25 | 27 | 24 | 23

1982 | Directed by Sydney Pollack | With Dustin Hoffman, Jessica Lange, Bill Murray, Teri Garr, Charles Durning | 119 minutes | Rated PG

"Cross-dressing doesn't get much better" than this "brilliantly funny" comedy about a long-"struggling actor" who finally achieves success – "as an actress"; though Hoffman might be "one ugly" broad, his "sublime", "think-out-of-the-box" performance mixing "humor with humanity" is beautiful, while a "slick" but "unpredictable script" and an "outstanding" supporting cast make this one a "keeper, not a renter."

⊠ Top Gun
22 | 18 | 20 | 24

1986 | Directed by Tony Scott | With Tom Cruise, Kelly McGillis, Val Kilmer, Anthony Edwards, Tom Skerritt | 110 minutes | Rated PG

"Sexy fighter pilots" populate this "'80s action icon", a roiling mix of "noise", "romance" and "aerial maneuvers"; Cruise "looks great in uniform" and that "volleyball scene" sure is "hot", but foes dis the "hokey" plot and "intermittent acting" and can't fathom why it's so "popular."

	OVERALL	ACTING	STORY	PROD.

☑ Top Hat ◑ 27 | 23 | 21 | 26

1935 | Directed by Mark Sandrich | With Fred Astaire, Ginger Rogers, Edward Everett Horton, Helen Broderick | 101 minutes | Not Rated

"Heaven, I'm in heaven" sigh fans of this "classic '30s musical" spotlighting the big-city charms of a "debonair Astaire" opposite a "feather"-gowned Rogers; sure, there's an "all-hit Irving Berlin score", "amazing production numbers" and a "witty French farce of a script", but in the end, it's "Fred and Ginger dancing cheek-to-cheek" that catapults it to "sublime"-ville.

Topkapi 24 | 22 | 25 | 21

1964 | Directed by Jules Dassin | With Melina Mercouri, Peter Ustinov | 119 minutes | Not Rated

Director "Dassin's '60s caper holds up well", managing to "avoid clichés the same way" its jewel-thief cast "avoid traps" as they engineer a heist in Istanbul; owing to a "clever script" and some "beautifully drawn characters" (like the "sophisticated" Mercouri and "priceless", "Oscar-winning" Ustinov), this "taut" thriller/comedy is reminiscent of an erstwhile *Mission: Impossible.*"

Topper ◑ 20 | 21 | 21 | 19

1937 | Directed by Norman Z. McLeod | With Roland Young, Constance Bennett, Cary Grant | 97 minutes | Not Rated

Grant and Bennett "never miss a beat" in this "smart" romantic comedy about a pair of martini-swilling, madcap ghosts who must do a good deed to go to heaven; expect lots of laughs when the "delightful" phantoms select uptight banker Cosmo Topper as the beneficiary of their largesse in this "lighthearted" bit of "whimsy."

Top Secret! 20 | 16 | 16 | 16

1984 | Directed by Jim Abrahams, David Zucker, Jerry Zucker | With Val Kilmer, Lucy Gutteridge | 90 minutes | Rated PG

The like-minded "follow-up to *Airplane!*", this "zany spoof" of "spy movies" and "teen-idol flicks" stars Kilmer ("before he got too serious") as an "Elvis Presley-ish" singer touring the Eastern Bloc who's drawn into a plot to reunite divided Germany; get ready for a "hilarious" string of "inside jokes", "one-liners" and "sight gags", notably that "cow in galoshes."

Topsy-Turvy 23 | 25 | 23 | 26

1999 | Directed by Mike Leigh | With Jim Broadbent, Allan Corduner | 160 minutes | Rated R

This "finely observed story about the stormy partnership of Gilbert and Sullivan" provides a "window into the Victorian age" as well as a "fascinating" glimpse into the "creative process" via a subplot about the first staging of *The Mikado*; "superb" acting (with an especially "grand Broadbent") and a "gorgeous production" make it a "joy to watch" for most, though a few yawn "boring."

Tora! Tora! Tora! 23 | 19 | 25 | 24

1970 | Directed by Richard Fleischer, Kinji Fukasaku, Toshio Masuda | With Martin Balsam, Jason Robards | 144 minutes | Rated G

Surveyors split on this "intricate" war chronicle of the "Japanese attack on Pearl Harbor": defenders say this "ultimate docudrama" is "well done historically", citing its "bilingual plotlines" and over-the-top "stunning" special effects, but curmudgeons counter it's a "comic-book" look at the tragedy.

Torch Song Trilogy
23 | 25 | 25 | 21

1988 | Directed by Paul Bogart | With Harvey Fierstein, Matthew Broderick, Anne Bancroft | 120 minutes | Rated R

A "faithful adaptation" of Fierstein's very "original" stage play, this "moving" account of a gay female impersonator's "need for family" was "very advanced for its time" and "still very entertaining" today; though a few feel it "doesn't translate well to the screen", there are kudos for the "boyish" Broderick and Bancroft's "outstanding" turn as an "archetypical Jewish mother."

Torn Curtain
23 | 24 | 23 | 22

1966 | Directed by Alfred Hitchcock | With Paul Newman, Julie Andrews, Lila Kedrova, Wolfgang Kieling | 128 minutes | Rated PG

This "compelling" Cold War spy thriller via Alfred Hitchcock concerns an American physicist who defects to East Germany, bent on espionage; while it "isn't the greatest Newman or Andrews" effort, it still "has is moments", notably the 'silent murder' sequence and Lila Kedrova's "compelling" supporting role as a down-and-out countess.

To Sir, With Love
22 | 23 | 24 | 20

1967 | Directed by James Clavell | With Sidney Poitier, Judy Geeson, Christian Roberts | 105 minutes | Not Rated

The "always-excellent" Poitier stars in this "nice piece of '60s" nostalgia as a "London high school teacher" giving life lessons to "inner-city punks"; "sweet" and "timeless", it deals with "still-relevant" issues – "race, family conflicts, respect for authority" – in a "genuinely moving" way, and Lulu's smashing rendition of the title song "makes the movie."

Total Recall
18 | 14 | 21 | 22

1990 | Directed by Paul Verhoeven | With Arnold Schwarzenegger, Rachel Ticotin, Sharon Stone | 113 minutes | Rated R

"One of Ah-nuld's better" efforts may be this "exciting sci-fi adventure" flick, one of those "is-it-all-a-dream" stories about a secret agent implanted with someone else's memory chip; filmed "just before the age of digital effects" dawned, this "visual tour de force" inspires diverse reactions – "original" vs. "mediocre" – though pacifists are peeved by all that "gratuitous violence."

Touch of Class, A ✉
22 | 24 | 20 | 20

1973 | Directed by Melvin Frank | With George Segal, Glenda Jackson, Paul Sorvino | 106 minutes | Rated PG

The "sublime" Jackson snagged her second Oscar for lending a "touch of magic" to this "funny yet thoughtful" depiction of extramarital bliss between a "sexy" divorcée and a "loosey-goosey" businessman; the "witty" repartee and "classy" treatment of "adult" issues "appeals to both genders", plus the picture also acts as a useful "guide to why you shouldn't cheat on your spouse."

Ⓩ Touch of Evil ◑
26 | 24 | 25 | 26

1958 | Directed by Orson Welles | With Charlton Heston, Janet Leigh, Orson Welles, Akim Tamiroff | 95 minutes | Rated PG-13

"Proof that Welles was more than a one-hit wonder", this "rococo" "pinnacle of film noir" stars the director as a "bloated" Texas border town cop feuding with his south-of-the-border counterpart (Heston in "Mexican blackface"); among its many memorable touches are the "sweeping" opening sequence and the "effortless scene-stealing" by Marlene Dietrich, who has the picture's best line: "lay off the candy bars"; P.S. the "restored version" is "much better" than the original release.

Towering Inferno, The 18 | 17 | 18 | 22

1974 | Directed by John Guillermin, Irwin Allen | With Steve McQueen, Paul Newman, William Holden | 165 minutes | Rated PG

"Make sure you know where all the exits are" before settling into this "big, bad '70s disaster" flick starring a skyscraper, a fire and a "rogues' gallery of great actors"; although the "passable" "special effects were top-drawer for its time", cynical sorts snort it's more of a "made-for-TV movie" by modern standards.

☑ Toy Story 27 | – | 25 | 28

1995 | Directed by John Lasseter | Animated | 81 minutes | Rated G

Ushering in a "new era of animation" with "breakthrough" computer-generated effects, this Pixar-produced "instant classic" is a bona fide "technical wonder"; its "humorous" storyline, "lovable characters" and the "great concept" of walking, talking toys add up to a picture that's not only "equally entertaining for adults and kids" but also "deserving of the franchise it started."

☑ Toy Story 2 26 | – | 24 | 28

1999 | Directed by John Lasseter, Ash Brannon, Lee Unkrich | Animated | 92 minutes | Rated G

"Not just another wind-up sequel", this "worthy successor" to "one of the best animated films" ever is a "marvel" in its own right, this time following the misadventures of Woody, a toy cowboy who's been "stolen by a greedy collector to be sold to the highest bidder"; Pixar's "wonderfully creative" CGI renderings work their usual magic so well that parents report "you almost don't mind watching it the 8,000 times that your kids request."

Trading Places 23 | 22 | 23 | 20

1983 | Directed by John Landis | With Dan Aykroyd, Eddie Murphy, Jamie Lee Curtis, Ralph Bellamy | 118 minutes | Rated R

This "hysterical" treatment of the "classic" "rags-to-riches" "switcheroo" has "pauper" Murphy turned into "prince" Aykroyd and vice-versa; "quickly paced and never boring", it's memorable for "early vintage" Eddie moments, some "funny" business from Dan and the spectacle of Jamie Lee's "exposed breasts."

Traffic 23 | 24 | 23 | 25

2000 | Directed by Steven Soderbergh | With Michael Douglas, Benicio Del Toro, Catherine Zeta-Jones | 147 minutes | Rated R

Maybe "more realistic than you want", this "eye-opening portrait of the drug wars" is "poignant, intelligent" and "troubling", using "multiple storylines" to create a "stunning" hybrid of "thriller" and "cautionary tale"; the "amazing use of color", "documentary-like handheld" camerawork and Del Toro's deft, Oscar-winning turn all get the green light, though the highest praise is reserved for its "absolutely brilliant" director.

	OVERALL	ACTING	STORY	PROD.

Training Day ✉   20   27   19   22

2001 | Directed by Antoine Fuqua | With Denzel Washington, Ethan Hawke, Scott Glenn, Tom Berenger | 120 minutes | Rated R

"Denzel shows his scary side" as a "profoundly bad" LA cop with "charisma" in his Oscar-winning role as a detective who has "one day to teach the ropes" to a "rookie" (played by a "holding-his-own" Hawke); the "twisting" plot "grabs you from the very beginning" and takes you on one "wild ride."

Trainspotting   22   22   20   22

1996 | Directed by Danny Boyle | With Ewan McGregor, Ewen Bremner, Robert Carlyle | 94 minutes | Rated R

"Giddy and witty" but also "harrowing and intense", this "graphic" British drama depicting the "daily life of drug addicts" has a "kinetic rawness" about it that "gets right under your skin"; while "not for everyone", its "quirky" cinematography and "outstanding" '80s pop score make for "reality-check" viewing, but bring an "interpreter" – the "Scottish accents are thick."

TransAmerica   24   28   23   22

2005 | Directed by Duncan Tucker | With Felicity Huffman, Kevin Zegers, Fionnula Flanagan | 103 minutes | Rated R

Huffman's "fearless", "dead-on" portrayal of an "uptight" male-to-female transsexual who "learns she has a son" provides this "original" gender-bender dramedy with plenty of "hilarious", "seat-squirming" moments mixed with "compelling", "raw emotion"; ok, it may "drag" in places, but at least its pro-"acceptance" message "pulls no punches."

Transformers   21   17   18   26

2007 | Directed by Michael Bay | With Shia LaBeouf, Megan Fox, Josh Duhamel | 144 minutes | Rated PG-13

An "over-the-top barrage" of "awesome" visuals and "booming", "earplug"-worthy audio heralds the live-action film debut of cartoondom's most beloved "robots from outer space" in this "fast-paced" action flick; it stars the "likable" LaBeouf, who fires off "funny one-liners" that bring relief when the plot – something about "saving the universe" – is at its most "mechanical."

ⓩ Treasure of the Sierra Madre, The ✉◑   27   27   26   24

1948 | Directed by John Huston | With Humphrey Bogart, Walter Huston, Tim Holt | 126 minutes | Not Rated

"Human nature poisoned by greed" is the theme of this "old-fashioned" "treasure hunt", a "wonderful adventure" that won Oscars for the father-and-son Hustons; Bogart exudes "masculine energy" showing "what gold will do to a man" in an "unforgettably powerful" performance that devolves into "paranoia" – and as for the "stunning" black-and-white photography, purists say "we don't need no stinkin' color."

Triplets of Belleville, The ⒡   24   -   23   26

2003 | Directed by Sylvain Chomet | Animated | 80 minutes | Rated PG-13

"Trippy and funny in a way that American animation isn't", this "art house" French cartoon sure "ain't Disney" with its "surreal" plot, "stylized" illustration and "nearly dialogue-free" soundtrack; having something to do with a kidnapped bicyclist rescued by his "grandmère", an "amazing" dog and the "wacky" Triplets of Belleville, it's both "innovative" and "offbeat", and probably more "for adults" than small fry.

Trip to Bountiful, The ✉ | 24 | 26 | 23 | 21 |
1985 | Directed by Peter Masterson | With Geraldine Page, John Heard, Carlin Glynn, Rebecca De Mornay | 108 minutes | Rated PG
An "elderly lady's wish" to relive her past by visiting her Texas hometown frames this "poignant" stage-to-screen adaptation, a journey through "memory and reality" featuring Page in an "exquisite", Oscar-grabbing turn; the "parable"-esque plot manages to strike "spiritual" chords, but it's the heroine's "suffocating situation" – an "all too common" dilemma for those "in their later years" – that will "haunt" you.

☒ Triumph of the Will ❶🄵 | 27 | - | 17 | 27 |
1935 | Directed by Leni Riefenstahl | Documentary | 114 minutes | Not Rated
"Perhaps the most powerful (and immoral) documentary" ever made, this "Leni Riefenstahl masterpiece" was commissioned to honor Germany's 1934 National Socialist Party Congress and the metaphorical "enthronement of Hitler"; the "superb" camerawork leads reluctant admirers to admit this "artful" propaganda piece is indeed a "triumph of filmmaking", if not subject matter.

Tron | 18 | 14 | 18 | 22 |
1982 | Directed by Steven Lisberger | With Jeff Bridges, Bruce Boxleitner, David Warner | 96 minutes | Rated PG
Wired types tout this "underappreciated forerunner to today's special-effects" extravaganzas by dubbing it the "first real geek movie", owing to a storyline that posits what could happen "if you got sucked into your Nintendo"; ok, it could be a tad "dated" now, but it was the "coolest thing since sliced bread when it came out."

Troy | 19 | 19 | 20 | 25 |
2004 | Directed by Wolfgang Petersen | With Brad Pitt, Orlando Bloom, Eric Bana | 163 minutes | Rated R
Homer's *Iliad* gets the "Hollywood treatment" in this "genuine epic" featuring lots of "oiled", "well-tanned" dudes in "miniskirts" engaged in battles that bear distinct "similarities to WWF wrestling"; wags say Brad's performance is the "only thing more wooden than the Trojan horse" ("too much buff, not enough substance"), but there's applause for the "action-packed" script and "excellent production values."

True Grit ✉ | 22 | 23 | 21 | 22 |
1969 | Directed by Henry Hathaway | With John Wayne, Glen Campbell, Kim Darby | 128 minutes | Rated G
"Another Western for your library", this "classic" oater is made "especially for Wayne fans" because the Duke took home his first (and only) Oscar here; otherwise, it's standard stuff about a vengeful lawman, though early-in-their-career performances by Dennis Hopper and Robert Duvall keep things lively.

True Lies | 19 | 16 | 20 | 22 |
1994 | Directed by James Cameron | With Arnold Schwarzenegger, Jamie Lee Curtis | 144 minutes | Rated R
"Arnold is Bond, James Bond" in this "tongue-in-cheek" spy flicker that's a "wonderful combo" of "comedy, action and intrigue"; as his

"frumpy wife" turned "drop-dead gorgeous" siren, Jamie Lee is "smoking", while Tom Arnold's a "gas" as the "not-so-super secret-agent sidekick"; throw in "lots of explosions and weapons" and you've got a true "blockbuster" "blastfest."

True Romance　　24　23　24　22

1993 | Directed by Tony Scott | With Christian Slater, Patricia Arquette, Dennis Hopper, Christopher Walken | 120 minutes | Rated R

Brace yourself for some "big-time gore" in this "ultraviolent" "true cult classic" about newlyweds on the run, scripted by a "pre–Pulp Fiction Quentin Tarantino" and featuring an "all-star" ensemble (including bits by Brad Pitt, Samuel L. Jackson and James Gandolfini "when they were little known"); sticklers note it "steals heartily from Badlands", but ultimately, it's "kinetic", "edgy", "weird" and just plain "cool"; best scene: the "showdown between Hopper and Walken."

Truly Madly Deeply　　23　25　23　22

1991 | Directed by Anthony Minghella | With Juliet Stevenson, Alan Rickman | 106 minutes | Rated PG

A "better British version of Ghost", this "deeply affecting" romance stars "sadly radiant" Stevenson as a Londoner who's "codependent with her husband" Rickman – even though he's recently deceased and "sticking around for unfinished business"; truly "stellar performances" transform the "odd" story into a "moving", sometimes "funny" meditation on the "nature of love" and "letting go."

Truman Show, The　　21　22　23　22

1998 | Directed by Peter Weir | With Jim Carrey, Laura Linney, Ed Harris | 103 minutes | Rated PG

This "original", "thought-provoking" fantasy/comedy offers a "departure" for Carrey, who's "unusually restrained" (i.e. "doesn't act like a moron") in the role of an unwitting star of a 24/7 reality TV show set in a "phony world"; though some lookers find "little content" among all the "hype", intellectuals enthuse that this "Big Brother"–ish allegory leaves you "questioning what reality is."

Truth or Dare　　15　-　14　17

1991 | Directed by Alek Keshishian | Documentary | With Madonna | 118 minutes | Rated R

"Ardent Madonna fanatics" say this "behind-the-scenes" documentary of her 1990 tour, a "warts-and-all" portrayal of the superstar "not striking a pose", is "better than it has any right to be"; but knockers claim this "self-absorbed" "vanity project" is just "mugging for the camera", save for the cameo by Warren Beatty, who "looks appropriately embarrassed as her latest boy toy"; most amusing scene: "talking to Daddy on the phone."

Tucker: The Man and His Dream　　20　21　23　21

1988 | Directed by Francis Ford Coppola | With Jeff Bridges, Joan Allen, Martin Landau | 110 minutes | Rated PG

For a "revealing look beneath the hood of the American auto industry", this "colorful", "stylish" film features a "terrific" Bridges in the sort of "true-ish story" of a "visionary '40s car maker and his sad defeat" at the hands of competitors and politicians; Coppola-ficionados say this "underrated" film "deserves more notice."

Tuck Everlasting
19 | 20 | 20 | 20

2002 | Directed by Jay Russell | With Alexis Bledel, Ben Kingsley, Sissy Spacek, Jonathan Jackson, William Hurt | 90 minutes | Rated PG

A "faithful", "Disneyfied version" of the "popular kids' book", this "picturesque" family flick features "rising star" Bledel as a girl befriended by a family of forest dwellers who have access to a fountain of youth; "heartwarming and all that stuff", it's "palatable" for "tweenagers" with "deep" enough themes to "hold adult interest."

Turning Point, The
23 | 25 | 22 | 23

1977 | Directed by Herbert Ross | With Shirley MacLaine, Anne Bancroft, Mikhail Baryshnikov | 119 minutes | Rated PG

Ascend to "chick-flick heaven" via this "moving" drama that sets the oft-told story of "women choosing between marriage and a career" in a "world-renowned ballet company"; as "longtime friends who took different paths" in life, Bancroft and MacLaine are "brilliant" (especially during that climactic "classic catfight" at Lincoln Center), though balletomanes only have eyes for "Baryshnikov's spectacular dance scenes."

☑ 12 Angry Men ◑
28 | 28 | 27 | 23

1957 | Directed by Sidney Lumet | With Henry Fonda, Martin Balsam, Lee J. Cobb, e.g. Marshall | 96 minutes | Not Rated

"Human nature at its best and worst" is on display in this "brilliant courtroom drama" depicting the "hidden agendas" of jurors deciding the fate of a murder defendant; thanks to its "taut" script and an "unforgettable Fonda", this "study of American democracy" is alternately "suspenseful and compelling."

Twelve Monkeys
22 | 23 | 24 | 23

1995 | Directed by Terry Gilliam | With Bruce Willis, Madeleine Stowe, Brad Pitt | 129 minutes | Rated R

Gilliam's "master-of-the-bizarre" status is reinforced by this "complex", "super-ingenious" time-travel tale about the "release of a deadly virus" followed by a "post-apocalyptic" attempt to "save the world"; the sets are "dazzling", Brad 'n' Bruce prove they can "actually act" and if the *Terminator*-meets-*Brazil* sci-fi storyline is "confusing", it's "wonderfully" so.

☑ Twelve O'Clock High ◑
26 | 25 | 26 | 23

1949 | Directed by Henry King | With Gregory Peck, Hugh Marlowe, Dean Jagger | 132 minutes | Not Rated

"Peck is marvelous" as a WWII Brigadier General "placing terrible pressure on young American pilots" in this "accurate" depiction of the "burdens of command" and the "human side of war"; a "perfect screenplay" "rooted in historical reality" "manipulates the tension" right up to the compelling climax.

28 Days Later
18 | 17 | 19 | 18

2003 | Directed by Danny Boyle | With Cillian Murphy, Naomie Harris | 113 minutes | Rated R

"Modern-day horror" gets some "low-budget twists" in this "seriously scary" British import that "reinvents the zombie flick for the new millennium" in its story of a "viral disaster" that threatens civilization;

while surveyors split on its digital video cinematography ("cool and grainy" versus "looks like it was shot with a bad camcorder"), most agree that the finale "wimps out" – although the DVD includes a number of "alternate endings."

28 Weeks Later
`19` `18` `20` `21`

2007 | Directed by Juan Carlos Fresnadillo | With Catherine McCormack, Robert Carlyle, Rose Byrne | 101 minutes | Rated R

"Gore, mutilation" and "frenetic action": "what else can you ask for" in a "zombie epidemic" flick?; those infected by this "action-packed" "shriekfest" deem it a "worthy follow-up" to Danny Boyle's original hit, but the immune suggest even the "fastest zombies in film history" can't outrun the "uneven acting" and "plot holes big enough to drive a truck through."

25th Hour
`21` `25` `20` `21`

2002 | Directed by Spike Lee | With Edward Norton, Philip Seymour Hoffman, Barry Pepper | 135 minutes | Rated R

A drug dealer "with one day left before prison turns to his friends for comfort" in this "captivating film that's even more poignant given its tribute to post-9/11 NYC"; it's "not your typical Spike Lee, but still one of his best" thanks to "superb ensemble acting"; still, some say "it seemed like it was 25 hours long."

21 Grams
`22` `27` `21` `21`

2003 | Directed by Alejandro González Iñárritu | With Sean Penn, Naomi Watts, Benicio Del Toro | 124 minutes | Rated R

"Not an easy watch", this "disturbing take on love and loss" details the lives of three people who meet as the result of a deadly accident; its "nonlinear storyline" told via "flashbacks and flashforwards" (à la *Memento* and *Pulp Fiction*") might be "intriguing" to some and "confusing" to others, but the "stellar" ensemble supplies enough "brain candy" to make for "compelling" viewing; in sum, be ready for an "emotionally draining downer" that's "moving, intelligent" and guaranteed to "keep you guessing."

27 Dresses
`17` `18` `16` `18`

2008 | Directed by Anne Fletcher | With Katherine Heigl, James Marsden, Edward Burns | 111 minutes | Rated PG-13

An "always-a-bridesmaid-never-a-bride" gal is the subject of this "cute" but "routine rom-com" that "charms" fans with its parade of "god-awful dresses" and "bizarre wedding rituals"; maybe the "predictable" script has been "done to death", but the palpable "chemistry" between the "endearing" Heigl and "appealing" Marsden makes for "harmless" viewing.

20,000 Leagues Under the Sea
`22` `18` `25` `23`

1954 | Directed by Richard Fleischer | With Kirk Douglas, James Mason, Peter Lorre | 127 minutes | Rated G

"Disney's live-action adaptation of the Jules Verne classic" is a "fabulous" undersea adventure starring a "singing", "tight shorts"–wearing Douglas as the heroic 19th-century seafarer who battles both Captain Nemo and a "scary giant squid" who "should have received an Oscar"; even though the special effects look "cheesy" today, overall it's a "real old-fashioned hoot."

Twins
15 | 15 | 15 | 15

1988 | Directed by Ivan Reitman | With Arnold Schwarzenegger, Danny DeVito, Kelly Preston | 105 minutes | Rated PG

For the ultimate "mismatch made in heaven", try this "far-fetched" laughfest about test-tube twins "separated at birth" and later reunited for "wacky" escapades; while the stars are "likable" enough and display relatively "good chemistry", for most this "guilty pleasure" lies somewhere between "ridiculous" and "dopey."

Twister
15 | 14 | 14 | 22

1996 | Directed by Jan de Bont | With Helen Hunt, Bill Paxton, Cary Elwes, Jami Gertz | 114 minutes | Rated PG-13

"Mother nature" runs amok in this "far-fetched disaster movie" about Midwestern meteorologists tracking tornados; though the "fancy computer effects" make the "awesome" twisters "look so real", the "sleepwalking" actors and "easily forgettable" story with "no concern for logic" lead some to snore "major bore."

Two for the Road
24 | 27 | 24 | 24

1967 | Directed by Stanley Donen | With Albert Finney, Audrey Hepburn | 111 minutes | Not Rated

"Love isn't always easy" in this "bittersweet travelogue of the ups and downs of a married couple" that "jumps back and forth in time" as they "find, lose and rekindle" their relationship; Audrey's at her "most charming" and "marvelous together" with Finney amid all that "unmatched European scenery"; meanwhile, the "mesmerizing, melodious" Mancini music "sustains the mood."

☒ 2001: A Space Odyssey
26 | 19 | 24 | 27

1968 | Directed by Stanley Kubrick | With Keir Dullea, Gary Lockwood, William Sylvester | 139 minutes | Rated G

The "Citizen Kane of science-fiction films", this "era-defining" Kubrick interpretation of an Arthur C. Clarke story "changed movies forever" with its "haunting view" of a future world of "machine domination"; sure, some modernists find it "slow" and "ponderous", but even those who have "no clue what it all means" say this "coldly magnificent" epic is "undeniably influential" – and add "you'll never hear Strauss' 'Blue Danube Waltz' the same way again"; P.S. "don't bother trying to figure out the ending."

2010
16 | 16 | 17 | 20

1984 | Directed by Peter Hyams | With Roy Scheider, John Lithgow, Helen Mirren, Bob Balaban | 114 minutes | Rated PG

"High-quality special effects" make this sequel to 2001 "relatively worthwhile", not to mention "less confusing", since a "more linear plot" "helps to explain the original storyline"; but foes insist it's "not in the same league at all", merely a "workmanlike" effort with "no transcendence", though admitting it "had an awful lot to live up to."

Two Weeks Notice
16 | 18 | 16 | 17

2002 | Directed by Marc Lawrence | With Sandra Bullock, Hugh Grant | 101 minutes | Rated PG-13

A "playboy" real estate tycoon and a "do-gooder" lawyer meet cute in this "soggy" romantic comedy, a "predictable" "bit of fluff" with an "obvious ending" and "only 10 minutes' worth of laughs"; further faults include a "flimsy script" and "no sense of true chemistry" between the otherwise "likable" leads – "no one in the real world behaves like this."

⚡ Two Women ✉❶🅵   25 | 28 | 25 | 24

1961 | Directed by Vittorio De Sica | With Sophia Loren, Eleanora Brown, Raf Vallone | 99 minutes | Not Rated

The "horror of war" from a "woman's viewpoint" is delineated in this "heartbreaking" Italian drama where a "protective mother and her daughter" bond after being "brutally raped" by a gang of soldiers; best remembered for Sophia's "riveting" performance, it's a "very emotional" film that's "seldom seen these days."

U-571   17 | 17 | 19 | 21

2000 | Directed by Jonathan Mostow | With Matthew McConaughey, Bill Paxton, Harvey Keitel | 116 minutes | Rated PG-13

This "tense" World War II "submarine flick" brings out plenty of "claustrophobia" in its story of a tightly quartered American crew duking it out with a German U-boat under high seas; while it's "no *Das Boot*" (given "so-so acting" and a "could-have-been-better" storyline "full of obvious holes"), it's still a "rousing", bona fide guy movie.

Umbrellas of Cherbourg, The 🅵   24 | 22 | 21 | 26

1964 | Directed by Jacques Demy | With Catherine Deneuve, Nino Castelnuovo | 87 minutes | Not Rated

Ultra-"bright Technicolor" and "captivating" music from Michel Legrand provide the uplift in this "sad story" of love in vain, an idiosyncratic French bonbon that's "entirely sung" (a "risky" proposition that ultimately "works"); starring a "fetching young Deneuve", it has the "courage" to turn a potentially "cheesy" premise into "inspiring" filmmaking.

Unbearable Lightness of Being, The   21 | 24 | 21 | 21

1988 | Directed by Philip Kaufman | With Daniel Day-Lewis, Juliette Binoche, Lena Olin | 171 minutes | Rated R

"Romance amid revolution" is the theme of this erudite picture about the "erotic" misadventures of a young Czech surgeon swept up in the '68 Russian invasion of Prague; while the light-headed like the "hottie" cast's "compelling" work, cynics sneer this "yawner" "leaves a lot to be desired" and suggest the title be cut to just plain "*Unbearable*."

Unbreakable   16 | 19 | 17 | 19

2000 | Directed by M. Night Shyamalan | With Bruce Willis, Samuel L. Jackson, Robin Wright Penn | 107 minutes | Rated PG-13

Ok, it's "hard to live up to *The Sixth Sense*", but this solid follow-up from the Shyamalan/Willis team "keeps you wondering all the time" with its "intriguing" story of a "man struggling with immortality"; though surveyors split on the end result (a "noble failure" vs. "terribly underrated"), holdouts insist it "warrants more than one viewing" to be fully appreciated.

Uncle Buck   17 | 18 | 17 | 17

1989 | Directed by John Hughes | With John Candy, Amy Madigan, Jean Louisa Kelly | 100 minutes | Rated PG

"Among John Candy's best", most "lovable" roles is his heavy-duty turn as a "derelict turned babysitter" in this lightweight comedy; while the "movie itself is just ok", the "funny dialogue" and heroic oafishness of the lead prevail – and an appearance by a pre–*Home Alone* Macaulay Culkin adds to its family appeal.

Under Siege

15 | 11 | 14 | 16

1992 | Directed by Andrew Davis | With Steven Seagal, Tommy Lee Jones, Gary Busey | 102 minutes | Rated R

Think "*Die Hard* on a battleship" to get the gist of this "graphically violent" Seagal vehicle where he "kicks some serious ass" to keep his "reputation afloat"; maybe the stealing-nukes plot is "moronic", but at least the "kill-first-ask-questions-later" sensibility is "entertainingly dumb."

Under the Tuscan Sun

19 | 20 | 18 | 22

2003 | Directed by Audrey Wells | With Diane Lane, Sandra Oh, Raoul Bova | 113 minutes | Rated PG-13

A newly divorced woman buys a house in "picturesque Tuscany" to start her life anew and "find herself" in this "coming-into-bloom" picture, a "feel-good" chick flick worth seeing for Lane's "warm, genuine performance" alone; ok, "it isn't *Enchanted April*" and there's "not much storyline", but it's still "sweet and fun."

Underworld

17 | 16 | 17 | 21

2003 | Directed by Len Wiseman | With Kate Beckinsale, Scott Speedman, Michael Sheen, Bill Nighy | 121 minutes | Rated R

It's "the vampires vs. the werewolves" in this "Goth" horror pic, a "noirish" mood piece in which "sexy vamp-babe" Beckinsale squares off against a pack of "evil" lycanthropes; but despite "cool effects" and "plenty of action", the underwhelmed say this "stylish fluff" "doesn't have any bite" and is "unscary" to boot.

Unfaithful

21 | 24 | 20 | 20

2002 | Directed by Adrian Lyne | With Diane Lane, Richard Gere, Olivier Martinez | 124 minutes | Rated R

Diane Lane is "spectacular" and "so convincing" as a modern housewife "torn between guilt and thrills as she embarks on an affair" with a "hot" stranger, and Richard Gere delivers the "most mature, nuanced performance of his career" as the "cuckold" in this "unexpectedly intense film" that's "disturbing in its credibility"; "now if only they'd found a better plot" and a less "lame" ending.

Unfinished Life, An

20 | 22 | 20 | 21

2005 | Directed by Lasse Hallström | With Robert Redford, Jennifer Lopez, Morgan Freeman | 107 minutes | Rated PG-13

"Strong" characters hold together this "moving" story of a rancher and his kin, struggling with "forgiveness" following a series of tragedies, ok, the script may be a bit "thin" and J. Lo's acting rather "stilted", but "great cinematography" and "good jobs" by the "believable" Freeman and "still-hot" Redford "save the movie."

☑ Unforgiven ✉

26 | 26 | 24 | 25

1992 | Directed by Clint Eastwood | With Clint Eastwood, Gene Hackman, Morgan Freeman | 131 minutes | Rated R

"Clint directs, Clint scores, Clint wins" a Best Picture statuette with this "grim" "anti-Western" that manages to "revise every convention and cliché of the genre" with a "superb script" and cast of "unforgivable" "unforgettable" characters; indeed, it's so "powerful" and "dark" you'll find "no white hats here."

	OVERALL	ACTING	STORY	PROD.

United 93
25 23 25 25

2006 | Directed by Paul Greengrass | With Christian Clemenson, Trish Gates, David Alan Basche | 111 minutes | Rated R

A "nightmarish subject" – the 9/11 hijacking of United flight 93 – is "handled with sensitivity" in this tribute to "spontaneous heroism" that's always "riveting" even though "you know the terrible outcome"; admittedly "tough to watch", it's "never overwrought", shot in a "real-time", "documentary" style and enacted by a "largely unknown cast" (along with "people who play themselves"); the end result is by turns "horrifying", "heartbreaking" and "exhausting."

Unmarried Woman, An
20 25 21 19

1978 | Directed by Paul Mazursky | With Jill Clayburgh, Alan Bates, Michael Murphy | 130 minutes | Rated R

This "very-much-of-its-time" portrait of a "New Yorkey" divorcée "in transition" offers a "thoughtful", "emotional" examination of a '70s "woman's lib"–style romance; the picture broke "new ground" when originally released, thanks to the "excellent" Clayburgh as the recently "single" gal, though postfeminists posit it may "seem dated now."

Unsinkable Molly Brown, The
21 20 20 21

1964 | Directed by Charles Walters | With Debbie Reynolds, Harve Presnell, Ed Begley | 128 minutes | Not Rated

"Think of it as the last big" MGM musical and "you'll be in for a good evening's entertainment" with this "rollicking" bio of a turn-of-the-century "bawdy broad who wants it all and gets it"; warblers adore the "rip-roarin'" Reynolds in the title role, who drowns all doubts about how "she got the name 'unsinkable.'"

Untouchables, The
22 22 22 22

1987 | Directed by Brian De Palma | With Kevin Costner, Sean Connery, Robert De Niro | 119 minutes | Rated R

"Sassy" '30s crime drama recounting the epic "good-vs.-evil" struggle between Eliot Ness and Al Capone, as interpreted by Costner and De Niro (wearing "amazing Armani suits"); while this "period piece" has "exciting action" and "style to spare", the most "compelling" work comes from the Oscar-winning Connery as a streetwise copper.

Up in Smoke
19 17 16 15

1978 | Directed by Lou Adler | With Cheech Marin, Tommy Chong, Zane Buzby | 86 minutes | Rated R

The "movie weed was made for", this "first and best" stoner comedy from "pot kings" Cheech and Chong rolls out the "herb"-addled duo's "smoke-laced" adventures around El Lay; despite "sophomoric" gags and "low production values", it's still regarded as a "rite of passage" for the "chemically altered" – "if only I could remember it, man."

Upside of Anger, The
22 26 21 22

2005 | Directed by Mike Binder | With Joan Allen, Kevin Costner, Erika Christensen, Evan Rachel Wood | 118 minutes | Rated R

"Rage and depression" grip an abandoned housewife when a "washed-up baseball player" steps up to the plate to "suffer by her side" in this "acute observation" of "real people"; it pairs the "amazing" Allen with a "hang-loose" Costner, but apart from the "great screen chemistry", there's a downside: that "difficult-to-swallow" "surprise" ending.

Uptown Girls
14 **16** **15** **15**

2003 | Directed by Boaz Yakin | With Brittany Murphy, Dakota Fanning | 92 minutes | Rated PG-13

"Don't set your expectations too high" before watching this "feel-good" story of a "spoiled rich girl" who goes broke and becomes a nanny for a "poor little trust fund" kid; as "mindless" chick flicks go, it's appropriately "shallow" and "cutesy-pie", though it does attempt to teach a lesson about the "power of friendship" that makes sentimental types "cry like a baby."

Urban Cowboy
18 **17** **16** **17**

1980 | Directed by James Bridges | With John Travolta, Debra Winger, Scott Glenn | 132 minutes | Rated PG

Travolta "in tight jeans" plays opposite Winger at her most "adorable" in this "highly watchable" honky-tonk romance about "beer-swigging", "mechanical bull-riding" men and the women who love them; although Debra nearly "steals the show", she's almost bested by an appealing Houston setting.

U.S. Marshals
18 **20** **18** **19**

1998 | Directed by Stuart Baird | With Tommy Lee Jones, Wesley Snipes, Robert Downey Jr. | 131 minutes | Rated PG-13

"Same main character, different storyline" sums up the pedigree of this "sequel of sorts" to *The Fugitive*, a "hard-hitting" action flick that brings back Jones' "straight-faced" lawman Sam Gerard for another "edge-of-your-seat" pursuit of a murder suspect; while most find "easy watching" with this "clever" follow-up, critics wonder "where's Harrison Ford?"

☒ Usual Suspects, The ✉
27 **28** **28** **25**

1995 | Directed by Bryan Singer | With Gabriel Byrne, Kevin Spacey, Benicio Del Toro, Stephen Baldwin | 106 minutes | Rated R

"Don't blink" or you'll risk missing one of the many "imaginative" twists in this "tricky-as-hell" "instant classic" that may be one of the finest "whodunit" "thrill rides" ever made; fans "watch it at least twice" to absorb the "brilliant" story, admire the "flawless" Spacey and figure out what the heck "Benicio's saying"; as for that "unpredictable finale", you'll "never see it coming."

Valley of the Dolls
17 **15** **18** **17**

1967 | Directed by Mark Robson | With Barbara Parkins, Patty Duke, Sharon Tate, Susan Hayward | 123 minutes | Rated PG-13

Based on Jacqueline Susann's "trashy" '60s best-seller, this "soapy", "schmaltzy" "cult classic" recounts the story of "racy" career girls seduced by the "glitter of showbiz" (and its attendant downsides, "pills and booze"); forget the "cheesy script", "bad wigs" and "Patty Duke chewing the scenery": the "high kitsch" factor alone makes for "camp perfection."

Valmont
20 **23** **21** **22**

1989 | Directed by Milos Forman | With Colin Firth, Annette Bening, Fairuza Balk, Henry Thomas | 137 minutes | Rated R

Forever known as "the 'other' adaptation of *Dangerous Liaisons*", this "elaborate" period piece stars a "charming" Firth as a "shallow" 18th-century nobleman of "questionable morality" who "connives" to wreck innocent lives; admirers aver this "subtle production" "has its moments", but admit it's a "pale competitor to the Glenn Close version."

	OVERALL	ACTING	STORY	PROD.

Van Helsing
15 | 15 | 14 | 21

2004 | Directed by Stephen Sommers | With Hugh Jackman, Kate Beckinsale | 132 minutes | Rated PG-13

"Superficially entertaining", this horror flick-cum-"thrill machine" about a bounty hunter hounding Dracula, Frankenstein and various werewolves should be "pure escapist fun" what with its "nonstop", "over-the-top" special effects, yet many call it a "big mess"; though Jackman "broods elegantly" in the title role, he's up against a "muddled storyline", Beckinsale's "awful accent" and an "overblown" production that seems more about "merchandising" than moviemaking.

Vanilla Sky
12 | 16 | 13 | 17

2001 | Directed by Cameron Crowe | With Tom Cruise, Penélope Cruz, Cameron Diaz, Kurt Russell | 136 minutes | Rated R

A "surreal" remake of a Spanish film, this "odd" romance "messes with your brain" as a "smug", "ultracool" Cruise is disfigured in a car crash only to undergo a *Twilight Zone*-worthy recovery (Cruz "reprises her role from the original" as the love interest); still, "annoyed" viewers find it nothing more than a "pretentious mishmash."

Vanity Fair
17 | 19 | 18 | 23

2004 | Directed by Mira Nair | With Reese Witherspoon, James Purefoy, Ramola Garai, Eileen Atkins | 141 minutes | Rated PG-13

A "visually beautiful" interpretation of Thackeray's "bitingly satirical" novel, this "opulent" romance tells the story of a "conniving" social climber trying to "elevate herself into society" in 19th-century Britain; but many say this "less than faithful adaptation" suffers most from a "miscast Reece", who's "more cutesy than cunning" and "never ages" in a story that unwinds over 30 years.

Van Wilder
14 | 13 | 13 | 13

2002 | Directed by Walt Becker | With Ryan Reynolds, Tara Reid, Tim Matheson, Kal Penn | 92 minutes | Rated R

"Immaturity in a college setting" and the National Lampoon imprimatur make for a Deltas "rehash" in this "party" comedy starring Reynolds as the "ultimate" campus troublemaker wielding a togaful of "gross" gags; it's "humorous" so long as "your expectations aren't too high", but most aren't wild about "regurgitated" material that's "unworthy of comparison to *Animal House*."

Velvet Goldmine
17 | 22 | 17 | 20

1998 | Directed by Todd Haynes | With Ewan McGregor, Jonathan Rhys Meyers, Christian Bale | 124 minutes | Rated R

This "ode to '70s glam rock", a "*Citizen Kane*"-like look at a "gender-bending", David Bowie-ish pop star, has "all the elements of a great film": "outstanding performances", a "spellbinding score", "full-frontal nudity", "fab hair and eye makeup"; yet due to an "insipid" script that "dips and drags", some call it "more a collection of wonderful ideas" than a coherent picture.

Venus
19 | 26 | 18 | 19

2006 | Directed by Roger Michell | With Peter O'Toole, Leslie Phillips, Jodie Whittaker, Vanessa Redgrave | 95 minutes | Rated R

O'Toole was "made for" the role of a "dying Lothario" in this "brilliant" if "twisted" dramedy about an "aging actor" whose "lecherous intentions" are stirred as he escorts the much younger Whittaker around London; the "creepy" "glorification of a dirty old man" may be "not for everyone", but there's "plausible pathos" in its "bittersweet mix of desire and desperation."

Vera Drake
24 | 28 | 25 | 23

2004 | Directed by Mike Leigh | With Imelda Staunton | 125 minutes | Rated R

Wherever you stand on Roe vs. Wade, it's "hard not to be moved" by this "devastating portrait" of a "well-meaning abortionist who runs afoul of the law" in '50s London; "delicate" direction by Leigh keeps the "polarizing" material in check, while "flawless" performances by a "magnificent" ensemble (particularly Staunton's "unforgettable" title turn) ensure there's "never a false moment."

Verdict, The
23 | 25 | 23 | 20

1982 | Directed by Sidney Lumet | With Paul Newman, Charlotte Rampling, Jack Warden | 129 minutes | Rated R

A "David-vs.-Goliath" legal struggle is the underpinning of this "underrated" courtroom drama about a "burned-out lawyer trying one last case to keep from going under"; Newman's "intense", "tour-de-force" turn is one of his "greatest" roles (leaving many "stunned" that the Oscar eluded him), while the "mesmerizing" Rampling "excels" as the love interest.

Veronica Guerin
21 | 25 | 22 | 20

2003 | Directed by Joel Schumacher | With Cate Blanchett, Gerard McSorley | 98 minutes | Rated R

"Versatile" Blanchett "shines" as a "determined" Dublin journalist "fighting the good fight" against drug kingpins in this "gripping" thriller based on a true but "tragic" story; if the thick brogues are "hard to follow" and the overall message skews toward "heavy-handedness", most feel it's Guerin-teed to "make you wonder" about some tough issues.

Z Vertigo
27 | 26 | 27 | 26

1958 | Directed by Alfred Hitchcock | With James Stewart, Kim Novak, Barbara Bel Geddes | 128 minutes | Rated PG

"Don't look down": this "dizzyingly complex" thriller offers lots of "twists and turns" as it details the "haunting" tale of an "obsessive" man who "tries to mold a woman into a vision of his lost love"; many call it "Hitchcock's crowning achievement" thanks to a Bernard Herrmann score that's "like perfume" as well as "spellbinding" work from a "bewitching Novak" and "Stewart at his darkest"; as for that "fever dream" of a plot, "it's not supposed to make sense."

Very Long Engagement, A ⊟
22 | 24 | 22 | 25

2004 | Directed by Jean-Pierre Jeunet | With Audrey Tautou, Gaspard Ulliel | 134 minutes | Rated R

Amélie's "dynamic duo" (director Jeunet and "radiant" actress Tautou) reunite for this "beautifully done" French war saga whose "graphic" depictions of WWI trenches are tempered by a "tearful" story of "lost love"; with "so many characters", the "complex storyline" can be "hard to follow" and "takes time" to develop, leaving some to retitle it "A Very Long Movie."

V for Vendetta

OVERALL	ACTING	STORY	PROD.
22	22	22	24

2006 | Directed by James McTeigue | With Natalie Portman, Hugo Weaving, Stephen Rea | 132 minutes | Rated R

"Reminiscent of *1984*" with its "dark" depiction of a "totalitarian" society, this "provocative" futuristic thriller relating the exploits of a "Guy Fawkes–like" rebel is "V for very good" thanks to "spine-tingling" visuals, "swiftly paced" action and "well-acted" characterizations by Portman and Weaving; flirting with the "controversial subject of terrorism", it strikes many as a "not-so-subtle" allusion to "current events."

Victor/Victoria

OVERALL	ACTING	STORY	PROD.
23	24	23	23

1982 | Directed by Blake Edwards | With Julie Andrews, James Garner, Robert Preston, Lesley Ann Warren | 132 minutes | Rated PG

"What a hoot!" holler fans who "never tire of watching" this "hilarious" musical farce about Parisian nightlife denizens in the '30s; "Andrews lights up the screen" as the titular double-crossed cross-dresser, while Leslie Ann Warren's fabulous floozie is deliciously "over-the-top"; in sum, this "fast-paced", "madcap" tale of "jazz-age gender bending" is "just plain fun."

Videodrome

OVERALL	ACTING	STORY	PROD.
▽ 17	17	20	19

1983 | Directed by David Cronenberg | With James Woods, Sonja Smits, Deborah Harry | 87 minutes | Rated R

"Made at the dawn of cable TV and home VCRs", this "seductive psychological thriller" about "how the media controls minds" has earned "cult classic" status thanks to Cronenberg's "weird", "icky-creepy touches" (like the "videotape inserted into Woods' abdomen"); maybe "it played better in 1983", though even then people still couldn't "figure out what it's all about."

View to a Kill, A

OVERALL	ACTING	STORY	PROD.
14	13	14	18

1985 | Directed by John Glen | With Roger Moore, Christopher Walken, Tanya Roberts, Grace Jones | 131 minutes | Rated PG

"Old" Moore caps his 12-year run as 007 – and "not in the best way" – with this "forgettable" installment pitting the secret agent against a psycho industrialist, whose scheme "to corner the world market in microchips" was a silly premise "even in 1985"; granted, it may have "some of the best stunts and title music" of the series and a "scary" Bond girl in Grace Jones, but the final view on this one is "clunker."

Village, The

OVERALL	ACTING	STORY	PROD.
16	19	17	19

2004 | Directed by M. Night Shyamalan | With Bryce Dallas Howard, Joaquin Phoenix, Adrien Brody | 108 minutes | Rated PG-13

Reminiscent of a "long episode of *The Twilight Zone*", this "unusual" thriller visits an isolated "countryside" hamlet where residents sport "period" threads and live under constant fear of "freaky monsters"; there's agreement on the "interesting concept", but director Shyamalan's "signature twist" at the end polarizes voters: buffs bet "you won't see it coming", whereas seen-it-alls sneer "hokey letdown."

Village of the Damned ◑

OVERALL	ACTING	STORY	PROD.
21	19	23	19

1960 | Directed by Wolf Rilla | With George Sanders, Barbara Shelley, Michael Gwynn | 78 minutes | Not Rated

An "unfortunate town" becomes host to an army of "alien children" with funny eyeballs in this "spooky" British sci-fi flick that "succeeds without a lot of fancy effects"; ever "cool" over 45 years later, it still "creeps out" viewers ("whoever thought kids could be so scary?") who advise "don't bother with the '95 version."

Virgin Suicides, The
20 | 21 | 20 | 20

2000 | Directed by Sofia Coppola | With Kirsten Dunst, James Woods, Kathleen Turner, Josh Hartnett | 97 minutes | Rated R

"Coppola's vision shines" in her virgin directorial outing, an "absorbing" dramedy about "melancholy" sibs in a "seemingly perfect family" driven to "deathly" measures by "suburban teenage angst"; a "sad, eerie story" of "imprisoned femininity", it's told with a "visually inventive" style that could be "even better than the book."

Viva Zapata! ◐
23 | 24 | 22 | 21

1952 | Directed by Elia Kazan | With Marlon Brando, Jean Peters, Anthony Quinn | 113 minutes | Not Rated

Elia Kazan directs a John Steinbeck screenplay in this "passionate" profile of Emiliano Zapata, the revolutionary hero who led a rebellion against Mexican dictator Porfirio Diaz; featuring an "unusual but expert turn" by Brando in the title role (as well as an Oscar-winning turn by Quinn), it's "historical" cinema "at its best" and, given the climate of its 1952 release, an "important political drama."

Volver 🅵
24 | 26 | 23 | 23

2006 | Directed by Pedro Almodóvar | With Penélope Cruz, Carmen Maura, Lola Dueñas | 121 minutes | Rated R

Spanish "master" Almodóvar "just gets better and better", coaxing a "luminously beautiful" performance from "luscious" "muse" Cruz ("no one writes for women the way Pedro does") in this "spellbinding" mother-daughter "family drama"; mixing "tragedy and laughter in the right amounts" with a splash of "Hitchcock", this "sentimental, emotional" concoction "has it all" for fans of cinema *maravillosa.*

🆉 Wages of Fear ◐🅵
27 | 26 | 27 | 24

1955 | Directed by Henri-Georges Clouzot | With Yves Montand, Charles Vanel | 148 minutes | Not Rated

"Fasten your seatbelts for a bumpy" ride via this "nerve-racking" "nail-biter" about "down-and-outers" racing a "nitroglycerine-loaded truck" across the mountains of South America; Clouzot's knack for "oh-my-God" suspense and "social commentary" makes it one of the "best art-house action" flicks around.

Wag the Dog
19 | 22 | 22 | 19

1997 | Directed by Barry Levinson | With Dustin Hoffman, Robert De Niro, Anne Heche, Denis Leary | 97 minutes | Rated R

Pundits praise this "biting black comedy" that "makes light (and dark) of media-oriented politics" via a "surreal" story about a "nonexistent war created by the government to divert attention" from a presidential scandal; though some wonder if it's a "documentary", others tout this "underrated" political satire for Hoffman and De Niro's "standout" turns.

Waiting for Guffman
25 | 26 | 24 | 23

1996 | Directed by Christopher Guest | With Christopher Guest, Eugene Levy, Fred Willard, Catherine O'Hara | 84 minutes | Rated R

"Anyone who loves the theater and loves to laugh" shouldn't miss this "hilarious" mockumentary about "community theater in the boonies" courtesy of "comic genius" Guest and his "usual incredibly talented ensemble"; it's a "laugh riot from the first frame to the last", with "classic" scenes you'll "quote lines from" – "I'm still searching for *My Dinner with Andre* action figures."

Waitress

24 | 26 | 23 | 23

2007 | Directed by Adrienne Shelly | With Keri Russell, Jeremy Sisto, Nathan Fillion, Andy Griffith | 107 minutes | Rated PG-13

With a "nod to *Alice Doesn't Live Here Anymore*", this "sweet-natured" comic confection about a "small-town" diner waitress "caught in a loveless marriage" has enough ingredients to "steal your heart", including an "outstanding" Russell, the "consummate" Griffith and, of course, those "delicious"-looking pies; indeed, many call this "uplifting" "little jewel" a "rallying cry for women everywhere."

Wait Until Dark

25 | 26 | 27 | 23

1967 | Directed by Terence Young | With Audrey Hepburn, Alan Arkin, Richard Crenna, Efrem Zimbalist Jr. | 107 minutes | Not Rated

This "unforgettable" thriller posits a "simple, nerve-shattering premise": a blind woman, all alone in her apartment, in a "game of cat-and-mouse" with a "brutal psychopath"; gird yourself for an "eerie Henry Mancini soundtrack" and a "twists-and-turns"–laden scenario with "one particularly electrifying moment" that's guaranteed to "have you out of your seat."

Walk the Line ✉

25 | 28 | 23 | 25

2005 | Directed by James Mangold | With Joaquin Phoenix, Reese Witherspoon, Ginnifer Goodwin | 136 minutes | Rated PG-13

The "Man in Black" walks again courtesy of this "evocative", "behind-the-music" biopic that pays "touching tribute" to country "legend" Johnny Cash and his "true love", June Carter, the "good woman" who "saved him" from a life of "drugs and temptation"; both Phoenix and Witherspoon are "phenomenal" (yep, "they do their own singing"), and the "foot-stomping" tunes "ain't bad", either; P.S. don't mind the unmistakable "similarity to *Ray*."

Walk to Remember, A

18 | 18 | 18 | 17

2002 | Directed by Adam Shankman | With Shane West, Mandy Moore, Peter Coyote | 101 minutes | Rated PG

"If you're in the mood for a good cry", this "teen" romance (via the Nicholas Sparks novel) is a "tear-inducing" remembrance of "young love" as a prim "preacher's daughter" and a bad-boy "heartthrob" find "redemptive power" in one another; yet even those "pleasantly surprised" by the "respectable" emoting acknowledge the story is pretty "sappy."

Wallace & Gromit in the Curse of the Were-Rabbit

24 | - | 22 | 27

2005 | Directed by Steve Box, Nick Park | Animated | 85 minutes | Rated G

Appearing in their first feature-length flick, "goofy" gadgeteer Wallace and his silently "expressive" pooch Gromit come to the neighborhood's rescue when a "mutated rabbit terrorizes its gardens" in this "jolly good", "for-all-ages" claymation comedy brimming with "Brit wit" and "inventive" visual spectacle; fans beg series creator Nick Park "please sir, may we have some more?"

| | OVERALL | ACTING | STORY | PROD. |

Wall Street ✉

22 | 23 | 22 | 21

1987 | Directed by Oliver Stone | With Michael Douglas, Charlie Sheen, Daryl Hannah, Martin Sheen | 125 minutes | Rated R

"Greed is good" in this "quintessential insider's view" of the "go-go '80s" as personified by "ruthless financier" Gordon Gekko, an "ever-so-cool" piece of "Wall Street slime", "brilliantly executed" by the Oscar-winning Douglas; the "world of high finance" in all its "money-making" excess is captured here "like in no other film."

WarGames

22 | 19 | 24 | 19

1983 | Directed by John Badham | With Matthew Broderick, Dabney Coleman, John Wood, Ally Sheedy | 114 minutes | Rated PG

A precocious high-school student "hacks into a Defense Department computer" with the potential to "start a nuclear war" in this "way-before-its-time" thriller that wags dub *Fail-Safe* in an '80s mall"; sure, it "seems very dated" today, with "primitive technology" and a "preachy ending", but overall the "thoughtful, incisive" script remains "urgently relevant."

War of the Roses, The

17 | 20 | 17 | 18

1989 | Directed by Danny DeVito | With Michael Douglas, Kathleen Turner, Danny DeVito | 116 minutes | Rated R

"You need a slightly off-color sense of humor" (namely, "black") to enjoy this "daring" comedy about the "disintegration of a marriage" and subsequent "over-the-top divorce shenanigans"; still, the "materialism, ego and folly" are played out with such a "mean-spirited", "venomous edge" that soft-hearted types find it "completely depressing and charmless."

War of the Worlds, The

23 | 16 | 24 | 23

1953 | Directed by Byron Haskin | With Gene Barry, Ann Robinson, Les Tremayne | 85 minutes | Rated G

Although the "Orson Welles radio broadcast" is "more famous", this "faithful" filming of the H.G. Wells "sci-fi classic" still clearly telegraphs its "frightening premise" of Martians run amok on Planet Earth; ok, it may be a bit "overstated" and "unintentionally funny today", but boob-tubers tune in "every time it's on television."

War of the Worlds

15 | 14 | 16 | 22

2005 | Directed by Steven Spielberg | With Tom Cruise, Dakota Fanning, Justin Chatwin | 116 minutes | Rated PG-13

"Stuff blows up" and "Tom runs away from it" in this "eye-popping", "big-budget" sci-fi remake about a "working-class loser dad" whose kids are threatened by extraterrestrial invaders; since Spielberg gives the plot a contemporary spin with the faintest "undertones of terrorism", many find it "pretty grim for a popcorn flick", capped by that "letdown of an ending"; as for the acting, Fanning's "incessant screaming" and Cruise's "unlikable" character leave some "rooting for the aliens."

Warriors, The

23 | 16 | 22 | 18

1979 | Directed by Walter Hill | With Michael Beck, James Remar, David Patrick Kelly | 93 minutes | Rated R

The "seedy cesspool that was NYC in the '70s" serves as the "dystopian" backdrop for this "intriguing" "gangland warfare" flick following a Coney Island crew's perilous trek across rival turf after they're pegged "for a murder they didn't commit"; boasting "great action", "fabulous production design" and even its own "video game", this movie has long enjoyed "cult classic" status – "can you dig it?"

Wayne's World

	OVERALL	ACTING	STORY	PROD.
	17	14	15	15

1992 | Directed by Penelope Spheeris | With Mike Myers, Dana Carvey, Rob Lowe | 95 minutes | Rated PG-13

"One of the few *Saturday Night Live* skits to soar in a longer format", this parody of local access cable TV shows is an "inventive", "mindless" romp that was one of the biggest box office comedies of the '90s; it's also the breakout for the pre–*Austin Powers* Myers, who gives an "awesome" rendition of "stupidity at its finest."

Way We Were, The

	24	25	25	23

1973 | Directed by Sydney Pollack | With Barbra Streisand, Robert Redford, Bradford Dillman | 118 minutes | Rated PG

"Still a tearjerker after all these years", this "improbable romance" pits a "brainy" Jewish girl opposite a "golden Wasp boy" and "tugs every heartstring available" in its "realistic" depiction of their "ill-fated" affair; Streisand and Redford "at their peak" are "beyond delicious" together, though the most indelible "memories" involve the "famous final scene" at the "Plaza Hotel" with that "sad", Oscar-winning song playing in the background.

We Are Marshall

	22	21	25	21

2006 | Directed by McG | With Matthew McConaughey, Matthew Fox, David Strathairn | 124 minutes | Rated PG

This "respectful" treatment of Marshall University's fabled "rise from the ashes" following the 1970 plane crash that claimed the school's entire football team runs the set play of many a sports film - "triumph against adversity" - and "does the story proud"; as for acting, McConaughey's "enthusiasm is contagious" in the role of embattled coach, giving "sentimental saps" more reason to recommend this "worthy two-hour investment."

Wedding Banquet, The 🄵

	22	21	25	21

1993 | Directed by Ang Lee | With Winston Chao, May Chin, Mitchell Lichtenstein | 106 minutes | Rated R

"Family dynamics" get a "touching" twist in this "gently told" Taiwanese tale about a "marriage of convenience" between a "gay man" hoping to make his parents happy and his green card–seeking bride; this "funny charade" comes to a climax at the titular feast, where "unconditional love" comes "out of the closet" in a "warmhearted" if "bittersweet finale."

Wedding Crashers

	21	21	20	21

2005 | Directed by David Dobkin | With Owen Wilson, Vince Vaughn, Christopher Walken | 119 minutes | Rated R

Fast becoming the "Lemmon and Matthau" of the "overgrown frat boy" set, Wilson and Vaughn play a pair of "opportunistic womanizers" who "prey on weddings" to "get their groove on" in this "deliciously vulgar" comedy; despite some "mushy" messing around with a "semi-serious love story", overall it delivers enough "flashes of hilarity" to make for "easy viewing."

	OVERALL	ACTING	STORY	PROD.

Wedding Singer, The
17 | 16 | 16 | 16

1998 | Directed by Frank Coraci | With Adam Sandler, Drew Barrymore | 96 minutes | Rated PG-13

Take a "blast to the past" via this romantic comedy set in the "suburban '80s" whose real stars are its rocking retro soundtrack and obligatory "tasteless fashion" parade; beyond that, it's a "cute if insipid" "chick flick" about a down-and-out wedding singer, "dejected love" and its "sweet" redemption.

We Don't Live Here Anymore
16 | 22 | 15 | 16

2004 | Directed by John Curran | With Mark Ruffalo, Naomi Watts, Laura Dern, Peter Krause | 101 minutes | Rated R

Marital infidelity "served raw" is the main course in this "intense" drama, a "small character study" built on a "strong quartet of performances" as "self-centered" academic couples "trade spouses" and "one emotion: angst"; it "tries hard", but contras say this "maudlin" "rip-off of *Who's Afraid of Virginia Woolf*" will make you "grateful for your relatively normal life."

Weekend at Bernie's
16 | 14 | 16 | 15

1989 | Directed by Ted Kotcheff | With Andrew McCarthy, Jonathan Silverman, Terry Kiser | 97 minutes | Rated PG-13

"So stupid it's funny", this "idiotic" comedy from the "classic '80s" canon serves up "nyuk-nyuks" aplenty when two shlubs "find their boss dead in his beach house but pretend he's alive" to continue "chasing chicks and partying"; it's the kind of picture that "revels in its ridiculousness" – right down to the steadfastly "deadpan" expression on the "actor playing the corpse."

Weird Science
19 | 15 | 19 | 17

1985 | Directed by John Hughes | With Anthony Michael Hall, Kelly LeBrock, Ilan Mitchell-Smith, Bill Paxton | 94 minutes | Rated PG-13

The "ultimate teen-geek fantasy", this "adolescent" comedy casts Hall and Mitchell-Smith as "horny nerds" who fabricate the "perfect woman" ("smoking hot" LeBrock) "from their computer"; sure, it all adds up to "cheesy nonsense", but for those "of a certain generation", this "'80s time capsule" just might "make you feel 16 again."

Welcome to the Dollhouse
22 | 21 | 21 | 19

1995 | Directed by Todd Solondz | With Heather Matarazzo, Matthew Faber, Eric Mabius | 88 minutes | Rated R

A "dead-on look at the horrors" of junior high, this "scathing" study of a "dorky adolescent" "hits close to home" thanks to an "eerily real" performance by Matarazzo as the "picked-on" protagonist; both "cruelly funny" and "disturbingly accurate", it makes some oldsters "worry about young people today."

⚡ West Side Story ✉
27 | 24 | 27 | 27

1961 | Directed by Robert Wise, Jerome Robbins | With Natalie Wood, Richard Beymer, Rita Moreno, George Chakiris | 151 minutes | Not Rated

Starting with that "opening bird's-eye view of Manhattan", this "remarkable musical" that transposes *Romeo and Juliet* to "urban" turf is "sheer perfection" thanks to "fiery acting", Robbins' "superb" streetwise choreography and the "dynamic" Leonard Bernstein/Stephen Sondheim score; sure, Beymer might be "miscast" and it's "too bad they wouldn't let Natalie sing", but otherwise this Oscar magnet – 10 statuettes including Best Picture – is "forever fabulous."

Westworld

1973 | Directed by Michael Crichton | With Yul Brynner, Richard Benjamin, James Brolin | 88 minutes | Rated PG

You can "see where *Jurassic Park* came from" in this sci-fi thriller whose "irresistible premise" involves a futuristic resort where vacationers live out their Wild West fantasies with robot stand-ins; though sharp-shooters say Brynner is "perfect" as an "android gunslinger" gone hay-wire, cynics ponder the idea of a "wooden actor playing an automaton."

We Were Soldiers

21 | 22 | 21 | 23

2002 | Directed by Randall Wallace | With Mel Gibson, Madeleine Stowe, Greg Kinnear, Sam Elliott | 138 minutes | Rated R

The "first ground battle of the Vietnam War" is "authentically repli-cated", "graphic violence" and all, in this "powerful" profile of the "hu-manity and courage" of America's soldiers in the thick of "intense action"; with a special salute going to Gibson's portrayal of a "religious man" turned "battlefield leader", some grunt this is "one of the most overlooked" combat pics around.

Whale Rider

25 | 26 | 24 | 24

2003 | Directed by Niki Caro | With Keisha Castle-Hughes, Rawiri Paratene, Vicki Haughton | 101 minutes | Rated PG-13

Featuring "no stars, no explosions and no CGI effects", this nonetheless "powerful" film tells the "captivating" story of a Maori girl's struggle to help her tribe balance "tradition and the 21st century"; a "refresh-ing", family-friendly slice of "edutainment" complete with "beautiful" New Zealand vistas and "phenomenal" work by "up-and-comer" Castle-Hughes, this "achingly sad" story will "leave your soul touched."

What About Bob?

18 | 19 | 18 | 17

1991 | Directed by Frank Oz | With Bill Murray, Richard Dreyfuss, Julie Hagerty | 99 minutes | Rated PG

Proving that "life is indeed baby steps", this "dark" comedy about a "shrink driven nuts" by a "psycho patient" pairs the "screwball" Murray with the "hilarious" Dreyfuss; though the picture might be "as irritat-ing as it is funny", your "sides will hurt" from laughter all the same.

What Dreams May Come

16 | 17 | 15 | 24

1998 | Directed by Vincent Ward | With Robin Williams, Cuba Gooding Jr., Annabella Sciorra | 113 minutes | Rated PG-13

"Extremely pleasing to the eye", this "beautiful fantasy of the afterlife" "based on the touching Richard Matheson novel" finds Williams des-perately trying to rescue his wife's soul from the underworld; but real-ists report a "sappy", "schmaltzy script" and sum this one up as "visually exquisite, but little else."

Whatever Happened to Baby Jane? ◐

22 | 25 | 23 | 21

1962 | Directed by Robert Aldrich | With Bette Davis, Joan Crawford, Victor Buono | 134 minutes | Not Rated

"Campy and creepy", this "classic" exercise in Grand Guignol is the last hurrah of Hollywood's "two queen bees" in a "frightening" story of the "hate-hate relationship" between a pair of movie-star sisters; ex-pect an "audacious" Crawford facing off against an "over-the-top"

Davis, whose "grotesque" appearance is "too scary to think about" for too long; most memorable scene: Joan's "rat à-la-carte" din-din.

What Lies Beneath

OVERALL	ACTING	STORY	PROD.
16	18	16	18

2000 | Directed by Robert Zemeckis | With Harrison Ford, Michelle Pfeiffer, Diana Scarwid | 126 minutes | Rated PG-13
This "chilling" "Hitchcockian" thriller about a "sinister ghost" at loose in the house is a "slick" endeavor, with enough "scary moments" to "make you jump" out of your seat; but foes find the "cable-TV-caliber script" "silly" and "predictable", and wonder what "A-list actors" are doing in this "overwrought", "C-list movie."

What's Eating Gilbert Grape

22	25	22	21

1993 | Directed by Lasse Hallström | With Johnny Depp, Juliette Lewis, Leonardo DiCaprio, Mary Steenburgen | 118 minutes | Rated PG-13
An "original" study of an ultra-"dysfunctional" family, this "weirdly winning" dramedy features a "quietly intense" Depp opposite a "brilliant" DiCaprio "before he became a celebrity teen idol"; its "loving look at two fringe groups – the obese and the mentally challenged" – turns this "quirky" "coming-of-age" tale into "surprisingly good" moviemaking.

What's Love Got to Do with It

22	26	22	21

1993 | Directed by Brian Gibson | With Angela Bassett, Laurence Fishburne | 118 minutes | Rated R
That Tina Turner "never did anything nice and easy" is plain to see in this "perfect" biopic depicting how a "gifted" gal "got the strength to move on" from an abusive marriage to super-duper stardom; in a picture that's "all about the acting", Bassett is "outstanding", but be warned that it can be "painful to watch."

What's Up, Doc?

21	20	21	20

1972 | Directed by Peter Bogdanovich | With Barbra Streisand, Ryan O'Neal, Madeline Kahn, Kenneth Mars | 94 minutes | Rated G
"Streisand's like butter" in this "zany" "modern screwball comedy" "reminiscent of *Bringing Up Baby*" wherein some "terrific Ryan-Babs chemistry" is brought to bear on a nutty storyline involving "igneous rocks", identical plaid suitcases and a "fantastic comic car chase through San Francisco"; P.S. "Kahn's a scream" in her film debut.

What Women Want

15	17	17	16

2000 | Directed by Nancy Meyers | With Mel Gibson, Helen Hunt, Marisa Tomei | 126 minutes | Rated PG-13
A misogynist is redeemed after becoming superhumanly "sensitized" to women's inner monologues in this "enjoyably light" chick flick; while it might "miss the mark" due to "predictable" plotting, it's an "original concept" that's "worth it just to see" "Mad Max Mel struggle with pantyhose."

☑ When Harry Met Sally . . .

26	25	25	24

1989 | Directed by Rob Reiner | With Billy Crystal, Meg Ryan, Carrie Fisher, Bruno Kirby | 96 minutes | Rated R
"Can a man and a woman be just friends?"; this romantic comedy – the "king of all date movies" – attempts to answer that question as it details a "terrific take on relationships" that "rings true for many"; written by Nora Ephron as an "ode to Manhattan", it stars an "adorable", "pre-pixie cut" Ryan opposite a "perfect" Crystal, both "forever remem-

bered" for the "infamous orgasm scene" in Katz's Deli that inspired one of the best lines in moviedom: "I'll have what she's having."

Where's Poppa?

`23` `25` `23` `21`

1970 | Directed by Carl Reiner | With George Segal, Ruth Gordon, Trish Van Devere, Ron Leibman | 82 minutes | Rated R

This "twisted" black comedy examines the "sick relationship" between a "senile" mom living with her "dutiful (up-to-a-point)" son; "painfully funny", it's acquired "cult" status over the years for set pieces like the "ape suit scene" and the "tush-biting" sequence; P.S. the jaw-dropping original ending, an extra on the DVD, is truly "insane."

While You Were Sleeping

`18` `19` `20` `18`

1995 | Directed by Jon Turteltaub | With Sandra Bullock, Bill Pullman, Peter Gallagher | 103 minutes | Rated PG

"Token-booth worker" Bullock "falls in love with two brothers" in this "tender" romantic comedy, an "engaging", "Cinderella"-like "fairy tale" trading on "mistaken identity"; sure, it's "feel-good fluff", but the "unique storyline", "sweet" performances and "great chemistry" between the leads add up to an "all-around cute movie."

☒ White Christmas

`25` `21` `22` `24`

1954 | Directed by Michael Curtiz | With Bing Crosby, Danny Kaye, Rosemary Clooney | 120 minutes | Not Rated

"It wouldn't be Christmas" without a peek at this "sentimental" favorite, a virtual holiday "requirement" with "all the trimmings": "wonderful dance numbers", "essential" Irving Berlin tunes and "Der Bingle" crooning "kringle jingles"; in short, this "classic" is so "charming", it's almost "un-American not to love it"; P.S. sticklers note that Bing originally "made the title song famous in *Holiday Inn.*"

☒ White Heat ◑

`25` `28` `24` `23`

1949 | Directed by Raoul Walsh | With James Cagney, Virginia Mayo, Edmond O'Brien | 114 minutes | Not Rated

One part "descent into madness", one part "valentine to mom", this schizophrenic, noirish thriller represents the "classic gangster film refined to the nth degree"; as a "homicidal nut job" "mama's boy", Cagney turns in one of his "greatest performances", though the flick's most remembered for the "best last line in movie history": 'made it, ma! top of the world!'

White Men Can't Jump

`13` `14` `13` `14`

1992 | Directed by Ron Shelton | With Wesley Snipes, Woody Harrelson, Rosie Perez | 115 minutes | Rated R

"It's no *Bull Durham*", but director Shelton's "combo of comedy and basketball action" scores some easy buckets with Woody and Wesley teaming up as "hot dog" hoopsters running a hustle based on Harrelson's implicit lack of skills; although ostensibly a look at "male mores", it's panned as a "painful" workout proving that one "white man can't act."

White Oleander

`18` `23` `19` `19`

2002 | Directed by Peter Kosminsky | With Michelle Pfeiffer, Renée Zellweger, Robin Wright Penn | 109 minutes | Rated PG-13

A "manipulating" mom in prison and a "conflicted teen" shunted from foster home to foster home are the protagonists of this "solid coming-of-age drama" based on the "offbeat", Oprah-endorsed best-seller; maybe it "falls short of being really great" (many say the "book was better"), but at least this "interesting tale of growth and change" is "perfectly cast."

Who Framed Roger Rabbit 24 | - | 23 | 27

1988 | Directed by Robert Zemeckis | Animated | With Bob Hoskins, Christopher Lloyd | 103 minutes | Rated PG

This "one-of-a-kind treat" featuring a "glorious mix of live action and animation" boasts an all-star cartoon cast, with appearances by every 'toon from Mickey to Woody (though the "seductive" Jessica Rabbit runs away with the picture); set in the Hollywood of yore, the "classic" noir plot has Hoskins investigating a murder case, with "wonderfully entertaining" results.

Who Killed the Electric Car? 23 | - | 25 | 21

2006 | Directed by Chris Paine | Documentary | 92 minutes | Rated PG

Sure to drive "environmentally conscious" sorts "mad" with rage at the "auto and oil industry fat cats" who "control our lives", this "informative" documentary (whose "title speaks for itself") illuminates a "fascinating" but "little-known" episode in eco-history; maybe the presentation veers toward "pedestrian", but overall most see a "great vehicle" for raising awareness and regret it "didn't get more airplay."

Whole Nine Yards, The 17 | 17 | 17 | 17

2000 | Directed by Jonathan Lynn | With Bruce Willis, Matthew Perry, Rosanna Arquette, Amanda Peet | 98 minutes | Rated R

A "fun waste of an hour-and-a-half", this "lightweight" crime comedy tells the story of a "hit man on the lam" in suburbia who moves next door to a "hyper-nervous dentist"; Willis and Perry sit ably atop the "big-budget cast", but it's the "hilarious" Peet who "shows her boobs" and "steals the movie" as a "gangster groupie."

☑ Who's Afraid of Virginia Woolf? ✉◑ 25 | 27 | 25 | 23

1966 | Directed by Mike Nichols | With Elizabeth Taylor, Richard Burton, George Segal, Sandy Dennis | 134 minutes | Not Rated

Maybe "Liz made up to look frumpy is a laugh", but otherwise this "scalding adaptation" of Edward Albee's "masterpiece" about an "unraveling marriage" is pretty serious stuff, "brilliantly acted" and "brutally honest"; it's "funny and mean and sad" all at once – "never has a play been converted into a movie" with such "power."

☑ Wild Bunch, The 27 | 26 | 25 | 27

1969 | Directed by Sam Peckinpah | With William Holden, Ernest Borgnine, Robert Ryan, Ben Johnson | 134 minutes | Rated R

Not for the faint of heart, this "blood-and-guts" Peckinpah "epic" is a "Western to end all Westerns" that "transcends the genre" with an "in-your-face style" that turns "violence into poetry"; starring Holden as the leader of a band of "honorable outlaws", it depicts a "changing world" at the "end of an era" in "unsentimental" terms and manages to be both "noble and perverse at the same time."

Wild Hogs 17 | 19 | 16 | 19

2007 | Directed by Walt Becker | With Tim Allen, John Travolta, Martin Lawrence, William H. Macy | 100 minutes | Rated PG-13

One "for the middle-aged set", this "silly" comedy maintains "men will be boys" as an all-star quartet confronts their "midlife crises" by "taking to the road on their Harleys" to "try and regain their youth"; it's "funnier than expected" (and "good-natured enough" to include a "Peter Fonda cameo"), but grouches grunt the uneasy ride is largely "forgettable."

Wild One, The ❶
22 | 24 | 19 | 20

1953 | Directed by László Benedek | With Marlon Brando, Mary Murphy, Lee Marvin | 79 minutes | Not Rated

"Brando on a motorcycle" in "tight black leather" sums up the appeal of this '50s cautionary tale about a gang of bikers that terrorizes a small town; sure, it's "dated" and "mild by today's standards", yet Marlon's "bad-boy attitude" alone keeps it "compelling"; most "unforgettable" exchange: "what are you rebelling against? – whaddya got?"

☑ Wild Strawberries ❶F
26 | 26 | 24 | 25

1959 | Directed by Ingmar Bergman | With Victor Sjöström, Bibi Andersson, Ingrid Thulin | 91 minutes | Not Rated

"Essential Bergman" that's not just for art movie mavens, this "elegiac" "road film about life, death and redemption" "continues to hold up well"; a "bittersweet" story of an "elderly doctor who learns how to love at the last minute of his life", it's ultimately "cathartic and hopeful", even if it occasionally displays the director's signature "depressive" streak.

Willow
20 | 18 | 20 | 22

1988 | Directed by Ron Howard | With Val Kilmer, Joanne Whalley, Warwick Davis | 130 minutes | Rated PG

"If you like *Princess Bride*", you'll like this "wonderfully escapist" fantasy featuring "appealing" characters in a sword-and-sorcery story that "seems familiar" to those who dub it a *Lord of the Rings* clone; "Kilmer's gorgeous" and there's plenty of "excitement", but some say that it's a "formulaic disappointment."

☑ Willy Wonka and the Chocolate Factory
26 | 22 | 26 | 26

1971 | Directed by Mel Stuart | With Gene Wilder, Jack Albertson, Peter Ostrum | 100 minutes | Rated G

Chocoholics cheer this "delicious family classic" adeptly adapted from the "brilliant Roald Dahl book" about an "underdog" kid who gets a "once-in-a-lifetime" chance to tour a "curious candy factory"; it's such a "blast to watch" (thanks to "psychedelic" sets, "imaginative" vignettes and "great songs") that it's almost become a "rite of passage" for the stroller set.

Wimbledon
15 | 16 | 15 | 17

2004 | Directed by Richard Loncraine | With Kirsten Dunst, Paul Bettany | 98 minutes | Rated PG-13

"Predictable but pleasant", this tennis-themed romantic comedy woos "teenage girls" with a "cute" court-ship and "sports movie" buffs with "exciting" match play enhanced by "inventive camera tricks"; still, a "far-fetched" premise and "poor" dialogue commit a "double fault" that mars the otherwise "diverting fluff."

Wind and the Lion, The
24 | 25 | 24 | 24

1975 | Directed by John Milius | With Sean Connery, Candice Bergen, Brian Keith | 119 minutes | Rated PG

This "old-fashioned, character-driven adventure" about an Arab chieftain's abduction of an American widow is loosely "based on a real incident during Teddy Roosevelt's presidency"; despite the "wonderful desert romance" that blooms between the "charismatic" Connery and "watchable" Bergen, there's "still enough action for the guys" in this "obscure history lesson."

Windtalkers

16 | 16 | 17 | 18

2002 | Directed by John Woo | With Nicolas Cage, Adam Beach, Christian Slater, Roger Willie | 134 minutes | Rated R

"Native American contributions" to the Allied war effort get "overdue" recognition in this "interesting" WWII action flick, starring Cage as a GI assigned to safeguard "Navaho code talkers" amid the "gruesome carnage" of combat; but foes fed up with the "graphic shooting and bombing" that "leaves behind a fine story" argue they "really blew this one."

☑ Winged Migration

26 | – | 21 | 28

2003 | Directed by Jacques Perrin, Jacques Cluzaud, Michel Debats | Documentary | 98 minutes | Rated G

"Soar with the birds" in this "breathtaking" documentary whose "amazing camerawork" puts you shoulder-to-wing with "flocks flying" around the globe on their "moving" migratory journeys; a "masterpiece" that will "awaken your appreciation" of nature's "avian heroes", it "should be required viewing" for budding environmentalists and cinematographers alike; P.S. one welcome feature: there's "no bad acting."

Wings of Desire ◑🅵

24 | 24 | 22 | 25

1988 | Directed by Wim Wenders | With Bruno Ganz, Solveig Dommartin | 127 minutes | Rated PG-13

A "charming meditation" about the "angels who watch over us", "longing to be human", this "haunting" German film "celebrates the human condition"; "dreamy cinematography" and an "amazing" cast elevate it to "pure poetry" – but don't "judge it by its self-conscious remake", Hollywood's "unfortunate" *City of Angels.*

Witches of Eastwick, The

17 | 20 | 18 | 18

1987 | Directed by George Miller | With Jack Nicholson, Cher, Susan Sarandon, Michelle Pfeiffer | 118 minutes | Rated R

Three small-town gals take on the devil himself in this "funny but disturbing" comedy, a variation on the "beauty-and-the-beast" theme based on the John Updike novel; no surprise, a "wicked Jack" walks away with the picture, triumphing over the occasionally "weird storyline" and "bizarre" denouement.

Witness ✉

23 | 24 | 23 | 22

1985 | Directed by Peter Weir | With Harrison Ford, Kelly McGillis, Lukas Haas | 112 minutes | Rated R

"One of Weir's finest", this "quiet" film offers a "sensitive portrayal" of a "small Amish community" that "collides with the violent outside world" in the aftermath of a murder; the actors have "perfect pitch" (particularly the "workmanlike" Ford, who "sizzles" against the "luminous McGillis"), and even if the story's somewhat "improbable", its overall "excellence sneaks up on you."

☑ Witness for the Prosecution ◑

27 | 28 | 28 | 25

1957 | Directed by Billy Wilder | With Tyrone Power, Marlene Dietrich, Charles Laughton | 116 minutes | Not Rated

Perhaps the "best murder mystery ever", this "Agatha Christie puzzler" is one of "Wilder's wiliest", featuring "two legends" – an "incredible" Laughton and an "outstanding" Dietrich – along with a courtroom-full of "compelling characterizations"; the dialogue "crackles" and the "plot twists and double twists" right up to the "still shocking ending."

Wiz, The
16 | 13 | 17 | 19

1978 | Directed by Sidney Lumet | With Diana Ross, Michael Jackson, Nipsey Russell, Ted Ross | 134 minutes | Rated G

The "timeless" *Wizard of Oz* is enacted by an all-black cast in this "lively" musical that transposes the action to 1970s NYC (with the "World Trade Center as the Emerald City"); the songs are "catchy" and it costars a "sane" Michael Jackson "before the lunacy", yet most find it "kinda boring" – Ross is "too long in the tooth" to play Dorothy, so it's "no threat to the Judy Garland version."

▲ Wizard of Oz, The
28 | 26 | 28 | 29

1939 | Directed by Victor Fleming | With Judy Garland, Ray Bolger, Jack Haley, Bert Lahr | 101 minutes | Rated G

A "star is born" – the "iconic" "Judy, Judy, Judy" – in this "time-less", "transporting" musical about a Kansas girl "off to see the Wizard" that's been "adored for decades" thanks to its "tremendous" cast, "glorious", "rainbow"-hued score and "inspired" moments involving a pair of "ruby slippers", a pack of "scary flying monkeys" and that "magical", "hello-Technicolor" transition; in Toto, this "landmark in family entertainment" is the ultimate proof that "there's no place like home."

Wolf
15 | 19 | 15 | 18

1994 | Directed by Mike Nichols | With Jack Nicholson, Michelle Pfeiffer, James Spader, Christopher Plummer | 125 minutes | Rated R

"Jack goes over the top and never looks back" in this "enjoyable" horror comedy, an "original take on the werewolf story" featuring Nicholson as a retiring book editor who morphs into an "alpha dog" with "way too much facial hair" when the moon is full; if the "stars outshine" the "weird" plotting, its "clever" premise still has some bite.

Wolf Man, The ◑
20 | 19 | 22 | 19

1941 | Directed by George Waggner | With Lon Chaney Jr., Claude Rains, Ralph Bellamy | 70 minutes | Not Rated

This "classic Universal monster" flicker set the "standard for fright" in its day with a hair-raising mix of ominous gypsies, howling werewolves and foreboding full moons; a "superb" Chaney stars as the fuzzy-faced lead, though a few howl about his "hammy" acting chops and "special effects that look damn silly" now.

▲ Woman of the Year ✉◑
27 | 28 | 26 | 26

1942 | Directed by George Stevens | With Katharine Hepburn, Spencer Tracy, Fay Bainter | 114 minutes | Not Rated

The "war between the sexes was never more fun" than in this first matchup of legendary duo Hepburn and Tracy in what some call the "best" of their eight films together; its Oscar-winning script pits the "right-on" Kate as an "ahead-of-her-time" foreign correspondent against Spence's laid-back sportswriter, but the hands-down winner in this battle of wills is clearly the audience.

| | OVERALL | ACTING | STORY | PROD. |

Woman Under the Influence, A
24 | 27 | 22 | 21

1974 | Directed by John Cassavetes | With Peter Falk, Gena Rowlands | 155 minutes | Rated R

"Raw, naturalistic performances" lie at the core of this "stunning", "hyper-real" drama about a "housewife's sad decline" into mental illness; a "heartbreaking" Rowlands plays the title role "like a Stradivarius", and even though some "overlong, meandering" scenes can be "difficult to watch", ultimately it's a "tender", "uncompromising" look at the "beautiful mess that is marriage."

☑ Women, The ◑
26 | 26 | 24 | 25

1939 | Directed by George Cukor | With Norma Shearer, Joan Crawford, Rosalind Russell, Paulette Goddard | 133 minutes | Not Rated

"Meow!": a "wonderful wallow" in "bitchy backstabbing", this "marvelous" MGM adaptation of Clare Boothe Luce's "snappy" stage play about high-society divorcées boasts an all-star, all-gal cast rattling off "extraordinary fast-paced" dialogue; though the constant "cattiness" can be a turnoff, it's still "required viewing" for "chick flick" and camp followers – "long live Jungle Red!"

Women in Love ✉
23 | 26 | 24 | 23

1970 | Directed by Ken Russell | With Alan Bates, Oliver Reed, Glenda Jackson, Jennie Linden | 131 minutes | Rated R

Ken Russell's "visually amazing", "erotically charged" take on the D.H. Lawrence novel "deals frankly" with two couples' struggle to conform to the marital and sexual conventions of 1920s England; it's a "sensual", "memorable" picture that's most renowned for Jackson's "strong", Oscar-winning turn and that notorious "nude male wrestling scene."

Women on the Verge of a Nervous Breakdown ☒
24 | 24 | 23 | 22

1988 | Directed by Pedro Almodóvar | With Carmen Maura, Antonio Banderas | 90 minutes | Rated R

Forget the "depressing" title: this "campy", "door-slamming farce" "put director Almodóvar on the map" and is one of the "funniest foreign films" ever made; a "wacky" story of "neurotic characters with different agendas", it also introduced "eye-candy Banderas to the Western world."

Wonder Boys
21 | 24 | 21 | 20

2000 | Directed by Curtis Hanson | With Michael Douglas, Tobey Maguire, Frances McDormand | 111 minutes | Rated R

Douglas shines in this "intelligent" if "overlooked" dramedy as a "humpy-shlumpy" college professor stultified by writer's block compounded by a "midlife crisis"; a "funny, smart and caring" piece of moviemaking, it supplies "many different interwoven storylines" – though calculators say its "parts prove greater than the sum of the whole."

Wonderland
16 | 21 | 17 | 17

2003 | Directed by James Cox | With Val Kilmer, Kate Bosworth, Lisa Kudrow, Josh Lucas | 104 minutes | Rated R

So "raw and violent" that it's "not for all audiences", this "dark", drug-drenched biopic recounts the alleged involvement of "desperate" porn star John Holmes in a notorious multiple murder; the underwhelmed find it alternately "depressing", "pointless" and "heavy-handed", noting that the same general idea was "done much better in *Boogie Nights*."

Woodsman, The

21 | 27 | 21 | 20

2004 | Directed by Nicole Kassell | With Kevin Bacon, Kyra Sedgwick | 87 minutes | Rated R

Venturing far afield from his *Footloose* beginnings, Bacon earns "high marks" for his "daring" turn as a "recovering pedophile" desperately "seeking a second chance" in this "honorably realistic" indie character study; fans warn if you're not in the mood to "feel sorry for" a "fragile" child molester, this one's gonna be "hard to watch."

Woodstock

24 | - | 21 | 23

1970 | Directed by Michael Wadleigh | Documentary | With Jimi Hendrix, The Who, Crosby, Stills & Nash, Santana | 184 minutes | Rated R

"Drop out, turn on and tune in" to this "seminal pop-culture event", a "groundbreaking" rockumentary about the fabled "peace-and-love" concert that's a "near-perfect snapshot" of the era, "minus the bad acid"; though ticked-off "tie-dyed flower children" sniff the "split-screen stuff gets old" and find "too much mud and not enough Hendrix", peaceniks maintain that this "marathon" movie provides "evidence that the summer of love was no pipe dream."

Wordplay

23 | - | 24 | 21

2006 | Directed by Patrick Creadon | Documentary | 94 minutes | Rated PG

"Word nerds" and even those who've "never completed a cross-word in their lives" are "spellbound" by this "excellent" documentary mining "real insights" from the "seemingly boring" world of *New York Times* "puzzle fanatics", whose "Sunday rituals" are an "American pastime"; celeb solvers like Jon Stewart, Bob Dole and Bill Clinton (in "one of his finer performances") add an extra-"fascinating" layer to the proceedings.

Working Girl

20 | 20 | 21 | 19

1988 | Directed by Mike Nichols | With Melanie Griffith, Harrison Ford, Sigourney Weaver, Joan Cusack | 109 minutes | Rated R

"Workplace revenge" was never funnier than in this "Cinderella-by-way-of-Wall-Street" "chick flick" that "empowers every woman who's had to put up with a difficult boss"; Griffith's at her "dumb girl/smart girl best", Weaver's "delightfully loathsome" and Ford's "adorable" "not playing an action hero for a change"; favorite line: "I've got a head for business and a bod for sin."

World According to Garp, The

21 | 23 | 22 | 19

1982 | Directed by George Roy Hill | With Robin Williams, Mary Beth Hurt, Glenn Close, John Lithgow | 131 minutes | Rated R

An "unforgettable", "modern-day fairy tale" full of "bizarre characters", this adaptation of John Irving's best-seller relates the "weird life" of T.S. Garp, beginning with his conception "when his mother sleeps with a man on his death bed"; though "unusual" is putting it mildly, this "unforgettable" tale is ultimately "affecting."

World Is Not Enough, The

19 | 19 | 18 | 21

1999 | Directed by Michael Apted | With Pierce Brosnan, Denise Richards | 128 minutes | Rated PG-13

Though admittedly "pure escapism", 007's 19th trip to the big screen divides voters: fans vow that Pierce is "as good as Sean", but foes growl that "gadgets have replaced characterization and plot" and snicker at the "ludicrous" Richards playing a "short-shorts-wearing nuclear physicist."

World Trade Center

| 20 | 21 | 22 | 23 |

2006 | Directed by Oliver Stone | With Nicolas Cage, Maria Bello, Michael Peña, Maggie Gyllenhaal | 129 minutes | Rated PG-13

A "monument to the rescue workers of 9/11", this "heartfelt" drama provides a "realistic portrayal of events" as Stone "reigns in his directorial eccentricities" for a "surprisingly compelling" portrait of "first responders caught under the rubble" after the attacks; a "painful true story" told with "sensitivity" that really "brings the tragedy home", it's an "uplifting" experience – "when you're ready."

Wrong Man, The ◑

| 22 | 24 | 24 | 21 |

1956 | Directed by Alfred Hitchcock | With Henry Fonda, Vera Miles, Anthony Quayle | 105 minutes | Not Rated

"Based on a true story" of a Stork Club musician "falsely accused" of armed robbery and the subsequent "pain his family goes through", this "unusual" Hitchcock drama is "less of a thriller" and more of a psychological study; but despite the "fine cast" and "solid" script, purists label it a "minor" work in the master's oeuvre, saying it just "isn't suspenseful" enough.

☑ Wuthering Heights ◑

| 27 | 27 | 27 | 24 |

1939 | Directed by William Wyler | With Laurence Olivier, Merle Oberon, David Niven | 103 minutes | Not Rated

This "Gothic romance" is a "charter" member of the "pantheon" of silver screen weepies and the "ultimate" adaptation of the Brontë tale; Olivier's "soulful brooding" as a spurned, lower-caste lover is so "brilliantly intense" that it's inspired generations of maidens to "waste away from heartbreak on the moors" ever after.

X-Files, The

| 17 | 17 | 16 | 19 |

1998 | Directed by Rob Bowman | With David Duchovny, Gillian Anderson, Martin Landau | 120 minutes | Rated PG-13

Both "fans and novices appreciate" this blockbuster adaptation of the TV series that's "just like the show" but with some "twists" and an "occasional dirty word" thrown in; it doesn't "answer any questions" and may be "muddled, disappointing" stuff to connoisseurs, but it does "serve as a bridge between seasons" with some "catchy" moments.

X-Men

| 19 | 18 | 18 | 23 |

2000 | Directed by Bryan Singer | With Patrick Stewart, Hugh Jackman, Ian McKellen, Halle Berry, James Marsden | 104 minutes | Rated PG-13

Even those "who've never read the comic book" chime in with their "ringing endorsement" of this "true-to-the-source" adaptation of the Marvel sci-fi series; most memorable for Jackman's "starmaking turn", it's such an obvious "setup for a franchise" that many "popcorn" eaters are hungrily "awaiting the sequels."

X-Men: The Last Stand

| 20 | 19 | 19 | 25 |

2006 | Directed by Brett Ratner | With Hugh Jackman, Halle Berry, Ian McKellen, Famke Janssen | 104 minutes | Rated PG-13

The "choice to be normal or true to themselves" confronts movieland's mutant superheroes as they battle "discrimination" and each other in this "big bang" finale to the franchise – or is it?; piling on more "spectacular" effects than ever (i.e. the "Golden Gate Bridge ripped from its base"), this "boisterous" juggernaut doesn't let up until the "last scene *after* the credits."

X2: X-Men United

2003 | Directed by Bryan Singer | With Patrick Stewart, Hugh Jackman, Ian McKellen, Halle Berry, Brian Cox | 133 minutes | Rated PG-13
"Finally, a sequel to sink your claws into": this "X-cellent" follow-up "tops the mediocre original" "in just about every way" – a "better storyline", "intriguing new characters", a "deservedly bigger role" for the "buff", "brooding" Jackman and "mega-cool special effects" . . . "what a bigger budget will do for a movie"; "can't wait for the next one – and there *will* be a next one."

XXX

2002 | Directed by Rob Cohen | With Vin Diesel, Asia Argento, Samuel L. Jackson | 124 minutes | Rated PG-13
"Check your brain at the door" and get snowed under by an avalanche of "terrific stunts" and "blowed-up stuff" in this "steroidal" refashioning of "James Bond" for the "slacker generation"; as for the acting, Vin's rendition of a "smartass" agent bent on "saving the world" is "kinda stupid", though some Diesel disciples still stand by their man – provided he "zips his flap."

Yankee Doodle Dandy ✉◑

1942 | Directed by Michael Curtiz | With James Cagney, Joan Leslie, Walter Huston | 126 minutes | Not Rated
"Flag-waving", "red-white-and-blue" musical bio of the "all-American" showman George M. Cohan, starring Cagney in full "hoofer" bloom; the story's "whitewashed", but after a few bars of its "patriotic tunes" you'll understand why the "4th of July wouldn't be the same without it."

Year of Living Dangerously, The

1983 | Directed by Peter Weir | With Mel Gibson, Sigourney Weaver, Linda Hunt | 117 minutes | Rated PG
An outbreak of "civil war" during the "Sukarno regime" in '60s Indonesia comes alive in this "captivating" "political" drama following a journalist who's covering the conflict; though the "compelling" Gibson and Weaver cast "steamy sparks", Hunt took home an Oscar for her "tour-de-force", "gender-bending role" in this "tense" thriller.

Yellow Submarine

1968 | Directed by George Dunning | Animated | 90 minutes | Rated G
"Contagiously fun", this "lighthearted" "hallucination" of a cartoon supplies "eye-popping" "psychedelic" imagery aplenty in recounting a story about the Fab Four's battle to save Pepperland from the Blue Meanies; though the "actual Beatles don't provide" the speaking parts, their performance on the "foot-tapping" soundtrack is "more than enough" – and the music "won't drive parents crazy."

Yentl ∅

1983 | Directed by Barbra Streisand | With Barbra Streisand, Mandy Patinkin, Amy Irving | 132 minutes | Rated PG
"La Streisand" does it all – "acts, sings and directs" – in this "underrated", "impeccably made" musical about a turn-of-the-century Jewish girl

masquerading as a "boy in order to study the Talmud"; though foes call it Babs at her "self-indulgent worst", fans counter her "incredible talent" and "amazing attention to detail" make this "emotionally stirring" picture "deserving of more credit."

Z Yojimbo OF | 28 | 27 | 26 | 26 |

1961 | Directed by Akira Kurosawa | With Toshiro Mifune, Tatsuya Nakadai | 110 minutes | Not Rated

"Kurosawa's classic samurai film" stars Mifune as the "ultimate anti-hero" who "plays both sides" of a village feud between a silk merchant and a sake merchant, and then watches as the depraved "warring factions" destroy each other; the "inspiration" for myriad remakes (*A Fistful of Dollars, Last Man Standing*, etc.), this "far superior" original clearly "shows how great this director really is."

You Can Count on Me | 23 | 26 | 22 | 20 |

2000 | Directed by Kenneth Lonergan | With Laura Linney, Mark Ruffalo, Rory Culkin, Matthew Broderick | 109 minutes | Rated R

Freshman director Lonergan "doesn't take a false step" in this "compelling", "character-driven" indie film about the "family bonds" between a "messed-up brother and sister" and the divergent paths their lives have taken; you can count on lots of "terrific acting" (with a "breakout performance from Linney") and a "lifelike lack of final resolution" that makes this a "sleeper with a heart."

You, Me and Dupree | 13 | 15 | 13 | 15 |

2006 | Directed by Anthony Russo, Joe Russo | With Owen Wilson, Kate Hudson, Matt Dillon, Michael Douglas | 108 minutes | Rated PG-13

The "relatable" scenario of a "freeloading friend from college" sustains this "light comedy" about a "shaggy, lovable doofus" – "Owen being Owen" – who crashes with married friends; it's "goofy fluff" that works for a "date night", but unless you're pree-pared for a "cringeable" series of "dud jokes", "don't waste your brain cells."

Z Young Frankenstein ◑ | 27 | 26 | 25 | 25 |

1974 | Directed by Mel Brooks | With Gene Wilder, Peter Boyle, Marty Feldman, Madeline Kahn, Cloris Leachman | 108 minutes | Rated PG

"Frankenstein Sr. would be proud" of this "insanely hysterical" "spoof of the Mary Shelley" horror classic that's Mel Brooks' "high-water mark" ("who else would have the monster" perform 'Puttin' on the Ritz' wearing a tuxedo?); Wilder is "pure genius" in the title role backed up by an "endlessly amusing" cast of characters spouting some of the "most quoted" dialogue in movie history; best line: a toss-up between "walk this way", "what knockers" and "hump? what hump?"; best song: Kahn's rendition of 'Ah! Sweet Mystery of Life', no contest.

Young Guns | 15 | 12 | 15 | 17 |

1988 | Directed by Christopher Cain | With Emilio Estevez, Kiefer Sutherland, Lou Diamond Phillips, Charlie Sheen | 107 minutes | Rated R

This "good Wild West romp 'n' stomp flick" featuring the "Brat Pack" in all their glory chronicles the beginnings of Billy the Kid's felonious career with his band of misfits, the Regulators; though "hardly the best movie ever", it works when you're in the mood for "interesting escapist fun."

	OVERALL	ACTING	STORY	PROD.

You Only Live Twice | 22 | 21 | 20 | 22 |

1967 | Directed by Lewis Gilbert | With Sean Connery, Mie Hama, Donald Pleasence | 117 minutes | Rated PG

"Despite the absurdity of a six-foot-plus Scotsman as a spy in Japan", diehards declare this espionage flicker one of the "better Connery Bonds", given its amusing "'60s Tokyo" settings and that "great Nancy Sinatra" theme song; ok, it might be "cheesy" and "doesn't age well", but camp followers claim that's what makes it "all the more fun now."

You've Got Mail | 18 | 20 | 18 | 18 |

1998 | Directed by Nora Ephron | With Tom Hanks, Meg Ryan, Parker Posey, Greg Kinnear, Jean Stapleton | 119 minutes | Rated PG

Manhattan's "Upper West Side looks like Paris" in this "feel-good" romantic comedy, a "remake of *The Shop Around the Corner*" updated to "today's techie, e-mail-ish world"; though a tad too "cutesy pie" and "predictable" for cynics, "chick flick" fans find it "enchanting" thanks to that "great chemistry between Hanks and Ryan."

Y Tu Mamá También 🄵 | 24 | 24 | 23 | 21 |

2002 | Directed by Alfonso Cuarón | With Maribel Verdu, Gael García Bernal, Diego Luna, Diana Bracho | 105 minutes | Rated R

Two "upper-middle-class Mexican boys" "learn the facts of life" and then some from a "sexy older woman" during a road trip "that takes some unexpected turns" in this *muy caliente* "coming-of-age" character study; some say "everything takes a back seat (no pun intended)" to the "very explicit sex scenes" – whew! –but more cerebral types see it more as a "passionate film about life, youth and love" that's "far greater than the sum of its parts."

Z ✉🄵 | 26 | 25 | 26 | 24 |

1969 | Directed by Costa-Gavras | With Yves Montand, Irene Papas, Jean-Louis Trintignant, Jacques Perrin | 127 minutes | Rated PG

Unfortunately all "too true", this fact-based account of the assassination of a left-leaning scientist in a right-wing country is a crackerjack "political thriller" that's "deeply affecting" and "not easy to watch"; Montand is "nothing less than superb" in the title role, while director Costa-Gavras makes this "documentary-like" "exposé" of corruption "captivating from the first scene."

Zelig ◑ | 20 | 20 | 21 | 21 |

1983 | Directed by Woody Allen | With Woody Allen, Mia Farrow | 79 minutes | Rated PG

What could be "Forrest Gump's ancestor" is the much "more charming (and neurotic) Zelig", a human chameleon who somehow manages to play a prominent role in 20th-century world events with "dryly comedic" results; it's an unusual, "technically complex" outing for the usually straightforward Allen that "warps history" by "digitally" inserting our hero into vintage "newsreel footage", but cynics say this "curiosity piece" has only "one clever idea" and "should have been funnier."

Ziegfeld Follies | 24 | 21 | - | 26 |

1946 | Directed by Vincente Minnelli et al | With Fred Astaire, Gene Kelly, Lena Horne, Judy Garland, Lucille Ball | 110 minutes | Not Rated

"Nearly every great star at MGM" is showcased in this "episodic" musical revue featuring "memorable" song-and-dance routines (like Fred

Astaire and Gene Kelly in their only appearance together) interspersed with "dated comedy skits"; overall, it may be a "mixed bag", but aficionados swoon over the "lavishly ridiculous" highlights: a "breathtaking" Judy Garland number, "rare footage of Fanny Brice" and "Lucille Ball as a glamour girl with a whip."

Zodiac

OVERALL	ACTING	STORY	PROD.
21	24	22	22

2007 | Directed by David Fincher | With Jake Gyllenhaal, Mark Ruffalo, Anthony Edwards, Robert Downey Jr. | 158 minutes | Rated R

The "stars align" for this "chilling" thriller about San Francisco's "never-solved" Zodiac killings of the '60s and '70s, with "special kudos" to Fincher's "artful reconstruction of the era" and to Gyllenhaal, Ruffalo and Downey Jr. for conveying the "frustration of a stalled murder investigation"; but the "fanatical" adherence to "realism" fires up foes, who fault the resulting "slow" pace and "lack of resolution."

Zoolander

16	16	15	16

2001 | Directed by Ben Stiller | With Ben Stiller, Owen Wilson, Will Ferrell | 89 minutes | Rated PG-13

Think "*Spinal Tap* for models" to get the gist of this "silly takeoff on the fashion industry" wherein a "cheek-sucking" male supermodel is brainwashed into being an assassin; sourpusses say its gleeful depiction of "narcissistic ninnies" reflects the general "dumbing down of America", though a few argue that this future "cult classic" redeems itself with "snarky cameos" and "physical shtick", i.e. Ben and Owen's infamous "walk-off."

Zorba the Greek ◑

25	27	25	23

1964 | Directed by Michael Cacoyannis | With Anthony Quinn, Alan Bates, Irene Papas, Lila Kedrova | 142 minutes | Not Rated

There's ex-zorba-tant praise for this "still-fresh" drama about an Englishman visiting Crete on an existential quest, only to fall under the spell of a "person full of passion", the "flamboyant" Zorba; Quinn's "breakout" performance, plus some "memorable" theme music and dancing, keep this "feel-good" "affirmation of life" so "exciting and entertaining" that repeaters faithfully "see it every year."

Zulu

24	24	25	24

1964 | Directed by Cy Endfield | With Stanley Baker, Jack Hawkins, Michael Caine | 138 minutes | Not Rated

The "true story of valor in the face of incredible odds", this "epic treatment of a 19th-century British military disaster" is played out against the "broad canvas of Africa" and features an "unknown Caine" in his "first big film"; "visually and viscerally stunning", it's "historically accurate without sacrificing dramatic appeal", and the "tension's unrelenting."

INDEXES

Years

Listings include Overall ratings. ⚡ indicates movies with the highest ratings, popularity and importance.

1910s/1920s

⚡ Birth of a Nation | 1915	25
⚡ Cabinet of Dr. Caligari | 1921	26
Cocoanuts, The | 1929	24
⚡ General, The | 1927	28
⚡ Gold Rush | 1925	28
Greed | 1925	28
Intolerance | 1918	27
⚡ Metropolis | 1927	27
⚡ Napoléon | 1929	28
Nosferatu | 1922	26
⚡ Potemkin | 1926	27
Thief of Bagdad | 1924	24

1930

⚡ All Quiet on Western Front	28
⚡ Animal Crackers	26
Anna Christie	26
Hell's Angels	24

1931

⚡ Blue Angel	25
⚡ City Lights	28
Dracula	24
Frankenstein	25
Front Page	24
Little Caesar	24
⚡ Monkey Business	26
Public Enemy	25

1932

Freaks	23
Grand Hotel	25
Horse Feathers	24
Mummy, The	24
Tarzan the Ape Man	21

1933

⚡ Dinner at Eight	27
⚡ Duck Soup	27
Flying Down to Rio	23
Footlight Parade	23
42nd Street	24
⚡ Gold Diggers of 1933	25
I'm No Angel	23
Invisible Man	22
⚡ King Kong	25
⚡ M	26
She Done Him Wrong	22

1934

Gay Divorcee	25
⚡ It Happened One Night	28
Scarlet Empress	24
Tarzan and His Mate	21
⚡ Thin Man	26

1935

⚡ Anna Karenina	26
Bride of Frankenstein	25
Captain Blood	23
⚡ David Copperfield	27
⚡ Mutiny on the Bounty	25
⚡ Night at the Opera	26
⚡ 39 Steps	27
⚡ Top Hat	27
⚡ Triumph of the Will	27

1936

Fury	25
Modern Times	28
Mr. Deeds Goes to Town	25
⚡ My Man Godfrey	25
⚡ Swing Time	26

1937

Awful Truth	25
⚡ Camille	26
⚡ Captains Courageous	25
Day at the Races	24
Lost Horizon	25
Nothing Sacred	23
Shall We Dance	25
⚡ Snow White	27
Stage Door	25
Topper	20

1938

Adventures of Robin Hood	25
Angels with Dirty Faces	24
⚡ Bringing Up Baby	27
Grand Illusion	28
⚡ Holiday	27
Jezebel	25
Lady Vanishes	25

1939

⚡ Alexander Nevsky	26
⚡ Beau Geste	25

YEARS

1947

☑ Beauty/Beast	28
Bishop's Wife	24
☑ Gentleman's Agreement	26
Ghost and Mrs. Muir	24
☑ Great Expectations	27
Kiss of Death	23
☑ Miracle on 34th Street	25
Monsieur Verdoux	25
Nightmare Alley	22
☑ Out of the Past	26

1948

Big Clock	25
Easter Parade	22
Fort Apache	23
☑ Hamlet	27
☑ Key Largo	26
Lady from Shanghai	25
Mr. Blandings	23
☑ Red River	26
☑ Red Shoes	26
Rope	22
Snake Pit	25
Sorry, Wrong Number	25
☑ Treasure of the Sierra Madre	27

1949

☑ Adam's Rib	26
☑ All the King's Men	25
☑ Bicycle Thief	27
Fountainhead, The	22
☑ Gun Crazy	27
☑ Heiress, The	27
I Was a Male War Bride	21
Letter to Three Wives	24
On the Town	23
She Wore a Yellow Ribbon	24
☑ Third Man	28
☑ Twelve O'Clock High	26
☑ White Heat	25

1950

☑ All About Eve	28
Asphalt Jungle	24
☑ Born Yesterday	26
Cheaper By the Dozen	22
☑ Cinderella	26
D.O.A.	22
Father of the Bride	23
Harvey	26
☑ Kind Hearts and Coronets	26
King Solomon's Mines	20
☑ Sunset Boulevard	28

1951

☑ African Queen	28
Alice in Wonderland	24
☑ American in Paris	26
Christmas Carol	27
Day the Earth Stood Still	25
☑ Lavender Hill Mob	25
Oliver Twist	25
☑ Place in the Sun	27
☑ Rashomon	29
Show Boat	23
☑ Strangers on a Train	26
☑ Streetcar Named Desire	27
Thing, The	23

1952

Bad and the Beautiful	24
☑ High Noon	28
Limelight	24
☑ Member of the Wedding	25
Moulin Rouge	21
☑ Quiet Man	27
☑ Singin' in the Rain	28
Viva Zapata!	23

1953

☑ Band Wagon	26
☑ Big Heat	25
5,000 Fingers of Dr. T.	20
☑ From Here to Eternity	26
Gentlemen Prefer Blondes	23
House of Wax	21
How to Marry a Millionaire	22
Kiss Me Kate	24
Lili	24
Niagara	21
Peter Pan	25
Pickup on South Street	23
Robe, The	22
☑ Roman Holiday	27
☑ Shane	26
☑ Stalag 17	27
War of the Worlds	23
Wild One	22

1954

Barefoot Contessa	24
Brigadoon	24
☑ Caine Mutiny	27
Carmen Jones	23
Country Girl	24
☑ Dial M for Murder	25
Johnny Guitar	19
Magnificent Obsession	22

Mr. Hulot's Holiday		25
🇿 On the Waterfront		28
🇿 Rear Window		28
Sabrina		25
Seven Brides/Seven Brothers		24
🇿 Star Is Born		25
Three Coins in the Fountain		21
20,000 Leagues Under Sea		22
🇿 White Christmas		25

1955

Bad Day at Black Rock	24
Blackboard Jungle	23
🇿 Diabolique	26
East of Eden	24
🇿 Guys and Dolls	24
Kiss Me Deadly	24
Lady and the Tramp	26
Love Is Many-Splendored...	22
Man with the Golden Arm	24
Marty	25
🇿 Mister Roberts	27
🇿 Night of the Hunter	27
Oklahoma!	24
Picnic	24
Rebel Without a Cause	24
Seven Year Itch	23
Summertime	23
To Catch a Thief	25
🇿 Wages of Fear	27

1956

Anastasia	23
Around the World in 80 Days	22
Baby Doll	20
Bad Seed	22
Bus Stop	21
Carousel	24
Forbidden Planet	25
Friendly Persuasion	24
Giant	24
Godzilla	16
High Society	23
Invasion/Body Snatchers	24
Killing, The	25
🇿 King and I	27
Ladykillers, The	21
🇿 La Strada	27
Lust for Life	23
Man Who Knew Too Much	24
🇿 Rififi	26
🇿 Searchers, The	27
🇿 Seven Samurai	29

🇿 Ten Commandments	24
Wrong Man	22

1957

🇿 Affair to Remember	26
🇿 Bridge on the River Kwai	28
Desk Set	25
Funny Face	24
Gunfight at O.K. Corral	20
Jailhouse Rock	18
Love in the Afternoon	24
Nights of Cabiria	27
Old Yeller	24
🇿 Paths of Glory	28
Peyton Place	20
🇿 Smiles of a Summer Night	26
🇿 Sweet Smell of Success	27
Three Faces of Eve	24
🇿 12 Angry Men	28
🇿 Witness for the Prosecution	27

1958

Auntie Mame	25
Bell, Book and Candle	22
🇿 Cat on a Hot Tin Roof	25
Damn Yankees	24
Fly, The	20
Gigi	24
🇿 I Want to Live!	24
🇿 Mon Oncle	26
No Time for Sergeants	23
🇿 Seventh Seal	27
7th Voyage of Sinbad	20
South Pacific	24
🇿 Touch of Evil	26
🇿 Vertigo	27

1959

🇿 Anatomy of a Murder	26
🇿 Ben-Hur	26
🇿 Black Orpheus	26
Diary of Anne Frank	23
🇿 400 Blows	27
Imitation of Life	21
Journey to Center of Earth	19
Mouse That Roared	23
🇿 North by Northwest	28
🇿 On the Beach	26
Operation Petticoat	19
Pillow Talk	20
Rio Bravo	24
Room at the Top	24
Sleeping Beauty	25
🇿 Some Like It Hot	28

Suddenly, Last Summer | 24
🅩 Wild Strawberries | 26

1960

Alamo, The | 18
Apartment, The | 25
Bells Are Ringing | 24
Butterfield 8 | 23
Elmer Gantry | 25
Exodus | 23
🅩 Hiroshima, Mon Amour | 25
🅩 Inherit the Wind | 26
🅩 Magnificent Seven | 26
Never on Sunday | 24
Ocean's Eleven | 16
🅩 Psycho | 28
🅩 Spartacus | 26
Swiss Family Robinson | 23
Time Machine | 22
Village of the Damned | 21

1961

Absent-Minded Professor | 19
🅩 Breakfast at Tiffany's | 26
Breathless | 25
Children's Hour | 24
El Cid | 19
Guns of Navarone | 23
Hustler, The | 25
🅩 Judgment at Nuremberg | 26
🅩 La Dolce Vita | 25
L'Avventura | 24
Misfits, The | 21
101 Dalmatians | 24
One, Two, Three | 23
Parent Trap | 23
Pit and the Pendulum | 22
🅩 Raisin in the Sun | 26
Splendor in the Grass | 25
🅩 Two Women | 25
🅩 West Side Story | 27
Yojimbo | 28

1962

🅩 Advise & Consent | 27
Birdman of Alcatraz | 22
🅩 Cape Fear | 25
Counterfeit Traitor | 25
🅩 Days of Wine and Roses | 27
Divorce Italian Style | 24
Experiment in Terror | 25
Gypsy | 20
Hatari! | 21
Jules and Jim | 24
🅩 Lawrence of Arabia | 29
Lolita | 24

Longest Day | 24
🅩 Manchurian Candidate | 27
🅩 Man Who Shot Liberty Valance | 25
Miracle Worker | 25
Music Man | 25
Mutiny on the Bounty | 22
🅩 Requiem for a Heavyweight | 26
Shoot the Piano Player | 25
Sweet Bird of Youth | 24
🅩 To Kill a Mockingbird | 29
Whatever Happened to... | 22

1963

Billy Liar | 22
Birds, The | 24
Bye Bye Birdie | 19
🅩 Charade | 26
Cleopatra | 19
Dr. No | 23
🅩 8½ | 26
🅩 Great Escape | 27
How the West Was Won | 23
🅩 Hud | 26
Irma La Douce | 21
It's a Mad Mad Mad World | 24
Knife in the Water | 24
Leopard, The | 25
🅩 Lilies of the Field | 25
Lord of the Flies | 23
Nutty Professor | 21
Servant, The | 25
Tom Jones | 25

1964

Americanization of Emily | 24
🅩 Becket | 26
Contempt | 25
🅩 Dr. Strangelove | 28
Fail-Safe | 24
From Russia With Love | 23
🅩 Goldfinger | 26
Hard Day's Night | 24
Hush... Hush, Sweet Charlotte | 24
Marnie | 21
🅩 Mary Poppins | 27
🅩 My Fair Lady | 27
Night of the Iguana | 23
Pink Panther | 24
🅩 Seven Days in May | 26
Shot in the Dark | 23
Topkapi | 24
Umbrellas of Cherbourg | 24
Unsinkable Molly Brown | 21
Zorba the Greek | 25
Zulu | 24

1965

Agony and the Ecstasy	23
Cat Ballou	21
Cincinnati Kid	24
Collector, The	23
Darling	22
☑ Doctor Zhivago	27
Flight of the Phoenix	25
Great Race	20
Help!	19
Ipcress File	24
Juliet of the Spirits	25
☑ Pawnbroker, The	26
Repulsion	25
Ship of Fools	23
☑ Sound of Music	28
Spy Who Came in from Cold	25
Thousand Clowns	25
Thunderball	22

1966

Alfie	22
☑ Blowup	26
Born Free	24
Endless Summer	24
Fahrenheit 451	21
Fantastic Voyage	19
Fortune Cookie	23
Funny Thing Happened...	22
Georgy Girl	23
Harper	21
☑ Man and a Woman	24
☑ Man for All Seasons	28
Our Man Flint	19
Russians Are Coming...	21
Sand Pebbles	24
☑ Shop on Main Street	27
Torn Curtain	23
☑ Who's Afraid of V. Woolf?	25

1967

Barefoot in the Park	23
☑ Battle of Algiers	28
Bedazzled	20
☑ Bonnie and Clyde	25
Camelot	21
☑ Cool Hand Luke	26
Dirty Dozen	21
Don't Look Back	25
Elvira Madigan	20
Fistful of Dollars	19
For a Few Dollars More	23
Good, the Bad and the Ugly	24
☑ Graduate, The	27
☑ Guess Who's Coming...	25

☑ In Cold Blood	25
In the Heat of the Night	24
Jungle Book	23
☑ King of Hearts	26
☑ Persona	27
Point Blank	21
Thoroughly Modern Millie	18
To Sir, With Love	22
Two for the Road	24
Valley of the Dolls	17
Wait Until Dark	25
You Only Live Twice	22

1968

Barbarella	13
☑ Belle de Jour	24
Bride Wore Black	25
Bullitt	22
Charly	21
Detective, The	20
Faces	22
Finian's Rainbow	21
☑ Funny Girl	26
☑ Heart Is a Lonely Hunter	25
☑ Lion in Winter	28
Night of the Living Dead	22
Odd Couple	25
Oliver!	24
Planet of the Apes	23
Producers, The	26
☑ Romeo and Juliet	26
Rosemary's Baby	24
Thomas Crown Affair	23
☑ 2001: A Space Odyssey	26
Yellow Submarine	22

1969

☑ Anne of the Thousand Days	26
Bob & Carol & Ted & Alice	17
☑ Butch Cassidy	26
Cactus Flower	21
Damned, The	23
Easy Rider	23
Goodbye, Columbus	19
Hello, Dolly!	20
Love Bug	18
☑ Midnight Cowboy	26
Once Upon a Time/West	25
On Her Majesty's/Service	19
Paint Your Wagon	18
Prime of Miss Jean Brodie	25
Sweet Charity	20
Take the Money and Run	21
They Shoot Horses...	21
True Grit	22

⊠ Wild Bunch	27		Deliverance	25
Z	26		Discreet Charm	24
			Everything You Wanted to Know...	21

1970

Airport	17		Frenzy	20
⊠ Catch-22	25		Fritz the Cat	16
Diary of a Mad Housewife	20		Getaway, The	22
Five Easy Pieces	24		⊠ Godfather, The	29
Gimme Shelter	25		Harold and Maude	25
Great White Hope	25		Heartbreak Kid	20
⊠ I Never Sang for My Father	27		High Plains Drifter	18
Little Big Man	24		Jeremiah Johnson	23
Love Story	19		Lady Sings the Blues	22
Man Called Horse	22		Pink Flamingos	18
⊠ MASH	26		Play It Again, Sam	22
My Night at Maud's	26		Poseidon Adventure	19
On a Clear Day You Can See...	20		Ruling Class	23
Out-of-Towners	20		1776	22
Owl and the Pussycat	17		Slaughterhouse-Five	22
⊠ Patton	27		Sleuth	25
Ryan's Daughter	22		⊠ Sorrow and the Pity	29
Satyricon	20		⊠ Sounder	26
Tora! Tora! Tora!	23		What's Up, Doc?	21
Where's Poppa?	23			
Women in Love	23			
Woodstock	24			

1973

			American Graffiti	24

1971

			⊠ Badlands	25
Andromeda Strain	20		Bang the Drum Slowly	23
Bananas	23		Cinderella Liberty	19
Carnal Knowledge	22		⊠ Day for Night	27
Claire's Knee	23		⊠ Day of the Jackal	25
⊠ Clockwork Orange	25		Don't Look Now	24
⊠ Conformist, The	26		Enter the Dragon	23
Death in Venice	24		Exorcist, The	25
Diamonds Are Forever	20		Harder They Come	25
Dirty Harry	21		Jesus Christ Superstar	21
⊠ Fiddler on the Roof	26		Last Detail	22
French Connection	25		Last Tango in Paris	17
Garden of the Finzi-Continis	25		Live and Let Die	19
Klute	20		Magnum Force	22
Last Picture Show	23		Mean Streets	24
McCabe & Mrs. Miller	23		Paper Chase	23
Play Misty for Me	22		Paper Moon	22
Shaft	17		⊠ Papillon	26
Straw Dogs	21		Save the Tiger	22
Summer of '42	21		Serpico	23
Sunday Bloody Sunday	24		Sisters	22
⊠ Willy Wonka	26		Sleeper	23
			⊠ Sting, The	27
			Touch of Class	22
			Way We Were	24
			Westworld	19

1972

Butterflies Are Free	21			
⊠ Cabaret	26			

1974

Candidate, The	20		Alice Doesn't Live Here	24
⊠ Cries and Whispers	26		Apprenticeship/Duddy Kravitz	22

Benji	19
Z Blazing Saddles	25
Z Chinatown	27
Conversation, The	25
Death Wish	16
Emmanuelle	16
Z Godfather Part II	29
Great Gatsby	22
Lenny	24
Longest Yard	17
Man with the Golden Gun	18
Murder on the Orient Express	23
Parallax View	24
Scenes from a Marriage	25
Sugarland Express	18
Texas Chainsaw Massacre	17
That's Entertainment!	25
Three Musketeers	22
Towering Inferno	18
Woman Under the Influence	24
Z Young Frankenstein	27

1975

Z Amarcord	26
Barry Lyndon	20
Day of the Locust	20
Dog Day Afternoon	24
Eiger Sanction	22
Funny Lady	15
Z Jaws	26
Z Man Who Would Be King	25
Z Monty Python/Holy Grail	26
Nashville	23
Z One Flew Over Cuckoo's...	27
Prisoner of Second Avenue	22
Rocky Horror Picture Show	21
Rollerball	19
Shampoo	16
Story of Adele H.	24
Sunshine Boys	21
Swept Away	24
Three Days of the Condor	24
Tommy	16
Wind and the Lion	24

1976

All the President's Men	25
Bad News Bears	18
Carrie	22
Car Wash	17
Cousin, Cousine	21
Freaky Friday	18
Front, The	23
Grey Gardens	25
Man Who Fell to Earth	18
Marathon Man	24
Missouri Breaks	16
Murder by Death	21
Network	24
Omen, The	21
Outlaw Josey Wales	25
Robin and Marian	20
Z Rocky	25
Z Seven Beauties	26
Silent Movie	20
Silver Streak	19
Z Taxi Driver	27

1977

Aguirre: The Wrath of God	25
Z Annie Hall	27
Black Sunday	19
Z Close Encounters	24
Deep, The	17
Eraserhead	21
Gauntlet, The	17
Goodbye Girl	21
High Anxiety	21
Julia	25
Looking for Mr. Goodbar	18
MacArthur	21
New York, New York	19
1900	22
Oh, God!	17
Pete's Dragon	20
Pumping Iron	17
Rescuers, The	23
Saturday Night Fever	22
Slap Shot	22
Smokey and the Bandit	16
Spy Who Loved Me	21
Z Star Wars	28
3 Women	25
Turning Point	23

1978

Z Animal House	24
Boys from Brazil	24
Buddy Holly Story	21
Coma	19
Coming Home	23
Dawn of the Dead	19
Days of Heaven	23
Death on the Nile	19
Z Deer Hunter	26
Every Which Way But Loose	16
Foul Play	21
Z Grease	23
Halloween	22
Heaven Can Wait	21

Interiors	23
Invasion/Body Snatchers	19
ℤ Last Waltz	26
Lord of Rings	15
Midnight Express	24
Pretty Baby	17
Same Time, Next Year	22
Superman	22
Unmarried Woman	20
Up in Smoke	19
Wiz, The	16

1979

ℤ Alien	25
All That Jazz	24
Amityville Horror	18
And Justice for All	23
ℤ Apocalypse Now	27
ℤ Being There	26
Black Stallion	24
Breaking Away	24
China Syndrome	22
Escape from Alcatraz	23
Great Santini	22
Hair	20
In-Laws, The	24
Jerk, The	22
Kramer vs. Kramer	23
La Cage aux Folles	24
Life of Brian	23
ℤ Manhattan	26
Marriage of Maria Braun	25
Meatballs	18
Moonraker	16
Muppet Movie	24
1941	14
Norma Rae	24
North Dallas Forty	19
Nosferatu the Vampyre	22
Onion Field	24
Picnic at Hanging Rock	24
Rose, The	19
Seduction of Joe Tynan	22
Starting Over	20
Star Trek	14
10	17
Time After Time	23
Warriors, The	23

1980

ℤ Airplane!	24
Altered States	19
American Gigolo	19
Atlantic City	24
Blues Brothers	22

ℤ Breaker Morant	27
Caddyshack	24
Caligula	12
Coal Miner's Daughter	24
Dressed to Kill	20
Elephant Man	24
Fame	21
Fog, The	17
Friday the 13th	16
Gloria	22
Heaven's Gate	14
Mad Max	20
Melvin and Howard	22
My Bodyguard	18
My Brilliant Career	25
9 to 5	18
Ordinary People	25
Popeye	13
Private Benjamin	17
ℤ Raging Bull	26
Shining, The	25
Stardust Memories	19
ℤ Star Wars V/Empire Strikes	26
Stir Crazy	20
Stunt Man	22
Tess	21
Tin Drum	23
Urban Cowboy	18

1981

Absence of Malice	21
American Werewolf/London	20
Arthur	20
Blow Out	19
Body Heat	24
Cannonball Run	17
ℤ Chariots of Fire	26
Clash of the Titans	18
Dragonslayer	18
Escape from New York	15
Excalibur	22
Eye of the Needle	23
Eyewitness	23
Fort Apache, The Bronx	21
For Your Eyes Only	18
Four Seasons	21
Fox and the Hound	18
French Lieutenant's Woman	22
Gallipoli	25
Ghost Story	21
Heavy Metal	20
History of the World: Pt. I	22
Howling, The	19
Last Metro	24
Mommie Dearest	17

Title	Rating
My Dinner with Andre	21
On Golden Pond	24
Pennies from Heaven	17
Polyester	19
Postman Always Rings...	20
Quest for Fire	17
Ragtime	21
☑ Raiders of the Lost Ark	28
Reds	21
Stripes	21
Taps	20
Time Bandits	21

1982

Title	Rating
Annie	19
Best Little Whorehouse in Texas	14
☑ Blade Runner	26
Cat People	16
Conan the Barbarian	16
Dark Crystal	24
☑ Das Boot	28
Dead Men Don't Wear Plaid	20
Deathtrap	22
Diner	25
Diva	24
Eating Raoul	18
☑ E.T.	26
Evil Dead	22
Fast Times/Ridgemont High	22
Firefox	17
First Blood: Rambo	18
☑ Fitzcarraldo	27
48 HRS.	19
Frances	23
☑ Gandhi	27
Midsummer Night's Sex	18
Missing	24
My Favorite Year	22
Night Shift	19
Officer and a Gentleman	22
Personal Best	15
Pink Floyd The Wall	23
Poltergeist	22
Porky's	14
Road Warrior	22
Secret of NIMH	24
☑ Sophie's Choice	26
Star Trek II	23
Thing, The	23
Tootsie	25
Tron	18
Verdict, The	23
Victor/Victoria	23
World According to Garp	21

1983

Title	Rating
All the Right Moves	16
Big Chill	23
Christine	17
☑ Christmas Story	26
Cujo	17
Dead Zone	21
Educating Rita	18
☑ Fanny and Alexander	26
Flashdance	16
Gorky Park	22
Hunger, The	20
King of Comedy	23
☑ Local Hero	26
Meaning of Life	24
Mr. Mom	18
National Lampoon's Vacation	22
Never Say Never Again	18
Octopussy	17
Outsiders, The	22
☑ Right Stuff	26
Risky Business	20
Scarface	22
Silkwood	22
Star 80	16
Star Wars VI/Return of Jedi	24
Sudden Impact	20
Tender Mercies	24
Terms of Endearment	25
Trading Places	23
Videodrome	17
WarGames	22
Year of Living Dangerously	24
Yentl	18
Zelig	20

1984

Title	Rating
Against All Odds	18
All of Me	21
☑ Amadeus	26
Beverly Hills Cop	20
Birdy	23
Broadway Danny Rose	22
Brother from Another Planet	23
Cotton Club	20
Dune	14
Firestarter	17
Footloose	17
Ghostbusters	21
Gods Must Be Crazy	22
Gremlins	19
Greystoke	15
☑ Indiana Jones/Temple of Doom	22
Karate Kid	19

Z Killing Fields	26
Moscow on the Hudson	19
Natural, The	23
Neverending Story	23
Nightmare on Elm Street	19
Once Upon a Time/America	24
Paris, Texas	22
Passage to India	25
Places in the Heart	20
Purple Rain	14
Red Dawn	17
Repo Man	17
Revenge of the Nerds	19
Romancing the Stone	20
Sixteen Candles	22
Z Soldier's Story	26
Splash	19
Starman	19
Stop Making Sense	25
Terminator, The	24
Z This Is Spinal Tap	26
Top Secret!	20
2010	16

1985

After Hours	21
Agnes of God	21
Back to the Future	23
Black Cauldron	19
Blood Simple	24
Brazil	24
Breakfast Club	22
Chorus Line	19
Cocoon	20
Z Color Purple	26
Desperately Seeking Susan	15
Falcon and the Snowman	21
Fletch	19
Goonies, The	23
Jagged Edge	22
Jewel of the Nile	19
Kiss of the Spider Woman	22
Ladyhawke	21
Legal Eagles	17
Lost in America	20
Mad Max/Thunderdome	17
Mask	21
Out of Africa	25
Pee-wee's Big Adventure	19
Prizzi's Honor	21
Purple Rose of Cairo	21
Z Ran	27
Runaway Train	21
Z Shoah	28
Silverado	24

Spies Like Us	16
St. Elmo's Fire	17
Teen Wolf	15
To Live and Die in L.A.	20
Trip to Bountiful	24
View to a Kill	14
Weird Science	19
Witness	23

1986

About Last Night...	17
Aliens	23
American Tail	21
Big Trouble in Little China	19
Blue Velvet	22
Brighton Beach Memoirs	22
Children of a Lesser God	23
Color of Money	16
Crimes of the Heart	21
Crocodile Dundee	17
Down and Out/Beverly Hills	17
Down by Law	24
Z Ferris Bueller's Day Off	23
Fly, The	16
F/X	21
Golden Child	14
Gung Ho	17
Hannah and Her Sisters	24
Heartburn	19
Highlander	19
Hoosiers	23
Labyrinth	22
Legend	18
Little Shop of Horrors	19
Manhunter	21
Mission, The	24
Money Pit	16
Mosquito Coast	16
My Beautiful Laundrette	23
Name of the Rose	22
9½ Weeks	15
Peggy Sue Got Married	19
Platoon	25
Pretty in Pink	19
Z Room with a View	26
Ruthless People	20
Salvador	21
She's Gotta Have It	21
Sid & Nancy	18
Something Wild	20
Stand by Me	24
Star Trek IV	21
Three Amigos	16
Z Top Gun	22

Indiana Jones/Last Crusade	24
License to Kill	14
Little Mermaid	24
Look Who's Talking	16
Major League	21
My Left Foot	25
Parenthood	22
Roger & Me	24
Say Anything	23
Sea of Love	20
Sex, Lies and Videotape	19
Shirley Valentine	24
Steel Magnolias	24
Uncle Buck	17
Valmont	20
War of the Roses	17
Weekend at Bernie's	16
☑ When Harry Met Sally...	26

1990

Akira	23
Alice	20
Avalon	24
Awakenings	22
☑ Cinema Paradiso	26
Cook, Thief, His Wife, Her Lover	20
Cry-Baby	17
Dances with Wolves	23
Dick Tracy	13
Edward Scissorhands	21
Flatliners	18
Freshman, The	21
Ghost	21
Godfather Part III	16
☑ Goodfellas	27
Grifters, The	22
Henry & June	20
Home Alone	19
Hunt for Red October	24
Internal Affairs	19
Jacob's Ladder	19
Longtime Companion	23
Metropolitan	20
Miller's Crossing	22
Misery	21
Paris is Burning	24
Postcards from the Edge	18
Presumed Innocent	20
☑ Pretty Woman	23
Pump Up the Volume	18
Reversal of Fortune	23
Sheltering Sky	16
Tie Me Up! Tie Me Down!	20
Total Recall	18

1991

Addams Family	17
Backdraft	18
Barton Fink	20
Beauty/Beast	26
Boyz N the Hood	23
Bugsy	18
Cape Fear	20
City Slickers	20
Commitments, The	24
Dead Again	22
Doors, The	20
Father of the Bride	20
Fisher King	21
Frankie & Johnny	20
Fried Green Tomatoes	23
Grand Canyon	18
Hook	17
JFK	19
La Femme Nikita	23
L.A. Story	20
My Girl	20
My Own Private Idaho	19
Naked Lunch	17
Prince of Tides	19
Regarding Henry	20
Robin Hood: Prince of Thieves	16
Rocketeer, The	18
☑ Silence of the Lambs	27
Sleeping with the Enemy	17
Terminator 2: Judgment Day	23
Thelma & Louise	23
Truly Madly Deeply	23
Truth or Dare	15
What About Bob?	18

1992

Aladdin	24
Basic Instinct	19
Batman Returns	16
Beethoven	16
Bob Roberts	22
Bodyguard, The	14
Chaplin	22
Crying Game	22
Damage	22
☑ Delicatessen	26
Dracula	20
☑ Enchanted April	24
Few Good Men	23
Glengarry Glen Ross	23
Hand That Rocks the Cradle	16
Hoffa	19
Honeymoon in Vegas	18

Howards End	22
Husbands and Wives	22
Indochine	23
Last of the Mohicans	22
League of Their Own	20
Malcolm X	23
Mambo Kings	20
Mediterraneo	21
Mighty Ducks	18
My Cousin Vinny	22
Noises Off	21
Patriot Games	21
Player, The	23
Prelude to a Kiss	16
Reservoir Dogs	24
River Runs Through It	22
Scent of a Woman	21
Single White Female	16
Sister Act	18
Under Siege	15
☑ Unforgiven	26
Wayne's World	17
White Men Can't Jump	13

1993

Age of Innocence	22
Army of Darkness	23
Benny & Joon	21
Carlito's Way	22
Cliffhanger	15
Cool Runnings	18
Dave	21
Dazed and Confused	22
Farewell My Concubine	25
Firm, The	17
Free Willy	17
Fugitive, The	23
☑ Gettysburg	25
Groundhog Day	22
Grumpy Old Men	21
Indecent Proposal	15
In the Line of Fire	20
In the Name of the Father	23
Joy Luck Club	25
Jurassic Park	22
Like Water for Chocolate	25
Manhattan Murder Mystery	21
Mrs. Doubtfire	20
Nightmare Before Christmas	24
Pelican Brief	16
Philadelphia	24
Piano, The	21
Remains of the Day	24
Rudy	23
☑ Schindler's List	29

Searching for Bobby Fischer	24
Short Cuts	22
Six Degrees of Separation	21
Sleepless in Seattle	21
Strictly Ballroom	23
This Boy's Life	21
Tombstone	21
True Romance	24
Wedding Banquet	22
What's Eating Gilbert Grape	22
What's Love Got to Do with It	22

1994

Ace Ventura	15
Adventures of Priscilla	23
Bullets Over Broadway	21
Clear and Present Danger	20
Clerks	23
Client, The	17
Crow, The	21
Dumb and Dumber	15
Eat Drink Man Woman	25
Ed Wood	20
☑ Forrest Gump	24
Four Weddings and a Funeral	21
Heavenly Creatures	24
☑ Hoop Dreams	26
Hudsucker Proxy	22
Interview with the Vampire	19
Last Seduction	22
Legends of the Fall	20
☑ Lion King	25
Little Women	21
Madness of King George	22
Mask, The	17
Maverick	18
Natural Born Killers	14
Professional, The	25
☑ Pulp Fiction	26
Quiz Show	21
Reality Bites	19
Santa Clause	19
☑ Shawshank Redemption	28
Speed	18
Stargate	18
True Lies	19
Wolf	15

1995

American President	21
Apollo 13	24
Babe	25
Basketball Diaries	22
Before Sunrise	23
Boys on the Side	15

Z Braveheart	26	Hunchback/Notre Dame	19
Bridges of Madison Co.	19	Independence Day	19
Brothers McMullen	19	James and the Giant Peach	20
Casino	21	Jerry Maguire	21
Casper	15	Kingpin	18
Celluloid Closet	25	**Z** Lone Star	25
Clueless	21	Long Kiss Goodnight	19
Crimson Tide	21	Michael Collins	21
Dead Man Walking	23	Mission: Impossible	16
Devil in a Blue Dress	19	Nutty Professor	15
Get Shorty	20	101 Dalmatians	18
GoldenEye	19	People vs. Larry Flynt	18
Heat	22	Phenomenon	18
Il Postino	24	Portrait of a Lady	16
Jumanji	18	Primal Fear	22
Leaving Las Vegas	20	Ransom	16
Little Princess	24	Rock, The	20
Mallrats	18	Romeo + Juliet	19
Mighty Aphrodite	18	Scream	20
Mr. Holland's Opus	21	Secrets & Lies	24
Muriel's Wedding	22	Shine	22
Net, The	16	Sleepers	22
Outbreak	16	Sling Blade	25
Pocahontas	17	Space Jam	16
Z Sense and Sensibility	26	Swingers	23
Seven	23	Time to Kill	18
Showgirls	5	Tin Cup	18
Strange Days	17	Trainspotting	22
To Die For	18	Twister	15
Z Toy Story	27	Waiting for Guffman	25
Twelve Monkeys	22		
Z Usual Suspects	27		
Welcome to the Dollhouse	22	**1997**	
While You Were Sleeping	18	Air Force One	18
		Amistad	21
1996		Anastasia	20
		As Good As It Gets	22
Antonia's Line	25	Austin Powers/Int'l Man	19
Basquiat	17	of Mystery	
Big Night	24	Boogie Nights	19
Birdcage, The	22	Chasing Amy	20
Bottle Rocket	22	Con Air	14
Breaking the Waves	23	Contact	20
Cable Guy	11	Cop Land	17
City Hall	18	Deconstructing Harry	16
Crucible, The	19	Devil's Advocate	19
Emma	22	Devil's Own	17
Z English Patient	22	Donnie Brasco	20
Eraser	14	Face/Off	18
Everyone Says I Love You	18	Fifth Element	19
Evita	19	Full Monty	22
Z Fargo	25	Game, The	22
First Wives Club	17	Gattaca	20
Fly Away Home	22	George of the Jungle	17
From Dusk Till Dawn	18	**Z** Good Will Hunting	24
Hamlet	24	Grosse Pointe Blank	22

subscribe to ZAGAT.com

YEARS

Mummy, The	19
Notting Hill	19
Office Space	25
Red Violin	24
Run Lola Run	23
🎬 Sixth Sense	26
Sleepy Hollow	17
South Park	20
Star Wars I/Phantom Menace	18
Straight Story	24
Stuart Little	19
Sweet and Lowdown	21
Talented Mr. Ripley	18
Tarzan	22
Three Kings	20
Topsy-Turvy	23
🎬 Toy Story 2	26
World Is Not Enough	19

2000

Almost Famous	23
American Psycho	19
Before Night Falls	22
Best in Show	24
Billy Elliot	25
Boiler Room	18
Boondock Saints	23
Bring It On	17
Cast Away	20
Charlie's Angels	13
Chicken Run	23
Chocolat	22
Contender, The	19
Crouching Tiger	24
Dancer in the Dark	22
Dinner Rush	23
Dinosaur	19
Emperor's New Groove	20
Erin Brockovich	21
Family Man	16
Finding Forrester	22
Frequency	19
🎬 Gladiator	23
Gone in Sixty Seconds	14
High Fidelity	21
How the Grinch Stole Xmas	17
Meet the Parents	19
🎬 Memento	26
Miss Congeniality	15
Mission: Impossible II	15
Nurse Betty	15
O Brother, Where Art Thou?	22
Patriot, The	21
Perfect Storm	16
Pitch Black	19

Pollock	22
Quills	22
Remember the Titans	20
Requiem for a Dream	25
Shadow of the Vampire	20
Snatch	21
Thirteen Days	22
Traffic	23
U-571	17
Unbreakable	16
Virgin Suicides	20
What Lies Beneath	16
What Women Want	15
Whole Nine Yards	17
Wonder Boys	21
X-Men	19
You Can Count on Me	23

2001

A.I.: Artificial Intelligence	16
Along Came a Spider	16
🎬 Amélie	26
🎬 Amores Perros	26
Anniversary Party	18
Atlantis	16
🎬 Beautiful Mind	26
Black Hawk Down	23
Blow	22
Bridget Jones's Diary	21
Donnie Darko	22
Enemy at the Gates	21
Ghost World	23
Gosford Park	23
Hannibal	15
🎬 Harry Potter/Sorcerer's	24
Hedwig and the Angry Inch	21
I Am Sam	21
In the Bedroom	22
Iris	24
Kate & Leopold	16
Kissing Jessica Stein	21
Knight's Tale	18
K-Pax	16
Lara Croft: Tomb Raider	13
Legally Blonde	19
🎬 Lord of Rings/Fellowship	27
Man Who Wasn't There	21
Monster's Ball	22
🎬 Monsters, Inc.	26
Moulin Rouge!	23
Mulholland Dr.	20
Mummy Returns	18
Ocean's Eleven	19
Others, The	23
Pearl Harbor	14

Barbarian Invasions	24	**Z** Mystic River	26
Bend It Like Beckham	26	Old School	20
Big Fish	22	Once Upon a Time/Mexico	15
Bringing Down the House	19	Open Range	21
Brother Bear	21	Peter Pan	20
Bruce Almighty	18	Phone Booth	18
Calendar Girls	23	Pieces of April	21
Cheaper By the Dozen	17	Pirates Caribbean/The Curse	24
Z City of God	26	Radio	22
Coffee and Cigarettes	18	Recruit, The	17
Cold Mountain	22	Runaway Jury	20
Company, The	19	Rundown, The	17
Confessions/Dangerous Mind	19	School of Rock	20
Confidence	18	Seabiscuit	25
Cooler, The	22	Secondhand Lions	22
Daredevil	14	Shanghai Knights	16
Dirty Pretty Things	23	Shattered Glass	21
Down with Love	18	Something's Gotta Give	23
Elephant	19	**Z** Spellbound	28
Elf	21	Station Agent	25
Fighting Temptations	17	S.W.A.T.	15
Z Finding Nemo	28	Swimming Pool	20
Fog of War	26	Sylvia	16
Freaky Friday	21	Tears of the Sun	18
Girl with a Pearl Earring	21	Terminator 3: Rise of Machines	16
Gothika	17	Thirteen	21
Holes	23	Triplets of Belleville	24
House of Sand and Fog	23	28 Days Later	18
How to Lose a Guy...	19	21 Grams	22
Hulk	12	Under the Tuscan Sun	19
Human Stain	18	Underworld	17
Identity	18	Uptown Girls	14
Z In America	26	Veronica Guerin	21
In-Laws, The	16	Whale Rider	25
Italian Job	22	**Z** Winged Migration	26
Kill Bill Vol. 1	23	Wonderland	16
Lara Croft Tomb Raider: Cradle	14	X2: X-Men United	24
Last Samurai	23		
Laurel Canyon	18	**2004**	
League of Extraordinary Gentlemen	12	After the Sunset	17
Legally Blonde 2	13	Alfie	12
Life of David Gale	21	Along Came Polly	15
Z Lord of Rings/Return	28	Anchorman	14
Lost in Translation	21	Assassination of Richard Nixon	18
Love Actually	22	Aviator, The	23
Magdalene Sisters	25	Bad Education	23
Master and Commander	23	Before Sunset	21
Matchstick Men	20	Being Julia	23
Matrix Reloaded	21	Beyond the Sea	19
Matrix Revolutions	15	**Z** Born into Brothels	27
Mighty Wind	23	Bourne Supremacy	21
Missing, The	18	Bridget Jones/Edge of Reason	14
Mona Lisa Smile	16	Butterfly Effect	17
Monster	24	Cellular	16

Chronicles of Riddick	14	Passion of the Christ	22
Clearing, The	16	Phantom of the Opera	21
Closer	19	Polar Express	21
Collateral	21	Princess Diaries 2	16
Dawn of the Dead	19	☑ Ray	26
Day After Tomorrow	16	Saw	18
De-Lovely	20	Sea Inside	25
Dodgeball	16	Shall We Dance?	17
Dogville	21	Shark Tale	19
Door in the Floor	19	Shaun of the Dead	22
Dreamers, The	17	☑ Shrek 2	26
Ella Enchanted	19	Sideways	23
Eternal Sunshine	23	Sky Captain/World Tomorrow	15
Fahrenheit 9/11	21	Spanglish	19
50 First Dates	18	Spider-Man 2	22
Finding Neverland	25	SpongeBob SquarePants	16
Friday Night Lights	21	Stage Beauty	20
Garden State	22	Starsky & Hutch	14
Harold & Kumar/White Castle	19	Stepford Wives	12
☑ Harry Potter/Prisoner	24	Super Size Me	24
Hellboy	16	Team America: World Police	18
Hero	25	Terminal, The	18
Hidalgo	20	13 Going on 30	19
Home at the End of World	18	Troy	19
☑ Hotel Rwanda	28	Van Helsing	15
House of Flying Daggers	24	Vanity Fair	17
I ♥ Huckabees	14	Vera Drake	24
☑ Incredibles, The	26	Very Long Engagement	22
In Good Company	19	Village, The	16
Intolerable Cruelty	15	We Don't Live Here Anymore	16
I, Robot	18	Wimbledon	15
Kill Bill Vol. 2	25	Woodsman, The	21
King Arthur	15		
Kinsey	22	**2005**	
Ladder 49	19	Assault on Precinct 13	16
Ladykillers, The	15	Batman Begins	23
Lemony Snicket	18	Because of Winn-Dixie	19
Life Aquatic/Steve Zissou	16	Breakfast on Pluto	19
Love Song for Bobby Long	19	Bride & Prejudice	20
Machinist, The	20	Brokeback Mountain	24
Manchurian Candidate	18	Broken Flowers	16
Man on Fire	21	☑ Capote	26
Maria Full of Grace	25	Casanova	16
Mean Girls	20	Charlie/Choc. Factory	18
Meet the Fockers	18	Chicken Little	19
Merchant of Venice	23	Chronicles of Narnia	23
☑ Million Dollar Baby	27	Cinderella Man	25
Miracle	24	Coach Carter	21
Motorcycle Diaries	23	Constant Gardener	23
Napoleon Dynamite	19	Constantine	16
National Treasure	19	Corpse Bride	20
Notebook, The	23	Crash	26
Ocean's Twelve	14	Derailed	16
Open Water	15	Diary of a Mad Black Woman	19

Gone Baby Gone	24	Savages, The	23
Great Debaters	25	Shooter	20
Grindhouse	21	Shrek the Third	20
Hairspray	21	Sicko	23
☑ Harry Potter/Order of Phoenix	24	Simpsons Movie	19
Hoax, The	21	Spider-Man 3	19
Hot Fuzz	24	Stardust	22
I Am Legend	19	Superbad	20
I'm Not There	17	Sweeney Todd	23
In the Valley of Elah	22	There Will Be Blood	23
Into the Wild	23	300	22
Juno	25	3:10 to Yuma	23
Kite Runner	24	Transformers	21
Knocked Up	19	28 Weeks Later	19
Lars and the Real Girl	22	Waitress	24
Last Mimzy	21	Wild Hogs	17
☑ La Vie en Rose	25	Zodiac	21
Live Free or Die Hard	20		
☑ Lives of Others	28	**2008**	
Meet the Robinsons	22		
Michael Clayton	24	Bank Job	23
Mighty Heart	21	Chronicles of Narnia: Caspian	23
Music and Lyrics	17	Forgetting Sarah Marshall	20
National Treasure/Book of Secrets	20	Horton Hears a Who!	23
No Country for Old Men	24	In Bruges	23
No Reservations	16	Indiana Jones/Crystal Skull	20
Ocean's Thirteen	17	☑ Iron Man	26
Once	25	Leatherheads	17
Pirates Caribbean/At World's End	21	Miss Pettigrew Lives for a Day	21
☑ Ratatouille	26	Other Boleyn Girl	19
Reign Over Me	20	Sex and the City	22
		27 Dresses	17

Genres/Special Features

Listings include Overall ratings. ☑ indicates movies with the highest ratings, popularity and importance.

ACTION/ADVENTURE

Adventures of Robin Hood	25
Aguirre: The Wrath of God	25
Apocalypto	19
Around the World in 80 Days	22
Assault on Precinct 13	16
Backdraft	18
Batman	20
Batman Begins	23
Batman Returns	16
Benji	19
Beverly Hills Cop	20
Big Trouble in Little China	19
Black Stallion	24
Blade	18
Blood Diamond	25
Bourne Identity	20
Bourne Supremacy	21
☑ Bourne Ultimatum	25
Brotherhood of the Wolf	18
Cannonball Run	17
Captain Blood	23
☑ Captains Courageous	25
Cast Away	20
Catch Me If You Can	23
Charlie's Angels	13
Chronicles of Narnia: Caspian	23
Chronicles of Narnia	23
Clash of the Titans	18
Cliffhanger	15
Con Air	14
Conan the Barbarian	16
Constantine	16
Contact	20
Count of Monte Cristo	19
Crimson Tide	21
Crocodile Dundee	17
Crouching Tiger	24
Daredevil	14
Day After Tomorrow	16
Deep, The	17
Deep Impact	15
Deliverance	25
Die Hard	23
Dragonslayer	18
Easy Rider	23
Eight Below	22
Enter the Dragon	23
Eragon	16

Eraser	14
Every Which Way But Loose	16
Evil Dead	22
Excalibur	22
Face/Off	18
Fantastic Four	14
Fantastic Four: Rise of Silver Surfer	15
Fantastic Voyage	19
Fearless	20
Fifth Element	19
First Blood: Rambo	18
☑ Fitzcarraldo	27
Flight of the Phoenix	25
Fly Away Home	22
Flyboys	18
Four Feathers	16
From Dusk Till Dawn	18
Gauntlet, The	17
Getaway, The	22
Ghost Rider	16
☑ Gladiator	23
Gods Must Be Crazy	22
Golden Child	14
Golden Compass	17
Goonies, The	23
☑ Great Escape	27
Great Race	20
Greystoke	15
Grindhouse	21
Guardian, The	18
Hatari!	21
Hellboy	16
Hell's Angels	24
Hero	25
Hidalgo	20
Highlander	19
House of Flying Daggers	24
Hulk	12
I Am Legend	19
Independence Day	19
Indiana Jones/Crystal Skull	20
Indiana Jones/Last Crusade	24
☑ Indiana Jones/Temple of Doom	22
I, Robot	18
☑ Iron Man	26
Jewel of the Nile	19
Journey to Center of Earth	19
Jumanji	18
Jurassic Park	22

GENRE/FEATURES

Hulk	12	Meet Joe Black	17
Human Stain	18	Merchant of Venice	23
I Am Legend	19	Michael Clayton	24
I ♥ Huckabees	14	Michael Collins	21
I'm Not There	17	Midnight in Garden of Good...	20
In Bruges	23	Mighty Ducks	18
Indiana Jones/Crystal Skull	20	Mighty Heart	21
Infamous	21	Miss Pettigrew Lives for a Day	21
In Good Company	19	Miss Potter	21
In-Laws, The (2003)	16	Monster House	20
Internal Affairs	19	Muriel's Wedding	22
In the Valley of Elah	22	Music and Lyrics	17
Into the Wild	23	Nacho Libre	12
☑ Iron Man	26	National Treasure/Book of Secrets	20
Island, The	16	Negotiator, The	20
Jackie Brown	21	Net, The	16
John Q	17	Neverending Story	23
Juno	25	Night at the Museum	19
Kate & Leopold	16	1941	14
Keeping Up with the Steins	17	No Country for Old Men	24
King Arthur	15	Noises Off	21
Kingdom of Heaven	18	No Reservations	16
Kingpin	18	Ocean's Thirteen	17
Kiss the Girls	20	Office Space	25
Kite Runner	24	Once	25
K-19: The Widowmaker	16	Onion Field	24
Knocked Up	19	Open Range	21
Ladyhawke	21	Open Season	18
Lady in the Water	14	Open Water	15
Lake House	16	Other Boleyn Girl	19
Land Before Time	20	Perfect Murder	19
Lara Croft Tomb Raider: Cradle	14	Planes, Trains/Automobiles	22
Lars and the Real Girl	22	Popeye	13
Last Holiday	19	Porky's	14
Last Mimzy	21	Prairie Home Companion	18
☑ La Vie en Rose	25	Predator	20
League of Extraordinary Gentlemen	12	Princess Diaries 2	16
Leatherheads	17	Pump Up the Volume	18
Legal Eagles	17	Quills	22
Legally Blonde 2	13	Racing Stripes	18
Les Misérables	21	☑ Ratatouille	26
Live Free or Die Hard	20	Red Dawn	17
Long Kiss Goodnight	19	Red Eye	16
Look Who's Talking	16	Regarding Henry	20
Lord of War	18	Reign Over Me	20
Lost Boys	21	Revenge of the Nerds	19
Machinist, The	20	Rocketeer, The	18
☑ Mad Hot Ballroom	27	Rocky Balboa	18
Magnum Force	22	Rollerball	19
Major League	21	Rumor Has It	14
Manhattan Murder Mystery	21	Rundown, The	17
Man of the Year	16	Sarah Silverman: Jesus Is Magic	18
Marie Antoinette	17	Savages, The	23
Matador, The	20	Saw III	17

Scanner Darkly	17	Virgin Suicides	20
School for Scoundrels	16	Walk to Remember	18
Science of Sleep	18	We Don't Live Here Anymore	16
Scoop	18	Weird Science	19
Sea Inside	25	White Men Can't Jump	13
Searching for Bobby Fischer	24	Wild Hogs	17
Sentinel, The	17	Windtalkers	16
Sex and the City	22	Wolf	15
Shanghai Knights	16	World Trade Center	20
Sherrybaby	18	You, Me and Dupree	13
Shooter	20		
☑ Shop on Main Street	27	**AMERICANA**	
Shortbus	18	Alamo, The	18
Sicko	23	☑ All the King's Men (1949)	25
Siege, The	19	All the King's Men (2006)	15
Simpsons Movie	19	American Graffiti	24
Skeleton Key	17	☑ Badlands	25
Sky Captain/World Tomorrow	15	☑ Best Years of Our Lives	28
Sky High	16	Blue Velvet	22
Snakes on a Plane	11	Bull Durham	22
Spies Like Us	16	Cheaper By the Dozen (1950)	22
Stage Beauty	20	☑ Christmas Story	26
Stardust	22	Dances with Wolves	23
Star Trek	14	Days of Heaven	23
Stranger Than Fiction	21	East of Eden	24
Straw Dogs	21	Elizabethtown	14
Sudden Impact	20	Far From Heaven	24
Superbad	20	☑ Forrest Gump	24
Superman Returns	18	Friendly Persuasion	24
Sweeney Todd	23	Giant	24
Sweet and Lowdown	21	☑ Grapes of Wrath	28
Talladega Nights	15	☑ It's a Wonderful Life	27
Team America: World Police	18	Kings Row	22
Tears of the Sun	18	Last Picture Show	23
Teen Wolf	15	League of Their Own	20
There Will Be Blood	23	☑ Meet Me in St. Louis	26
Thirteen Days	22	☑ Member of the Wedding	25
13 Going on 30	19	Miracle of Morgan's Creek	23
Three Amigos	16	Mr. Deeds Goes to Town	25
Three Burials/Estrada	22	☑ Mr. Smith Goes to Washington	26
3:10 to Yuma	23	Music Man	25
Top Secret!	20	Nashville	23
Transformers	21	Natural, The	23
Truly Madly Deeply	23	O Brother, Where Art Thou?	22
Tuck Everlasting	19	Oklahoma!	24
28 Weeks Later	19	Old Yeller	24
27 Dresses	17	Picnic	24
Underworld	17	Places in the Heart	20
Up in Smoke	19	Pleasantville	20
Valley of the Dolls	17	Radio Days	23
Valmont	20	Ragtime	21
Vanilla Sky	12	Seabiscuit	25
Van Wilder	14	1776	22
Venus	19	☑ Shadow of a Doubt	26

Stand by Me	24
Straight Story	24
Summer of '42	21
🔲 To Kill a Mockingbird	29
Trip to Bountiful	24
Truman Show	21
Tucker	20
Yankee Doodle Dandy	25

ANIMATED

(* Not for children)

Akira*	23
Aladdin	24
Alice in Wonderland	24
All Dogs Go to Heaven	17
American Tail	21
Anastasia (1997)	20
Ant Bully	18
Antz	20
Atlantis	16
🔲 Bambi	26
Beauty/Beast (1991)	26
Bee Movie	19
Black Cauldron	19
Brother Bear	21
Bug's Life	24
Cars	24
Chicken Little	19
Chicken Run	23
🔲 Cinderella	26
Corpse Bride	20
Curious George	19
Dinosaur	19
Dumbo	24
Emperor's New Groove	20
🔲 Fantasia	28
Fantasia 2000	24
🔲 Finding Nemo	28
Flushed Away	19
Fox and the Hound	18
Fritz the Cat*	16
Happy Feet	21
Heavy Metal*	20
Hercules	17
Hoodwinked	18
Horton Hears a Who!	23
Howl's Moving Castle	25
Hunchback/Notre Dame (1996)	19
Ice Age	23
Ice Age: The Meltdown	21
🔲 Incredibles, The	26
Iron Giant	24
James and the Giant Peach	20
Jungle Book (1967)	23

Lady and the Tramp	26
Land Before Time	20
Lilo & Stitch	23
🔲 Lion King	25
Little Mermaid	24
Lord of Rings	15
Madagascar	21
Meet the Robinsons	22
Monster House	20
🔲 Monsters, Inc.	26
Mulan	23
Nightmare Before Christmas	24
101 Dalmatians (1961)	24
Open Season	18
Over the Hedge	23
Peter Pan (1953)	25
Pete's Dragon	20
🔲 Pinocchio	26
Pocahontas	17
Polar Express	21
Prince of Egypt	19
🔲 Ratatouille	26
Rescuers, The	23
Robots	20
Secret of NIMH	24
Shark Tale	19
🔲 Shrek	26
🔲 Shrek 2	26
Shrek the Third	20
Simpsons Movie	19
Sleeping Beauty	25
🔲 Snow White	27
Song of the South	23
South Park*	20
Space Jam	16
Spirit: Stallion of Cimarron	21
🔲 Spirited Away	27
SpongeBob SquarePants	16
Tarzan	22
Team America: World Police*	18
🔲 Toy Story	27
🔲 Toy Story 2	26
Triplets of Belleville*	24
Wallace & Gromit	24
Who Framed Roger Rabbit	24
Yellow Submarine	22

BIOGRAPHIES

Agony and the Ecstasy	23
🔲 Alexander Nevsky	26
🔲 Amadeus	26
American Splendor	23
Anastasia (1956)	23
🔲 Anne of the Thousand Days	26

Antwone Fisher	23	Lenny	24
Auto Focus	16	Lust for Life	23
Aviator, The	23	MacArthur	21
Basquiat	17	Madness of King George	22
Z Becket	26	Malcolm X	23
Before Night Falls	22	Z Man for All Seasons	28
Beyond the Sea	19	Man on the Moon	16
Birdman of Alcatraz	22	Marie Antoinette	17
Z Bonnie and Clyde	25	Miracle Worker	25
Born Free	24	Miss Potter	21
Buddy Holly Story	21	Mommie Dearest	17
Bugsy	18	Mrs. Brown	22
Caligula	12	Z Napoléon	28
Z Capote	26	Z Patton	27
Casanova	16	People vs. Larry Flynt	18
Chaplin	22	Pocahontas	17
Cinderella Man	25	Pollock	22
Cleopatra	19	Pride of the Yankees	22
Coal Miner's Daughter	24	Z Queen, The	26
Confessions/Dangerous Mind	19	Z Raging Bull	26
De-Lovely	20	Z Ray	26
Diary of Anne Frank	23	Reds	21
Don't Look Back	25	Scarlet Empress	24
Doors, The	20	Sergeant York	25
Ed Wood	20	Sid & Nancy	18
Elephant Man	24	Song of Bernadette	22
Elizabeth	24	Star 80	16
Elizabeth: The Golden Age	21	Sylvia	16
Evita	19	Tucker	20
Finding Neverland	25	Unsinkable Molly Brown	21
Frances	23	Viva Zapata!	23
Frida	25	Walk the Line	25
Z Funny Girl	26	What's Love Got to Do with It	22
Funny Lady	15	Yankee Doodle Dandy	25
Z Gandhi	27	Young Guns	15
Gods and Monsters	23		
Gorillas in the Mist	19	**BLACK COMEDIES**	
Great White Hope	25	After Hours	21
Gypsy	20	American Psycho	19
Henry & June	20	Z Arsenic and Old Lace	26
Hoffa	19	Bad Santa	18
Hurricane, The	21	Beetlejuice	20
I'm Not There	17	Being John Malkovich	22
Infamous	21	Z Being There	26
Iris	24	Brazil	24
Julia	25	Cable Guy	11
Kid Stays in the Picture	21	Z Catch-22	25
Kinsey	22	Clerks	23
La Bamba	20	Cook, Thief, His Wife, Her Lover	20
Lady Sings the Blues	22	Death at a Funeral	20
Z Last Emperor	26	Z Delicatessen	26
Z Last King of Scotland	25	Discreet Charm	24
Z La Vie en Rose	25	Divorce Italian Style	24
Z Lawrence of Arabia	29	Z Dr. Strangelove	28

Eating Raoul	18
Ed Wood	20
Election	22
Fear and Loathing/Las Vegas	15
Fortune Cookie	23
Front, The	23
Go	20
Gremlins	19
Groundhog Day	22
Happiness	23
Harold and Maude	25
Heathers	21
Z Kind Hearts and Coronets	26
King of Comedy	23
Ladykillers, The (1956)	21
Ladykillers, The (2004)	15
Lars and the Real Girl	22
Life of Brian	23
Lolita	24
Z MASH	26
Meaning of Life	24
Monsieur Verdoux	25
Z Monty Python/Holy Grail	26
Night Shift	19
Nurse Betty	15
Pink Flamingos	18
Polyester	19
Prizzi's Honor	21
Producers, The (1968)	26
Producers, The (2005)	18
Royal Tenenbaums	20
Ruling Class	23
Russians Are Coming...	21
Ruthless People	20
Secretary	21
Slaughterhouse-Five	22
Something Wild	20
Stepford Wives	12
Stunt Man	22
Time Bandits	21
To Die For	18
Wag the Dog	19
War of the Roses	17
Weekend at Bernie's	16
Welcome to the Dollhouse	22
What About Bob?	18
Where's Poppa?	23

BLOCKBUSTERS

(Annual highest grossing movies with year of release)

Aladdin	1992	24
Armageddon	1998	15
Back to the Future	1985	23
Z Bambi	1942	26
Batman	1989	20
Bells of St. Mary's	1945	24
Z Ben-Hur	1959	26
Z Best Years of Our Lives	1946	28
Z Birth of a Nation	1915	25
Z Blazing Saddles	1974	25
Z Bridge on the River Kwai	1957	28
Z Butch Cassidy	1969	26
Cleopatra	1963	19
Z E.T.	1982	26
Exorcist, The	1973	25
Z Forrest Gump	1994	24
French Connection	1971	25
Z Funny Girl	1968	26
Ghostbusters	1984	21
Z Godfather, The	1972	29
Going My Way	1944	24
Z Gone with the Wind	1939	28
Z Graduate, The	1967	27
Z Grease	1978	23
Z Harry Potter/Sorcerer's	2001	24
Home Alone	1990	19
Honey, I Shrunk the Kids	1989	16
How the Grinch Stole Xmas	2000	17
Independence Day	1996	19
Z Jaws	1975	26
Jurassic Park	1993	22
Z King Kong	1933	25
King Solomon's Mines	1950	20
Kramer vs. Kramer	1979	23
Z Lawrence of Arabia	1962	29
Z Lord of Rings/Return	2003	28
Love Story	1970	19
Z Mary Poppins	1964	27
Z Mister Roberts	1955	27
Mrs. Miniver	1942	25
Z Night at the Opera	1935	26
Peyton Place	1957	20
Pirates Caribbean/Dead Man	2006	20
Z Raiders of the Lost Ark	1981	28
Rain Man	1988	25
Z Red River	1948	26
Robe, The	1953	22
Robin Hood: Prince of Thieves	1991	16
Z Rocky	1976	25
Z Saving Private Ryan	1998	26
Sergeant York	1941	25
Z Shrek 2	2004	26
Z Snow White	1937	27
Z Sound of Music	1965	28
South Pacific	1958	24
Z Spartacus	1960	26
Spider-Man	2002	21

Spider-Man 3 | 2007	19
☒ Star Wars | 1977	28
Star Wars I/Phantom Menace | 1999	18
Star Wars III/Revenge of Sith | 2005	23
☒ Star Wars V/Empire Strikes | 1980	26
Star Wars VI/Return of Jedi | 1983	24
☒ Ten Commandments | 1956	24
Terminator 2: Judgment Day | 1991	23
☒ Thin Man | 1934	26
Three Men and a Baby | 1987	16
Titanic | 1997	19
☒ Top Gun | 1986	22
☒ Toy Story | 1995	27
Twister | 1996	15
Under Siege | 1992	15
☒ West Side Story | 1961	27
☒ White Christmas | 1954	25

BUDDY FILMS

About a Boy	21
Analyze That	14
Analyze This	18
Auto Focus	16
Blues Brothers	22
Breaking Away	24
Brokeback Mountain	24
Bucket List	21
☒ Butch Cassidy	26
City Slickers	20
Down by Law	24
Easy Rider	23
48 HRS.	19
F/X	21
Ghost World	23
Gloria	22
☒ Gunga Din	25
Harold & Kumar/White Castle	19
Hot Fuzz	24
Lethal Weapon	21
☒ Man Who Would Be King	25
Matador, The	20
Mean Streets	24
Men in Black	21
Men in Black II	14
☒ Midnight Cowboy	26
Midnight Run	23
Motorcycle Diaries	23
Night Shift	19
North Dallas Forty	19
Odd Couple	25
Outrageous Fortune	15

Roger Dodger	18
Rush Hour	19
Rush Hour 2	17
Sahara	17
Shanghai Knights	16
Spies Like Us	16
Starsky & Hutch	14
Stir Crazy	20
Swingers	23
Thelma & Louise	23
Three Amigos	16
Wedding Crashers	21
White Men Can't Jump	13

CAMP CLASSICS

Adventures of Priscilla	23
Auntie Mame	25
Barbarella	13
Birdcage, The	22
Bride of Frankenstein	25
Caligula	12
Conan the Barbarian	16
Duel in the Sun	23
Eating Raoul	18
Evil Dead	22
Fly, The (1958)	20
Gentlemen Prefer Blondes	23
Godzilla	16
Hairspray (1988)	19
How to Marry a Millionaire	22
Hush... Hush, Sweet Charlotte	24
Imitation of Life	21
I'm No Angel	23
☒ I Want to Live!	24
Johnny Guitar	19
La Cage aux Folles	24
Little Shop of Horrors	19
☒ Mildred Pierce	26
Mommie Dearest	17
9½ Weeks	15
Pee-wee's Big Adventure	19
Peyton Place	20
Pillow Talk	20
Pink Flamingos	18
Poseidon Adventure	19
Rocky Horror Picture Show	21
Shaun of the Dead	22
Showgirls	5
Stepford Wives	12
Texas Chainsaw Massacre	17
Valley of the Dolls	17
Whatever Happened to...	22
☒ Women, The	26
Women on the Verge	24

CAPERS

Asphalt Jungle	24
Bank Job	23
Bourne Supremacy	21
Catch Me If You Can	23
Fish Called Wanda	23
Getaway, The	22
Inside Man	23
Italian Job	22
Killing, The	25
Ladykillers, The (1956)	21
Ladykillers, The (2004)	15
☒ Lavender Hill Mob	25
Lock, Stock and Two...	23
Matchstick Men	20
National Treasure	19
Ocean's Eleven (1960)	16
Ocean's Eleven (2001)	19
Ocean's Twelve	14
Ocean's Thirteen	17
Out of Sight	21
Pink Panther	24
Reservoir Dogs	24
☒ Rififi	26
Ronin	20
Ruthless People	20
Score, The	17
Silver Streak	19
Snatch	21
☒ Sting, The	27
Swordfish	15
Thomas Crown Affair	23
Topkapi	24

CHICK FLICKS

(See also Romance)

☒ Affair to Remember	26
☒ Amélie	26
Baby Boom	19
Beaches	22
Boys on the Side	15
☒ Breakfast at Tiffany's	26
Bridges of Madison Co.	19
Bridget Jones's Diary	21
Bridget Jones/Edge of Reason	14
Calendar Girls	23
Clueless	21
Crimes of the Heart	21
Dangerous Beauty	21
Desperately Seeking Susan	15
Devil Wears Prada	22
Dirty Dancing	21
Divine Secrets/Ya-Ya	16
Down with Love	18

Elizabethtown	14
☒ Enchanted April	24
☒ English Patient	22
Father of the Bride (1991)	20
First Wives Club	17
Four Weddings and a Funeral	21
Fried Green Tomatoes	23
Friends with Money	16
Funny Face	24
Ghost	21
How to Lose a Guy...	19
In Her Shoes	18
Joy Luck Club	25
Kissing Jessica Stein	21
Lake House	16
Legally Blonde	19
Legally Blonde 2	13
Letter to Three Wives	24
Little Women	21
Love Actually	22
Love Is Many-Splendored...	22
Love Story	19
Maid in Manhattan	14
Mean Girls	20
Miss Congeniality	15
Mona Lisa Smile	16
Muriel's Wedding	22
My Best Friend's Wedding	19
Mystic Pizza	17
Notebook, The	23
Notting Hill	19
☒ Now, Voyager	27
Officer and a Gentleman	22
Out of Africa	25
Outrageous Fortune	15
Peyton Place	20
☒ Pretty Woman	23
Pride and Prejudice (1940)	25
Princess Diaries	18
Princess Diaries 2	16
Private Benjamin	17
Real Women Have Curves	21
☒ Roman Holiday	27
Romy & Michele's/Reunion	14
☒ Sense and Sensibility	26
Sex and the City	22
Shakespeare in Love	24
Sisterhood/Traveling Pants	19
Sleepless in Seattle	21
Something's Gotta Give	23
Splendor in the Grass	25
Stage Door	25
Steel Magnolias	24
Sweet Home Alabama	17

GENRE/FEATURES

Whale Rider | 25
Willow | 20
 Willy Wonka | 26
Wiz, The | 16
⊠ Wizard of Oz | 28

CITY SETTINGS

LA
Adaptation | 22
American Gigolo | 19
Bad and the Beautiful | 24
Barfly | 18
Barton Fink | 20
Beverly Hills Cop | 20
⊠ Big Sleep | 27
⊠ Blade Runner | 26
Bodyguard, The | 14
Boyz N the Hood | 23
⊠ Chinatown | 27
Clueless | 21
Crash | 26
Day of the Locust | 20
D.O.A. | 22
Down and Out/Beverly Hills | 17
Ed Wood | 20
For Your Consideration | 17
Gods and Monsters | 23
Grand Canyon | 18
Jackie Brown | 21
Kiss Kiss Bang Bang | 20
⊠ L.A. Confidential | 26
L.A. Story | 20
Mulholland Dr. | 20
Player, The | 23
Postcards from the Edge | 18
⊠ Pretty Woman | 23
Reservoir Dogs | 24
Shampoo | 16
Short Cuts | 22
⊠ Singin' in the Rain | 28
Starsky & Hutch | 14
⊠ Sunset Boulevard | 28
Swingers | 23
To Live and Die in L.A. | 20

LAS VEGAS
Bugsy | 18
Casino | 21
Cooler, The | 22
Diamonds Are Forever | 20
Fear and Loathing/Las Vegas | 15
Honeymoon in Vegas | 18
Leaving Las Vegas | 20
Ocean's Eleven (1960) | 16

Ocean's Eleven (2001) | 19
Ocean's Thirteen | 17
Showgirls | 5

LONDON
About a Boy | 21
Alfie (1966) | 22
American Werewolf/London | 20
Bank Job | 23
Bedazzled | 20
⊠ Blowup | 26
Bridget Jones's Diary | 21
Bridget Jones/Edge of Reason | 14
Children of Men | 22
Elephant Man | 24
End of the Affair | 20
Fish Called Wanda | 23
Frenzy | 20
Gaslight | 26
Georgy Girl | 23
Ipcress File | 24
Lock, Stock and Two... | 23
Love Actually | 22
Man Who Knew Too Much | 24
⊠ Mary Poppins | 27
Match Point | 22
⊠ My Fair Lady | 27
Notting Hill | 19
Oliver! | 24
101 Dalmatians (1996) | 18
Patriot Games | 21
Scoop | 18
Secrets & Lies | 24
Snatch | 21
28 Days Later | 18
28 Weeks Later | 19

NEW YORK
⊠ Affair to Remember | 26
After Hours | 21
Age of Innocence | 22
Alice | 20
⊠ All About Eve | 28
All That Jazz | 24
Angels with Dirty Faces | 24
⊠ Annie Hall | 27
Apartment, The | 25
Arthur | 20
Barefoot in the Park | 23
Basquiat | 17
Bells Are Ringing | 24
Big | 23
⊠ Breakfast at Tiffany's | 26
Bright Lights, Big City | 15
Broadway Danny Rose | 22

Bullets Over Broadway	21	**Z** Miracle on 34th Street	25
Carlito's Way	22	Moonstruck	24
Changing Lanes	16	Moscow on the Hudson	19
Z Crimes and Misdemeanors	26	My Favorite Year	22
Crocodile Dundee	17	Network	24
Day After Tomorrow	16	New York, New York	19
Death Wish	16	Odd Couple	25
Desperately Seeking Susan	15	Once Upon a Time/America	24
Devil Wears Prada	22	On the Town	23
Dog Day Afternoon	24	**Z** On the Waterfront	28
Donnie Brasco	20	Out-of-Towners	20
Do the Right Thing	23	Owl and the Pussycat	17
Dressed to Kill	20	**Z** Pawnbroker, The	26
Elf	21	Pieces of April	21
Escape from New York	15	Pollock	22
Everyone Says I Love You	18	Prizzi's Honor	21
Eyewitness	23	Quiz Show	21
Fame	21	Radio Days	23
Fisher King	21	Ransom	16
Fort Apache, The Bronx	21	**Z** Rear Window	28
42nd Street	24	Rent	19
French Connection	25	Rosemary's Baby	24
Freshman, The	21	Saturday Night Fever	22
Gangs of New York	21	Serpico	23
Ghostbusters	21	Sex and the City	22
Gloria	22	Siege, The	19
Z Godfather, The	29	Six Degrees of Separation	21
Z Godfather Part II	29	Spider-Man	21
Guide to Recognizing Saints	18	Spider-Man 2	22
Z Guys and Dolls	24	Spider-Man 3	19
Hair	20	Sunshine Boys	21
Hannah and Her Sisters	24	**Z** Sweet Smell of Success	27
Hitch	21	**Z** Taxi Driver	27
Husbands and Wives	22	Tootsie	25
Hustler, The	25	25th Hour	21
Igby Goes Down	20	Unfaithful	21
Inside Man	23	Unmarried Woman	20
Interpreter, The	20	Wall Street	22
Kate & Leopold	16	Warriors, The	23
Z King Kong (1933)	25	**Z** West Side Story	27
King of Comedy	23	**Z** When Harry Met Sally...	26
Kissing Jessica Stein	21	Working Girl	20
Klute	20	World Trade Center	20
Madagascar	21	You've Got Mail	18
Maid in Manhattan	14		
Z Manhattan	26	**PARIS**	
Manhattan Murder Mystery	21	**Z** Amélie	26
Marathon Man	24	**Z** American in Paris	26
Marty	25	Before Sunset	21
Mean Streets	24	**Z** Belle de Jour	24
Melinda and Melinda	17	Bourne Identity	20
Metropolitan	20	Breathless	25
Z Midnight Cowboy	26	**Z** Charade	26
Mighty Aphrodite	18	**Z** Children of Paradise	28

subscribe to ZAGAT.com

GENRE/FEATURES

Bullets Over Broadway	21	Freshman, The	21
Cactus Flower	21	Full Monty	22
Caddyshack	24	Galaxy Quest	21
Car Wash	17	☑ General, The	28
Cat Ballou	21	George of the Jungle	17
Charlie's Angels	13	Get Shorty	20
Chasing Amy	20	Ghostbusters	21
Cheaper By the Dozen (1950)	22	Gods Must Be Crazy	22
Cheaper By the Dozen (2003)	17	☑ Gold Rush	28
City Slickers	20	Goodbye, Columbus	19
Clerks II	18	Goodbye Girl	21
Click	16	☑ Graduate, The	27
Clueless	21	☑ Great Dictator	26
Coming to America	18	Great Race	20
Cool Runnings	18	Gremlins	19
Crocodile Dundee	17	Grosse Pointe Blank	22
Crossing Delancey	23	Grumpy Old Men	21
Cry-Baby	17	Guess Who	16
Darjeeling Limited	17	Gung Ho	17
Dave	21	Hairspray (1988)	19
Dead Men Don't Wear Plaid	20	Harold & Kumar/White Castle	19
Deconstructing Harry	16	Harvey	26
Desk Set	25	Hatari!	21
Desperately Seeking Susan	15	Heartbreak Kid	20
Dirty Rotten Scoundrels	22	Heaven Can Wait (1943)	24
Dodgeball	16	High Anxiety	21
Down and Out/Beverly Hills	17	History of the World: Pt. I	22
Down with Love	18	Hitch	21
Dr. Dolittle	16	Hollywood Ending	15
Dumb and Dumber	15	Home Alone	19
Eat Drink Man Woman	25	Honey, I Shrunk the Kids	16
Elf	21	Honeymoon in Vegas	18
Emma	22	Hot Fuzz	24
Everyone Says I Love You	18	How to Lose a Guy...	19
Everything You Wanted to Know...	21	How to Marry a Millionaire	22
Failure to Launch	15	Hudsucker Proxy	22
Family Man	16	I'm No Angel	23
Fast Times/Ridgemont High	22	Importance of Being Earnest	21
Father of the Bride (1950)	23	In & Out	17
Father of the Bride (1991)	20	In-Laws, The (1979)	24
☑ Ferris Bueller's Day Off	23	In-Laws, The (2003)	16
Fever Pitch	20	Innerspace	15
50 First Dates	18	It's a Mad Mad Mad World	24
Fighting Temptations	17	I Was a Male War Bride	21
First Wives Club	17	Jackass: The Movie	13
Fish Called Wanda	23	Jerk, The	22
Fletch	19	Jungle Book (1967)	23
Forgetting Sarah Marshall	20	Just Like Heaven	19
40 Year Old Virgin	19	Keeping Up with the Steins	17
For Your Consideration	17	Kingpin	18
Foul Play	21	Kissing Jessica Stein	21
Four Weddings and a Funeral	21	Knight's Tale	18
Freaky Friday (1976)	18	Knocked Up	19
Freaky Friday (2003)	21	Kung Fu Hustle	23

La Cage aux Folles	24	My Cousin Vinny	22
L.A. Story	20	My Favorite Year	22
☑ Lavender Hill Mob	25	My Little Chickadee	23
Legal Eagles	17	Nacho Libre	12
Legally Blonde	19	Naked Gun	20
Legally Blonde 2	13	Napoleon Dynamite	19
Liar Liar	16	National Lampoon's Vacation	22
Little Big Man	24	1941	14
☑ Local Hero	26	9 to 5	18
Look Who's Talking	16	No Time for Sergeants	23
Lost Boys	21	Notting Hill	19
Lost in America	20	Nutty Professor (1963)	21
Love Actually	22	Nutty Professor (1996)	15
Love Bug	18	O Brother, Where Art Thou?	22
Maid in Manhattan	14	Odd Couple	25
Major League	21	Office Space	25
Mallrats	18	Oh, God!	17
☑ Manhattan	26	Old School	20
Manhattan Murder Mystery	21	One, Two, Three	23
Man Who Came to Dinner	26	Operation Petticoat	19
Married to the Mob	17	Out-of-Towners	20
Mask, The	17	Outrageous Fortune	15
Matador, The	20	Owl and the Pussycat	17
Matchstick Men	20	Parent Trap	23
Maverick	18	Pee-wee's Big Adventure	19
Mean Girls	20	Peggy Sue Got Married	19
Meatballs	18	Pillow Talk	20
Mediterraneo	21	Pink Panther	24
Meet the Fockers	18	Planes, Trains/Automobiles	22
Meet the Parents	19	Play It Again, Sam	22
Midnight Run	23	Popeye	13
Midsummer Night's Sex	18	Porky's	14
Mighty Aphrodite	18	Postcards from the Edge	18
Mighty Wind	23	Pretty in Pink	19
Miss Congeniality	15	☑ Pretty Woman	23
☑ Mister Roberts	27	Private Benjamin	17
Modern Times	28	Purple Rose of Cairo	21
Money Pit	16	Radio Days	23
☑ Monkey Business	26	Repo Man	17
☑ Mon Oncle	26	Revenge of the Nerds	19
Monster-in-Law	15	Risky Business	20
Mouse That Roared	23	Romy & Michele's/Reunion	14
Mr. Blandings	23	Roxanne	21
Mr. Deeds Goes to Town	25	Rush Hour	19
Mr. Hulot's Holiday	25	Rush Hour 2	17
Mr. Mom	18	Santa Clause	19
Mrs. Doubtfire	20	Sarah Silverman: Jesus Is Magic	18
Muppet Movie	24	School for Scoundrels	16
Murder by Death	21	School of Rock	20
Muriel's Wedding	22	Scoop	18
Music and Lyrics	17	Seven Year Itch	23
Must Love Dogs	16	Sex and the City	22
My Best Friend's Wedding	19	Shall We Dance?	17
My Big Fat Greek Wedding	23	Shampoo	16

GENRE/FEATURES

Shanghai Knights	16
Shaun of the Dead	22
She Done Him Wrong	22
She's Gotta Have It	21
Shirley Valentine	24
Shot in the Dark	23
Silent Movie	20
Silver Streak	19
Sister Act	18
Sixteen Candles	22
Slap Shot	22
Sleeper	23
Sleepless in Seattle	21
☑ Smiles of a Summer Night	26
Smokey and the Bandit	16
☑ Some Like It Hot	28
Something's Gotta Give	23
South Park	20
Spaceballs	18
Spies Like Us	16
Starsky & Hutch	14
Starting Over	20
Stir Crazy	20
Strictly Ballroom	23
Stripes	21
Sunshine Boys	21
Superbad	20
Swingers	23
Tadpole	19
Take the Money and Run	21
Talladega Nights	15
Team America: World Police	18
Teen Wolf	15
10	17
Thank You for Smoking	23
There's Something/Mary	21
☑ This Is Spinal Tap	26
Thousand Clowns	25
Three Amigos	16
Three Men and a Baby	16
Tie Me Up! Tie Me Down!	20
Tin Cup	18
Tom Jones	25
Tootsie	25
Topkapi	24
Topper	20
Top Secret!	20
Touch of Class	22
Trading Places	23
27 Dresses	17
Twins	15
Two for the Road	24
Two Weeks Notice	16
Uncle Buck	17

Unmarried Woman	20
Up in Smoke	19
Van Wilder	14
Waiting for Guffman	25
Waitress	24
Wayne's World	17
Wedding Banquet	22
Wedding Crashers	21
Wedding Singer	17
Weird Science	19
What Women Want	15
☑ When Harry Met Sally...	26
While You Were Sleeping	18
Whole Nine Yards	17
Wild Hogs	17
Wimbledon	15
Witches of Eastwick	17
☑ Woman of the Year	27
Working Girl	20
You, Me and Dupree	13
☑ Young Frankenstein	27
You've Got Mail	18
Zelig	20
Ziegfeld Follies	24
Zoolander	16

COMIC BOOK ADAPTATIONS

Addams Family	17
Akira	23
American Splendor	23
Annie	19
Barbarella	13
Batman	20
Batman Begins	23
Batman Returns	16
Blade	18
Casper	15
Constantine	16
Crow, The	21
Daredevil	14
Dick Tracy	13
Fantastic Four	14
Fantastic Four: Rise of Silver Surfer	15
Fritz the Cat	16
Ghost Rider	16
Ghost World	23
Heavy Metal	20
Hellboy	16
History of Violence	22
Hulk	12
☑ Iron Man	26
League of Extraordinary Gentlemen	12
Men in Black	21
Men in Black II	14

subscribe to ZAGAT.com

Eastern Promises	24	Natural Born Killers	14
Elephant	19	Negotiator, The	20
Experiment in Terror	25	No Country for Old Men	24
Fletch	19	Nurse Betty	15
Fort Apache, The Bronx	21	Ocean's Eleven (1960)	16
48 HRS.	19	Ocean's Eleven (2001)	19
French Connection	25	Ocean's Twelve	14
Freshman, The	21	Ocean's Thirteen	17
Gangs of New York	21	Once Upon a Time/America	24
Gauntlet, The	17	Onion Field	24
Getaway, The	22	☒ On the Waterfront	28
Get Shorty	20	Out of Sight	21
Gloria	22	Panic Room	18
☒ Godfather, The	29	Prizzi's Honor	21
☒ Godfather Part II	29	Public Enemy	25
Godfather Part III	16	☒ Pulp Fiction	26
Gone Baby Gone	24	☒ Rear Window	28
Gone in Sixty Seconds	14	Red Dragon	19
☒ Goodfellas	27	Reservoir Dogs	24
Grosse Pointe Blank	22	Road to Perdition	23
Harder They Come	25	Scarface	22
Harper	21	Score, The	17
Heat	22	Serpico	23
Heavenly Creatures	24	Shoot the Piano Player	25
History of Violence	22	Sleepers	22
Hoffa	19	Snatch	21
Hustle & Flow	23	☒ Sting, The	27
In Bruges	23	Sugarland Express	18
☒ In Cold Blood	25	Sweeney Todd	23
Inside Man	23	To Catch a Thief	25
In the Heat of the Night	24	To Live and Die in L.A.	20
I, Robot	18	Traffic	23
Italian Job	22	Training Day	20
☒ I Want to Live!	24	True Romance	24
Jackie Brown	21	25th Hour	21
Ladykillers, The (1956)	21	Untouchables, The	22
Ladykillers, The (2004)	15	☒ Usual Suspects	27
☒ Lavender Hill Mob	25	Whole Nine Yards	17
Lethal Weapon	21	Wonderland	16
Little Caesar	24		
Lock, Stock and Two...	23	**CULT FILMS**	
Lucky Number Slevin	21	Adventures of Priscilla	23
☒ M	26	After Hours	21
Magnum Force	22	Akira	23
Manhunter	21	☒ All About Eve	28
Married to the Mob	17	American Splendor	23
Matador, The	20	Army of Darkness	23
Matchstick Men	20	Baby Doll	20
Mean Streets	24	Barbarella	13
Midnight in Garden of Good...	20	Barfly	18
Miller's Crossing	22	Being John Malkovich	22
Monsieur Verdoux	25	Big Lebowski	20
Monster	24	Big Trouble in Little China	19
☒ Mystic River	26	Bill & Ted's	15

❷ Blade Runner	26	
Blair Witch Project	10	
Blue Velvet	22	
Boondock Saints	23	
Brazil	24	
❷ Breakfast at Tiffany's	26	
Breakfast Club	22	
Brother from Another Planet	23	
Caligula	12	
❷ Casablanca	29	
❷ Children of Paradise	28	
Clerks	23	
❷ Clockwork Orange	25	
Cook, Thief, His Wife, Her Lover	20	
Crow, The	21	
Crying Game	22	
Dawn of the Dead (1978)	19	
Dirty Dancing	21	
Donnie Darko	22	
Down by Law	24	
❷ Dr. Strangelove	28	
Dune	14	
Eating Raoul	18	
❷ 8½	26	
Enter the Dragon	23	
Eraserhead	21	
Eternal Sunshine	23	
Evil Dead	22	
❷ Fantasia	28	
Fear and Loathing/Las Vegas	15	
❷ Ferris Bueller's Day Off	23	
Fight Club	23	
5,000 Fingers of Dr. T.	20	
Fletch	19	
Forbidden Planet	25	
Freaks	23	
Friday the 13th	16	
From Dusk Till Dawn	18	
Go	20	
Gods Must Be Crazy	22	
❷ Grease	23	
Grey Gardens	25	
Grindhouse	21	
❷ Gun Crazy	27	
Harder They Come	25	
Harold and Maude	25	
Heathers	21	
Heavy Metal	20	
Hellraiser	19	
Highlander	19	
❷ It's a Wonderful Life	27	
Kill Bill Vol. 1	23	
Kill Bill Vol. 2	25	
❷ King of Hearts	26	

Life of Brian	23	
Little Shop of Horrors	19	
Lost Boys	21	
Mad Max	20	
❷ Manchurian Candidate (1962)	27	
Meaning of Life	24	
Melvin and Howard	22	
❷ Monty Python/Holy Grail	26	
Mulholland Dr.	20	
My Dinner with Andre	21	
Napoleon Dynamite	19	
Night of the Living Dead	22	
Office Space	25	
Pee-wee's Big Adventure	19	
Pink Flamingos	18	
Pink Floyd The Wall	23	
Polyester	19	
❷ Princess Bride	27	
Raising Arizona	23	
❷ Red Shoes	26	
Repo Man	17	
Repulsion	25	
Road Warrior	22	
Rocky Horror Picture Show	21	
Royal Tenenbaums	20	
Ruling Class	23	
Rushmore	23	
Serenity	23	
7th Voyage of Sinbad	20	
❷ Shawshank Redemption	28	
Showgirls	5	
Sin City	22	
❷ Sound of Music	28	
❷ Star Wars	28	
St. Elmo's Fire	17	
Stunt Man	22	
Texas Chainsaw Massacre	17	
Time Bandits	21	
Top Secret!	20	
True Romance	24	
28 Days Later	18	
Up in Smoke	19	
Valley of the Dolls	17	
Videodrome	17	
Village of the Damned	21	
Waiting for Guffman	25	
Warriors, The	23	
Welcome to the Dollhouse	22	
Where's Poppa?	23	
❷ Willy Wonka	26	
❷ Wizard of Oz	28	

DATE FLICKS

Along Came Polly	15	
❷ Amélie	26	

GENRE/FEATURES

☑ Annie Hall	27
Barefoot in the Park	23
Before Sunrise	23
Before Sunset	21
Big Chill	23
Bodyguard, The	14
Break-Up, The	15
Bride & Prejudice	20
Bull Durham	22
Butterflies Are Free	21
☑ Casablanca	29
Chocolat	22
Cocktail	16
Dirty Dancing	21
Eternal Sunshine	23
Fabulous Baker Boys	20
Failure to Launch	15
Fever Pitch	20
Forgetting Sarah Marshall	20
Four Weddings and a Funeral	21
Frankie & Johnny	20
Georgy Girl	23
Ghost	21
Good Year	16
High Fidelity	21
Holiday, The	19
How to Lose a Guy...	19
Jerry Maguire	21
Just Like Heaven	19
Kate & Leopold	16
Love Actually	22
Love Story	19
☑ Man and a Woman	24
Mediterraneo	21
Moonstruck	24
Music and Lyrics	17
My Big Fat Greek Wedding	23
No Reservations	16
Notting Hill	19
Officer and a Gentleman	22
Once	25
Prelude to a Kiss	16
☑ Pretty Woman	23
Prince of Tides	19
Romancing the Stone	20
☑ Roman Holiday	27
☑ Romeo and Juliet	26
Roxanne	21
Saturday Night Fever	22
Say Anything	23
Shakespeare in Love	24
Shopgirl	18
Sideways	23
Sleepless in Seattle	21

Sliding Doors	21
Something's Gotta Give	23
Starman	19
Strictly Ballroom	23
Summer of '42	21
Titanic	19
Truly Madly Deeply	23
Way We Were	24
Wedding Singer	17
What Women Want	15
☑ When Harry Met Sally...	26
Wimbledon	15
You've Got Mail	18

DISASTER FILMS

(See also End of the World)

☑ Airplane!	24
Airport	17
Backdraft	18
China Syndrome	22
Perfect Storm	16
Poseidon Adventure	19
Titanic	19
Towering Inferno	18
Twister	15

DOCUMENTARIES

☑ Born into Brothels	27
Bowling for Columbine	22
Buena Vista Social Club	25
Celluloid Closet	25
Don't Look Back	25
Endless Summer	24
Enron/Smartest Guys	25
Fahrenheit 9/11	21
Fog of War	26
Gimme Shelter	25
Grey Gardens	25
☑ Hoop Dreams	26
Inconvenient Truth	24
Kid Stays in the Picture	21
☑ Last Waltz	26
☑ Mad Hot Ballroom	27
☑ March of the Penguins	26
Murderball	25
Paris is Burning	24
Pumping Iron	17
Roger & Me	24
☑ Shoah	28
Sicko	23
☑ Sorrow and the Pity	29
☑ Spellbound (2003)	28
Stop Making Sense	25
Super Size Me	24
That's Entertainment!	25

GENRE/FEATURES

GENRE/FEATURES

EPICS

FANTASY

Donnie Darko	22
Edward Scissorhands	21
Enchanted	23
Eraserhead	21
Eternal Sunshine	23
Excalibur	22
Fantastic Voyage	19
Field of Dreams	22
Finian's Rainbow	21
Fisher King	21
5,000 Fingers of Dr. T.	20
Freaky Friday (1976)	18
Freaky Friday (2003)	21
Ghost	21
Ghost and Mrs. Muir	24
Golden Compass	17
Gremlins	19
☑ Harry Potter/Chamber	24
☑ Harry Potter/Goblet of Fire	24
☑ Harry Potter/Order of Phoenix	24
☑ Harry Potter/Prisoner	24
☑ Harry Potter/Sorcerer's	24
Harvey	26
Heaven Can Wait (1978)	21
Heavy Metal	20
Holes	23
Hook	17
How the Grinch Stole Xmas	17
Hunger, The	20
Juliet of the Spirits	25
Jumanji	18
☑ King Kong (1933)	25
King Kong (2005)	20
Labyrinth	22
Ladyhawke	21
Lady in the Water	14
League of Extraordinary Gentlemen	12
Legend	18
Lemony Snicket	18
Little Princess	24
Lord of Rings	15
☑ Lord of Rings/Fellowship	27
☑ Lord of Rings/Return	28
☑ Lord of Rings/Two Towers	27
Lost Horizon	25
Man Who Fell to Earth	18
☑ Mary Poppins	27
Mask, The	17
Meet Joe Black	17
☑ Miracle on 34th Street	25
Nanny McPhee	21
Neverending Story	23
Nightmare Before Christmas	24
☑ Pan's Labyrinth	27

Peggy Sue Got Married	19
Pete's Dragon	20
Phenomenon	18
Pirates Caribbean/Dead Man	20
Pleasantville	20
Polar Express	21
☑ Princess Bride	27
Purple Rose of Cairo	21
☑ Raiders of the Lost Ark	28
Repo Man	17
Scrooged	19
7th Voyage of Sinbad	20
Space Jam	16
☑ Spirited Away	27
Splash	19
Stardust	22
Stuart Little	19
Stuart Little 2	19
Superman	22
Time Bandits	21
Topper	20
☑ Toy Story	27
Truly Madly Deeply	23
Truman Show	21
Unbreakable	16
What Dreams May Come	16
Willow	20
☑ Willy Wonka	26
Wings of Desire	24
Witches of Eastwick	17
☑ Wizard of Oz	28

FILM NOIR

Against All Odds	18
Asphalt Jungle	24
Big Clock	25
☑ Big Heat	25
☑ Big Sleep	27
☑ Blade Runner	26
Blood Simple	24
Body Heat	24
☑ Cape Fear (1962)	25
Cape Fear (1991)	20
☑ Chinatown	27
Dead Again	22
Dead Men Don't Wear Plaid	20
D.O.A.	22
☑ Double Indemnity	28
☑ Fargo	25
Gilda	24
Good German	16
Grifters, The	22
☑ Gun Crazy	27
High Sierra	25

Hollywoodland	16
☑ Key Largo	26
Killers, The	25
Killing, The	25
Kiss Kiss Bang Bang	20
Kiss Me Deadly	24
Kiss of Death	23
☑ L.A. Confidential	26
Lady from Shanghai	25
Last Seduction	22
☑ Laura	27
Letter, The	25
☑ Maltese Falcon	28
Man Who Wasn't There	21
☑ Memento	26
☑ Mildred Pierce	26
Murder, My Sweet	24
Niagara	21
Nightmare Alley	22
☑ Night of the Hunter	27
☑ Out of the Past	26
Pickup on South Street	23
Point Blank	21
Postman Always Rings... (1946)	25
Postman Always Rings... (1981)	20
☑ Rififi	26
Scarlet Street	25
Seven	23
Sin City	22
Sorry, Wrong Number	25
☑ Strangers on a Train	26
☑ Sunset Boulevard	28
☑ Sweet Smell of Success	27
☑ Third Man	28
☑ Touch of Evil	26
☑ White Heat	25
Who Framed Roger Rabbit	24

FOOD-THEMED

☑ Babette's Feast	26
Big Night	24
Chocolat	22
Cook, Thief, His Wife, Her Lover	20
☑ Delicatessen	26
Diner	25
☑ Dinner at Eight	27
Dinner Rush	23
Discreet Charm	24
Eat Drink Man Woman	25
Fast Food Nation	18
Fried Green Tomatoes	23
Heartburn	19
Last Holiday	19
Like Water for Chocolate	25

My Big Fat Greek Wedding	23
Mystic Pizza	17
9½ Weeks	15
No Reservations	16
☑ Ratatouille	26
Spanglish	19
Super Size Me	24
Sweeney Todd	23
Tom Jones	25
Waitress	24
Wedding Banquet	22

FOREIGN FILMS

AUSTRALIAN

Adventures of Priscilla	23
Babe	25
☑ Breaker Morant	27
Crocodile Dundee	17
Gallipoli	25
Mad Max	20
Mad Max/Thunderdome	17
Muriel's Wedding	22
My Brilliant Career	25
Piano, The	21
Picnic at Hanging Rock	24
☑ Rabbit-Proof Fence	26
Road Warrior	22
Shine	22
Strictly Ballroom	23
Year of Living Dangerously	24

BRAZILIAN

☑ Central Station	26
☑ City of God	26
Motorcycle Diaries	23

BRITISH

About a Boy	21
Alfie (1966)	22
Amazing Grace	24
☑ Anne of the Thousand Days	26
Atonement	22
Bank Job	23
Barry Lyndon	20
☑ Becket	26
Bedazzled	20
Bend It Like Beckham	26
Billy Elliot	25
Billy Liar	22
☑ Blowup	26
Born Free	24
Brazil	24
Bride & Prejudice	20
☑ Bridge on the River Kwai	28

GENRE/FEATURES

Snatch	21
Spy Who Came in from Cold	25
Spy Who Loved Me	21
Sunday Bloody Sunday	24
☑ Third Man	28
☑ 39 Steps	27
Time Bandits	21
Tom Jones	25
Tommy	16
Tomorrow Never Dies	20
Topsy-Turvy	23
To Sir, With Love	22
Trainspotting	22
Truly Madly Deeply	23
28 Days Later	18
28 Weeks Later	19
Vanity Fair	17
Vera Drake	24
Village of the Damned	21
Wallace & Gromit	24
Wimbledon	15
Women in Love	23
World Is Not Enough	19
Yellow Submarine	22
You Only Live Twice	22
Zulu	24

CANADIAN

Apprenticeship/Duddy Kravitz	22
☑ Away From Her	26
Barbarian Invasions	24
Heavy Metal	20
Meatballs	18
Naked Lunch	17
Red Violin	24
Sweet Hereafter	24
Videodrome	17

CHINESE

Crouching Tiger	24
Curse of the Golden Flower	21
Farewell My Concubine	25
Fearless	20
Hero	25
House of Flying Daggers	24
Kung Fu Hustle	23

CZECHOSLOVAKIAN

☑ Shop on Main Street	27

DANISH

☑ Babette's Feast	26
Breaking the Waves	23
Dancer in the Dark	22
Dogville	21

DUTCH

Antonia's Line	25
☑ Black Book	26

FRENCH

☑ Amélie	26
☑ Au Revoir Les Enfants	27
Barbarella	13
☑ Beauty/Beast (1947)	28
☑ Belle de Jour	24
☑ Black Orpheus	26
Breathless	25
Bride Wore Black	25
Brotherhood of the Wolf	18
☑ Children of Paradise	28
Claire's Knee	23
Contempt	25
Cook, Thief, His Wife, Her Lover	20
Cousin, Cousine	21
☑ Day for Night	27
☑ Delicatessen	26
☑ Diabolique	26
Discreet Charm	24
Diva	24
☑ Diving Bell & the Butterfly	26
Emmanuelle	16
☑ 400 Blows	27
Grand Illusion	28
☑ Hiroshima, Mon Amour	25
Indochine	23
☑ Jean de Florette	27
Jules and Jim	24
☑ King of Hearts	26
La Cage aux Folles	24
La Femme Nikita	23
Last Metro	24
☑ La Vie en Rose	25
☑ Man and a Woman	24
☑ March of the Penguins	26
☑ Mon Oncle	26
Mr. Hulot's Holiday	25
My Night at Maud's	26
Name of the Rose	22
☑ Napoléon	28
Oliver Twist (2005)	20
Paris, Texas	22
☑ Pianist, The	28
Professional, The	25
Quest for Fire	17
☑ Rififi	26
☑ Rules of the Game	27
Science of Sleep	18
☑ Shoah	28
Shoot the Piano Player	25
☑ Sorrow and the Pity	29

Story of Adele H.	24	Fistful of Dollars	19
Swimming Pool	20	For a Few Dollars More	23
Tess	21	Garden of the Finzi-Continis	25
Triplets of Belleville	24	Good, the Bad and the Ugly	24
Umbrellas of Cherbourg	24	Il Postino	24
Valmont	20	Juliet of the Spirits	25
Very Long Engagement	22	☑ La Dolce Vita	25
☑ Wages of Fear	27	☑ La Strada	27
☑ Winged Migration	26	Last Tango in Paris	17
Z	26	L'Avventura	24
		Leopard, The	25
GERMAN		☑ Life Is Beautiful	27
Aguirre: The Wrath of God	25	Mediterraneo	21
☑ Blue Angel	25	Nights of Cabiria	27
☑ Cabinet of Dr. Caligari	26	1900	22
☑ Das Boot	28	Once Upon a Time/West	25
☑ Downfall	27	☑ Open City	28
☑ Fitzcarraldo	27	Satyricon	20
☑ Lives of Others	28	☑ Seven Beauties	26
☑ M	26	Swept Away	24
Marriage of Maria Braun	25	☑ Two Women	25
☑ Metropolis	27		
Neverending Story	23	**JAPANESE**	
Nosferatu	26	Akira	23
Nosferatu the Vampyre	22	Godzilla	16
Run Lola Run	23	Howl's Moving Castle	25
Tin Drum	23	☑ Ran	27
☑ Triumph of the Will	27	☑ Rashomon	29
Wings of Desire	24	☑ Seven Samurai	29
		☑ Spirited Away	27
GREEK		Yojimbo	28
Never on Sunday	24		
Zorba the Greek	25	**MEXICAN**	
		☑ Amores Perros	26
INDIAN		Like Water for Chocolate	25
Monsoon Wedding	24	Y Tu Mamá También	24
IRISH		**NEW ZEALAND**	
Breakfast on Pluto	19	Whale Rider	25
Commitments, The	24		
☑ In America	26	**RUSSIAN**	
In the Name of the Father	23	☑ Alexander Nevsky	26
Magdalene Sisters	25	☑ Potemkin	27
My Left Foot	25		
Once	25	**SOUTH AFRICAN**	
		Gods Must Be Crazy	22
ITALIAN			
☑ Amarcord	26	**SPANISH**	
☑ Battle of Algiers	28	All About My Mother	25
☑ Bicycle Thief	27	Bad Education	23
☑ Cinema Paradiso	26	Machinist, The	20
☑ Conformist, The	26	☑ Pan's Labyrinth	27
Damned, The	23	Sea Inside	25
Death in Venice	24	☑ Talk to Her	26
Divorce Italian Style	24	Tie Me Up! Tie Me Down!	20
☑ 8½	26		

GENRE/FEATURES

Volver	24
Women on the Verge	24

SWEDISH

☑ Cries and Whispers	26
Elvira Madigan	20
☑ Fanny and Alexander	26
My Life As a Dog	25
☑ Persona	27
Scenes from a Marriage	25
☑ Seventh Seal	27
☑ Smiles of a Summer Night	26
☑ Wild Strawberries	26

TAIWANESE

Eat Drink Man Woman	25
Wedding Banquet	22

GAY-THEMED

Adventures of Priscilla	23
Before Night Falls	22
Birdcage, The	22
Brokeback Mountain	24
Celluloid Closet	25
Children's Hour	24
Dying Gaul	17
Gods and Monsters	23
Hedwig and the Angry Inch	21
In & Out	17
Kissing Jessica Stein	21
Kiss of the Spider Woman	22
La Cage aux Folles	24
Longtime Companion	23
Love! Valour! Compassion!	21
☑ Notes on a Scandal	24
Paris is Burning	24
Personal Best	15
Philadelphia	24
Sunday Bloody Sunday	24
Torch Song Trilogy	23
Wedding Banquet	22

HIGH SCHOOL

All the Right Moves	16
American Graffiti	24
American Pie	19
Bill & Ted's	15
Blackboard Jungle	23
Breakfast Club	22
Bring It On	17
Carrie	22
Clueless	21
Coach Carter	21
Dazed and Confused	22
☑ Dead Poets Society	24

Donnie Darko	22
Election	22
Elephant	19
Fame	21
Fast Times/Ridgemont High	22
☑ Ferris Bueller's Day Off	23
Friday Night Lights	21
☑ Grease	23
Grosse Pointe Blank	22
Heathers	21
Mean Girls	20
My Bodyguard	18
Napoleon Dynamite	19
Porky's	14
Pretty in Pink	19
Remember the Titans	20
Romy & Michele's/Reunion	14
Rushmore	23
Save the Last Dance	17
Say Anything	23
Sixteen Candles	22
Sky High	16
Stand and Deliver	20
Superbad	20
Taps	20
Teen Wolf	15
Thirteen	21

HOLIDAY

CHRISTMAS

Bad Santa	18
Bells of St. Mary's	24
Bishop's Wife	24
Christmas Carol	27
☑ Christmas Story	26
Elf	21
Family Stone	16
Go	20
Holiday Inn	23
How the Grinch Stole Xmas	17
☑ It's a Wonderful Life	27
Meet John Doe	24
☑ Miracle on 34th Street	25
Nightmare Before Christmas	24
Polar Express	21
Santa Clause	19
Scrooged	19
☑ White Christmas	25

EASTER

Easter Parade	22
Last Temptation of Christ	22
Passion of the Christ	22
Robe, The	22

INDEPENDENCE DAY

Born on the 4th of July	20
Patriot, The	21
1776	22
Yankee Doodle Dandy	25

HORROR

American Werewolf/London	20
Amityville Horror	18
Army of Darkness	23
Blair Witch Project	10
Bride of Frankenstein	25
⚡ Cabinet of Dr. Caligari	26
Carrie	22
Cat People (1942)	23
Cat People (1982)	16
Christine	17
Constantine	16
Cujo	17
Dawn of the Dead (1978)	19
Dawn of the Dead (2004)	19
Descent, The	18
Dracula (1931)	24
Dracula (1992)	20
Evil Dead	22
Exorcist, The	25
Firestarter	17
Fly, The (1958)	20
Fly, The (1986)	16
Fog, The	17
Frankenstein	25
Freaks	23
Friday the 13th	16
Ghost Story	21
Godzilla	16
Gothika	17
Halloween	22
Hellraiser	19
House of Wax	21
Howling, The	19
Hunger, The	20
Hush... Hush, Sweet Charlotte	24
Identity	18
Interview with the Vampire	19
Invasion/Body Snatchers (1956)	24
Invasion/Body Snatchers (1978)	19
Invisible Man	22
Lost Boys	21
Mummy, The (1932)	24
Mummy, The (1999)	19
Mummy Returns	18
Nightmare on Elm Street	19
Night of the Living Dead	22
Nosferatu	26
Nosferatu the Vampyre	22

Omen, The	21
Pit and the Pendulum	22
Poltergeist	22
Ring, The	19
Rosemary's Baby	24
Saw	18
Saw II	19
Saw III	17
Scream	20
Shadow of the Vampire	20
Shaun of the Dead	22
Shining, The	25
Sisters	22
Sleepy Hollow	17
Texas Chainsaw Massacre	17
Thing, The (1951)	23
Thing, The (1982)	23
28 Days Later	18
28 Weeks Later	19
Van Helsing	15
Videodrome	17
Village of the Damned	21
Wolf Man	20
⚡ Young Frankenstein	27

INDIES

(See also Documentaries)

⚡ Akeelah and the Bee	26
American Psycho	19
American Splendor	23
Amityville Horror	18
Anniversary Party	18
Assassination of Richard Nixon	18
Assault on Precinct 13	16
Babel	22
Barfly	18
Basquiat	17
Before Night Falls	22
Being John Malkovich	22
Being Julia	23
Benji	19
Blair Witch Project	10
Blood Simple	24
Blue Velvet	22
Bobby	20
Boondock Saints	23
Breakfast on Pluto	19
Brokeback Mountain	24
Broken Flowers	16
Brother from Another Planet	23
Brothers McMullen	19
⚡ Capote	26
Cat's Meow	18
Clerks	23
Coffee and Cigarettes	18

Teen Wolf	15
Texas Chainsaw Massacre	17
☑ This Is Spinal Tap	26
Three Burials/Estrada	22
Torch Song Trilogy	23
Touch of Class	22
TransAmerica	24
Trip to Bountiful	24
21 Grams	22
Upside of Anger	22
Van Wilder	14
Velvet Goldmine	17
Virgin Suicides	20
Waitress	24
We Don't Live Here Anymore	16
Welcome to the Dollhouse	22
Whale Rider	25
Woman Under the Influence	24
Wonderland	16
Woodsman, The	21
You Can Count on Me	23

JAMES BOND

Casino Royale	23
Diamonds Are Forever	20
Die Another Day	19
Dr. No	23
For Your Eyes Only	18
From Russia With Love	23
GoldenEye	19
☑ Goldfinger	26
License to Kill	14
Live and Let Die	19
Living Daylights	14
Man with the Golden Gun	18
Moonraker	16
Never Say Never Again	18
Octopussy	17
On Her Majesty's/Service	19
Spy Who Loved Me	21
Thunderball	22
Tomorrow Never Dies	20
View to a Kill	14
World Is Not Enough	19
You Only Live Twice	22

LITERARY ADAPTATIONS

(Best of many)

Adventures of Robin Hood	25
☑ Advise & Consent	27
☑ All Quiet on Western Front	28
☑ All the King's Men (1949)	25
All the President's Men	25
☑ Anna Karenina	26

☑ Babette's Feast	26
☑ Beau Geste	25
☑ Beautiful Mind	26
☑ Beauty/Beast (1947)	28
☑ Being There	26
☑ Ben-Hur	26
☑ Big Sleep	27
☑ Blade Runner	26
☑ Bourne Ultimatum	25
☑ Breakfast at Tiffany's	26
☑ Bridge on the River Kwai	28
☑ Caine Mutiny	27
☑ Camille	26
☑ Captains Courageous	25
☑ Catch-22	25
Christmas Carol	27
☑ Christmas Story	26
☑ City of God	26
☑ Clockwork Orange	25
☑ Color Purple	26
☑ Day of the Jackal	25
Deliverance	25
☑ Diving Bell & the Butterfly	26
☑ Doctor Zhivago	27
Elmer Gantry	25
☑ Empire of the Sun	25
Exorcist, The	25
Forbidden Planet	25
For Whom the Bell Tolls	25
Frankenstein	25
☑ From Here to Eternity	26
☑ Gentleman's Agreement	26
☑ Godfather, The	29
☑ Goldfinger	26
☑ Gone with the Wind	28
☑ Goodbye, Mr. Chips	25
☑ Graduate, The	27
Grand Hotel	25
☑ Grapes of Wrath	28
☑ Great Expectations	27
☑ Gunga Din	25
☑ Hamlet (1948)	27
☑ Heart Is a Lonely Hunter	25
☑ Henry V	26
High Sierra	25
Hours, The	25
☑ Hud	26
☑ Hunchback/Notre Dame (1939)	26
☑ In Cold Blood	25
☑ Jane Eyre	25
☑ Jaws	26
☑ Jean de Florette	27
Joy Luck Club	25
Julia	25

GENRE/FEATURES

Purple Rose of Cairo	21
Shadow of the Vampire	20
☑ Singin' in the Rain	28
Stardust Memories	19
☑ Star Is Born	25
Stunt Man	22
☑ Sullivan's Travels	27
☑ Sunset Boulevard	28

MUSICALS

Across the Universe	22
All That Jazz	24
☑ American in Paris	26
Annie	19
☑ Band Wagon	26
Bells Are Ringing	24
Best Little Whorehouse in Texas	14
Beyond the Sea	19
Blues Brothers	22
Bride & Prejudice	20
Brigadoon	24
Buck Privates	22
Buddy Holly Story	21
Bye Bye Birdie	19
☑ Cabaret	26
Cabin in the Sky	24
Camelot	21
Carmen Jones	23
Carousel	24
☑ Chicago	27
Chorus Line	19
Commitments, The	24
Damn Yankees	24
Dancer in the Dark	22
De-Lovely	20
Dreamgirls	23
Easter Parade	22
Enchanted	23
Everyone Says I Love You	18
Evita	19
Fame	21
☑ Fiddler on the Roof	26
Fighting Temptations	17
Finian's Rainbow	21
5,000 Fingers of Dr. T.	20
Footlight Parade	23
42nd Street	24
Funny Face	24
☑ Funny Girl	26
Funny Lady	15
Funny Thing Happened...	22
Gay Divorcee	25
Gentlemen Prefer Blondes	23
Gigi	24

☑ Gold Diggers of 1933	25
☑ Grease	23
☑ Guys and Dolls	24
Gypsy	20
Hair	20
Hairspray (2007)	21
Hard Day's Night	24
Hedwig and the Angry Inch	21
Hello, Dolly!	20
Help!	19
High Society	23
Holiday Inn	23
Jailhouse Rock	18
Jesus Christ Superstar	21
☑ King and I	27
Kiss Me Kate	24
La Bamba	20
Little Shop of Horrors	19
Mambo Kings	20
☑ Mary Poppins	27
☑ Meet Me in St. Louis	26
Moulin Rouge!	23
Music Man	25
☑ My Fair Lady	27
New York, New York	19
Oklahoma!	24
Oliver!	24
On a Clear Day You Can See...	20
Once	25
On the Town	23
Paint Your Wagon	18
Pennies from Heaven	17
Phantom of the Opera	21
Pink Floyd The Wall	23
Popeye	13
Prairie Home Companion	18
Producers, The (2005)	18
Purple Rain	14
Rent	19
Rocky Horror Picture Show	21
Seven Brides/Seven Brothers	24
1776	22
Shall We Dance	25
Show Boat	23
☑ Singin' in the Rain	28
☑ Sound of Music	28
South Pacific	24
Sweeney Todd	23
Sweet Charity	20
☑ Swing Time	26
That's Entertainment!	25
Thoroughly Modern Millie	18
Tommy	16
☑ Top Hat	27

GENRE/FEATURES

OCCUPATIONS

DOCTORS

JOURNALISTS

LAWYERS

subscribe to ZAGAT.com

GENRE/FEATURES

Ⓩ Black Book	26	Educating Rita	18
Bourne Identity	20	Election	22
Bourne Supremacy	21	Emperor's Club	19
Ⓩ Bourne Ultimatum	25	Fame	21
Breach	23	5,000 Fingers of Dr. T.	20
Clear and Present Danger	20	Freedom Writers	22
Confessions/Dangerous Mind	19	Ⓩ Goodbye, Mr. Chips	25
Conversation, The	25	Great Debaters	25
Counterfeit Traitor	25	Ⓩ Harry Potter/Chamber	24
Donnie Brasco	20	Ⓩ Harry Potter/Goblet of Fire	24
Enigma	18	Ⓩ Harry Potter/Order of Phoenix	24
Eye of the Needle	23	Ⓩ Harry Potter/Prisoner	24
Falcon and the Snowman	21	Ⓩ Harry Potter/Sorcerer's	24
Foreign Correspondent	24	History Boys	22
Ⓩ General, The	28	In & Out	17
Good Shepherd	20	Ⓩ Inherit the Wind	26
Hunt for Red October	24	Ⓩ King and I	27
Ipcress File	24	Looking for Mr. Goodbar	18
La Femme Nikita	23	Miracle Worker	25
Man Who Knew Too Much	24	Mona Lisa Smile	16
Mission: Impossible	16	Mr. Holland's Opus	21
Ⓩ Notorious	27	Ⓩ My Fair Lady	27
No Way Out	20	Ⓩ Notes on a Scandal	24
Our Man Flint	19	Nutty Professor (1963)	21
Outrageous Fortune	15	Nutty Professor (1996)	15
Patriot Games	21	Oliver!	24
Recruit, The	17	Paper Chase	23
Siege, The	19	Piano, The	21
Spies Like Us	16	Prime of Miss Jean Brodie	25
Spy Game	19	Ⓩ Red Shoes	26
Spy Kids	19	Rushmore	23
Spy Kids 2	16	School of Rock	20
Spy Who Came in from Cold	25	Stand and Deliver	20
Sum of All Fears	16	Taps	20
Syriana	21	To Sir, With Love	22
Ⓩ 39 Steps	27	Wonder Boys	21
Torn Curtain	23		
True Lies	19	**OFFICE POLITICS**	
XXX	15	Apartment, The	25
		Baby Boom	19
TEACHERS		Broadcast News	23
Ⓩ Akeelah and the Bee	26	Desk Set	25
Anna and the King	19	Devil Wears Prada	22
Ⓩ Au Revoir Les Enfants	27	Front Page	24
Ⓩ Ball of Fire	26	Glengarry Glen Ross	23
Ⓩ Beautiful Mind	26	Ⓩ His Girl Friday	26
Billy Elliot	25	Hudsucker Proxy	22
Blackboard Jungle	23	In Good Company	19
Ⓩ Blue Angel	25	In the Company of Men	20
Charly	21	Michael Clayton	24
Children of a Lesser God	23	Network	24
Children's Hour	24	9 to 5	18
Coach Carter	21	Office Space	25
Ⓩ Dead Poets Society	24	Secretary	21
Ⓩ Diabolique	26		

Wall Street 22

Working Girl 20

OSCAR WINNERS

BEST PICTURE

☑ All About Eve | 1950 28

☑ All Quiet on Western Front | 28
1930

☑ All the King's Men | 1949 25

☑ Amadeus | 1984 26

☑ American Beauty | 1999 24

☑ American in Paris | 1951 26

☑ Annie Hall | 1977 27

Apartment, The | 1960 25

Around the World in 80 Days | 22
1956

☑ Beautiful Mind | 2001 26

☑ Ben-Hur | 1959 26

☑ Best Years of Our Lives | 1946 28

☑ Braveheart | 1995 26

☑ Bridge on the River Kwai | 1957 28

☑ Casablanca | 1943 29

☑ Chariots of Fire | 1981 26

☑ Chicago | 2002 27

Crash | 2005 26

Dances with Wolves | 1990 23

☑ Deer Hunter | 1978 26

☑ Departed, The | 2006 26

Driving Miss Daisy | 1989 24

☑ English Patient | 1996 22

☑ Forrest Gump | 1994 24

French Connection | 1971 25

☑ From Here to Eternity | 1953 26

☑ Gandhi | 1982 27

☑ Gentleman's Agreement | 1947 26

Gigi | 1958 24

☑ Gladiator | 2000 23

☑ Godfather, The | 1972 29

☑ Godfather Part II | 1974 29

Going My Way | 1944 24

☑ Gone with the Wind | 1939 28

Grand Hotel | 1932 25

☑ Hamlet | 1948 27

☑ How Green Was My Valley | 27
1941

In the Heat of the Night | 1967 24

☑ It Happened One Night | 1934 28

Kramer vs. Kramer | 1979 23

☑ Last Emperor | 1987 26

☑ Lawrence of Arabia | 1962 29

☑ Lord of Rings/Return | 2003 28

Lost Weekend | 1945 25

☑ Man for All Seasons | 1966 28

Marty | 1955 25

☑ Midnight Cowboy | 1969 26

☑ Million Dollar Baby | 2004 27

Mrs. Miniver | 1942 25

☑ Mutiny on the Bounty | 1935 25

☑ My Fair Lady | 1964 27

No Country for Old Men | 2007 24

Oliver! | 1968 24

☑ One Flew Over Cuckoo's... | 27
1975

☑ On the Waterfront | 1954 28

Ordinary People | 1980 25

Out of Africa | 1985 25

☑ Patton | 1970 27

Platoon | 1986 25

Rain Man | 1988 25

☑ Rebecca | 1940 27

☑ Rocky | 1976 25

☑ Schindler's List | 1993 29

Shakespeare in Love | 1998 24

☑ Silence of the Lambs | 1991 27

☑ Sound of Music | 1965 28

☑ Sting, The | 1973 27

Terms of Endearment | 1983 25

Titanic | 1997 19

Tom Jones | 1963 25

☑ Unforgiven | 1992 26

☑ West Side Story | 1961 27

BEST ACTOR

F. Murray Abraham

  ☑ Amadeus 26

Roberto Benigni

  ☑ Life Is Beautiful 27

Humphrey Bogart

  ☑ African Queen 28

Ernest Borgnine

  Marty 25

Marlon Brando

  ☑ Godfather, The 29

  ☑ On the Waterfront 28

Adrien Brody

  ☑ Pianist, The 28

Yul Brynner

  ☑ King and I 27

Nicolas Cage

  Leaving Las Vegas 20

James Cagney

  Yankee Doodle Dandy 25

Gary Cooper

  ☑ High Noon 28

  Sergeant York 25

Broderick Crawford

  ☑ All the King's Men (1949) 25

Bing Crosby

  Going My Way 24

Russell Crowe
Z Gladiator   23

Daniel Day-Lewis
My Left Foot   25
There Will Be Blood   23

Robert De Niro
Z Raging Bull   26

Robert Donat
Z Goodbye, Mr. Chips   25

Michael Douglas
Wall Street   22

Richard Dreyfuss
Goodbye Girl   21

Robert Duvall
Tender Mercies   24

Peter Finch
Network   24

Henry Fonda
On Golden Pond   24

Jamie Foxx
Z Ray   26

Clark Gable
Z It Happened One Night   28

Alec Guinness
Z Bridge on the River Kwai   28

Gene Hackman
French Connection   25

Tom Hanks
Z Forrest Gump   24
Philadelphia   24

Rex Harrison
Z My Fair Lady   27

Charlton Heston
Z Ben-Hur   26

Dustin Hoffman
Kramer vs. Kramer   23
Rain Man   25

Philip Seymour Hoffman
Z Capote   26

William Holden
Z Stalag 17   27

Anthony Hopkins
Z Silence of the Lambs   27

William Hurt
Kiss of the Spider Woman   22

Jeremy Irons
Reversal of Fortune   23

Ben Kingsley
Z Gandhi   27

Burt Lancaster
Elmer Gantry   25

Jack Lemmon
Save the Tiger   22

Fredric March
Z Best Years of Our Lives   28

Lee Marvin
Cat Ballou   21

Ray Milland
Lost Weekend   25

Paul Newman
Color of Money   16

Jack Nicholson
As Good As It Gets   22
Z One Flew Over Cuckoo's...   27

Laurence Olivier
Z Hamlet (1948)   27

Al Pacino
Scent of a Woman   21

Gregory Peck
Z To Kill a Mockingbird   29

Sean Penn
Z Mystic River   26

Sidney Poitier
Z Lilies of the Field   25

Cliff Robertson
Charly   21

Geoffrey Rush
Shine   22

Paul Scofield
Z Man for All Seasons   28

George C. Scott
Z Patton   27

Kevin Spacey
Z American Beauty   24

Rod Steiger
In the Heat of the Night   24

James Stewart
Z Philadelphia Story   27

Spencer Tracy
Z Captains Courageous   25

Jon Voight
Coming Home   23

Denzel Washington
Training Day   20

John Wayne
True Grit   22

Forest Whitaker
Z Last King of Scotland   25

BEST ACTRESS

Julie Andrews
Z Mary Poppins   27

Anne Bancroft
Miracle Worker   25

Kathy Bates
Misery   21

Ingrid Bergman
Anastasia (1956)   23
Gaslight   26

GENRE/FEATURES

Reese Witherspoon
   Walk the Line | 25

Joanne Woodward
   Three Faces of Eve | 24

BEST DIRECTOR

☒ All About Eve | 28
☒ All Quiet on Western Front | 28
☒ Amadeus | 26
☒ American Beauty | 24
☒ Annie Hall | 27
Apartment, The | 25
Awful Truth | 25
☒ Beautiful Mind | 26
☒ Ben-Hur | 26
☒ Best Years of Our Lives | 28
Born on the 4th of July | 20
☒ Braveheart | 26
☒ Bridge on the River Kwai | 28
Brokeback Mountain | 24
☒ Cabaret | 26
☒ Casablanca | 29
Dances with Wolves | 23
☒ Deer Hunter | 26
☒ Departed, The | 26
☒ English Patient | 22
☒ Forrest Gump | 24
French Connection | 25
☒ From Here to Eternity | 26
☒ Gandhi | 27
☒ Gentleman's Agreement | 26
Giant | 24
Gigi | 24
☒ Godfather Part II | 29
Going My Way | 24
☒ Gone with the Wind | 28
☒ Graduate, The | 27
☒ Grapes of Wrath | 28
☒ How Green Was My Valley | 27
☒ It Happened One Night | 28
Kramer vs. Kramer | 23
☒ Last Emperor | 26
☒ Lawrence of Arabia | 29
Letter to Three Wives | 24
☒ Lord of Rings/Return | 28
Lost Weekend | 25
☒ Man for All Seasons | 28
Marty | 25
☒ Midnight Cowboy | 26
☒ Million Dollar Baby | 27
Mr. Deeds Goes to Town | 25
Mrs. Miniver | 25
☒ My Fair Lady | 27
No Country for Old Men | 24

Oliver! | 24
☒ One Flew Over Cuckoo's... | 27
☒ On the Waterfront | 28
Ordinary People | 25
Out of Africa | 25
☒ Patton | 27
☒ Pianist, The | 28
☒ Place in the Sun | 27
Platoon | 25
☒ Quiet Man | 27
Rain Man | 25
Reds | 21
☒ Rocky | 25
☒ Saving Private Ryan | 26
☒ Schindler's List | 29
☒ Silence of the Lambs | 27
☒ Sound of Music | 28
☒ Sting, The | 27
Terms of Endearment | 25
Titanic | 19
Tom Jones | 25
Traffic | 23
☒ Treasure of the Sierra Madre | 27
☒ Unforgiven | 26
☒ West Side Story | 27

BEST FOREIGN LANGUAGE FILM

All About My Mother | 25
☒ Amarcord | 26
Antonia's Line | 25
☒ Babette's Feast | 26
Barbarian Invasions | 24
☒ Bicycle Thief | 27
☒ Black Orpheus | 26
☒ Cinema Paradiso | 26
Crouching Tiger | 24
☒ Day for Night | 27
Discreet Charm | 24
☒ 8½ | 26
☒ Fanny and Alexander | 26
Garden of the Finzi-Continis | 25
Indochine | 23
☒ La Strada | 27
☒ Life Is Beautiful | 27
☒ Lives of Others | 28
☒ Man and a Woman | 24
Mediterraneo | 21
☒ Mon Oncle | 26
Nights of Cabiria | 27
Sea Inside | 25
☒ Shop on Main Street | 27
Tin Drum | 23
Z | 26

BEST SCREENPLAY

☑ All About Eve	28
Almost Famous	23
☑ Amadeus	26
☑ American Beauty	24
☑ American in Paris	26
☑ Annie Hall	27
Apartment, The	25
Around the World in 80 Days	22
Bad and the Beautiful	24
☑ Beautiful Mind	26
☑ Becket	26
☑ Best Years of Our Lives	28
Breaking Away	24
☑ Bridge on the River Kwai	28
Brokeback Mountain	24
☑ Butch Cassidy	26
Candidate, The	20
☑ Casablanca	29
☑ Chariots of Fire	26
☑ Chinatown	27
Cider House Rules	22
☑ Citizen Kane	28
Coming Home	23
Country Girl	24
Crash	26
Crying Game	22
Dances with Wolves	23
Dangerous Liaisons	24
Darling	22
☑ Dead Poets Society	24
☑ Departed, The	26
Divorce Italian Style	24
☑ Doctor Zhivago	27
Dog Day Afternoon	24
Driving Miss Daisy	24
Elmer Gantry	25
Exorcist, The	25
☑ Fargo	25
☑ Forrest Gump	24
French Connection	25
☑ From Here to Eternity	26
☑ Gandhi	27
Ghost	21
Gigi	24
☑ Godfather, The	29
☑ Godfather Part II	29
Gods and Monsters	23
Going My Way	24
☑ Gone with the Wind	28
☑ Good Will Hunting	24
Gosford Park	23
☑ Guess Who's Coming...	25
Hannah and Her Sisters	24
Howards End	22

How the West Was Won	23
In the Heat of the Night	24
☑ It Happened One Night	28
☑ Judgment at Nuremberg	26
Julia	25
Juno	25
Kramer vs. Kramer	23
☑ L.A. Confidential	26
☑ Last Emperor	26
☑ Lavender Hill Mob	25
Letter to Three Wives	24
☑ Lion in Winter	28
Little Miss Sunshine	24
☑ Lord of Rings/Return	28
Lost in Translation	21
Lost Weekend	25
☑ Man and a Woman	24
☑ Man for All Seasons	28
Marty	25
☑ MASH	26
Melvin and Howard	22
☑ Midnight Cowboy	26
Midnight Express	24
☑ Miracle on 34th Street	25
Missing	24
Moonstruck	24
Mr. Mom	18
Mrs. Miniver	25
Network	24
No Country for Old Men	24
☑ One Flew Over Cuckoo's...	27
On Golden Pond	24
☑ On the Waterfront	28
Ordinary People	25
Out of Africa	25
☑ Patton	27
☑ Philadelphia Story	27
Piano, The	21
Pillow Talk	20
☑ Place in the Sun	27
Places in the Heart	20
Producers, The (1968)	26
☑ Pulp Fiction	26
Rain Man	25
☑ Roman Holiday	27
Room at the Top	24
☑ Room with a View	26
☑ Schindler's List	29
☑ Sense and Sensibility	26
Shakespeare in Love	24
☑ Silence of the Lambs	27
Sling Blade	25
Splendor in the Grass	25
☑ Sting, The	27

GENRE/FEATURES

☑ Sunset Boulevard	28
☑ Talk to Her	26
Tender Mercies	24
Terms of Endearment	25
Thelma & Louise	23
☑ To Kill a Mockingbird	29
Tom Jones	25
Traffic	23
☑ Treasure of the Sierra Madre	27
☑ Usual Suspects	27
Witness	23
☑ Woman of the Year	27

Paris, Texas	22
Planes, Trains/Automobiles	22
Smokey and the Bandit	16
Something Wild	20
Straight Story	24
Sugarland Express	18
Thelma & Louise	23
Three Burials/Estrada	22
TransAmerica	24
Up in Smoke	19
Wild Hogs	17
Y Tu Mamá También	24

RELIGION

Agnes of God	21
Agony and the Ecstasy	23
Bells of St. Mary's	24
☑ Ben-Hur	26
Bruce Almighty	18
Chronicles of Narnia	23
Dangerous Lives/Altar Boys	19
Da Vinci Code	19
Elmer Gantry	25
Exorcist, The	25
Going My Way	24
☑ Hunchback/Notre Dame (1939)	26
Intolerance	27
Jesus Christ Superstar	21
Last Temptation of Christ	22
Life of Brian	23
Magdalene Sisters	25
Name of the Rose	22
Oh, God!	17
Passion of the Christ	22
Prince of Egypt	19
Robe, The	22
Song of Bernadette	22
☑ Ten Commandments	24
Yentl	18

ROAD MOVIES

Adventures of Priscilla	23
Boys on the Side	15
Broken Flowers	16
Cannonball Run	17
☑ Central Station	26
Darjeeling Limited	17
Easy Rider	23
Gauntlet, The	17
Little Miss Sunshine	24
Lost in America	20
Midnight Run	23
Motorcycle Diaries	23
National Lampoon's Vacation	22

ROCK 'N' ROLL

Across the Universe	22
Almost Famous	23
Blackboard Jungle	23
Blues Brothers	22
Buddy Holly Story	21
Bye Bye Birdie	19
Commitments, The	24
Don't Look Back	25
Doors, The	20
Fame	21
Footloose	17
Gimme Shelter	25
☑ Grease	23
Hair	20
Hairspray (1988)	19
Hairspray (2007)	21
Hard Day's Night	24
Hedwig and the Angry Inch	21
Help!	19
High Fidelity	21
I'm Not There	17
Jailhouse Rock	18
Jesus Christ Superstar	21
La Bamba	20
☑ Last Waltz	26
Little Shop of Horrors	19
Pink Floyd The Wall	23
Purple Rain	14
Rocky Horror Picture Show	21
Rose, The	19
Saturday Night Fever	22
School of Rock	20
Sid & Nancy	18
Stop Making Sense	25
☑ This Is Spinal Tap	26
Tommy	16
Truth or Dare	15
Velvet Goldmine	17
Wayne's World	17
What's Love Got to Do with It	22

Woodstock	24
Yellow Submarine	22

ROMANCE

(See also Chick Flicks)

About Last Night...	17
Accidental Tourist	20
Adventures of Robin Hood	25
☒ African Queen	28
Alice	20
Almost Famous	23
Along Came Polly	15
☒ American in Paris	26
American President	21
Anna and the King	19
☒ Annie Hall	27
Apartment, The	25
Arthur	20
As Good As It Gets	22
Awful Truth	25
☒ Ball of Fire	26
Barefoot in the Park	23
Barry Lyndon	20
Before Sunrise	23
Before Sunset	21
Bell, Book and Candle	22
Bishop's Wife	24
Bodyguard, The	14
Breaking the Waves	23
Bride & Prejudice	20
☒ Brief Encounter	27
☒ Bringing Up Baby	27
Broadcast News	23
Broadway Danny Rose	22
Brokeback Mountain	24
Bull Durham	22
Bus Stop	21
Butterflies Are Free	21
Cactus Flower	21
Camelot	21
☒ Camille	26
Carousel	24
☒ Casablanca	29
☒ Charade	26
Chasing Amy	20
Children of a Lesser God	23
☒ Children of Paradise	28
Chocolat	22
Cinderella Liberty	19
Claire's Knee	23
Cocktail	16
Cold Mountain	22
Cooler, The	22
Cousin, Cousine	21

Crossing Delancey	23
Dangerous Liaisons	24
☒ Dark Victory	25
Days of Heaven	23
Desk Set	25
☒ Doctor Zhivago	27
Dracula (1992)	20
Easter Parade	22
Elvira Madigan	20
Emma	22
Emmanuelle	16
Enchanted	23
End of the Affair	20
Eternal Sunshine	23
Fabulous Baker Boys	20
Failure to Launch	15
Family Man	16
Family Stone	16
Farewell My Concubine	25
Far From Heaven	24
Fever Pitch	20
50 First Dates	18
Flashdance	16
Flying Down to Rio	23
Forgetting Sarah Marshall	20
40 Year Old Virgin	19
For Whom the Bell Tolls	25
Fountainhead, The	22
Frankie & Johnny	20
French Lieutenant's Woman	22
☒ From Here to Eternity	26
Garden State	22
Gay Divorcee	25
Georgy Girl	23
Ghost and Mrs. Muir	24
Gigi	24
☒ Gone with the Wind	28
Goodbye, Columbus	19
Goodbye Girl	21
Good Year	16
☒ Graduate, The	27
Great Gatsby	22
Hannah and Her Sisters	24
Harold and Maude	25
Heartbreak Kid	20
Heartburn	19
Hello, Dolly!	20
Henry & June	20
High Fidelity	21
☒ His Girl Friday	26
Hitch	21
☒ Holiday	27
Holiday, The	19
Holiday Inn	23

GENRE/FEATURES

10	17
Tess	21
Thomas Crown Affair	23
Three Coins in the Fountain	21
Titanic	19
To Catch a Thief	25
☑ To Have and Have Not	26
Tootsie	25
☑ Top Hat	27
Topper	20
Truly Madly Deeply	23
Two for the Road	24
Umbrellas of Cherbourg	24
Unbearable Lightness of Being	21
Upside of Anger	22
Urban Cowboy	18
Vanity Fair	17
Venus	19
☑ Vertigo	27
Waitress	24
Walk the Line	25
Walk to Remember	18
☑ West Side Story	27
What Dreams May Come	16
While You Were Sleeping	18
☑ White Christmas	25
Wimbledon	15
Witness	23
Women in Love	23
☑ Wuthering Heights	27
You, Me and Dupree	13

SCI-FI

Abyss, The	20
A.I.: Artificial Intelligence	16
Akira	23
☑ Alien	25
Aliens	23
Altered States	19
Andromeda Strain	20
Back to the Future	23
Barbarella	13
Batteries Not Included	19
☑ Blade Runner	26
Brother from Another Planet	23
Children of Men	22
Chronicles of Riddick	14
☑ Close Encounters	24
Cocoon	20
Contact	20
Day After Tomorrow	16
Day the Earth Stood Still	25
Deep Impact	15
Donnie Darko	22

Dune	14
Escape from New York	15
☑ E.T.	26
Fahrenheit 451	21
Fantastic Four	14
Fantastic Four: Rise of Silver Surfer	15
Fifth Element	19
Fly, The (1958)	20
Fly, The (1986)	16
Forbidden Planet	25
Frequency	19
Galaxy Quest	21
Gattaca	20
Ghostbusters	21
Godzilla	16
Grindhouse	21
Heavy Metal	20
Hitchhiker's Guide...	17
I Am Legend	19
Independence Day	19
Innerspace	15
Invasion/Body Snatchers (1956)	24
Invasion/Body Snatchers (1978)	19
I, Robot	18
☑ Iron Man	26
Island, The	16
Journey to Center of Earth	19
Jurassic Park	22
Man Who Fell to Earth	18
☑ Matrix, The	25
Matrix Reloaded	21
Matrix Revolutions	15
Men in Black	21
Men in Black II	14
☑ Metropolis	27
Minority Report	21
Mothman Prophecies	15
Nutty Professor (1996)	15
☑ On the Beach	26
Pitch Black	19
Planet of the Apes	23
Repo Man	17
RoboCop	16
Rollerball	19
Running Man	17
Scanner Darkly	17
Serenity	23
Signs	18
Sky Captain/World Tomorrow	15
Sleeper	23
Spaceballs	18
Stargate	18
Starman	19
Starship Troopers	15

GENRE/FEATURES

Star Trek	14	Miss Pettigrew Lives for a Day	21
Star Trek II	23	☑ My Man Godfrey	25
Star Trek IV	21	☑ Night at the Opera	26
☑ Star Wars	28	Noises Off	21
Star Wars I/Phantom Menace	18	Nothing Sacred	23
Star Wars II/Attack of Clones	17	Palm Beach Story	25
Star Wars III/Revenge of Sith	23	☑ Philadelphia Story	27
☑ Star Wars V/Empire Strikes	26	Raising Arizona	23
Star Wars VI/Return of Jedi	24	☑ Thin Man	26
Strange Days	17	What's Up, Doc?	21
Terminator, The	24	Women on the Verge	24

SILENT

Terminator 2: Judgment Day	23	☑ Birth of a Nation	25
Terminator 3: Rise of Machines	16	☑ Cabinet of Dr. Caligari	26
Thing, The (1951)	23	☑ City Lights	28
Thing, The (1982)	23	☑ General, The	28
Time After Time	23	☑ Gold Rush	28
Time Machine	22	Greed	28
Total Recall	18	Intolerance	27
Transformers	21	☑ Metropolis	27
Tron	18	Modern Times	28
Twelve Monkeys	22	☑ Napoléon	28
28 Days Later	18	Nosferatu	26
28 Weeks Later	19	☑ Potemkin	27
20,000 Leagues Under Sea	22	Silent Movie	20
☑ 2001: A Space Odyssey	26	Thief of Bagdad	24
2010	16		

SOUNDTRACKS

(See also Musicals;
* Best Score Oscar winner)

V for Vendetta	22	Adventures of Robin Hood*	25
Village of the Damned	21	Aladdin*	24
War of the Worlds (1953)	23	☑ Alexander Nevsky	26
War of the Worlds (2005)	15	Alfie (1966)	22
Weird Science	19	All That Jazz*	24
Westworld	17	Almost Famous	23
X-Files, The	19	☑ Amadeus	26
X-Men	19	☑ Amarcord	26
X-Men: The Last Stand	20	☑ American Beauty	24
X2: X-Men United	24	American Gigolo	19
		American Graffiti	24

SCREWBALL COMEDIES

		☑ American in Paris*	26
☑ Animal Crackers	26	☑ Anatomy of a Murder	26
Awful Truth	25	Around the World in 80 Days*	22
☑ Ball of Fire	26	Barry Lyndon*	20
☑ Born Yesterday	26	Basquiat	17
☑ Bringing Up Baby	27	Beauty/Beast (1991)*	26
Cocoanuts, The	24	Bells Are Ringing	24
Day at the Races	24	☑ Ben-Hur*	26
☑ Duck Soup	27	Beyond the Sea	19
☑ His Girl Friday	26	Big Chill	23
Horse Feathers	24	Blackboard Jungle	23
I ♥ Huckabees	14	☑ Black Orpheus	26
Intolerable Cruelty	15	Blue Velvet	22
☑ It Happened One Night	28		
☑ Lady Eve	28		
Leatherheads	17		
Miracle of Morgan's Creek	23		

GENRE/FEATURES

🅩 King and I*	27
La Bamba	20
Lady Sings the Blues	22
🅩 Last Emperor*	26
Last of the Mohicans	22
🅩 La Strada	27
Last Tango in Paris	17
🅩 Last Waltz	26
🅩 La Vie en Rose	25
🅩 Lawrence of Arabia*	29
🅩 Life Is Beautiful*	27
Lili*	24
Limelight*	24
🅩 Lion in Winter*	28
🅩 Lion King*	25
Little Mermaid*	24
🅩 Local Hero	26
Lock, Stock and Two...	23
🅩 Lord of Rings/Fellowship*	27
🅩 Lord of Rings/Return*	28
🅩 Lord of Rings/Two Towers	27
Lost Highway	16
Love Is Many-Splendored...*	22
Love Story*	19
🅩 Magnificent Seven	26
Magnolia	20
Mambo Kings	20
🅩 Man and a Woman	24
Man Who Knew Too Much	24
Man with the Golden Arm	24
Marie Antoinette	17
Mark of Zorro	22
🅩 Mary Poppins*	27
Mean Streets	24
Mediterraneo	21
🅩 Midnight Cowboy	26
Midnight Express*	24
Mighty Wind	23
Mission, The	24
Muriel's Wedding	22
Music Man*	25
🅩 My Fair Lady*	27
Nashville	23
Natural, The	23
Nightmare Before Christmas	24
🅩 Night of the Hunter	27
1900	22
🅩 North by Northwest	28
🅩 Now, Voyager*	27
O Brother, Where Art Thou?	22
Oklahoma!*	24
Oliver!*	24
Omen, The*	21
Once*	25

Once Upon a Time/West	25
On the Town*	23
Out of Africa*	25
Phantom of the Opera	21
Piano, The	21
Pink Floyd The Wall	23
Pink Panther	24
🅩 Place in the Sun*	27
Pleasantville	20
Pocahontas	17
Pretty in Pink	19
🅩 Princess Bride	27
🅩 Psycho (1960)	28
🅩 Pulp Fiction	26
Pump Up the Volume	18
Purple Rain*	14
🅩 Raiders of the Lost Ark	28
🅩 Ray	26
🅩 Red Shoes*	26
Red Violin*	24
Repo Man	17
Repulsion	25
Rescuers, The	23
🅩 Right Stuff*	26
🅩 Rocky	25
🅩 Romeo and Juliet	26
Romy & Michele's/Reunion	14
🅩 Room with a View	26
Rose, The	19
Run Lola Run	23
Rushmore	23
Saturday Night Fever	22
Say Anything	23
🅩 Schindler's List*	29
School of Rock	20
Seven Brides/Seven Brothers*	24
7th Voyage of Sinbad	20
Shaft	17
Shakespeare in Love*	24
Shall We Dance	25
Shine	22
🅩 Shrek	26
Sisters	22
Sleepless in Seattle	21
🅩 Snow White	27
Song of Bernadette	22
🅩 Sound of Music*	28
South Park	20
🅩 Spartacus	26
Spellbound (1945)*	24
🅩 Stagecoach*	27
Stand by Me	24
Star Trek II	23
🅩 Star Wars*	28

Ⓩ Star Wars V/Empire Strikes	26
Star Wars VI/Return of Jedi	24
St. Elmo's Fire	17
Ⓩ Sting, The*	27
Stop Making Sense	25
Strictly Ballroom	23
Summer of '42*	21
Ⓩ Sunset Boulevard*	28
Superman	22
Sweet and Lowdown	21
Ⓩ Sweet Smell of Success	27
Ⓩ Talk to Her	26
Tarzan	22
Ⓩ Taxi Driver	27
Ⓩ Third Man	28
Ⓩ This Is Spinal Tap	26
Thoroughly Modern Millie*	18
Thunderball	22
Tie Me Up! Tie Me Down!	20
Titanic	19
Ⓩ To Kill a Mockingbird	29
Tom Jones*	25
Tommy	16
Ⓩ Top Gun	22
To Sir, With Love	22
Ⓩ Touch of Evil	26
Trainspotting	22
Truth or Dare	15
Two for the Road	24
Ⓩ 2001: A Space Odyssey	26
Urban Cowboy	18
Ⓩ Vertigo	27
Victor/Victoria*	23
Wait Until Dark	25
Walk the Line	25
Way We Were*	24
Wedding Singer	17
Ⓩ West Side Story*	27
What's Love Got to Do with It	22
Ⓩ When Harry Met Sally...	26
Ⓩ Wild Bunch	27
Ⓩ Willy Wonka	26
Wind and the Lion	24
Ⓩ Wizard of Oz*	28
Woodstock	24
Yankee Doodle Dandy*	25
Yellow Submarine	22
Ⓩ Young Frankenstein	27
Zorba the Greek	25
Zulu	24

SPORTS

BASEBALL

Bad News Bears	18
Bang the Drum Slowly	23
Bull Durham	22
Damn Yankees	24
Eight Men Out	24
Fever Pitch	20
League of Their Own	20
Major League	21
Natural, The	23
Pride of the Yankees	22
Rookie, The	22

BASKETBALL

Basketball Diaries	22
Coach Carter	21
Ⓩ Hoop Dreams	26
Hoosiers	23
Space Jam	16
Teen Wolf	15
White Men Can't Jump	13

BOXING

Cinderella Man	25
Great White Hope	25
Hurricane, The	21
Ⓩ Million Dollar Baby	27
Ⓩ On the Waterfront	28
Ⓩ Raging Bull	26
Ⓩ Requiem for a Heavyweight	26
Ⓩ Rocky	25
Rocky Balboa	18

FOOTBALL

All the Right Moves	16
Any Given Sunday	17
Everybody's All-American	19
Fortune Cookie	23
Friday Night Lights	21
Gridiron Gang	19
Invincible	21
Jerry Maguire	21
Leatherheads	17
Longest Yard (1974)	17
Longest Yard (2005)	17
North Dallas Forty	19
Radio	22
Remember the Titans	20
Rudy	23
We Are Marshall	22

HOCKEY

Mighty Ducks	18
Miracle	24
Slap Shot	22

OTHER

Bend It Like Beckham	26
Blades of Glory	19

Cannonball Run	17	Children's Hour	24
☑ Chariots of Fire	26	Chorus Line	19
Color of Money	16	Cocoanuts, The	24
Cool Runnings	18	Country Girl	24
Dodgeball	16	Crucible, The	19
Dreamer	21	Damn Yankees	24
Endless Summer	24	Deathtrap	22
Hustler, The	25	Desk Set	25
Kingpin	18	☑ Dial M for Murder	25
Murderball	25	Diary of a Mad Black Woman	19
Nacho Libre	12	Diary of Anne Frank	23
Personal Best	15	☑ Dinner at Eight	27
Pumping Iron	17	Dreamgirls	23
Racing Stripes	18	Driving Miss Daisy	24
Rollerball	19	Educating Rita	18
Seabiscuit	25	Elephant Man	24
Talladega Nights	15	Evita	19
Tin Cup	18	☑ Fiddler on the Roof	26
Wimbledon	15	Finian's Rainbow	21
		Frankie & Johnny	20

STAGE ADAPTATIONS

		Front Page	24
About Last Night...	17	☑ Funny Girl	26
☑ Amadeus	26	Funny Thing Happened...	22
☑ Animal Crackers	26	Gaslight	26
Anna Christie	26	Gay Divorcee	25
☑ Anne of the Thousand Days	26	Glengarry Glen Ross	23
Annie	19	☑ Grease	23
☑ Arsenic and Old Lace	26	Great White Hope	25
Auntie Mame	25	☑ Guys and Dolls	24
Awful Truth	25	Gypsy	20
Bad Seed	22	Hair	20
Barefoot in the Park	23	Hairspray (2007)	21
☑ Becket	26	☑ Hamlet (1948)	27
Bell, Book and Candle	22	Hamlet (1996)	24
Bells Are Ringing	24	Harvey	26
Best Little Whorehouse in Texas	14	Heaven Can Wait (1943)	24
Biloxi Blues	21	Hedwig and the Angry Inch	21
Birdcage, The	22	☑ Heiress, The	27
☑ Born Yesterday	26	Hello, Dolly!	20
☑ Brief Encounter	27	☑ Henry V	26
Brigadoon	24	High Society	23
Brighton Beach Memoirs	22	☑ His Girl Friday	26
Bus Stop	21	History Boys	22
Butterflies Are Free	21	☑ Holiday	27
Bye Bye Birdie	19	☑ I Never Sang for My Father	27
☑ Cabaret	26	☑ Inherit the Wind	26
Cabin in the Sky	24	Irma La Douce	21
Cactus Flower	21	Jesus Christ Superstar	21
Camelot	21	Jezebel	25
Carmen Jones	23	☑ Key Largo	26
Carousel	24	☑ King and I	27
☑ Cat on a Hot Tin Roof	25	Kiss Me Kate	24
☑ Chicago	27	La Cage aux Folles	24
Children of a Lesser God	23	Letter, The	25

Z Lion in Winter	28
Z Little Foxes	26
Little Shop of Horrors	19
Love! Valour! Compassion!	21
Madness of King George	22
Z Man for All Seasons	28
Man Who Came to Dinner	26
Z Member of the Wedding	25
Merchant of Venice	23
Miracle Worker	25
Z Mister Roberts	27
Music Man	25
Z My Fair Lady	27
Night of the Iguana	23
Noises Off	21
Odd Couple	25
Oklahoma!	24
Oliver!	24
On a Clear Day You Can See...	20
One, Two, Three	23
On Golden Pond	24
On the Town	23
Owl and the Pussycat	17
Paint Your Wagon	18
Peter Pan (1953)	25
Peter Pan (2003)	20
Phantom of the Opera	21
Z Philadelphia Story	27
Picnic	24
Play It Again, Sam	22
Prelude to a Kiss	16
Prisoner of Second Avenue	22
Producers, The (2005)	18
Proof	18
Z Raisin in the Sun	26
Real Women Have Curves	21
Rent	19
Rocky Horror Picture Show	21
Z Romeo and Juliet	26
Romy & Michele's/Reunion	14
Rope	22
Roxanne	21
Ruling Class	23
Same Time, Next Year	22
1776	22
Seven Year Itch	23
She Done Him Wrong	22
Shirley Valentine	24
Shop Around the Corner	24
Show Boat	23
Six Degrees of Separation	21
Sleuth	25
Z Soldier's Story	26
Z Sound of Music	28

South Pacific	24
Stage Door	25
Z Stalag 17	27
Steel Magnolias	24
Z Streetcar Named Desire	27
Suddenly, Last Summer	24
Summertime	23
Sunshine Boys	21
Sweeney Todd	23
Sweet Bird of Youth	24
Sweet Charity	20
Thousand Clowns	25
Torch Song Trilogy	23
Trip to Bountiful	24
Unsinkable Molly Brown	21
Wait Until Dark	25
Z West Side Story	27
Z Who's Afraid of V. Woolf?	25
Z Witness for the Prosecution	27
Wiz, The	16
Z Women, The	26

SWASHBUCKLERS

Adventures of Robin Hood	25
Captain Blood	23
Count of Monte Cristo	19
Mark of Zorro	22
Mask of Zorro	18
Master and Commander	23
Z Mutiny on the Bounty (1935)	25
Mutiny on the Bounty (1962)	22
Pirates Caribbean/At World's End	21
Pirates Caribbean/Dead Man	20
Pirates Caribbean/The Curse	24
Robin and Marian	20
Robin Hood: Prince of Thieves	16
7th Voyage of Sinbad	20
Thief of Bagdad	24
Three Musketeers	22

THRILLERS

(See also James Bond)

Accused, The	23
Air Force One	18
Airport	17
Z Alien	25
Aliens	23
Along Came a Spider	16
Z Amores Perros	26
Angel Heart	18
Apollo 13	24
Apt Pupil	18
Armageddon	15
Assassination of Richard Nixon	18
Assault on Precinct 13	16

GENRE/FEATURES

Suspicion	25
Swimming Pool	20
Swordfish	15
Syriana	21
Talented Mr. Ripley	18
☑ Taxi Driver	27
Texas Chainsaw Massacre	17
☑ Third Man	28
☑ 39 Steps	27
Three Days of the Condor	24
Time After Time	23
To Catch a Thief	25
To Live and Die in L.A.	20
Torn Curtain	23
Towering Inferno	18
Training Day	20
Twelve Monkeys	22
Twister	15
Unbreakable	16
United 93	25
U.S. Marshals	18
Veronica Guerin	21
☑ Vertigo	27
Videodrome	17
Village, The	16
☑ Wages of Fear	27
Wait Until Dark	25
WarGames	22
Westworld	19
Whatever Happened to...	22
What Lies Beneath	16
X-Files, The	17
Z	26
Zodiac	21

WAR

CIVIL WAR

Cold Mountain	22
Dances with Wolves	23
Friendly Persuasion	24
☑ Gettysburg	25
☑ Glory	25
☑ Gone with the Wind	28
Good, the Bad and the Ugly	24

GULF WAR

Jarhead	17
Manchurian Candidate (2004)	18
Three Kings	20

KOREAN WAR

MacArthur	21
☑ Manchurian Candidate (1962)	27
☑ MASH	26

REVOLUTIONARY WAR

Patriot, The	21
1776	22

VIETNAM WAR

☑ Apocalypse Now	27
Born on the 4th of July	20
Casualties of War	20
Coming Home	23
☑ Deer Hunter	26
Fog of War	26
Full Metal Jacket	24
Good Morning, Vietnam	22
☑ Killing Fields	26
Platoon	25
Quiet American	24
We Were Soldiers	21

WWI

☑ All Quiet on Western Front	28
Flyboys	18
Gallipoli	25
Grand Illusion	28
Hell's Angels	24
☑ Lawrence of Arabia	29
☑ Paths of Glory	28
Sergeant York	25
Very Long Engagement	22

WWII

Americanization of Emily	24
Atonement	22
☑ Best Years of Our Lives	28
Biloxi Blues	21
☑ Black Book	26
☑ Bridge on the River Kwai	28
☑ Caine Mutiny	27
☑ Casablanca	29
☑ Catch-22	25
Counterfeit Traitor	25
Damned, The	23
☑ Das Boot	28
Diary of Anne Frank	23
Dirty Dozen	21
☑ Downfall	27
☑ Empire of the Sun	25
End of the Affair	20
Enemy at the Gates	21
☑ English Patient	22
Enigma	18
Eye of the Needle	23
Flags of Our Fathers	23
Garden of the Finzi-Continis	25
Good German	16
☑ Great Escape	27
Guns of Navarone	23

Hart's War	16
☑ Hope and Glory	26
I Was a Male War Bride	21
☑ Letters from Iwo Jima	27
Longest Day	24
MacArthur	21
Mediterraneo	21
☑ Mister Roberts	27
Mrs. Henderson Presents	23
Mrs. Miniver	25
1941	14
☑ Open City	28
Operation Petticoat	19
☑ Patton	27
Pearl Harbor	14
☑ Pianist, The	28
☑ Saving Private Ryan	26
☑ Schindler's List	29
☑ Seven Beauties	26
☑ Shop on Main Street	27
South Pacific	24
☑ Stalag 17	27
Thin Red Line	19
Tin Drum	23
☑ To Have and Have Not	26
Tora! Tora! Tora!	23
☑ Twelve O'Clock High	26
☑ Two Women	25
U-571	17
Windtalkers	16

OTHER

Alamo, The	18
☑ Alexander Nevsky	26
☑ Battle of Algiers	28
☑ Beau Geste	25
Black Hawk Down	23
☑ Braveheart	26
El Cid	19
For Whom the Bell Tolls	25
Four Feathers	16
☑ Gunga Din	25
☑ Henry V	26
Kingdom of Heaven	18
Last of the Mohicans	22
Master and Commander	23
☑ Napoléon	28
☑ Ran	27
Sand Pebbles	24
300	22
Troy	19

WEDDINGS

Bride Wore Black	25
Father of the Bride (1950)	23

Father of the Bride (1991)	20
Four Weddings and a Funeral	21
☑ Godfather, The	29
Honeymoon in Vegas	18
In-Laws, The (1979)	24
In-Laws, The (2003)	16
Monsoon Wedding	24
Monster-in-Law	15
Muriel's Wedding	22
My Best Friend's Wedding	19
My Big Fat Greek Wedding	23
☑ Philadelphia Story	27
Sex and the City	22
Sixteen Candles	22
Wedding Banquet	22
Wedding Crashers	21
Wedding Singer	17

WESTERNS

Alamo, The	18
☑ Blazing Saddles	25
☑ Butch Cassidy	26
Cat Ballou	21
City Slickers	20
Dances with Wolves	23
Destry Rides Again	25
Duel in the Sun	23
Fistful of Dollars	19
For a Few Dollars More	23
Fort Apache	23
Good, the Bad and the Ugly	24
Gunfight at O.K. Corral	20
Heaven's Gate	14
☑ High Noon	28
High Plains Drifter	18
How the West Was Won	23
☑ Hud	26
Jeremiah Johnson	23
Johnny Guitar	19
Legends of the Fall	20
Little Big Man	24
☑ Magnificent Seven	26
Man Called Horse	22
☑ Man Who Shot Liberty Valance	25
Maverick	18
McCabe & Mrs. Miller	23
Misfits, The	21
Missing, The	18
Missouri Breaks	16
☑ My Darling Clementine	25
My Little Chickadee	23
No Country for Old Men	24
Oklahoma!	24
Once Upon a Time/West	25

Open Range	21	Spirit: Stallion of Cimarron	21
Outlaw Josey Wales	25	Z Stagecoach	27
Z Ox-Bow Incident	27	Three Amigos	16
Paint Your Wagon	18	3:10 to Yuma	23
Z Red River	26	Tombstone	21
Rio Bravo	24	True Grit	22
Z Searchers, The	27	Z Unforgiven	26
Z Shane	26	Viva Zapata!	23
She Wore a Yellow Ribbon	24	Z Wild Bunch	27
Silverado	24	Young Guns	15